BRONZE AGE WORLDS

Bronze Age Worlds brings a new way of thinking about kinship to the task of explaining the formation of social life in Bronze Age Britain and Ireland.

Britain and Ireland's diverse landscapes and societies experienced varied and profound transformations during the twenty-fifth to eighth centuries BC. People's lives were shaped by migrations, changing beliefs about death, making and thinking with metals, and living in houses and field systems. This book offers accounts of how these processes emerged from social life, from events, places and landscapes, informed by a novel theory of kinship. Kinship was a rich and inventive sphere of culture that incorporated biological relations but was not determined by them. Kinship formed personhood and collective belonging, and associated people with nonhuman beings, things and places. The differences in kinship and kinwork across Ireland and Britain brought textures to social life and the formation of Bronze Age worlds.

Bronze Age Worlds offers new perspectives to archaeologists and anthropologists interested in the place of kinship in Bronze Age societies and cultural development.

Robert Johnston is a Senior Lecturer in Landscape Archaeology at the University of Sheffield. He has published articles and edited books on aspects of landscape archaeology and the later prehistory of Britain and northwest Europe. He currently researches landscape transformations in western Britain.

BRONZE AGE WORLDS

A Social Prehistory of
Britain and Ireland

Robert Johnston

Routledge
Taylor & Francis Group

LONDON AND NEW YORK

First published 2021
by Routledge
2 Park Square, Milton Park, Abingdon, Oxon OX14 4RN

and by Routledge
52 Vanderbilt Avenue, New York, NY 10017

Routledge is an imprint of the Taylor & Francis Group, an informa business

British Library Cataloguing-in-Publication Data
A catalogue record for this book is available from the British Library

Library of Congress Cataloging-in-Publication Data
A catalog record has been requested for this book

ISBN: 978-1-138-03787-8 (hbk)
ISBN: 978-1-138-03788-5 (pbk)
ISBN: 978-1-315-17763-2 (ebk)

Typeset in Bembo
by codeMantra

For Anna and Florrie

CONTENTS

ILLUSTRATIONS

Additional illustration and text credits

ACKNOWLEDGEMENTS

I benefited from the help and forbearance of many friends and colleagues during the writing of this book. The Department of Archaeology, University of Sheffield, provided me with time (two semesters of research leave), financial assistance (towards the production of illustrations) and a collegiate environment in which to work. I began writing the book in late 2016, when I had the good fortune to spend a short period as a visiting researcher at the Department of Archaeology, University College Dublin (UCD). Particular thanks to Graeme Warren for welcoming me to UCD, and for guiding me to some of the anthropological research that has influenced my thinking about kinship. It was while in Dublin that I approached Routledge with a book proposal. I am grateful to Matthew Gibbons at Routledge for the early encouragement and advice, and to Katie Wakelin for her editorial support.

Anna Badcock, Neil Carlin, Anwen Cooper, Oliver Davis, Chris Dwan, Duncan Garrow, Melanie Giles, Paul Halstead, Barry Heafield, Glynis Jones, Emily La Trobe Bateman, Ben Roberts and John Roberts were all kind enough to read and comment on drafts of chapters. Their suggestions were immensely helpful, and I hope I have reflected at least some of their wise feedback in the published text.

Rowan May (ArcHeritage) completed all the line drawings with her usual thoroughness and to a tight deadline. Bill Bevan shared a selection of his splendid photographs of monuments in Britain and Ireland (billbevanphotography. co.uk). John Wedgwood Clark and Julie Cruikshank permitted me to use quotations from their publications. Individuals, archaeological companies, archives and museums have kindly helped with images and permissions to reproduce illustrations: Adam Gwilt and Kay Kays (National Museum of Wales); Andy Jones (Cornwall Archaeological Unit); Ann Woodward; Billy O'Brien (University College Cork); Chris Chapman; Chris Evans, Andy Hall and Mark Knight

(Cambridge Archaeological Unit); Clare McNamara (National Museum of Ireland); Colchester Museums; Eva Bryant (Historic England Archive); Fraser Hunter, Matt Knight and Maggie Wilson (National Museum of Scotland); Gary Duckers (Clwyd-Powys Archaeological Trust); Gavin MacGregor (Northlight Heritage); Hazel Moore (EASE Archaeology); Jamie Quartermaine (Oxford Archaeology North); John Allan; Julie Curle; Kenny Brophy (University of Glasgow); Lisa Brown (Wiltshire Museum); Lyn Wilson (Historic Environment Scotland); Maria Medlycott (Essex County Council); Mark Gardiner (University of Lincoln); Martha Jasko-Lawrence (Museums Sheffield); Matt Brudenell (Oxford Archaeology East); Nigel Blackamore (y Gaer Museum, Art Gallery, Library—Brecon); Olivia Lelong; Penny Icke and Toby Driver (Royal Commission on the Ancient and Historical Monuments of Wales); Pippa Bradley (Wessex Archaeology); Sharon Webb and Aaron Watson (Kilmartin Museum); Stephen Carter; Stephen Weir (National Museums NI); Thomas Cadbury (Royal Albert Memorial Museum, Exeter); Wendy Mitchell (Tourism Ireland).

This book is dedicated to Anna and Florrie, my closest kin, and the ones who have given the most so that I could complete the writing.

1

INTRODUCTION

Dowris

Two men dig—it is the 1820s, in an unremarkable potato field in the middle of Ireland, close to the meeting of four townland boundaries on Lough Coura, County Offaly (Figure 1.1). Their spades turn up some broken and greened pieces of metal amongst the peaty earth. These first pieces give unexpected motivation to the men's labours, and rapidly a few objects become 'at least a horse-load of gold-coloured bronze antiquities' (Cooke 1847–1850, 424). The Dowris hoard, as the collection is now known, is the largest assemblage of Bronze Age metalwork from Ireland. The hoard comprises over 200 objects: swords and scabbard chapes, spearheads and a spear butt or butts, socketed axes and a hammer, gouges, knives and razors, cauldrons and buckets, horns and crotals, along with pieces of bronze and metalworking rubbing stones (Eogan 1983, 117–142). It was deposited in the tenth or ninth century BC (Becker 2012).

Published accounts of the Dowris discovery appeared a few decades after the event, with consequential divergences in reported facts and over its significance. Rev. Dr Thomas Robinson, an eminent academic astronomer, presented his account based on information from the Earl of Rosse, who held portions of the collection. Robinson placed the hoard in a cut-out bog where a Phoenician 'travelling merchant' had become stuck and forced to abandon his heavy load of commodities (Robinson 1847–1850, 242). Thomas Cooke, Crown Solicitor for County Offaly, claimed a first-hand account from one of the discoverers and, locating the discovery on dry ground, reasoned that the objects were the remains of a founder's workshop:

> In fine, the great quantity of things found, their variety, their being in an unfinished as well as in a finished state, the amorphous mass of spare metal, and the rub-stones, all tend to the conclusion that Dowris was the site of a manufactory of bronze utensils.
>
> *(Cooke 1847–1850, 439)*

FIGURE 1.1 An extract from the 1840 First Edition Ordnance Survey 6 inch map for County Offaly. The location of the Dowris find is marked with a star (information from Coles 1971). © Ordnance Survey Ireland/Government of Ireland; Copyright Permit No. MP 0001620.

Robinson and Cook's respective interpretations, the merchant's misfortune and the founder's safe-keeping, made common-sense of a wonderous assemblage.

A closed assemblage

Around the same time as the Dowris discovery, the curator of the Museum of Northern Antiquities in Copenhagen, Christian Thomsen, was classifying the museum's collection of artefacts into chronologically sequential groups defined by the technologies of working stone, bronze and iron (Rowley-Conwy 2007). The three-age system that Thomsen adopted was not a new idea. Lucretius, writing in the early first century BC, used the three ages to describe the development of human culture, and the scheme was reasserted by French and Danish scholars in the eighteenth century (Trigger 1989). The difference between these and Christian Thomsen's classification lay in the methodical way in which Thomsen approached the problems he faced: stone, bronze and iron were not utilised at the exclusion of one another, and there were many other materials, such as pottery, gold and wood, that occurred either intermittently or throughout prehistory. Thomsen began teasing these tangles apart by studying groups of objects that were found together in 'closed assemblages' such as graves or hoards. By comparing closed assemblages with one another, he was able to identify patterns in the variability of particular styles of artefacts within each period, and make a strong case for the integrity of the three-age model, which until then had been largely hypothetical.

The Dowris hoard provided a valuable closed assemblage with which prehistorians could apply Thomsen's approach and construct classifications and chronologies for the Bronze Age in Ireland and beyond (Figure 1.2). The term 'closed' was a misnomer, since the analysis required scholars to draw relations between the objects within the hoard and finds from elsewhere in Europe. Building on a century of scholarship, George Eogan (1964) defined the Dowris Phase through its metalwork styles and technologies, mainland European associations and ways of life. He observed plentiful links between the bronze and gold objects found in Ireland and examples from Britain, and northern and central Europe. The Dowris bucket, on stylistic grounds, originated from southeastern Europe. While some of the gold neck ornaments and sunflower pins found in other Dowris-type assemblages, Eogan interpreted as Irish manifestations of southern Scandinavian and German types.

However neatly woven Eogan's account of the Irish later Bronze Age, he had to accept that some threads lay looser around the edges of the pattern. Why was the metal placed in the ground? Eogan could not easily distinguish between utilitarian and spiritual purposes for hoarding, although he recognised the potential overlap between 'crisis and cults' (Eogan 1964, 311).

When Robinson and Cooke wrote their conflicting accounts of the Dowris discovery they appeared to at least agree on the utilitarian character of the hoard.

FIGURE 1.2 A small selection of the over 200 objects assembled at Dowris: including crotals, horns, swords, spearheads, axes and razors. © The Trustees of the British Museum. All rights reserved.

It was either a travelling merchant or the remains of a metalworking workshop. Vere Gordon Childe restated these same attributions a century later when he distinguished between hoards hidden during times of unrest by bands of 'travelling tinkers' or the remains of the 'village smithy' (Childe 1930, 45). George Eogan was less confident that hoards could be entirely explained as collections of objects hidden during periods of crisis, noting instead the ritual or cult functions that might be responsible. Nevertheless, he remained supportive of Dowris as a workshop (Eogan 1964, 311). The interpretative tide was turning, and a few years later John Coles presented the variety and unusual character of the objects found at Dowris as an accumulation of votive offerings in a sacred bog: 'the most convenient explanation of the objects from Dowris is that they represent a central offering place' (Coles 1971, 164). This idea was repeated and amplified in subsequent writing (Becker 2013, 238; Cooney and Grogan 1994, 166; Gerloff 2010, 69), and Dowris has settled as one of the 'unmarked natural locations in the landscape ... returned to for the enactment of ritual depositions over generations' (Leonard 2014, 69).

Dowris as kinwork

There are a variety of reasons to question the interpretation of Dowris as a gradual accumulation of offerings to a supernatural being. The designation of the findspot as a bog is problematic, since it is largely dependent on whose account you choose to believe. Thomas Cooke was especially clear on the matter, having been led to the location by a witness to the original discovery:

> the fact must be recorded that the Dowris relics were not found in what can be properly denominated bog, but in the centre of a potato garden extending down the slope of a rising ground between the paddock and the moorland. A cock of hay has been left during the last winter between the place of the finding and the bog, so little of wet or quagmire exists there even now.
>
> *(Cooke 1847–1850, 435)*

Unlike a river, a pool or a wetland, the bog-edge location would have made an unlikely spot for repeated offerings. Tellingly the objects were evidently recovered in a relatively tight group, given the short timeframe for their uncovering and removal from the field. While this does not preclude their deposition in a bog, it is less likely they were offerings made across years, decades or longer. By comparison, the finds from the Bog of Cullen, County Tipperary, which are also interpreted as an accumulative offering, were discovered during two centuries of turf cutting throughout the bog (Eogan 1983, 154).

I am also struck by curious symmetries in the Dowris assemblage that are difficult to interpret if the items accumulated over a long time period. There are 36 axes and 36 spearheads extant in museum collections, and the original estimate is that there were 44 spearheads and 43 axes. Of the 48 crotals (pendants), there are 20 with 12 neck ribs and 20 with 14 neck ribs. The fragments from five swords could be allied with the four large spearheads. Of the sheet-bronze vessels, there is one complete bucket and one complete cauldron. The horns are of two distinct types. The types have separate geographical distributions, divided between northeast and southwest Ireland. The single exception to this distribution is Dowris, where both types of horn were found together (Coles 1963).

These symmetries in the composition of the assemblage and the clustering of the objects in one location mean that Dowris was, at a time and place, a gathering of things and a gathering of persons. The spearheads and axes were the most numerous items in the hoard, and they were likely to have been everyday personal items—objects that people kept on their person. In support of this, the axes and spearheads have quite similar proportions of complete and slightly damaged examples. There is a logic to interpreting the 40 or so personal objects as the contributions from an equivalent number of persons with the hoard. It is a moot point whether or not the persons contributing axes and spearheads were individually present at the depositional event or if the hoard represented a process of collecting or gathering exchanges over time prior to deposition (e.g. Joy 2016). In a gift economy, things are parts of the persons that exchanged them ('things and people assume the social form of persons' (Strathern 1988, 145)), so the axes and spearheads at Dowris were co-present with the human persons with whom they were associated.

Animals were also amongst the relations gathered by the hoard, and they were present through some unusual objects: bronze horns and crotals. The graceful, curving horns, of which over 90 survive from Ireland, mimicked instruments made with cattle horns, which have not survived. John Coles (1963) classified the horns based on the slenderness of their form, the presence and style of decoration, and the ways in which they were played. The horns were used sufficiently frequently to become damaged, with two-thirds showing evidence for repairs. They were deposited in groups, up to 26 horns in the case of the Dowris hoard, and always in bogs. (Dowris may be the exception, if it was a bog-edge setting.) Coles (1965) suggested the horns formed an element in a wider 'bull cult' shared between communities as widespread as southern Scandinavia and Iberia. His key to linking this cult to Ireland was the 48 bronze crotals or pendants recovered from the Dowris hoard (Figure 1.3). The crotals are spherical or pear-shaped, hollow, and containing a small piece of bronze or stone, which rattles inside—or a 'feeble tinkling' according to Thomas Cooke (1847–1850, 431). They have a ring to enable them to be suspended, but few other clues to their function. To fit with the idea of a bull cult, John Coles argued the crotal might symbolise a bull's scrotum and so represent the animal's virility. John Waddell, while sceptical of the evidence for a 'bull cult', suggests the crotals might have been worn around the neck of a prize bull (Waddell 2010, 246), although the staples holding the suspension rings are not especially strong (Werner and Maryon in Eogan 1983, 136).

FIGURE 1.3　Three crotals from Dowris. The larger examples are c. 120 mm in length.

A reading of the early medieval Irish epic Táin Bó Cuailnge may influence these suggestions for the importance of the bull (Kinsella 1970). The stories centre on a raid by the armies of Connacht to steal the brown bull of Cuailnge. It is a misconception to imagine the animal as though it was the winner at a modern agricultural show. The bulls at the centre of the tales are begotten from two pig-herders who served their respective kings of Connact and Munster. The herders cast malign spells on each other's pigs in a quarrel that leads them to take the forms of first birds, then undersea creatures, stags, warriors, phantoms, dragons, maggots and, finally, the white and brown bulls. The principal human hero of the tales, Cúchulainn, is both human and otherworldly, and takes on multiple animal forms in his war-fuelled furies. In an analysis of the stories, Erik Larsen (2003, 182) suggests of one section that the 'ease by which the writers oscillate from man to cattle … indicates an identity ambivalent in its essence'. I am not using Táin Bó Cuailnge as an analogy for the tenth to ninth centuries BC, nor would I claim the stories have origins in the Bronze Age. The tales illustrate how the boundaries between humanity and animality may be porous: animals may act as humans, humans may act as animals. Animals may have characteristics of intentionality and personhood comparable with humans. Animals may be kin with humans. This brings a further category of actor, and kinfolk, to the assembly of the Dowris hoard: animals, possibly cattle, made present through the horns and crotals.

Assembling a world

If Dowris was partly a gathering of human and animal persons, it was also a gathering of the things and places that themselves made assemblies. The intact bucket and cauldron, both crafted from sheet bronze, were by virtue of their size best suited to preparing and sharing drink and food amongst a large gathering or long feasting event. Sabine Gerloff (2010, 64) estimates the capacity of Bronze Age cauldrons at 30–40 litres. The form and decorative elements on the base of the bucket are similar to examples from southeast Europe, and in hoards and burials elsewhere the buckets are associated with cups used in serving liquid from the vessels (Figure 1.4). The cauldron, on the other hand, is of an Irish type, round-based and with handles. The cauldrons are believed to have been suspended over a fire and used for cooking meat, with the contemporary flesh-hooks providing the means of serving food from the vessels (Needham and Bowman 2005). Both the Dowris vessels were well-used before deposition, with evidence of repairs to the bucket (Eogan 1983, 129–130) and the replacement of the cauldron's base (Gerloff 2010, 69). Their long lives may also be indicated by the period between their making and their deposition. Gerloff (1986) proposes that the bucket was made towards the end of the second millennium BC, and that the Tulnacross-type cauldrons (of which Dowris is an example) began being deposited early in the first millennium BC. This makes the bronze vessels around a century older than the other objects in the assemblage (Becker 2012), which is conceivable given their wear and repair.

FIGURE 1.4 The bronze-handled vessel found in boggy ground at Corrymuck-loch, Perthshire. The vessel is 153 mm in diameter. Image © National Museums Scotland.

The consensus amongst scholars is the cauldrons, flesh-hooks, buckets and cups were the accoutrements for prestigious feasting customs that operated throughout Atlantic Europe (Coombs 1975; Needham and Bowman 2005), and which may have derived inspiration if not identical meanings from practices in central Europe and the eastern Mediterranean (Gerloff 1986, 107). These feasts are imagined as exclusive affairs, either where a select and high status few practised elite dining rituals or a chief (usually figured as male—Brück 2019) distributed largesse upon his kinsfolk. These interpretations take account of the distant associations of the feasting practices and the styles of the feasting equipment. Distance equated with high social status, which was individualised in a chief.

Inspired by Mary Helms's writing (Helms 1988), Kristian Kristiansen and Thomas Larsson explain how chiefs acquired their elevated status within Bronze Age society:

> Magical powers and heroic fame were gained through participating in distant travels and expeditions, where chiefs could meet and compete about their skills, mythical stories and heroic deeds, and return with new knowledge, skills and fame, and with esoteric goods to symbolise their social and ritual standing.
>
> *(Kristiansen and Larsson 2005, 39)*

A vertical scale plays a pivotal role in these accounts. The chiefly class, or 'elites', at the top of the social hierarchy operated on a different spatial level to those at the bottom of the hierarchy. Elites travelled long distances and, sometimes through proxies, acquired objects and materials from outside their regions. People of lower status were defined through their labours, and the animals, grain and local resources they contributed to the wealth of chiefdoms. Within this framework, there were dependencies between high social status, inter-regional travel and exchange, and rare materials or objects. Earle and Kristiansen (2010) present a vivid contrast between the closed nature of the local and the open nature of the distant. The local is conceived as something static and inward looking: 'archaeologists should leave the safe harbours and homesteads of local processual and contextual studies and enter the roads and seaways that were travelled numerous times during the Bronze Age and beyond' (Kristiansen and Larsson 2005, 369).

The cauldrons and buckets from Dowris are large vessels that could provide for tens of participants in a feast. They also had long lives, outlasting any single individual within a community. That does not preclude them being prestigious and distantly connected objects. It does mean that in their lives they enabled the formation of a great many relations as the sources of the drink and food that bonded persons together at gatherings. These gatherings offered a variety of means for making and sustaining relations. Rather than placing the agency for these occasions with 'chiefs', I would suggest we interpret the vessels as the creators of the relations that were made during collective feasting events. As participants in these events, the vessels were in kinship with the human participants. Like the human participants, the vessels' relations stretched out geographically and through time by virtue of their long biographies.

The Dowris hoard was created through exchanges between kin and with a place. Persons were present in the hoard through their weapons, tools, and perhaps also in the contributions of their craft. Animal kin participated through the horns and crotals, which were more than representations of animals—they brought essences of the cattle to the assemblage. The collective practices of kinship were present in the feasting equipment, which included a complete bucket and a complete cauldron, alongside further fragments of vessels. The assembly was also defined by the place itself. Dowris is less than 10 kilometres east from the River Shannon, Ireland's longest river, and the location that would later take on political significance as the confluence of three of Ireland's four provinces. Yet the hoard was not placed in or by the river. The participants gathered at a bog-edge location, topographically indistinct, in a landscape otherwise empty of late Bronze Age activity. This marginality played an important role in facilitating kinwork—the practices that made and sustained kinship. All the participants may have recognised shared kinship before the assembly of the hoard. My preferred interpretation is that the hoard was an assembling of existing and new kin relations. The hoard made kin with a place: an assembly of relations that was made by and made a place in the Irish landscape.

This is not a critique of the idea of distance or an attempt to localise and close-down the Bronze Age. The point I am making is that the local was shaped by the distant, and the distant was constituted from the local. This seems to favour a flatter and relational conception of scale. It is one in which the local and the distant mutually constitute one another, rather than representing separate, hierarchically organised and perhaps contrary realities. Doreen Massey (1993) argued against the conceptualisation of places as easily determinable, bounded and spatial. She conceived of places as intersections in the networks of relations between people and things in space that transform and 'flow' with time.

Sallie Marston and colleagues (2005) draw inspiration from Doreen Massey in their theoretical critique of scale. They argue that their academic field, human geography, should dispense with scale altogether and adopt a 'flat ontology'. Attempts to conceive of scales relationally in horizontal terms, or as hybrids of horizontal and vertical, cannot escape from the fundamental hierarchies and intrinsic inequalities of concepts such as global and local, macro and micro:

> social practices are cordoned off in their respective localities (or even homes), thereby eviscerating agency at one end of the hierarchy in favour of such terms as 'global capitalism', 'international political economy', 'larger scale forces' and 'national social formations', while reserving for the lower rungs examples meant to illustrate the 'unique manifestations' of these processes in terms of local outcomes and actions, such as 'the daily sphere of the local', 'the urban as the scale of experience' and 'the smaller scale of the local'.
>
> *(Marston et al. 2005, 421)*

Discarding a scale requires less rather than more vocabulary. Terms like place and landscape, body and home, region and world can all apply in the same domains of social life. Human experiences may be said to be 'scale-insensitive', what Marilyn Strathern (2000, 53) refers to as the 'extensibility of the environment': 'values retain their relationships...and thus their significance, across different domains of life regardless of the dimensions of an event'. Throughout this book I will work from the position that places like Dowris are of a particular time and place, and simultaneously of accumulated times and places. We can address social orders in all forms through the study of places and localities. Worlds were the accumulated webs of practices and orders that humans made and inhabited through social life—'a knot in motion' (Haraway 2003, 6). Worlding, as Marisol de la Cadena (2015, 291 n4) explains it: 'is the practice of creating relations of life in a place and the place itself'.

A social prehistory

My interpretation of the Dowris metalwork emphasises the relations that brought the assemblage into being. I use the terms 'kinship' and 'kinwork' to describe the relations and the activities that made them. I did not place hard boundaries between the humans, animals and things that composed the Dowris assemblage. With the remainder of this chapter I will present an argument for the approach to kinship that guides the book's narrative. I begin with my use of the adjective 'social' in the book's title. Why not simply 'prehistory' (cf. Webmoor and Witmore 2008)? *Social* directs attention to the associations that emerge as humans inhabit their worlds. These associations make persons, create collectives, and bring lives and meanings to things, places and events. My approach is influenced by Bruno Latour's (2005) 'sociology of associations'. Latour argues that research should begin with the proposition we do not know what the social is made from. Researching social life involves a slow process of identifying the participants and following the associations. This approach differs from methods that claim to know from the beginning 'roughly what the social world is made of' (Latour 2005, 160). If the social is too closely constrained within models and categories, then we (researchers, prehistorians) in turn constrain our capacities to recognise diversity and difference. We struggle with recognising our mistranslations, gaps in knowledge and the incompatibilities of our theories. The categories used to describe social life occupy and determine the beginning, the middle and the end of the inquiries.

In accounts of Bronze Age societies, social life is often composed with theories about group and individual identities that exist independently of the material evidence from the past. Prehistories begin with households, families, lineages, clans, chiefdoms and polities already in mind. Individuals become present through their roles as warriors and wives, farmers, miners, shamans, smiths, chiefs and adventurers. Prehistorians use these identities, and the concepts they represent, for different reasons. The personal and collective identities populate a coherent framework for writing about society. They bring explanatory power to material that is difficult to comprehend because of its immense distance from our present-day experiences and worldviews. They connect our present with a Bronze Age past using familiar language. Often enough we shortcut the task of describing social life by using terms that are ready to hand: 'elite', both as noun and adjective, is one such shortcut. The language and the concepts carry many assumptions that constrain our narratives.

A model of society and pre-defined identifiers are not necessary for researching past social life. Some archaeologists have worked steadily and effectively to introduce new ways of thinking that undermine the assumptions we bring as modern humans encountering ancient material culture (as with Brück 2019; Conneller 2012; Lucas 2012). These empirical and theoretical investigations question the separations of rituals from everyday practices, people from environments and things, experience from meaning. They share a critique of the binary categorisations of the world that seem intrinsic to modern worldviews. Amongst the catalysts are relational ways of thinking that describe worlds as assemblages (DeLanda 2006), actor-networks (Latour 2005), meshworks (Ingold 2011), entanglements (Hodder 2012) and ontologies (Holbraad and Pedersen 2017). These ideas appear in different guises, whether non-representational theory, assemblage theory, new materialism or the 'ontological turn'. Their influence on archaeology is well documented (Hamilakis and Jones 2017; Harris and Cipolla 2017; Jervis 2019). Whatever the metaphors, styles and distinctions, the common framework can be defined broadly as *relational*.

Thinking through relations (or associations) allows social life to remain complicated, ephemeral and messy (Law 2004), while offering a means of tracing the formation and significances of persons, ideas and institutions. It acknowledges flow, and offers means (the connector, association or line) that temporarily holds participants (whether human or not) in place and for their relative locations to be mapped. It decentres humans, so that they remain part of although never entirely in control of, or makers of, the worlds they inhabit. In Theodore Schatzki's (2002, 123) words:

> Social life transpires through human activity and is caught up in orders of people, artefacts, organisms, and things. As such, it is not just immersed in a mesh of practices and orders, but also exists only as so entangled. The mesh of practices and orders is the site where social life takes place.

A relational approach accounts for the infinite ways in which things, places and persons may be constituted, while offering a method for describing and comparing. It brings multiple ways of configuring how humanity and nature are constituted (Strathern 1988; Viveiros de Castro 2015).

Relational approaches have met with plentiful criticism. They do not offer a theory of the world, rather they provide methods for building theories about worlds. They appear better at describing than explaining. Their specificities can lead to close engagements with practices and things, while wider observations about regularities in how social life is organised are absent. But the descriptions, however geographically or historically defined, can appear similar to one another. An example is the 'dividual' person, conceived in Hindu Indian and Melanesian ethnographies (Marriott 1976; Strathern 1988), deftly and imaginatively applied to the interpretation of early Bronze Age burials (Brück 2006) and subsequently becoming the consensus about the formation of personhood in the British Bronze Age. An approach (a relational study of personhood) evolves into a theory (persons are divisible) and then an instance (Bronze Age persons were dividual), without sufficient disruption and qualification from the observations prehistorians make about material culture (Sørensen 2010).

Decentring humans within social life returns symmetry in the relations between people and things (Henare et al. 2005) recognises the influences and vibrancies of materials (Bennett 2010), and disperses agency (the capacity to act intentionally) across collectives. This exercise plays to archaeology's strengths in attending to and understanding things and substances. Unlike anthropology, where humans are subjects of enquiry and co-participants in research, people's voices and much of their presence are absent from prehistoric research. It might well be asked whether a 'return to things' means much in an academic field that cannot move for things. Prehistorians were criticised for giving things undue priority in social processes long before object biographies and vibrant matter were in vogue. John Barrett (2016) identifies what he terms 'a new antiquarianism' in archaeology's ontological turn or its 'return to things'. He challenges the claim that description is sufficient. By emphasising the descriptions of assemblages, relational approaches have exorcised depth and humanness from narratives of prehistory. There is similarity here with Paolo Heywood's entreaty for relational approaches to be purposeful. To mean anything distinctive, relational studies have to be clear about what they wish to achieve (Heywood 2018, 233).

In this book I follow a relational approach to composing the synthesis. Relations connected people with one another, with objects, and with substances, places, animals and beings from other worlds. I describe things, architectures and places emerging and acting in relation with humans. While seeking to retain a relational approach within the synthesis, I am mindful of the criticisms I outlined earlier. How do I retain an attention on humanity in a prehistory of associations? Are there ways to give priority to certain kinds of associations, and therefore bring a theoretical discrimination to the process of synthesis? How do I identify and represent the depth and persistence of certain relations through time?

Kinship and the genealogical method

My response to the questions I pose above is to situate kinship at the core of this book's narratives. I regard kinship as a distinct form of relation, and kinwork as a distinct practice of relating. The distinctions that elevate kinship from other forms of relatedness are in degrees of intensity and mutuality. Following Marshall Sahlins (2013), I define kinship as a 'mutuality of being', or what Stasch (2009, 129) calls an 'intersubjective belonging'. Kinship describes the close relations and practices of relating that constitute humans as persons and groups. These relations include those generated through procreation and established through the many varied acts of naming, co-presence, gift exchange and sharing substances that have been documented amongst societies worldwide.

This definition moves away from the genealogical method that dominated kinship studies for much of the twentieth century. A biological theory of kinship, or the genealogical method, gave primacy to the relations of birth (nature) onto which categories and systems (culture) were then applied: 'the elements of the physical pattern are essentially simple and universal, whilst the social patterns imposed on it are highly diversified and complex' (Gellner 1960, 193). For societies without state-structures, kinship provided the basis for the political economy and the genealogical method mapped kinship and the organisation of authority. This enabled societal organisation to be comprehended in its entirety through levels and degrees of connection and separation, which in diagrammatic form had 'the sterile austerity of an electrical circuit board' (Ingold 2007, 111) or 'a totality present in simultaneity' (Bourdieu 1977, 38). Prehistorians benefited from the societal models that emerged from anthropology's obsession with kinship. It may not have been possible to 'dig up a kinship system' as Gosden (1999, 4) characterised Lewis Binford's (1962, 218) position on the matter. However, it was possible to apply principles derived from anthropology to the interpretation of archaeological material (Ellison 1981; Rowlands 1980).

The biological theory of kinship was transformed through accumulated ethnographic studies and anthropological critiques during the later decades of the twentieth century. A key shift came in new conceptualisations of nature and culture, which challenged the binary relationship that underpinned the genealogical method. In her ethnography written while researching the Hagen in Papua New Guinea, Marilyn Strathern (1980) argues that the strict dualistic pattern of male:wild female:tamed is not a universal structural principle to which all humans adhered. The concepts of nature and culture, so fundamental to modern European thought, are contingent on who as well as where they are applied. David Schneider (1984) directed a similar critique at the idea of kinship and anthropology's reliance on kinship. Schneider argued that the priority given to biological relations represented a Western assumption about the primacy of sexual reproduction. He observed that the genealogical method will always find kinship structures at the core of small-scale political economies because it starts with the categories of relation already pre-formed: 'The genealogical method cannot but confirm that genealogical relations constitute the basis of the notions of relatedness in all societies' (Holy 1996, 146).

The anthropology of kinship gradually emerged from this critique in different forms and with a more diverse theoretical literature. A form of the traditional, genealogical method persisted or 'metamorphized' (Godelier 2011). Domains that had earlier taken prominence in kinship studies found new expressions in studies of personhood and domestic life (Busby 1997; Joyce and Gillespie 2000). The impacts of new reproductive technologies on sexual relationships, families and communities formed a further focus for attention (Bamford 2007). Archaeologists have contributed to the reconceptualising of kinship through their contributions on personhood and houses (Casella and Fowler 2006; González-Ruibal and Ruiz-Gálvez 2016), and in shaping discussions around the deep history of kinship structures (Ensor 2011; Trautmann et al. 2011).

Biomolecular and genetic analyses can now define the biological relatedness of ancient human remains with remarkable precision. The power of these methods and richness of the data offers potential for reconstructing biological relatedness across populations and between individuals. Palaeogenetics borrows its terms for relatedness from anthropology: patrilineal, matrilineal, lineage, clan and so on (Sánchez-Quinto et al. 2019; Zeng et al. 2018). Its network diagrams representing genetic diversity and connectedness parallel those produced from ethnographic studies. Palaeogenetic research is 'big science': in the amount of funding, in the size of datasets and in the ambition and appeal of the explanations it presents about the past. The disciplinary conventions, ambition and status of science require publication of short-form papers in a handful of prestigious journals. These formats leave no space for longer, contextual expositions on either the archaeological evidence or theories of relatedness, mobility and culture (Booth 2019, 593). The risk is that reductive historical narratives are heard most clearly within academic and public contexts. And that kinship returns to being a synonym for biological relatedness, and all the theoretical 'heavy-lifting' of recent decades is over-shadowed by a more widely heard genealogical method.

Kinship in five premises

Several reasons emerge for foregrounding kinship in my synthesis of Bronze Age Ireland and Britain. Kinship prioritises certain kinds of associations, and brings a theoretical discrimination and explanatory power to a relational synthesis. Kinship places the emphasis on humanity and humanness in a prehistory of associations. The transformation, or reinvention, of kinship theory during the last two decades has broadened the realms and practices of kinship. It now informs and is informed by broadly relational approaches that share considerable ground with archaeological theorising. This forms part of a wider rebalancing in what might be called an asymmetry in the relations between archaeological and anthropological theory (Yarrow 2010).

A different asymmetry is emerging in kinship research, this time between the life and social sciences. Biomolecular and genetic analyses now define the biological relatedness of ancient human remains with extraordinary precision. Bioarchaeology and palaeogenetics are applying methods that 'excavate' kinship. The risk is that we take this literally, and the biological relations identified through palaeogenetic analysis become kinship facts, around which we then fashion an interpretative culture. The response must be to keep the dialogue open between the fields within the natural and social sciences, and focus on the means, theoretical and empirical, for integrating accounts of social life (Johnson 2019; Johnson and Paul 2016; Nash 2018). Explanations will be reductive where this integration fails to account for advancements of social theory and biological science.

I embed kinship and kinwork throughout this book's narratives. Kinship is the lens through which I view the task of writing a social prehistory of Bronze

Age Britain and Ireland. Kinship describes the close relations and practices of relating that constitute humans as persons and groups. The distinctions that define kinship from other forms of relating are in degrees of intensity, mutuality and belonging. I will close this theoretical discussion by describing the scope of my relational theory of kinship in five premises.

Kinship creates personhood and collective belonging. Kinship is both a constituent of persons and networks of persons. Kinsfolk are 'persons who belong to one another, who are parts of one another, who are co-present in each other, whose lives are joined and interdependent' (Sahlins 2013, 21). In this respect, kinship is much the same as a partible theory of personhood: persons are the 'plural and composite site of the relationships that produced them' (Strathern 1988, 13). Persons embody their kin relations, and those relations comprise the myriad ways in which persons participate in others' lives. Kinship is a transpersonal way of belonging. Kinship is 'intrinsic to the person, but also capable of overcoming the boundedness of particular bodies and persons' (Carsten 2004, 107). In Alan Rumsey's (2000) study of the pronoun 'I' in Polynesia and Melanesia, he observed that a speaker can use 'I' in reference to a variety of social configurations, including themselves, their kin group or an ancestor. Kinship provides a means of going beyond the constitution of persons, and considers the formulation of groups, places, ancestries and so forth. It represents the different ways that people belong: to one another, to places and to histories.

Kinship associates people with nonhuman beings, things and landscapes. Kin may be animals; supernatural entities; and persons, things and places. Peoples may describe their descent from gods and seek kinship with ancestral beings. In Maori sagas, humans share descent with a variety of other beings: from flies and whales to trees and canoes (Johansen 1954). Kinship is created through gift exchange, with gifts taking on the roles of persons or parts of persons existing within gifts (Gregory 2015). Exchange extends the distances across which kinship may be maintained, with things participating in the formation and maintenance of kinship alongside and as parts of persons.

> Perhaps the most serious of the many weaknesses of [kinship] diagrams ... is that they only include people: occasionally a god or an ancestor-turned-animal may be admitted as a quasi-human circle or triangle, but only on the condition that we recognise them as quasi-kin. There is no symbol for a spring, river, mountain, mist or whale. In divorcing the humanity from the materiality of kinship, these charts reinforce an understanding of kinship as ultimately transcendent when what we should be seeking is a deeper understanding of the ways in which the humanity and materiality of kinship are implicated in each other's emergence.
>
> *(Sissons 2013, 373)*

The multiple ways in which animals were incorporated alongside humans in Bronze Age funerary assemblages illustrate how these relations could be assembled

(Brück 2019). Land and places played their parts: 'the land is very much alive and enters directly into the constitution (generation) of persons' (Leach 2003, 30). During the Bronze Age, kinmaking with living places can be recognised by the deposition of metalwork as votive offerings and the persistence of landmarking with monuments and boundaries.

Kinship is historically constituted, territorialised and codified. Kinship has structural attributes by virtue of its persistence through time, culture, materiality and beings: whether in language, habits, rituals, houses, things and bodies. DeLanda (2006) uses the terms territorialisation and codification to describe the ways that assemblages stabilise, consolidate and constrain social life. These processes are properties of the assemblages and not external structures that impose an order from without. Territorialisation and codification offer expressions of the 'depth' or historical conditions that Barrett (2016) argues are lacking from relational approaches in archaeology. 'Descent' has been used to describe the way that some forms of kinship can accumulate through time, endure across generations and stretch into mythic time. Descent may distinguish kinship that is reproduced in political and public practices, rather than in the co-presences of daily life. The linear arrangements of barrows built during the nineteenth and eighteenth centuries BC provide an example of how the material conditions for lines of descent were created and mobilised in the legitimation of authority.

Kinship is made through the sharing of substances and presences. A biological theory of kinship essentialises sexual reproduction and the affinal relations (through institutions like marriage) that enable reproduction. Other relations are recognised within a biological theory as either fictive or lying outside the proper domain of kinship. A relational theory of kinship accommodates kinmaking through the sharing of substances, including though not exclusively through procreation: human blood, milk, bone, food and soil can all contribute. Kin may share the same bones (Bloch 1992, 75), consume one another's flesh (Fausto 2007) or be made in the meals cooked from a shared hearth (Carsten 1997). Francesca Merlan and Alan Rumsey (1991, 43) describe how the Ku Waru (New Guinea) derive their kinship from the soil, which contains *kopong*, the matter that gives life to all beings: 'a kind of *nutritive* substance, whether extracted directly from the gardens, channelled through man's reproductive organs, woman's breast, or stored and consumed in the flesh of a pig'. A sharing of substances may be equated with co-presences of bodies and in spaces. Kinship emerges from a mutuality of existence and the affectivity that emanates from proximities—'to live with kin is life itself' (Gow 1991, 119). Janet Carsten (2004, 35) writes that the 'qualitative density of experiences' is what makes houses important for kinmaking. The times spent in one another's presence, sharing knowledge, labour, food and nurture, contribute to the affective qualities of kinship.

Kinship is creative, performative and political. Kinship can be unstable and need work to sustain it. Mark Nuttall (2000) describes how Greenlanders choose many of their kin according to circumstance. Naming plays a key part in this process, with a shift from using personal to kin names providing the means of framing particular associations as kin-based. Obligations and rights constrain the fluidity of these relations; they are flexible, not formless. Stefano Boni (2010) drew similar conclusions from his study of funeral ledgers in the Akan area of West Africa. Funeral offerings are a means of making and severing kinship, although it is not a process of unconstrained invention. Norms and sanctions control creativity. Kinship may be core to destructive and contestable relations (Sahlins 2013, 53–57). Marriage exchanges within exogamous societies create inequalities between the affinal groups, for which bride-wealth and dowry may operate as recompense. Descent and inheritance create opportunities for theft as well as gift (Lambek 2011). The arenas for creating powerful kin during the Bronze Age varied through time, and from the personal to the collective: in lavish funerary offerings, intimate and rare gifts to gods, the labours gathered at monuments and hilltop enclosures and the violence of raids and inter-personal conflict.

The five premises map a relational approach to kinship: collective belonging, plurality of relations, historical, commensal and creative. They constitute kinship but they do not determine how it is manifest in particular settings. If kin relations connect different domains of life and life's many participants, human and otherwise, then, Marshall Sahlins (2013) contends, kinship is cultural not biological relatedness. Eduardo Viveiros de Castro phrases this same idea in a different way when describing the formation of kinship in Amazonia: 'kinship is what you have when you "do without" a biological theory of relationality' (Viveiros de Castro 2009, 241). This broader conceptualisation of kinship is worth defending as new methods sharpen the potential of biological relations. If we break from a genealogical model, then different dimensions become possible within kinship. Kinwork maps out some of the variations in how persons, groups, things and places are constituted.

Gifts, Dwellings, Landmarks

This book brings kinship to the task of explaining the formation of social life in Bronze Age Britain and Ireland. The book divides into three parts, each comprised of two chapters: Gifts, Dwellings and Landmarks. These are convenient compartments within which to organise the narrative. Gifts, Dwellings and Landmarks are distinguishable and closely connected aspects of past social life. The parts are ordered chronologically so that they present independent historical narratives. I have not used established schemes for organising the Bronze Age, whether the quadripartite system (Chalcolithic, Early, Middle and Late Bronze Age) or periodisations based on artefacts. In their place, I have followed centennial, and occasionally decadal where available, timescales, which are more sensitive to the different resolutions of archaeological chronologies and historical processes. A calendrical framework can better accommodate the different rhythms, resolutions and asynchronies of change. As a consequence of these asynchronies and the different precisions within archaeological timescales, the paired chapters within each part are divided at different times during the Bronze Age and with differing degrees of overlap.

Part I, *Gifts*, examines human mortuary rites and the deposition of metalwork and other valued objects in the landscape. These were the practices through which persons and things were exchanged within and between worlds. Prehistorians have recognised similarities and differences in the ways things and people were treated at the ends of their lives. The differences depended on the exclusion of certain types of objects from one domain (axes were absent from human burials) compared with another (axes were frequently left in unmarked places throughout the landscape). Similarities are recognisable in the ways that things were treated as persons (carefully arranged for burial within a barrow or cairn) and humans were transformed and used like other materials (when cremated bone was used as votive offerings within settlements). Gifts, with the dead and in the landscape, were important and creative kinwork. They were exchanges amongst persons and with supernatural beings, and they offer glimpses of how kinship was constituted through time. The chapters' chronological sequence is divided at around the time that cremation returned as a widespread practice throughout Britain and Ireland, which occurred during the twentieth to eighteenth centuries BC.

In Part II, *Dwellings*, I consider the archaeological remains of domestic life. I discuss the changing architecture of house and of settlements, the ways that daily life left traces in places even when people did not live in durable buildings and the rituals that took place within domestic settings. Settlements were the places where people shared meals and shared their lives. The accumulations of food waste, pottery and burnt stone within settlements are evidence for the intensities, durations and richness of inhabitation. Settlements were places where some of the deepest bonds of kinship were formed. They hosted large gatherings and selective feasts, and provided the stages for performing life-cycle rites. The distinctions were blurred between these practices and the depositional events I discuss in Part I. The chapters in Dwellings overlap by two centuries and are divided at around the time that settlements took on more powerful and intense roles in social life, during the thirteenth and twelfth centuries BC. The overlap between the chapters is around two centuries, and it could have been more. Settlements were long-lived, and it is difficult to establish archaeological chronologies from the accumulated residues of everyday life.

The chapters in Part III, *Landmarks*, are concerned with the different ways that people's relations with land and sky shaped the places of Bronze Age Britain and Ireland. Landmarking includes a breadth of building and ritual practices, encompassing barrows, cairns and circles, rock art, cairnfields and field systems. These were places where people's labours and performances made kin between themselves and other selves who inhabited a living land and vibrant sky. Changes in landmarking mattered because they were part of how persons and kindred were constituted. The practices defined in Gifts and in Dwellings are blended throughout Landmarks: in the mortuary deposits within monuments, and in the shared labours involved in creating hilltop enclosures. The chapters in Landmarks overlap across seven centuries during 2200–1500 BC. The narrative dismantles the categorical barriers that prehistorians have placed between monumental and agricultural landscapes. The animate land remained an important aspect of kinship throughout the Bronze Age, even if the associations and the practices of kinmaking changed.

I conclude the book by reviewing the long-term processes that transformed social life during the twenty-fifth to eighth centuries BC. Kinship was not a stable category within social life. Kin were made from blends of processes that we define as biological and cultural. The early centuries of the Bronze Age were characterised by a fluidity of kin relations that absorbed unfamiliar populations and cultures into social life. Localisation describes the process through which people increasingly belonged to landscapes and places. This occurred alongside and shaped the growing distinctions between regions in Ireland and Britain. A gradual empowerment of domestic life occurred as houses replaced monuments as landmarks. The performative and public aspects of kinmaking were founded on relations with the supernatural, in personal and communal rituals, and in acts of raiding, collective labour and feasting. The differences in kinwork across Ireland and Britain brought textures to social life and the formation of Bronze Age worlds.

References

Bamford, Sandra C. 2007. *Biology unmoored: Melanesian reflections on life and biotechnology.* University of California Press, Berkeley.

Barrett, John C. 2016. The new antiquarianism? *Antiquity* 90(354):1681–1686.

Becker, Katharina. 2012. The dating of Irish Late Bronze Age Dowris phase metalwork—a pilot study. *Journal of Irish Archaeology* 21:7–15.

Becker, Katharina. 2013. Transforming identities – new approaches to Bronze Age deposition in Ireland. *Proceedings of the Prehistoric Society* 79:225–263.

Bennett, Jane. 2010. *Vibrant matter: a political ecology of things.* Duke University Press, London.

Binford, Lewis R. 1962. Archaeology as anthropology. *American Antiquity* 28(2):217–225.

Bloch, Maurice. 1992. *Prey into hunter: the politics of religous experience.* Cambridge University Press, Cambridge.

Boni, Stefano. 2010. Brothers 30,000, sisters 20,000; nephews 15,000, nieces 10,000: Akan funeral ledgers' kinship and value negotiations, and their limits. *Ethnography* 11(3):381–408.

Booth, Thomas. 2019. A stranger in a strange land: a perspective on archaeological responses to the palaeogenetic revolution from an archaeologist working amongst palaeogeneticists. *World Archaeology* 51(4):586–601.

Bourdieu, Pierre. 1977. *Outline of a theory of practice,* translated by Richard Nice. Cambridge University Press, Cambridge.

Brück, Joanna. 2006. Homing instincts: grounded identities and dividual selves in the British Bronze Age. In *The archaeology of plural and changing identities,* edited by Eleanor Conlin Casella and Chris Fowler, pp. 135–160. Springer, Boston, MA.

Brück, Joanna. 2019. *Personifying prehistory: relational ontologies in Bronze Age Britain and Ireland.* Oxford University Press, Oxford.

Busby, Cecilia. 1997. Permeable and partible persons: a comparative analysis of gender and body in South India and Melanesia. *Journal of the Royal Anthropological Institute* 3(2):261–278.

Carsten, Janet. 1997. *The heat of the hearth: the process of kinship in a Malay fishing community.* Clarendon Press, Oxford.

Carsten, Janet. 2004. *After kinship.* Cambridge University Press, Cambridge.

Casella, Eleanor Conlin and Chris Fowler (editors). 2006. *The archaeology of plural and changing identities.* Springer, Boston, MA.

Childe, V G. 1930. *The Bronze Age.* Cambridge University Press, Cambridge.

Coles, John. 1963. Irish Bronze Age horns and their relations with northern Europe. *Proceedings of the Prehistoric Society* 29:326–356.

Coles, John. 1965. The archaeological evidence for a 'bull cult' in Late Bronze Age Europe. *Antiquity* 39(155):217–219.

Coles, John. 1971. Dowris and the Late Bronze Age of Ireland: a footnote. *Journal of the Royal Society of Antiquaries of Ireland* 101(2):164–165.

Conneller, Chantal. 2012. *An archaeology of materials: substantial transformations in early prehistoric Europe.* Routledge, London.

Cooke, Thomas L. 1847–1850. On bronze antiquities found at Dowris, in the King's County. *Proceedings of the Royal Irish Academy* 4:423–440.

Coombs, David G. 1975. Bronze Age weapon hoards in Britain. *Archaeologia Atlantica* 1:49–81.

Cooney, Gabriel and Eoin Grogan. 1994. *Irish prehistory: a social perspective.* Wordwell, Dublin.

de la Cadena, Marisol. 2015. *Earth beings: ecologies of practice across Andean worlds.* Duke University Press, London.

DeLanda, Manuel. 2006. *A new philosophy of society: assemblage theory and social complexity.* Bloomsbury, London.

Earle, Timothy and Kristian Kristiansen. 2010. Introduction. In *Organizing Bronze Age societies: the Mediterranean, central Europe and Scandinavia compared*, edited by Timothy Earle and Kristian Kristiansen, pp. 1–33. Cambridge University Press, Cambridge.

Ellison, Ann. 1981. Towards a socio-economic model for the Middle Bronze Age in southern England. In *Patterns of the past: studies in honour of David Clarke*, edited by Ian Hodder, Glynn Isaac and Norman Hammond, pp. 413–438. Cambridge University Press, Cambridge.

Ensor, Bradley E. 2011. Kinship theory in archaeology: from critiques to the study of transformations. *American Antiquity* 76(2):203–227.

Eogan, George. 1964. The later Bronze Age in Ireland in the light of recent research. *Proceedings of the Prehistoric Society* 30:268–351.

Eogan, George. 1983. *The hoards of the Irish Later Bronze Age.* University College Dublin, Dublin.

Fausto, Carlos. 2007. Feasting on people: eating animals and humans in Amazonia. *Current Anthropology* 48(4):497–530.

Gellner, Ernest. 1960. The concept of kinship: with special reference to Mr. Needham's "Descent systems and ideal language". *Philosophy of Science* 27:187–204.

Gerloff, Sabine. 1986. Bronze Age class A cauldrons: typology, origins and chronology. *Journal of the Royal Society of Antiquaries of Ireland* 116:84–115.

Gerloff, Sabine. 2010. *Atlantic cauldrons and buckets of the Late Bronze Age and Early Iron Age in western Europe.* Prähistorische Bronzefunde II/18, Stuttgart.

Godelier, Maurice. 2011. *The metaphorses of kinship.* Verso, London.

González-Ruibal, Alfredo and Marisa Ruiz-Gálvez. 2016. House societies in the ancient Mediterranean (2000–500 BC). *Journal of World Prehistory* 29:383–437.

Gosden, Chris. 1999. *Anthropology and archaeology: a changing relationship*. Routledge, London.

Gow, Peter. 1991. *Of mixed blood: kinship and history in Peruvian Amazonia*. Clarendon Press, Oxford.

Gregory, Christopher A. 2015. *Gifts and commodities (second edition)*. Hau, Chicago, IL.

Hamilakis, Yannis and Andrew Meirion Jones. 2017. Archaeology and assemblage. *Cambridge Archaeological Journal* 27(1):77–84.

Haraway, Donna. 2003. *The companion species manifesto: dogs, people and significant otherness*. Prickly Paradigm Press, Chicago, IL.

Harris, Oliver J T and Craig N Cipolla. 2017. *Archaeological theory in the new millennium: introducing current perspectives*. Routledge, London.

Helms, Mary. 1988. *Ulysses' sail: an ethnographic odyssey of power, knowledge, and geographical distance*. Princeton University Press, Princeton, NJ.

Henare, Amiria, Martin Holbraad and Sari Wastell (editors). 2005. *Thinking through things: theorising artefacts ethnographically*. Routledge, London.

Heywood, Paolo. 2018. The ontological turn: school or style. In *Schools and styles of anthropological theory*, edited by Matei Candea, pp. 224–235. Routledge, London.

Hodder, Ian. 2012. *Entangled: an archaeology of the relationships between humans and things*. John Wiley, Chichester.

Holbraad, Martin and Morten Axel Pedersen. 2017. *The ontological turn: an anthropological exposition*. Cambridge University Press, Cambridge.

Holy, Ladislav. 1996. *Anthropological perspectives on kinship*. Pluto, London.

Ingold, Tim. 2007. *Lines: a brief history*. Routledge, London.

Ingold, Tim. 2011. *Being alive: essays on movement, knowledge and description*. Routledge, London.

Jervis, Ben. 2019. *Assemblage thought and archaeology*. Routledge, London.

Johansen, Jørgen Prytz. 1954. *The Maori and his religion*. Munksgaard, Copenhagen.

Johnson, Kent M. 2019. Opening up the family tree: promoting more diverse and inclusive studies of family, kinship, and relatedness in bioarchaeology. In *Bioarchaeologists speak out: deep time perspectives on contemporary issues*, edited by Jane Buikstra, pp. 201–230. Springer, Cham.

Johnson, Kent M and Kathleen S Paul. 2016. Bioarchaeology and kinship: integrating theory, social relatedness, and biology in ancient family research. *Journal of Archaeological Research* 24:75–123.

Joy, Jody. 2016. Hoards as collections: re-examining the Snettisham Iron Age hoards from the perspective of collecting practice. *World Archaeology* 48(2):239–253.

Joyce, Rosemary A and Susan D Gillespie (editors). 2000. *Beyond kinship: social and material reproduction in house societies*. University of Pennsylvania Press, Philadelphia.

Kinsella, Thomas. 1970. *The Táin: translated from the Irish epic Táin Bó Cuailnge*. Oxford University Press, Oxford.

Kristiansen, Kristian and Thomas Larsson. 2005. *The rise of Bronze Age society: travels, transmissions and transformations*. Cambridge University Press, Cambridge.

Lambek, Michael. 2011. Kinship as gift and theft: acts of succession in Mayotte and Ancient Israel. *American Ethnologist* 38(1):2–16.

Larsen, Erik. 2003. Cú Chulainn: god, man, or animal? *Proceedings of the Harvard Celtic Colloquium* 23:172–183.

Latour, Bruno. 2005. *Reassembling the social: an introduction to actor-network theory*. Oxford University Press, Oxford.

Law, John. 2004. *After method: mess in social science research*. Routledge, London.

Leach, James. 2003. *Creative land: place and procreation on the Rai Coast of Papua New Guinea*. Berghahn Books, Oxford.

Leonard, Katherine. 2014. *Ritual in Late Bronze Age Ireland: material culture, practices, landscape setting and social context*. PhD thesis, National University of Ireland, Galway.

Lucas, Gavin. 2012. *Understanding the archaeological record*. Cambridge University Press, Cambridge.

Marriott, McKim. 1976. Hindu transactions: diversity without dualism. In *Transaction and meaning: directions in the anthropology of exchange and symbolic behavior*, edited by Bruce Kapferer, pp. 109–142. Institute for the study of human issues, Philadelphia, PA.

Marston, Sallie A, John Paul Jones and Keith Woodward. 2005. Human geography without scale. *Transactions of the Institute of British Geographers* 30(4):416–432.

Massey, Doreen. 1993. Power-geometry and a progressive sense of place. In *Mapping the futures: local cultures, global change*, edited by John Bird, Barry Curtis, Tim Putnam and Lisa Tickner, pp. 59–69. Routledge, London.

Merlan, Francesca and Alan Rumsey. 1991. *Ku Waru: language and segmentary politics in the Western Nebilyer Valley*. Cambridge University Press, Cambridge.

Nash, Catherine. 2018. Making kinship with human remains: repatriation, biomedicine and the many relations of Charles Byrne. *Environment and Planning D: Society and Space* 36(5):867–884.

Needham, Stuart and Sheridan Bowman. 2005. Flesh-hooks, technological complexity and the Atlantic Bronze Age feasting complex. *European Journal of Archaeology* 8(2):93–136.

Nuttall, Mark. 2000. Choosing kin: sharing and subsistence in a Greenlandic hunting community. In *Dividends of kinship: meanings and uses of social relatedness*, edited by Peter P Schweitzer, pp. 33–60. Routledge, London.

Robinson, Thomas R. 1847–1850. On the contents of an ancient bronze vessel found in the King's county. *Proceedings of the Royal Irish Academy* 4:237–246.

Rowlands, Michael. 1980. Kinship, alliance and exchange in the European Bronze Age. In *Settlement and society in the British later Bronze Age*, edited by John C Barrett and Richard Bradley, pp. 59–72. BAR British Series, 83. British Archaeological Reports, Oxford.

Rowley-Conwy, Peter. 2007. *From Genesis to prehistory: the archaeological three age system and its contested reception in Denmark, Britain, and Ireland*. Oxford University Press, Oxford.

Rumsey, Alan. 2000. Agency, personhood and the 'I' of discourse in the Pacific and beyond. *Journal of the Royal Anthropological Institute* 6(1):101–115.

Sahlins, Marshall. 2013. *What kinship is—and is not*. University of Chicago Press, Chicago, IL.

Sánchez-Quinto, Federico, Helena Malmström, Magdalena Fraser, Linus Girdland-Flink, Emma M Svensson, Luciana G. Simões, Robert George, Nina Hollfelder, Göran Burenhult, Gordon Noble, Kate Britton, Sahra Talamo, Neil Curtis, Hana Brzobohata, Radka Sumberova, Anders Götherström, Jan Storå and Mattias Jakobsson. 2019. Megalithic tombs in western and northern Neolithic Europe were linked to a kindred society. *Proceedings of the National Academy of Sciences* 116(19):9469–9474.

Schatzki, Theodore R. 2002. *The site of the social: a philosophical account of the constitution of social life and change*. Pennsylvania State University Press, University Park, PA.

Schneider, David M. 1984. *A critique of the study of kinship*. University of Michigan Press, Ann Arbor.

Sissons, Jeffrey. 2013. Reterritorialising kinship: the Māori "hapū". *Journal of the Polynesian Society* 122(4):373–391.

Sørensen, Marie Louise Stig. 2010. Bronze Age bodiness – maps and coordinates. In *Body parts and bodies whole: changing relations and meanings*, edited by Katharina Rebay-Salisbury, Marie Louise Stig Sørensen and Jessica Hughes, pp. 54–63. Oxbow, Oxford.

Stasch, Rupert. 2009. *Society of others: kinship and mourning in a West Papuan place*. University of California Press, Berkeley.

Strathern, Marilyn. 1980. No nature, no culture: the Hagan case. In *Nature, culture and gender*, edited by Carol P MacCormack and Marilyn Strathern, pp. 174–222. Cambridge University Press, Cambridge.

Strathern, Marilyn. 1988. *The gender of the gift: problems with women and problems with society in Melanesia*. University of California Press, Berkeley.

Strathern, Marilyn. 2000. Environments within: an ethnographic commentary on scale. In *Culture, landscape, and the environment: the Linacre Lectures 1997*, edited by Kate Flint and Howard Morphy, pp. 44–71. Oxford University Press, Oxford.

Trautmann, Thomas R, Gillian Feeley-Harnik and John C Mitani. 2011. Deep kinship. In *Deep history: the architecture of past and present*, edited by Andrew Shyrock and Daniel Lord Smail, pp. 160–188. University of California Press, Berkeley.

Trigger, Bruce. 1989. *A history of archaeological thought*. Cambridge University Press, Cambridge.

Viveiros de Castro, Eduardo. 2009. The gift and the given: three nano-essays on kinship and magic. In *Kinship and beyond: the geneaological model reconsidered*, edited by Sandra C Bamford and James Leach, pp. 237–268. Berghahn, New York.

Viveiros de Castro, Eduardo. 2015. *The relative native: essays on indigenous conceptual worlds*. Hau, Chicago, IL.

Waddell, John. 2010. *The prehistoric archaeology of Ireland*. Wordwell, Dublin.

Webmoor, Timothy and Christopher L Witmore. 2008. Things are us! A commentary on human/things relations under the banner of a 'social' archaeology. *Norwegian Archaeological Review* 41(1):53–70.

Yarrow, Thomas. 2010. Not knowing as knowledge: asymmetry between archaeology and anthropology. In *Archaeology and anthropology: understanding similarity, exploring difference*, edited by Duncan Garrow and Thomas Yarrow, pp. 13–27. Oxbow, Oxford.

Zeng, Tian Chen, Alan J Aw and Marcus W Feldman. 2018. Cultural hitchhiking and competition between patrilineal kin groups explain the post-Neolithic Y-chromosome bottleneck. *Nature Communications* 9(1):1–12.

PART I
Gifts

2

A PATINA OF JOURNEYS

2500–1700 BC

Early autumn 1976 brought a storm to the island of Coll, on Scotland's west coast (Figure 2.1). The winds whipped through the sands below Cnoc Mór, near Sorisdale, shifting the dunes and exposing human bones and an adjacent arc of stones (Richie and Crawford 1977/1978). The stones formed a low wall that was probably the edge of a domestic structure. There were floor deposits within the arc of stones; a midden containing coarse pottery and limpet shells had accumulated outside. The bones lay within a grave dug through the midden and marked with an upright stone.

The grave contained a slightly built, young woman and parts of a small ceramic vessel: an all-over-cord beaker, which was decorated and shaped in a similar style to vessels from the Middle Rhine region, western Germany (Needham 2005, 179). A calibrated radiocarbon measurement on a sample of the woman's bone placed her death during the twenty-fourth or twenty-third century BC (Jay et al. 2019, 54). This date is amongst the earliest for burials accompanied by beakers in Britain. Strontium isotopic analysis on one of the woman's teeth showed that she spent her early childhood outside the region of gneiss bedrock and calcareous sands where she was buried (Montgomery et al. 2019, 395). She may have grown up in eastern Ireland, eastern England or mainland northern and western Europe. Her genetic ancestry predominantly lay to the east, originating from populations in the Eurasian steppe (Olalde et al. 2018).

The circumstances of the woman's burial at Sorisdale and her biography and ancestry mean it is likely she travelled from the western European lowlands to Britain. She participated in cultural and population changes that began in the late decades of the twenty-fifth century BC and eventually affected all of Britain and Ireland. And she is one of very few 'first-generation migrants' that have been recognised amongst the individuals buried during the twenty-fourth century BC in Britain.

FIGURE 2.1 Coll's northern shore: the beaker-accompanied burial was uncovered amongst dunes close to the beach on the lower right side of the photograph. © Crown copyright: HES.

As compelling as the woman's biography and journey might be, there is more to say about her kinship and her place in Coll's landscape. The excavators did not find the woman's bones in anatomical order: the bones of her right arm lay below her pelvis; her femora were correctly aligned yet rotated by 180 degrees; the majority of her hand and feet bones had not survived or were missing from the grave (Richie and Crawford 1977/1978, 76). The beaker was incomplete too. It lacked its base, and roughly half the body was missing. The grave may have been revisited, the bones moved and reordered and sherds removed from the beaker. Alternatively, the woman's bones and a large fragment of pot were carried from another location and re-interred within a midden, by a house. The redeposited bones were laid, without too much precision, in the shape of a body. The pit's unusual key-hole shape might have reflected the need to create a space like a body in which the bones could be arranged.

The reordering and reburial of the woman's bones at Sorisdale represented a performance that differed from the mortuary rites undertaken immediately after her death. Following her death, her body and identities were transformed during rites of passage and incorporation. At Sorisdale, the woman's bones were uncovered, collected and moved. They became an offering within a midden, and a means of connecting living and dead kin with a contemporary settlement. A connection between the midden and the burial can be made because the pottery sherds found within the midden were also beaker, although of coarser fabric than the burial beaker and undecorated. Like the mortuary deposit, the midden was also assembled from fragments of former lives. These fragments were created from the domestic debris that accumulated when people were temporarily living at Sorisdale. The wider landscape of communities living amongst Scotland's west coast and islands is evidenced by numerous beaker-associated sites, including examples from Coll (Sharples 2009).

The assembling of human body, ceramic vessel and the place drew on different, although connected, forms of kinship. The all-over-cord beaker had a role in the assemblage that was intrinsic with the woman's body. Kinship extended through the bodies of the pot and the woman. When the woman's bones were moved, the vessel was also disturbed and this was possibly the time when a portion was removed. Perhaps the pot's base and body sherds were left in the woman's original grave. Alternatively, the sherds were kept and deposited elsewhere. The beaker's shape and decoration, and perhaps the ways it was used, recognisably related it with continental European traditions, and complemented the journeys taken by the human dead. Long-distance kinship was carried in the bodies of the person and vessel. People's kinship was also composed from the more routine journeys around the landscapes of the western Scottish coastlines. The redeposition of the woman and the beaker in a midden show that people did not make the same categorical distinctions between funerary rituals and domestic life that are prevalent in the modern world. The fragments of daily life and the parts of well-travelled bodies were brought together to compose the kinship of a beaker-using community on Coll.

In this chapter, I trace novel ways of assembling people and objects during the twenty-fifth to eighteenth centuries BC. The process began when beaker pottery, metalworking and incoming populations from continental Europe were incorporated within and transformed social life in Ireland and Britain. The inhumation of human remains at the close of mortuary rites formed one strand within these social transformations. From the twenty-third century BC, the mortuary rites that accompanied beakers were widely adopted and translated into different regional traditions and with varying levels of conformity and ostentation. Many objects held sufficient potency and value to be worthy of deposition as votive offerings without associating with the human dead. Offerings of objects crafted from copper, gold, bronze and stone were, in the absence of human bodies, performed with care and a knowledge of the proper way to do things. They were exchanges between humans and other nonhuman beings who occupied places and supernatural realms. By examining the interplay between mortuary rites and votive exchanges, it becomes possible to trace the evolving vibrancy of things and identify the different kin, human and nonhuman, who participated in social life.

Ancestry and mobility in the twenty-fourth century BC

During the late twenty-fifth to twenty-third centuries BC, people in Ireland and Britain encountered new materials, objects and mortuary rites. Distinctive pots called beakers (or Bell Beakers) were placed in some graves, and used in votive exchanges and in domestic settings. In Britain, mainly in eastern and midland regions, beakers accompanied small numbers of human burials, objects made from copper and gold were occasionally left with the dead and mourners dressed corpses uniformly for graves. Aspects of these mortuary rites, particularly the gifts of ceramic vessels and the adornment of the body within a stone or timber-lined grave, remained important for many centuries and developed as a widespread tradition.

Beakers took different forms, which varied depending on whether they were used in funerary rites, in votive exchanges or in domestic settings. At their finest, beakers looked and felt different to the vessels people made in the ceramic traditions of Britain and Ireland during the third millennium BC. The source of the differences lay in continental Europe, since similarities existed in the beakers across a large region that stretched from the Atlantic and Mediterranean coasts, east as far as Moravia in the Czech Republic (Vander Linden 2007). The earliest beakers in Britain tended to have a carination (or ridge) low in the vessels' profiles, with horizontal decoration made either with cords or by combs impressed into the clay (Figure 2.2). Where present, the other objects that people placed in early beaker graves varied relatively little: stone bracers and arrowheads, copper daggers and gold ornaments. Mourners followed a recurring set of rites when dealing with the dead person. They placed the dead in a flexed position, knees drawn up tightly to their chests, laid on one side or on their backs, and sometimes within timber-lined chambers that remained accessible for a time after the burial.

FIGURE 2.2 An all-over-cord beaker that was excavated from a timber-lined grave, along with fragments of two other beakers, at Upper Largie, Argyll. KHM 2016.1088. © Kilmartin Museum Company Ltd.

Prehistorians' earliest explanations for the apparent uniformity of the pottery and the burial rites focussed on the expansion of people—the 'beaker folk'—across continental and island Europe either through migration or by forceful invasion. Researchers have challenged this interpretation on many occasions by criticising the assumptions it carries about personal and ethnic identity, even if the themes of mobility and homelands have retained currency throughout decades of research (Vander Linden 2013). The direct dating of human bones accompanying beakers has countered claims for a complicated sequence of invasions and migrations from the mainland into Britain and Ireland (Healy 2012; Jay et al. 2019). Stuart Needham (2005; 2012a) organised the adoption and use of beakers into three phases: an introduction of the pottery style into Britain (and Ireland, where the situation is slightly different because beakers were rarely deposited with human remains) in the mid-third millennium BC (2450–2250 BC): a period when the styles of beaker pottery became more diverse and the burial rite flourished (2250–1950 BC): and a final phase when beaker burials were uncommon (1950–1800 BC). Prehistorians have revised the ways that the identities of the burials are interpreted. Researchers have moved from a straightforward reading of ethnic origin and identity on the basis of the grave goods accompanying the burials, and replaced this with interpretations emphasising the importance of the mourners in constructing the identities of the deceased during the burial ceremony and the symbolic roles of the beaker assemblage in marking particular ideals of identity.

Alongside these theoretical advances, geneticists and bioarchaeologists have made progress in understanding the diet, mobility and ancestry of the people buried with beaker pottery. The ancient DNA sequenced from British beaker burials includes distinctive genetic markers in the Y-chromosome and mitochondrial DNA of the sampled individuals that originated from populations in the Eurasian steppe and which appeared in populations in central Europe at around 3000 BC (Olalde et al. 2018). The researchers propose that for central and western Europe, and for Britain especially, the 'expansion of the beaker complex was driven to a substantial extent by migration' (Olalde et al. 2018, 194). In support of this interpretation, the genetic markers associated with steppe ancestry remained dominant in the DNA of burials sampled from throughout the Bronze Age in Britain and continues as a presence within today's populations. By comparison, the genetic markers defining Neolithic ancestry were rare in the Bronze Age burials in Britain (and probably Ireland too: Cassidy et al. 2015), suggesting a substantial turnover in people's genetic inheritance initiated during 2450–2300 BC.

The analysis of ancient DNA maps the extent in time and space of genetic markers, but it alone does not explain the processes through which steppe ancestry became prevalent in the populations of Britain and Ireland (Furholt 2018). Isotope ratios measured in human teeth add complexity to the interpretation of human mobility. In a major study, Mike Parker Pearson and colleagues (2016; 2019) analysed the isotope ratios in the teeth of 257 burials from Britain dating to the period 2450–1500 BC, and 41 percent were interpreted by the research team as 'movers'. The movers were individuals whose isotope ratios are statistically different to the regional burial environment, meaning they were buried in a location that was geologically differ-ent from the region where they spent their childhood. While this might seem to support the demographic expansion indicated by the genetics, almost all the mobil-ity in the study can be explained as movement between geological regions within, not outside, Britain. There are several individuals (Amesbury—Wiltshire—and Bee Low—Derbyshire—are two examples) where the isotopic differences are best ex-plained as movement from continental Europe to Britain. There are notable regional differences in the proportions of movers amongst the population, with the Peak Dis-trict and northern Scotland exhibiting a high number (52–63 percent) and central England an example of a lower proportion of movers (33 percent). The study shows limited differences in the proportion of movers between male and female burials, and the results were relatively consistent through time when comparing 2450–2300 BC, 2300–2150 BC and 2150–1500 BC.

Researchers using genetic evidence propose that populations from continental Europe migrated into Britain and Ireland at the same time as the adoption of beaker pottery and funerary rites. The isotopic evidence supports the idea that inter-regional mobility was a characteristic of some though not all people's lives, but it does not indicate frequent long-distance cross-continental migration. The genetics and the isotopes measure different ancestries, and with differing levels of exactitude. This helps explain their divergence. A genetic marker will be carried by individuals from one generation to the next as part of their biological inheritance. Isotope ratios depend on where individuals were born and spent their childhood, and on the distinctiveness or otherwise of the regional burial environment. Only first-generation migrants who spent their early lives in dis-tinctively non-British or Irish environments would have both steppe ancestry and continental European isotope ratios. The radiocarbon dates, at least from Ireland, do not support a model of a rapid, large population increase during the twenty-fourth and twenty-third centuries (McLaughlin et al. 2016). The conti-nuities and changes in culture during the same period also point to complex and diverse historical processes (Carlin 2018). We can only adequately describe the changes as an interplay of genetic ancestry, mobility and culture.

Uncommon ideals: early beaker burials in Britain, 2450–2250 BC

Archaeologists from Wessex Archaeology worked into the night, aided with torches and vehicle headlights, to excavate and record the most impressive of the early beaker burials found in Britain (Fitzpatrick 2011). The burial pit lay on the lower, west-facing slopes of Boscombe Down, near Amesbury, Wiltshire, several kilometres to the southwest of Stonehenge. The man in the grave was middle-aged (35–45 years old) when he died during the twenty-fourth century BC (Figure 2.3). The mourners placed his body in a timber-lined pit, crouched and lying on his left side facing north. The man, named by the excavators as the 'Archer', was accompanied by an unusually large number and variety of

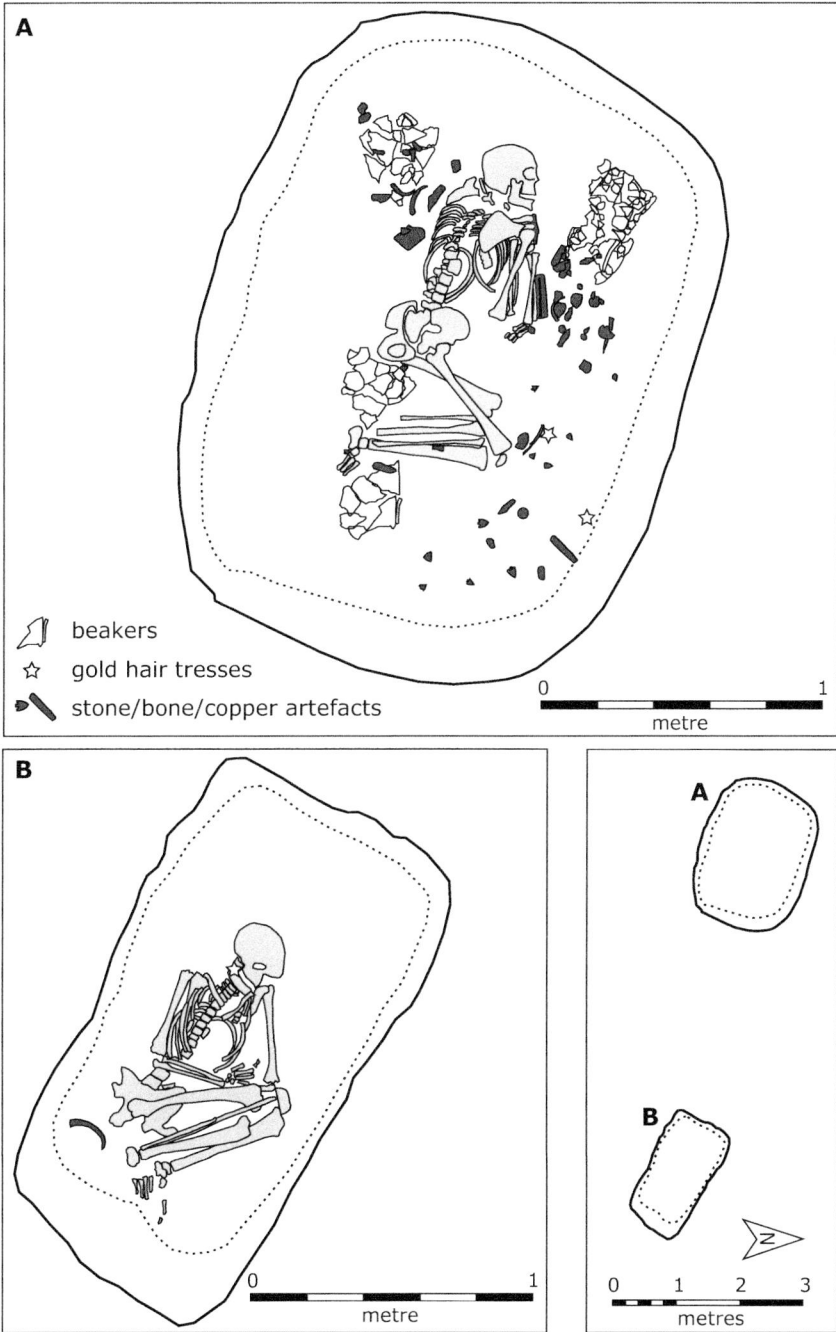

FIGURE 2.3 The graves of the 'Archer' and 'Companion' at Amesbury, Wiltshire. Adapted from Fitzpatrick 2011.

grave goods. These included five beakers, two stone bracers, a copper dagger and two copper knives, a pair of gold basket-shaped ornaments (or 'hair tresses'), numerous flint tools and arrowheads, a bone pin, a pendant made from an oyster shell, boar tusks and a cushion stone for metalworking. Probably around the same time or within a couple of generations of the Archer's burial, a younger man (20–25 years old) was buried in a smaller grave a short distance to the east of the Archer. Jaqueline McKinley's (2011, 80) osteological analysis of both burials identified a rare condition in their feet that is normally inherited between first degree relatives (for example, father to son and then grandson). The younger man, who the excavation team named the 'Companion', was buried with fewer grave goods: a single boar tusk was put next to the body, and a pair of gold ornaments, similar to those found with the Archer, either were placed in his mouth or had fallen there as his body decomposed.

The burials on Boscombe Down are located in a region of southwest England, Wessex, that has produced some of the earliest dates for beakers and is estimated to be the first region to have adopted the burial rites (Parker Pearson et al. 2019, 78). There are similar early burials, although less richly provisioned with grave goods, from elsewhere in Britain. At Upper Largie, Kilmartin Glen, a timber-lined grave enclosed by a ring ditch contained the remains of three beakers, all with strong similarities to continental European examples (Cook et al. 2010). A barrow on a limestone knoll at Kirkhaugh, in the valley of the South Tyne, Northumberland, contained an all-over-cord beaker, barbed and tanged arrowheads, a whetstone and two gold basket-shaped ornaments (Fitzpatrick 2015; Maryon 1936). Bodies did not survive in the graves at Upper Largie and Kirkhaugh. At Thomas Hardye School, Dorchester, Dorset, a man was buried, crouched and on his left side, in a timber-lined pit with a copper dagger by his head, a beaker at his feet and a bracer on his left forearm (Gardiner et al. 2007, 38). A bone toggle, perhaps for fastening a bag, also lay by the man's left arm, and there were three arrowheads at his back.

Stuart Needham (2005) interprets the exclusivity of these (predominately male) early beaker burials and their relative isolation (widely and thinly distributed around Britain—Garwood 2012, 299) as evidence for a phase when beakers established distinctive identities for the dead either ethnically, as incomers, or in terms of their alliances within wider beaker networks. Humphrey Case (2007) interpreted the archery equipment and daggers as symbolic hunting equipment, which was gifted to the most privileged dead as weapons they might use for protecting the living from malevolent spirits. Andrew Fitzpatrick (2011) interprets the burial rites of the Amesbury Archer as ascribing the status of warrior (blades, bracers and arrowheads) to a metalworker who held exceptionally high social status. The man's esteem emerged from his knowledge of and skill as a metalworker, his foreign origins and his maturity.

These interpretations read both literal and symbolic identities in the beaker grave assemblages. The dead took on persona that accentuated attributes and roles that they held in life. The stone bracers are understood to have been wristguards that archers wore to prevent the bowstring from wounding the inside of their arm. The presence of bracers in graves identified the dead by their former skills as archers, hunters and warriors. Some of the bracers are highly ornate, made with materials such as jet and decorated with gold-capped rivets that would have caught on the bowstring. Frequently, they were placed on the outside of the forearm, on the opposite side to where they would provide effective wrist protection. Ann Woodward and colleagues note a poor correlation between the presence of bracers and other aspects of archery equipment in British beaker burials (Woodward et al. 2006, 540). Some 'archer' burials were individuals whose ailments or deformities would have prevented them from using a bow (Shepherd 1986). The bracer could have employed archery as a metaphor, perhaps a martial one, for particular qualities of a person's identity (Fokkens et al. 2008). From this perspective, the beaker assemblage may have been as much about the construction of a symbolic persona through the inclusion of emblems associated with ideals linking archery with status and gender.

These interpretations helpfully blend practices and symbolism that might have defined the dead person in life and death. They explain the recurring grave goods and form of the burials, which share similarities with adjacent areas of mainland Europe. These ideals of personhood were codified through the infrequent though repeated assembly and performance of bodies and things in the grave. The performance of the burial and the roles of the kinfolk at the graveside are worthy of further consideration. We might also reflect on how social categories defined in Classical and European history, such as archer and warrior, have been applied as identities to the dead.

Returning to the Archer burial at Amesbury, the man was placed in a timber-lined chamber considerably larger than would have been required to contain just his body. Only a few of the grave goods might have been attached to the body. The other items were laid in groups around the body (Figure 2.3). The dead man wore a copper dagger, a black stone bracer and a bone pin. Two beakers, boar tusks, a copper knife, a perforated oyster shell, a nodule of iron pyrites and some antler and flint tools were placed in front of the man's head and chest. Another beaker, boar tusks, more flint tools and a cushion stone for metalworking were laid behind his back. One more beaker was placed behind his legs and another by his feet. A red stone bracer, a copper knife, a shale belt ring and two gold basket-shaped ornaments were placed in front of the body, arranged as though around a missing body by the man's feet. Finally, a sheaf of arrows was either laid, scattered or thrown into the grave.

The timber chamber enabled a narrative to unfold as the dead man's kinfolk assembled new relations with the resting body, between one another and with the objects chosen as grave goods. Each group of gifts laid in the grave was distinct from the others and shared similarities with the grave goods from contemporary beaker burials: the copper knife, basket-shaped ornaments and bracer in front of the man's legs; the beaker, cushion stone and boar tusks behind the man's head. The groups together formed an assemblage through their differences and similarities with one another: the boar tusks (all from the right side of male animals) were placed either side of the upper body, and the copper blades and bracers were in front of the body. The five beakers are especially interesting in their relations with one another. In her analysis of the pots, Rosamund Cleal (2011) identifies two pairs of vessels based on similarities in their decoration and fabric. One pair was worn through use and might have been a few years old before the burial. The other pair was made from local clays and had been inadequately fired, making the fabric fragile. This pair of pots may have been crafted specially for the mortuary rites (a feature recognised in other beakers: Boast 1995), and they were laid together in front of the man's head. The worn vessels were assembled behind the body and at the feet. Rather than interpreting the Archer's assemblage as the expression of a powerful individual, the assemblage shows us some of the relations emerging within and constituting a kin group: their relations between one another, with the dead man and other beings in their world (Brück 2019).

The beaker pots are important in archaeological narratives because they play the primary role in relating widely dispersed grave assemblages, and grouping the rites and people within a shared culture. There is an interesting complication to the pots' geographic association. The beakers comprised localities that were local and distant. The pottery was in daily use in settlements, and it was made specially for mortuary events and deposition in graves (Gibson 2019). Beakers were commonly made from clays local to the place of deposition (Carlin 2018, 40; Vander Linden 2007). This relationship with the localities of the pots' deposition contrasts with the distant associations of the styles in which the pots were made. In the case of Upper Largie, Argyll, Alison Sheridan suggests close links for the quality, style and decoration of the three locally made pots in the grave lay in the Netherlands (Cook et al. 2010). There are similarities, and there are differences, which make the case for simple and short-term connections through human migration unlikely on the basis of the funerary assemblages alone (Fokkens 2012, 117–118). All three of the Upper Largie vessels contain a grog temper (that is the crushed remains of pottery). Grog was first widely used as a temper in beaker ceramics in Britain, Ireland and western Europe. The grog fulfilled the tasks of strengthening the clay and making it more resilient to firing. As the clay for new vessels contained the broken remains of old pots, Ann Woodward suggests (2002, 1041) the 'essence of important pots belonging to significant individuals or families could be preserved and passed down through the generations'. Given the ubiquity of grog in making beakers, I would interpret it differently. Its presence was not a distinction of status. It was a routine means of retaining connecting with localities and traditions within the vessels. At Ewanrigg, Cumbria, one of the two beakers found during the excavations was made in a fine, non-local fabric, and contained grog within the grog (Ian Freestone in Bewley et al. 1992). Pots, like people, were composed through shared substances. This might have been expressed through the instances where a paste of burnt, ground bone was impressed into the pots' decoration, creating a contrast between the white inlay and the ceramic's reddish surface—a beaker made from flesh and bone (Curtis and Wilkin 2019, 231).

Interpreting people and pots as composite, made of relations near and far, can be supplemented by examples of human bodies that were incomplete or disassembled, like the woman's burial from Sorisdale that opens this chapter. These examples further challenge the individual integrity of the beaker dead. The Archer and his 'companion' excavated at Amesbury were both typical early beaker male burials. While the bodies were mostly intact, someone had removed one of the Archer's left ribs, and the sediment around the companion's skull included an infant's milk tooth (McKinley 2011). Around 600 metres from the Archer's burial, on Boscombe Down, Wessex Archaeology excavated a timber-lined grave containing the remains up to nine individuals, along with the broken remains of eight beaker vessels (Fitzpatrick 2011). The latest burials in the chamber, a male adult and a child, were articulated and buried flexed on their sides. The other bodies were disarticulated and incomplete: two adult crania were by the feet of the adult flexed inhumation, several long bones lay across his middle. These disarticulated bones were the incomplete remains of four or five adult males, a subadult (15–18 years) and a child. At Barrow Hills, Radley, grave 919 contained the partial remains of a four- to five-year-old child accompanied by a small beaker, a bone disc and three copper rings (Barclay and Halpin 1999, 55–57). Sometime later, people disturbed the grave of the earlier burial; they removed some of the child's bones and added another beaker. This beaker contained a few pieces of cremated bone from a young child and the skeleton of a newborn baby, which must have been partially disarticulated or a collection of loose bones to fit in the vessel. The disassembly, reassembly and removal of bones were common to all these examples. At Chilbolton, Hampshire, the primary burial of an adult male, with a typical if generous variety of beaker grave goods, was disturbed and the bones reordered when a later burial was added to the chamber: the man's head was inverted, and other bones were collected in groups or rearranged (Russel 1990) (Figure 2.7).

The disassembled and incomplete bodies in early beaker graves counter the idea that the mortuary rites and grave goods straightforwardly attributed esteem and idealised identities to hunters, warriors and metalsmiths. The beaker person was assembled by kinfolk for the grave. The mortuary rites that were performed before and at the graveside connected distant ideas and kin with a locality. The distant emerged through the styles of pottery, in the craft needed to make the vessels, in the metal items and knowledge of their making and in totemic beings, such as boars or pig and cattle. The journeys that kin had taken to the localities were present in the biographies of the persons and the things in the graves. The presence of grog and bone in the fabric of the pots provided one instance of these biographies, as did the worn and sometimes fragmented objects that were chosen as grave goods.

The beaker 'complex' existed across Europe because of consistencies across its local manifestations. The consistencies in early beakers existed because there was a fair degree of mobility amongst populations. More speculatively, this mobility existed to retain and was enabled by widely dispersed kin networks. Mortuary rituals, and particularly rites of incorporating the dead, localised and performed expressions of kinship that were distant and near at hand.

The adoption of beaker pottery, metallurgy and flexed inhumation burial rites during the twenty-fourth to twenty-second centuries BC began and progressed with journeys. These journeys created kinship between places, people and things that would persist in social networks for centuries. The ways that kinship held places and people together, even over great distances, can be illustrated by Anne Salmond's (2005) eloquent account of the first journeys that European sailors took between the Polynesian islands guided by local navigators. The Polynesian navigators' abilities to use ocean currents, stars and the sun to guide the ships many days from land-fall impressed the European sailors. Salmond's account tells of a world bound together through kinship:

> For the Tahitians, an ancestral relationship had to be established before the navigators could share their knowledge with the strangers. This was achieved by forging a *taio*, or ceremonial friendship, in which part of the being of each was bound into the other. By the ritual presentation of names and gifts, the *taio* shared part of each other's identities, including kinship networks and alliances. Through this exchange of personhood, and perhaps only in this way, the gift of navigational information to the Europeans could be accomplished.
>
> *(Salmond 2005, 181)*

Journeys made kin and were made from kin. Kinship was the relation through which navigational knowledge could be transmitted.

Kinship was the relatedness that shaped mortuary ceremonies and grave assemblages, and the conduit along which beliefs, technologies, materials, things, people and other animals were exchanged and moved. Archaeologists have long-recognised complex webs of relatedness across continental and island Europe during the third millennium BC in ceramic styles, metallurgy and burial rites. Ancient DNA (aDNA) illustrates the webs of biological relatedness that accompanied these material connections. It is a mistake to characterise one of these sources, the aDNA, as kin-based, and the other, the material culture, not. They were all forms of relatedness and evidence of kinwork. Given the extent of shared genetic ancestry across western and central Europe at this time, it is reasonable to imagine varied kinship links covering long distances that could have been maintained or re-mobilised when needed.

Performances at gravesides retold journeys and connected kin. They prepared the dead for journeys across and into other worlds. During the twenty-fifth to twenty-third centuries BC, these journeys were, for reasons we do not know, more commonly performed by and with the bodies of men. They were the ones most suitable for this kinwork. Within a few centuries, the burials assembled people of different genders and ages, a larger repertoire of things and in many more places throughout the landscape. Burial remained the assembling of beings in readiness for journeys, with their crouched position in the grave an embryonic allusion to birth.

The flows and alloys of early metals, 2450–2000 BC

For Ireland and Britain there was a correspondence, within a century, between the appearance of beaker ceramics, objects of copper and gold either in or out of graves and the exploitation of metal ores. This was different to western Europe as a whole, where metallurgy was both earlier and more widespread than the use of beaker ceramics (Roberts 2008, 366). We cannot describe the adoption of metals solely through the knowledge and journeys of the people buried with beakers, since so much of the assimilation of the technology drew upon traditions and relations pre-existing within Ireland and Britain.

The Archer burial at Amesbury offers a unique example in Britain of the coincidence of beakers, copper and goldwork, and an item associated with metalworking—the cushion stone. The man's oxygen and strontium isotope ratios indicate he spent his childhood outside Wessex and probably in the Alpine region, possibly western Germany (Chenery and Evans 2011). His journey to southern Britain took him from and through regions where copper metallurgy was established by the middle of the third millennium BC. This makes the Archer a representative for the flows of people and ideas that transferred metallurgical knowledge into Ireland and Britain. While we know from genetics and the compositional studies of metals that these flows occurred, the burial is unique in Britain as an individual demonstrably from mainland Europe and associated with metal and, more speculatively, metalsmithing.

The early copper objects that have survived from Ireland and Britain (c. 2450–2250 BC) are primarily blades of one or other form: axes, daggers, knives, halberds, along with awls and ingots (Needham 1996, 124–127), with axes the most common in archaeological collections. In Ireland, which has produced more copper objects than Britain, 939 artefacts were found singly and 143 in groups of two or more objects (Becker 2013, 231). Although copper axes are rarer finds in Britain, Mike Parker Pearson (2009, 104) has proposed that the widespread and early availability of copper axes might be underestimated, based on the interpretation of metal axe marks on chalk quarried from the ditch at the great henge at Durrington Walls dating to the twenty-fifth century BC. The earliest copper axes were cast in a simple, flat form with a trapezoidal shape and a thick butt. Their form is similar to examples from Iberia and France, which is one basis for arguing for an Atlantic origin for metallurgy in Ireland (Sheridan 1983).

Travel along the Atlantic coastline may have provided both the inspiration for the objects and knowledge of metallurgy. Small numbers of the early copper objects recorded from Britain and Ireland were made with metal from sources beyond the islands, including the blades in the Amesbury burial. This 'Bell-Beaker copper' includes high traces of arsenic and smaller amounts of antimony and nickel copper, which may originate from Iberia and France (Needham 2002). Whatever the ex-insular origins, native ores from mines in southwest Ireland and, with less certainty, southwest England were the important sources of metal for most surviving copper objects (Bray 2012). The evidence for a Cornish source for early copper has emerged during the past 20 years of compositional analyses. The direct traces of contemporary mining have not been found and are likely entirely destroyed by historic ore extraction.

More than two-thirds of the early copper artefacts in Ireland and Britain have distinctive arsenic, antimony and silver impurities that are peculiar to southwest Ireland (Bray and Pollard 2012; Northover 1980; Rohl and Needham 1998) (Figure 2.4). The source of this arsenical copper ore was Ross Island, located on a peninsula on the east side of Lough Leane, County Kerry. The calibrated radiocarbon dates for mining at Ross Island span 2400–1900 BC, and the associated occupation and smelting remains produced beaker ceramics (O'Brien 2004).

Copper-bearing deposits are found across the western and northern parts of Ireland and Britain, yet Ross Island and Cornwall appear to be the only insular sources accessed before the twenty-first century BC (Rohl and Needham 1998, 86–88). Ross Island and Cornwall produced arsenical copper ores. Peter Bray (2012, 856)

FIGURE 2.4 The copper halberd with a surviving portion of its wooden haft, which was excavated from a ring ditch near Trecastell, Powys (Needham 2015). The copper is 'A-metal' sourced from Ross Island, County Kerry. BRCNM 2013.19.08 y Gaer Museum, Art Gallery, Library—Brecon; image copyright: Phil Parkes.

noted that the ores share a similar grey colour and the traces of arsenic give off a faint garlic smell when crushed. The smelters searching for suitable rock used attributes such as smell and colour to identify ore. It was several more centuries before the characteristics of the chalcopyrite ores in north and west Wales and the English midlands were recognised as copper sources (Timberlake and Marshall 2018). The chemical analysis of metal composition, stylistic studies of objects and excavations at mines reveal the rapidly evolving and complex network of prospecting and metal flows that linked the British and Irish islands with Atlantic and western Europe.

Axes were familiar emblems and tools (Bradley 1990). Polished stone axes had, during the preceding 1,500 years, served as one of the archetypes and commonplace objects in people's lives. Metal axes were treated in a similar way to stone axes, in that both types were deposited as votive offerings and they rarely accompanied burials. The physical appearances of both stone and metal axes were enhanced in ways that emphasised the surface qualities of the materials. With stone axes, this involved polishing the entire surface of the axe, which enhanced the colour and accentuated patterns in the stone (Cooney 2002). Some metal axes were, after 2200 BC, decorated with incised patterns reminiscent of the designs found on contemporary ceramics. Others were coated in a thin tin layer, giving them a silvery-grey colour that might have been intended to reproduce the silverish hue of earlier arsenical copper axes (Kinnes et al. 1979). Tin-coated axes were more commonly present when axes were deposited in groups (Coles 1969). Decorated axes were treated similarly.

Most stone axes were made from material sourced at a relatively few locations, with some quarries and mines proving especially important: Rathlin Island and Tievebulliagh in Ulster, Graig Lwyd in north Wales, Langdale in Cumbria and Grimes Graves in Norfolk. The movement of axes from these dispersed sources occurred through individuals' journeys and the repeated gift exchange of the axes (Bradley and Edmonds 1993). A few of the axe sources retained or regained importance during the twenty-fourth century with the use of fine-grained stone for the production of bracers, with Langdale tuff and Ulster porcellanite both utilised (Roe and Woodward 2009; Woodward and Hunter 2011). Of the 74 bracers examined from Britain, a quarter derived from a volcanic tuff from Langdale, Cumbria (Woodward and Hunter 2011). The stone is a distinctive light green with a rust-coloured mottling. The rock's structure enabled it to be worked in any direction, meaning that craftworkers could make distinctive bracers that curved around a wrist. Possible roughouts for bracers have been located at stone sources overlooking the Langdale Valley, so it appears that people returned to the same sources of tuff that had previously been quarried for stone axes (Mark Edmonds in Woodward and Hunter 2011, 35–36). Some bracers may be reworked stone axes (Harding and Healy 2007, 252), with one powerful object transforming into another. The distribution of the Langdale bracers overlaps with the distribution of polished stone axes from Langdale, with a small cluster of the bracers in Yorkshire and a bias towards eastern Scotland. As with axes, the craftworkers selected stone for the bracers from a limited range of sources and colours. Fiona Roe and Ann Woodward (2009) observed that the British bracers were usually in shades of blue-grey or green-grey, and those from Ireland used a red jasper or stones in shades of near-black, grey or brown.

Familiar and ancient associations enabled metal axes and bracers to find their places in the social life of the twenty-fourth and twenty-third centuries BC. Metals were in part understood through past forms of making and valuing objects. Even important differences between stone and metal seem to have been softened. Metal could be recycled into fresh forms, in ways that stone resisted. Early smiths did not work the material in this way. Axes show subtle differences between one another because moulds were not repeatedly reused (Roberts 2008, 363). Recycling began in an exclusive way, with limited mixing, reflecting something of the wholeness of objects as learnt from stone. Peter Bray re-analysed the compositional data from copper and bronze objects from the British and Irish early Bronze Age (Bray and Pollard 2012). He identified less recycling of metal in the objects found closer to the ore sources, which is perhaps unsurprising. He also noted increasing levels of recycling and mixing with time, and especially from the twentieth century BC. It appears that there was a 'gradually increasing recognition, social acceptance and exploitation of metal's mutability' (Bray and Pollard 2012, 862).

A copper-alloy, tin-bronze, was used for making objects in Ireland and Britain from around the twenty-third and twenty-second centuries BC, at broadly the same time as elsewhere in Europe and worldwide (O'Brien 2015). Stylistic changes in objects occurred alongside the use of bronze: with riveted rather than tanged daggers, thin-butted axes and symmetrically bladed halberds. The only insular source of tin was in southwest England, and the nearest continental sources also lie on the Atlantic coastline, in Brittany and northwest Iberia (Penhallurick 1986; Timberlake 2017). These sources were close to the areas where copper ore was found, and the proximity of tin to established copper mines might explain the rapidity with which tin-bronze was taken up in Ireland and Britain. Subsequent working of tin from the medieval period onwards removed the evidence for Bronze Age activity or buried it beneath large volumes of sediment. During the nineteenth century AD, tin miners found Bronze Age metalwork several metres down, at the base of medieval tin working sediments (Shell 1978). Tin was understood as a material in relation with copper and bronze, and not solely as a constituent of bronze. A thin coating of tin was applied to small numbers of bronze axes, with a concentration of finds in northern Britain (Needham 2004, 235). Other examples of pure tin include the studs and beads associated with a cremation burial on Whitehorse Hill, Dartmoor (Jones 2016), as an inlay in a jet button from Rameldry Farm (Baker et al. 2003), and a possible wire under the rim of a gold armlet from Lockington (Hughes 2000, 29).

The flows of tin reinforced the networks along the Atlantic coast that connected kin with copper and gold sources in Cornwall and Ireland. Gold and copper objects were deposited together in some early beaker graves. Metalsmiths crafted the thin gold sheet into basket-shaped ornaments, small decorated discs and plaques (Figure 2.5). Somewhat later, from the twenty-third and twenty-second centuries BC, new objects were made in gold, including crescent-shaped lunulae and armlets. There were many potential sources of the gold as it occurs in native form in locations around Ireland and Britain (Timberlake 2017). Lead isotope analysis has supported the suggestion that the gold in Irish objects originated from southwest England (Standish et al. 2015).

The relations between communities along the Atlantic coast contributed to the distribution of gold lunulae. The crescent-shaped objects were made from thin sheet gold with incised or impressed geometric designs around the edges and horns of the crescents. The geometric decoration shares features with the patterns on beaker pottery, and the crescent shape corresponds with the forms of jet, shale and amber spacer-plate necklaces (Frieman 2012). Most of the lunulae have been found in Ireland, with a smaller number from Britain, northwest France and northern Portugal (Eogan 1994; Taylor 1980). The pattern matches the Irish Sea and Atlantic distribution of gold, copper and tin sources. Two lunulae were found along with a bronze flat axe in a stone cist at Harlyn Bay on the north Cornish coast. The style of the lunulae suggests Irish origins,

FIGURE 2.5 A slate die for making gold 'sun discs', recovered from Hackets-town, County Waterford (Cahill 2016). The motif is 25 mm across. Image. Copyright of the National of Museum of Ireland.

and one lunula closely resembles examples from Kerivoa and St Potan on the north coast of Brittany. Joan Taylor (1980) proposed that the decoration on all three was fashioned using the same distinctive tool, and potentially by one goldsmith.

Metals and metallurgy were new participants in the social life of Britain and Ireland by the twenty-fourth century BC. They were embodied in novel objects, in the people who carried and wore the objects, and those who knew how to smelt and smith metal. Objects, people and ideas moved considerable distances around coastal and continental Europe on journeys and as gifts. The archaeological distributions of early objects like thick-butted flat axes are the traces of these journeys and exchanges.

Metals and metallurgy changed the geographic orientation and extent of networks as the sources of copper ore, gold and subsequently tin made southwest Ireland and southwest Britain important places to visit, live and be connected with. The networks that evolved were blended with long-established relations with places and things. The stone sources used for axes were visited again, albeit on a smaller scale, for the materials for bracers, which retained or regained the importance of relations with these places. The craftworkers selected rocks like red jasper because of the colour, how the stone flaked and, derived from these and other qualities, what the stone meant. Copper axes found a place in partial relation to stone. Stone and copper axes were both deposited in similar ways at the ends of their lives, and there may have been comparable understandings of the immutability of objects, as recycling and mixing of metals took several centuries to emerge as a widespread practice. The adoption of metals and metallurgy into social life emerged, like the relations with beakers, in blends of novelty and tradition.

Creative relations with the dead: beaker and food vessel burials, 2250–1900 BC

The twenty-fourth century formed the prelude for an impressive diversity of craft and burial assemblages. After 2250 BC, around the same time that tin-bronze became available, burial was emerging as an increasing feature of mortuary rites. The frequency of burials and their diversity makes it feasible to recognise burial assemblages throughout Ireland and Britain and define regional traditions (Cleary 2016). The few tens of excavated burials dated to the twenty-fourth and twenty-third centuries BC are a tiny fraction of the numbers who died. Most people were buried in ways that meant their remains did not survive within archaeological deposits. This situation began changing from the late twenty-third century BC, when more of the population were buried at the close of mortuary rites, and with greater proportions of female and child burials than had been the case during the preceding centuries. These changes coincided with diverse and regionalised styles of beakers, and a new ceramic style, the food vessel, which was widespread in Ireland and became common in Britain from around 2100 BC (Brindley 2007; Wilkin 2014).

Stuart Needham (2005, 209) characterises 2250–1950 BC as a period of acculturation and diversification, in which the exclusive rites associated with early beaker burials were adopted throughout Britain. This process began, Needham proposes, with a 'fission horizon' lasting around a century when there was rapid diversification both in burial practices and in the styles of the pottery vessels, with the pots and accompanying objects having a less exclusive association with European networks and ideas. The bracers, which seemed so important for male burials in the preceding century, were rarely included as grave goods. Flint daggers and jet buttons, on the other hand, were a feature of burials after 2250 BC. The inhumation burial beneath Irthlingborough Barrow 1, Northamptonshire, offers an example of both earlier and later beaker objects assembled together (Harding and Healy 2007). Sometime during the twenty-second or twenty-first century BC, kin buried an adult male in an oak-lined grave with a collection of objects at the man's feet: a long-necked beaker, jet buttons and a flint dagger, together with a boar tusk and a bracer made from Langdale tuff. The bracer was a heavily worn fragment and the calibrated radiocarbon measurement on the boar tusk makes it at least three centuries older than the burial.

The emergence of regional traditions constrained by British and Irish shores can be miscategorised as a form of insularity. People maintained relations both along the Atlantic coast and eastwards onto mainland Europe. Comparable representations of the sun appear in motifs on gold, bronze and ceramics across western and northern Europe, and the sun was referenced in the alignments of burials and monuments (Cahill 2015; Carlin 2018, 209–211). Catherine Frieman argues that the flaked-stone daggers, which have a markedly eastern distribution in Britain during 2250–2000 BC, were either derived from or emulated Dutch examples (Frieman 2014). In this respect they were a means of connecting with an 'ancestral' beaker identity and situating the daggers' wearers (living and dead) within a wider value-system signified by daggers.

Regionalisation takes different forms. Burials with beakers are found in notable clusters in Wessex, the Thames Valley, the Peak District and northeast Scotland. In the regions where beakers were less visible, there was an early adoption of bowl-shaped food vessels: north and east Ireland and the west coast of Scotland. The food vessels accompanied both inhumation and cremation burials, some single-graves and others with multiple interments, placed in stone cists and pits, and sometimes in flat cemeteries and mounds. The University of Groningen's programme of radiocarbon dating concluded that the burials accompanied by bowls span 2150–1950 BC (Brindley 2007). The vessels are small and ornately decorated with a variety of complex designs, which the potters impressed into the clay using a comb or small triangular implement. Their forms may have derived inspiration from earlier impressed wares and contemporary organic containers (Wilkin 2014, 49).

Keenoge, County Meath, is a large cemetery with early food vessel burials (Mount 1997) (Figure 2.6). Twenty-six individuals were buried in fourteen graves, both pits and stone-built cists, which were dug into a low, natural mound. The people inhumed at Keenoge were placed in the graves on their sides and tightly flexed, with the bowls, where present, by their heads. This arrangement has parallels with beaker burials in Britain. The majority of the burials were adult men and women. A few children were represented but only one was the primary burial in a grave. A greater proportion of the male burials contained bowls, and more of the cremated remains were male (Mount 1997).

The age and sex of the dead contributed to subtle distinctions between individual assemblages (Haughton 2018). When beaker vessels were present in graves, there were codified ways to treat men and women during mortuary rites and these varied somewhat between regions. Joanna Sofaer analysed the beaker

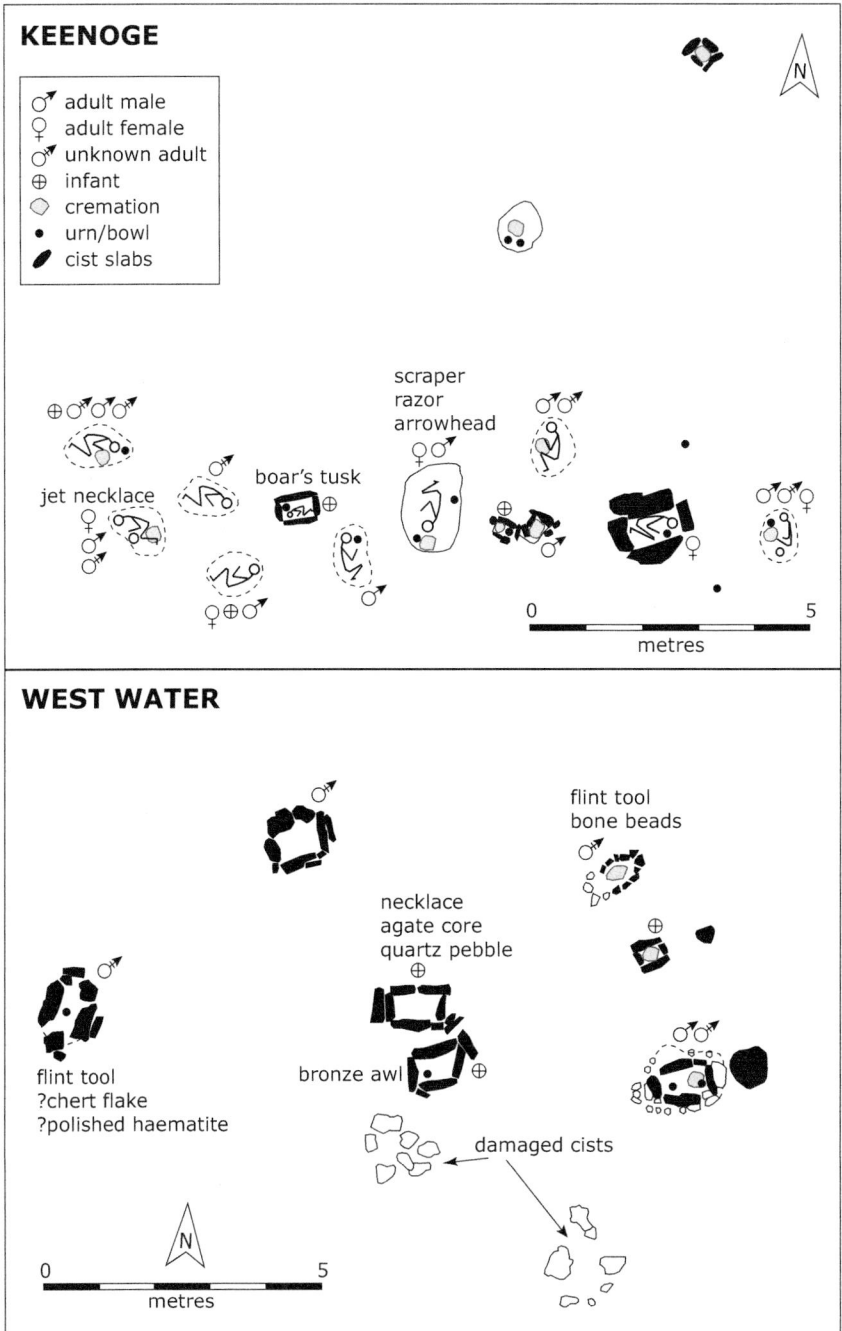

FIGURE 2.6 Plans of the excavated cist cemeteries at Keenoge, County Meath, and West Water, Peeblesshire. Adapted from Hunter 2000 and Mount 1997.

burials in the Thames Valley and identified differences between the ways the graves of men and women were assembled (Sofaer Derevenski 2002). Men were buried both in flat graves and in round barrows, laid on their left side and oriented to the north or northwest, in grave cuts of a common shape and size, and located either in the centre or completely outside monuments. The lack of variability in the form of burial, according to Sofaer, indicates that male identities were relatively fixed by sexual characteristics. The ways of expressing masculinity in mortuary rituals were limited and inflexible. Burials sexed as female, by comparison, were almost always within monuments and in a variety of positions, with a tendency for older individuals to be buried in more peripheral locations. The shapes of the grave cuts were also more variable than for men, with no pattern in the orientation of the graves, although there were strong preferences for laying bodies on their right sides. Sofaer argues that female identities were constructed in multiple ways, with greater complexity and potential for variability than male gender. The grave was not a passive reflection of a person's identity; it was a mediator through which identities were defined.

Alexandra Shepherd (2012) studied the beaker burials from east Yorkshire and northeast Scotland. Here the burials followed an east-west alignment, differing from the north-south arrangements in southern Britain and amongst beaker graves in western Europe: the women were laid on their right sides, with their heads to the west, and men on their left sides with heads to the east, both women and men facing south. There were small differences in this pattern. A quarter of the male burials in east Yorkshire (4 out of 16) were laid on different orientations. Otherwise the principles were reproduced consistently. Alexandra Shepherd proposed that the pots accompanying the burials were made or chosen in relation with the sex of the dead person. The shorter, squatter pots were more commonly placed with females (particularly children), and the pots placed with males tended to be taller. Shepherd accepted the patterns were far from clear or consistent. Biological sex, as defined by osteological analysis, formed an aspect of how genders were created. At Broomend of Crichie, Aberdeenshire, one of the cists contained a male and an infant, with the taller, broader pot accompanying the man. Another cist included two males, laid alongside one another and with their heads oriented in opposing directions. The pots accompanying the men were a complementary pair: one taller and the other squatter.

Shepherd (2012, 262) compared her results with the food vessel-accompanied burials in east Yorkshire. The bodies with food vessels were arranged in more diverse alignments when compared with the beaker-accompanied burials. There remained a slight preference for east-west alignments with the bodies facing towards the south, with more variability than burials with beakers. The positions of the pots in the graves differed depending on whether the bodies were buried with beakers or food vessels: beakers were behind the head, and food vessels were placed in front (Lucas 1996, 110). In Ireland, where small numbers of inhumation burials were accompanied by bowl food vessels in cists, there are no discernible patterns in the arrangement of the bodies (Waddell 1990, 18–19). Chris Fowler and Neil Wilkin (2016) noted variability in the arrangement of the bodies that were accompanied by food vessels in north-east England and south-east Scotland. They propose that choices about the orientations of cists and the bodies they contained were made according to local distinctions and connections with regions elsewhere. The north-south aligned burials in the north and east Cheviot Hills are one example of a local tradition. The predominately older male burials with copper-alloy daggers and knife-daggers in northern Britain form a wider regional grouping (Baker et al. 2003).

Along with sex, age is another biological characteristic that can be estimated through the analysis of human bone. Like gender, age emerged from the unfolding relations between kin and cultural traditions. Estimates of childhood mortality in prehistory place it at around 50 percent, meaning that half or more of a population would have been under 18 years of age (Lucy 2005). It is on these terms that some accounts of the Bronze Age have treated the burial of children as unproblematic and an expected albeit poignant 'fact of life' (Burgess 1980, 162). Despite the common occurrences of childhood death, during the twenty-fourth and twenty-third centuries only a few children were chosen for formal burial in ways that have become archaeologically visible, and it was rare for these children to be either female or infants. From the twenty-second century, people buried children's remains more frequently and made distinctions during the mortuary rites according to the children's ages. The age categories were not nearly as clearly defined as they were for gender. The decisions about when to enact the formal burial of children, as with other categories of people, were defined historically and culturally.

Barra Ó Donnabháin and Anna Brindley's (1989/1990) review of the human remains, most cremated, from burials with miniature cups in Ireland shows that children under the age of 14 were not accorded individual burial with grave goods, but were in all but one case (Rathlin Island—inhumation of a child of about six years old in a cist (Wiggins 2000)) interred with an adult. Ó Donnabháin and Brindley suggest that the change at around the age of 14 marked the transition to adulthood. Paul Garwood (2007) identified changes through time in the ways children were treated at death during the early Bronze Age in southern England. He suggests that during 2400–2150 BC, children were not buried as individuals memorialised in death, but rather treated as offerings or part of the grave assemblage accompanying an adult: as at Boscombe Down, described above, and at Hemp Knoll, Wiltshire, where the body of a three-year-old child was placed on the ground surface next to the pit in which an adult male with a beaker was buried (Robertson-Mackay 1980). During 2150–1800 BC, burials of children, particularly infants and young children, were more common. These included many examples of children buried as individual persons, occasionally with grave goods. The types of artefacts associated with the burials varied according to the age of the child, with infants most commonly accompanied by a pot such as a handled beaker or food vessel, and children aged four to six years old buried with flint objects. Burials of children older than 13 or 14 were rarer during 2150–1800 BC, and all were found in secondary contexts within the burial monument. The few older children that were buried with grave goods seem to have been treated as adults. Children could be mourned and remembered in similar ways to adults, with puberty probably the important threshold into adulthood.

A child (five to nine years old) was buried in a cist at Doune, Perth and Kinross, accompanied by a miniature battle axe, a small food vessel and an abraded sherd from a larger food vessel (McLaren 2004). Dawn McLaren interprets the presence of the miniature battle axe as an indication that the child was a significant member of the community. Miniature versions of artefacts were as common in adult burials as they were with children. At Barbrush, Perthshire, the complete remains of a necklace made from local cannel coal beads with a jet fastener were sized to fit a juvenile or child (Holden and Sheridan 2001). A nearby cist contained the inhumation burial of a 9–12-year-old child accompanied with a food vessel. At West Water Reservoir, in the Scottish Borders, all the human remains that could be assigned an age were under 25 years old, and the youngest child, perhaps 3–5 years old, was buried with a disc bead necklace with a second strand of lead beads (Hunter 2000) (Figure 2.6).

Paul Garwood (2007) interprets the increase in burials of children in southern England during 2150–1800 BC and their common inclusion within barrows with multiple, related phases of burial as deliberate attempts to re-order relations amongst the living and ensure the successful reproduction of communities. The placement of burials in vertical alignment, one above the other, in the same mounds signalled a concern to symbolise continuity and growth, perhaps at times when communities were in other regards unstable or vulnerable (Figure 2.7). In a study of the beaker and food vessel inhumation burials in east Yorkshire, Gavin Lucas (1996) notes that more than half of the beaker-accompanied graves contained multiple burials, and this practice was less common with the food vessel burials. Across all types of interment, more than two-thirds of the primary burials in the sequences of multiple interments were male. The sex ratios were more equal for the subsequent, secondary, burials. The male burials, Lucas suggests, were founding events for constructing kinship histories during the mortuary rites. Commenting on the same east Yorkshire burials as Lucas, Koji Mizoguchi (1993) proposes that the sequence of male burials followed by a wider variety of persons narrated an idealised narrative for how a society was organised, and which materialised relations of dominance between different social categories.

The greater numbers of male burials compared with females and young people could have reproduced a 'relation of dominance' for masculinity in society (Mizoguchi 1993). The more common sequence for multiple burials in some regions to begin with an adult male might have meant that kinship narratives were founded on senior male ancestors (Lucas 1996). These interpretations miss out the important precondition for the patterns, which was the tradition of

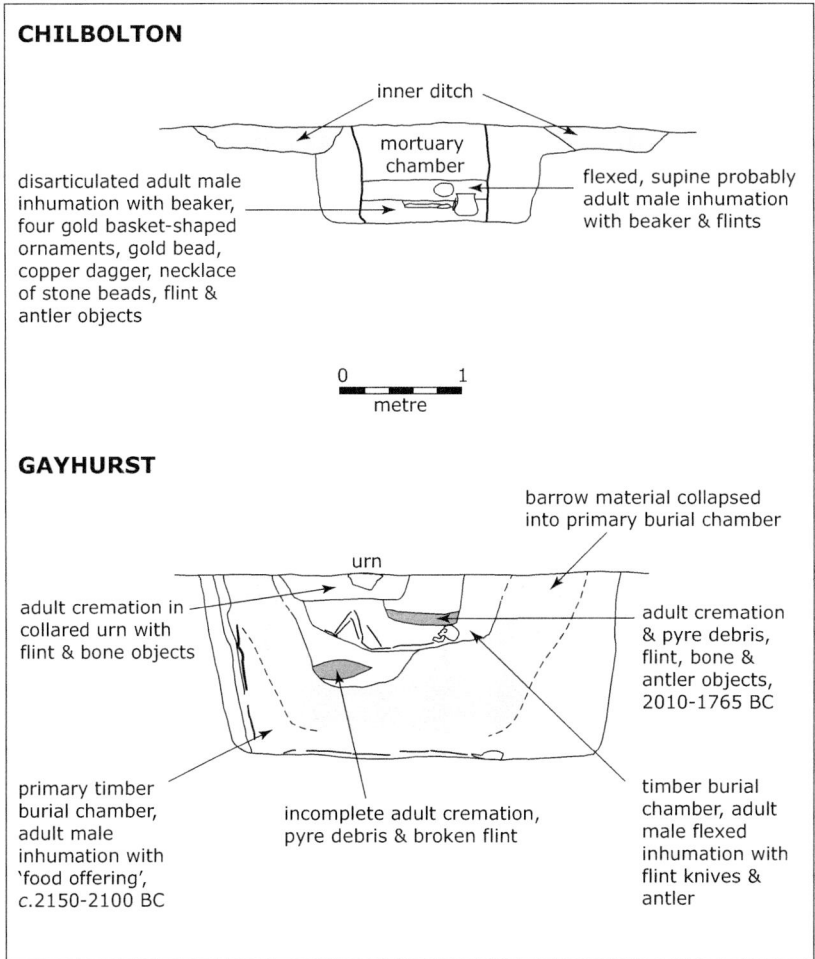

FIGURE 2.7   The vertical placements of burials at Chilbolton, Hampshire and Gayhurst, Buckinghamshire. Adapted from Chapman 2007 and Russel 1990.

assembling graves around male burials began in the early beaker period. The male dead played prominent roles in grave assemblages after 2200 BC in the same regions, east Yorkshire being one, that beakers were important. The reproduction of beaker burial traditions required that the burials of women and men were assembled in difference with one another. In comparison, the food vessels in graves changed the conformity of the assemblages, and there was more variability in how male and female burial rites were performed.

The juxtaposition of burial deposits and their proximity to the centre or the principal alignments of the monuments will have enabled the dead to be placed with reference to existing social orders and to play a part in reproducing those orders. The excavation of a round barrow at Barnack in Cambridgeshire produced an exceptional but by no means unique series of burials, which Jonathan Last (1998) argues were spatially associated with one another in ways that defined each person's individuality and built up a genealogical narrative for the community (Figure 2.8). The first person to be buried was a 40-year-old man. He was accompanied by a large finely made beaker, a copper or bronze dagger, a bracer decorated with gold and a bone pendant. The subsequent burial events within the monument took place over about 200 years, and each retained references to and created differences with the preceding interments. There was a tension between selves and community. There was perhaps a desire to deal with short-term concerns of mourning and remembrance, while also placing the dead within a longer history that projected the ongoing success of the community.

From the late twenty-third and twenty-second centuries BC, burial became an increasingly common rite. Burial occurred alongside other funerary rites, which are hinted at by the occasional finds of human bone in places such as caves and rivers. A dozen human skulls and other bones, fragments of wickerwork and animal bone were excavated in a former channel of the River Trent, and interpreted as the remains of an excarnation structure dated to the late third millennium BC (Garton et al. 1997). As burials became more frequent and geographically widespread, the assemblages increased in their diversity, with women

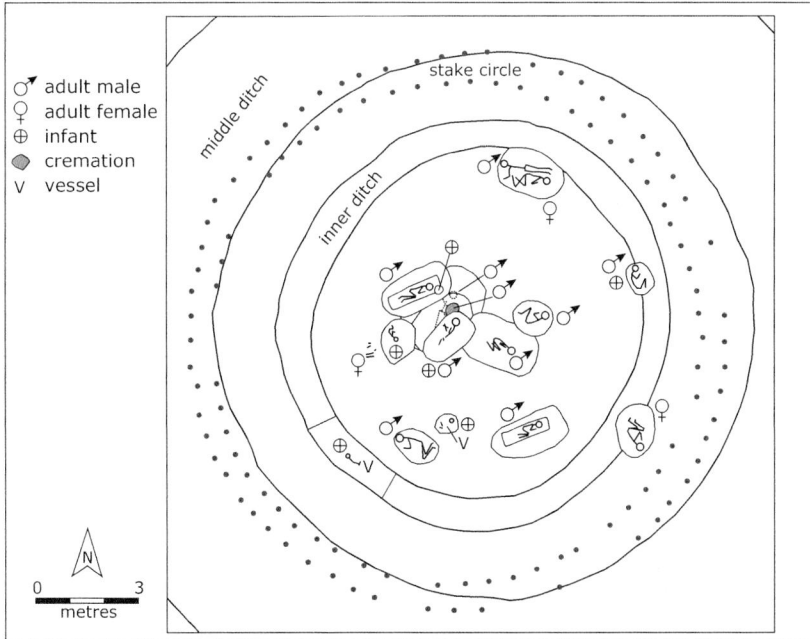

FIGURE 2.8   A plan of the burials within a barrow at Barnack, Cambridgeshire. Adapted from Donaldson 1977.

and young people more commonly buried, and new pottery styles included in the graves. It was around this time that cremation became visible as a mortuary practice, most notably in Ireland. Cremation was probably practised routinely in preceding centuries, with the main change around 2200 BC being that the cremated bone was more commonly buried in a cist in a similar manner to inhumation burials. This larger and more diverse burial dataset has meant that prehistorians have reconstructed different categories of objects and persons, relating to sex and age, for instance, and the social order as it was represented in mortuary monuments.

Votive exchanges, 2450–2000 BC

In Ireland, beakers and associated objects were rarely incorporated into human burial assemblages (Carlin 2018). People did not assemble the characteristic grave goods that occur in some British early beaker burials and in continental examples. Bracers, goldwork, v-perforated buttons and copper daggers are found instead in other contexts and rarely with beakers. The pottery is common in pits and spreads of occupation material, and occasionally in earlier, Neolithic monuments such as chambered tombs, timber circles and enclosures. Over 100 bracers are known from Ireland. Almost all lack contextual information about their findspots (Carlin 2018, 181–185), which indicates that most were deposited singly and not with human burials. Those few bracers for which there is information were found in wet ground, with spreads of occupation debris and with cremation burials. An assemblage of objects in a wooden box recovered from a bog at Corran, County Armagh, included two bracers, gold plates or discs, and jet beads (Eogan 1994, 21). The deposit has aspects in common with early beaker burials in Britain. It illustrates the similarities and differences that structured the relations between grave goods and other forms of depositional activity.

The scale of deposition is apparent from Katharina Becker's (2013) review of deposited artefacts in Ireland. She assigns 2051 copper and bronze axes, 162 halberds and 114 stone battle axes to the period 2400–1500 BC. The majority (92 percent) of these objects were single finds, without any association with either burials or other objects. There is an expected bias in collections towards resilient materials. Perhaps in the Bronze Age this resilience was valued for deposited objects, although the rare survivals of textiles and animal skins from burials would suggest otherwise (Harris 2019). A small number of wooden objects found in bogs and lakes have been dated to the later third millennium BC. These include six polypod bowls (Earwood 1991/1992), which were like ceramic examples known from Ireland and common in beaker assemblages in central Europe (Carlin 2018, 177–179).

Copper, gold and bronze could have been recycled into new objects. Aside from unfortunate losses, objects such as axes, daggers, halberds and lunulae need never have been left for modern generations to find and curate. Patterns in the distribution and contexts for these artefacts underpin claims for rules that governed depositional practices (Bradley 1990; Needham 1988). A recurring though flawed distinction that structures these analyses is between single finds, where an individual item of metalwork is found in isolation, and hoards, where two or more objects are recovered together. The distinction between one or more objects being found together was sustainable when single finds were interpreted as chance losses and hoards were the outcome of deliberate acts of deposition. This interpretation has been eroded by evidence for patterning in the selection of both individual and collections of objects for deposition, which shows there were patterns recurring across all forms of deposition. I am using the terms 'votive exchange' and 'votive offering' to describe the deposition of material culture outside mortuary rites and human burial assemblages.

Viewed in broad terms, there were notable differences in the types of objects that were deposited in graves, individually and in groups. There were regional differences in the numbers of individual and group offerings, in the ways they were constituted and in the locations where they were deposited. In north Leinster, the majority of copper and bronze flat axes were found singly and in wet ground, while in Munster most axes were recovered in groups on dryland (Cooney and Grogan 1994). Other patterns cut across these regional distinctions. Axes and halberds rarely accompanied burials, and they were mutually exclusive in votive exchanges (Needham 1988). Of the small numbers of axes known from graves, the early examples are all from northern Britain. Later axes in graves were commonly atypical in size or shape. Small, flanged axes accompanied the cremation burials at Llanddyfnan, Anglesey (Lynch 1991). Both daggers and knives were deposited in graves in Britain and rarely with burials in Ireland. One of these Irish exceptions was discovered in a large cist excavated close to Derry-Londonderry (McConway and Donnelly 2006). The man's body was laid on a bed of quartz, with a bronze dagger in a decorated organic sheath placed on his chest.

Decorated discs and basket-shaped ornaments, which are amongst the earliest items of goldwork, come almost exclusively from human burials in Britain, and in Ireland they were deposited singly and in groups without any associations with human bone (Figure 2.9). These differences shaped distinctive mortuary traditions in Ireland and Britain during the twenty-fifth to twenty-third centuries BC. The lunulae were deposited somewhat later, after 2250 BC, although the dating is tentative (Needham 2000a; O'Connor 2004, 210). They were offered individually or more occasionally in groups of up to four and almost never in association with other objects. While lunulae very rarely accompanied burials, their supposed equivalents in other materials, necklaces crafted from jet, shale and amber beads were usually deposited as grave goods. This difference has been explained as a distinction between personal items (necklaces as grave goods) and communal property (lunulae as regalia and votive offerings) (Eogan 1994, 34). The binary categorisation of individuals and communities is not helpful. Persons were constituted relationally, through their kin and the things that were shared and exchanged: 'The flow of objects constituted the person not as an

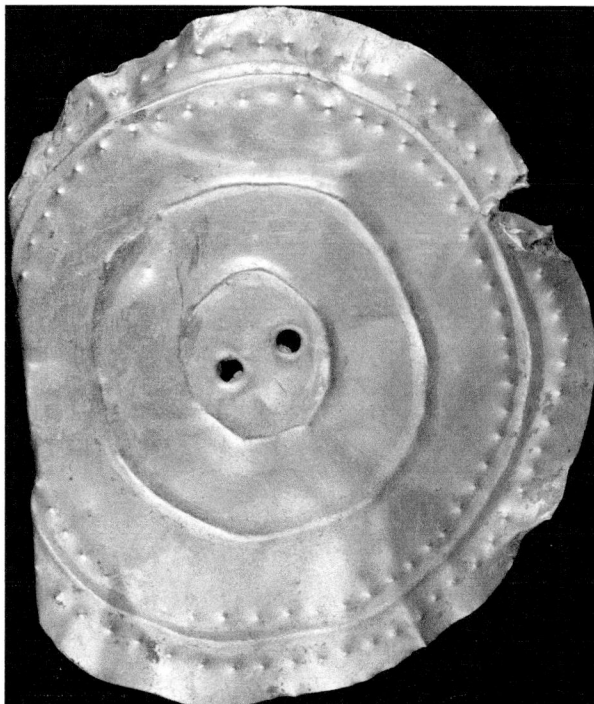

FIGURE 2.9 The Banc Tynddol gold disc recovered from a probable grave close to the Copa Hill copper mine, Ceredigion (Timberlake 2003). The disc is 39 mm across. Copyright: National Museum of Wales.

"individual" but as relationally embedded and profoundly sociocentric' (Brück 2019, 235). Although a few complete necklaces are known from burials, many more are incomplete, comprise only a few beads or are composites of beads made from different materials and with varying degrees of wear and damage. Ann Woodward's (2002) interpretation of this phenomenon is that the beads, and particularly the spacer plates, were treated as powerful objects that were passed on as gifts between generations. Through these transactions the objects acquired important biographies and became communal heirlooms.

The examples I have described illustrate how human burials and votive exchanges were exclusionary domains. They were related through their differences. Looking beyond the categorisation of objects, there were similarities that connected depositional practices with or without human remains. As convention, archaeologists present plans of human burials showing the arrangement of the body (or bodies) and the grave goods. Comparable plans are rarely available for groups of objects that lack an association with human bone (Lockington is one of the exceptions: Hughes 2000, 13). Textual descriptions of the arrangements of objects in the ground indicate they were assembled with the same care and formality afforded grave goods (Barber 2003, 53–63). These arrangements reflected a skilled and knowledgeable concern to treat the objects in the correct manner (Pollard 2001). A group of 10 or 11 flat axes from Carhan, County Kerry, were found in a stone-covered hollow in a large rock (Harbison 1968/1969, 43–44). The rock was a stepping stone across a small river, next to boggy ground, and the axes were arranged in a circle with the blades facing outwards and around some remains of wood ash and fragments of animal bone—possibly deer. Seven copper halberds from Hillswood, County Galway, were found in a shallow bog 'stuck in a bunch in the ground, with the points down' (Hemans 1850, 566). Seven flat axes from Colleonard Farm, Banff, Aberdeenshire, nested within a small pottery vessel in a stone-lined pit. The axes, two of which were incomplete and four with decorated surfaces, had been set upright with their blades uppermost in the pot (Coles 1969, 104). Two or three centuries later, on Arreton Down, the Isle of Wight, 11 spearheads, 4 flanged axes and 2 daggers were 'ranged in a regular order, the axes laid on the spear-heads about a foot deep on the brow of a hill' (Franks 1855, 326).

Ceramic and timber vessels, small pits and rock clefts were sometimes used to contain and conceal items of metalwork, as with the examples from Corran and Colleonard Farm (Coles 1969, 33). Five axes and an armlet were placed in the cleft of a rock face at Port Murray, Ayrshire, and subsequently discovered in 1883 (Cowie 2004, 250). Two flat axes were recovered from a cleft in a limestone quarry at Clontoo, County Kerry, and four axes were found under a large rock at Glenalla, County Donegal (Harbison 1968/1969). The presentation of objects in hollows and clefts, in ceramic vessels or in timber boxes provided a means of keeping items together, protected, concealed and potentially recoverable if required. Human burials and grave goods were sometimes wrapped in textiles and hides, and buried in timber- and stone-lined pits, and accompanied by pottery vessels and organic containers. These coverings served as means of controlling the assembly and deposition of objects, notably by protecting them from view as they were committed to the ground (Brück 2004, 318). Around 2150–1900 BC, in Strath Oykel, Easter Ross, a young woman's kin wrapped her body in a cattle hide, before lowering her into a carefully built cist, and covering her with woven material (Lelong 2014).

Cists, cairns and barrows, which usually contained human burials, also occasionally included separate deposits of metalwork. Excavations by William O'Brien at Toormore wedge tomb, County Cork, uncovered a bronze flat axe and two pieces of raw copper. The objects were placed in a hollow by an upright stone to one side of the tomb's entrance (O'Brien et al. 1989/1990). The two lunulae and the bronze axe from Harlyn Bay, Cornwall, were placed in a stone cist within a barrow; human remains had not survived or were never present (Jones et al. 2011). At Lockington, Leicestershire, two gold armlets; an unusual, large copper dagger; and two beakers (missing their upper bodies and rims, inverted and nested inside one another) were placed in a scoop just beyond the edge of a ring ditch and barrow (Hughes 2000) (Figure 2.10). Armlets and blades were more commonly deposited as grave goods, although there were no indications of human remains, nor space for them in the pit at Lockington.

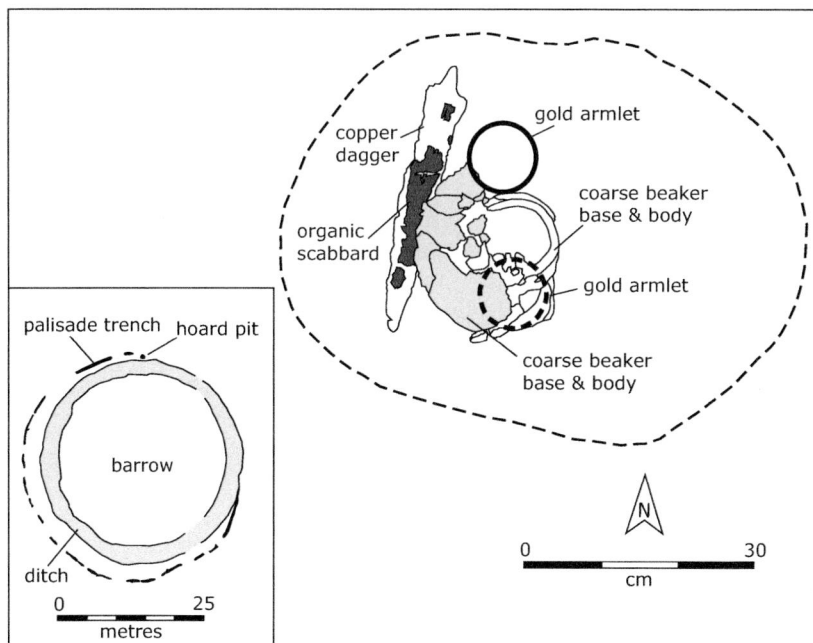

FIGURE 2.10 A plan of the pit at Lockington, Leicestershire, containing a copper dagger, gold armlets and fragments of beaker vessels. Adapted from Hughes 2000.

The association with mortuary architecture, specifically barrows and cairns, may have been made in another way through the use of natural mounds as locations for the deposition of metalwork (Needham 1988, 241 and 244). Three clusters of metalwork were recovered from Dail na Caraidh, Lochaber, on a prominent glacial mound close to the River Lochy and on the lowland northwest of Ben Nevis (Barrett and Gourlay 1999). The objects included whole and fragments of flat (Migdale-type) axes and blades (daggers and knives). John Barrett and Robert Gourlay (1999, 185) suggest the metalwork accumulated at Dail na Caraidh during exchanges between people and a well-used and venerated place in the landscape. The place may have acquired some of its significance alongside a prominent routeway across Scotland and as a location where the mid-winter sun could be observed rising from behind Ben Nevis (Bradley 2016, 193–197). Through votive exchanges of metalwork, individuals entangled their biographies with the place's 'unchanging practical, moral and sacred orders' (Barrett and Gourlay 1999, 185).

People deposited large numbers of objects in contexts outside graves. In Ireland during 2400–2100 BC, only 13 of the 1,215 copper and gold objects that Katharina Becker (2013, 231) recorded in her research were grave goods. Axes were, by long tradition, rarely associated with human remains in graves, and this tradition perpetuated through depositional practices. The ubiquity of axes in archaeological collections and their absence from graves might make us, as archaeologists, objectify or de-culture the axes: a disposable, alienable material. Part of the logic for treating grave goods as more important, as a greater contributor to culture, comes from the primacy we give to the human body in depositional acts.

Categories in the Bronze Age world emerged through the associations that people and things created during depositional events (Brück 2019). These associations may further disrupt archaeological categorisations of persons, objects and materials. Amongst the wooden artefacts recovered from wetlands are two anthropomorphic wooden figures dated to 2350–1950 BC, one

from marshland on the north bank of the Thames at Dagenham, Greater London, and the other from a crannog excavated at Lagore, County Meath (Coles 1990). Both figures are close to half a metre tall, the Dagenham figure made from pine and the Lagore one from oak (Figure 2.11). The wood-people were probably deposited in a similar manner to many, though not most, metal objects: on their own and in wet ground.

Axes and rare objects like the figures were related through the manner and places of their burial. The depositions of metalwork and other materials were, like grave goods and human bodies, performed with care and a knowledge of the proper way to do things. Depositional practices sometimes closely overlapped with mortuary rites in their shared use of mounds and monuments. They were also related through their differences, as some categories of object emerged depending upon whether they were excluded from or included in graves. Assemblages without and with human bodies were selective; they respected and created traditions; and they socialised people, places and objects. They were acts of exchange that brought beings and things into relation. They created kin and categories of kinship.

FIGURE 2.11 The wooden figure from Dagenham, Essex, made from pine and 495 mm in height. Image copyright: Colchester Museums.

The vibrant dead, 2000–1700 BC

The Bronze Age metalwork in museums has accumulated through thousands of individual discoveries. Commonly, objects have a provenance limited to a placename or fieldname, a parish or a county. Of the 115 lunulae that George Eogan (1994) identified in his review of Irish and British goldwork, the findspots of 33 are known only as 'Ireland'. Most depositional acts during 2450–1700 BC involved the exchange of a single commonplace item (an axe or a spearhead) in an unremarkable location. Similarly, most human burials during the same period appear to us as modest depositional events. In Chris Fowler's (2013) review of 355 burials in northeast England and the National Museum of Ireland's publication of rescue excavations of 167 graves throughout the country (Cahill and Sikora 2011), around a third of the burials they list lacked grave goods. This likely underestimates the original proportions.

Votive exchanges of metalwork occasionally involved elaborate and creative assemblages. When quarrying—with explosives—a granite knoll close to Loch Migdale, Sutherland, the workers revealed a group of objects dating to around the twenty-second and twenty-first centuries BC: two flat axes, sheet-bronze beads and armlets, fragments of bronze basket-shaped ornaments and six shale or jet buttons (Anderson 1900). Such groups were rare when compared with the objects deposited individually. Similarly, grave assemblages, although usually modest, were occasionally comprised of large numbers of goods, including distinctive and rare objects. During one of his many excavations of barrows in Derbyshire, Thomas Bateman (1848, 91–95) uncovered a cist at Cow Low, near Buxton, which contained the bodies of an adult and child. They were buried with 2 necklaces totalling over 100 jet beads and spacer plates.

A long-recognised group of burials from the twentieth to sixteenth centuries BC are the so-called 'Wessex' graves. These were inhumation (1950–1700 BC) and cremation (1750–1500 BC) burials found beneath and within barrows and accompanied by large numbers of uncommon grave goods including ornate bronze daggers and objects made from gold, amber and faience (Needham, Parker Pearson, et al. 2010; Woodward 2000, 101–122; Woodward et al. 2015). Stuart Piggott (1938) defined the burials as different in the 1930s. He interpreted them as incoming warrior aristocrats, who were buried with distinctive bronze daggers with links to Armorica, northwest France, and faience, which was then understood to originate in the eastern Mediterranean. The majority of the burials identified in Stuart Piggott's study were located in Wiltshire and Dorset, and he termed the phenomenon the 'Wessex Culture'.

Three of the better-known examples of these burial assemblages are 'Bush Barrow' (sited amongst the Normanton group of barrows overlooking Stonehenge), the 'Manton Barrow' (Preshute Down, on the Ridgeway, above the great henge at Avebury), and the 'Golden Barrow' (Upton Lovell, on the southwest edge of Salisbury Plain). In Bush Barrow, the central burial comprised three bronze daggers and an axe, a gold belt hook, two decorated gold lozenges, an ornate macehead and the crouched body of a mature man laid on his side (Needham, Lawson, et al. 2010). Maud Cunnington and her husband excavated the barrow at Manton in 1906, having noticed that ploughing was gradually destroying the mound (Cunnington 1907). They found an inhumation burial, possibly a woman, laid on her side in a flexed position. The grave goods arranged around and on her body included an amber disc bound in gold, a shale button also bound in gold, two small ceramic vessels, a dagger, three bronze awls, a necklace of shale and amber beads and a miniature halberd with a gold-covered haft. The woman was lying upon and was covered by separate woven textiles (Harris 2019). The Golden Barrow at Upton Lovell included two cremation burials, one of which was centrally placed beneath the barrow (Hoare 1812, 98). A group of objects were found within the barrow, although it is unclear if these accompanied a human burial. They included 13 gold beads, a gold plate, a shale button bound in gold, 2 gold cones and an amber necklace comprising up to a 1,000 beads.

The Wessex graves were expressions of a widespread tradition for burying the human dead with objects made from rare materials, especially gold, jet, amber and faience. These objects have been recovered from a small number of burials widely distributed in Ireland and Britain (Woodward et al. 2015). Some of the burials show similarities with the examples from Wessex, as at Towthorpe, North Yorkshire, which included a macehead and dagger (Gerloff 1975). In a barrow near Mold, Flintshire, the body was accompanied by a large number of amber beads, textiles and a unique embossed gold 'cape' (Needham 2012b; Powell 1953). A young person, around 14–15 years, was buried with faience, amber, bronze and jet beads, and a bronze blade and awl on the Mound of the Hostages, Tara, in the seventeenth century BC (O'Sullivan 2005; Sheridan et al. 2013).

By the 1970s, interpretations had disconnected the burials from direct Armorican and Mediterranean influences. They served a new role as evidence for the evolution of 'an individualising chiefdom society' whose leaders communicated their status through the acquisition and display of exotic material culture (Renfrew 1973, 224). The splendour and rarity of the grave goods are unquestionable. The burials were important and memorable events, and it is feasible that there were correlations between the influences of the dead in the graves and the ostentation of the grave goods and the burial monuments. The bronze, gold, amber and other materials can be described as 'riches' and as evidence of the 'wealth' of the deceased. These terms ascribe a narrow and recognisably modern system of value to the objects. The contexts in which the objects were used, and the knowledge associated with their use, broadened their means for defining identities and authority.

The shale, amber and gold cups found in a few graves, are comparable with rare examples from western Europe, and may have played a role in rituals where liquids were consumed or offered as libations (Needham et al. 2006). The vessels and the practices associated with their use derived from relations with and travel to distant places. They were redolent of journeys across the British and

Irish islands and to the European continent. Such journeys enabled travellers to acquire unusual and exotic things and gave them access to specialist forms of knowledge about the world, which may have been held in higher regard than the objects themselves (Kristiansen and Larsson 2005; Needham 2000b). In concluding their analysis of the grave goods from early Bronze Age burials, Ann Woodward and John Hunter propose that the objects were paraphernalia and special costumes worn during rituals, and that the dead in the graves were recognised as ritual specialists (Woodward et al. 2015, 559). This echoes Stuart Piggott's (1962) suggestion that the elderly man buried in a barrow at Upton Lovell, Wiltshire, held a role comparable with that of a shaman. He was interred with, amongst other objects, stone battle axes, polished flint axes and wearing a costume perhaps fringed at the base with bone points.

In addition to the roles and 'spheres of involvement' that the deceased held in a community, the grave assemblages were the consequence of kinfolk's efforts to reconfigure their social positions during important moments of change (Sørensen 2004). In such terms, the burials accompanied by rare grave goods may have been people who played important roles in life, while their positions in death were mediated through the actions of the kin who assembled the grave goods and enacted the funeral rites. It was the relations amongst the kin performing the mortuary rites that determined the extent to which the dead were buried with rare, sacred and supernatural objects. Necklaces made from jet, shale, amber, bone and ceramics were occasionally placed as grave goods (Figure 2.12). The beads in the necklaces may have been assembled during the life of the wearers through the exchanges in which they participated (Barrett 1994, 121–123) and symbolised the personal relations that contributed to the wearers' identities: the necklaces were a stringing together of kin (Brück 2004, 314). Commonly only a few beads were present in burials, and necklaces may have been buried incomplete or with parts of several necklaces buried together (Woodward 2002). Mortuary rites involved the fragmentation, exchange and recirculation of parts of the dead person, including the objects through which they were constituted, in order to recompense the losses that death brought to living kin: 'the giving of gifts at funerals allows kin groups to channel death into regeneration and turn loss to potential social gain' (Brück 2006, 87). The necklaces may have revealed how kinship was formed through the burial assemblages, with little direct regard for the relations that the dead had accumulated during their lives.

Powerful grave assemblages incorporated places into their performances. The large cairn at Rillaton, Cornwall, contained a gold cup accompanied by an inhumation burial with a bronze dagger, a pottery vessel and faience beads. The cairn is located on the crest of a ridge on the southeast edge of Bodmin Moor and close to a group of stone circles. In a study of the locations of barrows around Stonehenge, Frances Peters (2000) argues that the 'Wessex' burials, with finer and rarer grave goods, were more likely to be placed in large barrows in more conspicuous locations. This is a distinction that could be made in other parts of Britain and Ireland, as around Arbor Low, Derbyshire (Rogers 2013), and where

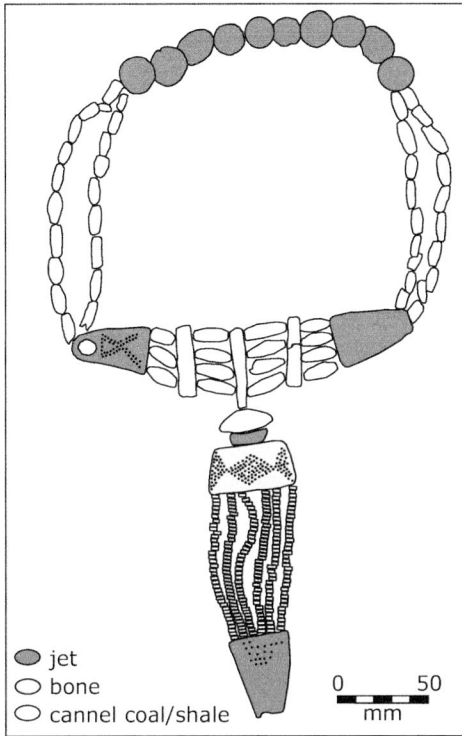

FIGURE 2.12 The Middleton Moor spacer plate necklace excavated by Thomas Bateman from a barrow near Arbor Low henge, Derbyshire. The necklace accompanied the burials of an adult and a child. It is comprised from pieces of six necklaces, showing variation in material and wear amongst the beads and spacer plates (Woodward et al. 2015, 313). Drawing based on an image in Woodward et al. 2015, with permissions of Ann Woodward and Museums Sheffield.

there were traditions of locating burial mounds on the crests of ridges and hill tops. The inhumation from a cist within the large cairn on Topped Mountain, County Fermanagh, was accompanied by a finely made bronze dagger, along with a gold band that probably decorated the dagger's pommel (Waddell 1990).

The distinctions between humans, objects and places can be softened by recognising multiple beings—human and nonhuman—creatively assembled as kin during the mortuary rites. A few objects and materials easily lend themselves to this perspective. The macehead from the Clandon Barrow, Wiltshire, is especially vivid (Needham and Woodward 2008). The polished piece of jet is inset with five circular studs made from shale which, in three cases, retain delicate gold covers. Four of the studs are arranged in pairs. The pair that retain their gold covers appear as wide contemplative eyes looking characterfully from the dark macehead. It does not matter whether or not this ocular effect was intended by the person crafting the object. The assembling of gold with other materials changed the vibrancy of the objects. Amber and jet were materials reserved for deposition during exceptional burial events, and both are notable for their electro-static properties, which have contributed to their long-standing use for jewellery, charms and amulets (Davis 2018). They may have imbued the wearers with quasi-magical properties or served to protect the dead during their journey to the afterlife (Sheridan and Shortland 2004). Alternatively, following the line of interpretation I used with gold, the materials carried a vibrancy that contributed to the potency of objects: 'An assemblage owes its agentic capacity to the vitality of the materialities that constitute it' (Bennett 2010, 34).

Rather than selecting grave goods that might protect the deceased in another world, the kin assembled composite persons, from respected, wise humans and powerful things, which now related would make a difference together in other worlds. Like the humans in the assemblages, the objects were chosen for their biographies and their kin. The analysis of the grave goods undertaken by Ann Woodward, John Hunter and colleagues demonstrates that many graves contained heirlooms (Woodward et al. 2015). Heirlooms were well-used things that had passed between hands and across generations, outliving the people who made them. In some cases the heirlooms were only fragments of objects, as with the amber bead recovered along with a large urn and a miniature cup from near Dromara, County Down (Kavanagh 1977), the pieces of a stone battle axe assembled with the inhumation at Upton Lovell, Wiltshire, and the pieces of an older sheet gold object that accompanied the gold cape from Mold, Flintshire (Needham 2012b). Other heirlooms were composite necklaces comprising beads of various materials and degrees of wear (Woodward et al. 2015, 389–460). The beads and spacer plates in the necklaces included many vibrant materials—gold, jet, faience, amber, fossils and bone—and the beads were formed into a variety of shapes, some mimicking forms in other materials. The necklace accompanying a burial at South Newton, Wiltshire, comprised an amber bead and 18 split and pierced teeth: 2 of dog and 16 of wolf.

If objects exhibited biographies and vibrancy, then they also held the capacities to tell and be the subjects of stories. In her ethnography of personal objects and narratives in Indonesia, Janet Hoskins (1998, 2) realised that she could not separate the histories of objects and persons: 'People and the things they valued were so complexly intertwined they could not be disentangled'. Given the sometime rarity, ancestry and vibrancy of the assemblages in some graves, Janet Hoskins's observation could be inverted: it was the things and the humans they valued that were intertwined and could not be untangled. The human beings in these assemblages were important although not essential in performing the story at the graveside and bringing the assemblage into being. This may help explain the lack of a human body with the objects in the Clandon Barrow on the Dorset Ridgeway, and the positions of the objects, fragmented, on top of the cairn that in normal circumstances would likely have covered an inhumation: a bronze dagger, amber cup, gold lozenge, small ceramic vessel and the remarkable jet macehead inlaid with gold (Needham and Woodward 2008). The person was the assemblage of things, unusually though not uniquely, without a human body (Cooper et al. 2020).

Conclusion

Chilling air and frozen ground dusted with snow greeted the archaeologists who excavated a cist at Langwell Farm, Strath Oykel, Easter Ross (Lelong 2014) (Figure 2.13). The procurator fiscal had directed local police to remove the human bones before the archaeologists arrived at the site. Fortunately, the driver of a mechanical excavator who had accidently disturbed the cist took photographs. The images show a tightly flexed body partially shrouded in a woven material. The body was a young, slender adult woman. She had lived in the region during her early childhood and died in her late 20s, sometime during the twenty-second to twentieth centuries BC. The cist was carefully built with large slabs, perhaps quarried from exposed bedrock in the River Oykel, nearby. The cist lay in peaty ground in the river's floodplain. The damp ground preserved organic materials that accompanied the woman's body: she was wrapped in the hide of a light to mid-coloured brown cow or bull, a hazel stick was laid on her knees, woven material covered her lower body and head and it may have extended across her entire body. An immense rock slab was hefted over the cist.

We could imagine the woman being laid as though she were sleeping in her stone box-bed, wrapped in a warming cow-skin. As Olivia Lelong (2014, 123) observes, this conjures a reassuring, though probably false, image of the woman prepared for awakening into an afterlife. The image is probably false because mites were recovered from surviving animal fibres from the hide. The mites had likely lived on the cow or bull just before it was killed and skinned. The hide was untreated, fresh, still bloodied, when it was wrapped around the body. The woman's body was not fresh. Decomposition had been arrested soon after her death, which limited the bacterial impact on the bones. Tom Booth (in Booth et al. 2015; Lelong 2014) argues that this process can have involved deliberate preservation or mummification of the corpse. There is therefore the possibility that the woman had died some time before she was committed to the cist. The woman's kin preserved her body and waited for the correct time of year for the completion of mortuary rites, or until their journeys brought her body to the proper place for burial.

Death was the end of a life and not the end of living. People treated the dead in ways that recognised and maintained their continued vibrancy in the world. In doing so, the living created new forms of person and new kin. At Langwell Farm, a near-living cattle hide was wrapped around the curated dead woman's body. The skin had a generative power that transformed and augmented the woman's personhood. Cattle were important livestock for meat, milk and wealth (Serjeantson 2011). The lives of beasts and people were intrinsic to one another,

FIGURE 2.13 The setting and excavation of the cist at Start Oykel, Easter Ross. Images courtesy of Olivia Lelong.

they were mutually constituted—they were kin. The mortuary rites performed at Langwell Farm reflected and reproduced this mutuality between human and animal kin. The young woman buried with a beaker at Sorisdale, which opens this chapter, offers a different expression of this process. The woman's body was interred, uncovered and reburied. Each of these acts created and transformed relations between kin and with a place or places. The people that gathered during mortuary rites recognised kinship with the dead and through the object(s) that accompanied her body. The beaker vessel was respected alongside the human body. It too was uncovered and reburied like the woman, and its fragments may have been distributed amongst living kin or left buried elsewhere. Both the woman and the beaker carried complex genealogies that related them to Coll and to distant 'homelands'.

This perspective brings into question ideas that beakers formed part of immutable ethnicities or identities—a Beaker People. Unquestionably, palaeo-genetic research has provided a fresh clarity to explanations of the impacts of population mobility on human ancestry during the third millennium BC. Combined with isotopic studies, we can now identify a few of the persons, the woman buried at Sorisdale being one, who travelled from the mainland to Britain and formed a part of these transformations. We can wonder at how the woman buried at Sorisdale and her kin found their ways to the Inner Hebrides, and how the knowledge of metallurgy and metal rapidly found a place in social life. A part of the answer is that kinship was a fluid and creative domain of social life during the twenty-fifth to twenty-third centuries BC. Networks were mutable, and people's lives were defined by mobilities rather than place-bound genealogical histories. Metal was absorbed into and then transformed ways of valuing and exchanging stone. This mutability enabled unfamiliar ancestries and cultures to rapidly associate and blend with places, things and kin in the landscapes of Ireland and Britain.

Distinctive, European, mortuary rites were followed for small numbers of the dead during the twenty-fourth and twenty-third centuries BC. These were noteworthy events, but their primary importance lay in their influence on the future trajectory of mortuary customs. Burial evolved as an increasingly complex and important rite of incorporation within mortuary rituals. Cemeteries developed as the inhumations and cremated remains of women and men, both young and old, were gathered in places. Monuments created histories of association and descent that localised aspects of kinship. Funerary assemblages were distinguished in part through their variability, as different rites and combinations of things and persons were gathered and performed at the grave. Burials became more ostentatious and creative, especially during and after the twentieth century BC. These provided new arenas with which to make powerful persons assembled from the dead and vibrant, biographical objects.

References

Anderson, Joseph. 1900. Notice of a hoard of bronze implements and ornaments, and buttons of jet, found at Migdale, on the estate of Skibo, Sutherland, exhibited to the Society by Mr Andrew Carnegie of Skibo. *Proceedings of the Society of Antiquaries of Scotland* 35:266–275.

Baker, Louise, Alison Sheridan and Trevor Cowie. 2003. An Early Bronze Age 'dagger grave' from Rameldry Farm, near Kingskettle, Fife. *Proceedings of the Society of Antiquaries of Scotland* 133:85–123.

Barber, Martyn. 2003. *Bronze and the Bronze Age: metalwork and society in Britain c. 2500–800 BC.* Tempus, Stroud.

Barclay, Alistair and Claire Halpin. 1999. *Excavations at Barrow Hills, Radley, Oxfordshire. Volume 1: the Neolithic and Bronze Age monument complex.* Oxbow Books, Oxford.

Barrett, John C. 1994. *Fragments from antiquity: an archaeology of social life in Britain, 2900–1200 BC.* Blackwell, Oxford.

Barrett, John C and Robert B Gourlay. 1999. An early metal assemblage from Dail na Caraidh, Inverness-shire, and its context. *Proceedings of the Society of Antiquaries of Scotland* 129:161–187.

Bateman, Thomas. 1848. *Vestiges of the antiquities of Derbyshire, and the sepulchural usages of its inhabitants: from the most remote ages to the reformation.* J R Smith, London.

Becker, Katharina. 2013. Transforming identities – new approaches to Bronze Age deposition in Ireland. *Proceedings of the Prehistoric Society* 79:225–263.

Bennett, Jane. 2010. *Vibrant matter: a political ecology of things,* Duke University Press. London.

Bewley, Robert, Ian Longworth, Sue Browne, Jacqueline Huntley and Gill Varndell. 1992. Excavation of a Bronze Age cemetery at Ewanrigg, Maryport, Cumbria. *Proceedings of the Prehistoric Society* 58:325–354.

Boast, Robin. 1995. Fine pots, pure pots, Beaker pots. In *'Unbaked urns of rudely shape': essays on British and Irish pottery for Ian Longworth,* edited by Ian Kinnes and Gill Varndell, pp. 69–80. Oxbow, Oxford.

Booth, Thomas, Andrew Chamberlain and Mike Parker Pearson. 2015. Mummification in Bronze Age Britain. *Antiquity* 89(347):1155–1173.

Bradley, Richard. 1990. *The passage of arms: an archaeological study of prehistoric hoards and votive deposits.* Cambridge University Press, Cambridge.

Bradley, Richard. 2016. *A geography of offerings: deposits of valuables in the landscapes of ancient Europe.* Oxbow, Oxford.

Bradley, Richard and Mark Edmonds. 1993. *Interpreting the axe trade: production and exchange in Neolithic Britain.* Cambridge University Press, Cambridge.

Bray, Peter J. 2012. Before $_{29}$Cu became copper: tracing the recognition and invention of metalleity in Britain and Ireland during the 3rd millennium BC. In *Is there a British Chalcolithic? People, place and polity in the late third millennium BC,* edited by Michael J Allen, Julie Gardiner and Alison Sheridan, pp. 56–70. Prehistoric Society Research Papers, 4. Prehistoric Society/Oxbow, Oxford.

Bray, Peter J and A Mark Pollard. 2012. A new interpretative approach to the chemistry of copper-alloy objects: source, recycling and technology. *Antiquity* 86(333):853–867.

Brindley, Anna. 2007. *The dating of Food Vessels and Urns in Ireland.* Department of Archaeology, National University of Ireland, Galway, Galway.

Brück, Joanna. 2004. Material metaphors: the relational construction of identity in Early Bronze Age burials in Ireland and Britain. *Journal of Social Archaeology* 4(3):307–333.

Brück, Joanna. 2006. Death, exchange and reproduction in the British Bronze Age. *European Journal of Archaeology* 9(1):73–101.

Brück, Joanna. 2019. *Personifying prehistory: relational ontologies in Bronze Age Britain and Ireland.* Oxford University Press, Oxford.

Burgess, Colin B. 1980. *The age of Stonehenge.* Dent, London.

Cahill, Mary. 2015. Here comes the sun…. *Archaeology Ireland* 29(1):26–33.

Cahill, Mary. 2016. A stone to die for. *Archaeology Ireland* 30(3):26–29.

Cahill, Mary and Maeve Sikora (editors). 2011. *Breaking ground, finding graves: reports on the excavations of burials by the National Museum of Ireland, 1927–2006.* Wordwell, Dublin.

Carlin, Neil. 2018. *The Beaker phenomenon? Understanding the character and context of social practices in Ireland 2500–2000 BC.* Sidestone Press, Leiden.

Case, Humphrey. 2007. Beakers and Beaker culture. In *Beyond Stonehenge: essays in honour of Colin Burgess,* edited by Christopher Burgess, Peter Topping and Frances Lynch, pp. 237–254. Oxbow, Oxford.

Cassidy, Lara M, Rui Martiniano, Eileen M Murphy, Matthew D Teasdale, James Mallory, Barrie Hartwell and Daniel G Bradley. 2015. Neolithic and Bronze Age migration to Ireland and establishment of the insular Atlantic genome. *Proceedings of the National Academy of Sciences* 113(2):368–373.

Chapman, Andy. 2007. A Bronze Age barrow cemetery and later boundaries, pit alignments and enclosures at Gayhurst Quarry, Newport Pagnell, Buckinghamshire. *Records of Buckinghamshire* 47(2):81–211.

Chenery, Carolyn A and Jane A Evans. 2011. A summary of the strontium and oxygen isotope evidence for the origins of Bell Beaker individuals found near Stonehenge. In *The Amesbury Archer and the Boscombe Bowmen: Bell Beaker burials at Boscombe Down, Amesbury, Wiltshire,* edited by Andrew P Fitzpatrick, pp. 185–190. Wessex Archaeology, Salisbury.

Cleal, Rosamund. 2011. Pottery. In *The Amesbury Archer and the Boscombe Bowmen: Bell Beaker burials at Boscombe Down, Amesbury, Wiltshire,* edited by Andrew P Fitzpatrick, pp. 140–154. Wessex Archaeology, Salisbury.

Cleary, Kerri. 2016. Burial practices in Ireland during the late third millennium BC: connecting new ideologies with local expressions. In *Celtic from the West 3. Atlantic Europe in the metal Ages: questions of shared language,* edited by John Koch and Barry Cunliffe, pp. 139–178. Oxbow, Oxford.

Coles, Bryony. 1990. Anthropomorphic wooden figures from Britain and Ireland. *Proceedings of the Prehistoric Society* 56:315–333.

Coles, John. 1969. Scottish Early Bronze Age metalwork. *Proceedings of the Society of Antiquaries of Scotland* 101:1–110.

Cook, Martin, Clare Ellis and Alison Sheridan. 2010. Excavations at Upper Largie Quarry, Argyll & Bute, Scotland: new light on the prehistoric ritual landscape of the Kilmartin Glen. *Proceedings of the Prehistoric Society* 76:165–212.

Cooney, Gabriel. 2002. So many shades of rock: colour symbolism and Irish stone axeheads. In *Colouring the past: the significance of colour in archaeological research,* edited by Andrew Meirion Jones and Gavin MacGregor, pp. 93–107. Berg, Oxford.

Cooney, Gabriel and Eoin Grogan. 1994. *Irish prehistory: a social perspective.* Wordwell, Dublin.

Cooper, Anwen, Duncan Garrow and Catriona Gibson. 2020. Spectrums of depositional practice in later prehistoric Britain and beyond: grave goods, hoards and deposits 'in between'. *Archaeological Dialogues* 27(2).

Cowie, Trevor. 2004. Special places for special axes? Early Bronze Age metalwork from Scotland in its landscape setting. In *Scotland in ancient Europe: the Neolithic and Bronze Age of Scotland in their European context,* edited by Ian A G Shepherd and Gordon J Barclay, pp. 247–261. Society of Antiquaries of Scotland, Edinburgh.

Cunnington, Maud E. 1907. Notes on the opening of a Bronze Age barrow at Manton, near Marlborough. *The Reliquary and Illustrated Archaeologist* 13:28–46.

Curtis, Neil and Neil Wilkin. 2019. Beakers and bodies in north-east Scotland: a regional and contextual study. In *The Beaker people: isotopes, mobility and diet in prehistoric Britain*, edited by Mike Parker Pearson, Alison Sheridan, Mandy Jay, Andrew Chamberlain, Michael P Richards and Jane Evans, pp. 211–252. Prehistoric Society Research Papers, 7. Prehistoric Society/Oxbow, Oxford.

Davis, Glynn. 2018. Rubbing and rolling, burning and burying: the magical use of amber in Roman London. In *Material approaches to Roman magic: occult objects and supernatural substances*, edited by Adam Parker and Stuart McKie, pp. 69–83. Oxbow, Oxford.

Donaldson, Peter. 1977. The excavation of a multiple round barrow at Barnack, Cambridgeshire 1974–1976. *Antiquaries Journal* 57(2):197–231.

Earwood, Caroline. 1991/1992. A radiocarbon date for Early Bronze Age wooden polypod bowls. *Journal of Irish Archaeology* 6:27–28.

Eogan, George. 1994. *The accomplished art: gold and gold working in Britain and Ireland during the Bronze Age (c. 2300–650 BC)*. Oxbow, Oxford.

Fitzpatrick, Andrew P. 2011. *The Amesbury Archer and the Boscombe Bowmen: Bell Beaker burials at Boscombe Down, Amesbury, Wiltshire*. Wessex Archaeology, Salisbury.

Fitzpatrick, Andrew P. 2015. The Kirkhaugh cairn: an old find and a new tale. *Past* 79:4–6.

Fokkens, Harry. 2012. Dutchmen on the move? A discussion of the adoption of the Beaker package. In *Is there a British Chalcolithic? People, place and polity in the late third millennium BC*, edited by Michael J Allen, Julie Gardiner and Alison Sheridan, pp. 115–125. Prehistoric Society Research Papers, 4. Prehistoric Society/Oxbow, Oxford.

Fokkens, Harry, Yvonne Achterkamp and Maikel Kuijpers. 2008. Bracers or bracelets? About the functionality and meaning of Bell Beaker wrist-guards. *Proceedings of the Prehistoric Society* 74:109–140.

Fowler, Chris. 2013. *The emergent past: a relational realist archaeology of Early Bronze Age mortuary practices*. Oxford University Press, Oxford.

Fowler, Chris and Neil Wilkin. 2016. Early Bronze Age mortuary practices in north-east England and south-east Scotland: using relational typologies to trace social networks. In *Prehistory without borders: the prehistoric archaeology of the Tyne-Forth region*, edited by Rachel Crellin, Chris Fowler and Peter Topping, pp. 112–135. Oxbow, Oxford.

Franks, Augustus W. 1855. Notes on bronze weapons found on Arreton Down, Isle of Wight. *Archaeologia* 36:326–331.

Frieman, Catherine J. 2012. *Innovation and imitation: stone skeuomorphs of metal from 4th–2nd millennia BC northwest Europe*. BAR International Series, 2365. Archaeopress, Oxford.

Frieman, Catherine J. 2014. Double edged blades: re-visiting the British (and Irish) flint daggers. *Proceedings of the Prehistoric Society* 80:33–65.

Furholt, Martin. 2018. Massive migrations? The impact of recent aDNA studies on our view of third millennium Europe. *European Journal of Archaeology* 21(2):159–191.

Gardiner, Julie, Michael J Allen, Andrew Powell, Phil Harding, Andrew J Lawson, Emma Loader, Jacqueline I McKinley, Alison Sheridan and Chris Stevens. 2007. A matter of life and death: Late Neolithic, Beaker and Early Bronze Age settlement and cemeteries at Thomas Hardye School, Dorchester. *Proceedings of the Dorset Natural History and Archaeological Society* 128:17–52.

Garton, Daryl, Andrew Howard and M Pearce. 1997. Archaeological investigations at Langford Quarry, Nottinghamshire 1995–6. *Tarmac Papers* 1:29–40.

Garwood, Paul. 2007. Vital resources, ideal images and virtual lives: children in Early Bronze Age funerary ritual. In *Children, childhood and society*, edited by Sally Crawford and Gillian Shepherd, pp. 63–82. BAR International Series, 1696. Archaeopress, Oxford.

Garwood, Paul. 2012. The present dead: the making of past and future landscapes in the British Chalcolithic. In *Is there a British Chalcolithic? People, place and polity in the late third millennium BC*, edited by Michael J Allen, Julie Gardiner and Alison Sheridan, pp. 298–316. Prehistoric Society Research Papers, 4. Prehistoric Society/Oxbow, Oxford.

Gerloff, Sabine. 1975. *The Early Bronze Age daggers in Great Britain and a reconsideration of the Wessex Culture*. Beck'sche Verlagsbuchhandlung, München.

Gibson, Alex (editor). 2019. *The Bell Beaker settlement of Europe: the Bell Beaker phenomenon from a domestic perspective*. Prehistoric Society Research Papers, 9. Prehistoric Society/ Oxbow, Oxford.

Harbison, Peter. 1968/1969. Catalogue of Irish Early Bronze Age associated finds containing copper or bronze. *Proceedings of the Royal Irish Academy* 67C:35–91.

Harding, Jan and Frances Healy. 2007. *The Raunds Area Project: a Neolithic and Bronze Age landscape in Northamptonshire*. English Heritage, London.

Harris, Susanna. 2019. The challenge of textiles in Early Bronze Age burials: fragments of magnificence. In *The textile revolution in Bronze Age Europe*, edited by Serena Sabatini and Sophie Bergerbrant, pp. 154–196. Cambridge University Press, Cambridge.

Haughton, Mark. 2018. Social relations and the local: revisiting our approaches to finding gender and age in prehistory. A case study from Bronze Age Scotland. *Norwegian Archaeological Review* 51(1/2):64–77.

Healy, Frances. 2012. Chronology, corpses, ceramics, copper and lithics. In *Is there a British Chalcolithic? People, place and polity in the late third millennium BC*, edited by Michael J Allen, Julie Gardiner and Alison Sheridan, pp. 144–163. Prehistoric Society Research Papers, 4. Prehistoric Society/Oxbow, Oxford.

Hemans, George W. 1850. A letter on presenting some antiquities to the Academy. *Proceedings of the Royal Irish Academy* 4:565–566.

Hoare, Richard C. 1812. *The ancient history of South Wiltshire*. William Miller, London.

Holden, Timothy G and Alison Sheridan. 2001. Three cists and a possible Roman road at Barbrush Quarry, Dunblane, Perthshire. *Proceedings of the Society of Antiquaries of Scotland* 131:87–100.

Hoskins, Janet. 1998. *Biographical objects: how things tell the stories of people's lives*. Routledge, London.

Hughes, Gwilym. 2000. *The Lockington gold hoard: an Early Bronze Age barrow cemetery at Lockington, Leicestershire*. Oxbow, Oxford.

Hunter, Fraser. 2000. Excavation of an Early Bronze Age cemetery and other sites at West Water Reservoir, West Linton, Scottish Borders. *Proceedings of the Society of Antiquaries of Scotland* 130:115–182.

Jay, Mandy, Michael P Richards and Peter Marshall. 2019. Radiocarbon dates and their Bayesian modelling. In *The Beaker people: isotopes, mobility and diet in prehistoric Britain*, edited by Mike Parker Pearson, Alison Sheridan, Mandy Jay, Andrew Chamberlain, Michael P Richards and Jane Evans, pp. 43–80. Prehistoric Society Research Papers, 7. Prehistoric Society/Oxbow, Oxford.

Jones, Andy M. 2016. *Preserved in the peat: an extraordinary Bronze Age burial on Whitehorse Hill, Dartmoor, and its wider context*. Oxbow, Oxford.

Jones, Andy M, Jane Marley, Henrietta Quinnell and Steve Hartgroves. 2011. On the beach: new discoveries at Harlyn Bay, Cornwall. *Proceedings of the Prehistoric Society* 77:89–109.

Kavanagh, Rhoda M. 1977. Pygmy cups in Ireland. *Journal of the Royal Society of Antiquaries of Ireland* 107:61–95.

Kinnes, Ian, Paul T Craddock, Stuart Needham and Janet Lang. 1979. Tin-plating in the Early Bronze Age: the Barton Stacey axe. *Antiquity* 53(208):141–144.

Kristiansen, Kristian and Thomas Larsson. 2005. *The rise of Bronze Age society: travels, transmissions and transformations.* Cambridge University Press, Cambridge.

Last, Jonathan. 1998. Books of life: biography and memory in a Bronze Age barrow. *Oxford Journal of Archaeology* 17(1):43–53.

Lelong, Olivia. 2014. Wrappings of power: a woman's burial in cattle hide at Langwell Farm, Strath Oykel. *Proceedings of the Society of Antiquaries of Scotland* 144:65–131.

Lucas, Gavin. 1996. Of death and debt: a history of the body in Neolithic and Early Bronze Age Yorkshire. *Journal of European Archaeology* 4(1):99–118.

Lucy, Sam. 2005. The archaeology of age. In *The archaeology of identity: approaches to gender, age, status, ethnicity and religion,* edited by Margarita Díaz-Andreu, Sam Lucy, Staša Babić and David N Edwards, pp. 43–66. Taylor and Francis, London.

Lynch, Frances. 1991. *Prehistoric Anglesey: the archaeology of the island to the Roman conquest.* The Anglesey Antiquarian Society, Llangefni.

Maryon, Herbert. 1936. Excavation of two Bronze Age barrows at Kirkhaugh, Northumberland. *Archaeologia Aeliana* 13:207–217.

McConway, Cia and Emma Donnelly. 2006. Daggers at dawn. *Archaeology Ireland* 20(2):5.

McKinley, Jacqueline I. 2011. Human remains (graves 1236 and 1289). In *The Amesbury Archer and the Boscombe Bowmen: Bell Beaker burials at Boscombe Down, Amesbury, Wiltshire,* edited by Andrew P Fitzpatrick, pp. 77–87. Wessex Archaeology, Salisbury.

McLaren, Dawn. 2004. An important child's burial from Doune, Perth and Kinross, Scotland. In *From sickles to circles: Britain and Ireland at the time of Stonehenge,* edited by Alex Gibson and Alison Sheridan, pp. 289–303. Tempus, Stroud.

McLaughlin, T Rowan, Nicki J Whitehouse, Rick J Schulting, Meriel McClatchie, Philip Barratt and Amy Bogaard. 2016. The changing face of Neolithic and Bronze Age Ireland: a big data approach to the settlement and burial records. *Journal of World Prehistory* 29:117–153.

Mizoguchi, Koji. 1993. Time in the reproduction of mortuary practices. *World Archaeology* 25(2):223–235.

Montgomery, Janet, Jane Evans and Jacqueline Towers. 2019. Strontium isotopic analysis. In *The Beaker people: isotopes, mobility and diet in prehistoric Britain,* edited by Mike Parker Pearson, Alison Sheridan, Mandy Jay, Andrew Chamberlain, Michael P Richards and Jane Evans, pp. 369–424. Prehistoric Society Research Papers, 7. Prehistoric Society/Oxbow, Oxford.

Mount, Charles. 1997. Adolf Mahr's excavations of an Early Bronze Age cemetery at Keenoge, County Meath. *Proceedings of the Royal Irish Academy* 97C(1):1–68.

Needham, Stuart. 1988. Selective deposition in the British Early Bronze Age. *World Archaeology* 20(2):229–248.

Needham, Stuart. 1996. Chronology and periodisation in the British Bronze Age. *Acta Archaeologica* 67:121–140.

Needham, Stuart. 2000a. The development of embossed goldwork in Bronze Age Europe. *Antiquaries Journal* 80(1):27–65.

Needham, Stuart. 2000b. Power pulses across a cultural divide: cosmologically driven acquisition between Armorica and Wessex. *Proceedings of the Prehistoric Society* 66:151–207.

Needham, Stuart. 2002. Analytical implications for Beaker metallurgy in north-west Europe. In *The beginnings of metallurgy in the old world,* edited by Martin Bartelheim, Ernst Pernicka and Rüdiger Krause, pp. 99–133. Forschungen zur Archäometrie und Altertumswissenschaft, Rahden.

Needham, Stuart. 2004. Migdale-Marnoch: sunburst of Scottish metallurgy. In *Scotland in ancient Europe: the Neolithic and Bronze Age of Scotland in their European context,* edited by Ian A G Shepherd and Gordon J Barclay, pp. 217–245. Society of Antiquaries of Scotland, Edinburgh.

Needham, Stuart. 2005. Transforming Beaker culture in north-west Europe: processes of fusion and fission. *Proceedings of the Prehistoric Society* 71:171–217.

Needham, Stuart. 2012a. Case and place for the British Chalcolithic. In *Is there a British Chalcolithic? People, place and polity in the late third millennium BC*, edited by Michael J Allen, Julie Gardiner and Alison Sheridan, pp. 1–26. Prehistoric Society Research Papers, 4. Prehistoric Society/Oxbow, Oxford.

Needham, Stuart. 2012b. Putting capes into context: Mold at the heart of a domain. In *Reflections on the past: essays in honour of Frances Lynch*, edited by William J Britnell and Robert J Silvester, pp. 210–236. Cambrian Archaeological Association, Welshpool.

Needham, Stuart. 2015. A hafted halberd excavated at Trecastell, Powys: from undercurrent to uptake – the emergence and contextualisation of halberds in Wales and north-west Europe. *Proceedings of the Prehistoric Society* 81:1–41.

Needham, Stuart, Andrew J Lawson and Ann Woodward. 2010. 'A noble group of barrows': Bush Barrow and the Normanton Down Early Bronze Age cemetery two centuries on. *Antiquaries Journal* 90:1–39.

Needham, Stuart, Keith Parfitt and Gill Varndell (editors). 2006. *The Ringlemere Cup: precious cups and the beginnings of the Channel Bronze Age*. British Museum, London.

Needham, Stuart, Mike Parker Pearson, Alan Tyler, Mike Richards and Mandy Jay. 2010. A first 'Wessex 1' date from Wessex. *Antiquity* 84(324):363–373.

Needham, Stuart and Ann Woodward. 2008. The Clandon barrow finery: a synopsis of success in an Early Bronze Age world. *Proceedings of the Prehistoric Society* 74:1–52.

Northover, Peter. 1980. The analysis of Welsh Bronze Age metalwork. In *Guide catalogue to the Bronze Age collections in the National Museum of Wales*, edited by Hubert N Savory, pp. 229–243. National Museum of Wales, Cardiff.

Ó Donnabháin, Barra and Anna L Brindley. 1989/1990. The status of children in a sample of Bronze Age burials containing pygmy cups. *Journal of Irish Archaeology* 5:19–24.

O'Brien, William. 2004. *Ross Island: mining, metal and society in early Ireland*. National University of Ireland, Galway, Galway.

O'Brien, William. 2015. *Prehistoric copper mining in Europe: 5500–500 BC*. Oxford University Press, Oxford.

O'Brien, William, Peter Northover and Esther Cameron. 1989/1990. An Early Bronze Age metal hoard from a wedge tomb at Toormore, Co. Cork. *Journal of Irish Archaeology* 5:9–17.

O'Connor, Brendan. 2004. The earliest Scottish metalwork since Coles. In *Scotland in ancient Europe: the Neolithic and Bronze Age of Scotland in their European context*, edited by Ian A G Shepherd and Gordon J Barclay, pp. 205–216. Society of Antiquaries of Scotland, Edinburgh.

O'Sullivan, Muiris. 2005. *Duma na nGiall: the Mound of the Hostages, Tara*. Wordwell in association with the UCD School of Archaeology, Bray.

Olalde, Iñigo, Selina Brace, Morten Allentoft, E and et al. 2018. The Beaker phenomenon and the genomic transformation of northwest Europe. *Nature* 555(7695):190–196.

Parker Pearson, Mike. 2009. The Earlier Bronze Age. In *The archaeology of Britain: an introduction from earliest times to the twenty-first century*, edited by John Hunter and Ian Ralston, pp. 103–125. Routledge, London.

Parker Pearson, Mike, Andrew Chamberlain, Mandy Jay, Mike Richards, Alison Sheridan, Neil Curtis, Jane Evans, Alex Gibson, Margaret Hutchison, Patrick Mahoney, Peter Marshall, Janet Montgomery, Stuart Needham, Sandra O'Mahoney, Maura Pellegrini and Neil Wilkin. 2016. Beaker people in Britain: migration, mobility and diet. *Antiquity* 90(351):620–637.

Parker Pearson, Mike, Alison Sheridan, Mandy Jay, Andrew Chamberlain, Michael P Richards and Jane Evans (editors). 2019. *The Beaker people: isotopes, mobility and diet in prehistoric Britain.* Prehistoric Society Research Papers. Prehistoric Society/Oxbow, Oxford.

Penhallurick, Roger D. 1986. *Tin in antiquity: its mining and trade throughout the ancient world with particular reference to Cornwall.* Institute of Metals, London.

Peters, Frances. 2000. Two traditions of Bronze Age burial in the Stonehenge landscape. *Oxford Journal of Archaeology* 19(4):343–358.

Piggott, Stuart. 1938. The Early Bronze Age in Wessex. *Proceedings of the Prehistoric Society* 4:52–106.

Piggott, Stuart. 1962. From Salisbury Plain to Siberia. *Wiltshire Archaeological and Natural History Magazine* 58:93–97.

Pollard, Joshua. 2001. The aesthetics of depositional practice. *World Archaeology* 33(2):315–333.

Powell, Terrence G E. 1953. The gold ornament from Mold, Flintshire, North Wales. *Proceedings of the Prehistoric Society* 29:161–179.

Renfrew, Colin. 1973. Wessex as a social question. *Antiquity* 47(187):221–224.

Richie, J N Graham and John Crawford. 1977/1978. Excavations at Sorisdale and Killunaig, Coll. *Proceedings of the Society of Antiquaries of Scotland* 109:75–84.

Roberts, Benjamin. 2008. Creating traditions and shaping technologies: understanding the earliest metal objects and metal production in western Europe. *World Archaeology* 40(3):354–372.

Robertson-Mackay, M E. 1980. A 'head and hooves' burial beneath a round barrow, with other Neolithic and Bronze Age sites, on Hemp Knoll, near Avebury, Wiltshire. *Proceedings of the Prehistoric Society* 46:123–176.

Roe, Fiona and Ann Woodward. 2009. Bits and pieces: early Bronze Age stone bracers from Ireland. *Internet Archaeology* 26.

Rogers, Alice. 2013. The afterlife of monuments in the English Peak District: the evidence of Early Bronze Age burials. *Oxford Journal of Archaeology* 32(1):39–51.

Rohl, Brenda M and Stuart Needham. 1998. *The circulation of metal in the British Bronze Age: the application of lead isotope analysis.* British Museum Occasional Paper 102. The British Museum, London.

Russel, Andrew D. 1990. Two beaker burials from Chilbolton, Hampshire. *Proceedings of the Prehistoric Society* 56:153–172.

Salmond, Anne. 2005. Their body is different, our body is different: European and Tahitian navigators in the 18th century. *History and Anthropology* 16(2):167–186.

Serjeantson, Dale. 2011. *Review of animal remains from the Neolithic and Early Bronze Age of southern Britain (4000 BC–1500 BC).* Research Department Report Series. English Heritage, Portsmouth.

Sharples, Niall. 2009. Beaker settlement in the Western Isles. In *Land and People: papers in memory of John G Evans,* edited by Michael J Allen, Niall Sharples and Terry O'Connor, pp. 147–158. Prehistoric Society Research Papers, 2. Prehistoric Society/Oxbow Books, Oxford.

Shell, Colin. 1978. The early exploitation of tin deposits in south west England. In *The origins of metallurgy in Atlantic Europe: proceedings of the fifth Atlantic Colloquium,* edited by Michael Ryan, pp. 251–263. Stationery Office, Dublin.

Shepherd, Alexandra. 2012. Stepping out together: men, women and their Beakers in time and space. In *Is there a British Chalcolithic? People, place and polity in the late third millennium BC,* edited by Michael J Allen, Julie Gardiner and Alison Sheridan, pp. 257–280. Prehistoric Society Research Papers, 4. Prehistoric Society/Oxbow, Oxford.

Shepherd, Ian A G 1986. *Powerful pots: Beakers in north-east prehistory.* Anthropological Museum, University of Aberdeen, Aberdeen.

Sheridan, Alison. 1983. A reconsideration of the origins of Irish metallurgy. *Journal of Irish Archaeology* 1:11–19.

Sheridan, Alison, Mandy Jay, Janet Montgomery, Maura Pellegrini and Jacqueline Cahill Wilson. 2013. 'Tara Boy': local hero or international man of mystery? In *Tara. From the past to the future: towards a new research agenda*, edited by Muiris O'Sullivan, Christopher Scarre and Maureen Doyle, pp. 207–232. Wordwell, Dublin.

Sheridan, Alison and Andrew Shortland. 2004. '…beads which have given rise to so much dogmatism, controversy and rash speculation': faience in Early Bronze Age Britain and Ireland. In *Scotland in ancient Europe: the Neolithic and Early Bronze Age of Scotland in their European context*, edited by Ian A G Shepherd and Gordon J Barclay, pp. 263–279. Society of Antiquaries of Scotland, Edinburgh.

Sofaer Derevenski, Joanna. 2002. Engendering context: context as gendered practice in the early Bronze Age of the Upper Thames Valley, UK. *European Journal of Archaeology* 5(2):191–211.

Sørensen, Marie Louise Stig. 2004. Stating identities: the use of objects in rich Bronze Age graves. In *Explaining social change: essays in honour of Colin Renfrew*, edited by John Cherry, Chris Scarre and Stephen Shennan, pp. 167–176. McDonald Institute for Archaeological Research, Cambridge.

Standish, Christopher D, Bruno Dhuime, Chris J Hawkesworth and Alistair W G Pike. 2015. A non-local source of Irish Chalcolithic and Early Bronze Age gold. *Proceedings of the Prehistoric Society* 81:149–177.

Taylor, Joan. 1980. *Bronze Age goldwork of the British Isles.* Cambridge University Press, Cambridge.

Timberlake, Simon. 2003. *Excavations at Copa Hill, Cwmystwyth (1986–1999).* British Archaeological Reports British Series 348. Archaeopress, Oxford.

Timberlake, Simon. 2017. New ideas on the exploitation of copper, tin, gold, and lead ores in Bronze Age Britain: the mining, smelting, and movement of metal. *Materials and Manufacturing Processes* 32(7–8):709–727.

Timberlake, Simon and Peter Marshall. 2018. Copper mining and smelting in the British Bronze Age: new evidence of mine sites including some re-analyses of dates and ore sources. In *Mining for ancient copper: essays in memory of Beno Rothenberg*, edited by Erez Ben-Yosef, pp. 418–434. Eisenbrauns, Winona Lake, Indiana.

Vander Linden, Marc. 2007. What linked the Bell Beakers in third millennium BC Europe? *Antiquity* 81(312):343–352.

Vander Linden, Marc. 2013. A little bit of history repeating itself: theories on the Bell Beaker phenomenon. In *The Oxford handbook of the European Bronze Age*, edited by Harry Fokkens and Anthony Harding, pp. 68–81. Oxford University Press, Oxford.

Waddell, John. 1990. *The Bronze Age burials of Ireland.* Galway University Press, Galway.

Wiggins, Kenneth. 2000. A rescue excavation on Rathlin Island, County Antrim. *Ulster Journal of Archaeology* 59:47–70.

Wilkin, Neil. 2014. *Food Vessel pottery from Early Bronze Age funerary contexts in northern England: a typological and contextual study.* PhD thesis, University of Birmingham.

Woodward, Ann. 2000. *British barrows: a matter of life and death.* Tempus, Stroud.

Woodward, Ann. 2002. Beads and beakers: heirlooms and relics in the British Early Bronze Age. *Antiquity* 76:1040–1047.

Woodward, Ann and John Hunter. 2011. *An examination of prehistoric stone bracers from Britain.* Oxbow, Oxford.

Woodward, Ann, John Hunter, David Bukach, Stuart Needham and Alison Sheridan. 2015. *Ritual in Early Bronze Age grave goods: an examination of ritual and dress equipment from Chalcolithic and Early Bronze Age graves in England.* Oxbow, Oxford.

Woodward, Ann, John Hunter, Rob Ixer, Fiona Roe, Philip Potts, Peter Webb, John Watson and Michael Jones. 2006. Beaker age bracers in England: sources, function and use. *Antiquity* 80(309):530–543.

3

DISPERSED LIVES

2000–700 BC

Whitehorse Hill is a high and now bleak part of Dartmoor, Devon, reserved as a military training area. A young adult's cremated remains were buried in the hill's mantle of peat in the late eighteenth or seventeenth century BC (Jones 2016) (Figure 3.1). The peat preserved the organic objects accompanying the burial and the colours and textures of the mortuary rites.

FIGURE 3.1 The cist emerges from the peat on Whitehorse Hill, Dartmoor. Copyright: Cornwall Archaeological Unit.

The person died in early adulthood. Their body was wrapped in a fine textile and burnt on a pyre of oak timber. The incompleteness of the cremated remains and their containment in a bear's pelt, probably secured with a bronze pin, could mean the cremation took place some distance from Whitehorse Hill and the cremated remains were carried to the cist. A lidded basket was used to collect and conceal jewellery accompanying the burial: a braided cattle-hair bracelet with small tin studs (Figure 3.2); a necklace of clay, shale, amber and tin beads; two pairs of turned-wood studs that might have been worn in ears and lips. The pelt-wrapped bone and the basket were placed on a piece of fine textile with a decorative fringe of animal-hide. Purple moor grasses, possibly incorporating meadowsweet flowers, softened the rough stone floor of the cist. The grasses were collected locally and probably late in the summer when they would have been easier to pull up and the meadowsweet was in flower. A similar shroud of grasses may have covered the burial.

Aspects of the Whitehorse Hill burial were exceptional for the time: the bronze pin, composite necklace and the tin-studded bracelet. Other elements such as the textiles and animal pelt may also have been, although too little survives from elsewhere to judge this confidently. Plants and flowers accompanied contemporary burials (Tipping 1994), and acts of containment and concealment were common (Cooper et al. 2019). The grave gathered local materials and textures into its construction: earthy, damp peat; the granular, weathered granite slabs in the cist; the bed of moor grasses and meadowsweet. Kinship was constituted during mortuary rites in the company of things, animals and places. This chapter traces the gradual erosion of these elaborate grave assemblages. They were replaced with dispersed fragments and substances entangling people and things deeply with the landscape.

FIGURE 3.2 The braided cattle-hair bracelet with tin studs from Whitehorse Hill, after conservation. Copyright: Wiltshire Conservation Centre.

Cremation, 2000–1600 BC

People cremated some of the dead throughout much of the Neolithic and Bronze Age in Ireland, with the rite appearing less frequently in Britain. This difference might be because in Britain cremated human remains were not commonly buried in chambered tombs or in the ground during the third millennium, and they have not survived for archaeologists to excavate. Our knowledge is also biased by a long-held understanding that cremation was a Bronze Age mortuary rite, and therefore, cremated human remains unaccompanied by grave goods were assumed to be of Bronze Age date. This position has changed as scientific dating is more routinely applied during excavation projects. At Yarnton, Oxfordshire, small quantities of cremated bone were identified in pits dating to the late fourth and early third millennia BC (Hey et al. 2016, 88–89). A pit containing a larger quantity (620 g) of cremated human and possibly sheep bone was found amongst a group of later Neolithic pits. Cemeteries of later Neolithic cremation burials have now been recognised at more than 12 locations within Britain: Dorchester-on-Thames, Stonehenge, Imperial Sports Ground and Forteviot are several examples (Noble and Brophy 2017).

Cremation is more visible in archaeological material dated after 2000 BC and appears as the dominant rite throughout Ireland and Britain from 1800 BC. The many exceptions within this pattern indicate that cremation and inhumation were contemporary rites. Three infants were inhumed at Low Grounds, Over, Cambridgeshire, and their bodies stacked above two earlier beaker-accompanied burials at a time after cremation was adopted as a rite in a neighbouring barrow (Garrow et al. 2014). Two graves at Barns Farm, Fife, contained inhumations and deposits of cremated bone, with accompanying food vessels (Watkins 1982, 70–77). John Waddell (1990, 20) identified multiple instances of cremated and unburnt human remains in close proximity or within the same graves. At Cuillare, County Mayo, the unburnt fragments of a man's body were placed on top of a cist containing a cremation (Waddell 1990, 121). The unburnt remains of at least nine individuals were buried around a cairn at Cnip Headland, Isle of Lewis, during the eighteenth and seventeenth centuries BC (Lelong 2018). Four inhumations were placed beneath a cairn in Longniddry, East Lothian, in the middle of the second millennium BC (Baker 2003). In reviewing Neolithic mortuary traditions in Ireland, Gabriel Cooney (2016) recognised varying combinations of cremation and inhumation rites that reflected choices made by kin in the ways they distinguished the dead. This same observation could apply to the early and middle centuries of the second millennium BC.

The styles of vessels that people sometimes selected to accompany mortuary deposits changed during the period that cremation became more widely practised. In Ireland, vase forms began replacing bowl food vessels, with the latter more strongly associated with inhumation burials. Enlarged food vessels, also termed food vessel urns, form the earliest Bronze Age ceramic style routinely deposited with cremation burials in Britain: in east Yorkshire, where over half of the food vessels in Britain have so far been found, cremations only commonly accompany food vessel urns (Manby et al. 2003). Collared urns and cordoned urns were the other widespread types of ceramic vessels made during 2050–1500 BC, and they were associated exclusively with cremation burials (Law 2008). Collared urns take their name from a decorated, raised collar around the upper third of the vessel, and cordoned urns are characterised by raised, horizontal cordons that encircle the vessel, dividing it into two or more sections. Smaller vessels, variously known as accessory, incense and pygmy cups, accompanied some burials (Allen and Hopkins 2000). Some are perforated, and many have decorated bases. The cups can show traces of intense heat, and one suggestion that has retained currency since the 1800s is that the vessels held embers that were carried to the pyre (Stanley and Way 1868, 289). The cups undoubtedly played varied roles (Gibson 2004). Robert Law (2008, 106) argues that all the urn forms that were current during 2050–1500 BC were stylistically and technologically

FIGURE 3.3   A ceramic vessel from an inhumation burial in a barrow near Folkton, North Yorkshire, which shows affinities with both collared urns and food vessels (Wilkin 2014, 301). The vessel is 216 mm in height. © The Trustees of the British Museum. All rights reserved.

inter-related. Potters began with similar templates and made minor changes to the vessels' forms to develop distinctive styles like the collared urn (Figure 3.3).

Alongside the ceramic vessels that accompanied some cremation burials, kin provided objects and animals to accompany bodies on the pyres and for the burial rites (Medina-Pettersson 2013, 148–150). Toggles, buttons and beads that acted as fastenings on clothing or wrappings were present with cremation deposits, just as they were alongside inhumation burials (as at Ewanrigg, Cumbria: Bewley et al. 1992). Dressing, wrapping or covering the body were important actions during the mortuary rites, irrespective of whether or not the body would be cremated. A familiar variety of grave goods accompanied small numbers of cremation burials. Bronze earrings, a bone belt hook and pin and probably a battle axe too were pyre goods accompanying a cremation with a collared urn at Stanbury, West Yorkshire (Richardson and Vyner 2011). Chris Fowler notes that, in northeast England, flint and bronze knives were rarely burnt with the body but were placed with the person after cremation (Fowler 2013, 162 and 239). In this context, they may, Fowler suggests, be metaphors for the cutting loose of the dead from the living or directly employed in the preparation of the corpse. Small bronze knives or razors were found burnt and unburnt along with cremations and cordoned urns in Ireland and Scotland (Kavanagh 1991). Joanna Brück (2004) interprets the burnt and unburnt objects with the cremated human remains in a collared urn at Bedd Branwen, Anglesey (Lynch 1971, 26), as a distinction between things chosen to accompany the corpse and items deposited at the time of burial. The burnt objects, a bone bead and pommel, were placed on the man's body before it was cremated, while the unburnt objects, made up of jet-like and amber beads, may have been presented as gifts at the graveside. The burnt bone objects lay amongst the human bone, with the beads on top of the cremated material.

The human bodies on the pyres were, in select instances, accompanied by rarer objects crafted from materials such as bronze, gold, amber and faience. In the nineteenth or eighteenth century BC, at Grange, Tulsk, County Roscommon, a young adult male was cremated with an Armorica-British dagger and bone pommel, and the remains collected into a vase urn and placed in the top of a cairn (Ó Ríordáin 1997). Around a similar time, amber beads and decorated gold discs were buried with cremated human remains in a large barrow at the Knowes of Trotty, Mainland, Orkney (Clarke et al. 1985, 282). Two or more centuries later, at Camerton, Somerset, a cremated body was accompanied by a small ceramic vessel, a perforated stone, a bronze dagger (Camerton-Snowshill type) and a bulb-headed pin. The bronze pin is intricately decorated and polished through use (Woodward et al. 2015, 177–178). Another unique and well-worn bronze pin, headed by two pairs of interlinked rings, was buried in a timber-lined pit with cremated human remains, a small pottery vessel and a Camerton-Snowshill dagger at Collingbourne Ducis, Wiltshire (Piggott 1938, 105) (Figure 3.4). Richard Colt Hoare excavated Collingbourne Ducis and the barrow at Wilsford G8, Wiltshire, where he found a cremation burial lying on the

FIGURE 3.4 A bronze ring-headed dress pin from Collingbourne Ducis, Wiltshire. The pin is 161 mm in length and very worn from use. Copyright: Wiltshire Museum, Devizes.

surface below the mound, along with a perforated ceramic cup and a group of pendants made from gold, amber, bronze, bone and shale (Woodward et al. 2015, 450–451). The fine collection of 23 faience beads accompanying the cremated remains of a woman and an unborn or newly born infant from Findhorn, Moray, were all burnt (Shepherd and Shepherd 2001) (Figure 3.5). The differential effects of burning on the cremated bone from Findhorn is interpreted as evidence

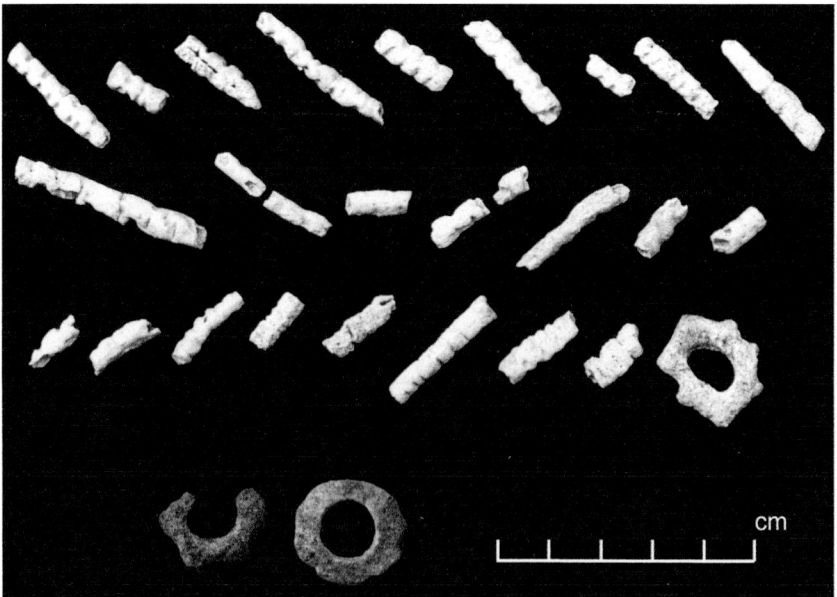

FIGURE 3.5 The segmented, quoit and star-shaped faience beads from Findhorn, Moray. Image © National Museums Scotland.

that the woman was laid on her right side and perhaps flexed, as was common in earlier inhumation burials.

The few centuries after 2000 BC were defined by the increasing visibility of cremation as a rite within mortuary ceremonies. The pyre offered a new setting around which relations between kin, objects and places could be assembled. Sometimes the goods accompanying cremated human bone were burnt on the pyre, and on other occasions things were held from the fire and committed to the grave. Cremation became a preferred and proper way for the treatment of the human dead. Sometimes more extravagant offerings of things and cremated human bone were assembled, including metalwork. To pick up on the ideas I develop in the last chapter, cremation did not initially affect the potential for assembling powerful persons composed of vibrant things and dead humans.

Gatherings of the dead, 2000–1600 BC

The woman, child and faience beads buried at Findhorn, Moray, appear to be an isolated deposition on a sand bank by the bay's edge. Isolated burials were common, although roughly equal in frequency to the gathering of burials in clusters (or 'cemeteries') (Waddell 1990, 27). Cemeteries were sometimes marked by barrows, cairns and enclosures. At other times, kin used ancient landmarks, such as chambered tombs and henges, and natural mounds as places for burying the cremated dead. At Raunds, Northamptonshire, the excavations uncovered the remains of 26 individuals (13 inhumations and 13 cremations) buried in the 6 excavated barrows, spanning 2300–1500 BC (Harding and Healy 2007). The sequences of burial events were in some cases contemporary with the enlargement and elaboration of the barrows. Jan Harding and Frances Healy (2007, 216) interpret these sequences as the efforts of small kin groups to maintain genealogical continuities and 'renew their relations of inheritance, obligation and affinity with the dead'. Fraser Hunter (2000) proposes a similar interpretation for the nine cist graves clustered around the southern side of a flat-topped knoll at West Water, Peeblesshire. Both unburnt and cremated human remains were buried in the cists, and the dead were mostly young people, no older than 25 and in one case a child of 3–5 years.

The durations over which the dead were gathered into cemeteries help to distinguish between kinwork within and between generations and relations made across longer gaps of time. At Barrow 5, Raunds, Northamptonshire, the excavators proposed that a beaker-accompanied inhumation burial located centrally within the barrow was disinterred several centuries later and cremated along with two further individuals (Harding and Healy 2007, 141). The remains of all three bodies were then placed in a pit cut into the top of the original grave, and beneath an inverted collared urn. At Low Grounds, Over, Cambridgeshire, the sequence of interments in each of the barrows followed a pattern (Garrow et al. 2014). At least two of the barrows were built after one another, with the sequence beginning only once burials had finished in the adjacent barrow. The founding burial in each of the three turf barrows was a cremation, accompanied by a pot and placed on or alongside the pyre. The subsequent burials broadly followed a similar order in the type of burial, even if there were variations in the styles of urns, which led the excavators to argue that memory 'functioned extremely well over the 200 or so years of the site's use for cremation burial; the variability observed appears to have been a deliberate creation of difference' (Garrow et al. 2014, 232). At Armadale Bay, Isle of Skye, the cremated remains of more than 20 people were buried in cists and pits clustered around and within an earlier timber and stone circle (Krus and Peteranna 2016) (Figure 3.6). The Bayesian modelling of the radiocarbon dates from Armadale estimates a likely duration for the mortuary deposition of two or three centuries, during the twenty-first to eighteenth centuries BC. Anthony Krus and Mary Peteranna (2016) suggest there were one or two burials during each human generation. The memory of the burial ground and the manners of the mortuary rites persisted irrespective of its infrequent use.

On occasions, people returned to monuments that were centuries and sometimes more than a millennium old for interring human remains. The Armadale Bay cemetery was sited within 50 metres of a Neolithic chambered tomb. In other cases, the relationship was more direct. At the early Neolithic tomb at Cairnderry, Dumfriesshire, cremation burials dated to the nineteenth and eighteenth centuries

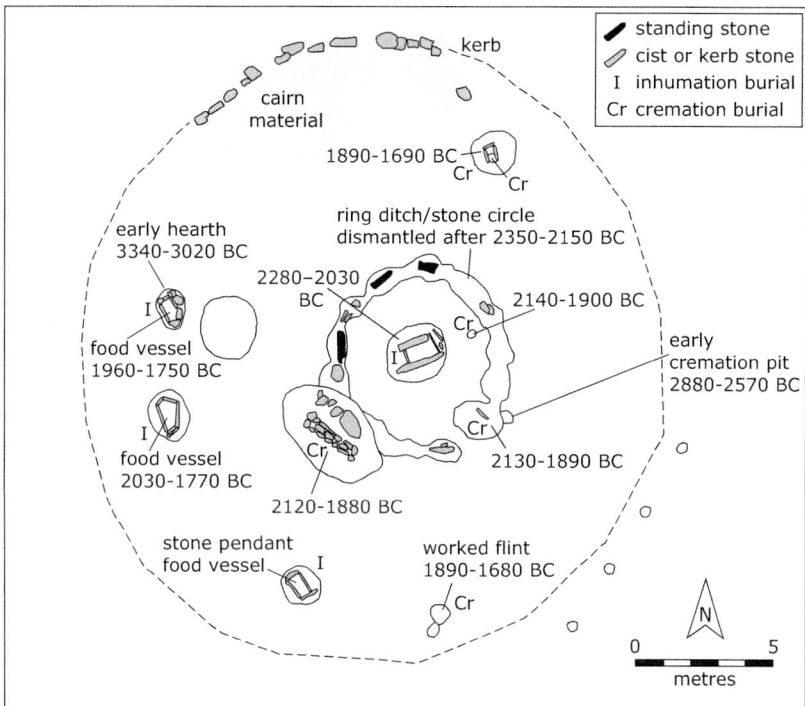

FIGURE 3.6 A plan of the burials within a cairn at Armadale Bay, Isle of Skye. Adapted from Krus and Peteranna 2016.

BC were placed against the outside edge of the kerb enclosing the cairn (Cummings and Fowler 2007). A further cremation burial was found in a pit adjacent to the entrance to the tomb. It was accompanied by a collared urn, a miniature cup and a stone battle axe. Contemporary burials were recovered from the nearby chambered tomb at Bargrennan. More than 1000 years passed between the construction of the chambered tombs and the subsequent deposition of cremated human remains and objects during the early second millennium BC.

In several Irish examples, layers of material were added to the mounds covering Neolithic chambered tombs, and cremation burials were placed into the revitalised mounds. The cairn at Poulawack sits on a raised plateau of limestone in the Burren, County Clare. First excavated in 1934 by the Harvard Archaeological Expedition in Ireland (Hencken and Movius 1935), the human remains were subsequently radiocarbon dated and the cairn's structure reinterpreted by Anna Brindley and Jan Lanting (1991/2) (Figure 3.7). Poulawack's life began in the mid-fourth millennium BC. A large cist was used for the burial of unburnt human remains and covered by a cairn, the edges of which were retained by a drystone wall. In the twenty-first century BC, people returned to the monument and interred further unburnt and cremated human remains in cists excavated deeply into the stone. In the sixteenth century BC, perhaps later, the mound was enlarged, with the edge now retained by upright limestone slabs. A further four burial events occurred in association with the larger monument. At the Mound of the Hostages, County Meath, the cairn-covered passage tomb was a focus of cremation and inhumation burials around 3000 BC (O'Sullivan 2005). From the twenty-third or twenty-second century BC, people began using the monument again for the deposition of human bone. The earliest of these burials were placed within the chambers of the passage tomb, where they joined an 'enormous mass' of centuries-old cremated and unburnt human bone (O'Sullivan 2005, 121). During the following three or four centuries, a further 19 burials, all but one comprising cremated bone, were placed in the mound. It is probable that the cairn was covered with a metre's depth of clay before the burials were deposited.

Monuments gathered burials. Places gathered monuments. The term 'cemetery' could apply to the groups of burials placed within individual mounds and to the clusters of mounds that were built together (Figure 3.8). The most ordered of these groupings are the linear barrow and ring ditch cemeteries known from various areas of southern England, and dating to the nineteenth to seventeenth centuries BC (Garwood 2007). At Barrow Hills, Oxfordshire, the linear cemetery was built after 1850 BC and comprised single-phase monuments overlying individual central burials (Barclay and Halpin 1999). The barrows followed a northeast-southwest alignment defined by earlier monuments, most notably a pair of barrows that formed one terminal of the linear group. The linear arrangements may have formed the structure for processional rituals undertaken amongst the monuments (Garwood 2007; Healy and Harding 2007). The lines of barrows offered physical expressions of lineages and the stages for performing those lineages. Histories and genealogies connected the living with the recent

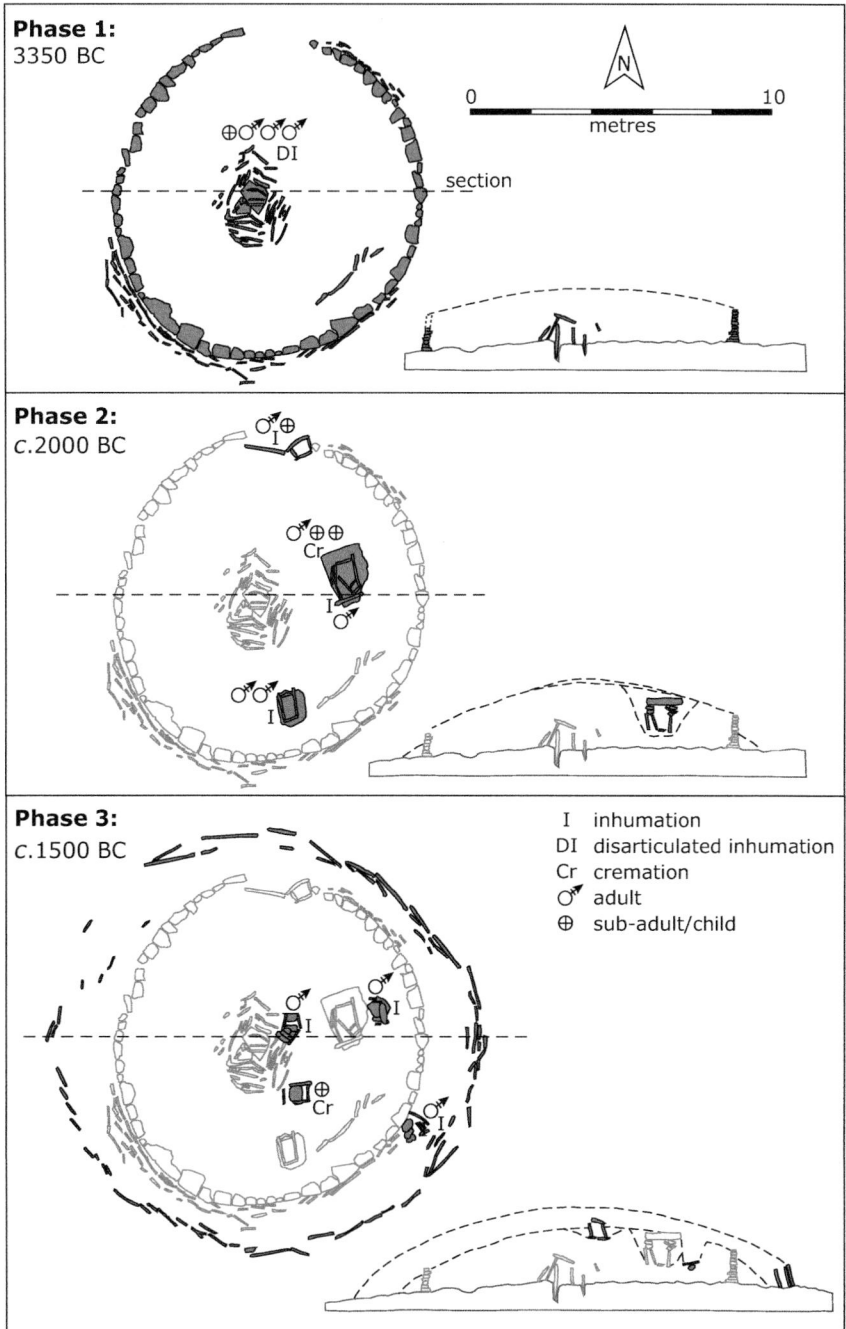

FIGURE 3.7 Three phases of burials and elaboration of the cairn at Poulawack, County Clare. Adapted from Brindley and Lanting 1991/2.

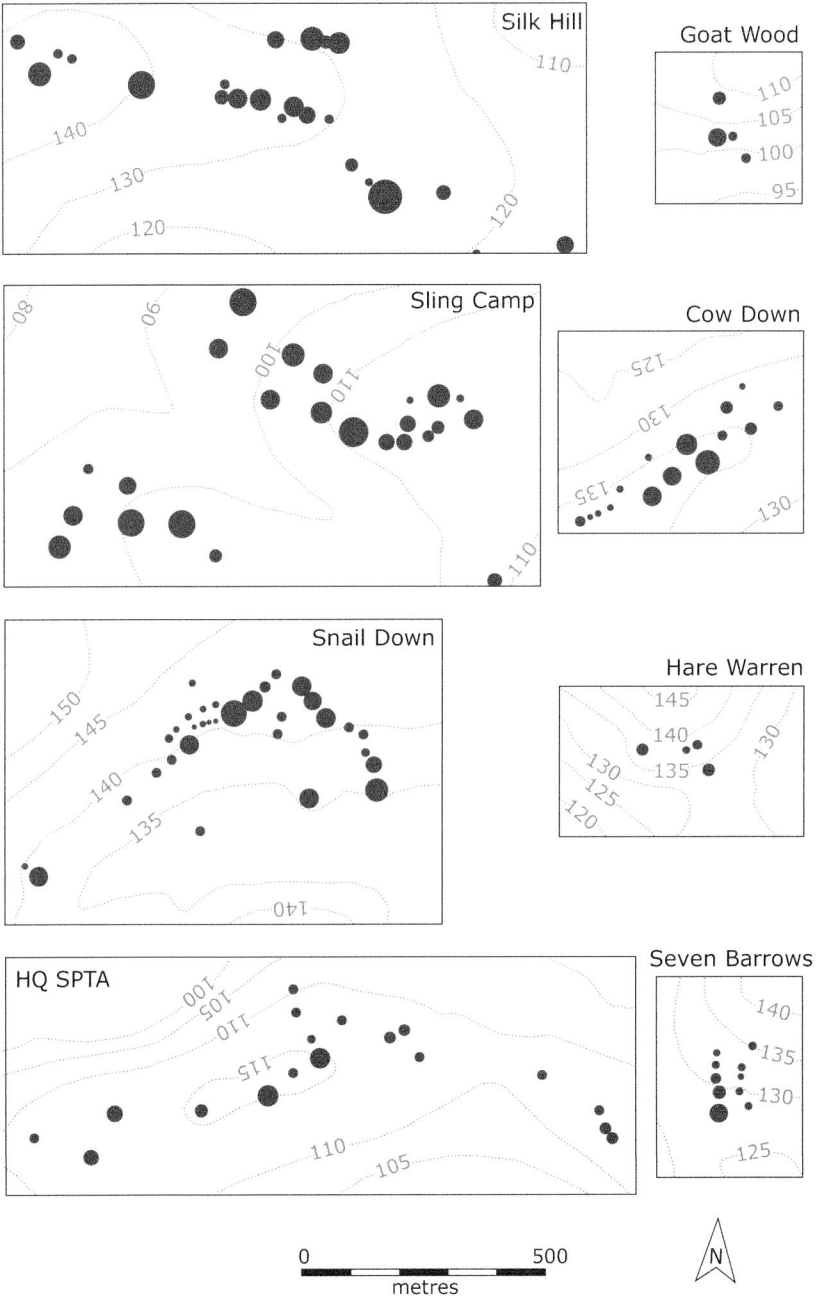

FIGURE 3.8 Examples of barrow groups on Salisbury Plain, Wiltshire. Adapted from McOmish et al. 2002. Cartographic data: © Crown copyright and database rights 2020 Ordnance Survey (100025252).

and the long dead: 'inaccessible and heroic figures…who now lay buried beneath the massive turf and chalk-capped tumuli' (Barrett 1994, 127–128).

This interpretation is persuasive in the way it takes account of the linearity of some cemeteries and the ostentatious grave goods occasionally assembled within burials. I find it less compelling when considering that gatherings of burials manifested in a multitude of ways across Ireland and Britain. There were lines and clusters of burials and monuments; burials sometimes gathered in mounds and sometimes not. Burials accumulated in caves and rock shelters, in a similar manner to the re-used chambered cairns (Barnatt and Edmonds 2002). At Skilmafilly, Aberdeenshire, the cremated remains of up to 42 adults and children were deposited in pits, some with collared and cordoned urns (Johnson and Cameron 2012) (Figure 3.9). The pits formed lines, clusters and a rough arc. They did not intersect one another, although some pits were recut. In one, a child (aged nine) was added to a pit already containing two adults. The child's cremated remains were accompanied by two talons from a golden eagle.

When excavators have the resources to invest in detailed scientific dating programmes, the estimates for the durations of sustained deposition within cemeteries were two or three centuries, sometimes less. These might be genealogical histories, perhaps eight generations, memorable within an oral story-telling tradition, and made familiar through their presence in the landscape. At times there were gaps between periods of sustained mortuary deposition, as places seem to have lost and then regained their powers to gather the dead. The burials of humans and objects, along with the building and modification of monuments,

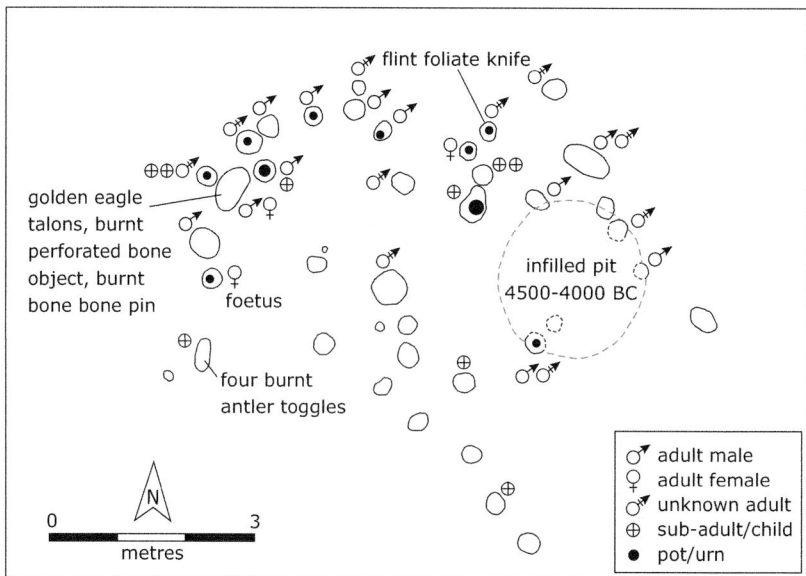

FIGURE 3.9 A plan of the cremation cemetery at Skilmafilly, Aberdeenshire. Adapted from Johnson and Cameron 2012.

entangled lives, deaths and stories of kin into places. Through these processes, kinship was made with and flowed through places. I would interpret the gatherings of the dead during the twentieth to sixteenth centuries BC as kinwork that tied people into the landscape. Through the deposition of the dead, kinfolk invited places to participate in the formation of histories.

Bodies transformed, 1800–1600 BC

Fire consumes the form of the individual, destroying or fragmenting much of the bone, and limiting its potential for osteological analysis (Appleby 2012). Yet cremation makes a transformation within the mortuary process archaeologically detectable (Williams 2008). Fire leaves traces as it consumes. The remnants of the pyre may survive both 'in situ' and incorporated with the burial. Archaeologists can distinguish between the things that were burnt alongside the body and objects kept from the pyre, then added to the grave along with the cremated bone. Cremation created different practices, substances and places within burial rites.

When Jane Downes observed a Balinese cremation ceremony, she did so from an ethno-archaeological perspective (Downes 1999). This meant she took a special interest in the physical details of the mortuary rituals, particularly their setting, architecture and technology. The ceremony took place in a wooded cemetery, where an earthen mound marked the location of the pyre, spaces were set aside for other rituals, and graves were dug for the inhumed remains of the dead awaiting cremation. The cemetery offered little indication of the elaborate and protracted character of Hindu mortuary rituals.

The day-long ceremony was a colourful, noisy occasion. A procession made its way from the family's house to the cemetery, led by a large and richly decorated wooden bull. The bull became the container for the body on the pyre. The women attending the ceremony, including the widow of the dead man, undertook many of the funeral rites: they used holy water to cleanse the body before the pyre was ignited; they collected and cleaned the cremated bones before briefly re-assembling them into the shape of the body; finally, they transferred the man's remains into a silver vessel and took them for disposal in the river, from where they continued their journey to the sea. The dead man's soul returned to his house and resided with the ancestors in the family-temple. Now polluted, the objects used by the women during the ceremony were not re-used or removed from the cemetery. The women broke the pots that had contained water or bone, burnt the bamboo and timber structures and finally buried the residues of all this activity in pits within the cemetery.

Dressing and wrapping the dead person were moments of intimacy when only a small number of people and things contributed to the mortuary rites. Other practices involved greater numbers of participants: harvesting timber, constructed pyres, building cists and monuments and participating in processions or other rituals such as feasts. Once lit, the pyre formed a spectacle around which further rites might have been enacted (Barrett 1990). Pyre sites are less frequently discovered when compared with the thousands of recorded cremation burials. Most pyres were discovered because they lay close to and in some cases underlay burial monuments. Other pyre sites were sited further away from the burial location, and accordingly the cremation may have taken place days, weeks or more before the remains were buried.

In some cases, the remains of the pyres, including charcoal and bone, were collected and deposited in pits and barrow ditches (McKinley 1997). At Urbalreagh, County Antrim, the excavators identified a cremation pyre where fragments of cremated bone lay within an area of intense burning, which had shortly afterwards been cut by a ring ditch (Waterman 1968). The cremated body of a mature adult was buried in an inverted cordoned urn in the centre of the area defined by the ring ditch. Two further cremation burials followed this. At Twyford Down, Hampshire, seven deposits of pyre material, comprising burnt bone, ash and charcoal, were recovered from the fill of a ring ditch (Walker and Farwell 2000). The deposits were in the eastern and southern segments of the ditch, roughly overlying the inhumation burials of 13 individuals who had been buried about 150 years earlier. The excavation team were able to relate some pyres to specific cremation burials in the ditch, and in a few cases these seem to have involved the cremation of more than one individual.

The ordering of materials transformed by the pyre have been reconstructed by Jane Downes (2005; 2009) as a consequence of her excavations at Linga Fiold, Orkney, where she uncovered large numbers of cremation burials, pyre sites and structures associated with mortuary rituals. At one mound, the sequence began with a central stone cist containing cremated human bone that had been burnt in an immediately adjacent pyre (Figure 3.10). The pyre had been carefully sorted and transferred to the cist, with the layers inverted so that the bone was placed at the bottom and overlain with pyre debris. The remains of pyre debris collected in dumps elsewhere on the site seem to show that sorting the material into its constituent elements was a distinct stage during the mortuary rituals. Downes interprets this sorting and inversion of the pyre as an effort to maintain a cultural order in which the dead were required to lie axially between the earth and the

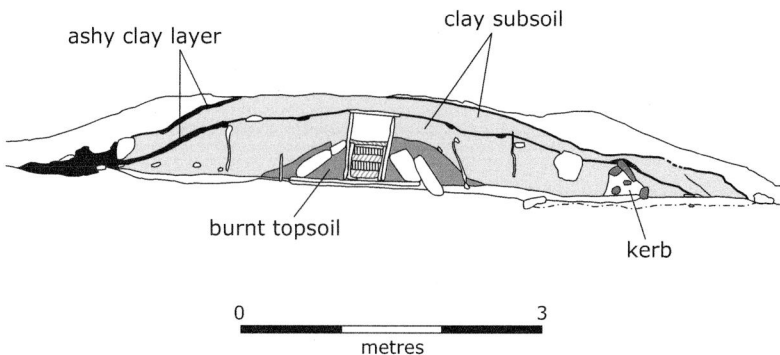

FIGURE 3.10 A section through one of the excavated barrows at Linga Fiold, Mainland, Orkney. Adapted from Downes 2005.

living. This inversion of deposits was also adopted when the covering mound was built over the cist. The lowest part of the mound contained pyre debris; this was then covered with freshly cut turves, top soil and subsoil, laid in the reverse order to which they were extracted. The dead, Downes goes on to argue, had generative and perhaps dangerous powers that may have been controlled within their inverted world.

As cremation rites increased in popularity, the vessels accompanying or containing the cremated remains were more commonly inverted in the graves. In reviewing the early Bronze Age burials in Ireland and western Britain, Elise Fraser documents a change from burials with food vessels and vase urns, where more than half the examples were upright in the graves or on their sides, and encrusted, collared and cordoned urns, which were inverted in the graves in 80–95 percent of cases (Fraser 2013, 299). Inversion does not directly correlate with the practice of cremation, as vase food vessels were commonly associated with cremated remains and were placed upright in more than half of the recorded burials. One of the graves at Ballinchalla, County Mayo, was a bipartite cist, with the chambers containing cremated human remains representing an adult male, adult female and an adolescent, and vase food vessels, one of which was lidded and exquisitely decorated (Cahill and Sikora 2011, 294–295; 2014) (Figure 3.11). The majority of the cremated bone was placed around the vessels, with a small quantity inside each pot. When collared and cordoned urns accompanied cremated bone, they were commonly inverted on top of the cremation deposit. When upright, the vessels containing cremated bone were sometimes sealed with a stone or a piece of wood. At Skilmafilly, Aberdeenshire, nine of the ten complete urns were inverted (Johnson and Cameron 2012). At Eaglestone Flat, Derbyshire, only three of the seven urn-accompanied cremation burials were inverted (Barnatt 1994). Of the upright urns, two were capped with stone slabs and the tops of the others were lost through damage. Two of the inverted urns rested on stone slabs. At Birkside Fell, Northumberland, a burning or burnt split timber was laid on top of the pit containing an upright collared urn (Tolan-Smith 2005).

The inversion or the capping of the vessels may have empowered the pots to contain a vibrant, perhaps unstable and malign, material. In rare cases, two or more vessels were nested and inverted over the cremated material. Elise Fraser (2013, 226–230) identifies seven examples of nested vessels in Ireland. In southern Britain, at a barrow on Gallibury Down, Isle of Wight, a food vessel urn was inverted over a second, upright, urn containing the cremated bones of an adult male, a bronze pin and a handled vessel with a burnished haematite surface (Tomalin 1988). The burnished vessel is a *vase à anse*, which was perhaps made in northwest France, and of which only a handful are known from southern Britain. The Gallibury Down *vase à anse* had a long life before it was buried with cremated human bone: its rim is heavily worn, its handle lost and a hole had been drilled through the surviving handle stump.

Only a proportion, sometimes a small proportion, of the cremated bone and pyre material was buried during mortuary rites. Studies of cremation estimate

FIGURE 3.11   The lidded vase food vessel from Ballinchalla, County Mayo. The vessel is c. 220 mm in height. Image copyright of the National of Museum of Ireland.

that an adult's body would produce around 1,600 grams (range 1,000–2,400 grams) of cremated bone (McKinley 1993). At two examples I described earlier, Eaglestone Flat and Skilmafilly, most deposits of single cremated individuals were smaller than 1,600 grams. At Skilmafilly, the cremated bone in vessels was greater in quantity compared with the un-urned bone (averaging 1,462 grams in an urn and 905 grams without an urn) (Johnson and Cameron 2012, 21). At

Eaglestone Flat, the mean weight of cremated bone in the seven vessels was 588 grams, with 233 grams the mean weight of cremated bone in seven pits without vessels (Barnatt 1994, 338). Jaqueline McKinley (1997, 142) observes that larger, more complete, burials of cremated bone were commonly primary within cemeteries. She offers the suggestion that the completeness of the body reflected the social standing of the dead person and the care that kin were prepared to take in recovering cremated bone from the pyre site. The identification of 'primary' burials may not always be straightforward. The decision to bury most or all of the recoverable cremated material might be in relation to the purpose of the burial and not the personal standing of the deceased. In her analysis of human burials in Neolithic and Bronze Age Wales, Geneviève Tellier (2015, 208) documents a reduction in the size of cremation burials from the early to the middle Bronze Age (before and after 1500 BC). This coarse chronological resolution hides a lot of diversity, and probably a gradual change towards the deposition of smaller amounts of cremated bone.

In reviewing cremation practices in Bronze Age and Iron Age Europe, Katharina Rebay-Salisbury (2010, 70) concludes that '[f]ragments of cremated bodies can stand metonymically for whole bodies and can be used for dispersal and enchainment'. Rebay-Salisbury interprets the ceramic vessels that contained some cremation deposits as new bodies for the dead. The urns, which took human forms in some parts of Europe in the first millennium BC, reconstituted whole bodies and were the contrary of the fragmented and dispersed dead. This idea might be applied to the examples I introduced earlier—Eaglestone Flat and Skilmafilly—where the quantity of cremated bone in a burial was usually greater when contained within a vessel.

A different interpretation of this evidence is that through cremation and dispersal, cremated human bone had different agencies within assemblages. Bodies took on a different form of humanness. Cremation was a technology for the transformation of the body (Downes 2009; Williams 2008). Cremation changed the substance and agency of humanness. Joanna Brück (2006b; 2019) makes connections between cremation and other transformative technologies, such as firing ceramics or metalworking. The sorting and breaking of the bone, and perhaps its grinding down, also had parallels with processing plants, particularly grain. Through these practices the transformation from life to death was controlled within relations of reproduction or regeneration.

The changed nature of human bone after cremation can be explored through its absence from some assemblages, where charcoal instead of bone was placed in pits, vessels and monuments. Deposits containing primarily charcoal, whether from cremation pyres or other fires, were assembled in similar ways to burials of cremated human bone. On Shaugh Moor, Devon, two of the ring cairns and two small cairns contained pits that were rich in charcoal (Wainwright et al. 1979). One pit was filled in the eighteenth or seventeenth century BC in the manner of a funerary deposit, all it lacked was cremated bone: seven faience beads and an incomplete small pot lay in the pit's base, overlain by a sediment rich in oak charcoal, then subsoil and finally capped with a stone slab. Elsewhere on Dartmoor, excavation of a cairn at Metheral revealed a central pit filled with charcoal and covered by a slab (Worth 1937). On Farway Hill, 2 adjacent ring cairns were associated with 38 pits filled with charcoal along with 3 deposits of cremated bone in a cist (Pollard 1971). The excavation of a ring cairn at Cefn Coch, Gwynedd, revealed a small collared urn in a pit on the inside edge of the inner kerb (Griffiths 1960). The urn contained earth and charcoal that seems to have come from a fire that had burnt around and in the pit before the urn was deposited. The only human bone from the monument was a small amount of cremated bone, which someone had pushed into a small gap between the stones on the inside edge of the kerb. Similar practices took place at the ring cairn excavated at Brenig, Denbighshire (Lynch 1993). Fires of birch and hazel were burnt against the inside edge of the cairn, and the charcoal, in some cases carefully selected and cleaned, was buried within pits. The burial of cremated human remains in collared urns did not occur until late in the history of the monument, though these followed the pattern of the charcoal pits in being located against the inside edge of the cairn (Cooper et al. 2020).

From the eighteenth century BC, as cremation was widely practised during mortuary rites, the burial of human remains blended with a range of practices, materials and places. In addition to the deposits of cremated bone placed in mounds and in flat cemeteries, a wide variety of circular or near-circular monuments became places for the deposition of cremated bone, charcoal and a variety of objects, notably pottery vessels, that formerly constituted grave assemblages. Stone circles, cairn circles, ring cairns and cremation cemeteries were amongst the variants within the broad category of stone-built circular monuments. The deposition of cremated bone tied living kin into the landscape by inviting places to participate in the formation of social histories.

This simplifies the process by assuming that human bone remained related to living or recently dead people after cremation. There were characteristics of the assemblages that upset this perspective. The quantities of cremated human bone that were incorporated into burials decreased, and it became more common to deposit small proportions from a cremation deposit. Presumably, the bone from a cremation was assembled in varied ways, which sometimes included partial burial, with or without a ceramic vessel. There was a gradual erosion of burial as a part of mortuary rites as a broader spectrum of depositional practices was used for the correct treatment of cremated material, including both human bone and charcoal. Cremated bone was, in some assemblages, a potent or unstable material that was controlled through containment in inverted vessels, sealed by pyre and stone. Cremation changed the substance of human bone, altering its humanness.

Calming the dead, 1600–1150 BC

The practices I described in the previous sections continued into the middle and later centuries of the second millennium BC. Barrows, ring ditches and cairns were built, although they were fewer in number and tended to be smaller than their predecessors. Monuments, both ancient and more recently built, were re-used. Cremated human bone was commonly deposited in unmarked pits, both isolated and in clusters of burials. Occasionally cemeteries became relatively large, numbering more than 50 burials. Human bone was sometimes deposited within settlements and houses. The quantities of human bone were commonly small, representing a minor proportion of the cremated remains. Inhumation burials seem to have been rare, although the more routine scientific dating of inhumation burials without grave goods is revealing more examples (Mays et al. 2018).

A number of new ceramic styles, all quite large, flat-based, decorated vessels, were in use at about this time, from the seventeenth century BC onwards: notably Trevisker and Deverel-Rimbury pottery. The pottery in use in northern Britain differs by being more coarsely made and with limited or no decoration. It is referred to as flat-rimmed ware or 'bucket urns', and it lacks the chronological sensitivity of ceramics from southern and midland Britain (Burgess 1995; Sheridan 2003). In Ireland, the later Bronze Age ceramics are coarse, usually undecorated, flat-based vessels, whose form derived from cordoned urns. Overall, ceramic vessels remained important as containers for human bone, as had been the case with collared and cordoned urns. Other objects were less common than they were in the earlier half of the second millennium. Only 137 out of the 3,133 burials in Caswell and Roberts's (2018) Britain-wide study were accompanied by objects other than pottery. Metal-work was rarely deposited with cremation burials and an occasional few inhumations (Burgess 1976). The archaeological contexts in which metalwork is most commonly found are either wet areas, such as bogs or rivers, or buried in a variety of dryland locations in the landscape, sometimes in association with settlements.

The burials of human remains in northern Britain and in Ireland, although fewer in number compared with southern and midland Britain, show evidence for a continuity in practices throughout the last seven or eight centuries of the second millennium and the early first millennium BC. Alison Sheridan (2003) identifies examples of cremated burials in bucket urns dating from the sixteenth to ninth centuries BC. Many were found in cists, cairns and cemetery mounds: as at Largs and Ardeer Sands, North Ayrshire; Upper Largie, Argyll; and Sanaigmhor, Islay. Burials were late insertions in recumbent stone circles in northeast Scotland, with an example from Old Keig dated to 1050–900 BC. Cremation burials in stone circles were a feature of the mortuary practices in southwest Ireland after 1500 BC, as at Drombeg, Bohonagh and Reanascreena, all in County Cork. There was also a continued use of mounds in Ireland, although smaller quantities of cremated remains tended to be deposited along with only fragments of ceramic vessels (Grogan 2004). One of the pits at the remains of a Neolithic tomb at Altanagh, County Down, contained pyre debris, a small amount of cremated bone, and over 20 burnt flints; it was radiocarbon dated to the fifteenth or fourteenth century BC (Williams 1986). The excavation of a low stone and earth mound at Knockast, County Westmeath, produced over 40 burials, of which two-thirds were accompanied by either a few sherds of pottery or, in most cases, no vessel at all (Hencken and Movius 1934).

Development-led excavations have revealed equivalent groups of burials unmarked by monuments (Cooney 2017). Covering a transect 335 kilometres from east to west through the middle of Ireland, archaeologists working in advance of the gas 'Pipeline to the West' excavated 62 deposits of cremated bone from 19 locations (Grogan et al. 2007). The cremated remains were generally placed in shallow pits. Only small amounts of cremated bone were present in the pits, with 80 percent of the deposits containing less than 100 grams of cremated material and 50 percent containing less than 10 grams. The largest quantity of cremated bone from a single individual amounted to just 781 grams. At Kiltenan South, County Limerick, the pits were in two clusters, with several outliers. They contained small amounts of cremated bone together with charcoal and charred cereal presumed to be from the pyre. Two of the pits were 'sealed' with a layer of clay subsoil. Rathcannon, County Limerick, comprised a tight cluster of pits containing cremated bone, charcoal and charred cereals. Stakeholes close to and in the base of some pits might have been the traces of small posts marking the pits' locations. A rare example of a large number of cremation deposits at one location was excavated in advance of road improvements on the N8 at Templenoe, County Tipperary (McQuade et al. 2009, 130–133; O'Donnell 2016) (Figure 3.12). Of the tight cluster of over 70 pits, 57 contained cremated bone and in 13 cases a clay capping survived on the top of the pits.

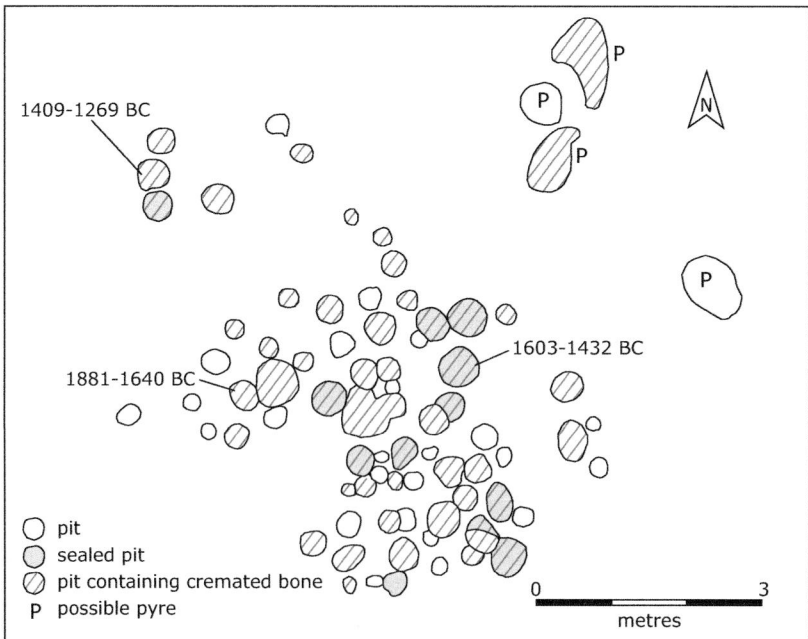

FIGURE 3.12 A plan of the cremation cemetery at Templenoe, County Tipperary. Adapted from McQuade et al. 2009.

Aspects of these same traditions can be traced in the midland and southern counties of Britain. At Twyford Down, Hampshire, a ring ditch, centred on a single cremation contained in a collared urn, was the focus for first inhumation and then cremation burials associated with Deverel-Rimbury ceramics (Walker and Farwell 2000). Comparable sequences have been identified at sites in Northamptonshire (Chapman 2003). While further north, at Catfoss, east Yorkshire, the cremation burials, some in coarse bucket urns, were arranged within and adjacent to a small penannular ditch (McInnes 1968).

One noticeable difference in the evidence from southern Britain is that some of the cemeteries contained large numbers of burials. A group of five barrows was excavated at Simons Ground, Dorset; each barrow comprised a low mound with an outer ring ditch with a break in the southeast side (White 1982). The ditches enclosed centrally buried urns, and in some cases, mortuary structures associated with patches of burning. Nearly 300 urns, about 40 percent containing small amounts of cremated human bone, were placed in pits both pre- and post-dating the construction of the barrows. They were distributed in clusters, in one case forming a linear band about 30 metres in length, usually around the southern half of the ring ditches. A few urns had been inserted into the mound or into the ring ditch. Aside from the clusters, there was no obvious spatial patterning in the styles of urns, the presence of objects accompanying the burials or the age or sex of individuals being buried. The burials at Knighton Heath, Dorset, were also placed in a barrow (Petersen 1981). As at Simons Ground, although the burials were clustered in groups, there were no discernible criteria determining the positions of the burials, the quantities of cremated bone or the styles of the urns.

Eye Kettleby, Leicestershire, was different (Figure 3.13). The team analysing the cremation burials recognised correlations between the ages at which people had died, the presence or absence of an urn and the species of timber used to fuel the pyre (Finn 2011). As at Simons Ground and Knighton Heath, the burials were spatially clustered in groups of varying numbers. In the largest cluster, comprising 44 burials and deposits of pyre debris enclosed by a ring ditch, adults were more likely to be buried in urns, while children were generally buried without an urn. The burials in urns were more commonly cremated on pyres fuelled by a single species of timber: usually oak, but also alder or ash. The cremation pyres for children were of mixed species and oak was excluded (a pattern somewhat similar to that recognised in contemporary cremation deposits at Raunds: Campbell and Robinson 2007, 32). These distinctions marked the ways the mortuary ceremonies were constituted and enacted, with choices partly conditioned by aspects of the identities of the dead. The spatial clusters were marginally different, whether in the proportions of urned to unurned burials, the treatment of pyre debris, or in the ways in which urns were placed within the burial pits.

An interpretation of the presence of 'clusters' of burials is that they formed cemeteries for a household or small kin group (Ellison 1980). This idea is supported by the, usually, small size of the cemeteries, the mix of people of different ages

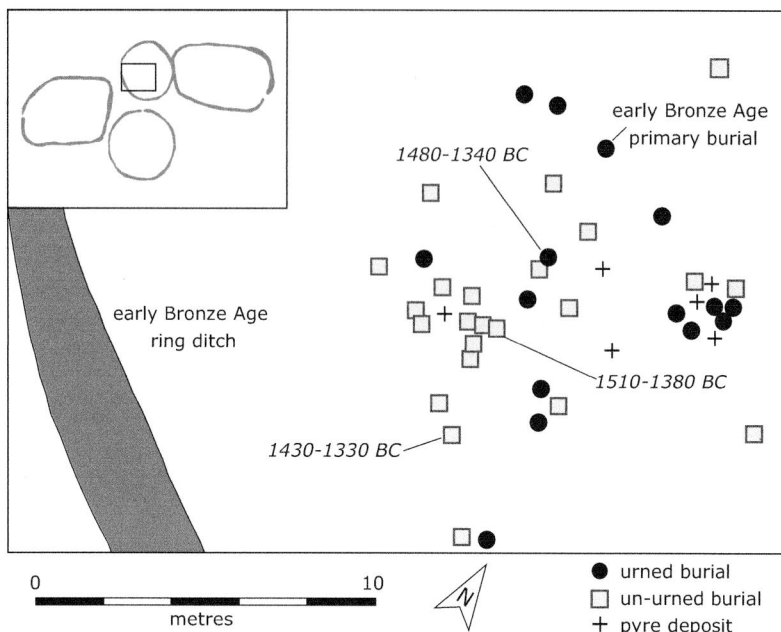

FIGURE 3.13 The largest cluster of cremation burials amongst the funerary structures excavated at Eye Kettleby, Leicestershire. Adapted from Finn 2011.

and genders within each cemetery and also the incidences where cemeteries were in close proximity to contemporary settlements. The two most cited examples of cemeteries directly associated with settlements are in southern Britain, at Itford Hill and South Lodge. At Itford Hill, Sussex, the excavated barrow was approximately 30 metres north from a contemporary settlement of roundhouses (Ellison 1980; Holden 1972). A sherd of pottery from one of the phases of the settlement came from part of the rim of a distinctive handled vessel containing cremated human bone buried next to the barrow. At South Lodge, Dorset, a group of six barrows were broadly contemporary with an area of settlement located 100 metres to the south (Barrett et al. 1991). Both the barrows and the settlement were sited amongst an existing field system. In their review of cremation burials dating to 1600–1150 BC, Edward Caswell and Benjamin Roberts (2018, 15–17) explain that the association, based on spatial proximity, between cemeteries and settlements is weak when analysed across the whole of Britain. On this basis, they dismiss the interpretation of the cemeteries as burial grounds of a locally based population.

Defining settlements is not straightforward. I will expand on this observation in Chapter 4, so at this point I will offer a simple assertion: traces of domestic life, whether inhabitation, craft or agriculture, were distributed in varying intensities throughout landscapes. More durable architecture emerged in domestic assemblages, especially from the eighteenth and seventeenth centuries BC, and sometimes boundaries were built around settlements and fields. Cremated human bone was incorporated into these new structures and places. The densities and quantities of cremated bone were lower around inhabitation areas and in fields when compared with the burials in cemeteries.

At Caltragh, County Sligo (Danaher 2007), deposits of cremated bone were found underneath a burnt mound and close to a group of three roundhouses. At O'Connell Ridge, Over Narrows, Cambridgeshire, a cremation burial with a Deverel-Rimbury urn and two inhumation burials were excavated amongst an area of contemporary settlement activity (Evans et al. 2016, 253). At Heathrow Terminal 5, seven pits with cremated human bone or, in one case, pyre debris were excavated close to one of the settlements (Lewis et al. 2010, 202–203). The pits were distributed in three locations in the fields surrounding the settlement, and in one case within the settlement enclosure. This makes it difficult to interpret the burials as a definable cemetery or to connect them with the settlement. Similarly, at Yarnton, Oxfordshire, a small number of cremation deposits was dispersed across the large excavated area, without any obvious correlation with settlements or clustering in cemeteries (Hey et al. 2016, 88–90).

The large numbers of people represented in the interments at some cemeteries and round barrows and the relative proportions of adults and children of both sexes indicate that the burials reflected a broad spectrum of the dead population. Distinctions between burials were made based on their locations within the cemeteries, the quantities of cremated bone in the deposits and the styles of pottery vessels chosen to accompany the bone. These variables generally fail (excepting Eye Kettleby, above) to correlate with measurable biological attributes such as age or sex. A logical inference from this evidence is that the clusters of burials represented small egalitarian communities such as close kin groups or households, and that social differences were either unmarked during funerary rites or defined in non-material ways.

I am wary of following this line of argument for the same reasons that I gave in the previous section. It assumes that the dead retained some or all of their capacities as human or human-like agents from cremation through to burial. The evidence from the centuries after 1800 BC would suggest that increasingly cremation transformed the human nature of the dead. Cremated bone was a new substance and a new agency in the world, which could be substituted for or had equivalence with other materials transformed through the pyre. The decrease in the quantities of cremated bone within burial deposits was maintained in the centuries after 1800 BC. Geneviève Tellier's (2015, 208) analysis of the cremated bone from prehistoric burials in Wales shows a decrease in the mean weight from 978 grams in the early Bronze Age to 391 grams on the middle Bronze Age. Tellier's sample of 12 burials for 1600–1150 BC corresponds with Caswell and Roberts's (2018, 339) review of 859 burials in Britain. They calculated a mean weight of 375 grams and a median of 140 grams. Most burials comprised only a small fraction of the cremated individual. On occasions, cremated animal bone has been identified amongst the human material. At Templenoe, County

Tipperary, dog and possible sheep/goat were identified in 2 of the 57 pits containing cremated bone (McQuade et al. 2009, 146).

The burial of cremated bone was not about the memorialising of individuals or creating communities. It defined histories of association with places using a material transformed from humans. Deposits of cremated bone were not beings, nor were they assembled as beings (in the way that some earlier burials were treated). If assemblages of humans and powerful things existed in another world after their death, they reached it through other means, probably through the transformative effects of the pyre and the rituals undertaken before and during the cremation. The residue that remained was perhaps unstable and dangerous because it no longer retained the characteristics and the relations that gave it humanity. Consequently, the living kin made efforts to bring the cremated bone into relation with other places and things. This was a process of territorialisation, stabilising the potency of cremated bone by weaving it into places and the land.

Votive exchanges, 1700–1150 BC

The widespread adoption of cremation within funerary rites occurred alongside a decline in the assembling of metalwork with human bone in burials. By the sixteenth century BC, grave goods with the exception of pottery vessels were rare. This coincided, coarsely defined, with an increase in the deposition of metalwork elsewhere in the landscape. In her review of Bronze Age metalwork finds from throughout Ireland, Katharina Becker (2013) assigned 1,362 objects to 2000–1500 BC and 2,785 to 1500–1150 BC. The collections from both periods are dominated by single finds rather than groups of objects. Normalising the data based on the duration of each period, metalwork deposition was nearly three times more prolific during 1500–1150 BC compared with 2000–1500 BC. This pattern is replicated in Britain. The database of the Portable Antiquities Scheme, which records finds made by the public in England and Wales, holds entries for nearly three times more copper alloy objects ascribed to 1500–1150 BC compared with 2200–1500 BC.

The majority of the metalwork consists of single personal items, axes and spearheads, deposited in unremarkable locations. Metalwork researchers have recognised and attempted to place categorical order on the considerable diversity of styles and forms in axes and spearheads. The axe typologies focus primarily on the methods used to haft the axes onto handles (Schmidt and Burgess 1981). Flanges on the side and a 'stop' towards the blade enabled the axes to sit more securely on the haft and without splitting the timber. The axes' blades were sometimes enlarged and splayed, with decoration on the flanges and blades. The large flanged axe from Bannockburn, Stirlingshire, has a wide and gracefully curved blade with a decorative scheme comprising angled lines and dots covering the outside of the flange (Coles 1963, 90). At some point, probably around the sixteenth century BC, metalworkers began employing a design in which the flange and stop were fused to form a continuous ridge on each side of the axe. These axes are termed palstaves, based on the comparison that nineteenth-century archaeologists drew between the form of the axes and an Icelandic digging tool termed a *paalstab*. Like axes, spearheads display a somewhat bewildering variability in forms and sizes. They were designed with a socket and loops that enabled the spearhead to be mounted and bound securely to a shaft. The blades were lozenge, leaf and triangular in shape, with some reaching exceptional lengths. A spearhead recovered from a bog at Knockenbaun, County Sligo, is 46 centimetres in length (Eogan 1983, 149–150).

Axes and spearheads were commonly deposited individually, in locations that lack obvious archaeological associations. While this generalisation stands, multiple objects were sometimes placed together in ways that echo the aesthetics of earlier depositional practices. In the summer of 1915, amongst the steep hills bordering Glen Trool, Dumfries and Galloway, a military officer called Captain Dinwiddie spotted a piece of metal protruding from mossy ground beneath an overhanging boulder (Callander 1920/1921). The captain's excavations and those of a local gamekeeper uncovered a flanged axe, spearhead, rapier, razors, chisels, a torc and amber beads. Five palstaves were recovered from an alignment of equally spaced pits at Lower Hardres, Kent (Chestnutt and Wilkin 2013). The axes were laid flat and respecting the same northeast-southwest alignment as the pits. The blades of the axes in two adjacent pits 'faced' each other. In another pit, which contained two axes, the axes were set perpendicular to one another.

In a study of the spatial distributions of Bronze Age metalwork in northeast England, Andrew Poyer (2015) found that axes and spearheads did not exhibit clear patterning in the locations where they were found. Their topographic settings and proximities to watercourses were comparable with a simulated random distribution of findspots. This does not mean that distributions were an accumulation of thoughtless acts or clumsy losses. The preponderance of axes and spearheads in archaeological collections indicates a degree of selectivity. Certain personal things were suitable for exchange, and it might have been their close associations with individuals that made them appropriate as gifts. The Horridge Common palstave can act as an example (Fox and Britton 1969). While revising the Ordnance Survey mapping in 1965, a surveyor happened upon a palstave, 13 centimetres in length, lying in loose soil by the edge of a recently built track on Horridge Common, Dartmoor (Figure 7.13). The style of axe, with a distinctive v-shaped flange, was unique in Britain at the time of its discovery although a more common find in continental and particularly central Europe. The axe had been left, probably buried, near the middle of a contemporary field and around 50 metres from a group of roundhouses.

Other items of metalwork were generally reserved for deposition in a more restricted range of locations, whether in bogs, lakes or rivers, or near to watercourses. Based on researching the metalwork from northeast England, Andrew Poyer (2015) concludes that bladed weapons (dirks, rapiers and swords) were most commonly recovered from within or close to major rivers and their tributaries. These practices were replicated elsewhere, in the Thames (York 2002) and Trent (Davis 1999; Scurfield 1997) in Britain, and the Shannon, Bann, Blackwater and Barrow in Ireland (Bourke 2001). Ninety percent of the rapiers and dirks that Colin Burgess and Sabine Gerloff (1981, 41) examined showed patina derived from burial in a wet environment, with many of the blades from Britain coming either from the Thames or the East Anglian Fenland. The deposition of blades concentrated on specific locations along the rivers. On the River Tyne, the stretch that flows between Newcastle upon Tyne and Gateshead has produced a dagger, two rapiers, two swords and three spearheads (Poyer 2015). A concentration of metalwork finds is recorded at Toome, County Antrim, where the Lower Bann begins its journey northwards from Lough Neagh: a knife and a razor, two axes, two spearheads and seven swords or sword fragments (Bourke 2001, 167–174). Dredging of rivers during recent centuries has biased the recovery of metalwork. Dredging extended further along the rivers than the locations where concentrations of Bronze Age material have been found, indicating there were focal places for the deposition of some categories of metalwork.

Blades may have needed to undertake long journeys to reach a suitable location or region for their deposition. These journeys might explain why we identify concentrations of blades in places such as the lower reaches of the Shannon and the Thames. The rivers were not foci for economic wealth. Their waters were the culminations of multiple journeys and the starting points for subsequent journeys that the blades made into other worlds. Certain rivers were places where multiple lines of kinship became knotted. They held significance in the landscape, and that significance thickened as more relations across geographies and time became entangled. The convention is to interpret concentrations of metalwork as wealth, destroyed or consumed through deposition, in ways that empowered elites (Yates 2007). I would instead suggest that if there was wealth it was the social wealth of shared kinship with powerful places (Fontijn 2020).

Contemporary with the dirks, rapiers and earliest swords (1300–1125 BC) are a number of bronze and organic shields, which have been found throughout Britain and Ireland (Coles 1962; Uckelmann 2012). The shields are round and made from a thin sheet of beaten bronze. This was then strengthened and decorated with bosses and ribs, which formed complex concentric patterns. The shields from Yetholm, on the north side of Cheviot Hills, Roxburghshire, and Moel Hebog, Snowdonia, are examples of the most common style of British shields (Figure 3.14). Each is decorated with concentric rings of bosses separated by a circular rib; there are equal numbers of boss rings and ribs on each shield. The shield from Auchmaliddie, Aberdeenshire, has a more unusual design: two concentric ribs surround four further ribs executed in a 'meander' pattern. Two of the meanders are open, with terminals that may be stylised snakes or birds' heads. Rare examples of both wooden and hardened animal-hide shields are known from Ireland, with the only animal-hide shield found in a bog at Clonbrin, County Longford (Armstrong 1909). The organic shields were decorated with concentric designs like those on their metal counterparts, including distinctive V- and U-shaped notches in the ribs that are otherwise only found on shields in northern and southwest Europe.

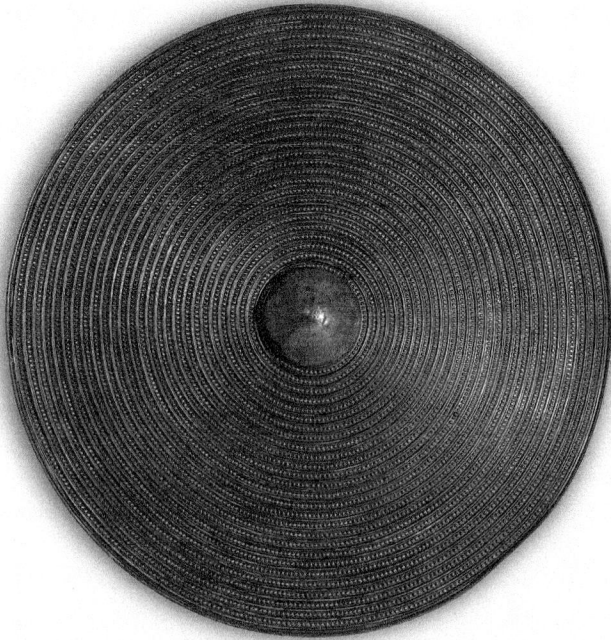

FIGURE 3.14 The bronze shield recovered during peat-cutting near Moel Hebog, Gwynedd. The shield is 640 mm in diameter. © The Trustees of the British Museum.

It is unsurprising that the organic shields have been recovered from bogs, given that these provided the only conditions in which they would have been preserved. The bronze shields too have almost all been recovered from bogs or rivers (32 out of 35 examples whose provenance is known, Coles et al. 1999). In a few cases there is evidence that there was a careful and deliberate arrangement of the shields when they were deposited. Two of the three shields recovered from Yetholm Bog, Roxburghshire, were placed upright and on their edges in what was probably a bog (Cowie et al. 2016). At Beith, Ayrshire, five or six shields were recovered from two metres deep in a peat bog, where they had been arranged, probably set vertically, in a circle. The surviving Beith shield was damaged by a sharp object or objects that had been pushed though the bronze. This may have been caused during recovery, although similar damage was inflicted on the shield from South Cadbury, which was found in the upper levels of a right-angled ditch below a prominent hilltop enclosure (Coles et al. 1999; Needham et al. 2012). A sharp stake had been driven into and then removed from the damp clay in the right-angle corner of the ditch. Then the shield, whose rim had been broken, was laid front-face down with the central boss in the hole left by the stake. Finally, the stake or a similar implement was driven through the shield in three places. The date for the shield's destruction may be after the mid-eleventh century, which was a century or two later than the currently accepted date for bronze shields (Needham et al. 2012, 489).

Axes and spearheads were usually deposited as individual offerings at places throughout the landscape. Weapon blades and, more rarely, shields were offered on a less frequent basis and in a restricted range of locations, which were usually defined by water. Ornaments form a third category of material in archaeological collections dating to the fourteenth to twelfth centuries BC. They comprise a variety of gold and bronze objects that people probably wore on their wrists, arms, ankles and necks, or used as decorative items on hair and clothing. In mainland Europe, ornaments were generally placed as grave goods. In Ireland and Britain, where mortuary rites did not involve the burial of unburnt human remains, ornaments were deposited individually and in groups, commonly at dryland locations (Wilkin 2017). One of the exceptions was discovered at Duff House, Banffshire, and reported in the early nineteenth century. Several gold armlets and rings were deposited together with cremated bone under an inverted urn (Coles 1963, 150).

The groups of ornaments have been studied more thoroughly than the single finds. Benjamin Roberts (2007) identifies two categories of ornament groups based on his research in southern Britain. The first consists of twisted and cast bronze rings, bracelets, torcs and pins, which are restricted to a dense distribution in southern and eastern England and to the period 1400–1275 BC. The second, overlapping in date with the first and possibly continuing later, until the twelfth century BC, comprises gold rings, bracelets and torcs, and with a distribution thinly scattered throughout Ireland and Britain. The bronze and gold ornaments were made in novel ways, working bars and wire, and the styles had currencies that spanned large areas of continental Europe (Sørensen 1997). The gold bar torcs or neck-rings, some with elaborate expanded and spiral terminals, were deposited across midland and eastern Ireland, Wales, southeastern England, northwest France and Iberia (Eogan 1994, 71). Other forms had distinctly local distributions. Metalworkers created Sussex loops, which were worn as bracelets or arm-rings, by doubling-over a narrow bronze bar and twisting it so that one end provided a loop and the other a hook. Sussex loops are tightly distributed on England's south coast, with a few examples from adjoining areas.

When groups of ornaments were deposited together, they were either composed of a single type of object or a variety of ornaments and sometimes other items (particularly sickles and axes) were included in the assemblage. Single-type assemblages predominate amongst the small number from Ireland and are either formed from torcs or bracelets (Becker 2013, 242; Eogan 1983, 13). A local boy found three bar torcs in a 'mound or bank' on the Hill of Tara, County Meath, in 1810 (Herity 1969, 21). One of the two surviving torcs is especially large: it comprises 852 grams of gold and its opened-out length would be 1.7 metres. The terminal of the smaller torc curves delicately into a spiral. An assemblage of different ornament types was discovered four metres deep in a bog in Derrinboy,

County Offaly: two gold bracelets with elaborate repoussé decoration, two hair tresses, a necklace made from a sewn leather core tightly wound in thin gold wire and piece of copper wire (Raftery 1961).

Combinations of object types are more common amongst the assemblages in southern Britain. Neil Wilkin (2017) groups the assemblages into three commonly occurring combinations: bracelets/arm-rings with tools (axes or sickles), bracelets/arm-rings with torcs, torcs with tools. There is considerable variability within these broad patterns, which emerge out of some notable localised idiosyncrasies. A feature of some groups is a combination of ornaments with either axes or sickles. The bronze objects found carefully arranged in a low mound on Hollingbury Hill, Brighton, fall in this category: three rings were threaded onto a torc before it was placed, flat, in the ground; four Sussex loops were arranged regularly around the torc; finally, a palstave was placed centrally on top of the torc. In 2004, three metal detectorists discovered a group of gold ornaments, palstaves and a chisel at Burton, Wrexham (Gwilt et al. 2007) (Figure 3.15). The objects had probably been arranged in a ceramic vessel, of which only a portion survived plough damage. The gold items included gold beads and a pendant, rings, a torc and an unusual twisted wire bracelet for which the nearest parallel is from northwest France.

FIGURE 3.15 The gold ornaments, palstaves, chisel and ceramic vessel from Burton, Wrexham. Copyright: National Museum of Wales.

Wilkin (2017, 28–29) notes a symmetry in the numbers of ornaments and tools or weapons that were assembled in some groups. Of the 47 examples, 13 have equal numbers of ornaments and tools or weapons. These groups might, Wilkin suggests, have been assembled in ways to balance differing or opposed associations, such as male and female. Using the example of two palstaves and two torcs deposited together at Spaxton in the Quantock Hills, Somerset, Stuart Needham (2001, 292) speculates that the equal numbers of axes and ornaments sealed a marriage alliance between kin groups.

A man found the Quantock torcs and axes in December 1794 when digging a drain through marshy ground: 'six feet beneath the surface, two rings, one lying on the other; within each of which was placed a celt [axe]' (Harford 1803, 94). The careful setting of the objects within the assemblage, with the torcs stacked on top of each other and encircling the axes, echoes the more elaborate arrangement of the rings, torc, Sussex loops and palstave at Hollingbury Hill. Neil Wilkin (2017, 29–34) identifies many instances amongst the ornament assemblages of conjoined and stacked objects, and objects that were tightly coiled and sometimes broken prior to deposition. Wilkin likens these arrangements to the intertwining of ornaments, limbs and bodies. In the case of the Hollingbury Hill assemblage: 'the torc "wears" the finger-rings while the positioning of the palstave evokes the neck and head and the pairing and separation of Sussex Loop bracelet/arm-rings are arranged as if worn by four absent limbs' (Wilkin 2017, 33). The group of bronze ornaments excavated from a field ditch at Hopton on Sea, Norfolk, references a body in a different way (Cooper 2018, 4). The two torcs, two ring-headed pins and two bracelets were laid out in the ditch as though they were dressing a human body.

Absent human bodies influence researchers' interpretations of both the ornament assemblages and the weapons deposited in rivers, lakes and bogs (Bradley 2019, 216). Metal objects were assembled and deposited in the landscape instead of as grave goods with the dead or as part of mortuary rites that were reserved for certain categories of people. This explains the change from depositing daggers in graves early in the Bronze Age to the practice of placing dirks, rapiers and then swords in watery places. The idea accounts for the differences between insular and continental practices of ornament deposition, whether or not they were in graves. Supporting the association between weapon deposition and mortuary rites, Colin Burgess and Sabine Gerloff (1981, 42) noted the example of a dirk recovered alongside some skull fragments from the River Wreake, Syston, Leicestershire. These interpretations present things as proxies for the people who carried, wore and deposited them. Gold and bronzework was the wealth that defined the value and status of persons, whether or not the humans were present in the assemblages.

What if things were themselves participating in kinwork with people, and were at times more powerful than and as alive as humans? A blade, a shield, a torc: these were actors in stories and participants in journeys, and their presence in the landscape a means of consolidating kinship with places. This was not the displacement of human mortuary rites. Instead, it might be understood as the mortuary rites for vibrant things. Assemblage and emplacement in the landscape were the means through which things could participate in this and other worlds. The careful arrangement of objects in the ground was not undertaken in the absence of a human body. People were present at the depositional events, just as they were present during human mortuary rites. The things were bodies, and they were assembled as composite persons, as kin. It is not that things were parts of humans—their proxies. Through gift exchange, 'things and people assume the social form of persons' (Strathern 1988, 145). Viveiros de Castro (2009) makes an instructive comparison between kin relations and gift exchange. Kinship is made through the exchange of inalienable persons, things and substances, whether that be food, blood, bone or semen in relations of consanguinity or marriage partners and names in relations of affinity. These are, to use Christopher Gregory's definition, gifts: 'the personal relations between people that the exchange of things in certain social contexts creates' (Gregory 2015, lxii). Within gift exchange, the entities that are the objects of the transaction become persons, if they are not so already. We might say that as a process of personification—making and relating persons—gift giving and kinship are one and the same. Gift exchange is kinwork.

Metalwork offerings during the sixteenth to twelfth centuries BC were characterised by their intimacy: limited relations were assembled at the events. Single items predominate and assemblages, more visible from the fourteenth century, mostly comprise small numbers of items. This was not because large quantities of metal items were never accumulated. Over 350 objects, including many median-winged axes otherwise unknown from Britain, were recovered by divers from the shallows of Langdon Bay, Kent (Muckelroy 1981; Needham et al. 2013). The assemblage is interpreted as a wrecked boat or a crew's desperate efforts to save a troubled vessel sometime in the thirteenth century BC.

In contrast to the chaotic moments when assemblages were caught-out in the flux of their lives, the depositions of metalwork in the landscape were intimate, careful and concealed acts of kinwork. In these regards and in their simplicity, there were parallels between the treatments of metalwork and of human bodies. A girl on a school trip to Argyll in June 1979 found a small dirk on the edge of Loch Glashan (O'Connor and Cowie 1995, 350–351). The blade had broken at its point, and then been reshaped and sharpened. It was placed beneath a stone in peat by the loch's edge, where a stream joined the loch from the surrounding boggy ground of Mòine Ghlas. There were many small acts of deposition throughout the landscape, which were cumulatively significant to archaeologists and individually important to the people that made them.

'All-remembering', 1150–700 BC

The evidence for mortuary practices during 1150–700 BC is varied (Brück 2017; Cooney 2017). It is possible to trace mortuary and burial rites that carried forward from preceding centuries. Cremation remained important and small quantities of cremated human bone were deposited in pits, domestic settings and monuments. Unburnt bone and inhumation burials provide examples of defleshing, dismemberment, curation and biases in the deposition of body parts, notably skulls. The fragmentation of human bodies was echoed in the metalwork evidence, where the deposition of broken objects and parts of objects dominates some assemblages. Rivers, bogs and lakes continued as important locations for depositing metalwork along with other materials and bodies. Metalwork deposition, overall, increases as a practice, with more and larger assemblages of objects dating to the later centuries of the Bronze Age. There were instances of individual inhumation burials, which maybe drew on archaic traditions (Brück 1995, 273–276; Burgess 1976). At Rylstone, North Yorkshire, a log coffin dated to 840–790 BC contained an inhumation wrapped in woollen textile (Melton et al. 2016). Infant inhumation burials, perhaps up to five, were inserted in an earlier cairn or barrow on The Bostle, Balsdean, East Sussex, during the tenth to ninth centuries BC (McKinley 2004).

People retained small quantities of cremated human bone for deposition in monuments and clusters of unmarked pits. Richard Bradley has recognised instances where cremated bone was deposited and pyres set in centuries-old circular monuments during the later Bronze Age in Scotland (Bradley 2016, 122–124). Burning and scattered cremated bones were the residues of pyres within the recumbent stone circle at Tomnaverie, Aberdeenshire (Bradley 2005, 26). There was a scatter of cremated bone within the interior of the monument at Croftmoraig, Perth and Kinross, with four pieces recovered during the recent excavations (Shapland 2016). Cremation deposits have been excavated within stone circles in southwest Ireland, as at Reanascreena South and Drombeg, County Cork (O'Brien 2004). Unlike the northeast Scottish circles, the circles in southwest Ireland could be contemporary with the cremation burials. At Reanascreena South, radiocarbon measurements from the cremation burial and charcoal beneath the monument's outer bank span the twelfth to ninth centuries BC.

Ring ditches provided foci for cremation burials throughout the first millennium BC in Ireland (McGarry 2009). Barry Raftery excavated burials and pyre deposits dating to the twelfth to eleventh centuries within a ring ditch at Rathgall, County Wicklow (Becker 2010; Raftery 1973) (Figure 3.16). A cremation pyre took place within a prepared hollow screened on three sides by timbers (comprising 1,500 stakeholes), with the open side facing east. The cremated remains of a young adult were deposited on a stone slab in the base of a pit within the timber structure. A second cremation of a woman and child were buried with a coarseware vessel. Katherina Becker (2014) interprets a large rectangular pit containing a rectangular setting of four posts, charred material and stone as the base for a cremation pyre. Five equivalent pits were excavated within the adjacent, larger, enclosure. Some pits within the small ring ditch included pyre material and small quantities of cremated bone. Another contained an assemblage of three bronze objects, which complemented the large quantities of metalworking moulds and crucibles from the adjacent enclosure.

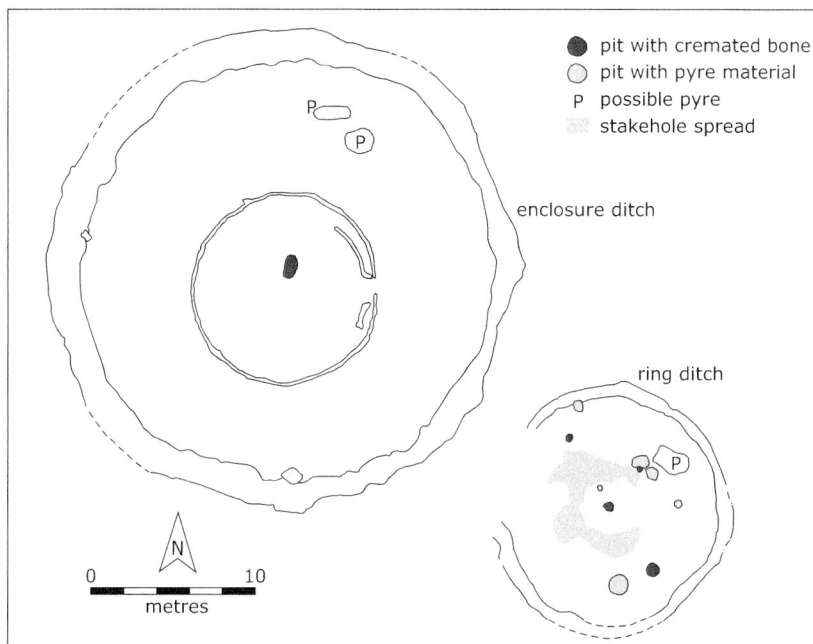

FIGURE 3.16   The funerary deposits within the ring ditch and enclosure at Rathgall, County Wicklow. Adapted from Becker 2010 and 2014.

Continuities in practices from the middle to later centuries of the Bronze Age were strongest in the small deposits of cremated human bone recovered from isolated and clusters of pits, sometimes accompanied by vessels. Several examples post-dating 1150 BC were excavated during the 'Pipeline to the West' (Grogan et al. 2007, 104). The bone was deposited in smaller quantities that preceding centuries and the pits lacked evidence for capping. At Kiltenan South, County Limerick, the pits containing tenth- and ninth-century cremated bone were amongst and in alignment with a cluster of pits containing cremated human bone dated to the sixteenth to fourteenth centuries BC (Grogan et al. 2007, 292–293). The corridor investigated during the construction of the Carlow bypass was 18.5 kilometres. The archaeologists excavated 39 burials of cremated human bone, of which 10 were dated after 1100 BC, compared with 17 attributed to 1600–1100 BC (Troy 2015). The size of the deposits remained small, averaging 210–260 grams. Like the 'Pipeline to the West', the groups of pits containing cremated bone appear to have gathered over centuries rather than decades. At Ballyhade, the excavations revealed a cluster of six pits containing small amounts of cremated human bone and broken pottery (Baker et al. 2015, 19–20). The five calibrated radiocarbon dates span 1350–850 BC. Two adjacent pits, one containing an adult and the other an adolescent, had similar radiocarbon estimates and may have been deposited together during the tenth or ninth century BC.

Cremated human bone was deposited within and close to agricultural and domestic features. In her review of the human bone from late Bronze Age Britain, Joanna Brück (1995) identifies over 40 examples of human bone, most unburnt, recovered during settlement excavations. Benefiting from recent decades of development-led excavations in Ireland, Kerri Cleary (2018) lists 16 locations in Ireland where human bone was excavated from domestic features, including houses, boundaries and burnt mounds. As in Britain, the material is fragmentary and both unburnt and cremated remains are represented in the assemblages. Cleary notes five locations where cremated human bone was present in settlement features. It was generally found in features near or on thresholds.

The excavations at South Hornchurch, Essex, identified 14 deposits of cremated bone amongst the boundaries, enclosures and settlements dating to the tenth to eighth centuries BC (Guttmann and Last 2000). While all the deposits were small, a few comprised 50–180 grams of cremated human bone and two of these were in pits set a short way from the domestic structures. The other deposits of cremated bone comprised at most 8 grams and in many cases less than a gram, making them too small for certain identification as human (Tony Waldron in Guttmann and Last 2000, 346). The small amounts meant that half the deposits were only recognised when sediments were bulk sampled and sieved. They were found in or close to entranceways to buildings and enclosures. The excavators identified 'special deposits' of pottery that were placed in similar contexts and on several occasions in association with cremated bone.

At Stone Hall, Essex, two groups of pits containing cremated human bone, pottery and pyre debris, dated to 1200–920 BC, were sited adjacent to a contemporary boundary and waterhole (Timby et al. 2007). In two sites, Ongar Hall and Grange Lane, excavated as part of the same project, the arrangement of the cremation deposits indicated they either followed or underlay a boundary. At Ongar Road, one pit in a dispersed group forming a curving line of five features contained the cremated remains of a mature man, dated to the ninth century BC. At Grange Lane, a further 3 kilometres east, the cremated remains of a girl and an adult female were in separate pits, which formed a straight line with a third pit containing pottery, animal bone (including red deer), fired clay, burnt stone, charcoal and worked flint.

At South Hornchurch and Grange Lane the deposition of cremated human bone occurred in similar contexts to, though kept apart from, other materials derived from domestic life: broken pottery, burnt or worked stone and animal bone. At Toll House, Broom, Bedfordshire, cremated human and animal bones were intermingled with settlement debris associated with a roundhouse, storage structures and pits (Edmonds and Cooper 2007, 112–113). The animal and human bones were indistinguishable from one another in their cremated and fragmented state. An exception might have been a largish fragment (9 grams) from a maybe-human cremated femur in an entrance posthole to the roundhouse. In reviewing the cremated bone from Toll House, Matt Brudenell and Anwen Cooper (2008) propose that its abraded state, mixed with occupation debris, indicates its derivation from middens—accumulations of occupation de-bris. Human bone was incorporated into middens in places as far apart as Pot-terne and All Cannings Cross, Wiltshire, and at Manish Strand, Ensay, Western Isles—where two complete inhumations were interred in pits in an earlier mid-den (Simpson et al. 2003). At Cliffs End Farm, Kent—a site I will return to in this chapter's conclusion—burnt human bone was excavated in both a midden and the fill of a nearby mortuary pit (McKinley et al. 2014). Whatever the pro-cesses that led to the midden debris returning to the pits and postholes at Toll House, Brudenell and Cooper (2008, 30) suggest 'the specific histories of the people represented … and even their presence in the material being deposited, may not have been clear'.

A difference in the treatment of human remains from the preceding cen-turies is that a greater proportion of the human bone is unburnt, though dis-articulated, with skull and long-bone fragments forming a larger than might be expected part of the assemblages (Brück 1995; K. Cleary 2018; Cooney and Grogan 1994, 146–148). At Inchagreenoge, County Limerick, a young man's skull (radiocarbon dated to 1250–1000 BC) was placed in peaty ground next to a spring (Grogan et al. 2007, 282). The skull and the spring were then covered with a layer of large stones. An individual's skull, vertebrae and right leg bones recovered from peat in a palaeochannel at Watermead, Leicestershire, date from the eleventh to ninth centuries BC. Cut marks on the vertebrae indicate the individual's neck had been sliced with a metal blade from the front and back, and the injuries may be peri- rather than post-mortem (Jill Cook in Ripper and Beamish 2011, 193–195). Within tenth- to ninth-century midden deposits of the coastal settlement of Brean Down, excavations uncovered 15 pieces of human bone (Bell 1990). Seven of the pieces were skulls or skull fragments. The upper portion of an infant's skull was found in the base of a stone-lined pit within an oval house at Knockadoon, County Limerick (R. Cleary 2018, 191–192). Frag-ments of skull, burnt and unburnt, were excavated in a field bank elsewhere on Knockadoon; radiocarbon measurements of charcoal from within the bank lie within the fourteenth to twelfth centuries BC (R. Cleary 2018, 161). Hugh O'Neil Hencken (1942) excavated the portions of three adult skulls from beneath the lake settlement at Ballinderry, County Offaly. The frontal portions of two skulls had been removed, and the third was represented by the upper portion of the cranium. From his examination of the skulls, William Howells (in Hencken 1942, 17–20) proposed that the skulls were modified post-mortem with a knife and by breaking off bone fragments.

The manipulation and curation of human remains and their incorporation into domestic spaces are illustrated by the exceptional findings at Cladh Hallan, South Uist (Parker Pearson et al. 2005). The excavation of a group of round-houses revealed the burials of two adults and two children beneath the earliest floor levels, which the excavators interpreted as foundation deposits for the buildings. The skeleton of one of the adults, a man, comprised the bones of three different individuals: the postcranial body from one person, the head of another and the mandible of a third. The woman's body had been altered after death when two of her front teeth were removed and placed in each of her hands. A comparison of the radiocarbon dates obtained from the burials with the chronology of the houses indicates that the bodies of the woman and one of the children may have been buried up to a century after their death. The 'bodies' of the man had been dead long before they were buried beneath the floor of the house, probably by a few centuries. Other analytical techniques were applied in the study of the skeletons from Cladh Hallan with the conclusion that the bodies had undergone some form of mummification process to preserve the soft tissue component, probably involving burial in peat (Booth et al. 2015). At some stage the decision was taken to inter the dead, assembling them with the houses. It is likely that the bodies, partial and composite, buried beneath the settlements were loosely based on memories of living persons. In the case of the composite body at Cladh Hallan, 10–12 generations had passed between its deaths and interment.

In settlements and middens, human bones and bodies were assembled with varied other materials derived from domestic life. Human bones and bodies, along with animal bone and pottery, were also deposited in rivers, bogs, lakes and caves. These were the same places that were chosen for offerings of metalwork. Limited excavation of an artificial pool, called the King's Stables, located close to the contemporary enclosure of Haughey's Fort, County Armagh, produced the broken remains of clay moulds used for making swords, fragments of a human skull, red deer antlers and the partially articulated remains of dogs, cattle and pigs (Lynn 1977). The human bone was the facial portion of a young man's skull, which had been deliberately separated from the cranium. The poor preservation of the bone suggested it had been curated elsewhere before deposition in the pool. The dredging of Duddingston Loch, below Arthur's Seat in Edinburgh, produced a large collection of broken sword blades and spearheads, and a fragment from a cauldron, all of which were possibly associated with human skulls and animal bones found in the same area (Callander 1922). Skulls dated to the Bronze Age have been recovered from the Thames and its tributaries, leading Richard Bradley and Ken Gordon (1988) to interpret them as votive deposits along with metalwork, also recovered in large quantities from the river. More recent analysis and scientific dating of the skulls has confirmed the importance of deposition of skulls, mostly adults and of both sexes, in the eleventh to seventh centuries BC, within a longer duration of skull deposition that spanned the second millennium BC to first millennium AD (Edwards et al. 2009; Schulting and Bradley 2013).

Caves, too, were suitable for the deposition of human remains and material culture. Marion Dowd (2015) has gathered evidence for the human use of caves throughout Ireland. A quarter (24) of her sites included Bronze Age material, with the early and late Bronze Age most commonly represented. The Bronze Age was characterised by human presence in deeper, more restrictive and dangerous parts of cave systems. In Brothers' Cave, County Waterford, people negotiated a vertical drop of eight metres from a circular swallow hole to the cave beneath (Dowd 2015, 145–146). During the late Bronze Age, objects were then placed deep within the cave: 25 metres inside the cave, more than 50 amber beads were deposited in a place where water pooled after heavy rainfall; an axe, chisel and sickle were laid together 50 metres along the passage. A cave accessed from the side of the Glencurran Valley, County Clare, contained archaeological material dated to 1600–700 BC (Dowd 2009). The area of later deposition was excavated 45 metres from the cave's main entrance. It contained the disarticulated and partial remains of at least six individuals, young and old, along with broken pottery and perforated shells. There was also a large quantity of fragmented animal bones, with domestic sheep, cattle and horse (especially neonatal individuals) and wild species, notably hare.

Sculptor's Cave is accessed from a beach on the southern shore of the Moray Firth. It provided material culture, including ceramics and metalwork, animal and human bone attributed to the late Bronze Age (Armit et al. 2011; Cowie 1988). The human bone is dominated by postcranial fragments, with smaller numbers of cranial bones. Striations on one child's skull indicate post-mortem modification of the bone. Following their excavations in the 1970s, Ian and Alexandra Shepherd suggested the presence of mandibles around the entrance could have resulted from skulls suspended in the cave's entrance (Shepherd 1995). The most recent analysis shows more variation in the ages of the dead and the body parts represented in the assemblage, with calibrated radiocarbon dates placing this deposition in the eleventh to tenth centuries BC (Armit et al. 2011). The metalwork comprises small gold and bronze rings and bronze bracelets (Benton 1931). The objects were found alongside the human bone and stylistically could be contemporary with the bone or a century or two later.

In the assemblages I discussed above distinctions existed between fragmented and whole bodies, whether humans, animals, ceramic vessels and metalwork. The metalwork recovered during excavations at Flag Fen, Peterborough, offers a stronger and consistent pattern of objects, particularly weapons, being subjected to forceful destruction before their deposition (Pryor 2001). The structures at Flag Fen comprised an alignment of vertical and horizontal timbers, possibly forming a causeway, that led for nearly 1 kilometre from dry ground into the marshy fenland, where it joined with a large timber platform. Metalwork, animal and human bone, timber objects and querns were recovered from the area around the alignment and from the platform. This activity spanned the duration of the time when the timber structures were built and maintained, 1300–900 BC, and continued into the middle of the first millennium BC. Of the seven weapon blades (dirks, rapiers and swords), only one was complete and undamaged. The other examples had been deliberately broken or bent before deposition. The dagger and knife blades were also all broken before deposition. Bronze pins were the other objects consistently damaged, broken into pieces and bent. These practices were not applied to quernstones, spears and rings, which were generally deposited complete and undamaged. The remains of humans and animals were found fragmented, although the bone was not processed and included some paired and articulated elements of the skeletons. Amongst the animals were at least 14 dogs, which were all large in stature for the period (Halstead et al. 2001).

The connection between broken objects and water can be paralleled at other places broadly contemporary with Flag Fen. At Duddingston Loch, Edinburgh, the objects were found together and partly fused through heating, with the swords showing evidence that they were deliberately burnt and then broken (Callander 1922). Jill York's (2002) study of the Bronze Age metalwork from the non-tidal stretch of the River Thames identified an increase in the proportion of deliberately damaged objects in the late Bronze Age, with large numbers of both spearheads and swords being destroyed before deposition in the river. By comparison, most of the swords recovered from the River Trent were complete, while the majority of weapons recovered from the river were spearheads (Davis 1999; Scurfield 1997). This corresponds with the pattern in the River Blackwater, Ulster, in which one sword, an almost complete example, was identified during recent drainage operations, compared with 11 late Bronze Age spearheads (Ramsey et al. 1991/2). Susan Bridgford's (1997) analysis of the swords from Ireland shows that the swords recovered from wet contexts, such as bogs, rivers and lakes, are more likely to be complete and less likely to show damage due to use.

One interpretation of the breaking of objects is to see this as a form of 'ritual killing', turning blades from physically and socially dangerous objects into material commodities that could be safely exchanged (Bradley 1990). Alternatively, the transformation into parts made the objects suitable for exchange with supernatural beings (Barrett and Needham 1988). This social interpretation of fragmentation and exchange is illustrated by the discovery of two halves of the same sword, which were deposited on inter-visible hilltops, 3 kilometres apart, and on either side of the River Trent (Bradley and Ford 2004). The two pieces of the blade fitted together, although the lower section showed greater wear on the broken surface, indicating it had been handled and perhaps been in circulation longer. Richard Bradley and Deborah Ford (2004) interpret this as an example of 'enchainment' (Chapman 2000), whereby the parts of the sword were retained by different people as tokens of a social connection. This may have been a debt of some kind, which was materially closed by the mutual burial of the sword's fragments.

The parallels between the treatments of humans and objects would seem to be important for furthering an understanding of assemblages in fragments (Brück 2006b). I argued in the previous section that blades and other objects were participants with people in events and journeys. Offerings of objects to places such as rivers and bogs were rites of passage that enabled things to transition from one world into another. The exchanges brought things, people and places into kinship with one another. Assembling and placing things in the landscape enabled them to participate in this and other worlds. From the eleventh and tenth centuries, things were more frequently deposited in fragments and parts of humans more commonly joined the fragments of things. A world of fragments was a world of relations. The circulation and exchanges of parts through the world and into other worlds occurred alongside the assembling of vibrant substances, bodies and their relations throughout the landscape.

During the later centuries of the second millennium BC, fragmentation became the means for facilitating exchanges and materialising the relations that emerged through metalwork exchanges. The thirteenth-century sunken cargo in Langdon Bay, Kent, which I described earlier, is an example of objects accumulated through exchanges and suitable for recrafting. Fragmentation was the practical way that metal could move between kin and be transformed into new objects. During the tenth and ninth centuries BC, broken objects began to dominate some metalwork assemblages from dryland contexts, and these practices occur around the same time in near and distant continental Europe (Dietrich 2014; Fontijn 2020). The assemblages that living kin accumulated and exchanged were, especially during the tenth and ninth centuries, assembled as offerings in the landscape.

In his analysis of metalwork in southwest England, Matthew Knight (2018) identifies many more incomplete objects in late Bronze Age collections, with most representing a quarter or less than the original artefacts. Two-thirds of the objects that Knight analysed had been broken deliberately, with ingots and socketed axes making up the majority of these. An assemblage of 50 objects, including broken axes, swords and ingots, was deposited on the tidal island at St Michael's Mount, Cornwall. One of the axes was deliberately broken and its socket plugged with fragments from other broken items. While the commonly occurring objects in the assemblage were broken, the two unusual items—a chape and a buckle—were deposited whole. The objects at St Michael's Mount were assembled with a local landmark: a rocky promontory and tidal island close to Cornwall' western tip. Two assemblages were found near one another at Southchurch, Essex, on England's east coast (Turner 1998, vol. 2, 196–216). Workers quarrying gravel in 1924 uncovered an assemblage of metal and a ceramic vessel. The six small pieces from copper ingots were arranged around the shoulder of the pot. A second larger assemblage was discovered at a nearby brickworks: a pottery vessel contained more than 60 fragments of axes, tool, blades and ingots.

The assemblage at Isleham, Cambridgeshire, is the largest metalwork deposit recovered from Britain or Ireland (Britton 1960). The 6,500 pieces of bronze, weighing over 90 kilograms, were contained in a large ceramic vessel and buried in the ground. All the objects were fragmentary, with large numbers of broken weapons, the raw metal and casting debris resulting from metalworking, the remains of sheet-metal containers (cauldrons or buckets) and items of horse gear. The well-studied group of objects from Petters, in the Thames Valley, provides another perspective (Needham 1990). Here the metalwork, comprising a similar range of items to the Isleham find, was deposited in two caches in the upper fills of a ditch terminal, which was itself adjacent to the remains of a contemporary settlement site. Although assemblages similar to these are most common in southern England, there are examples from other regions. The group from Glascoed, Monmouthshire, consists of complete and fragmentary axes, spearheads, swords and casting material (Gwilt 2004) (Figure 3.17). The 200 broken

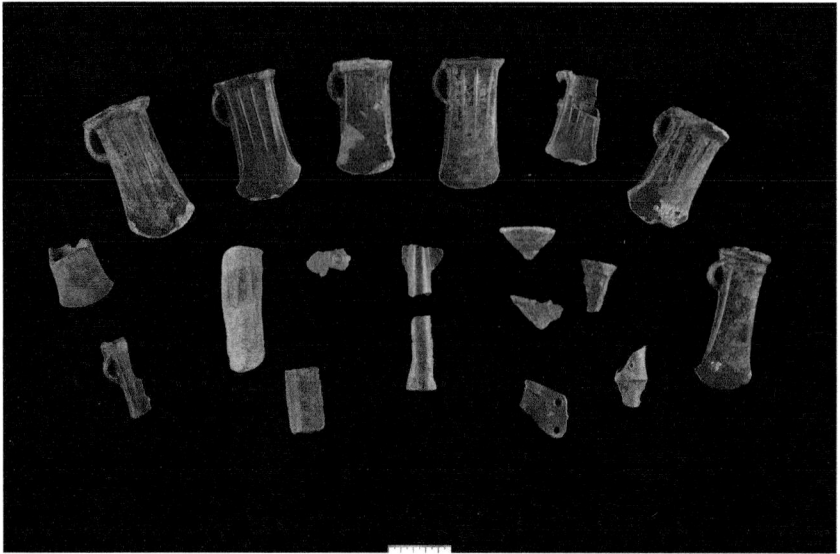

FIGURE 3.17 The broken objects from Glascoed, Gwent, include socketed axes, a sickle, knife, sword, spearhead, casting jets and a bronze cake. Copyright: National Museum of Wales.

bronze objects and waste pieces of bronze from an unknown location in County Roscommon are an example from Ireland (Eogan 1983, 47–49).

These assemblages of predominately broken material have been interpreted as hoards of raw material—commodities—accumulated by metalworkers, deposited for safe-keeping and never retrieved. There are reasons to question this categorisation (Brück 2016; Fontijn 2020; Turner 2010). Fragments of things were incorporated in many metalwork assemblages and deposited throughout the landscape, in rivers, bogs, caves and settlements. Fragmentation, as a process, was applied to different materials, not just metalwork, and it was frequently an important precondition for deposition. Fragments retained properties of the whole and retained relations with each other and with the places and beings involved in exchange. Joanna Brück (2006a) offers the suggestion that the recycling of metal fragments was a means of introducing the genealogy of old objects into the lives of the new. In these terms, she interprets the collections of material in the enclosure ditch at Petters as 'items with transformative and rejuvenating properties … buried at a location where social distinctions (and perhaps links between social groups) were marked out in space' (Brück 2006a). Following a study of the late Bronze Age metalwork assemblages from Essex and Kent, Louise Turner (2010) argues that the material was collected selectively in order to symbolise metalworking and related processes, including the agricultural cycle.

As important as this symbolism might have been, the links with the assemblages that living kin accumulated and exchanged might be interpreted in a more direct way. Fragmentation became the means through which vibrant beings and substances were controlled, exchanged and dispersed. The roots of these traditions could be traced centuries back to the early second millennium BC as cremation became a normal mortuary rite and the cremated bone was treated as a potent material that was incorporated into varied places and events. This process was understood alongside and in relation with other transformative processes, such as metalworking and ceramic production (Brück 2006b). By the tenth and ninth centuries, metal was widely and commonly exchanged in its fragmented states. This should not be confused with a process of commodification. Exchange remained, fundamentally, kinwork that created and maintained relations between people. A change in depositional assemblages occurred when the fragments that circulated amongst living kin were gathered and offered in exchanges with places, continuing a practice of votive or sacrificial offerings that stretched back for millennia. A characteristic of some assemblages was their size, sometimes including hundreds or even thousands of items. These drew large numbers of relations together into a single assemblage. They marked moments of collective kinwork and exchange at a time, as I will discuss in later chapters, when people and animals were periodically gathering in large numbers for feasts, fairs and collective labour projects.

The creativity of fragmentation and association is illustrated from Downpatrick, County Down (Figure 3.18). In the 1950s, two groups of gold objects were recovered when digging graves for the cemetery on Cathedral Hill (Proudfoot 1955; 1957; Warner and Cahill 2012). Both groups were arranged above one another in pits and covered with stones. The assemblages were dominated by penannular bracelets of a common Irish type dating to around the mid-tenth or ninth century BC. Three objects were at least two centuries older, of an Atlantic-style (Berzocana/Marne) and had travelled from further afield, perhaps Iberia. They included a penannular bracelet with decorated terminals and a fragment of a decorated neck-ring. The larger assemblage was carefully arranged. Nine penannular bracelets were stacked in the hole first. They were covered with two centimetres of charcoal-flecked sediment, before the three larger, older pieces were added and then capped with stones. Richard Warner and Mary Cahill's (2012) analytical research indicates that the younger bracelets were surfaced in gold from the older, foreign objects. Katharina Becker (2013, 255) interprets the assemblage as deliberately refencing the objects' transformation from a foreign into a local style. Maybe so, although the distinction might have been between relations that were distant (in time and geography, rather than 'foreign') and those that were close. The objects were assembled in a way that acknowledged their connections and, through the shallow lens of sediment that separated them, respected their differences.

I selected the title for this section from a long poem called 'Processing Plant' by John Wedgwood Clarke in his collection *Landfill*: 'a solid fog of stuff / all-remembering in its dismemberments, / hidden from sight' (Clarke 2017, 41). 'Nothing's more real than this', Clarke writes, of the rubbish that accumulates in a modern town's clay-capped landfill. During the eleventh to ninth centuries BC, the fragments of

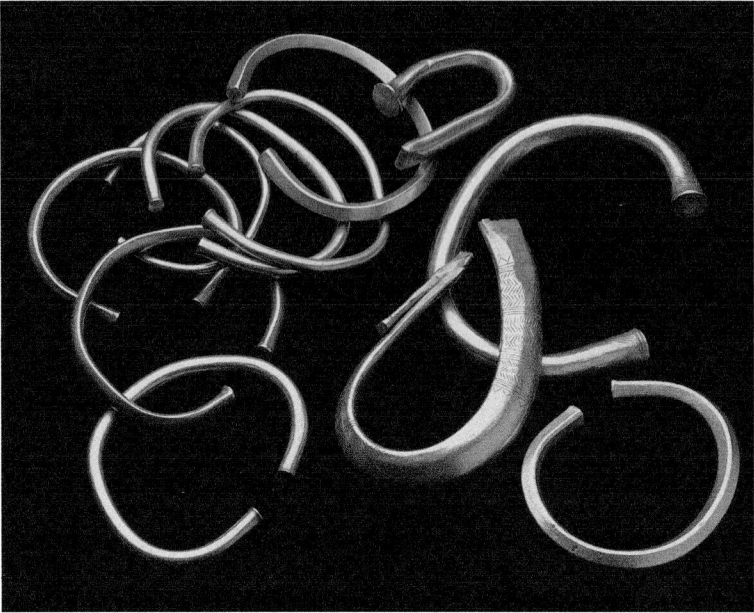

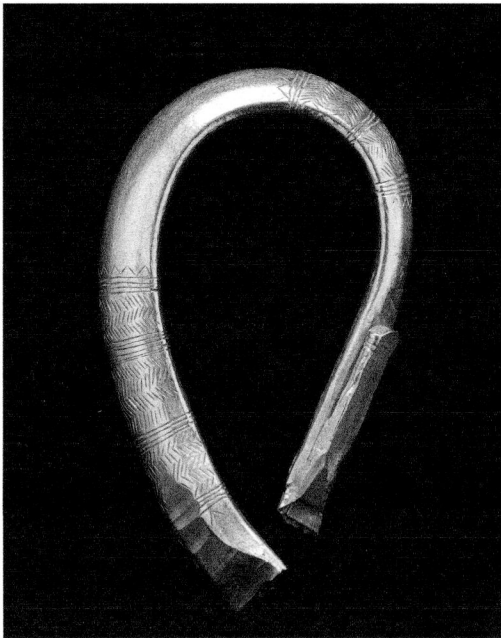

FIGURE 3.18 Gold penannular bracelets and the decorated neck-ring (shown in both images) from Downpatrick, County Down. The neck-ring is c. 95 × 55 mm. BELUM.AL.D1.12, Downpatrick Hoard; © National Museums NI, Collection Ulster Museum.

everyday life and lives were assembled as offerings in the landscape. Fragments had become a means of transforming and controlling substances. They were also a means of exchange, through which widening relations were created and bound together. Sometimes these depositions were exceptional. At Heathery Burn cave, located deep in the North Pennine dales, County Durham, nineteenth-century mineworking and quarrying uncovered hundreds of items of bronze and goldwork, worked bone and pottery, human and animal bone (Britton and Longworth 1968). At other times deposits were routine and the fragments could be almost homeopathic in their quantities. The debris deposited in pits amongst domestic structures at South Hornchurch and Broom was a substance assembled from the past-lives of humans, animals and things. Always, depositional assemblages continued practices of exchange that operated amongst living kin. To paraphrase John Wedgwood Clarke—hidden from sight, there was nothing more real than this.

Conclusion—Dartmoor to the Isle of Thanet

I opened this chapter with the burial of a young person's cremated remains on Whitehorse Hill, Dartmoor. The burial continued practices from the earlier second millennium BC, as kin assembled vibrant things along with the dead and contained them in a bear's pelt, a lidded basket and a stone chamber. The young person was cremated before their interment and only a portion of their body reached the grave. These practices of transformation, fragmentation and dispersal would come to dominate mortuary practices over the coming centuries. By the tenth century BC, fragments of humans, animals and things mixed and combined into new substances, and formed the currencies for exchanges in this and other worlds.

Compared with Dartmoor, the Isle of Thanet, Kent, offered a quite different setting for human burials. It is at England's southeastern tip, facing both the North Sea and the Channel. During later prehistory, the Wantsum Channel separated Thanet from the mainland and provided a navigable waterway from the English Channel into the Thames Estuary. In the tenth or ninth centuries BC, the body of an elderly woman was placed in a large pit at Cliffs End, on the south side of the island (McKinley et al. 2014). The woman died following four blows to the back of her head from a sharp blade, probably a sword. Her kin laid her in the pit on her left side, lower hand holding a chalk lump to her mouth and right arm flexed with her index finger extended to the southwest (Figure 3.19). The bodies of two neonatal lambs lay across her pelvic area. The base of the pit already contained the bodies of two foetal lambs, and layers of burnt occupation debris, including human bone, which was possibly midden from an adjacent enclosure. Further human and animal remains were added to the pit after the woman. These included two juveniles and a young adult. The head of the young adult rested on a fleshed cattle skull—the animal's atlas vertebra was still attached. The head of one of the juveniles was twisted upright, post-mortem though while still

FIGURE 3.19 A view of the mortuary deposit at Cliffs End, Kent: the elderly woman holds a chalk lump to her mouth and gestures with her other arm; the juvenile in front of the woman is missing its skull and right hand; the head of the sub-adult to the right of the woman rests on a cattle skull. © Wessex Archaeology.

fleshed, in order to face a pottery vessel that lay behind the young person's head. The bundled, perhaps bagged, and partially decomposed remains of a man's head and the left side of his body were deposited on the other side of the pit, across from the elderly woman. The backfilled lenses of sediment in the pit included further disarticulated human bones, along with animal bone and pottery.

The burials at Cliffs End are exceptional for the quantities of late Bronze Age human bone that the excavators recovered across the site and the variation in the post-mortem treatment of the bodies within the pit. The weapon trauma on the woman's skull is also a rare discovery for Britain and Ireland. Elsewhere in Europe, there is more ample evidence for violent deaths (Jantzen et al. 2011). Setting aside these exceptional characteristics, there is a lot at Cliffs End that fits with our understanding of mortuary practices and deposition. The manipulation and curation of corpses was evidenced in a direct way by the mummified and composite body from Cladh Hallan, South Uist. The many more discoveries of modified crania offer further examples for curation and deposition of body parts. The burials at Cliffs End were unusual for their completeness. The majority of the dead people were represented by fragments of bone recovered from occupation debris or midden within the pit and from the nearby enclosures. This reflects a widespread practice.

Human bone was frequently recovered during excavations of settlement middens. Unusual examples of inhumation burials were excavated at Manish Strand, Ensay, Western Isles, where two individuals were interred, flexed and on their sides, in pits inserted within an earlier midden (Simpson et al. 2003).

Despite the gap of seven or eight centuries and the markedly different mortuary rites, there were similarities between the burials on Whitehorse Hill and at Cliffs End. The dead were assembled in ways that enabled them to influence and act upon a world, whether this world or another. The cremated remains on Whitehorse Hill were buried in the manner of the vibrant dead, provided with grave goods and contained in a cist. The elderly woman at Cliffs End was manipulated into a position of action: consuming chalk and with a finger pointing southwesterly. There were human and other-than-human bodies in the graves at both Cliffs End and on Whitehorse Hill. The elderly woman lay with two lambs across her hips and a cattle skull offered support for the young adult's head. Wrapped in a bear's pelt and accompanied by a cattle-hair bracelet, the cremated human bone on Whitehorse Hill was also assembled in relation with animals. Both burial deposits were composed of near and distant relations. The cist on Whitehorse Hill, softened with grasses from the surrounding peatland, contained objects made from amber and tin that reflected the connections southwest England had within the wider Atlantic world. At Cliffs End, 7 of 13 sampled Bronze Age individuals produced non-local isotopic ratios. Of the burials in the pit, the bundled and incomplete remains of the man were from colder, northern, Scandinavian regions and one of the juveniles grew up in a warmer, southern region. In his review of the site's significance, Stuart Needham (in McKinley et al. 2014, 219) describes Thanet as at the fulcrum between two major 'maritime highways of north-western Europe': the Channel and the North Sea.

The cremated bone carried to and deposited in the cist on Whitehorse Hill represented around half or less of the individual's remains from the pyre (Mays in Jones 2016, 42–43). Most areas of the young person's body were represented, although there were smaller than expected numbers of cranial and long bone fragments. The missing fragments might have remained at the pyre, been collected and deposited elsewhere or curated and exchanged amongst the living. During the thousand years of prehistory covered by this chapter, fragmentation became a dominant aspect of depositional practices. Fragments had figured in earlier assemblages, as abraded sherds of pottery and incomplete necklaces in burials. By the tenth and ninth centuries BC, fragmented material was widespread and came to dominate some assemblages.

In fragments, things and beings could be exchanged and retained, their potencies and relations dispersed throughout the landscape. Fragmentation was translated from one domain of practice to another: it enabled metalwork to be transformed and exchanged amongst the living, and it was the means of exchange with other worlds. Fragmentation enabled substances and relations to combine turning parts into hybrid wholes. The term *'ayllu'* is used in

Andeanist ethnography for 'a group of humans and other-than-human persons related to each other by kinship ties, and collectively inhabiting a territory' (de la Cadena 2015, 43). One of de la Cadena's (2015, 44) informants explained *ayllu* through the metaphor of weaving: 'all the beings in the world—people, animals, mountains, plants etc.—are like the threads, we are part of the design. The beings in this world are not alone, just as a thread by itself is not a weaving'. The Bronze Age world emerged in a similar way, as the fragments and hybrid substances that related beings and things amongst the living becoming knitted into the landscape. Kinwork created an ever-denser cloth woven into places and the land, which slowly gathered patterns and folds through time, and in patches became faded and bare as relations were forgotten and kinwork moved on.

References

Allen, Carol and David Hopkins. 2000. Bronze Age accessory cups from Lincolnshire: Early Bronze Age pot? *Proceedings of the Prehistoric Society* 66:297–317.

Appleby, Jo. 2012. Temporality and the transition to cremation in the late third millennium to mid second millennium BC in Britain. *Cambridge Archaeological Journal* 23(1):83–97.

Armit, Ian, Rick Schulting, Christopher Knüsel and Ian Shepherd. 2011. Death, decapitation and display? The Bronze and Iron Age human remains from the Sculptor's Cave, Covesea, north-east Scotland. *Proceedings of the Prehistoric Society* 77:251–278.

Armstrong, Edmund C R. 1909. Prehistoric leather shield found at Clonbrin, County Longford. *Proceedings of the Royal Irish Academy* 27C:259–262.

Baker, Louise. 2003. A Bronze Age burial ground at Longniddry, East Lothian. *Proceedings of the Society of Antiquaries of Scotland* 133:125–136.

Baker, Louise, Tessa Bolger and Lyndsey Clark. 2015. Site summaries. In *A journey along the Carlow corridor: the archaeology of the M9 Carlow bypass*, edited by Tessa Bolger, Colm Moloney, and Damian Shiels, pp. 11–76. NRA Scheme Monographs, 16. National Roads Authority, Dublin.

Barclay, Alistair and Claire Halpin. 1999. *Excavations at Barrow Hills, Radley, Oxfordshire. Volume 1: the Neolithic and Bronze Age monument complex*. Oxbow Books, Oxford.

Barnatt, John. 1994. Excavation of a Bronze Age unenclosed cemetery, cairns, and field boundaries at Eaglestone Flat, Curbar, Derbyshire, 1984, 1989–1990. *Proceedings of the Prehistoric Society* 60:287–370.

Barnatt, John and Mark Edmonds. 2002. Places apart? Caves and monuments in Neolithic and Earlier Bronze Age Britain. *Cambridge Archaeological Journal* 12(1):113–129.

Barrett, John C. 1990. The monumentality of death: the character of Early Bronze Age mortuary mounds in southern England. *World Archaeology* 22(2):179–189.

Barrett, John C. 1994. *Fragments from antiquity: an archaeology of social life in Britain, 2900–1200 BC*. Blackwell, Oxford.

Barrett, John C, Richard Bradley and Martin Green. 1991. *Landscape, monuments and society: the prehistory of Cranborne Chase*. Cambridge University Press, Cambridge.

Barrett, John C and Stuart Needham. 1988. Production, circulation and exchange: problems in the interpretation of Bronze Age bronzework. In *The archaeology of context in the Neolithic and Early Bronze Age: recent trends*, edited by John C Barrett, and Ian Kinnes, pp. 127–140. Sheffield University Department of Archaeology and Prehistory, Sheffield.

Becker, Katharina. 2010. Heritage Guide No. 51: Rathgall, Co. Wicklow. *Archaeology Ireland* 24(4).

Becker, Katharina. 2013. Transforming identities – new approaches to Bronze Age deposition in Ireland. *Proceedings of the Prehistoric Society* 79:225–263.

Becker, Katharina. 2014. Token explanations—Rathgall and the interpretation of cremation deposits in later prehistoric Ireland. *Archaeology Ireland* 28(1):13–15.

Bell, Martin. 1990. *Brean Down: excavations 1983–87.* English Heritage, London.

Benton, Sylvia. 1931. The excavation of the Sculptor's Cave, Covesea, Morayshire. *Proceedings of the Society of Antiquaries of Scotland* 65:177–216.

Bewley, Robert, Ian Longworth, Sue Browne, Jacqueline Huntley and Gill Varndell. 1992. Excavation of a Bronze Age cemetery at Ewanrigg, Maryport, Cumbria. *Proceedings of the Prehistoric Society* 58:325–354.

Booth, Thomas, Andrew Chamberlain and Mike Parker Pearson. 2015. Mummification in Bronze Age Britain. *Antiquity* 89(347):1155–1173.

Bourke, Lorraine. 2001. *Crossing the Rubicon: Bronze Age metalwork from Irish rivers.* Department of Archaeology, NUI Galway, Galway.

Bradley, Richard. 1990. *The passage of arms: an archaeological study of prehistoric hoards and votive deposits.* Cambridge University Press, Cambridge.

Bradley, Richard. 2005. *The moon and the bonfire: the investigation of three stone circles in north-east Scotland.* Society of Antiquaries of Scotland, Edinburgh.

Bradley, Richard. 2016. Histories of reuse. In *The use and reuse of stone circles: fieldwork at five Scottish monuments and its implications*, edited by Richard Bradley, and Courtney Nimura, pp. 122–133. Oxbow, Oxford.

Bradley, Richard. 2019. *The prehistory of Britain and Ireland (second edition).* Cambridge University Press, Cambridge.

Bradley, Richard and Deborah Ford. 2004. A long distance connection in the Bronze Age: joining fragments of a Ewart Park sword from two sites in England. In *From megaliths to metal: essays in honour of George Eogan*, edited by Helen Roche, Eoin Grogan, John Bradley, John Coles, and Barry Raftery, pp. 174–177. Oxbow, Oxford.

Bradley, Richard and Ken Gordon. 1988. Human skulls from the River Thames, their dating and significance. *Antiquity* 62(236):503–509.

Bridgford, Susan. 1997. Mightier than the pen? An edgewise look at Irish Bronze Age swords. In *Material harm: archaeological studies of war and violence*, edited by John Carman, pp. 95–115. Cruithne Press, Glasgow.

Brindley, Anna and Jan Lanting. 1991/2. Radiocarbon dates from the cemetery at Poulawack, Co. Clare. *Journal of Irish Archaeology* 6:13–17.

Britton, Dennis. 1960. The Isleham hoard. *Antiquity* 34(136):279–282.

Britton, Dennis and Ian H Longworth. 1968. *Late Bronze Age finds in the Heathery Burn Cave, Co. Durham.* Inventaria Archaeologica, GB 55. British Museum, London.

Brück, Joanna. 1995. A place for the dead: the role of human remains in Late Bronze Age Britain. *Proceedings of the Prehistoric Society* 61:245–277.

Brück, Joanna. 2004. Material metaphors: the relational construction of identity in Early Bronze Age burials in Ireland and Britain. *Journal of Social Archaeology* 4(3):307–333.

Brück, Joanna. 2006a. Death, exchange and reproduction in the British Bronze Age. *European Journal of Archaeology* 9(1):73–101.

Brück, Joanna. 2006b. Fragmentation, personhood and the social construction of technology in Middle and Late Bronze Age Britain. *Cambridge Archaeological Journal* 16(3):297–315.

Brück, Joanna. 2016. Hoards, fragmentation and exchange in the European Bronze Age. In *Raum, Gabe und Erinnerung: weihgaben und heiligtümer in prähistorischen und antiken gesellschaften,* edited by Svend Hansen, Daniel Neumann, and Tilmann Vachta, pp. 75–92. Universität Berlin und der Humboldt-Universität zu Berlin, Berlin.

Brück, Joanna. 2017. Reanimating the dead: the circulation of human bone in the British later Bronze Age. In *Engaging with the dead: exploring changing human beliefs about death, mortality and the human body,* edited by Jennie Bradbury, and Chris Scarre, pp. 138–148. Oxbow, Oxford.

Brück, Joanna. 2019. *Personifying prehistory: relational ontologies in Bronze Age Britain and Ireland.* Oxford University Press, Oxford.

Brudenell, Matt and Anwen Cooper. 2008. Post-middenism: depositional histories on later Bronze Age settlements at Broom, Bedfordshire. *Oxford Journal of Archaeology* 27(1):15–36.

Burgess, Colin B. 1976. Burials with metalwork of the later Bronze Age in Wales and beyond. In *Welsh antiquity: essays mainly on prehistoric topics presented to H N Savory upon his retirement as keeper of archaeology,* edited by George C Boon, and J M Lewis, pp. 81–104. National Museum of Wales, Cardiff.

Burgess, Colin B. 1995. Bronze Age settlements and domestic pottery in northern Britain: some suggestions. In *'Unbaked urns of rudely shape': essays on British and Irish pottery,* edited by Ian Kinnes, and Gill Varndell, pp. 145–158. Oxbow, Oxford.

Burgess, Colin B and Sabine Gerloff. 1981. *The dirks and rapiers of Great Britain and Ireland.* Prähistorische Bronzefunde IV/7, Munich.

Cahill, Mary and Maeve Sikora (editors). 2011. *Breaking ground, finding graves: reports on the excavations of burials by the National Museum of Ireland, 1927–2006.* Wordwell, Dublin.

Cahill, Mary and Maeve Sikora. 2014. More evidence for Bronze Age body-piercing. *Archaeology Ireland* 28(2):30–31.

Callander, J Graham. 1920/1921. A Bronze Age hoard from Glen Trool, Stewartry of Kirkcudbright. *Proceedings of the Society of Antiquaries of Scotland* 55:29–37.

Callander, J Graham. 1922. Three Bronze Age hoards. *Proceedings of the Society of Antiquaries of Scotland* 56:351–364.

Campbell, Gill and Mark Robinson. 2007. Environment and land use in the valley bottom. In *The Raunds Area Project: a Neolithic and Bronze Age landscape in Northamptonshire,* edited by Jan Harding, and Frances Healy, pp. 18–36. English Heritage, London.

Caswell, Edward and Benjamin Roberts. 2018. Reassessing community cemeteries: cremation burials in Britain during the Middle Bronze Age (c. 1600–1150 cal BC). *Proceedings of the Prehistoric Society* 84: 329–357.

Chapman, Andy. 2003. Three Bronze Age burial sites in Northamptonshire. *Northamptonshire Archaeology* 31:1–14.

Chapman, John. 2000. *Fragmentation in archaeology: people, places and broken objects in the prehistory of south eastern Europe.* Routledge, London.

Chestnutt, Caroline and Neil Wilkin. 2013. KENT-FE9DB2: a Bronze Age hoard https://finds.org.uk/database/artefacts/record/id/570344, accessed 30/01/20.

Clarke, David V, Trevor G Cowie and Andrew Foxon. 1985. *Symbols of power: at the time of Stonehenge.* National Museum of Scotland, Edinburgh.

Clarke, John Wedgwood. 2017. *Landfill.* Valley Press, Scarborough.

Cleary, Kerri. 2018. Broken bones and broken stones: exploring fragmentation in Middle and Late Bronze Age settlement contexts in Ireland. *European Journal of Archaeology* 21(3):336–360.

Cleary, Rose M. 2018. *The archaeology of Lough Gur.* Wordwell, Dublin.

Coles, John. 1962. European Bronze Age shields. *Proceedings of the Prehistoric Society* 28:156–190.

Coles, John. 1963. Scottish Middle Bronze Age metalwork. *Proceedings of the Society of Antiquaries of Scotland* 97:82–156.

Coles, John M, Peter Leach, Steve C Minnitt, Richard Tabor and Andrew S Wilson. 1999. A later Bronze Age shield from South Cadbury, Somerset, England. *Antiquity* 73(279):33–48.

Cooney, Gabriel. 2016. Pathways to ancestral worlds: mortuary practice in the Irish Neolithic. In *The Neolithic of mainland Scotland*, edited by Kenneth Brophy, Gavin MacGregor, and Ian Ralston, pp. 79–94. Edinburgh University Press, Edinburgh.

Cooney, Gabriel. 2017. Pathways for the dead in the Middle and Late Bronze Age in Ireland. In *Cremation and the archaeology of death*, edited by Jessica Cerezo-Román, Anna Wessman, and Howard Williams, pp. 117–129. Oxford University Press, Oxford.

Cooney, Gabriel and Eoin Grogan. 1994. *Irish prehistory: a social perspective*. Wordwell, Dublin.

Cooper, Anwen. 2018. The regional historic environment research framework for the east of England: Early to Middle Bronze Age 2500–1150 BC. ALGAO East of England http://eaareports.org.uk/algao-east/regional-research-framework-review/, accessed 07/04/20.

Cooper, Anwen, Duncan Garrow and Catriona Gibson. 2020. Spectrums of depositional practice in later prehistoric Britain and beyond: grave goods, hoards and deposits 'in between'. *Archaeological Dialogues* 27(2).

Cooper, Anwen, Duncan Garrow, Catriona Gibson and Melanie Giles. 2019. Covering the dead in later prehistoric Britain: elusive objects and powerful technologies of funerary performance. *Proceedings of the Prehistoric Society* 85:223–250.

Cowie, Trevor. 1988. *Magic metal: early metalworkers in the north-east*. Anthropological Museum, University of Aberdeen, Aberdeen.

Cowie, Trevor, Brendan O'Connor and Marion Uckelmann. 2016. Yetholm revisited: old and new finds of high-quality Late Bronze Age metalwork. In *Prehistory without borders: the prehistoric archaeology of the Tyne-Forth region*, edited by Rachel Crellin, Chris Fowler, and Peter Topping, pp. 168–178. Oxbow, Oxford.

Cummings, Vicki and Chris Fowler. 2007. *From cairn to cemetery: an archaeological investigation of the chambered cairns and early Bronze Age mortuary deposits at Cairnderry and Bargrennan White Cairn, south-west Scotland*. Archaeopress, Oxford.

Danaher, Ed. 2007. *Monumental beginnings: the archaeology of the N4 Sligo inner relief road*. NRA Scheme Monographs, 1. National Roads Authority, Dublin.

Davis, Richard. 1999. Bronze Age metalwork from the Trent Valley: Newark, Notts, to Gainsborough, Lincs. *Transactions of the Thoroton Society of Nottinghamshire* 103:25–48.

de la Cadena, Marisol. 2015. *Earth beings: ecologies of practice across Andean worlds*. Duke University Press, London.

Dietrich, Oliver. 2014. Learning from 'scrap' about Late Bronze Age hoarding practices: a biographical approach to individual acts of dedication in large metal hoards of the Carpathian Basin. *European Journal of Archaeology* 17(3):468–486.

Dowd, Marion. 2009. Middle and Late Bronze Age funerary and ritual activity at Glencurran Cave, Co. Clare. In *Bann Flakes to Bushmills: papers in honour of Peter C. Woodman*, edited by Nyree Finlay, Sinead McCartan, Nicky Milner, and Caroline Wickham-Jones, pp. 86–96. Oxbow, Oxford.

Dowd, Marion. 2015. *The archaeology of caves in Ireland*. Oxbow, Oxford.

Downes, Jane. 1999. Cremation: a spectacle and a journey. In *The loved body's corruption: archaeological contributions to the study of human mortality*, edited by Jane Downes, and Tony Pollard, pp. 19–29. Cruithne, Glasgow.

Downes, Jane. 2005. *Cremation practice in Bronze Age Orkney*. PhD thesis, University of Sheffield.

Downes, Jane. 2009. The construction of barrows in Bronze Age Orkney—an 'assuagement of guilt'. In *Land and people: papers in memory of John G Evans*, edited by Michael

J Allen, Niall Sharples, and Terry O'Connor, pp. 126–135. Prehistoric Society Research Papers, 2. Prehistoric Society/Oxbow Books, Oxford.

Edmonds, Mark and Anwen Cooper. 2007. *Past and present: excavations at Broom, Bedfordshire 1996–2005.* Cambridge Archaeological Unit, Cambridge.

Edwards, Yvonne H, Alison Weisskopf and Derek Hamilton. 2009. Age, taphonomic history and mode of deposition of human skulls in the River Thames. *Transactions of the London and Middlesex Archaeological Society* 60:35–51.

Ellison, Ann. 1980. Deverel-Rimbury urn cemeteries: the evidence for social organisation. In *Settlement and society in the British later Bronze Age,* edited by John C Barrett, and Richard Bradley, pp. 115–126. BAR British Series, 83. British Archaelogical Reports, Oxford.

Eogan, George. 1983. *The hoards of the Irish Later Bronze Age.* University College Dublin, Dublin.

Eogan, George. 1994. *The accomplished art: gold and gold working in Britain and Ireland during the Bronze Age (c. 2300–650 BC).* Oxbow, Oxford.

Evans, Christopher, Jonathan Tabor and Marc Vander Linden. 2016. *Twice-crossed river: prehistoric and palaeoenvironmental investigations at Barleycroft Farm/Over, Cambridgeshire.* McDonald Institute for Archaeological Research, Cambridge.

Finn, Neil. 2011. *Bronze Age ceremonial enclosures and cremation cemetery at Eye Kettleby, Leicestershire.* University of Leicester Archaeological Services, Leicester.

Fontijn, David. 2020. *Economies of destruction: how the systematic destruction of valuables created value in Bronze Age Europe, c. 2300–500 BC.* Routledge, London.

Fowler, Chris. 2013. *The emergent past: a relational realist archaeology of Early Bronze Age mortuary practices.* Oxford University Press, Oxford.

Fox, Aileen and Dennis Britton. 1969. A continental palstave from the ancient field system on Horridge Common, Dartmoor, England. *Proceedings of the Prehistoric Society* 35:220–228.

Fraser, Elise. 2013. *The regionality of Bronze Age burial traditions around the Irish Sea.* PhD thesis, University of Reading.

Garrow, Duncan, John Meadows, Christopher Evans and Jonathan Tabor. 2014. Dating the dead: a high-resolution radiocarbon chronology of burial within an Early Bronze Age barrow cemetery at Over, Cambridgeshire. *Proceedings of the Prehistoric Society* 80:207–236.

Garwood, Paul. 2007. Before the hills in order stood: chronology, time and history in the interpretation of Early Bronze Age round barrows. In *Beyond the grave: new perspectives on barrows,* edited by Jonathan Last, pp. 30–52. Oxbow, Oxford.

Gibson, Alex. 2004. Small but perfectly formed? Some observations on the Bronze Age cups of Scotland. In *From sickles to circles: Britain and Ireland at the time of Stonehenge,* edited by Alex Gibson, and Alison Sheridan, pp. 270–288. Tempus, Stroud.

Gregory, Christopher A. 2015. *Gifts and commodities (Second Edition).* Hau, Chicago, IL.

Griffiths, W E. 1960. The excavation of stone circles near Penmaenmawr, North Wales. *Proceedings of the Prehistoric Society* 26:303–339.

Grogan, Eoin. 2004. Middle Bronze Age burial traditions in Ireland. In *From megaliths to metal: essays in honour of George Eogan,* edited by Helen Roche, Eoin Grogan, John Bradley, John Coles, and Barry Raftery, pp. 61–71. Oxbow, Oxford.

Grogan, Eoin, Lorna O'Donnell and Penny Johnston. 2007. *The Bronze Age landscapes of the Pipeline to the West: an integrated archaeological and environmental assessment.* Wordwell, Bray.

Guttmann, Erika B and Jonathan Last. 2000. A Late Bronze Age landscape at South Hornchurch, Essex. *Proceedings of the Prehistoric Society* 66:319–359.

Gwilt, Adam. 2004. Late Bronze Age societies (1150–600 BC): tools and weapons. In *The Gwent County History. Volume 1: Gwent in prehistory and early history*, edited by Miranda Aldhouse-Green, and Ray Howell, pp. 111–139. University of Wales Press, Cardiff.

Gwilt, Adam, Mark Lodwick and Mary Davis. 2007. Burton, Wrexham: Middle Bronze Age hoard of gold adornments and bronze tools with a pot. In *Treasure Annual Report 2004*, edited by Fi Hitchcock, pp. 198–199. Department for Culture, Media and Sport, London.

Halstead, Paul, Ellen Cameron and Stephen Forbes. 2001. Non-human and human mammalian bone remains from the Flag Fen platform and Power Station post alignment. In *The Flag Fen Basin: archaeology and environment of a fenland landscape*, edited by Francis Pryor, pp. 330–350. English Heritage, Swindon.

Harding, Jan and Frances Healy. 2007. *The Raunds Area Project: a Neolithic and Bronze Age landscape in Northamptonshire*. English Heritage, London.

Harford, Charles Joseph. 1803. An account of some antiquities discovered on the Quantock Hills, in Somersetshire, in the year 1794. *Archaeologia* 14:94–98.

Healy, Frances and Jan Harding. 2007. A thousand and one things to do with a round barrow. In *Beyond the grave: new perspectives on barrows*, edited by Jonathan Last, pp. 53–71. Oxbow, Oxford.

Hencken, Hugh O'Neill. 1942. Ballinderry Crannog No. 2. *Proceedings of the Royal Irish Academy* 47C:1–76.

Hencken, Hugh O'Neill and Hallam L Movius. 1934. The cemetery cairn of Knockast. *Proceedings of the Royal Irish Academy* 41C:232–284.

Hencken, Hugh O'Neill and Hallam L Movius. 1935. A cairn at Poulawack, County Clare: with a report on the human remains. *Journal of the Royal Society of Antiquaries of Ireland* 5(2):191–222.

Herity, Michael. 1969. Irish antiquarian finds and collections of the early nineteenth century. *Journal of the Royal Society of Antiquaries of Ireland* 99(1):21–37.

Hey, Gill, Christopher Bell, Caroline Dennis and Mark Robinson. 2016. *Yarnton: Neolithic and Bronze Age settlement and landscape*. Thames Valley Landscapes, 39. Oxford University School of Archaeology, Oxford.

Holden, Eric W. 1972. A Bronze Age cemetery-barrow on Itford Hill, Beddingham, Sussex. *Sussex Archaeological Collections* 110:70–117.

Hunter, Fraser. 2000. Excavation of an Early Bronze Age cemetery and other sites at West Water Reservoir, West Linton, Scottish Borders. *Proceedings of the Society of Antiquaries of Scotland* 130:115–182.

Jantzen, Detlef, Ute Brinker, Jörg Orschiedt, Jan Heinemeier, Jürgen Piek, Karlheinz Hauenstein, Joachim Krüger, Gundula Lidke, Harald Lübke, Reinhard Lampe, Sebastian Lorenz, Manuela Schult and Thomas Terberger. 2011. A Bronze Age battlefield? Weapons and trauma in the Tollense Valley, north-eastern Germany. *Antiquity* 85(328):417–433.

Johnson, Melanie and Kirsty Cameron. 2012. An Early Bronze Age unenclosed cremation cemetery and Mesolithic pit at Skilmafilly, near Maud, Aberdeenshire. *Scottish Archaeological Internet Reports* 53.

Jones, Andy M. 2016. *Preserved in the peat: an extraordinary Bronze Age burial on Whitehorse Hill, Dartmoor, and its wider context*. Oxbow, Oxford.

Kavanagh, Rhoda M. 1991. A reconsideration of razors in the Irish Earlier Bronze Age. *Journal of the Royal Society of Antiquaries of Ireland* 121:77–104.

Knight, Matthew. 2018. *The intentional destruction and deposition of Bronze Age metalwork in south west England*. PhD thesis, University of Exeter.

Krus, Anthony and Mary Peteranna. 2016. Bayesian modeling of an Early Bronze Age cemetery at Armadale, Isle of Skye, Scotland. *Radiocarbon* 58(3):693–708.

Law, Robert. 2008. *The development and perpetuation of a ceramic tradition: the significance of Collared Urns in Early Bronze Age social life.* PhD thesis, University of Cambridge.

Lelong, Olivia. 2018. Fluid identities, shifting sands: Early Bronze Age burials at Cnip Headland, Isle of Lewis. *Scottish Archaeological Internet Reports* 75.

Lewis, John, Matt Leivers, Lisa Brown, Alex Smith, Kate Cramp, Lorraine Mepham and Chris Phillpotts. 2010. *Landscape evolution in the Middle Thames Valley: Heathrow Terminal 5 excavations. Volume 2.* Framework Archaeology, Oxford and Salisbury.

Lynch, Frances. 1971. Report on the re-excavation of two Bronze Age cairns in Anglesey: Bedd Branwen and Treiorwerth. *Archaeologia Cambrensis* 120:64–72.

Lynch, Frances. 1993. *Excavations in the Brenig Valley: a Mesolithic and Bronze Age landscape in North Wales.* Cambrian Archaeological Association, Bangor.

Lynn, Chris J. 1977. Trial excavations at the King's Stables, Tray Townland, County Armagh. *Ulster Journal of Archaeology* 40:42–62.

Manby, Terry G, Alan King and Blaise Vyner. 2003. The Neolithic and Bronze Age: a time of early agriculture. In *The archaeology of Yorkshire: an assessment at the beginning of the 21st century*, edited by Terry G Manby, Stephen Moorhouse, and Patrick Ottaway, pp. 35–116. Yorkshire Archaeological Society, Leeds.

Mays, Simon, David Roberts, Peter Marshall, Alistair W G Pike, Vivian van Heekeren, Christopher Bronk Ramsey, Elaine Dunbar, Paula Reimer, Bethan Linscott, Anita Radini, Abigail Lowe, Adam Dowle, Camilla Speller, John Vallender and Jon Bedford. 2018. Lives before and after Stonehenge: an osteobiographical study of four prehistoric burials recently excavated from the Stonehenge World Heritage Site. *Journal of Archaeological Science: Reports* 20:692–710.

McGarry, Tiernan. 2009. Irish late prehistoric burial ring-ditches. In *Relics of old decency: festschrift for Barry Raftery. Archaeological studies in later prehistory*, edited by Gabriel Cooney, Katharina Becker, John Coles, Michael Ryan, and Susanne Sievers, pp. 413–423. Wordwell, Bray.

McInnes, Isla J. 1968. The excavation of a Bronze Age cemetery at Catfoss, East Yorkshire. *East Riding Archaeologist* 1(1):1–10.

McKinley, Jacqueline. 1993. Bone fragment size and weights of bone from modern British cremations and its implications for the interpretation of archaeological cremations. *International Journal of Osteoarchaeology* 3:283–287.

McKinley, Jacqueline. 1997. Bronze Age 'barrows' and funerary rites and rituals of cremation. *Proceedings of the Prehistoric Society* 63:129–145.

McKinley, Jacqueline. 2004. Archaeological investigations at The Bostle, Bronze Age and Anglo-Saxon barrow cemeteries, Balsdean, East Sussex, 1997. *Sussex Archaeological Collections* 142:25–44.

McKinley, Jacqueline, Matt Leivers, Jörn Schuster, Peter Marshall, Alistair Barclay and Nick Stoodley. 2014. *Cliffs End Farm, Isle of Thanet, Kent: a mortuary and ritual site of the Bronze Age, Iron Age and Anglo-Saxon period.* Wessex Archaeology, Salisbury.

McOmish, David, David Field and Graham Brown. 2002. *The field archaeology of the Salisbury Plain Training Area.* English Heritage, Swindon.

McQuade, Melanie, Bernice Molloy and Colm Moriarty. 2009. *In the shadow of the Galtees: archaeological excavations along the N8 Cashel to Mitchelstown road scheme.* NRA Scheme Monographs, 4. National Roads Authority, Dublin.

Medina-Pettersson, Cecilia. 2013. *Bronze Age urned cremation burials of mainland Scotland: mortuary ritual and cremation technology.* PhD thesis, University of Edinburgh.

Melton, Nigel, Janet Montgomery, Benjamin Roberts, Gordon Cook and Susanna Harris. 2016. On the curious date of the Rylstone log-coffin burial. *Proceedings of the Prehistoric Society* 82:383–392.

Muckelroy, Keith. 1981. Middle Bronze Age trade between Britain and Europe: a maritime perspective. *Proceedings of the Prehistoric Society* 47:275–297.

Needham, Stuart. 1990. *The Petters Late Bronze Age metalwork: an analytical study of Thames Valley metalworking in its settlement context.* British Museum, London.

Needham, Stuart. 2001. When expediency broaches ritual intention: the flow of metal between systemic and buried domains. *Journal of the Royal Anthropological Institute* 7(2):275–298.

Needham, Stuart, Peter Northover, Marion Uckelmann and Richard Tabor. 2012. South Cadbury: the last of the bronze shields? *Archäologisches Korrespondenzblatt* 42(4):473–492.

Needham, Stuart, Dave Parham and Catherine J Frieman. 2013. *Claimed by the sea: Salcombe, Langdon Bay, and other marine finds of the Bronze Age.* Council for British Archaeology, York.

Noble, Gordon and Kenneth Brophy. 2017. Cremation practices and the creation of monument complexes: the Neolithic cremation cemetery at Forteviot, Strathearn, Perth & Kinross, Scotland, and its comparanda. *Proceedings of the Prehistoric Society* 83:213–245.

Ó Ríordáin, Breandán. 1997. A Bronze Age cemetery mound at Grange, Co. Roscommon. *Journal of Irish Archaeology* 8:43–72.

O'Connor, Brendan and Trevor Cowie. 1995. Middle Bronze Age dirks and rapiers from Scotland: some finds old and new. *Proceedings of the Society of Antiquaries of Scotland* 125:345–367.

O'Brien, William. 2004. (Con)Fusion of tradition? The circle henge in Ireland. In *From sickles to circles: Britain and Ireland at the time of Stonehenge*, edited by Alex Gibson, and Alison Sheridan, pp. 323–338. Tempus, Stroud.

O'Donnell, Lorna. 2016. The power of the pyre—a holistic study of cremation focusing on charcoal remains. *Journal of Archaeological Science* 65:161–171.

O'Sullivan, Muiris. 2005. *Duma na nGiall: the Mound of the Hostages, Tara.* Wordwell in association with the UCD School of Archaeology, Bray.

Parker Pearson, Mike, Andrew Chamberlain, Oliver Craig, Peter Marshall, Jacqui Mulville, Helen Smith, Carolyn Chenery, Matthew Collins, Gordon Cook, Geoffrey Craig, Jane Evans, Jen Hiller, Janet Montgomery, Jean-Luc Schwenninger, Gillian Taylor and Timothy Wess. 2005. Evidence for mummification in Bronze Age Britain. *Antiquity* 79(305):529–546.

Petersen, Fredric. 1981. *The excavation of a Bronze Age cemetery on Knighton Heath, Dorset.* BAR British Series, 98. British Archaeological Reports, Oxford.

Piggott, Stuart. 1938. The Early Bronze Age in Wessex. *Proceedings of the Prehistoric Society* 4:52–106.

Pollard, Sheila H M. 1971. Seven prehistoric sites near Honiton, Devon. Part II: three flint rings. *Proceedings of the Devon Archaeological Society* 29:162–180.

Poyer, Andrew. 2015. *The topographic setting of Bronze Age metalwork deposits in north east England.* PhD thesis, University of Sheffield.

Proudfoot, Bruce. 1955. *The Downpatrick gold find: a hoard of gold objects from Cathedral Hill.* Archaeological Research Publications, Belfast.

Proudfoot, Bruce. 1957. A second gold find from Downpatrick. *Ulster Journal of Archaeology* 20:70–72.

Pryor, Francis. 2001. *The Flag Fen Basin: archaeology and environment of a fenland landscape.* English Heritage, Swindon.

Raftery, Barry. 1973. Rathgall: a Late Bronze Age burial in Ireland. *Antiquity* 47(188):293–295.

Raftery, Joseph. 1961. The Derrinboy Hoard, Co. Offaly. *Journal of the Royal Society of Antiquaries of Ireland* 91(1):55–58.

Ramsey, Greer, Cormac Bourke and Deirdre Crone. 1991/2. Antiquities from the River Blackwater I: Bronze Age metalwork. *Ulster Journal of Archaeology* 54/55:138–149.

Rebay-Salisbury, Katharina. 2010. Cremations: fragmented bodies in the Bronze and Iron Ages. In *Body parts and bodies whole: changing relations and meanings*, edited by Jessica Hughes, Katharina Rebay-Salisbury, and Marie Louise Stig Sørensen, pp. 64–71. Oxbow, Oxford.

Richardson, Jane and Blaise Vyner. 2011. An exotic Early Bronze Age funerary assemblage from Stanbury, West Yorkshire. *Proceedings of the Prehistoric Society* 77:49–63.

Ripper, Susan and Matthew Beamish. 2011. Bogs, bodies and burnt mounds: visits to the Soar wetlands in the Neolithic and Bronze Age. *Proceedings of the Prehistoric Society* 78:173–206.

Roberts, Benjamin. 2007. Adorning the living but not the dead: understanding ornaments in Britain c. 1400–1100 cal BC. *Proceedings of the Prehistoric Society* 73:135–167.

Schmidt, Peter and Colin Burgess. 1981. *The axes of Scotland and northern England*. Prähistorische Bronzefunde IX/7, Munich.

Schulting, Rick and Richard Bradley. 2013. 'Of human remains and weapons in the neighbourhood of London': new AMS ^{14}C dates on Thames 'river skulls' and their European context. *Archaeological Journal* 170(1):30–77.

Scurfield, Christopher. 1997. Bronze Age metalwork from the River Trent in Nottinghamshire. *Transactions of the Thoroton Society of Nottinghamshire* 101:29–57.

Shapland, Fiona. 2016. Bone. In *The use and reuse of stone circles: fieldwork at five Scottish monuments and its implications*, edited by Richard Bradley, and Courtney Nimura, pp. 68. Oxbow, Oxford.

Shepherd, Ian A G. 1995. The Sculptor's Cave, Covesea, Moray: from Bronze Age ossuary to Pictish shrine? *Proceedings of the Society of Antiquaries of Scotland* 125:1194–1195.

Shepherd, Ian A G and Alexandra N Shepherd. 2001. A Cordoned Urn burial with faience from 102 Findhorn, Moray. *Proceedings of the Society of Antiquaries of Scotland* 131:101–128.

Sheridan, Alison. 2003. New dates for Scottish Bronze Age cinerary urns: results from the National Museums of Scotland *Dating Cremated Bone Project*. In *Prehistoric pottery: people, pattern and purpose*, edited by Alex Gibson, pp. 201–226. British Archaeological Reports International Series 1156. Archaeopress, Oxford.

Simpson, Derek D A, Richard A Gregory and Eileen Murphy. 2003. Excavations at Manish Strand, Ensay, Western Isles. *Proceedings of the Society of Antiquaries of Scotland* 133:173–189.

Sørensen, Marie Louise Stig. 1997. Reading dress: the construction of social categories and identities in Bronze Age Europe. *Journal of European Archaeology* 5(1):93–114.

Stanley, William Owen and Albert Way. 1868. Ancient interments and sepulchral urns found in Anglesey and North Wales. *Archaeologia Cambrensis (Third Series)* 55:218–293.

Strathern, Marilyn. 1988. *The gender of the gift: problems with women and problems with society in Melanesia*. University of California Press, Berkeley.

Tellier, Geneviève. 2015. *The analysis of funerary and ritual practices in Wales between 3600–1200 BC based on osteological and contextual data*. PhD thesis, University of Bradford.

Timby, Jane, Richard Brown, Edward Biddulph, Alan Hardy and Andrew Powell. 2007. *A slice of rural Essex: archaeological discoveries from the A120 between Stansted Airport and Braintree.* Oxford Wessex Archaeology, Oxford and Salisbury.

Tipping, Richard. 1994. Ritual floral tributes in the Scottish Bronze Age—palynological evidence. *Journal of Archaeological Science* 21(1):133–139.

Tolan-Smith, Christopher. 2005. A cairn on Birkside Fell: excavations in 1996 and 1997. *Archaeologia Aeliana* 34:55–65.

Tomalin, David. 1988. Armorican *vases à anses* and their occurrence in southern Britain. *Proceedings of the Prehistoric Society* 54:203–221.

Troy, Camelita. 2015. Contextualising cremations: evidence from prehistoric burials. In *A journey along the Carlow corridor: the archaeology of the M9 Carlow bypass*, edited by Tessa Bolger, Colm Moloney, and Damian Shiels, pp. 131–144. NRA Scheme Monographs, 16. National Roads Authority, Dublin.

Turner, C E Louise. 1998. *A re-interpretation of the Late Bronze Age metalwork hoards of Essex and Kent.* PhD thesis, University of Glasgow.

Turner, C E Louise. 2010. *A re-interpretation of the Late Bronze Age metalwork hoards of Essex and Kent.* British Archaeological Reports, Oxford.

Uckelmann, Marion. 2012. *Die Schilde der Bronzezeit in Nord-, West- und Zentraleuropa.* Prähistorische Bronzefunde III/4, Stuttgart.

Viveiros de Castro, Eduardo. 2009. The gift and the given: three nano-essays on kinship and magic. In *Kinship and beyond: the genealogical model reconsidered*, edited by Sandra C Bamford, and James Leach, pp. 237–268. Berghahn, New York.

Waddell, John. 1990. *The Bronze Age burials of Ireland.* Galway University Press, Galway.

Wainwright, Geoffrey J, Andrew Fleming and Ken Smith. 1979. The Shaugh Moor Project: first report. *Proceedings of the Prehistoric Society* 45:1–33.

Walker, Karen E and David E Farwell. 2000. *Twyford Down, Hampshire: archaeological investigations on the M3 motorway from Bar End to Compton, 1990–93.* Hampshire Field Club and Archaeological Society, Winchester.

Warner, Richard and Mary Cahill. 2012. The Downpatrick hoards: an analytical reconsideration. In *Of things gone but not forgotten: essays in archaeology for Joan Taylor*, edited by Jonathan R Trigg, pp. 95–108. BAR International Series, 2434. Archaeopress, Oxford.

Waterman, Dudley M. 1968. Cordoned urn burials and ring-ditch at Urbalreagh, Co. Antrim. *Ulster Journal of Archaeology* 31:25–32.

Watkins, Trevor. 1982. The excavation of an Early Bronze Age cemetery at Barns Farm, Dalgety, Fife. *Proceedings of the Society of Antiquaries of Scotland* 112:48–141.

White, David A. 1982. *Bronze Age cremation cemeteries at Simons Ground, Dorset.* Dorset Natural History and Archaeological Society, Dorchester.

Wilkin, Neil. 2014. *Food Vessel pottery from Early Bronze Age funerary contexts in northern England: a typological and contextual study.* PhD thesis, University of Birmingham.

Wilkin, Neil. 2017. Combination, composition and context: readdressing British Middle Bronze Age ornament hoards (c. 1400–1100 cal. BC). In *Dress and society: contributions from archaeology*, edited by Toby Martin, and Rosie Weetch, pp. 14–47. Oxbow, Oxford.

Williams, Brian B. 1986. Excavations at Altanagh, County Tyrone. *Ulster Journal of Archaeology* 49:33–88.

Williams, Howard. 2008. Towards an archaeology of cremation. In *The analysis of burned human remains*, edited by Chistopher Schmidt, and Steven Symes, pp. 239–269. Academic Press, London.

Woodward, Ann, John Hunter, David Bukach, Stuart Needham and Alison Sheridan. 2015. *Ritual in Early Bronze Age grave goods: an examination of ritual and dress equipment from Chalcolithic and Early Bronze Age graves in England.* Oxbow, Oxford.

Worth, R Hansford. 1937. 13th report of the Dartmoor Exploration Committee. *Report and Transactions of the Devonshire Association* 69:147–150.

Yates, David T. 2007. *Land, power and prestige: Bronze Age field systems in southern England.* Oxbow, Oxford.

York, Jill. 2002. The life cycle of Bronze Age metalwork from the Thames. *Oxford Journal of Archaeology* 21(1):77–92.

PART II

Dwellings

4

HOME GROUND

2500–1200 BC

The stone slabs forming the walls of the Bronze Age roundhouses at Kestor, Devon, were positioned with a precision and delicacy belying their size. Aileen Fox (1954) excavated at Kestor in the early 1950s. The local workers helping with the excavations knew from years of experience how to shift the hefty pieces of granite. Fox observed two men gradually raising a fallen slab, 'trigging' it up on a growing pile of small stones and then 'walking' it into its former position (Figure 4.1). This experience remained a strong memory for Aileen Fox. She recounted it in her autobiography, published 50 years later, alongside a photograph of the 'trigging' (Fox 2000, 118).

Granite orthostats formed the walls of the roundhouses at Kestor. The spaces inside the largest buildings were 11 metres in diameter, with walls raised a metre above the floors. The apexes of the conical timber roofs will have reached at least 3 metres higher. The houses were solid structures that took time, care and co-operation to build. They were products of a knowledgeable crafting of land and stone. Aileen Fox captured a minor aspect of this craft when she described the ways the workers on her excavations handled heavy stones.

After three and a half millennia, the Kestor roundhouses have weathered into the landscape. The walls and floors are softened with turf and grass. Where it can, the bracken's yearly invasion obscures the terraces and the fieldwalls. In spite of these processes, the architecture endures and the Bronze Age 'domestic landscape' retains a presence and familiarity. Dartmoor's present-day field systems and dispersed hamlets seem like a continuity from the second millennium BC. Our landscape began taking shape with theirs. When Aileen Fox cleaned the excavated interior of a roundhouse at Dean Moor, on the southern side of Dartmoor from Kestor, she 'often thought of other women who had swept it in the Bronze Age' (Fox 2000, 119).

There are risks with this familiarity and sense of connection. Prehistorians describe Bronze Age worlds that were little different to their own, or at least a

FIGURE 4.1 Aileen Fox's photographs of a stone being 'trigged' into position during her excavations at Kestor, 1952. Copyright: Royal Albert Memorial Museum & Art Gallery, Exeter.

version of their recent rural past. Households were composed in familiar ways, inhabited by several generations of a family. Houses and settlements are described in terms of economy, production and reproduction. The durability of domestic architecture is unproblematic and inevitable.

A photograph taken during the Cambridge Archaeological Unit's excavations at Whittlesey Brick Pits shows the ring gully, pits and postholes of a later prehistoric roundhouse (Cooper et al. 2004) (Figure 4.2). Within the circle, one of the archaeologists stands ironing a shirt, someone else sits in an armchair reading a newspaper, and a vacuum cleaner lies to one side. Transposing the mid-twentieth-century home into the plan of a roundhouse gently mocks reconstructions of later prehistoric life. Its exaggeration draws attention to the assumptions we normalise when writing about domestic spaces: settlements were inhabited by multi-generational families; settlements were the reproductive and productive centres of daily life. Hoovering the floor of a 3,000-year-old roundhouse in a Cambridgeshire clay pit should make us more attentive to the partial

FIGURE 4.2   'House beautiful' (Cooper et al. 2004). Image courtesy of Mark Knight.

connections we have with that Bronze Age world. It was the world where, I have argued, things and people flowed as gifts, not commodities. Practices of fragmentation gave life to places, objects and persons. Kinfolk were sent on journeys into other worlds, assembled from vibrant materials and the parts of multiple beings. Why should the daily lives of the people inhabiting Bronze Age worlds be familiar to us? 'There is nothing easily graspable when trying to understand how people lived their lives in the past' (Cooper et al. 2004, 101).

Fragile architecture, 2500–1700 BC

The evidence from settlements dating to the early part of the Bronze Age, before the seventeenth century BC, disrupts archaeologists' efforts to categorise and explain domestic life. Finding the traces of people spending time at places is not a problem. This survives as the remains of hearths and burnt debris associated with cooking, deposits of pottery and stone tools, and more rarely the traces of lightly built domestic buildings. It is what is often lacking that causes complexity. There are few examples of houses dating to 2500–1700 BC, roughly contemporary with the use of beakers, food vessels and early urns. Houses are commonly isolated and with limited evidence for associated materials and traces of everyday life: cultivation, crafts, and preparing and cooking food. The insubstantiality of the archaeological evidence for domestic activity contrasts with prominent and durable monuments—the barrows, chambered tombs, cairns and circles—that were built during the same period.

This difference is illustrated by examples where domestic structures were excavated in association with funerary monuments. At Cefn Caer Euni, Meirionnydd, a settlement that preceded the construction of a kerb cairn comprised a layer of occupation debris, including coarse beaker-like ceramics, a hearth and some stakeholes (Lynch 1986). A layer of clay sealed the domestic debris and the cairn was constructed on top. The location of the cairn at Cefn Caer Euni did not replicate precisely the earlier occupation. It was a knowledgeable re-use of a place that was modified physically and culturally through settlement. The cairn was the feature that drew archaeological interest to the site, as the remains of settlement left no above-ground trace. At Snail Down, Wiltshire, a few arcs of stakeholes associated with beaker pottery and a patch of burnt flints seem to have been the remains of settlement on the slopes below Sidbury Hill before the construction of a barrow cemetery (Thomas 2005). The structures were located close to the boundaries of a field that predated the barrows.

At Belle Tout, East Sussex, in the base of a dry valley, a number of slight, stake-built domestic structures were associated with both beaker and food vessel pottery (Bradley 1970). Mike Allen (2005) has identified other beaker-associated settlements buried beneath colluvium in similar, dry valley, locations. Although occupation deposits remain common in the examples Allen cites, including evidence for ploughing, there are few examples of structures. An exception is Holywell Coombe, Kent, where a hollow-way, fencelines, middens and ardmarks were associated with a large assemblage of beaker pottery (Bennett et al. 1998). At Sutton Hoo, Suffolk, ditched boundaries, groups of pits and a roundhouse were dated on the basis of an association with beaker pottery (Carver 2005). The excavations in advance of a new runway at Manchester Airport (Oversley Farm, Cheshire) uncovered two small oval structures located near a contemporary hollow-way (Garner 2007). One of the buildings was defined by posts with a possible porch and the other by a shallow ditch. Calibrated radiocarbon dates from the structures spanned 2130–1750 BC. Dan Garner interprets the structures as permanent dwellings, noting the presence of occupation debris, including cereals—emmer wheat and naked barley.

At Over, Cambridgeshire, a circle of pits on O'Connell Ridge could be the truncated remains of a small roundhouse associated with a nearby cluster of pits containing beaker pottery (Evans et al. 2016, 241). On the opposite side of a river channel from O'Connell Ridge, on Godwin Ridge, the team from Cambridge Archaeological Unit excavated a further round building, in this case associated with collared urn pottery (Evans et al. 2016, 138–144). It comprised six postholes forming a circle 5 metres in diameter. Spreads of material culture and a cluster of pits lay close to the building. The postholes cut through an area of cultivation remains—interpreted as hand-dug 'lazy beds'—forming four or five unbounded fields. A similar arrangement of pits, interpreted as postholes, forming a circle 4 metres in diameter, was excavated on the fenedge at Fengate, Peterborough (Evans et al. 2009, 136–138). The postholes and adjacent pits contained a variety of burnt and unburnt occupation debris, including bone, lithics, collared urn pottery, and charred cereal grains and flax.

The circular arrangements of postholes probably formed the internal supports for roofed buildings with relatively insubstantial outer walls. Andy Jones offers this interpretation for a sub-circular structure dating to the early second millennium BC at Tremough, Cornwall (Jones et al. 2015, 169–172). Based on the fragility of the structure, Jones envisages short-term occupation of the site by a group that practised a degree of residential mobility. At Stackpole Warren, on the south coast of Pembrokeshire, Dyfed Archaeological Trust excavated three round structures associated with beaker and collared urn pottery (Benson et al. 1990) (Figure 4.3). The better preserved of the three structures was in a hollow 5 metres in diameter. A structure had possibly burnt down on one occasion and been rebuilt using more substantial posts. The radiocarbon measurements on the burnt material are ambiguous, unfortunately, as calibrated they span 2100–1450 BC. An earlier second millennium BC date is more likely based on the associated pottery.

These examples, widely dispersed around Britain, were primarily single, small round or oval buildings, rarely more than 5 or 6 metres across. They were built from organic materials, and in most cases, the hearths and other internal features do not survive. The pottery, worked stone and other midden material suggest

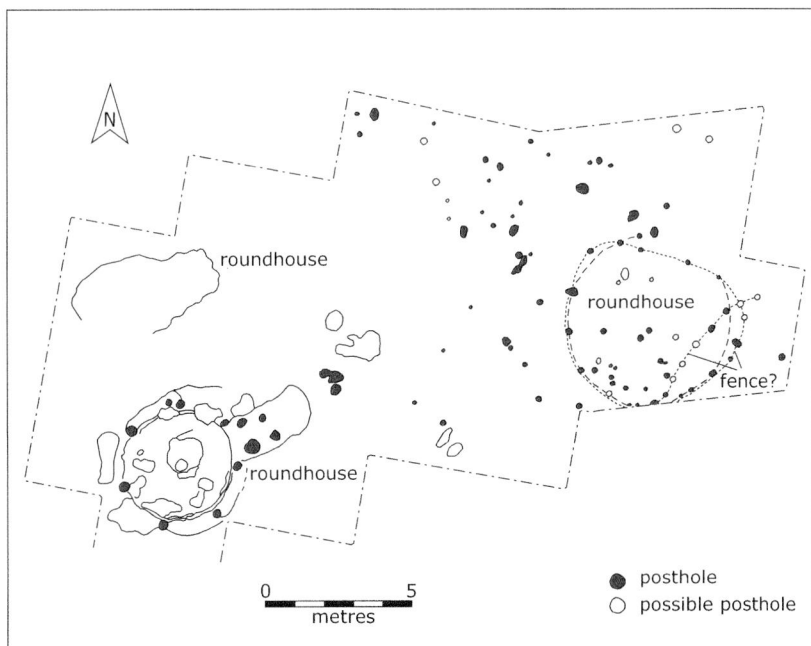

FIGURE 4.3   The roundhouses at Stackpole Warren, Dyfed. Adapted from Benson et al. 1990.

that the buildings had roles in domestic life. Assuming the buildings formed the sheltered living-spaces for co-resident kin, then the groups were small and they did not, in any durable way, set aside spaces for different activities. People, perhaps some animals too, all gathered together under a roof. These practices left slight evidence of how life was organised around or within the buildings.

The duration of settlement in locations is unclear. Some excavators use the presence of cereals, cultivation features and boundaries as evidence for year-round occupation. Others interpret the relatively slight architecture of dwellings as indicators of residential, perhaps seasonal, mobility. The excavations undertaken around Kilmacthomas, County Waterford, uncovered two locations with domestic occupation and structures associated with beaker pottery (Johnston et al. 2008). John Tierney and colleagues (2008) interpret the concentric rings of stakeholes, hearth and pits with occupation debris at Graigueshoneen as evidence for a seasonally occupied camp (Figure 4.4). The cereals they found (barley and wheat) were processed before charring, and there were few weed seeds, which might have been present if the material was grown and processed nearby. The emerging picture across Ireland and Britain is of variation in occupation practices, with some groups moving on and others settling down.

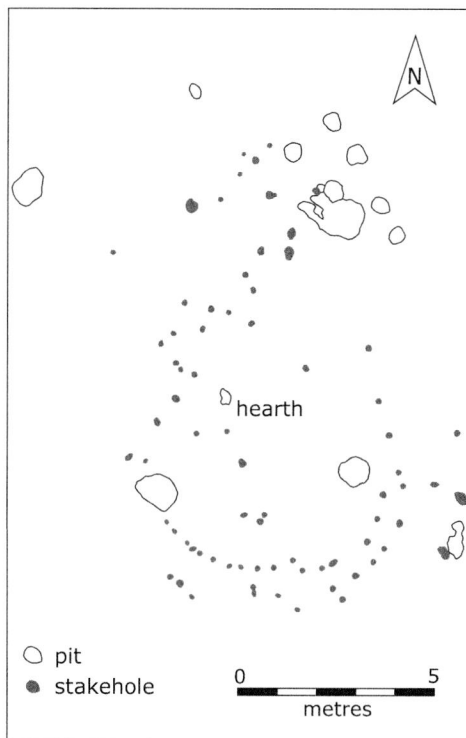

FIGURE 4.4 A domestic structure associated with beaker ceramics excavated at Graigueshoneen, County Waterford. Adapted from Tierney et al. 2008.

A distinction between tangible and intangible architecture existed amongst the settlements in the Western Isles of Scotland. Eighteen beaker-associated settlements have been identified on the islands, and some of these indicate that occupation was occasionally long-lived if not necessarily year-round (Sharples 2009). A curious aspect of the evidence is the lack of substantial houses even though there are well-defined settlement areas, occupation debris and evidence of cultivation. Large oval structures have been identified in several places, such as Dalmore on Lewis. The structures were hollows dug into the sand and revetted with stone. The structures which stood within these hollows were probably quite light, impermanent shelters. The early beaker burial at Sorisdale on Coll (discussed in Chapter 2) was placed in a midden of occupation debris containing beaker pottery (Richie and Crawford 1977/1978). The midden was associated with the putative remains of a structure cut into the sand, which the excavator suggested might have been a stone-lined hollow within which a tent or light structure might have stood. A similar sequence was excavated at Northton on the Isle of Harris, where a beaker burial in a cist was placed in the upper levels of a midden (Simpson et al. 2006). An oval, stone structure within the midden provided a sheltering wall for a lightly built dwelling with evidence of both a hearth and a small number of stakeholes. Perhaps, the excavators suggested, shelter might have been provided beneath an upturned boat—the midden was located, as with all the early settlements in the region, on the sandy coastal plain, termed 'machair'. The structure was occupied at least twice, separated by a layer of wind-blown sand, and the laminated character of the midden was interpreted as evidence for repeated short-lived visits.

The recognition of a group of settlements at Roughan Hill in the limestone karst landscape of the Burren, County Clare, offers an unusually well-preserved example of the organisation of settlements (Jones 1998; 2019), yet again the evidence for houses is poorly preserved. The occupation at Roughan Hill was located within roughly oval stone-built enclosures, up to 50–70 metres in size, within which there were middens and some fragmentary remains of stone structures. The assemblages comprised animal bone (mainly cattle, with sheep/goat and pig), pottery and stone tools. The settlement enclosures formed part of a larger network of walled fields. These are fragmentary in many places. It is possible to distinguish small irregular plots close to the settlements and a few longer, axial boundaries, including the distinctive double banks of trackways, towards the periphery of the survey area. It is tempting to interpret the settlements, fields and monuments at Roughan Hill as contemporary with one another, but it is notable that there were differences in the ceramic assemblages from the settlements—one settlement produced mainly beaker ceramics and another only food vessels, and the calibrated radiocarbon dates span the twenty-third to fifteenth centuries BC (Jones 2016). The large numbers of wedge tombs (14 in all) is also suggestive of a relatively sustained use of the landscape, perhaps over several centuries, within which time there would have been considerable scope for the construction, abandonment and reoccupation of settlement enclosures.

What were notably missing from Roughan Hill were the remains of domestic dwellings contemporary with the beaker ceramics and late third millennium BC calibrated radiocarbon dates, which would be expected given the substantial character of the enclosures and surrounding fields. One explanation is that the boundaries and enclosures are of a later second millennium BC date, and fortuitously incorporate earlier spreads of occupation debris (Carlin 2018, 56). If we accept the excavator's chronology, then the traces of any stone, timber or turf structures that might have stood within the enclosures have gone. And a contrast emerges between the substantial and lasting qualities of the stone-built enclosures, fields and monuments, and the more fragile, at least in the long-term, architecture of dwellings.

Reviewing these examples together, there is plentiful if thinly scattered evidence for the material culture and structures created through domestic occupation in the centuries up to 1700 BC. Domestic buildings, which for simplicity's sake I will call houses, were relatively insubstantial, even fragile in archaeological terms, by comparison with the monuments that surrounded them in the landscape. This fragility emerged from the materials that were used to construct houses, with fewer and lighter timbers, and less structural complexity: the buildings tend not to have porches, prepared floors, definable hearths or pits.

The fragility of buildings need not have equated with a fragility or instability in the kin that lived together. Nor did it mean that people's lifestyles were always seasonally mobile and with a weak commitment to places. At times, groups cultivated fields and occasionally bounded the fields with ditches and fences; they accumulated the debris from settlement in middens; they practised mortuary rites and buried the dead within and around monuments across several generations. Kinwork shaped and was shaped by domestic life, yet houses were only weakly associated within these processes and consequently were not enduring assemblages.

Marking time with scatters and pits, 2500–1700 BC

It is problematic to limit the account of domestic life to locations where houses have been excavated. Excavations at many sites provided little or no evidence for buildings. The traces of domestic life are pits, hearths, midden material or spreads of material culture, such as ceramics or lithics. The kinwork of living and eating together was marked through the accumulation, curation and deposition of material. These pits and scatters marked the time spent at places and the relations that were assembled during settlement.

A valuable source of evidence comes from the material culture, mostly flaked stone, that archaeologists have systematically collected from the surfaces of ploughed land during fieldwalking. The chronological control of the material is relatively coarse, to the extent that it is commonly only feasible to make broad distinctions between periods, with later Neolithic and early Bronze Age technologies usually treated together, spanning a period over more than a millennium. Nonetheless, the evidence is sufficient to demonstrate the locations and intensities of domestic life, and to grasp the ways in which occupation made places in the landscape.

Benjamin Chan (2003) analysed the flint assemblages collected around Stonehenge, Wiltshire. The traces of episodic activities look unstructured over the long-term and 'wash up to' and over the landscape's monuments. These patterns are evidence for intermittent and relatively intensive occupation of the landscape, especially focussed at times when the monuments were being built and during their use for ceremonies. The densities of the lithic scatters around Stonehenge are greater than contemporary material collected from elsewhere in Britain, leading Chan to conclude that the 'size of these gatherings would have far exceeded those that would have occurred in almost all other contemporary landscapes' (Chan 2003, 310). A high intensity of occupation was also recognised by Conor Brady (2007) in his study of the lithic distributions around the later Neolithic monuments at Brú na Bóinne, County Meath.

In less intensively inhabited landscapes it is possible to identify how parts were preferentially used for domestic occupation over the long-term. Killian Driscoll (2013) used fieldwalking to locate concentrations of later Neolithic and early Bronze Age flaked stone working at two locations on the eastern edge of Galway Bay. In the Exe Valley, Devon, Olaf Bayer (2011) observed a preference for the valley floor and the higher ground on the valley's western edge throughout the Mesolithic to early Bronze Age, with the intensity and extent of the lithic scatters increasing with time. This pattern of increasing intensity and extent of occupation areas during the third and early second millennia BC is recognised in other well-studied assemblages of field-collected flaked stone (Gardiner 1988). In a review of lithic scatters in the Furness Peninsula, Cumbria, Helen Evans (2008) interprets the lithic scatters as evidence for a narrowing and intensifying of occupation to a smaller number of places.

This evidence for an increase in the size of flaked stone assemblages could have resulted from larger numbers of people living together within residential groups, a longer duration of settlement at locales or some combination of both these factors. These certainly seem reasonable inferences to make for areas around large monuments, which continued to represent major building projects and the focus for large ceremonies into the Bronze Age. Mark Edmonds and colleagues offer an alternative viewpoint derived from their study of a large lithic scatter at Soham, Cambridgeshire (Edmonds et al. 1999). They suggest the size and diffuse character of the scatter results from a 'succession' of intermittent, small-scale occupations spanning the Neolithic and Bronze Age. Small groups of people repeatedly returned to and briefly occupied this promontory of higher ground that jutted out into the fenland marsh.

Most excavated domestic evidence comprises surface midden material and small groups of pits. Neil Carlin (2018) thoroughly and critically reviewed the evidence for beaker-associated domestic activity from Irish excavations. He concludes that pits were the most common feature to be securely associated with domestic activity. The excavators usually found the pits isolated or in small groups, with only one or two pits within the groups containing beaker ceramics. Although of varied sizes, the pits were frequently bowl-shaped, and they were filled soon after they were dug. The contents of the pits comprised material that might be expected to result from domestic life, and particularly the preparation and consumption of food: broken pottery, flaked and ground stone objects, and sometimes the charred remains of cereals and animal bone. A circular pit at Rathdown, County Wicklow, was filled with a variety of burnt and unburnt material, including sherds from seven beaker pots, flaked stone debitage and tools and charred plant remains (hazelnuts, barley and wheat) (Eogan and O'Brien 2005). Most pits comprised a single episode of infilling with sherds from a few vessels, and in half of the pits that Neil Carlin reviewed only a single vessel was represented. In a few cases, the pits contained the fragments from many pots and multiple layers of fill. The archaeologists working on the motorway bypassing Drogheda, County Meath, excavated three groups of pits along 500 metres of the road corridor in Rathmullan. In one group, a small pit set apart from the others contained oak and hazel charcoal, flaked stone and 224 sherds from up to 20 fine and coarse beaker vessels (Nelis 2011, 5–6). The sizes of the sherds and the lack of wear on the edges mean that the pottery was probably deliberately fragmented before it was incorporated into the pit. Similar pits have been excavated during many of the road schemes across Ireland, with pottery and radiocarbon dates indicating their creation continued throughout the Bronze Age (Baker et al. 2015; Eogan and Shee Twohig 2011).

The things and substances gathered within the pits were the residues from domestic life, and predominately those residues which were sufficiently robust to remain recognisable after four millennia in the ground: burnt animal bone, charred plant remains and wood; fragmentary pottery and worked stone. These materials also accumulated in mounds and spreads, and the spreads may have been a source for the cultural debris in the pits. Some of the largest of the spreads were excavated around the passage tombs at Knowth and Newgrange, Brú na Bóinne, County Meath, with others surviving in places where they avoided being degraded by later land use. Five spreads of material were identified at Knowth, with the largest covering an area 21 by 12.5 metres and containing over 2000 beaker sherds representing 104 vessels (Eogan 1984, 245–322; Eogan and Roche 1997, 223–260). A little over 8 kilometres east from Knowth, along the Boyne Valley, the excavations at Mell provide an example of a smaller accumulation (McQuade 2005). Three layers of occupation debris (charred wood and plant remains, lithics and pottery) accumulated to a depth of 0.4 metres in a hollow above an earlier stone surface.

The Irish evidence is similar to sites in Britain. In his review of beaker domestic sites, which predated the increase in data generated during development-led excavations, Alex Gibson (1982) identified 'domestic' beaker pottery associated with many monuments, including chambered tombs, causewayed enclosures and henges. Large-scale excavations have recurrently uncovered groups of pits and spreads of occupation debris (Figure 4.5). Two tight clusters of pits excavated

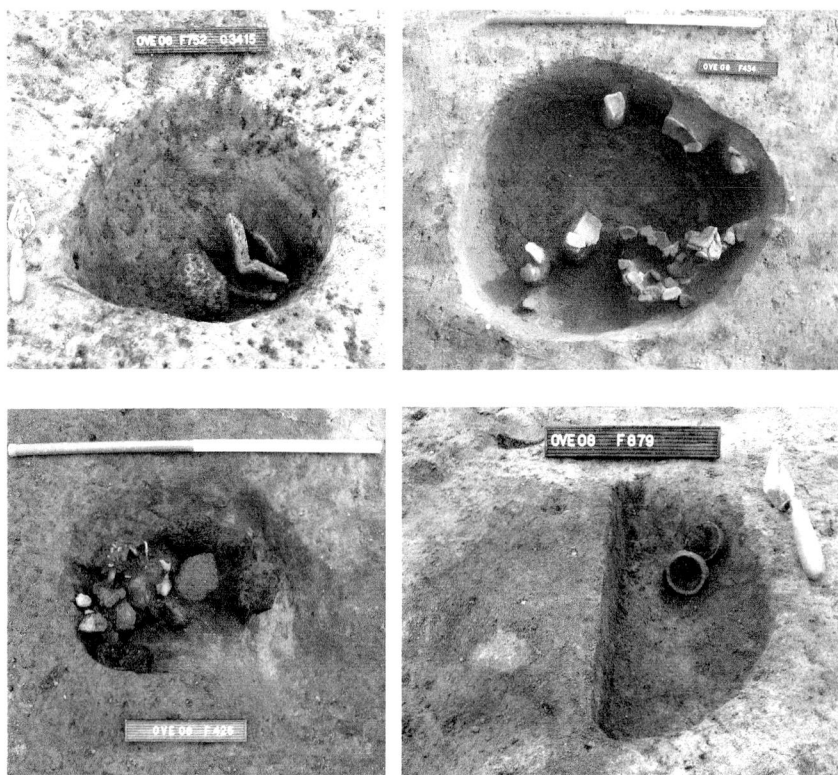

FIGURE 4.5 'A miscellany of pits' containing beaker (top left) and collared urn (top right and bottom) pottery excavated at Godwin Ridge, Cambridgeshire (Evans et al. 2016). Image. Copyright Cambridge Archaeological Unit.

at Gravelly Guy, Oxfordshire, contained small amounts of broken beaker pottery, worked flint, along with charred plant and animal remains (Lambrick and Allen 2004, 35–45). One pit, dug in a fairly regular bowl shape, was filled with charcoal-rich sediment, followed by the broken remains from five or six beakers, worked flint, including knives and an arrowhead, and the bones from two piglets. Another pit in a nearby cluster contained two fragments of a saddle quern along with an assemblage of worked flint, including knives and scrapers.

Less than 10 kilometres northeast from Gravelly Guy, Oxford Archaeology excavated more than 300 pits at Yarnton, with a chronology spanning the Neolithic and Bronze Age (Hey et al. 2016, 72–79). Digging pits was most prevalent in the Yarnton landscape during the late fourth and third millennia BC, up to and including associations with beaker pottery. The pollen and plant macrofossils recovered during the excavations show that the landscape was relatively clear of woodland and kept open through grazing and small areas of cultivation. It was surrounded by dense woodland, dominated by alder and oak. Pit groups were rarer in the early second millennium BC, before becoming a feature again, associated with houses and other settlement evidence, after 1600 BC.

The beaker-associated pits at Yarnton contained pottery, some of which was unusual and quite distinct from the styles placed in nearby barrows, flintwork, burnt stone and fired clay. They contained more cultivated species, wheat and barley, compared with the later Neolithic pits, with burnt hazelnut shells still the most common plant remains. People selected and perhaps even made fresh tools to place in the pits, notably knives and scrapers. In one example (Hey et al. 2016, 180–184), a regular-shaped and deep pit was first filled with small quantities of ash and charcoal-rich soil, flint, animal bone and pottery fragments. Someone then backfilled the remainder of the pit, placing some broken pieces from a large and a few smaller beakers in the middle, and surrounding these with animal bone from a variety of domesticated and wild species: mostly sheep or goat, and also cattle, pig, dog, bird and red deer. The main fill of the pit contained burnt cereals and hazelnut shells, a piece of quartz crystal and worked flint. As a final act, the body of a neonatal infant was buried in the uppermost layer of the pit.

Pits formed important repositories for the debris of daily life. Like time-capsules, they gathered and preserved degrading assemblages from the surface. In collecting the materials for a pit, cohabitants—kinfolk who lived together—chose the stuff and relations that accumulated during their domestic life and gave, or returned, them to the soil: pots, tools, animals, the burnt remains of cooking fires and meals. Occasionally, people selected unusual items to accompany the more mundane material in a pit, such as the disc beads from Cloghers or the grooved ware vessel placed in a beaker pit at Rathmullan (Carlin 2018). The pits marked times during the inhabitation of a place, which were perhaps events in the yearly cycle, moments of departure or arrival or changes in the relations amongst kinfolk. Curiously, even though above-ground traces of domestic life were vulnerable to collapse and decay, the pits were rarely intercut or disturbed. The digging and filling of pits were commemorations of habitation that perpetuated a millennia-old tradition of kinwork and placemaking.

Depositing material in pits may have been an irregular rather than routine occurrence, at least in some regions. Having studied the beaker-accompanied pits in East Anglia, Duncan Garrow (2006, 137–138) concludes that the pottery had spent sufficient time on the surface to become abraded and fragmented. There was also a limited amount of animal bone in the pits, which might mean the material had lain exposed for some time. The numbers of vessels represented amongst the pottery sherds were higher compared with earlier centuries, which Garrow suggests was a consequence of longer or more persistent use of places for settlement. These occupations led to the large accumulation of domestic debris, from which small quantities of fragmentary material were occasionally gathered for deposition.

Settlement debris marked the times people spent living together with their animals, tending cultivated ground, crafting objects, preparing and sharing food, raising children. Durable domestic architecture was rarely a part of these assemblages. Presence and absence were marked by the ways that people accumulated, selected and buried the residues of kinwork. Geographies grew through accumulations and deposition. They emerged from a slow making and eroding of places.

Making time with mounds, 2500–1200 BC

Inhabitation made its marks on the landscape. The above-ground traces of domestic life were largely fragile, degraded or rapidly transformed. There were prolific exceptions to this observation: through survey and excavation archaeologists have recorded many thousands of burnt-stone mounds or, in Ireland, *fulachtaí fiadh*—fulacht fiadh is Gaelic for 'cooking place'. The mounds were generally accompanied by troughs, sometimes lined with timber, wattle or stone, and usually a hearth. The troughs in the burnt mounds are presumed to have contained water that was heated using hot stones from the hearth. The water may then have been used for cooking, bathing, processing textiles, or one of the many suggestions that have been put forward in explanation for the sites. Like depositing domestic debris in pits, the practice of accumulating mounds of burnt stone and the use of burnt stone technology had a long chronology that predated and out-lasted the Bronze Age.

There were periods when active burnt mounds were most common in the landscape. In their survey of radiocarbon dates from prehistoric contexts in Ireland, Rowan McLaughlin and colleagues (2016, 130–131) identified a 'major phase of construction and use' of *fulachtaí fiadh* during 2500–1900 BC, comprising half of the dated sites, with the majority of the remaining dates falling within the second millennium BC. Robert Chapple's (2019) database of Irish radiocarbon dates includes more than 1,000 measurements from burnt mounds. The sum probability of these calibrated dates indicates the intensive creation and use of burnt mounds spanned 2500–700 BC. This supports Alan Hawkes's (2014; 2018) analysis of the chronology of *fulachtaí fiadh*, although he places the early development of the technology in Ireland during the Neolithic. Jane Kenney came to similar conclusions following her review of 44 scientifically dated burnt mounds in northwest Wales: people began creating burnt mounds from around 2500 BC, and they continued with the practice until the end of the Bronze Age (Kenney 2012).

The densities of *fulachtaí fiadh* in the Irish landscape can be appreciated from the many hundreds uncovered by recent excavations in advance of road schemes and pipelines. Alan Hawkes (2018) considered around 1,000 excavated examples in his review of the Irish evidence. The N5 road scheme through Mayo and Roscommon identified 39 burnt mounds along a narrow 15-kilometre transect (Gillespie 2007). The densest concentration of burnt mounds was 10 within 40 metres. Most of the *fulachtaí fiadh* consisted of rectangular troughs lined with timber and moss or occasionally with stone. In one, an oval pit was lined with wicker and moss. At another, a series of oval and round ditches perhaps formed the remains of buildings. Some animal bones and a biconical tin bead were recovered. At Caltragh, County Sligo, the calibrated radiocarbon dates from six of the burnt stone mounds spanned the twenty-second to fifteenth centuries BC, and another was dated to the tenth or ninth century BC (Danaher 2007, 21–25). The mounds dating to the middle of the second millennium BC lay close to three roundhouses, but the earlier sites may at first have been isolated in the landscape. The mounds and troughs formed important foci in the landscape. At Magheraboy, a sequence of 14 pits was excavated, some of which were certainly used as troughs while others may have been hearths (Danaher 2007, 25–31). The entire complex was covered by a layer of burnt stone and ash.

Archaeologists have expended considerable energies searching for evidence that burnt mounds had a specific function. The emerging picture after hundreds of excavations is diverse. A variety of activities created burnt mounds and seem to have included cooking, craftwork and cleansing. The few instances where light timber structures enclose the troughs may indicate their use as sweat houses or for bathing. A stone-lined trough at Scartbarry, County Cork, was enclosed by an oval slot-trench that probably supported a timber wall with a narrow entrance (O'Neil 2013). A hearth was located outside the structure, and the area was covered in burnt mound material. Alan Hawkes (2015) makes the case for Irish *fulachtaí fiadh* being primarily associated with the cooking and consumption of meat. About a quarter of the 1,165 excavated *fulachtaí fiadh* in Hawkes's study produced animal bone. Cattle made up the largest proportion of identifiable bone (67 percent), with sheep/goat, pig, deer, dog and horse accounting for the rest. At Inchagreenoge, County Limerick, cattle bone was recovered from the base of the trough, along with large stones that the excavators interpreted as the traces from the trough's last use during 2200–1950 BC (Grogan et al. 2007, 281).

Examining environmental and structural evidence from eight *fulachtaí fiadh*, Tony Brown and colleagues (2016) conclude that textile processing, including dyeing, was an important purpose of the troughs. In one trough, they identified plants that can be used as dyes: red fruit and alder catkins (as a green dye). Raised levels of heavy metals in two troughs, Brown and colleagues suggest, resulted from ash or urine used for preserving animal hides. The shallow troughs, which self-filled from ground water and used materials such as sand and moss to filter the water, were suited to processing wool and plant textiles. As with the animal bone, the environmental indicators for the uses of burnt mounds do not provide clear and consistent answers. The presence of alder catkins is to be expected as the mounds are normally located near water sources. The forms of the troughs vary considerably in their shapes, depths and linings.

Burnt mounds are found singly and in clusters, mostly in proximity to a water source, whether a stream, spring or marshy ground. A study of the distribution of excavated and unexcavated *fulachtaí fiadh* in lowland County Galway concluded that nearly three quarters of mounds were located within 1 kilometre of another mound (Delaney and Tierney 2011, 37–39). Mounds contain multiple layers of burnt and fractured stone, and radiocarbon dating at some sites estimates centuries-long chronologies of episodic use. It is more common that the deposition within a mound is of shorter and more intensive duration, even when burnt mounds might have accumulated in the locality over a long time.

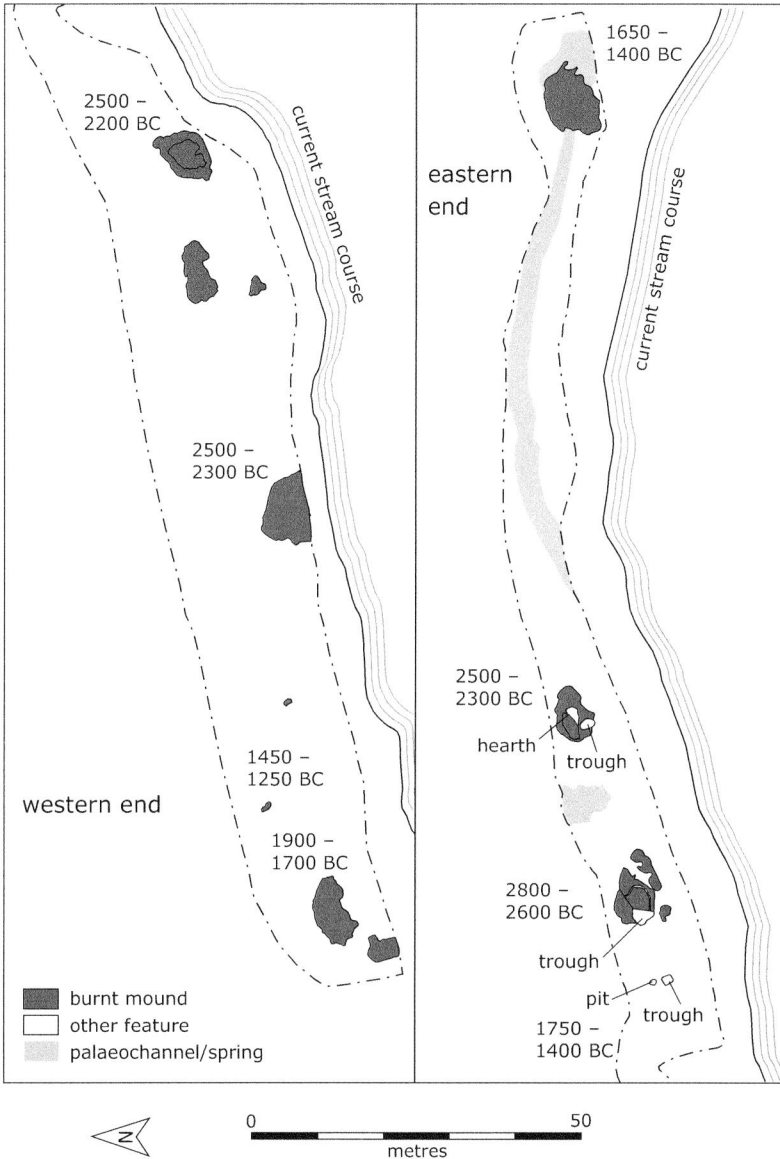

FIGURE 4.6 Burnt stone mounds and troughs distributed along a stream-edge at Glan-rŷd Bridge, Pembrokeshire, annotated with simplified chronological information based on the project's programme of radiocarbon dating and chronological modelling. Adapted from Hart et al. 2014.

A programme of radiocarbon dating and Bayesian modelling for the eight burnt mounds at Glan-rŷd Bridge, Pembrokeshire, estimated that activity began during the early to mid-third millennium BC and continued until the fourteenth to twelfth centuries BC (Figure 4.6) (Hart et al. 2014). The results from three of the mounds were statistically consistent, and could represent a short phase of activity during 2450–2300 BC. At Soar, Leicestershire, the Bayesian modelling of the site's 48 radiocarbon determinations estimated burnt mound activity lasted up to 100 years and was more likely (68 percent probability) 1–40 years, during the twenty-second to twenty-first centuries BC (Ripper and Beamish 2011). In reporting the excavation of a *fulacht fiadh* at Killoran Bog, County Tipperary, John Ó Néill (2005) estimated that the mound's 300 cubic metres of sandstone and limestone could have served up to 4,000 'firings' for the trough's maximum capacity of 1245 litres. Ten years' daily use could account for this volume of material, although a less frequent and perhaps seasonally varied estimate of duration would seem more likely. During the same project, analysis of the timber from three excavated *fulachtaí fiadh* determined the seasons of cutting in autumn at one mound, spring another and mixed seasons at the third (Gowen et al. 2005).

At Ballygawley, County Tyrone, the research team analysed the environmental evidence from a group of 23 mounds and 10 troughs distributed amongst an area of infilled stream channels (Mighall et al. 2018; Wheeler et al. 2016). The creation of the mounds spanned the late fourth millennium BC to the thirteenth century AD, with most created during the third and second millennia BC. During the late third and second millennia BC, the burnt mounds were in partially open and grazed wet pasture at the woodland's edge. The charcoal and preserved timber in the mounds and troughs was derived from alder and hazel branches, which were species that dominated the immediate woodland. People used the woodland with sufficient care that there were no impacts on the proportions of arboreal taxa in the pollen record. Only the early first millennium BC brought an appreciable reduction in the local alder carr, although some opening up began in the seventeenth century BC. The burnt mounds accompanied small-scale clearance of the woodland around the edges of wetland, and these clearings could have stayed open through grazing animals and continuing burnt mound activity.

Prehistorians frequently employ the term 'enigmatic' when describing burnt mounds. The inscrutability of the mounds explains the unresolved, and perhaps unresolvable, debates about their functions that bubble-up periodically. The reasons prehistorians struggle are because the mounds do not fit into familiar categories, the material is ambiguous or the material they search for is absent. The problem lies with archaeological categories, not with the material or its absence. Dry and wet heat served many purposes, which included cooking and craftwork. Bathing and steam might have cleansed human and other-than human bodies. These activities do not necessarily correlate with the archaeologically recovered structure of the burnt mounds. Attempts to categorise them have highlighted variability and a lack of chronological, spatial and functional patterning (Ó Néill 2009). The lack of coherent categorisation may confound archaeologists, but it is consistent with the material excavated from contemporary domestic contexts: the structures, scatters, pits and spreads that I describe above. These too are difficult to categorise. They are difficult to draw boundaries around. They are hard to place.

Domestic life accumulated as layers in places. The debris from food, craft and shelter changed the shape of places. Felling trees and clearing undergrowth, bringing animals to graze, and digging-over soil changed the textures of flora and land. The soil gradually absorbed the waste left by animals and humans. Sometimes people gathered occupation debris and placed it in pits—as gifts, perhaps—in practices reminiscent of burials of metalwork and human bone. The soil did not absorb burnt and fractured stone with the same haste. Burnt mounds accumulated when people used places and they marked times spent in places. The mounds were distinctive, readily recognisable monuments during the Bronze Age and they remain so today.

House culture, 1700–1200 BC

The preceding discussion explored the evidence for people's dwelling in parts of the landscape, where they lived, cooked and ate, made objects, tended to gardens and animals. A recurring characteristic of these descriptions is their intangibility or inscrutability. Throughout many regions, settlements changed during the middle centuries of the second millennium BC, from the seventeenth century, with the widespread adoption of durable domestic buildings. The houses varied in shape, size and materials. Most were round or oval, constructed with timber or wattle and daub walls with internal timber posts to support a roof. Turf, clay and stone were also used. The presence of artefacts, hearths and pits within well-preserved houses is evidence that many buildings were dwellings for people, although they served a variety of purposes and their roles changed during their lives. The houses are found in small groups, singly and occasionally as part of settlements comprising large numbers of dwellings.

The change can be quantified. Martin Doody's (2002) review of the evidence from Ireland identified 8 Bronze Age houses predating and 53 houses postdating c. 1600 BC. Publishing a decade after Doody and with access to many more development-led excavations, Victoria Ginn (2012) collated the evidence for high-quality scientific dates from Bronze Age settlements with houses, placing five sites during 2100–1700 BC and 36 during 1700–1325 BC. The inclusion of settlements with less secure chronologies almost doubles the numbers and only marginally affects the ratio of 2100–1700 BC (12) to 1700–1325 BC (68) sites. In her studies of Bronze Age settlements in Wessex, Sussex and the Thames Valley, Joanna Brück discusses 25 locations with evidence of early Bronze Age (before 1600 BC) occupation and 53 middle Bronze Age (after 1600 BC) sites (Brück 1999a; 1999b). Brück documents a consistent difference between early Bronze Age sites where there were no houses and middle Bronze Age settlements that comprised a variety of round, oval and rectangular structures; ponds; fencelines; enclosures; and fields. Rachel Pope studied the roundhouses in northern Britain (Pope 2003). She describes a small increase in the numbers of roundhouses during the second millennium BC, with a trend towards larger and more architecturally complex structures. Eleanor Ghey and colleagues' (2007) review of roundhouses in Wales identifies a small number of buildings that might date before 1500 BC and these where isolated buildings excavated beneath funerary monuments. Although still few in number, the roundhouses after 1500 BC were more substantial than the earlier buildings, larger, and built from timber, stone and clay.

At places where settlement spanned the early and middle second millennium BC, it is feasible to trace changes in the substance and durability of domestic architecture. John F.S. Stone (1941) excavated a small enclosure on Thorny Down, Wiltshire, during the few years prior to the Second World War. He identified more than 250 post and stakeholes cut into the chalk within the enclosure, and he interpreted the features as nine post-built houses. Stone kept meticulous records of his excavations, and these provided Ann Woodward (née Ellison) with sufficient evidence to reinterpret Thorny Down's post and stakeholes (Ellison 1987). She proposes that some of the buildings predated the use of Deverel-Rimbury pottery and the enclosure's bank and ditch. The earliest buildings were simple oval and circular structures, a little under 6 metres in diameter, and defined by single lines of postholes. The later buildings, contemporary with the boundary around the settlement, were associated with Deverel-Rimbury pottery. Two substantial roundhouses dominated the enclosure. They were 7 to 8 metres in diameter, supported by concentric rings of posts and stakes, and with prominent southeast facing porches. During the time that the roundhouses were occupied, the enclosure was bisected by a fence and there were various slighter structures that formed working areas and storage.

The character of houses is difficult to appreciate from postholes alone. Sometimes the superstructures of buildings survive because they were made from stone or the environment has fortuitously preserved organic material, as with the ninth-century pile-dwelling settlement at Must Farm, Cambridgeshire (Knight et al. 2019). At Teigncombe, on the northeastern side of Dartmoor, Devon, Sandy Gerrard (2016) uncovered a roundhouse built and inhabited in the mid-second millennium BC, re-occupied in the mid-first millennium BC and briefly used in the second century AD. The builders dug out and partially quarried a platform, 14 metres in diameter, to provide a stance for the building. They raised large slabs of granite onto their edges to form an orthostatic wall. Against the hillslope, the wall was laid with horizontal courses of granite slabs to a height of 1.3 metres. A carefully bedded threshold stone sat across the southeast-facing entrance, and flagstones surfaced the well-used parts of the floor. Gerrard calculated that the roof's apex was over 4 metres above floor level in a building around 9 metres across. Stake and postholes, pits and a hearth attested to the building's use for a variety of activities. Radiocarbon measurements of organic residues on pottery dated the building's Bronze Age use to the fifteenth and fourteenth centuries BC. There are similarly large roundhouses, built on platforms and with orthostatic granite walls amongst the field walls a short distance north of the

Teigncombe building. They are overlooked by Kestor Rock: an 8-metre high dome of weathered granite.

In 1951, Aileen Fox excavated one of the large roundhouses amongst the Kestor fields (Fox 1954). Internally 8 metres across, the house's orthostatic stone wall sat on a constructed terrace. Fox returned to Kestor the following year and investigated another building nearby (the scene for the trigging shown in Figure 4.1). This is the largest roundhouse amongst the 27 then mapped within the field systems: over 11 metres across internally, with orthostatic walls surviving over a metre high. The building's size is exaggerated by a surrounding stone enclosure 33 metres across and divided internally by four radial lines of stones that link the enclosure's wall with the roundhouse. The enclosure is accessed off a walled trackway through a narrow gap on the west side. The entrance to the roundhouse is on the southeast, with a 'passageway' lined with upright slabs and steps down to the house's interior. The megalithic granite slabs ensured that the Kestor buildings persisted in the landscape: early Iron Age and medieval pottery was recovered alongside the Bronze Age Trevisker ware; a furnace within the building was radiocarbon dated to the fifth or sixth century AD (Henrietta Quinnell in Gerrard 2016, 41–43).

The roundhouses at Kestor are scattered amongst contemporary field systems, which have survived because the boundaries, like the houses, were built from granite. Accumulated memories of domestic settlement elaborated the landscape, signified relations and remain visible today. Stone walls might have endured where timber, clay and turf did not. Organic structures persisted in a different way: through rebuilding. At Peterhead, Aberdeenshire, a timber roundhouse was rebuilt five times on roughly the same footprint probably sometime during the fifteenth to thirteenth centuries BC (Strachan and Dunwell 2003). At Kintore, also in Aberdeenshire, open area excavation recorded the foundations of 44 circular buildings ranging in date from 1800 BC to the beginning of the first millennium AD (Cook and Dunbar 2008). The clustering of roundhouses on the site and identifiable changes in their architecture through time would suggest the settlement formed during periodic, at times continuous, occupation by relatively small groups. The timber roundhouses on the steep slopes above the River Clyde in Lanarkshire, at Lintshie Gutter and Bodsberry Hill, were built on constructed platforms (Figure 4.7). Over 30 platforms have been recorded, with excavations indicating repeated re-use of the same platforms from the nineteenth or eighteenth century BC until the eleventh century BC (Ashmore 2001; Terry 1993; 1995). At Green Knowe, Peeblesshire, the house platforms were built upon small terraces whose edges were defined by low boundaries of field-cleared stone (Jobey 1981). One of the excavated house platforms, which was sited next to an agricultural terrace, was occupied by a sequence of three roundhouses, calibrated radiocarbon dates from which span the second half of the second millennium BC.

The durability of architecture and its persistence in the landscape accounts for the scale of the change that I quantified at the beginning of this section. Houses became a common, widespread if not ubiquitous part of daily life. Built,

FIGURE 4.7 Aerial photograph of the 'platform settlement' at Lintshie Gutter, Lanarkshire. The earthworks are highlighted by light snow and low sunlight in the fields right of the road. © Crown copyright: HES.

lived, abandoned, rebuilt, their architectures became synonymous with settlement. Long-lived buildings were a component in the assemblages of practices and structures that gathered within domestic life.

Giving life to houses, 1700–1200 BC

The roundhouse was an assembly of vibrant materials and beings whose character changed with time, tasks and weather: fire in the hearth, pots with food and stored grain, livestock tethered by a post, and kinfolk sharing drink and stories. The intensity of relations around dwellings, and their duration, made them fundamental to processes of socialisation, and to the making and defining the closeness of kin. The Malays claim kinship is made in houses and, as in many areas of southeast Asia, rice is the common relation between people, houses and soil:

> The consumption of rice meals cooked in the hearth not only strengthens existing ties of kinship between household members, it can actually

create such ties with those who have recently come to share residence, such as foster children or in-marrying affines … As the inhabitants live together in one house over time and eat meals together, their blood becomes progressively more similar—and this is especially true of the blood of brothers and sisters, which is said to be more alike than that of other categories of kin.

(Carsten 2004, 40)

The solidity of roundhouses in the centuries after 1700 BC made aspects of kin-work more stable, more durable. Houses and people were more intimately associated than before. They shared a mutuality of being. Houses were co-constituents in domestic life. They became kin.

Houses were brought into life through their participation in daily life. They also took life from their places in the landscape. At Green Park and Reading Business Park, Oxfordshire, the houses built amongst field systems respected the dominant alignments of the land boundaries, while the houses nearby that were not amongst fields showed greater variability in their entrance alignments (Lambrick 2009, 142). The entrances of Bronze Age buildings were commonly oriented within an arc between east and south. This increased the interiors' access to direct sunlight and protected them from westerly and northerly weather (Pope 2006). This was a partial association. The sun was important in other spheres of culture. The same sun that contributed light and warmth to houses appeared as representations on metalwork and pottery (Cahill 2015), and was incorporated into the alignments of some circular monuments and human burials. It is fruitless to attempt an unpicking of the tangled associations between atmosphere, cosmology and houses. The sun brought life into dwellings literally as light and as a spiritual being. Houses took their orientations from the land and the sky. They were assembled from without and within.

Houses were given life during acts of making, inhabitation, growth and decay. Timothy Mitchell (1988, 51) describes the house as 'not an object or a container but a charged process, an inseparable part of a life that grows flourishes, decays and is reborn'. In exploring the idea of living dwellings, Tim Ingold paraphrased the writing of Portuguese architect Alvaro Siza (1997): 'Rainwater drips through the roof where the wind has blown off a tile, feeding a mould that threatens to decompose the timbers, the gutters are full of rotting leaves' (Ingold 2013, 48). The gathering processes of accumulation and decay can be punctuated by moments of chaotic violence. Margaret Leigh lived in a croft on Scotland's west coast in the 1940s. She described a terrifying night in winter 1943:

In a momentary lull between waves, I heard a sighing far up in the air, which passed over the house and died away. Then came a clap of wind, which increased till there was a great clamour; and after that, I was aware of something that was neither wind nor sea. Trembling with ancient fears, I fumbled for matches and lit the candle. The thin flame drew up, guttering in the draught and casting faint, wavering shadows. A moment later, the world outside dissolved in chaos: flash on flash, crash after crash, with wind in screaming crescendo; and then, drowning all else, a bombardment of hailstone on ninety-six yards of galvanised iron.

(Leigh 2018, 65–66)

Margaret Leigh hated her croft's sheet-iron roof. She dreaded being in the house during storms. Eventually, after the roof had thinned and rotted, she had the means to replace the iron with thatch. The traditional material insulated the house from heat, cold and storms. It offered protection that was akin with the metre-thick stone walls, whose rounded corners made the building a 'stream-lined' cave providing 'warmth, shelter and silence' (Leigh 2018, 67).

Prehistorians may dream of chances to study living houses. The stories we can reconstruct for excavated houses are often the stories of their abandonment. This changes, not diminishes, their importance. Jacqueline Nowakowski (1991) led the excavations of a settlement at Trethellan Farm, Cornwall, during 1987's hot summer. The settlement comprised seven roundhouses, both residential and ancillary structures, occupied during the fifteenth to thirteenth centuries BC, and which had been maintained and rebuilt throughout the life of the settlement. Nowakowski (2001) argues that the abandonment of the settlement took place in a formal way. The buildings were dismantled, some timbers were removed from the ground and the holes left by the posts were backfilled. Other posts were cut off at the base and slate slabs placed on top. The interiors of the houses were then filled with levelling deposits of earth, stone and occupation debris, including large amounts of broken pottery and stone tools. This material culture may not have been randomly selected. The ceramics from one building were considered to represent all the possible pot types that might have been expected to be present on the settlement. In another case, a quernstone was burnt and broken before being spread throughout the levelling layer. At Penhale Moor, also in Cornwall, a small bronze spearhead was found piercing the ground at an acute angle in one of the buildings after it was levelled and before a phase of rebuilding (Nowakowski and Johns 2015, 136). The fragment of a second spearhead lay adjacent to the first. Perhaps, Nowakowski (2001, 145) suggests, the spearhead was used to 'kill the house'.

One of the abandoned houses at Bestwall Quarry, Dorset, was the focus for the accumulation of ceramics and a burnt mound associated with feasting (Ladle and Woodward 2009). Two bronze bracelets were placed in separate locations within the building and on the same alignment as the doorway. Towards the close of activity within the enclosure at South Lodge, Dorset, a deposit of cat-tle bone was placed in a shallow pit in one roundhouse and a mound of broken pottery, topped with a broken quern, was spread on the second building (Barrett et al. 1991, 183). At Ballyprior Beg, Island Magee, County Antrim, the freshly broken mid-section of an otherwise pristine palstave was buried in a pit cut into a final occupation deposit (Suddaby 2003). The palstave may have been found or inherited and curated, as it was made in a style dated two or three centuries older than the building. The occupation layer into which the pit was dug contained the broken blade of a polished porcellanite axe, which is likely to have been up to a millennium older than the building. Following the abandonment of the roundhouses at Broom and Broomfield, the left-hand sides of the buildings were dismantled and the right-hand sides formed the focus for the deposition of large amounts of broken pottery, some of it abraded and perhaps the remains of middens and others recently and deliberately fragmented (Webley 2007). The pottery had in many cases been packed in pits and around the decayed bases of the surviving structural posts.

There were recurring practices associated with the abandonment of roundhouses. One of these is the use of occupation debris to 'close' the buildings. Another is the selection and deposition of individual objects. In a few cases these are metal items. More frequently, querns or their fragments were selected (Cleary 2018). The querns at Caltragh, County Sligo, were recovered from pits either face-down or turned inwards towards the sides of the pit, leading the excavator to suggest this placement symbolised the end of the querns' lives and the life of the dwelling (Danaher 2007, 84–85). At Ballybrowney, County Cork, fragments of querns were only found in the substantial postholes at the entrances of the enclosures (Cleary 2006).

Fire may have been important in transforming the lives of buildings. Of the 13 Bronze Age roundhouses excavated at Kintore, Aberdeenshire, 5 produced evidence they were burnt prior to abandonment (Cook and Dunbar 2008, 338). These were also the buildings with the largest assemblages of artefacts. In house 26, a deposit of burnt bone, pottery fragments and charcoal formed a final deposition above the hearth. Ten quernstones, nine lying face down, were recovered from building's internal ring ditch. One of the excavated buildings, on Tormore Hill, Arran, tells a different story (Barber 1997, 7–11) (Figure 4.8). The building was relatively substantial: 10 metres in diameter, with stone facing on the outside of the bank, and hazel wattlework on the inside. Four phases of construction within the bank, and numerous pits and postholes within the interior, point to repeated renovation or rebuilding. Fire destroyed the building sometime during the later centuries of the second millennium BC. Amongst the charred remains inside the rear of the building, the excavators recovered large quantities of timber and cleaned barley grains, and the burnt articulated remains of a bovine calf. The wood, mostly oak, with smaller quantities of alder and hazel comprised poles, rods and brushwood, some of which seemed to have been sorted and were therefore in the building for storage rather than being structural. Close to the building's entrance, the burnt cereals were the 'reject dross' from grain processing, while the charcoal was smaller and more degraded compared with the well-preserved and larger roundwood from the building's interior (Fairweather and McCullagh 1997, 19). The building appears caught unexpectedly by the fire.

Objects, such as querns and pottery, and processes, such as burning, that accompanied the end of buildings' lives might not have constituted formal

FIGURE 4.8 Excavations progressing through the burnt layers within the roundhouse at Tormore, Arran. © Crown copyright: HES.

abandonments (Brudenell and Cooper 2008; Seager Thomas 1999). The dismantlement and destruction of houses may not have been acted out by either the inhabitants or their near kin. It is plausible to interpret such acts as superstitions followed by people confronted with an abandoned or 'failed' settlement.

Accepting these caveats and ambiguities, it still seems reasonable given the large number of examples that the abandonment of houses was practised in more or less formal ways. In her interpretation of the evidence from Cornwall, Jacqueline Nowakowski (2001) suggests that the abandonment of houses paralleled the sequence at earlier round barrows where the use of the place was discontinued with the closure of the ground surface with a mound of turves or stone. In both cases the mounds or the dismantled and buried houses became landmarks and material memories for the people that were buried or had lived in the houses. Andy Jones (2008) comes to similar conclusions in his review of sites in Cornwall. He proposes that abandoned timber roundhouses in lowland settings were transformed to resemble earthen barrows, and stone roundhouses in the uplands were constructed to resemble ring cairns. They began life as open monuments, often as a circle of timber posts or stakes, and were closed with earthen mounds, perhaps incorporating stone kerbs, as at the roundhouse at Callestick, where the outline of the abandoned building was marked out with a kerb of quartz blocks.

FIGURE 4.9 The low stone wall constructed around the infilled roundhouse at Scarcewater, Cornwall. Copyright: Cornwall Archaeological Unit.

At Scarcewater, the interiors of the hollow-set roundhouses were infilled with what was probably midden from the settlement (Jones 2015). A low wall was built around one infilled structure, changing its orientation and appearance to match the alignments in nearby funerary cairns (Figure 4.9). Jones interprets these actions as maintaining a connection with the past, represented by earlier monument forms, at a time when significant changes were taking place in the organisation of people's lives—specifically, the construction of houses and field systems.

In her interpretation of the settlements in southern Britain, Joanna Brück connects the lifecycles of households, houses, pots and querns (Brück 1999a; 2001; 2006). These categories of material were treated in similar ways, involving burning and fragmentation, as part of rituals associated with fertility and regeneration. Pottery vessels and querns were sometimes deliberately broken and burnt before burial in similar ways to human bodies, which were cremated and perhaps further fragmented before being buried. Houses too were sometimes dismantled, burnt and buried. These similarities meant that the lives of houses, pottery vessels and querns could represent or act as metaphors for the human lifecycle. They needed to be treated like human bodies, where cremation and fragmentation were important symbols of breaking ties with the past, the regeneration of new social relationships and ensuring the continuity of the community.

Rather than houses offering metaphors for the human lifecycle, the lives of houses were just that: meaningful lives. Houses became durable assemblages in

Bronze Age worlds and participants in kinwork. Kinfolk were persons who, to paraphrase Marshal Sahlins (2013, 28), lived each other's lives and died each other's deaths. At times, through their durability and intrinsic relationality with everyday life, houses made kin and were recognised as kin. At the end of their dwelling-life, some houses were re-assembled: processes of dismantling, burning, burial and entombment might all have played their parts. These processes transformed the buildings for their future roles in the landscape, perhaps ensuring that as dead kinfolk their intervention in the living world remained benign.

In defining houses as intrinsic to kinwork and as kinfolk, I am accepting a porosity between things and persons. They were mutually constituted through their relations with one another. This mutuality constituted kinship. I do not mean that all things became kinfolk through their interactions with people, though all things were one way or another intrinsic to kinwork. Houses nurtured people's lives. They were the places where food was prepared and consumed, animals raised and killed. Things and people were made in and around houses. Houses too had lives: in their making and upkeep; their connections through place and alignment with the sky and the land; the warping, slipping, splitting and slow rot of their materials; the midden gathering outside and the hollows and hearths within; in the finality of their abandonment and their continuing life in the landscape.

The kindred of places, 1700–1200 BC

Houses need not have been isolated dwellings. As in the example of Trethellan Farm, Cornwall, buildings of different sizes, shapes and purposes clustered together. Settlements could be stable and durable, retaining their order over decades and longer. Buildings were rebuilt, sometimes time and again on the same footprint. The evidence from the seventeenth century BC onwards includes diverse settlement forms. Buildings were isolated, dispersed and clustered, sometimes enclosed by boundaries and other times not, lived in year-round or only for parts of the year. This diversity meant that kinship within resident groups varied in how it was constituted. I will explore some of this diversity in this and the following section.

The chalklands of Wessex and the South Downs provide many excavated examples of Bronze Age settlements. Ann Woodward interprets the settlements as the farms of extended family groups following a mixed agricultural economy (Ellison 1981). Each settlement comprised usually one or sometimes more main roundhouses, associated with an ancillary, smaller, roundhouse and other structures such as ponds and yards. At Thorny Down, Wiltshire, the second phase of the settlement comprised two 'units': a large timber-built roundhouse with a prominent porch and a series of ancillary structures (Ellison 1987). The entire settlement area was enclosed by an earthen bank and ditch, with the units separated by a timber fence and accessed by separate entrances. Joanna Brück (1999b) develops Woodward's model further by suggesting that the settlements were usually occupied by a kin group for only one generation. If settlement continued, then this involved the entire re-ordering of the layout and the construction of new buildings in different locations.

At Black Patch, on the South Downs in East Sussex, each phase of settlement on one of the excavated platforms comprised two houses, a pond and traces of a fenced enclosure (Drewett 1982; Russell 1996). The rebuilt houses did not substantially overlap, with the consequence that the earlier buildings' footprints remained. The artefacts recovered by Peter Drewett and his team during their excavations were distributed differently amongst and within the buildings. This surprised Drewett (1982, 338) as he had expected the material on the house floors to have been affected by subsequent, and especially twentieth-century, activity—the area was a military artillery range and later the platforms were bulldozed and ploughed. Two of the buildings lacked many artefacts aside from worked stone. The others contained burnt food remains, pottery, loom weights, worked stone and small bronze items. Some of the materials clustered within areas of the buildings: the loom weights found close to the wall of one house were interpreted as a space used for weaving; the clustering of burnt and fractured flint marked the locations of hearths. This was an insight, Drewett suggested, into the way daily life was organised within and amongst the houses. Houses had specific roles within the settlement that were perhaps associated with different members of an extended family group.

The settlements at Black Patch were dispersed amongst field systems, whose boundaries existed prior to the construction of the settlement platforms and enclosures. The boundaries survive as lynchets, which formed when sediment on cultivated land eroded from the surface and accumulated downslope. The excavators recovered charred cereal from the settlements, with two pits within houses at separate settlements being notable for each containing 20 kilograms of charred seed (Peter Hinton in Drewett 1982, 382–390). Hulled barley was the most common cereal grain, along with emmer and spelt wheat. Small numbers of beans were also recovered. Animal bones did not survive well at Black Patch. The relatively few bones that were identified were predominately cattle, with smaller numbers of sheep/goat and few pig and red deer (Terry O'Connor in Drewett 1982, 378–379).

The variety and relative proportions of domesticated animals and plants at Black Patch are matched at comparable settlements excavated prior to the construction of the Brighton bypass (Rudling 2002). Clusters of roundhouses were identified at four locations along the bypass route. As at Black Patch, the settlements were occupied in an increasingly open landscape, with mature woodland nearby. From the food remains recovered from the settlements, cattle dominated the livestock, with sheep/goat of lesser importance. Barley was the most intensively cultivated cereal, with wheat and beans present in smaller quantities. Large shallow hollows excavated at settlements on the South Downs were possibly ponds. These might have served as water storage for the human residents of the settlement, although it is as likely if not more so that they provided water for animals. The two ponds at Black Patch lay within the same fenced enclosures as the roundhouses. Animals were part of the settlement space alongside people.

Excavations in subsequent decades have uncovered further examples of paired and small clusters of buildings. At Yarnton, Oxfordshire, both the earlier and later Bronze Age houses were round and oval post-built structures, with the early examples (pre-1700 BC) generally smaller than the later examples (Hey et al. 2016, 63–67). At one of the Yarnton sites (Site 1), on raised and drier ground adjacent to a palaeochannel, six later Bronze Age oval houses were arranged in pairs (Figure 4.10). One building in each pair contained finds of pottery, worked stone and food remains, the other did not. It is likely the pairs represent sequential, rather than contemporary, settlement. People dug waterholes into palaeochannels in order to access water for livestock. These were not sited adjacent to buildings, and the floodplain lacked evidence for bounded fields.

At Caltragh, County Sligo, a cluster of three houses was excavated on a gentle south-facing slope above a wetland and a group of *fulachtaí fiadh* (Danaher 2007, 83–87). Two of the houses were sited so close together that it seems unlikely they were contemporary. New houses were constructed alongside abandoned or dismantled buildings. Short lengths of ditch lay next to the buildings and might have marked small garden plots or fields. In the north of Scotland, at Allt na Fearna quarry, Sutherland, the use of the site during c. 1600–1200 BC might have comprised paired structures separated by earthen enclosure banks (McCullagh and Tipping 1998) (Figure 4.10). The large houses replaced earlier, adjacent domestic structures, both roughly oval in plan and dating to 1800–1600 BC. After it was abandoned one house was reused as a pen and then later a small cultivated garden plot. Cultivation seems to have continued in the vicinity of the settlements throughout their occupation, with six row barley forming the principal cultivated plant remains recovered from the houses. Other species present, such as fat hen, sheep's sorrel and corn spurrey, may have been gathered.

On occasions the roundhouses and settlement area were enclosed or partially enclosed by a ditch and bank or palisade. Excavations at North Shoebury, Essex, uncovered clusters of pits and postholes associated with Deverel-Rimbury pottery and within two rectangular ditched enclosures (Wymer and Brown 1995). At Stansted, Essex, a group of four roundhouses occupied a roughly rectangular, fenced enclosure during 1700–1500 BC (Cooke et al. 2008, 37–52). The settlement then extended across a larger area, still enclosed by fences, and the number of roundhouses increased to six. It was abandoned with some formalities, including offerings in a waterhole and burial of large sarsen stone block.

At South Lodge, Dorset, a settlement developed within the uncultivated corner of a field and was enclosed by a ditch and bank late in its occupation (Barrett et al. 1991, 153–168). Shortly after the ditch was dug, a pottery vessel, a bronze razor and an awl were placed in the bottom and the ditch was partially backfilled. The razor and the awl marked the enclosure's northeast and southwest corners. Three metal objects were placed near one another on top of the backfilled layer and towards the enclosure's northeast corner. Although the ditch was 2 metres deep and steep-sided, it was quickly backfilled with nearly a metre of chalk rubble, there was no substantive bank or fence surrounding the site, and no evidence

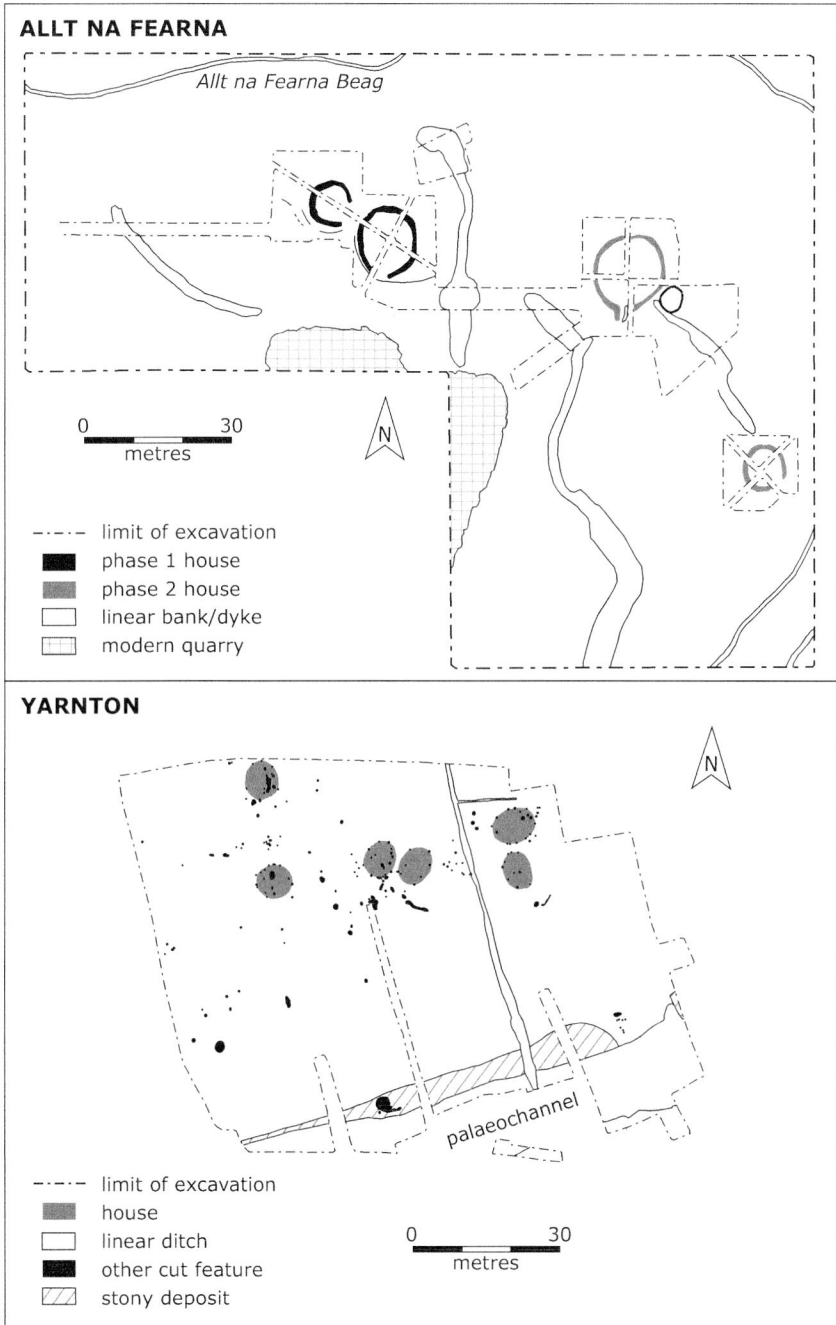

FIGURE 4.10 Plans of paired roundhouses within the settlements at Allt na Fearna, Sutherland, and Yarnton Site 1, Oxfordshire. Adapted from Hey et al. 2016, and McCullagh and Tipping 1998.

for a gate structure in the entrance. The metalwork and pottery vessel seem unlikely casual loses and are more convincingly interpreted as offerings associated with forming and backfilling the boundary. The razor, awl and urn were objects that in other circumstances would have accompanied the burial of cremated human bone. It is possible that they and the ditch marked a transitional event in the settlement's history, and perhaps even its death. The contemporary settlement at Down Farm, located nearby, was initially unenclosed, then bounded by a timber palisade, and finally the eastern and southern sides of the enclosure were defined with a bank and ditch (Barrett et al. 1991, 183–211). As at South Lodge, key points along the ditch were the focus for deposits of material culture. In the case of Down Farm these were the southwestern terminal and the southeastern corner.

The Llŷn Peninsula is the long arm of land that reaches into the Irish Sea below Anglesey, on Wales's northwest coast. It is now predominately grazing land enclosed within fields. There were areas of pasture and heathland during the later centuries of the second millennium BC, when roundhouse settlements were appearing for the first time in the landscape. There is evidence that cereals were cultivated (Smith et al. 2017, 31). A team from Gwynedd Archaeological Trust excavated one of the settlements, at Meyllteyrn Uchaf, where two circuits of ditches enclosed clay-walled roundhouses (Ward and Smith 2001) (Figure 4.11).

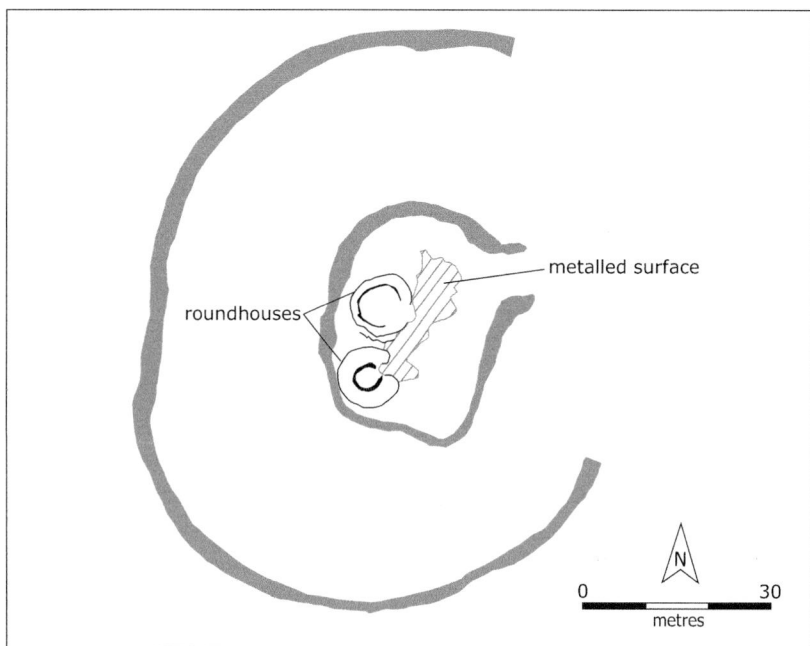

FIGURE 4.11 The concentric enclosures and roundhouses at Meyllteyrn Uchaf, Gwynedd. Adapted from Ward and Smith 2001.

The outer enclosure was 80 metres across. The sub-rectangular ditch of the inner enclosure, over 30 metres at its largest extent, surrounded three roundhouses, with the footprints of the two largest roundhouses overlapping. The inner enclosure and the buildings were arranged together. The enclosure's out-turned entrance on the east side was mimicked in form and alignment by the entrance to the first of the two large roundhouses. The entrance of the smaller round-house faced towards the enclosure's entrance, and the enclosure's southwestern corner appears to curve around and respect the edge of the roundhouse. While the order in which the structures were built is unknown, the inter-dependence of the inner enclosure and two of the roundhouses reflects a shared architecture and a sociality. Sometime later, a third roundhouse replaced the larger building, the inner enclosure was recut and stone metalling laid across the entrances to the roundhouses and towards the enclosure entrance. The settlement retained its architectural integrity and sociality. Layers of burnt stone and charcoal overlay the abandoned buildings.

Martin Doody (2008) excavated an oval enclosure at Chancellorsland, County Tipperary. The two concentric ditches and palisade at Chancellorsland enclosed an area 34 by 51 metres. The ditches survived to 1 metre in depth and up to 3 metres wide. A line of stakeholes inside the line of the inner bank might have been a palisade or formed a revetment for a bank. Doody used the stratigraphy to interpret three phases to the enclosure: the outer ditch, replaced by the inner ditch, followed by a recut outer ditch and a palisade. Nearly 70 percent of the excavated pottery (21 kilograms) and most of the animal bone (cattle, pig and sheep) came from the lower fill of the inner ditch, with much of this material found in a trench by the enclosure's eastern entrance. The pottery and bone were mixed with a variety of debris that included charred plants, worked wood, fragments of human skull and an amber bead. The excavations inside the enclosure revealed large numbers of postholes and stakeholes, pits and hearths. There were both rectangular structures and sub-oval dwellings, which overlapped demonstrating relative longevity of occupation. Features were uncovered outside the ditches, though not excavated. The radiocarbon chronology placed the occupation sometime during the sixteenth to fourteenth centuries BC.

Chancellorsland was a long-lived and intensively inhabited settlement. Buildings were rebuilt on multiple occasions, their locations overlapping and leaving scatters of post- and stakeholes. The enclosure's shape remained stable. It did not substantially enlarge, contract, nor were annexes added. The inhabitants reinforced the enclosure's identity by digging an inner ditch, raising a palisade and recutting the outer ditch. At Meyllteyrn Uchaf, one of the roundhouses was replaced and the layout changed, though the new buildings retained a spatial alignment with the enclosure's entrance and the enclosure's shape was maintained and the ditch recut. At Downsview, one of the settlements excavated during the construction of the Brighton bypass, around 12 structures were built and occupied during the sixteenth to ninth centuries BC (Rudling 2002, 200). The buildings were constructed on terraces cut into the steep slopes at the head of a dry valley. The activity was never enclosed by an earthwork or palisade, yet it remained clustered within an area less than half a hectare in extent.

These settlements exemplify the intensity and entangling of the daily lives of humans, livestock, houses and things that emerged in the centuries after 1700 BC. The settlements were closer in size to a farmstead than a village, with one, two or perhaps several buildings grouped together. There were spaces where livestock might live alongside people; probably, they sometimes occupied the same buildings. Food was prepared and eaten. Architecture played an important role in the formation of these assemblages and their longevity. Houses were akin with their human inhabitants. Settlements were generative places. They outlasted the lives of humans and houses. Living in the same places as previous generations, even if not in the same houses, was a means of generating kinship and establishing kindred. The boundaries around some settlements contained these generative processes and intensified them. If houses and people were kin, settlements were sites of kindred.

Seasons for dwelling together and apart, 1700–1200 BC

The formation of kindred settlements was an uncertain, faltering process. The examples I chose for the previous section offered degrees of clarity that are frequently absent. George Lambrick (2009, 150) reviewed more than 100 excavated Bronze Age houses in the Upper and Middle Thames Valley. He identified contemporary pairs and clusters of buildings in a handful of examples. For regions as far apart as the Outer Hebrides, Essex, East Anglia and the West Midlands, houses were rare or absent until late in the second millennium BC. In reviewing the evidence from East Anglia, Matt Brudenell (2012) notes a scarcity of evidence for settlement predating 1200 BC in spite of the plentiful traces of large-scale land enclosure. In much of Essex, the majority of occupation is defined by clusters of pits associated with domestic debris. Work on the A120 road scheme showed this contrast, with Bronze Age settlement that comprised just pits and a few field boundaries, and the very substantial evidence for Iron Age roundhouses and enclosures (Timby et al. 2007).

The limitations of development-led fieldwork contribute to this pattern. Excavations do not extend beyond the developed area, whether that be a road or rail corridor, the limits of a housing or commercial estate, or the extension to a quarry. Modern development predominately occurs on land subjected to centuries of intensive use and the degradation of surfaces and structures. Development is unevenly distributed around the islands, with the east and south of both Ireland and Britain the subject of greater levels of development-led fieldwork. Unspectacular and poorly preserved settlements are not widely reported. They make poor case studies with which to write narratives of domestic life during the second millennium BC. The evidence for Bronze Age settlement identified during the development of the A1–M1 link road near Leeds, West Yorkshire, was slight and impoverished in comparison with the extensive later Iron Age landscapes

(Roberts et al. 2001). Only two Bronze Age roundhouses, located at Swillington Common, were found during the evaluations along the 40 kilometres of the road scheme. They dated to the sixteenth or fifteenth century BC and only the bases of deeply dug features survived because the site was heavily disturbed by later ploughing.

A way to explain the variation in settlement evidence around Britain and Ireland is to correlate the presence of roundhouses with people living together year-round. The settlements were sited amongst the lands where crops grew and animals grazed. However wide the networks and however interdependent the lives of neighbouring kindred, settlements retained a longevity and individuality engendered by years and generations tending a place. For John Barrett (1994, 147), these ways of living led to a 'landscape viewed from the centre of a domain'—the household—which was distinct from the 'outside world of others'. Joanna Brück (2000) interprets organised domestic spaces as responses to a wider fracturing of large community formations. By defining households and making daily life more structured and routine, settlements brought ontological security and stability to a world in flux (Brück 2000, 294).

In regions where settlements were rare or the evidence for domestic occupation lacks buildings, prehistorians have assumed that settlement was transitory and seasonal, and that mobility remained important in lifeways. David Mullin (2003) reviewed the evidence for Bronze Age settlement in the diverse landscapes of the northern Midlands of England. He explains that for much of the second millennium BC communities practised a degree of residential mobility and did not dwell in substantial houses or settlements. Excavations undertaken as part of major road developments failed to find much evidence of Bronze Age settlement, with burnt mounds providing the most durable indications of occupation during the second millennium BC. This corresponds with Willy Kitchen's (2001) interpretation of the Bronze Age landscapes of the Peak District. Here too, the evidence for year-round settlement of places is equivocal, and it seems more likely that the fertile limestone plateau of the White Peak and the sandstone Eastern Moors around its periphery were used by the same communities at different times of year. The result may have been a more fluid sense of tenure over places than seems likely for regions where year-round settlement was more common.

Earlier in this chapter I queried the idea that slight remains of settlement and a lack of durable domestic buildings correlated with a single model of mobility. The presence of cereals and cultivation, small stake- and post-built buildings, accumulations of midden material indicated stays of months and probably years in some locations. Large spreads of material culture and accumulations of burnt mounds emerged during repeated, often brief, inhabitations of locales. The multiple human burials in barrows, cairns and cemeteries, which I described in the previous chapters, documented long memories of places and created complex, layered geographies. Houses do not, in themselves, demonstrate year-round settlement, more intensive use of landscape and the formation of independently productive households—settling down rather than moving around.

Strat Halliday (2000; 2007) questions the assumption that roundhouses equated with long-lived, year-round settlement. Using evidence from northern Britain and building on work by John Barber and Anne Crone (2001), Halliday identifies examples of single-phase relatively simple structures and the repeated rebuilding of houses on the same 'footprint'. These could have been short-term, discontinuous uses of places either during cycles of movement within the landscape or as part of temporary expansions and contractions to and from more 'marginal' areas.

Halliday uses a roundhouse excavated by Jack Stevenson (1984) at Cúl a'Bhaile, on the island of Jura, as one of his examples. Close to the coast and shadowed by Jura's impressive rock-strewn peaks, the house lies within an enclosure formed by a low stone bank or wall. With poor precision, sadly, the calibrated radiocarbon dates place the building's use during the middle and late centuries of the second millennium BC. Stevenson (1984, 134) proposed that the building was occupied continuously and for sufficiently long to require three major rebuilds, with the earth and stone bank steadily widening and the repeated replacement of timber posts supporting the roof and the porch. Strat Halliday (2007, 52) offers a different interpretation of the structural sequence: a timber building was built on recently cultivated ground; it was replaced by an earth and stone-banked roundhouse; this was replaced again by a thickened earth and stone-banked roundhouse within which multiple rings of posts indicated repeated refurbishment. With a surveyor's eye for surface and slope, Halliday observes that the initial thickening of the house's ring-bank occurred on the downslope edge of the building, as though the structure had collapsed a little before being rebuilt.

Cúl a'Bhaile's use was short-term and discontinuous, with periods when it was left to decay before being repaired and re-occupied. The limited artefactual evidence from the building's interior supports this interpretation, as does the hearth made from a simple stone slab laid on the floor. The pollen analysed from turves in the roundhouse bank and the sediment in the postholes included 'different floristic elements', suggesting 'remodelling and even rebuilding of the house along with some repair work' (Graeme Whittington in Stevenson 1984, 157).

There are examples of settlements in the uplands that may only have been occupied seasonally, perhaps while tending grazing animals or mining. A temporary shelter was identified during the excavation of an ore processing area at one of the Mount Gabriel copper mines, County Cork (O'Brien 1994, 102–116). At Llyn Morwynion, Meirionnydd, a late third millennium BC radiocarbon date was obtained for the peat overlying a small roundhouse located at an altitude of 400 metres (Caseldine et al. 2001). The pollen from the peat showed that the roundhouse was built in a landscape of pasture and mixed woodland. At Bracken Rigg, County Durham, a stone and timber roundhouse was built within a larger irregularly shaped stone enclosure; there is only one radiocarbon date for the house, calibrated to 1590–1350 BC (Coggins and Fairless 1984). The building is an exposed, upland location, and there is relatively little material culture or a recognisable hearth. Chronologically later (radiocarbon dated to 1150–900 BC) is the small stone 'hut' and associated enclosure at Graig Fechan, located at an altitude of over 400 metres on the Denbigh Moors (Manley 1990).

Altitude and isolation need not determine seasonality, as with the settlement at Shaugh Moor, Devon (Wainwright and Smith 1980). In plan, it fits the model of a small group of roundhouses with paired residential and ancillary structures, defined late in its history by an enclosing boundary. Yet it was sited on the fringes of Dartmoor where, the excavators argued, it was probably occupied seasonally in order to take advantage of upland pasture during the summer months, per- haps in combination with the exploitation of nearby metal ores. The evidence for seasonal use is ambiguous: there were no hearths within the buildings, and the material culture recovered during the excavations was meagre. Radiocarbon dates obtained from the site calibrated to 1850–850 BC. These were not from particularly reliable samples, and the pottery supports a more constrained chro- nology of a few hundred years.

The enclosure on Shaugh Moor was only one of numerous settlements that have been identified within the Plym Valley and across Dartmoor, many of which were enclosed. Some of the settlements comprise clusters of two to five build- ings, and others are much larger (Figure 4.12). At Legis Tor, there are four enclo- sures and over 40 buildings within a distance of 800 metres on the south facing

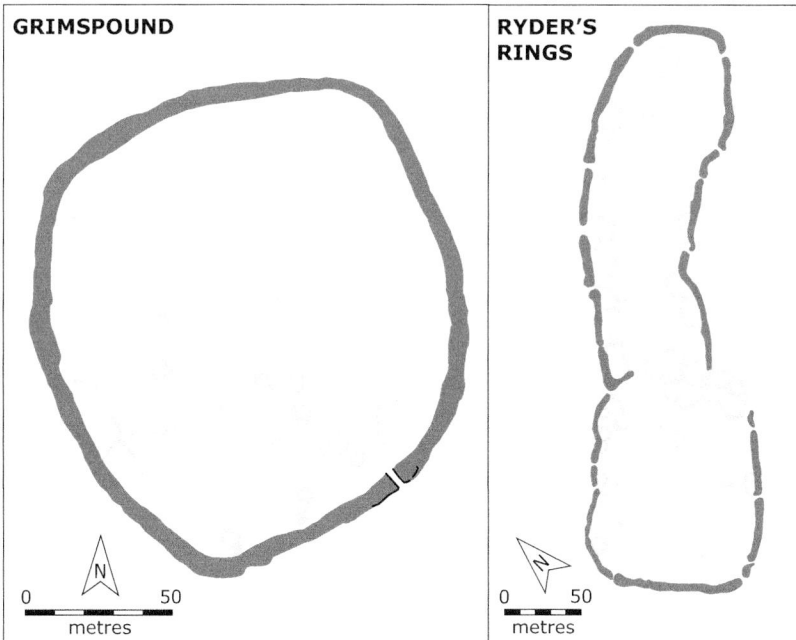

FIGURE 4.12 Examples of enclosed roundhouse settlements on Dartmoor, Devon. Ryder's Rings was a similar size to Grimspound before a second en- closure was appended and infilled with pens and roundhouses. Adapted from Newman 2011.

slopes above the river, while at Whittenknowles Rocks a single large enclosure contains 38 roundhouses (Butler 1994). As with Shaugh Moor, the setting and morphology of the settlements seems to fit the idea of seasonal use of pasture. It is likely that the settlements have complex histories and so will not all have been occupied concurrently. Instead, imagine the settlements as places where graziers would arrive each spring, repair and rebuild their houses or establish new structures. The settlements' populations fluctuated year to year and decade to decade with the changing fortunes of the kinfolk, their herds and the land.

Similar large blocks of Bronze Age settlement are known from Bodmin Moor, Cornwall (Johnson and Rose 1994). These include Blacktor, where there are 96 roundhouses, and Leskernick Hill, where about 50 houses were built into a hillside of surface stone, locally termed 'clitter'. The archaeologists who most recently surveyed and excavated the settlements at Leskernick interpret a strong symbolic order in the ways people lived amongst the stone of the hillside: both the incorporation of large earthfast stones into houses and the modification of stones in the wider landscape may point to animistic beliefs about the spiritual powers of stone (Bender et al. 2007). Calibrated radiocarbon dates from the excavated houses place their use during the fifteenth to thirteenth centuries BC, with later occupation of at least one structure with rebuilding and hearth dating to 1030–810 BC. Careful survey revealed complex re-working of the landscape as enclosures were appended and others went out of use.

Barbara Bender, Sue Hamilton and Christopher Tilley (2007) regard the cosmological ordering of space within the settlement and the substantial architecture of the buildings as evidence for year-round and long-term inhabitation of Leskernick. Their presumption is that the immutability of stone was matched by a continuity of the household. What if, as I argued earlier, houses were living kin and houses' presence in the landscape marked continuities that need not be matched by the co-presence of their human inhabitants? Houses need not be lived in year-round, though their presence retains kinship with a place and access to grazing for related people and animals.

There are parallels for the large clusters of roundhouses on Dartmoor and Bodmin Moor, albeit geographically distant. At Corrstown, County Derry, on the north coast of Ireland, 74 structures, including round, oval and rectangular buildings, were excavated within an area of 1.75 hectares (Ginn and Rathbone 2012). The calibrated radiocarbon dates appear to show one or two houses in use in the first half of the second millennium BC, before the majority of the buildings were occupied during the fifteenth to thirteenth centuries BC. As with the stone-built settlements in southwest England, there were only a small number of instances where the Corrstown houses intercut one another and there is evidence for patterning in the layout of the settlement. In one area, the houses were arranged along the edge of a surfaced track, which itself avoided one of the buildings with an early radiocarbon date.

Wetlands present different evidence for temporary and sometimes seasonal use of places. Research on the Severn Estuary is particularly illustrative. Fieldwork

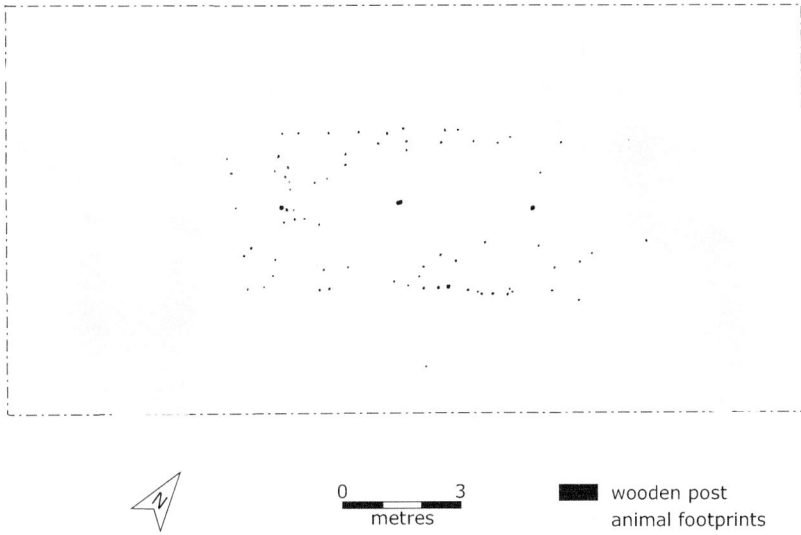

FIGURE 4.13   Excavation plan of Redwick 'Building 2', Severn Estuary. Adapted from Bell 2013.

identified a range of buildings and other structures related to what was probably seasonal use of the raised bog from 1500 BC up until the later first millennium BC (Bell 2013; Bell et al. 2000). Roundhouses have so far been excavated in three areas, while excavations at Redwick uncovered up to five rectangular buildings radiocarbon dated to 1500–900 BC. Two of the structures at Redwick were sufficiently well-preserved for most of the outlines of the walls to survive either as shallow gullies or as timber posts, along with a central line of three larger posts, presumably to support the roof (Figure 4.13). The buildings were 9–12 metres long and 3.5–5 metres wide, and in one case there were internal sub-divisions. The presence of cattle footprints preserved in the peat around the buildings offers some indication of the purpose of living on the estuarine pasture. There were relatively few artefacts recovered from the buildings, although they were not fully excavated. Bronze Age pottery from elsewhere along the estuary, including in association with the houses, is similar to the ceramics from the settlement at Brean Down (Bell 1990). The houses may only form one element of people's use of the landscape, albeit a visible one. For instance, about 200 metres from the buildings, a scatter of charcoal and a wooden stake driven into the ground at an angle appears to be the remains of a temporary encampment. Similar ephemeral traces of settlement recovered elsewhere, including charcoal, a few burnt flints, pottery and angled stakes, with scientific dates that overlapped with those from the buildings: 1300–920 BC.

The investigation of wetland environments has much to offer in Ireland, where an extraordinary range of material has been recovered from raised bogs, lakes and estuaries (O'Sullivan 2007). These include extensive areas of trackways across the bogs and evidence for estuarine structures on the Shannon estuary, similar to those from the Severn. Settlements dating to the second millennium BC are known from a number of lakeside settings, as at Cullyhanna, County Armagh (Hodges 1958). The felling of one of the timbers used in the construction of the settlement was dated to 1526 BC using dendrochronology (Mallory and McNeill 1991, 108). The settlement was enclosed by a simple palisade, and it comprised two circular structures defined by clay and stone mounds 'floating' on timbers laid within peaty lakeside sediments. Both mounds had central hearths, and one was certainly the stance for a roundhouse. The excavator interpreted the settlement as a hunting camp (the enclosure being too wet for penning animals), but the range of artefacts from comparable settlements may indicate they were at least occupied quite intensively.

Aidan O'Sullivan (2007) argues that distinctive identities emerged from the labours, routines and cultural histories of dwelling in wetlands. The same observation might be made for the small and large settlements in the uplands of western and northern Britain. Households and houses need not have been stable assemblages. Eugene Costello (2018) reviewed short distance transhumance in the recent history of northern Europe. He recognises a preponderance of young people, especially young women, tended animals on summer pasture. This arrangement brought the women freedoms from the ties of life around family farms.

Settlements were constituted through varied lifeways and durations of inhabitation during the centuries after 1700 BC. John Barrett (1994) draws attention to the different senses of time and history that people might have experienced living year-round, over decades in one location. While this change may have occurred in some regions, there were other experiences of places and alternative social configurations. The temporary shelters and seasonal dwellings on salt marsh and moorland created different kin compared with the clusters of roundhouses occupied year-round at Trethellan Farm or Chancellorsland. Seasonally occupied settlements did not weaken kinship with places. People returned time and again. Houses stayed. If houses could be kin, then relations were retained with a place even when the people and animals were away. The clusters of tens of roundhouses in settlements on Dartmoor and Bodmin Moor created unusual intensities of kinship and life with a place and a land. These assemblages were far removed from the small households that have tended to dominate our narratives of Bronze Age social life.

Conclusion—living ruins

Imagine a place where a dozen or more people and their animals had lived for a year or a few and then left during the early second millennium BC. There would be collapsed remnants of benders, bare earth and dried animal dung; faded axe-marked stumps on nearby trees and boughs; nettles growing on turned earth and colonising mounds of discarded debris; middens that warmed the soil; and a subtle smell of decay and burning that would freshen with rain. You would find the place easily enough by following the trodden ways left by people's and animals' routines or crossing paths with a feral dog or pig. Were you familiar with the landscape, the likelihood is you would know the people and animals who had lived there and where they had gone. You might learn something about the duration and time of their dwelling from the fragments of pottery, worked wood and stone. The place would have a name, perhaps, and stories of death, birth, affiliation.

For five or six centuries, until the seventeenth century BC, there appears an intangibility to the archaeological evidence for domestic architecture and the tasks of daily life. Scatters of stone tools, clusters of pits, mounds of cracked and burnt stone and midden spreads were dispersed around the landscape. This did not mean that settlements were unimportant or that dwelling was an ephemeral or marginal aspect of life. Generations returned to some locales. Accumulations of the debris of daily life attest to these durations. Inhabitation left unstable materials and traces that lived on after the people and animals had left. Selected pottery, flint, animal and human remains were gifted in pits. The fractured stones used to heat troughs of water were piled next to the troughs, in layers that accumulated through years of use. These were the living ruins and residues of dwelling and of kinwork.

People rarely built substantial dwellings during the early centuries of the Bronze Age. The excavated round and oval structures appear to be simple and found individually or perhaps with one or two others. They were not the structures where most people lived. Some may have had unusual purposes or carried novel or archaic connotations. From the seventeenth century, durable houses were increasingly commonplace. The pace of this change is elusive because the chronologies, beyond handfuls of well-dated sites, are imprecise. The cumulative change can be quantified. I began this chapter with the examples of stone-built roundhouses on Dartmoor. Jeremy Butler (1997, 141) identified about 4,000 roundhouses in the surveys he completed of the moor, and a great many of these are likely to originate in the middle and late centuries of the second millennium BC.

As Dartmoor illustrates, the roundhouses were more substantial than the buildings that preceded them. They were capable of surviving a couple of decades with maintenance, and could have been repaired and replaced over longer time spans. Houses came to life through their participation in the lives of people and animals. They also took life from their materials and their placement in the landscape. The easterly to southerly alignments of most houses related architecture, place and sky. The beginnings and abandonments of houses were marked by the depositions of things and substances. A spearhead pierced the floor of a roundhouse at Penhale Moor; burnt stone and charcoal overlay the abandoned buildings at Meyllteyrn Uchaf. Houses lived and died with persons and as kin.

The organisation of daily life in and around the buildings is mostly lost to us. The houses and settlements were formed through a variety of activities, and associated with commonplace tasks such as the preparation and consumption of food. Clusters of houses, fenced yards and gardens, ponds and waterholes attest to longer and more intensive use of places. The places were sometimes enclosed by palisades, banks, ditches and walls. Longevity brought senses of kindred and place emerging from domestic spaces.

Kinship was generated from living places, and houses were amongst the kindred of a place. Countering what Diana Coole (2010) termed 'the inertia of matter and the generativity of flesh', dwelling places were vibrant and generative. They accumulated and folded kin into their fabric. The intensity of lives in these places gave them a flow and a process, a folding and forming, that gradually or abruptly, carefully or carelessly, ended.

The assembling of durable domestic architecture did not emerge uniformly throughout Ireland and Britain, nor was it accompanied by a proscribed way of living within similar configurations. People built durable houses in places that they only inhabited for parts of the year. In some regions, settlements moved periodically within landscapes. There were other regions where houses have remained rare archaeological discoveries—where houses did not come to life. This was not straightforwardly a consequence of retaining some aspect of residential mobility that made durable houses unnecessary. Houses had remained fragile during the earlier Bronze Age when people were living year-round in places. People built durable houses in locations that they only inhabited for the seasons when their stock grazed upland and coastal pastures. Durable houses and settlements were a way of life, a way of kinwork and a durable association with place and land. Dwelling places without durable houses might have been conscious acts made by kindred to remain outside established ways for living together. Maybe it provided a means of retaining a certain fluidity in relation with the landscape. This mosaic brought particular identities to communities and differences in how they are organised.

References

Allen, Michael J. 2005. Beaker settlement and environment on the chalk downs of southern England. *Proceedings of the Prehistoric Society* 71:219–245.

Ashmore, Patrick. 2001. Settlement in Scotland during the second millennium BC. In *Bronze Age landscapes: tradition and transformation*, edited by Joanna Brück, pp. 1–8. Oxbow, Oxford.

Baker, Louise, Tessa Bolger and Lyndsey Clark. 2015. Site summaries. In *A journey along the Carlow corridor: the archaeology of the M9 Carlow bypass*, edited by Tessa Bolger, Colm Moloney, and Damian Shiels, pp. 11–76. NRA Scheme Monographs, 16. National Roads Authority, Dublin.

Barber, John (editor). 1997. *The archaeological investigation of a prehistoric landscape: excavations on Arran 1978–1981.* Scottish Trust for Archaeological Research, Edinburgh.

Barber, John W and B Anne Crone. 2001. The duration of structures, settlements and sites: some evidence from Scotland. In *Recent developments in wetland research*, edited by Barry Raftery, and Joyce Hickey, pp. 69–86. Department of Archaeology, University College Dublin, Dublin.

Barrett, John C. 1994. *Fragments from antiquity: an archaeology of social life in Britain, 2900–1200 BC*. Blackwell, Oxford.

Barrett, John C, Richard Bradley and Martin Green. 1991. *Landscape, monuments and society: the prehistory of Cranborne Chase*. Cambridge University Press, Cambridge.

Bayer, Olaf. 2011. *Lithic scatters and landscape: the Mesolithic, Neolithic and Early Bronze Age inhabitation of the lower Exe valley, Devon*. PhD thesis, University of Central Lancashire.

Bell, Martin. 1990. *Brean Down: excavations 1983–87*. English Heritage, London.

Bell, Martin. 2013. *The Bronze Age in the Severn Estuary*. Council for British Archaeology, York.

Bell, Martin, Astrid Caseldine and Heiki Neumann. 2000. *Prehistoric intertidal archaeology in the Welsh Severn Estuary*. Council for British Archaeology, London.

Bender, Barbara, Sue Hamilton and Chris Tilley. 2007. *Stone worlds: narrative and reflexivity in landscape archaeology*. Left Coast Press, Walnut Creek, Ca.

Bennett, Paul, Steve Ouditt and Jon Rady. 1998. The prehistory of Holywell Coombe. In *Late Quaternary environmental change in north-west Europe: excavations at Holywell Coombe, south-east England*, edited by Richard C Preece, and David R Bridgland, pp. 261–314.

Benson, Don G, John G Evans, George H Williams, Timothy Darvill and Andrew David. 1990. Excavations at Stackpole Warren, Dyfed. *Proceedings of the Prehistoric Society* 56:179–245.

Bradley, Richard. 1970. The excavation of a Beaker settlement at Belle Tout, East Sussex, England. *Proceedings of the Prehistoric Society* 36:312–379.

Brady, Conor. 2007. *A landscape survey of the Newgrange environs: earlier prehistoric settlement at Brú na Bóinne, Co. Meath*. PhD thesis, University College Dublin.

Brown, Antony G, Steven R Davis, Jackie Hatton, Charlotte O'Brien, Fiona Reilly, Kate Taylor, Emer Dennehy, Lorna O'Donnell, Nora Bermingham, Tim Mighall, Scott Timpany, Emma Tetlow, Jane Wheeler and Shirley Wynne. 2016. The environmental context and function of burnt-mounds: new studies of Irish *fulachtaí fiadh*. *Proceedings of the Prehistoric Society* 82:259–290.

Brück, Joanna. 1999a. Houses, lifecycles and deposition on Middle Bronze Age settlements in southern England. *Proceedings of the Prehistoric Society* 65:145–166.

Brück, Joanna. 1999b. What's in a settlement? Domestic practice and residential mobility in Early Bronze Age southern England. In *Making places in the prehistoric world: themes in settlement archaeology*, edited by Joanna Brück, and Melissa Goodman, pp. 52–75. UCL Press, London.

Brück, Joanna. 2000. Settlement, landscape and social identity: the Early–Middle Bronze Age transition in Wessex, Sussex and the Thames Valley. *Oxford Journal of Archaeology* 19(3):273–300.

Brück, Joanna. 2001. Body metaphors and technologies of transformation in the English Middle and Late Bronze Age. In *Bronze Age landscapes: tradition and transformation*, edited by Joanna Brück, pp. 149–160. Oxbow, Oxford.

Brück, Joanna. 2006. Fragmentation, personhood and the social construction of technology in Middle and Late Bronze Age Britain. *Cambridge Archaeological Journal* 16(3):297–315.

Brudenell, Matt. 2012. *Pots, practice and society: an investigation of pattern and variability in the Post-Deverel Rimbury ceramic tradition of East Anglia*. PhD thesis, University of York.

Brudenell, Matt and Anwen Cooper. 2008. Post-middenism: depositional histories on later Bronze Age settlements at Broom, Bedfordshire. *Oxford Journal of Archaeology* 27(1):15–36.

Butler, Jeremy. 1994. *Dartmoor atlas of antiquities. Volume 3: the south-west*. Devon Books, Exeter.

Butler, Jeremy. 1997. *Dartmoor atlas of antiquities. Volume 5: the second millennium BC.* Devon Books, Exeter.

Cahill, Mary. 2015. 'Here comes the sun…'. *Archaeology Ireland* 29(1):26–33.

Carlin, Neil. 2018. *The Beaker phenomenon? Understanding the character and context of social practices in Ireland 2500–2000 BC.* Sidestone Press, Leiden.

Carsten, Janet. 2004. *After kinship.* Cambridge University Press, Cambridge.

Carver, Martin. 2005. *Sutton Hoo: a seventh-century princely burial ground and its context.* British Museum Press, London.

Caseldine, Astrid E, George Smith and Catherine J Griffiths. 2001. Vegetation history and upland settlement at Llyn Morwynion, Ffestiniog, Meirionnydd. *Archaeology in Wales* 41:21–33.

Chan, Benjamin. 2003. *Understanding the inhabitation of the Stonehenge environs: the interpretative potential of ploughsoil assemblages.* PhD thesis, University of Sheffield.

Chapple, Robert M. 2019. Catalogue of radiocarbon determinations and dendrochronology dates (August 2019 release). Oculus Obscura Press https://sites.google.com/site/chapplearchaeology/irish-radiocarbon-dendrochronological-dates, accessed 13/11/19.

Cleary, Kerri. 2006. Intriguing discoveries at Ballybrowney, County Cork. *Past* 53:12–14.

Cleary, Kerri. 2018. Broken bones and broken stones: exploring fragmentation in Middle and Late Bronze Age settlement contexts in Ireland. *European Journal of Archaeology* 21(3):336–360.

Coggins, Denis and Ken Fairless. 1984. The Bronze Age settlement site of Bracken Rigg, Upper Teesdale, Co Durham. *Durham Archaeological Journal* 1:5–21.

Cook, Murray and Lindsay Dunbar. 2008. *Rituals, roundhouses and Romans: excavations at Kintore, Aberdeenshire 2000–2006. Volume 1: Forest Road.* Scottish Trust for Archaeological Research, Edinburgh.

Cooke, Nicholas, Fraser Brown and Christopher Phillpotts. 2008. *From hunter gatherers to huntsmen: a history of the Stansted landscape.* Framework Archaeology, Oxford and Salisbury.

Coole, Diana. 2010. The inertia of matter and the generativity of flesh. In *New materialisms: ontology, agency, and politics*, edited by Diana Coole, and Samantha Frost, pp. 92–115. Duke University Press, Durham and London.

Cooper, Anwen, Duncan Garrow, Mark Knight and Lesley McFadyen. 2004. The pot, the flint and the bone and house beautiful. In *Substance, memory, display: archaeology and art*, edited by Colin Renfrew, Chris Gosden, and Elizabeth DeMarrais, pp. 97–102. McDonald Institute for Archaeological Research, Cambridge.

Costello, Eugene. 2018. Temporary freedoms? Ethnoarchaeology of female herders at seasonal sites in northern Europe. *World Archaeology* 50(1):165–184.

Danaher, Ed. 2007. *Monumental beginnings: the archaeology of the N4 Sligo inner relief road.* NRA Scheme Monographs, 1. National Roads Authority, Dublin.

Delaney, Finn and John Tierney. 2011. *In the lowlands of south Galway: archaeological excavations on the N18 Oranmore to Gort national road scheme.* NRA Scheme Monographs, 7. National Roads Authority, Dublin.

Doody, Martin. 2002. Bronze Age houses in Ireland. In *New agendas in Irish prehistory: papers in commemoration of Liz Anderson*, edited by Angela Desmond, Gina Johnson, Margaret McCarthy, John Sheenan, and Elizabeth Shee Twohig, pp. 135–159. Wordwell, Bray.

Doody, Martin. 2008. *The Ballyhoura Hills Project.* Wordwell, Bray.

Drewett, Peter. 1982. Later Bronze Age downland economy and excavations at Black Patch, East Sussex. *Proceedings of the Prehistoric Society* 48:321–400.

Driscoll, Killian. 2013. Coastal communities in earlier prehistoric Ireland: ploughzone survey and the Tawin/Maree stone axes, Galway Bay. *Proceedings of the Royal Irish Academy* 113C:29–65.

Edmonds, Mark, Christopher Evans and David Gibson. 1999. Assembly and collection— lithic complexes in the Cambridgeshire fenlands. *Proceedings of the Prehistoric Society* 65:47–82.

Ellison, Ann. 1981. Towards a socio-economic model for the Middle Bronze Age in southern England. In *Patterns of the past: studies in honour of David Clarke*, edited by Ian Hodder, Glynn Isaac, and Norman Hammond, pp. 413–438. Cambridge University Press, Cambridge.

Ellison, Ann. 1987. The Bronze Age settlement at Thorny Down: pots, post-holes and patterning. *Proceedings of the Prehistoric Society* 53:385–392.

Eogan, George. 1984. *Excavations at Knowth, vol. 1: smaller passage tombs, Neolithic occupation and Beaker activity.* Royal Irish Academy, Dublin.

Eogan, George and Helen Roche. 1997. *Excavations at Knowth 2: settlement and ritual sites of the fourth and third millennia BC.* Royal Irish Academy, Dublin.

Eogan, James and Richard O'Brien. 2005. *Final report of excavations at Rathdown Upper, Greystones, Co. Dublin.* Archaeological Development Services Ltd, Dublin.

Eogan, James and Elizabeth Shee Twohig (editors). 2011. *Cois tSiúire: nine thousand years of human activity in the lower Suir Valley. Archaeological excavations on the route of the N25 Waterford City bypass. Volume 1.* NRA Scheme Monographs. National Roads Authority, Dublin.

Evans, Christopher, Emma Beadsmore, Matt Brudenell and Gavin Lucas. 2009. *Fengate revisited: further fen-edge excavations, Bronze Age fieldsystems and settlement and the Wyman Abbott/Leeds archives.* Cambridge Archaeological Unit, Cambridge.

Evans, Christopher, Jonathan Tabor and Marc Vander Linden. 2016. *Twice-crossed river: prehistoric and palaeoenvironmental investigations at Barleycroft Farm/Over, Cambridgeshire.* McDonald Institute for Archaeological Research, Cambridge.

Evans, Helen. 2008. *Neolithic and Bronze Age landscapes of Cumbria.* BAR British Series, 463. Archaeopress, Oxford.

Fairweather, Alan D and Rod McCullagh. 1997. Carbonised plant remains. In *The archaeological investigation of a prehistoric landscape: excavations on Arran 1978–1981*, edited by John Barber, pp. 13–21. Scottish Trust for Archaeological Research, Edinburgh.

Fox, Aileen. 1954. Excavations at Kestor, an Early Iron Age settlement near Chagford, Devon. *Report and Transactions of the Devonshire Association* 86:21–62.

Fox, Aileen. 2000. *Aileen—a pioneering archaeologist: the autobiography of Aileen Fox.* Gracewing, Leominster.

Gardiner, Julie. 1988. *The composition and distribution of Neolithic surface flint assemblages in central southern England.* PhD thesis, University of Reading.

Garner, Dan J. 2007. *The Neolithic and Bronze Age settlement at Oversley Farm, Styal, Cheshire. Excavations in advance of Manchester Airport's second runway.* BAR British Series 435. Archaeopress, Oxford.

Garrow, Duncan. 2006. *Pits, settlement and deposition during the Neolithic and Early Bronze Age in East Anglia.* BAR British Series, 414. Archaeopress, Oxford.

Gerrard, Sandy. 2016. Archaeology and bracken: the Teigncombe prehistoric roundhouse excavation. *Proceedings of the Devon Archaeological Society* 74:1–63.

Ghey, Eleanor, Nancy Edwards, Robert Johnston and Rachel Pope. 2007. Characterising the Welsh roundhouse: chronology, inhabitation and landscape. *Internet Archaeology* 23 https://doi.org/10.11141/ia.23.1.

Gibson, Alex. 1982. *Beaker domestic sites: a study of the domestic pottery of the late third and early second millennia BC in the British Isles*. BAR British Series, 107. British Archaeological Reports, Oxford.

Gillespie, Richard. 2007. Prehistory and history on the N5 Charlestown bypass in counties Mayo and Roscommon. In *New routes to the past: proceedings of a public seminar on archaeological discoveries on national road schemes, August 2006*, edited by Jerry O'Sullivan, and Michael Stanley, pp. 11–24. National Roads Authority, Dublin.

Ginn, Victoria. 2012. *Settlement structure in Middle–Late Bronze Age Ireland*. PhD thesis, Queen's University Belfast.

Ginn, Victoria and Stuart Rathbone. 2012. *Corrstown, a coastal community: excavations of a Bronze Age village in Northern Ireland*. Oxbow, Oxford.

Gowen, Margaret, John Ó Néill and Michael Phillips (editors). 2005. *The Lisheen Mine a rchaeological project, 1996–8*. Wordwell, Bray.

Grogan, Eoin, Lorna O'Donnell and Penny Johnston. 2007. *The Bronze Age landscapes of the Pipeline to the West: an integrated archaeological and environmental assessment*. Wordwell, Bray.

Halliday, Strat P. 2000. Hut-circle settlements in the Scottish landscape. In *'We were always chasing time': papers presented to Keith Blood*, edited by Paul Frodsham, Peter Topping, and David C Cowley, pp. 49–65. Northern Archaeology 17/18 (1999). Northumberland Archaeology Group, Newcastle upon Tyne.

Halliday, Strat P. 2007. Unenclosed round-houses in Scotland: occupation, abandonment, and the character of settlement. In *Beyond Stonehenge: essays in honour of Colin Burgess*, edited by Christopher Burgess, Peter Topping, and Frances Lynch, pp. 49–56. Oxbow, Oxford.

Hart, Jonathan, James Rackham, Seren Griffiths and Dana Challinor. 2014. Burnt mounds along the Milford Haven to Brecon gas pipeline, 2006–07. *Archaeologia Cambrensis* 163:133–172.

Hawkes, Alan. 2014. The beginnings and evolution of the *fulacht fia* tradition in early prehistoric Ireland. *Proceedings of the Royal Irish Academy* 114C:89–139.

Hawkes, Alan. 2015. *Fulachtaí fia* and Bronze Age cooking in Ireland: reappraising the evidence. *Proceedings of the Royal Irish Academy* 115C:47–77.

Hawkes, Alan. 2018. *The archaeology of prehistoric burnt mounds in Ireland*. Archaeopress, Oxford.

Hey, Gill, Christopher Bell, Caroline Dennis and Mark Robinson. 2016. *Yarnton: Neolithic and Bronze Age settlement and landscape*. Thames Valley Landscapes, 39. Oxford University School of Archaeology, Oxford.

Hodges, Henry W M. 1958. A hunting camp at Cullyhanna Lough, near Newtown Hamilton, County Armagh. *Ulster Journal of Archaeology* 21:7–13.

Ingold, Tim. 2013. *Making: anthropology, archaeology, art and architecture*. Routledge, London.

Jobey, George. 1981. Green Knowe unenclosed platform settlement and Harehope cairn, Peeblesshire. *Proceedings of the Society of Antiquaries of Scotland* 110:72–113.

Johnson, Nicholas and Peter Rose. 1994. *Bodmin Moor: an archaeological survey. Volume 1— the human landscape to c.1800*. English Heritage, London.

Johnston, Penny, Jacinta Kiely and John Tierney. 2008. *Near the bend in the river: the archaeology of the N25 Kilmacthomas realignment*. NRA Scheme Monographs, 3. National Roads Authority, Dublin.

Jones, Andy M. 2008. Houses for the dead and cairns for the living: a reconsideration of the Early to Middle Bronze Age transition in south-west England. *Oxford Journal of Archaeology* 27(2):153–174.

Jones, Andy M. 2015. Ritual, rubbish or everyday life? Evidence from a Middle Bronze Age settlement in mid-Cornwall. *Archaeological Journal* 172(1):30–51.

Jones, Andy M, James Gossip and Henrietta Quinnell (editors). 2015. *Settlement and metalworking in the Middle Bronze Age and beyond: new evidence from Tremough, Cornwall.* Sidestone, Leiden.

Jones, Carleton. 1998. The discovery and dating of the prehistoric landscape of Roughan Hill in Co. Clare. *Journal of Irish Archaeology* 9:27–44.

Jones, Carleton. 2016. Dating ancient field walls in karst landscapes using differential bedrock lowering. *Geoarchaeology* 31(2):77–100.

Jones, Carleton. 2019. Climate change and farming response in a temperate oceanic zone—the exploitation of a karstic region in western Ireland in the third and second millennia BC. *Journal of Island and Coastal Archaeology.* DOI: 10.1080/15564894.2019.1614115

Kenney, Jane. 2012. Burnt mounds in north-west Wales: are these ubiquitous features really so dull? In *Reflections on the past: essays in honour of Frances Lynch*, edited by William J Britnell, and Robert J Silvester, pp. 280–302. Cambrian Archaeological Association, Welshpool.

Kitchen, Willy. 2001. Tenure and territoriality in the British Bronze Age. In *Bronze Age landscapes: tradition and transformation*, edited by Joanna Brück, pp. 110–120. Oxbow, Oxford.

Knight, Mark, Rachel Ballantyne, Iona Robinson Zeki and David Gibson. 2019. The Must Farm pile-dwelling settlement. *Antiquity* 93(369):645–663.

Ladle, Lilian and Ann Woodward. 2009. *Excavations at Bestwall Quarry, Wareham 1992–2005. Volume 1: the prehistoric landscape.* Dorset Natural History and Archaeological Society, Dorchester.

Lambrick, George. 2009. Hearth and home: buildings and domestic culture. In *The Thames through time: the archaeology of the gravel terraces of the Upper and Middle Thames. The Thames Valley in late prehistory: 1500 BC–AD 50*, edited by George Lambrick, and Mark Robinson, pp. 133–178. Oxford Archaeology, Oxford.

Lambrick, George and Tim Allen. 2004. *Gravelly Guy, Stanton Harcourt, Oxfordshire: the development of a prehistoric and Romano-British community.* Thames Valley Landscapes, 21. Oxford University School of Archaeology, Oxford.

Leigh, Margaret. 2018. *Spade among the rushes.* Birlinn Origin, Edinburgh.

Lynch, Frances. 1986. Excavation of a kerb circle and ring cairn on Cefn Caer Euni, Merioneth. *Archaeologia Cambrensis* 135:81–120.

Mallory, James P and Tom E McNeill. 1991. *The archaeology of Ulster: from colonisation to plantation.* Institute of Irish Studies, Belfast.

Manley, John. 1990. A Late Bronze Age landscape on the Denbigh Moors, northeast Wales. *Antiquity* 64:514–526.

McCullagh, Rod and Richard Tipping (editors). 1998. *The Lairg Project 1988–1996: the evolution of an archaeological landscape.* Scottish Trust for Archaeological Research, Edinburgh.

McLaughlin, T Rowan, Nicki J Whitehouse, Rick J Schulting, Meriel McClatchie, Philip Barratt and Amy Bogaard. 2016. The changing face of Neolithic and Bronze Age Ireland: a big data approach to the settlement and burial records. *Journal of World Prehistory* 29:117–153.

McQuade, Melanie. 2005. Archaeological excavation of a multi-period prehistoric settlement at Waterunder, Mell, Co. Louth. *Journal of the County Louth Archaeological and Historical Society* 26(1):31–66.

Mighall, Tim, Scott Timpany, Jane Wheeler, L Bailey, Mike Bamforth, L Gray and Maisie Taylor. 2018. Vegetation changes and woodland management associated with a prehistoric to medieval burnt mound complex at Ballygawley, Northern Ireland. *Environmental Archaeology* 23(3):267–285.

Mitchell, Timothy. 1988. *Colonising Egypt*. University of California Press, Berkeley, CA.

Mullin, David. 2003. *The Bronze Age landscapes of the northern English Midlands*. BAR British Series 351. Archaeopress, Oxford.

Nelis, Dermot. 2011. *M1 northern motorway Gormanston–Monasterboice (Drogheda bypass) Platin to Oldbridge. Chainage 21600–24800. Contract 7. 01E0390: Rathmullan 9. Final report*. Irish Archaeological Consultancy Ltd, Bray.

Newman, Phil. 2011. *The field archaeology of Dartmoor*. English Heritage, Swindon.

Nowakowski, Jacqueline A. 1991. Trethellan Farm, Newquay: the excavation of a lowland Bronze Age settlement and Iron Age cemetery. *Cornish Archaeology* 30:5–242.

Nowakowski, Jacqueline A. 2001. Leaving home in the Cornish Bronze Age: insights into planned abandonment processes. In *Bronze Age landscapes: tradition and transformation*, edited by Joanna Brück, pp. 139–148. Oxbow Books, Oxford.

Nowakowski, Jacqueline A and Charles Johns. 2015. *Bypassing Indian Queens, archaeological excavations 1992–1994: investigating prehistoric and Romano-British settlement and landscapes in Cornwall*. Cornwall Archaeological Unit, Truro.

O'Brien, William. 1994. *Mount Gabriel: Bronze Age mining in Ireland*. Galway University Press, Galway.

Ó Néill, John. 2005. Killoran 240. In *The Lisheen Mine Archaeological Project, 1996–8*, edited by Margaret Gowen, John Ó Néill, and Michael Phillips, pp. 267–269. Wordwell, Bray.

Ó Néill, John. 2009. *Burnt Mounds in northern and western Europe: a study in prehistoric technology and society*. VDM Verlag Dr. Müller, Saarbrücken.

O'Neil, Tara. 2013. Scartbarry 1—*fulacht fia*/sweat lodge. In *Generations: the archaeology of five national road schemes in County Cork. Volume 1: prehistoric sites*, edited by Ken Hanley, and Maurice F Hurley, pp. 105–110. NRA Scheme Monographs, 13. National Roads Authority, Dublin.

O'Sullivan, Aidan. 2007. Exploring past people's interactions with wetland environments in Ireland. *Proceedings of the Royal Irish Academy* 107C:147–203.

Pope, Rachel E. 2003. *Prehistoric dwelling: circular structures in north and central Britain c. 2500 BC – AD 500*. PhD thesis, University of Durham.

Pope, Rachel E. 2006. Ritual and the roundhouse: a critique of recent ideas on domestic space in later British prehistory. In *The Earlier Iron Age in Britain and the near continent*, edited by Colin C Haselgrove, and Rachel E Pope. Oxbow Books, Oxford.

Richie, J N Graham and John Crawford. 1977/1978. Excavations at Sorisdale and Killunaig, Coll. *Proceedings of the Society of Antiquaries of Scotland* 109:75–84.

Ripper, Susan and Matthew Beamish. 2011. Bogs, bodies and burnt mounds: visits to the Soar wetlands in the Neolithic and Bronze Age. *Proceedings of the Prehistoric Society* 78:173–206.

Roberts, Ian, Andrea Burgess and David Berg (editors). 2001. *A new link to the past: the archaeological landscape of the M1–A1 link road*. West Yorkshire Archaeology Service, Leeds.

Rudling, David (editor). 2002. *Downland settlement and land-use: the archaeology of the Brighton bypass*. Archetype and English Heritage, London.

Russell, Miles. 1996. Problems of phasing: a reconsideration of the Black Patch MBA "nucleated village". *Oxford Journal of Archaeology* 15(1):33–38.

Sahlins, Marshall. 2013. *What kinship is—and is not*. University of Chicago Press, Chicago.

Seager Thomas, Mike. 1999. Stone finds in context: a contribution to the study of later prehistoric artefact assemblages. *Sussex Archaeological Collections* 137:39–48.

Sharples, Niall. 2009. Beaker settlement in the Western Isles. In *Land and people: papers in memory of John G Evans*, edited by Michael J Allen, Niall Sharples, and Terry O'Connor, pp. 147–158. Prehistoric Society Research Papers, 2. Prehistoric Society/Oxbow Books, Oxford.

Simpson, Derek D A, Eileen M Murphy and Richard A Gregory. 2006. *Excavations at Northton, Harris*. BAR British Series, 408. Archaeopress, Oxford.

Siza, Alvaro. 1997. *Alvaro Silza: writings on architecture*. Skira Editore, Milan.

Smith, George, Astrid E Caseldine, Catherine J Griffiths, Inga Peck, Nigel Nayling and David Jenkins. 2017. An Early Bronze Age burnt mound trough and boat fragment with accompanying palaeobotanical and pollen analysis at Nant Farm, Porth Neigwl, Llŷn Peninsula, Gwynedd. *Studia Celtica* 51(1):1–63.

Stevenson, Jack B. 1984. The excavation of a hut circle at Cul a'Bhaile, Jura. *Proceedings of the Society of Antiquaries of Scotland* 114:127–160.

Stone, John F S. 1941. The Deverel-Rimbury settlement on Thorny Down, Winterbourne Gunner, S. Wilts. *Proceedings of the Prehistoric Society* 7:114–133.

Strachan, Richard and Andrew Dunwell. 2003. Excavations of Neolithic and Bronze Age sites near Peterhead, Aberdeenshire, 1998. *Proceedings of the Society of Antiquaries of Scotland* 133:137–171.

Suddaby, Ian. 2003. The excavation of two Late Bronze Age roundhouses at Ballyprior Beg, Island Magee, County Antrim. *Ulster Journal of Archaeology* 62:45–91.

Terry, John. 1993. Bodsberry Hill unenclosed platform settlement, near Elvanfoot, Strathclyde. *Glasgow Archaeological Journal* 18:49–63.

Terry, John. 1995. Excavation at Lintshie Gutter unenlosed platform settlement, Crawford, Lanarkshire, 1991. *Proceedings of the Society of Antiquaries of Scotland* 125:369–427.

Thomas, Nicholas. 2005. *Snail Down, Wiltshire: the Bronze Age barrow cemetery and related earthworks, in the parishes of Collingbourne Ducis and Collingbourne Kingston. Excavations, 1953, 1955 and 1957*. Wiltshire Archaeological and Natural History Society, Devizes.

Tierney, John, Margot Ryan and Áine Richardson. 2008. Beaker settlement: Area 2, Graigueshoneen TD. Licence no. 98E0575. In *Near the bend in the river: the archaeology of the N25 Kilmacthomas realignment*, edited by Penny Johnston, Jacinta Kiely, and John Tierney, pp. 33–38. NRA Scheme Monographs, 3. National Roads Authority, Dublin.

Timby, Jane, Richard Brown, Edward Biddulph, Alan Hardy and Andrew Powell. 2007. *A slice of rural Essex: archaeological discoveries from the A120 between Stansted Airport and Braintree*. Oxford Wessex Archaeology, Oxford and Salisbury.

Wainwright, Geoff J and Ken Smith. 1980. The Shaugh Moor Project: second report—the enclosure. *Proceedings of the Prehistoric Society* 46:65–122.

Ward, Michael and George Smith. 2001. The Llŷn Crop Marks Project. Aerial survey and ground evaluation of Bronze Age and Romano-British settlement and funerary sites in the Llŷn Peninsula of north west Wales: excavations by Richard Kelly and Michael Ward. *Studia Celtica* 35:1–87.

Webley, Leo. 2007. Using and abandoning roundhouses: a reinterpretation of the evidence from Late Bronze Age–Early Iron Age southern England. *Oxford Journal of Archaeology* 26(2):127–144.

Wheeler, Jane, Scott Timpany, Tim Mighall and L Scott. 2016. A palaeoenvironmental investigation of two prehistoric burnt mound sites in Northern Ireland. *Geoarchaeology* 31(6):506–529.

Wymer, John J and Nigel R Brown. 1995. *Excavations at North Shoebury: settlement and economy in south-east Essex, 1500 BC–AD 1500*. East Anglian Archaeology Report, 75. Essex County Council Archaeology Section, Chelmsford.

5

LIVING AND GATHERING

1400–700 BC

On a visit to the stone fort at Dún Aonghasa one summer, I lay down near the cliff's edge and inched forward until my head and arms hung over the sea. I looked 90 metres vertically down to the silent waves. Even now, seated by a desk in Sheffield, whenever I think about the experience my legs grow heavy with vertigo. Dún Aonghasa sits in an extraordinary position in an extraordinary landscape—the island of Árainn or Inis Mór, off Ireland's west coast (Figure 5.1).

FIGURE 5.1 Dún Aonghasa, on the south coast of Árainn—the figures are standing on *an bord*. © Gareth McCormack.

The fort's three circuits of walls were constructed in the eleventh or tenth century BC at a place above Árainn's highest cliffs. The walls were originally one to two metres in height, with subsequent enlargement and modern reconstructions raising them into higher and grander structures. Claire Cotter's (2012) excavations in the early- and mid-1990s uncovered plentiful evidence for Bronze Age occupation within both the middle and inner enclosures. Sheep and cattle, guillemots and shags, seals, wrasse and bream were the inhabitants' food from land and the sea. A wide scatter of clay crucible fragments and broken moulds lay within the more sheltered, western lee of the inner enclosure. The moulds were used for making a sword, spearheads, knives, bracelets, pins and axes. A large hearth in the enclosure's northwest corner might have been where metalworking took place.

The bedrock within the inner enclosure was quarried and levelled except for a low rectangular platform by the cliff's edge. The platform sits proud of its surrounding limestone and it is known as *an bord*, the table. It is a curious feature. One story, retold by Tim Robinson (1990), might help in thinking about how *an bord* relates to the enclosure and its setting. An excursion of 70 from the British Association's Ethnological Section visited Dún Aonghasa in 1857. In the manner of such events and of the time, the speeches began after the party had enjoyed the fine dinner and sherry they had carried up the hill in hampers. The Reverend Dr MacDonnell, Provost of Trinity College, Dublin, then took a position on *an bord*, a convenient dais from which he chaired the proceedings.

Dún Aonghasa was somewhere people dwelt, consumed food, and worked stone, bone and metal. It can be described as a settlement. The three walls enclose almost 6 hectares, with narrow entrances that controlled the routeway onto the hill. The walls limited access, and protected and projected the status of the enclosure's inhabitants. Dún Aonghasa meets the definition of a stone fort. It is and was a spectacular location, perched on land's edge, high above the Atlantic Ocean. *An bord*, the table or platform, was a stage with the western sky as its backdrop or audience. It is a position from which the significance of the place might have been performed into being. The juxtaposition of food, craft, architecture and performance was important. The materials and beings of everyday life were drawn to, transformed and consumed in a powerful place. The kin that were made and affirmed at Dún Aonghasa were distinct and powerful because of their association with the place.

This chapter describes the creation of places like Dún Aonghasa through the changes and continuities in how people dwelt in landscapes from the twelfth to eighth centuries BC. I examine the connections between three processes that define the transformation of dwelling places across the centuries of the late Bronze Age: intensity, gathering and performance. Dwelling places acquired a greater intensity of relations as more aspects of daily life and craftworking happened in and close to houses. Tasks and technologies, like pottery production and metalworking, appeared more frequently in domestic assemblages. People collaborated in building hilltop enclosures that required immense efforts and resources. The banks, ditches, palisades and walls accentuating the hills' topographies both physically and culturally, and they empowered the kindred who built and occupied them. The hilltop enclosures structured access and movement within and through landscapes. At a small number of enclosures, there is evidence of more intensive occupation comprising large gatherings and feasting. These were locations where metalworking occurred, and they were near to places where votive exchanges were performed at lakes, rivers and bogs. The performative characteristics of the enclosures were accentuated by elaborate architectural forms: circuits of water-filled ditches; dramatic cliff edge settings; circular ditches, banks and palisades and large central buildings. By the final centuries of the Bronze Age, a sophisticated culture of domestic life had emerged that blended performance, control, community and an intense connection with places.

Settlement tradition and flux, 1400–700 BC

There were similarities in the forms that dwelling places took through the eight centuries of the later Bronze Age. At Meadowend Farm, near the River Forth in Clackmannanshire, small groups of individual roundhouses were built and occupied intermittently from 1650–900 BC (Jones et al. 2018) (Figure 5.2). Throughout that time, there were few differences in how the settlement areas were organised or in the architecture of the roundhouses. The occupants utilised a mix of oak and hazel timber and cultivated naked barley. At Yarnton, Oxfordshire, the middle and late Bronze settlements had similar characteristics: pairs or single roundhouses dispersed across the landscape, along with pits, waterholes and fencelines (Hey et al. 2016). Cattle, sheep and, to a lesser degree, pigs were the primary livestock, with cattle forming the highest proportion of the later assemblages. Spelt and emmer wheat, naked barley and flax were cultivated.

Heathrow, Middlesex, offers an alternative example of this continuity. Excavations were completed ahead of the building of Terminal 5, on the western side of the airport, and at Imperial College Sports Ground and RMC Land, to the north (Lewis et al. 2010; Powell et al. 2015). The occupation spanning 1600–750 BC was located amongst hedged fields and tracks. At both Terminal 5 and Imperial College Sports Ground, the excavators had difficulty defining settlements among the fields because there were few clear buildings. Instead, they used occupation debris from pits, waterholes, wells and ditches, and environmental indicators such as pollen and plant remains, to define the foci for domestic life within the landscape. These foci were the places where people had dwelt among the field systems, tending crops and keeping animals. The lack of roundhouses at Terminal 5 could be explained by a twentieth-century sludge works that truncated the archaeological layers. Despite this, a large cluster of Iron Age roundhouses and four-posters survived across the middle of the excavation area, demonstrated the persistence of settlement features in at least parts of the site. The Bronze Age dwelling places in the Heathrow landscape were less durable than their later, Iron Age, counterparts, relatively short-lived and shifting, perhaps, from one location to another depending on access to waterholes and the uses to which particular fields were put (Lambrick 2009, 74).

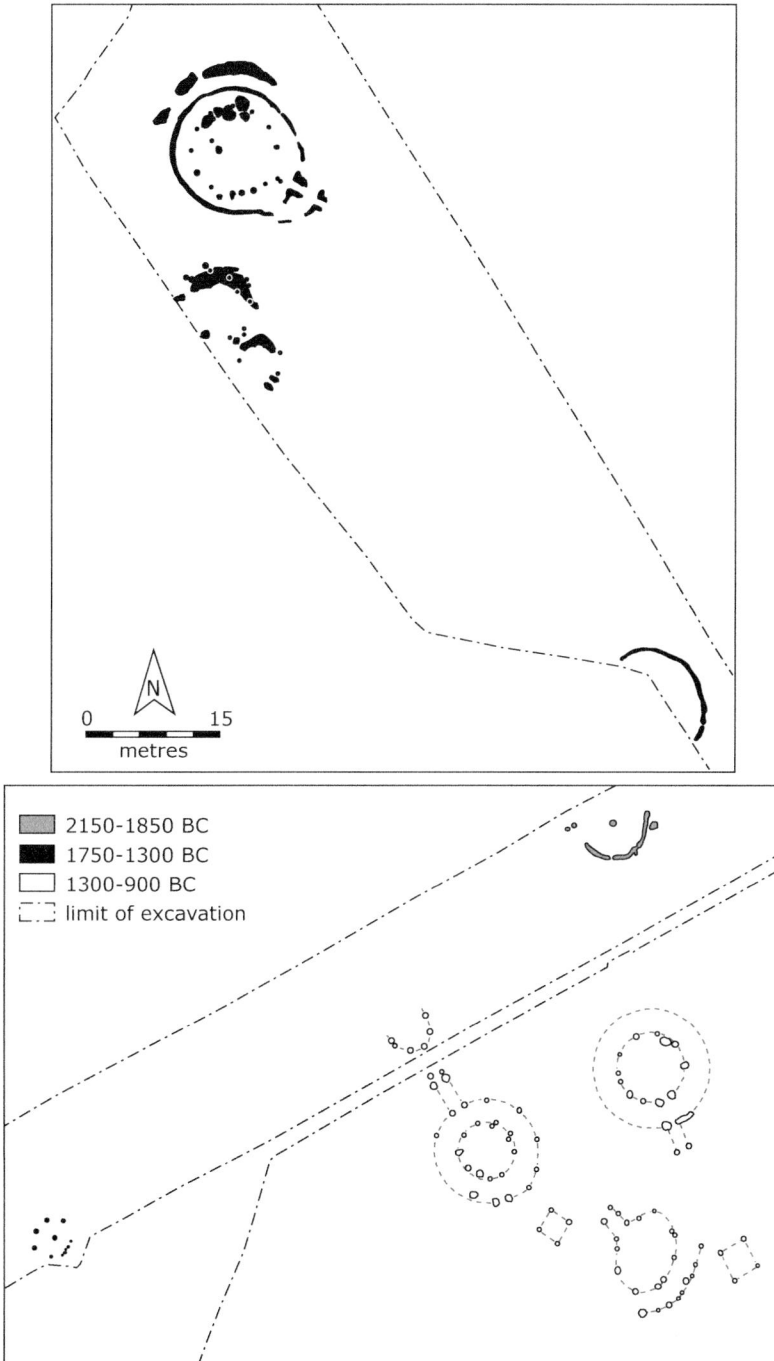

FIGURE 5.2 Plan of the Bronze Age domestic structures at Meadowend Farm, Clackmannanshire. Adapted from Jones et al. 2018.

Dwelling gradually transformed locales to varying intensities. In southern and midland Britain, excavations have uncovered late Bronze Age settlement activity dispersed across several hectares. As with the examples of large settlements I introduce in Chapter 4, the late Bronze Age locales emerged over decades and usually centuries of inhabitation. Rather than ordered, nucleated 'villages', these were places where generations occupied the same locale, with the locations of houses shifting periodically. The residues and memories of earlier dwellings contributed to a locale's kinship.

The excavations at Dunch Hill on Salisbury Plain uncovered four roundhouses spaced along a distance of 330 metres within what was probably a more extensive area of settlement, perhaps 4–5 hectares—the excavations were confined to a corridor 12 metres wide (Andrews 2006; Bradley et al. 1994). A group of four-post structures were also excavated, and these were the only features associated with charred cereals (emmer wheat and hulled barley), supporting their interpretation as raised grain storage. A group of fenced enclosures located beyond the roundhouses might have served as pens for livestock, probably sheep. Environmental evidence indicated a landscape of open pasture with the possibility of some arable cultivation nearby. At Tower Hill, on the Berkshire Downs, the roundhouses and four-post structures, which were occupied during the eighth century BC, formed a settlement covering an area of up to 4 hectares (Miles et al. 2003).

A pattern of shifting settlement areas is visible in the excavated remains at Cassington, on the western edge of the Yarnton landscape (Figure 5.3). A field team from Oxford Archaeology excavated 14 roundhouses, several D-shaped and rectangular buildings and up to 20 four-post structures (Hey et al. 2016, 47–49). Some of the structures intercut one another, indicating that they were not all in use concurrently, and scientific dates span 1000–850 BC. The roundhouses were relatively dispersed around the settlement area, while the four-post structures were located in two clusters and the waterholes formed a rough alignment on the eastern edge of the excavated area. A similarly large, though widely dispersed, area of settlement was excavated at Shorncote, Gloucestershire, by Wessex Archaeology (Hearne and Adam 1999).

In parts of East Anglia and the English Midlands, more durable domestic architecture appears in the archaeological record for the first time during the twelfth and eleventh centuries. Open settlements of roundhouses were occupied amongst abandoned field systems (for example, Godwin Ridge, Over Narrows: Evans, Tabor, et al. 2016, 151). For the Midlands, the excavations at Huntsman's Quarry, near Kemerton, Worcestershire, identified eleventh-century settlement in an already established field system (Jackson 2015), in a region that otherwise lacks evidence for durable Bronze Age settlements (Hurst 2011).

Huntsman's Quarry lies on gently sloping glacial gravels, about 1 kilometre from where the ground rises towards Bredon Hill (Jackson 2015). During the eleventh century BC, the landscape was grazed grassland, partly enclosed with thorny hedges, with some cultivated ground and nearby stands of woodland.

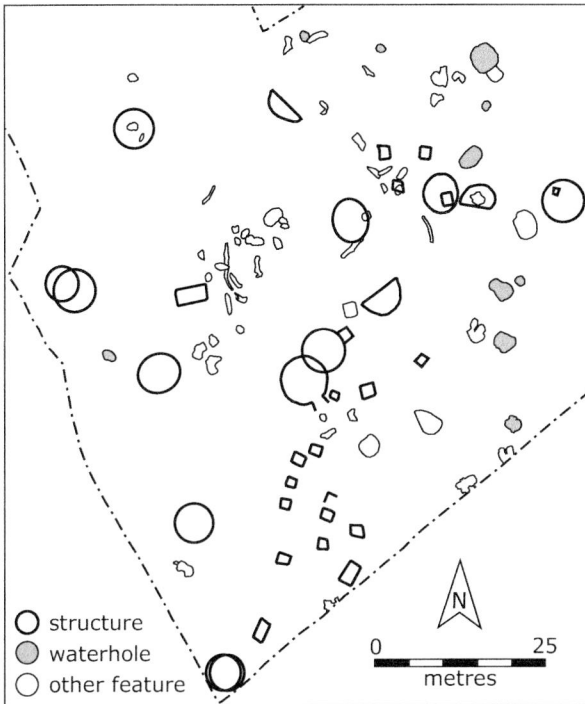

FIGURE 5.3   Plan of the tenth- to ninth-century structures at Cassington, Oxfordshire. Adapted from Hey et al. 2016.

The excavated Bronze Age occupation covered more than 8 hectares and dated
within the range 1130–960 BC. The waterholes, buildings and pits were set
amongst boundary ditches that were reorganised on one occasion, although their
chronological relationship with the settlement is unclear. One group of three
post-built roundhouses, arranged in a line, sat alongside a smaller rectangular
building and a large fenced enclosure. A further fenced enclosure lay 70 metres
away, with two waterholes and a rectangular 'pen' in its interior. This central
zone formed the most coherent part of the excavated area. The greatest quantities of cultural material were excavated from pits and the upper layers of waterholes. These included large quantities of burnt stone, worked flint, undecorated
post-Deverel-Rimbury pottery and animal bone. The domestic faunal remains
comprised cattle, sheep, pigs and dogs, and there was some evidence for the cultivation of cereals and flax. Robin Jackson (2015, 156) argues in the conclusion to
the publication of Huntsman's Quarry that the domestic occupation of the landscape periodically shifted between several locations around the landscape during
at most 160 years. The deposition of cultural material in large pits and waterholes
marked events in the lifecycle of each settlement's inhabitants.

The investigations at Reading Business Park, east of the Berkshire Downs, in
the Kennet Valley, uncovered a cluster of 15 roundhouses (Brossler et al. 2004;

Moore and Jennings 1992). There was relatively little evidence for repair of the buildings, and only two of the post-rings partially overlapped, which might indicate some contemporaneity of the buildings. The post-Deverel-Rimbury ceramics collected from the settlement tell a different story. The pottery includes both undecorated and decorated forms, with the decorated wares more common on later sites. The decorated pottery was more prevalent on the western side of the occupied area, leading Elaine Morris (2004, 80) to propose that the domestic buildings in the eastern area were abandoned when a large mound of burnt flint began accumulating. The variation in the pottery indicates a longer duration than the life of an unrepaired building, therefore contemporaneity of the roundhouses does not seem likely. As with Kemerton, the settlements were small, and occupied year-round for a short duration before shifting elsewhere.

If we accept the iterative, shifting character of the domestic occupation in these examples, then the difficulty we have is understanding over what durations the groups of buildings were occupied. At Bestwall Quarry, on the edge of Poole Harbour, Dorset, the domestic buildings and occupation areas were sited within an established network of grazed and cultivated fields (Ladle and Woodward 2009). During 1500–1200 BC, the houses were sited apart from one another, dispersed amongst the fields. The chronological modelling estimates that the houses stood for less than a century, with two of the buildings standing for longer than this—up to two centuries (Bayliss et al. 2009, 126–153). After 950 BC, and with a change to the use of post-Deverel-Rimbury ceramics, houses were more obviously clustered, including a pair and a group of three buildings. The post-950 BC clusters shifted southwards between three locations during a period of 50–140 years, and the buildings were occupied for shorter durations than the pre-1200 BC houses. The northernmost, smallest and earliest post-950 BC occupation ('settlement 1') spans 15–50 years. The other two settlements are each estimated to have been occupied for longer, perhaps two or even three human generations. This difference could be a consequence of the fewer radiocarbon measurements from 'settlement 1'; the numbers of buildings and pits increased as the settlements moved southwards.

The tenth to ninth-century settlement areas at Bestwall are likely to have outlasted a human generation. Some roundhouses were maintained for longer than the life of the individuals who first built and inhabited them. If we accept some interdependence between the lifecycles of the roundhouses and the kinfolk who were their inhabitants (Brück 1999), then there was some generation-to-generation inheritance of domestic spaces. There were moments when the kinship with a settlement area ended. New dwellings were built close by and kindred with and inhabitation of the wider locale continued. The three settlements were spread across 400 metres and occupied sequentially. Ruinous settlements remained visible and remembered within the fields that animals grazed and people cultivated. Even robbed of reusable materials, a building remained a decaying tumble of timbers and roof matter. After years of trampling and neglect, posthole hollows and reed-filled pits and waterholes would be part of the localities.

In Scotland's Western and Northern Isles, substantial domestic buildings appear again during the twelfth and eleventh centuries BC having been rare since the later third millennium. At Cladh Hallan, South Uist, a 'terrace' of at least three buildings was well-preserved by an overburden of sand (Parker Pearson et al. 2004). The floors of the buildings were relaid on up to 14 occasions, and the excavators interpret the calibrated radiocarbon dates as evidence for 700 years of occupation, between 1100 and 400 BC. In Orkney, settlements have been excavated at Links of Noltland on Westray and Tofts Ness on Sanday (Dockrell 2007). The buildings at Links of Noltland are paired, comparable with examples from Shetland, and the excavators infer from the dating evidence that they were occupied earlier—from the mid-second millennium BC (Moore and Wilson 2011, 38) (Figure 5.4).

A distinctive feature of these settlements is the middens accompanying the houses. At Tofts Ness, a raised arable soil surrounded the buildings. It was formerly a midden, first cultivated in the Neolithic, and then extended and enriched with waste from the settlement, including night soil (Guttmann 2005; Simpson et al. 1998). Houses were excavated at various locations on Shetland, including Sumburgh and Jarlshof, located towards the south of the islands (Downes and Lamb 2000). There is good evidence at both locations that the buildings were divided between living space and stalls for animals, probably cattle. At

FIGURE 5.4 A conjoined pair of Bronze Age houses at Links of Noltland, Westray, Orkney. Photography by Graeme Wilson; copyright EASE Archaeology.

Sumburgh, craft activities were focussed around the southwest side of the central hearth within an area that seems to have been partially screened off with stone orthostats. The Shetland houses were commonly in pairs of main and ancillary structures or showed a marked bipartite division of space with an inner dwelling and outer 'courtyard'.

Arjun Appadurai (1996, 181) observed that '[l]ocality is ephemeral unless hard and regular work is undertaken to produce and maintain its materiality'. This work, through inhabitation, was a characteristic of later Bronze Age dwelling places. Over years, decades, sometimes centuries and through the lives of people, animals and houses, locales acquired their kindred. As domestic life in one group of houses ended, a new house cluster was established close by. This territorialisation of kin extended the 'household' in time and space and maintained a relationship between kindred and land. The medieval Welsh concept *gwely* can offer inspiration for this interpretation (Jones 1996). *Gwely*, literally 'bed', was the term used for a deep lineage and for the land and properties held within the lineage. *Gwely* was a place or territory and a kindred. Where archaeologists have excavated and scientifically dated late Bronze Age domestic occupation across landscapes like Kemerton, Bestwall Quarry and Yarnton, they have identified these shifting households. Through small generational movements, kindred built a deep attachment to land.

Making households, 1150–700 BC

For all the elements of continuity that I stressed in the previous section, the formation of dwelling places gradually, subtly changed during the later centuries of the second millennium BC. The process can be illustrated by Gwithian, on Cornwall's north coast, close to Land's End. Gwithian was settled and farmed during the eighteenth to tenth centuries BC, through which time the character of occupation intensified (Nowakowski 2009). An enlarged settlement of six buildings arranged around a yard was established after the twelfth century BC. This settlement produced evidence for an intensity of domestic life that was not present previously at Gwithian. Grain storage, pottery production, tools for working leather, textiles and metal were all evidenced in this area of the site.

The process exemplified by Gwithian occurred more widely across Britain and Ireland. In her review of material from southern Britain, Joanna Brück (2007) recognises a greater artefactual range amongst settlements dated after the twelfth century BC. Items of worked bone and metalwork were more common. The crafting of ceramics, metalwork, textiles and shale is visible in archaeological collections. The evidence is not as clear for Ireland, where Ginn (2012, 188) documents an increase in 'potential exchange valuables'. These were primarily items of metalwork, along with glass and amber. The so-called 'four-post' structures recorded during many excavations of later settlements are interpreted as raised storage, probably for cereal or fodder, and as racks on which pots or textiles might be dried. Rachel Sites (2015) identifies a marked increase in the numbers and size of storage structures (pits and four-post structures) from the twelfth century, which corresponds with regional reviews of the evidence (Robinson and Lambrick 2009, 271–272).

The traces of craftwork and making took varied forms, some of which were dependent on locality. Brean Down is a narrow high promontory that reaches into the Bristol Channel (Bell 1990). For a time during the twelfth to tenth centuries BC (the pottery is early within this range), salt production took place within one and maybe two adjacent roundhouses on the promontory's south side, where its slopes joined the mainland. The briquetage (a term used for the coarse ceramics used in salt-making) comprised broken pedestals and evaporation trays. They were concentrated on the east of the building's hearth, where brine carried up from the nearby shoreline could be evaporated with heat from the fire. The small excavated area makes it difficult to judge the intensity of salt-making that happened at Brean Down. It was associated with the houses and, Martin Bell (1990, 260–262) proposes in his conclusion to the excavation report, salt-making was one of the household's several seasonal activities. At Reading Business Park (introduced above) an area was set aside for processing textiles from plants which may have been grown in fields close by (Moore and Jennings 1992). Large pits, arranged in a line, were dug deep enough to fill with groundwater and contained the seeds of cultivated flax together with nettle and several other species. The excavators interpret this as evidence the pits were used for retting the fibres from the flax and possibly nettle too.

Craft, salt production, stored grain and fodder broadened and intensified the activities that occurred within and close to houses. These materials and tasks were drawn in from the surrounding landscape, where earlier in the Bronze Age they had occurred in weaker associations with houses and households. Their proximity to domestic life during the late Bronze Age enabled new forms of kinwork within settlements. The relations outward from dwelling places into the landscape changed as well. Clay, metal, brine, plants and animals flowed through and were transformed within dwelling places. Crafted objects and substances carried the places and the kin into the wider world. Households and living places intensified their roles in transforming materials and as the origins of things and people.

Bestwall Quarry, Dorset, offers an example of this shift in relations (Ladle and Woodward 2009). Evidence for pottery production was recovered from beaker, Deverel-Rimbury and post-Deverel-Rimbury contexts. In the fifteenth to eleventh centuries BC, the features associated with pottery production were isolated or amongst groups of pits sited away from buildings. Pits were generally more scattered during this period. It was only during the tenth and ninth centuries BC that the features associated with ceramic production and other craft activities were consistently sited amongst roundhouses and settlement debris.

While the forms of vessels changed during a millennium of pottery production at Bestwall, and people made use of different local clay sources, there was a continued preference for grog as a filler (Ladle and Woodward 2009, 313). Grog was used in the post-Deverel-Rimbury pottery at Bestwall, when elsewhere in southern Britain there was a shift to using white stone such as calcite and limestone. Grog is broken and ground ceramics—recycled pots. Its use throughout the Bronze Age at Bestwall connected generations of potters through their materials and their craft. Grog persisted even as the place of craft shifted from being dispersed and apart from roundhouses to being closely associated with house-life.

Tinney's Lane, Sherborne, is 40 kilometres inland from Bestwall and sited close to the River Yeo. Excavations in 2002 uncovered twelfth- to tenth-century BC buildings and exceptional evidence for pottery production, which were protected by a layer of colluvium up to 0.5 metre in depth (Best and Woodward 2011). The settlement was occupied for no more than 220 years (probably briefer), when it was surrounded by an open landscape and, judging by the faunal remains, grazed by sheep and cattle. The excavators identified seven activity areas, where pottery was made and fired, some of which comprised separate phases of occupation on the same location (Figure 5.5). Clay was extracted at Tinney's Lane and brought in from nearby sources. There were pits for holding water, bone tools for smoothing and decorating the pots' surfaces, and racks and stone slabs for drying the vessels. The potters fired the vessels in bonfires of ash, oak and maple, which left patches of heavily burnt stone and bedrock. They sometimes used pits for the firings, with perforated clay objects providing spacers between the stacked pots. Single post-built roundhouses stood within 15 metres of most of the activity areas. There were close spatial associations between the dwellings and craft practice.

The excavators recovered 98 kilograms of post-Deverel-Rimbury jars, bowls and cups from Tinney's Lane, representing more than 1,000 vessels. The broken pottery recovered from the activity areas comprised pots that failed during the firing process (wasters) and others that were broken accidently (Figure 5.6). Based on the quantity of broken pots, which might account for 5–10 percent of the fired vessels, Joanne Best and Ann Woodward (2011, 246) estimate that 550–1100 vessels were made during the occupation of each activity area and its associated dwelling. This goes beyond the production of pottery for the households at Tinney's Lane. Similar fabrics were found at South Cadbury, 7.5 kilometres distant and not further afield, which is a pattern of local production, use and deposition that characterises most post-Deverel-Rimbury pottery assemblages (Morris 1994). Like Bestwall Quarry, Tinney's Lane illustrates the mutuality of dwelling and making, household and craft. Tinney's Lane differs in the intensities and quantities of pottery making that have survived—the protective blanket of colluvium offers only a partial explanation. It was a place especially defined by its craft.

Pottery production was the most visible though not the only pyro-technology practised at Tinney's Lane and Bestwall. Both excavations produced evidence for bronze casting in the form of clay moulds (at both sites), crucible fragments (Bestwall) and pieces of hearth lining and a tuyère (bellows-connecting rod)

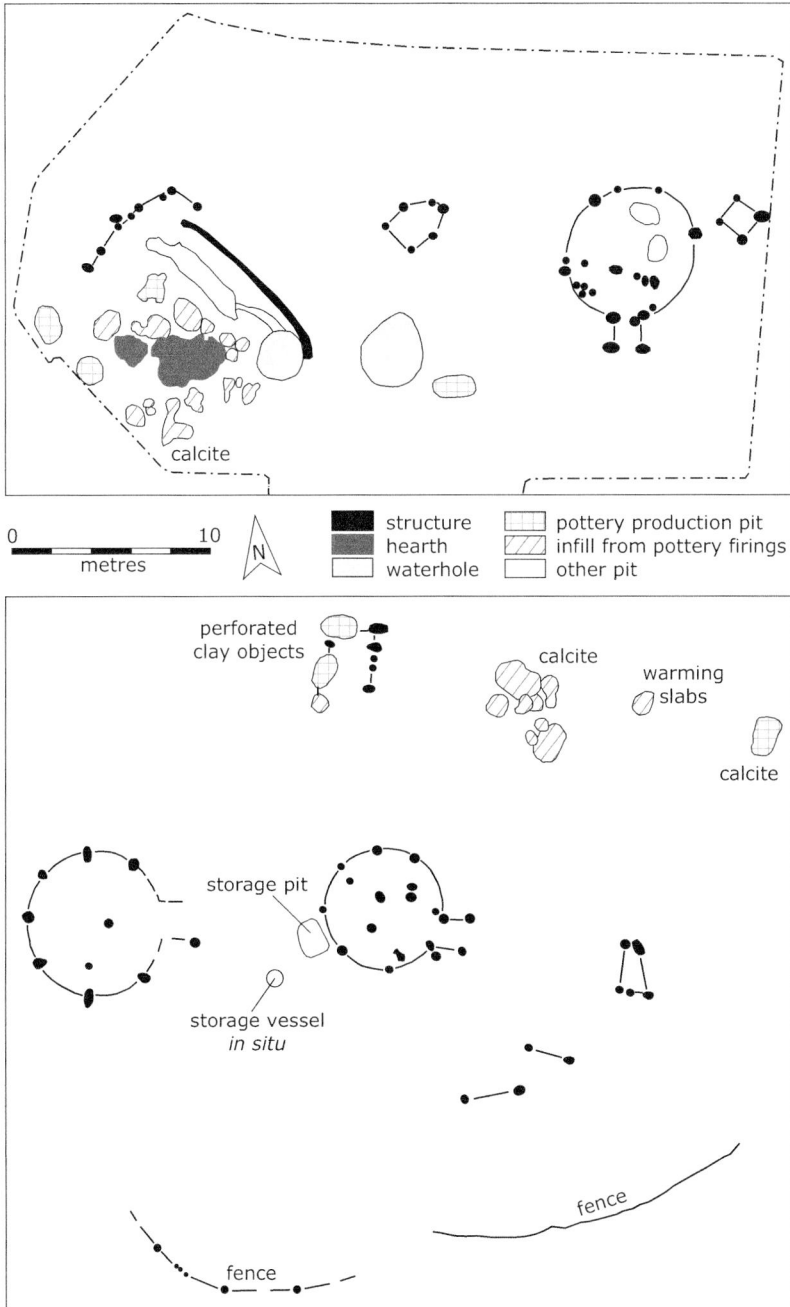

FIGURE 5.5   Two spatially separate examples of how pottery production was organised within the settlement at Tinney's Lane, Dorset. Adapted from Best and Woodward 2011.

FIGURE 5.6 Pottery within a pit at Tinney's Lane, Dorset, including wasters, cup and spindle whorl. Copyright: Exeter Archaeology.

(Tinney's Lane). The refractory debris was only present in post-Deverel-Rimbury contexts (tenth and ninth centuries) at Bestwall and found within pits amongst the settlement areas. The chronological distribution matches the pattern in Britain. Tremough, Cornwall, is an exception (Pearce 2015). Nine stone moulds and a fragment of clay mould were recovered from an infill deposit of the roundhouse at Tremough. Andy Jones (2015, 195) interprets the moulds as offerings marking the building's abandonment. The moulds were placed directly on the floor around an area of scorched clay and the hearth, where geochemical analysis identified enrichment with copper (Marshall and Solman 2015, 109). Taking the radiocarbon dates and stylistic analysis together, Susan Pearce (2015, 99) concludes that the moulds were most likely deposited late in the fourteenth and early thirteenth centuries BC.

There was a knowledgeable association between metalworking and the life of the settlement at Tremough that is usually absent from settlements until the twelfth century BC. Joanna Brück (2007, 34–35) identified materials associated with metalworking at a quarter of the 68 late Bronze Age settlements she reviewed in southern Britain. Refractory debris comprising fragments of moulds and crucibles, raw copper or furnace lining was excavated at around a fifth of the open settlements and the majority of middens and ringworks. This pattern continues elsewhere in Britain (Hunter et al. 2006, 53) and, to a lesser extent, in Ireland (Ginn 2012, 296). Stuart Needham and Susan Bridgford (2013, 69–71) list 36 finds of late Bronze Age refractory waste from Britain. With few exceptions, these were recovered from pits, ditches, middens and waterholes.

The refractory debris excavated amongst settlement remains could be evidence that metal casting occurred within or nearby to dwellings. A closer contextual study of the material indicates that metalworking debris, and perhaps metalworking as practice, occurred within peripheral associations (in time or space) with settlements. When synthesising the evidence from the houses at Jarlshof,

Shetland, John Hamilton (1956, 23) interpreted the final phase of occupation in one building (dwelling III—following Hamilton's numbering) as a 'smithy'. Finds from the building included broken clay moulds for casting swords and axes, and there was a hearth and a pit with sand that the excavator, Alexander Curle (1932/1933, 92) suggested held moulds during casting. Small numbers of broken clay moulds were scattered within deposits in two of the buildings and in the middens at Jarlshof (Figure 5.7). As with Tremough, the refractory assemblage accumulated once the use of the buildings ended. In dwelling III, stone slabs were placed on top of the hearth and the sand-filled pit, and then cultural material was scattered or accumulated on the floor. Many of the mould fragments, for casting swords and axes, were excavated from a small blocked-off chamber on the southeast side of the entrance (Curle 1931/1932, 120) (Figure 5.8). In dwelling IV, two stone-lined, sand-filled boxes were sunk into the floor blocking access to one of the chambers (Curle 1933/1934, 234). Parts of an unused clay sword mould were placed in the boxes together with animal bones. Curle recovered a few mould fragments from the building's floor deposits. Like dwelling III, the main concentration of refractory waste was in a small blocked recess on the building's southeast side.

The refractory waste and, less assuredly, the hearths and pits within the buildings demonstrate that swords, axes and spearheads were cast at Jarlshof. Defining

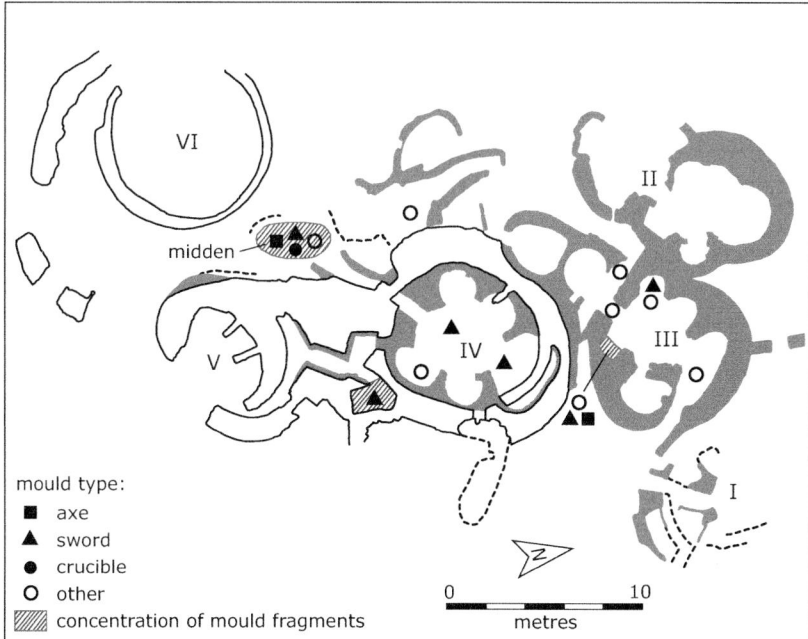

FIGURE 5.7   A plan of the buildings at Jarlshof, Shetland, showing the distribution of mould and crucible fragments. Adapted from Hamilton 1956.

FIGURE 5.8 Excavation photograph during Alexander Curle's excavations at Jarlshof in 1932—the blocked niche in the top left of the image was the focus for the deposition of metalworking moulds in Building III. © Courtesy of HES (Early photographs of sculptured stones).

the buildings as smithies or workshops is more problematic. Mould fragments were distributed within the deposits above the floors of two dwellings. These were also the places where Curle found numerous pieces of worked sandstone and slate, worked animal bone and small amounts of broken pottery. These were items of waste, though far from being inert, they drew powerful and valuable relations into the dwelling when a period of occupation ended. Some of these relations are discernible. The 'roughly-fashioned stone implements' (Curle 1933/1934, 308) included many examples of what are now recognised as mattocks and ard shares (Clarke 2006). The stones' connection with breaking ground and tillage led to their deposition around the edges of early Bronze Age burial monuments in the Northern Isles. Jane Downes suggests they continued to have associations with regeneration or renewal when incorporated in the closing deposits of dwellings (Downes and Lamb 2000, 126). The refractory debris took on a similar role. The difference between the agricultural implements and the refractory debris was that the latter's deposition concentrated in blocked recesses on the southeast sides of the buildings. This was not an exclusive pattern, although it is sufficient to suggest the refractory debris had a particular potency that meant it was treated differently to worked stone.

The associations of metalworking with the buildings at Jarlshof were peripheral in time (amongst the abandonment layers) and in space (concentrated in niches and in a midden). Elsewhere, the debris was placed in ditches and pits on the peripheries of settlement areas. At Kemerton, Worcestershire, clay mould fragments were excavated from a large pit and several waterholes. The majority of the mould fragments came from a bowl-shaped pit located outside the entrance to a fenced enclosure and 50 metres from the nearest roundhouses (Jackson 2015, 42). The pit lay open for sufficiently long for silt to gather in its base. Then it was backfilled with several kilograms of domestic debris: pottery, animal bone, charcoal and burnt stone, flaked stone, fragments of clay moulds and hearth lining. Radiocarbon measurements and chronological modelling date the material to the eleventh century BC. The debris was collected from elsewhere at Kemerton and deposited within the pit. Similar deposits were placed in waterholes at Kemerton. In three instances, the waterholes contained metalworking debris that, along with larger quantities of pottery, animal bone and flaked stone, were deposited once the waterholes went out of use. The incorporation of pieces from moulds and crucibles changed the properties of the materials with which it mixed. Its potency was more suitable for peripheries or thresholds, set apart from dwellings.

Miltor Mator Common, near Dainton, Devon, offers a different setting for the deposition of refractory material. Dainton is a place where fragments of later prehistoric field boundaries and cairns survive on the limestone hills of south Devon. Quarrying largely destroyed the fields and cairns on Miltor Mator Common. A small area of the damage was mitigated through excavation in the mid-1970s (Silvester 1980). The excavations recovered pottery, worked stone and refractory waste, and no evidence for dwellings. Most of the refractory waste, comprising parts of clay moulds and crucibles, was packed tightly within a small pit in the limestone bedrock. Stuart Needham (1980) recognised three casting episodes, based on the composition of the clay in the mould fragments. The moulds from the castings produced three spearheads, two ferrules, two swords and rings, in styles that fit with a date in the tenth century BC. The crucibles resulted from a longer duration of metalworking. They had been relined on several occasions, representing up to six castings (Needham 1980, 213), before their breakage and deposition.

None of the moulds or crucibles were deposited in their entirety within the pit at Dainton, and they were in varying states of wear and fragmentation. Some material was scattered through the soil overlying the pit, although this does not account for all the absent fragments. It is likely that the material accumulated elsewhere, probably nearby given the fragility of the broken moulds, and then a proportion was deposited in the pit. There was a degree of selectivity: half of the largest crucible was present in the pit, and there was equal representation of moulds in each of the two main clay fabrics. The pit was created by prising out slabs of limestone to make an irregular hole in the bedrock (Silvester 1980, 20). There were no other pits or postholes in the excavated areas, and the pit's only purpose was for the deposition of the refractory debris. Occupation debris— pottery, worked stone and animal bone—was scattered throughout the soil and in nearby cairns. Wherever the metalworker crafted the objects at Dainton, some of the residue from the craftwork was gathered and placed in the ground.

Three locations (Lough Gur, Galmisdale and Lough Eskragh) place metal-working apart from, though in proximity with, settlement. Beginning in 1936, Seán Ó Ríordáin committed 16 years to excavating sites around Lough Gur, County Limerick (Grogan and Eogan 1987). Of the 14 later prehistoric 'habita-tion sites' Ó Ríordáin investigated, 3 produced evidence for Bronze Age metal-working (R. Cleary 2018). 'Circle K' is a near-circular stone-walled enclosure on the hillside overlooking the lough. Thirty metres across, its entrance on the southeast arc of the circle was flanked by two pairs of large postholes. Clay mould fragments, possibly from making a sword blade, were recovered in a deposit im-mediately outside the enclosure's wall. A bronze awl, broken pieces of bronze, including casting waste, and blue-glass beads were found inside the enclosure. There were no definite contemporary buildings, although early Neolithic houses did survive. Two hundred and fifty metres from Circle K, close to Lough Gur's shore, Ó Ríordáin (1954, 415–425) excavated an isolated rectangular structure and field wall adjoining a low crag. The structures were historic, perhaps medi-eval, in date. Fortuitously, the wall adjacent to the crag preserved a hearth, late Bronze Age pottery and a collection of a 100 or so clay mould fragments. Traces of looped spearheads and rapier blades could be discerned in the larger mould pieces. Of the locations at Lough Gur where metalworking debris was excavated, only one produced definite evidence for domestic occupation. If metalworking occurred at the sites, then it was peripheral to the main areas of settlement on Knockadoon Hill and around the lough.

Galmisdale on Eigg, part of the Small Isles on Scotland's west coast, offers a second example of metalworking apart from though within the proximity of dwellings (Cowie 2001; RCAHMS 2003). In 2001, an islander, the late Brigg Lancaster, chose a prominent boulder on the hillside near his house to bury a cat. While digging a hole in the lee of the boulder, he turned up broken clay moulds and crucible fragments. The moulds were used to make at least two socketed axes, a knife and other objects that cannot be reconstructed because the fragments are too small. The boulder had long been a local landmark: a cache of third millennium BC worked flint was found during further investigations by the National Museum of Scotland. A large roundhouse sits 50 metres away from the boulder, and it may be contemporary with the metalworking. Even if the roundhouse were contemporary, as with Lough Gur, the metalworking at Galmisdale took place some way apart from the dwelling.

Lough Eskragh lies to the west of Dungannon, County Tyrone. Lowered water levels in the lough in 1953 and 1973 exposed later prehistoric timber struc-tures at several locations (Collins and Seaby 1960; Williams 1978). Radiocarbon measurements placed one of the structures in the twelfth to tenth centuries BC. It was a roughly circular platform, nine metres in diameter, and comprised of timber and brushwood. Its edge was defined by piles and the presence of burnt daub might indicate a continuous wall or fence. The excavators recovered refractory debris (fragments of crucibles and clay moulds for blades and axes), a few small pieces of bronze, broken querns and a peck-marked boulder, which they interpreted as an anvil. The platform was constructed on waterlogged ground on the lough's margin. Was this small enclosed space chosen for metalworking? Alternatively, like Galmisdale, were the residues from metalworking taken to a peripheral setting for deposition?

The debris from casting metal, commonly mould and crucible fragments, has been excavated frequently within or near to dwelling places. These associations were peripheral though no less important for their status as 'edgelands'. At Jarlshof, Shetland, Alexander Curle excavated refractory waste from buildings and middens. The concentrations of material were in specific locations, which were blocked recesses or cells close to the buildings' entrances. The mixture of refractory and domestic waste at Jarlshof was present at Kemerton, Worcestershire, where again the refractory waste was treated differently to other materials. Its deposition was restricted and on the margins, at the entrance to an enclosure and away from dwellings. In differing respects, Lough Gur, Dainton, Galmisdale and Lough Eskragh reproduce this pattern. The places for casting, or the places where casting debris was deposited, may have been nearby to dwellings though not within or immediately adjacent to them. At Lough Eskragh, this was edgeland, on made-ground by the lake. At Galmisdale, it was a large boulder a few 100 metres from the nearest roundhouse. These places betray a familiarity with localities. The clay used for making the moulds at Dainton was sourced locally. Hillary Howard (in Needham 1980, 194) concludes her analysis of the clays by observing that the craftspeople were 'sufficiently familiar with the working properties of the many diverse nearby deposits to select clays adequate for their specialized requirement'.

Considering the variety of crafts and substances that were assembled in dwelling places during the late Bronze Age, settlements became sites that were more complex and knotted with relations, drawn tighter and more intensely into domestic life. The peculiar circumstances of the ninth-century Must Farm pile dwelling's destruction offers an insight into daily life that is extraordinary for its detail and variety (Knight et al. 2019). Within a year of their construction, a catastrophic fire consumed the settlement's buildings and their contents, which then collapsed into a slow-moving river channel, where the water quenched the fire and the wet silts protected organic materials. Mark Knight and colleagues from the Cambridge Archaeological Unit excavated the settlement's 'material intensity': 'wooden artefacts, pottery sets, bronze tools and weapons, fabrics and fibres, querns, loom weights, spindle whorls, articulated and butchered animal remains, charred plants and seeds' (Knight et al. 2019, 655). The spools of twine and the textiles, 90 pieces of metalwork and over 100 pottery vessels, some with their contents intact, are traces of life stilled by the silts.

There was differentiation in the process by which dwelling places increased in their complexity and importance for social life. Some making—ceramics and salt are examples—took place in or next to houses and the residues accumulated with limited sorting and separation. Metalworking created residues that were potent and perhaps dangerous. They were sometimes incorporated into domestic spaces, or at least their peripheries. Through the increased intensity of their relations, dwelling places were themselves more powerful and therefore able to contain, control and benefit from metalworking's residues. This may not have been a change in the status of metal casting. Metalworking, as a craft and through the persons practising the craft, may have associated with different domains of kinship that were kept at a social distance from daily life.

Marking in and out, 1150–700 BC

Settlements were inconsistently enclosed in Ireland and Britain during the later Bronze Age, with clusters of enclosed sites in some regions. For Ireland, Vicky Ginn identified enclosures at around 35 percent of the 192 excavated settlements she reviewed, with the majority of these dating before 1150 BC (Ginn 2012, 195). I described the enclosures at Chancellorsland and the lakeside enclosed settlement at Cullyhanna in the previous chapter, although these are amongst the best examples of what is often ambiguous evidence for settlement boundaries. In East Anglia, there are examples of large rectangular enclosures that may pre-date the twelfth century (Gilmour et al. 2014). Stone walls enclosed some of the settlement areas, known as pounds, on Dartmoor, and they are broadly later Bronze Age based on the pottery and a handful of scientifically dated sites (Wainwright and Smith 1980). Joanna Brück (1997) reviewed the Deverel-Rimbury Bronze Age settlements in the Thames Valley and Wessex, where she found that two-thirds were enclosed at some stage in their lives. In some case it can be shown that the enclosing boundaries came late in the settlement's history, as at South Lodge (Barrett et al. 1991).

The substantial enclosure of settlements spaces became widespread and the boundaries more substantial from the fourteenth century BC and especially from the twelfth century BC. A trench created by a timber palisade enclosed an oval area up to 25 metres across at Treanbaun, County Galway (Muñiz-Pérez and Bermingham 2014). The palisade's timbers were replaced on multiple occasions. The interior contained pits and a short arc of trench that might have contained a timber screen or formed the truncated remnants of a building. The radiocarbon measurements from charcoal and grain from the palisade and the pits indicate at least two phases of activity: one in the sixteenth to fifteenth centuries BC and another during the twelfth to tenth centuries BC. Further pits and a structure were clustered 30 metres from the enclosure. The palisaded enclosure cannot be securely associated with either the earlier or the later occupation at Treanbaun. The occupation within the enclosure at Meyllteyrn Uchaf, on the Llŷn Peninsula, Gwynedd, spanned the fourteenth to ninth centuries BC, without a clear hiatus apparent in the radiocarbon measurements (Ward and Smith 2001).

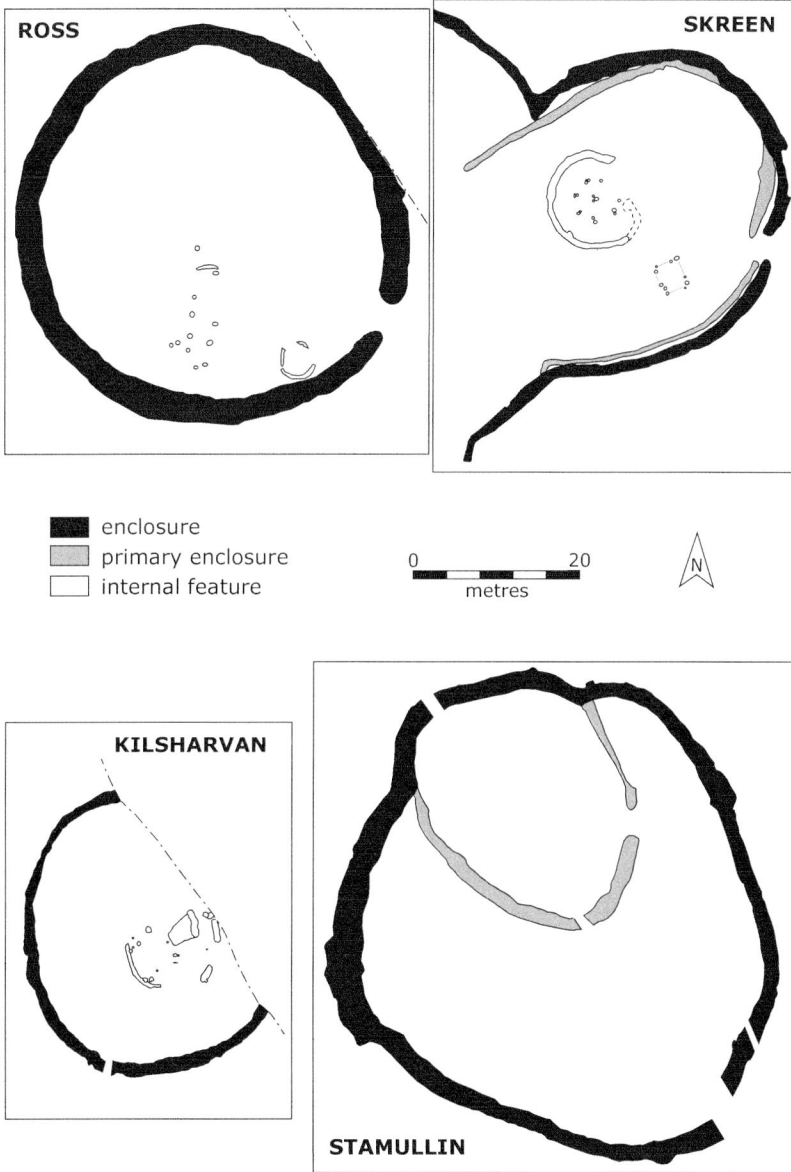

ROSS

SKREEN

■ enclosure
▨ primary enclosure
☐ internal feature

0 _____ 20
metres

N

KILSHARVAN

STAMULLIN

FIGURE 5.9 Plans of eleventh- to ninth-century BC enclosures from eastern and midland Ireland. Adapted from Ní Líonáin 2007, O'Neil 2009, Russell and Cocoran 2001 and Wiggins et al. 2009.

The rebuilding of roundhouses and recutting of the enclosure ditch could easily have occurred following a period of abandonment.

A group of eleventh- to ninth-century enclosures has been excavated during development-led fieldwork in eastern and midland Ireland (Figure 5.9). At Stamullin, during the tenth and ninth centuries BC an oval ditched enclosure was enlarged by a second ditch enclosing an area 58 by 47 metres across (Ní Líonáin 2007). The excavations did not uncover evidence for domestic buildings within the enclosures, although the ditch did produce pottery, whole quernstones, animal bone and human skull fragments (see also K. Cleary 2018). At Lagavooren, southwest of Drogheda, the oval enclosure was 50 metres across and defined by a ditch up to 5 metres in width and 1.5 metres in depth (Murphy and Clarke 2001). There were rectangular and circular buildings within the enclosure, and the enclosure's entrance lay on the southeast side. Animal bone from the ditch gave a radiocarbon measurement calibrated to 1040–810 BC. Other oval or circular enclosures were excavated at Skreen and Ross, where entrances were, as at Lagavooren, within the southeastern arcs of the enclosures (O'Connell 2013, 52–53). At Skreen, the ditch enclosed two buildings, one roundhouse and a smaller, rectangular four-post structure (O'Neil 2009). At Kilsharvan 16, the enclosure was 33 metres in diameter, with an oval timber building in the interior (Russell and Cocoran 2001). The ditch at Kilsharvan included broken pottery and animal bone, which the excavator used to support an interpretation of domestic use of the site.

The enclosure at Clonfinlough, County Offaly in the Irish Midlands, was a similar size (40 by 50 metres) and shape (oval) to the enclosures further east, although its fenland setting meant it was palisaded, not ditched, and subsequent waterlogging resulted in the preservation of timbers (Moloney 1993). Clonfinlough was discovered when Bord na Móna drained and then stripped peat from a raised bogland southwest of Fin Lough. Today, Fin Lough has disappeared and the bogland is scarred and empty. During the late tenth century BC (917–899 BC), the enclosure was built on a drier hummock of fen peat by the lakeside. The palisade of close-set ash poles surrounded the settlement on three sides, with the lake-edge defining the fourth side. The two roundhouses in the interior, both with central hearths, had wattlework walls built on elaborate deep foundations of laid timbers and stone. The larger of the two dwellings sat somewhat isolated, close to the lakeshore. The smaller building was sited next to two further constructed platforms, one of which had a wattle wall and may have been roofed. Two paddles or oars were laid lengthways from the entrance to the second roundhouse, forming the base for a brushwood path. The paddles were crafted from ash roundwood; one had a surviving U-shaped handle and the other a blade with paired round and oval perforations. If occupation layers had survived within or around the buildings, they were subsequently destroyed by the modern mechanised removal of the peat. The excavators recovered small quantities of coarseware pottery, fragmentary animal bone (mainly from cattle), wooden objects and two amber beads.

On Knockadoon Hill by the shore of Lough Gur, County Limerick, surveys and excavations have identified six enclosed settlements dating to the later centuries of the second and early first millennia BC (Cleary 1995; 2003; Grogan and Eogan 1987). The settlements vary in their forms, with both small, irregular enclosures making use of the outcropping limestone, and near-circular enclosures around 30 metres across. They were enclosed with low limestone walls, perhaps covered with scrubby bushes. Knockadoon Hill is locally prominent and, before drainage schemes in the 1700s and 1800s, was almost entirely enclosed by the waters of Lough Gur. The effect was for the dwelling places to be encircled twice: first by their stone walls and again by the lake, which separated Knockadoon from the surrounding land.

The Traprain Law Environs Project identified a group of twelfth- to ninth-century enclosures in the coastal lowlands east of Edinburgh (Haselgrove 2009). Traprain Law is a steep dome of igneous rock overlooking the coastal plain, and it is known as the site of a tenth- to ninth-century hilltop enclosure. The surprise for the Traprain Law Environs Project was that some of the enclosed settlements they investigated around the hill were of similar date: Standingstone, Whittingehame Tower and East Linton. Standingstone's curving ditch, incomplete in the northwest arc, enclosed an area roughly 44 metres across. A palisade, set a few metres beyond the ditch's inside edge, might have retained a bank that limited the interior to around 36 metres across. The modelled radiocarbon determinations placed the construction and use of the enclosure during a short period (most likely within 30 years) during the late tenth and early ninth centuries BC. Modern ploughing truncated the ground surface, and there were few surviving features and no structures contemporary with the enclosure. At Whittingehame Tower, an arc of multiple circuits of ditches, banks and palisades enclosed 0.26 hectares above a ravine. East Linton also used the steep side of a gorge to complete its circuit, when it was enclosed by first a palisade and then a ditch. Both Whittingehame and East Linton produced twelfth- to eleventh-century BC radiocarbon measurements, although only a few samples were successfully dated from the boundaries and they cannot be attributed to the Bronze Age with the same confidence as Standingstone. David Cowley's (in Haselgrove 2009, 205–223) survey of cropmarks in the environs of Traprain Law identified a scattering of more than 20 enclosures similar to the Bronze Age examples excavated by the project.

While geographically dispersed, the enclosures I described share some characteristics. They are of equivalent sizes: around a third of a hectare, up to 60 metres across. Their boundaries formed substantial barriers. There were buildings within the interiors, limited to a few roundhouses at most, with ancillary structures—comparable with contemporary open settlements. The enclosures' size enabled livestock to shelter alongside the human inhabitants. Where there is precise scientific dating, the duration of occupation within the enclosures is less than a century and likely to have been briefer. This is supported by the limited repair and rebuilding of houses and the enclosure boundaries. Based on dendrochronology, the Clonfinlough enclosure was likely built during 917–899 BC, with a repair to one platform in 886 BC (Moloney 1993, 61). The replacement of hearths in the buildings might show that occupation was discontinuous, even within the decade or two suggested by the dendrochronology. The variety of material culture does not differ between enclosed and open settlements. The dwelling places, whether or not they were enclosed, seem to have been assembled in similar ways.

Prehistorians have used differences in the forms of settlement to reconstruct hierarchical models for social organisation. Based on a study of the distributions of later Bronze Age material in north Munster, Eoin Grogan (2005b) concluded that the hilltop enclosures and enclosed settlements reflected different levels in regional polities or chiefdoms. I will return to the hilltop enclosures later in the chapter. The excavated evidence from enclosed homesteads, as I interpret it, does not accommodate hierarchical levels or stable relations. Enclosures were inconsistently parts of settlement assemblages in time and space. Households enclosed their settlements or built new enclosed settlements according to localised and short-term imperatives. Enclosed homesteads reproduced traditions in open sites, employing comparable house architecture and configurations of buildings. Enclosure may have been a shorter-term response to conditions within close networks: episodes of raiding, threats of supernatural and malign forces.

Philippe Descola's (1997) account of a 'house at war' illustrates the ways that kinship can be transformed through enclosure. Descola spent two years undertaking ethnographic fieldwork while living with a family of Achuar, in the Amazonian jungle of Ecuador. During a long exploratory journey into the jungle with his hosts, Descola visited the 'house at war', where six households were gathered inside a palisaded settlement. They were protecting themselves from neighbours whose shaman they had killed. This was primarily a dispute between shamans, into which near and distant relations had been drawn. Descola described his walk towards the fortified house. He and his companions passed through abandoned settlements and gardens, where the houses lay empty of belongings, their inhabitants having retreated to the new, defended location. On reaching the palisade, they first announced their presence by blowing across the top of a rifle barrel and then each called out loudly. They encountered a 'glacial' welcome. The house's inhabitants were tense and suspicious. Vendettas might last two or three years, during which time households that would normally live apart found themselves cramped together, fenced in. Their trips into the forest to tend gardens and gather food were perilous and therefore infrequent. Descola (1997, 289) recounted how jealousies surface and envies abound 'as the exceptional circumstances encourage exploits of all kinds and emphasize natural disparities in courage, cunning, strength and skill'. The experience is corrosive and consolidating. Vendettas require a charismatic leader to transform relations of affinity into 'ideal bonds of consanguinity': it 'tightens links that have slackened amongst kindred' (Descola 1997, 290–291).

I suggest this example is helpful for thinking about the changes that occurred within Bronze Age enclosed homesteads. Enclosure required different skills in cooperation and dwelling together. It did this by changing the social configurations and proximities that had been commonplace when settlements were not bounded. Enclosure affected permeability and the relations beyond and within the household. Enclosure distorted kinwork and enabled new forms of kinship. The kindred who resided together in homesteads might have been unchanged from those that lived in an unenclosed setting. And yet the addition of the enclosure did alter their relations with one another and the world beyond the palisades, ditches or walls. The character of those differences eludes us for enclosed homesteads, even if accounts like Philippe Descola's can help with imagining what those differences might have been like.

Gathering to the hills, 1250–700 BC

Standing on Gardom's Edge, Derbyshire, provides an expansive view across the Derwent Valley and westward towards the Peak District's limestone plateau. The 'edge' is a low, discontinuous sandstone crag. The wooded ground below the edge drops rapidly to the valley; the land above forms a shelf that slopes gently southwards. At a time during the twelfth to tenth centuries BC, people began gathering surface stones and piling them into a low bank that stretched for 600 metres (Barnatt et al. 2017, 39–58). The bank enclosed the eastern side of a broad ridge of ground above Gardom's Edge, with the steep crag providing a boundary on the west. The bank's form varied as it wove its way amongst the large earthfast boulders that littered the ridge. In places it was a low unstructured heap of stones. Elsewhere, the builders elaborated the bank's outer, eastward-facing side with a façade of stone slabs. In one section, archaeologists identified a line of timber posts within the bank and a second dump of stones that followed a fire on the bank's internal, west, face. Five entrances survive through the bank. There may have been more. The 6 hectares enclosed by the bank were never cleared of stone and contain no visible roundhouses or platforms where houses might have stood. It seems unlikely that people lived within the enclosure.

John Barnatt, Bill Bevan and Mark Edmonds (2017) grappled with the difficulties of interpreting the enclosure they excavated on Gardom's Edge: the bank's segmented character; the lack of occupation within the interior; the striking location and the bank's alignment on the Eagle Stone, an isolated outcrop of sandstone that landmarks the shelf on the opposite side of the valley. These factors suggested the enclosure was built in the fourth millennium BC, in the tradition of earlier Neolithic enclosures. The scientific dating disproved this idea and placed the enclosure in the twelfth to tenth centuries BC. Barnatt and colleagues (2017, 56) conclude the enclosure was a place where kin could gather their livestock at times during the year. Corralled stock could be sorted, exchanged and perhaps protected. The enclosure's multiple entrances offered access from different directions and ways to distinguish the animals and people who entered and left the enclosure: 'the moving and even mingling of herds bound communities together in both a literal and a metaphoric sense'. The place for these gatherings mattered. Prominent yet inaccessible from the west, Gardom's Edge had a history. There were monuments that marked its importance to people in the centuries before work began on the bank: burial mounds, standing stones and rock art. Gardom's Edge was defined by its use as a gathering place for animals and people, the presence of a large stone-banked enclosure and the more sacred histories inscribed on the land as rock art and monuments.

FIGURE 5.10 A distant view of the hilltop enclosure on Mam Tor, Derbyshire. Copyright: Bill Bevan.

A journey of 20 kilometres from Gardom's Edge, following the River Derwent upstream first north and then west, leads to another enclosure, on Mam Tor (Figure 5.10). At an altitude 230 metres higher that Gardom's Edge, Mam Tor is a vertiginous ridge dividing the Edale and Hope valleys. The location is made more dramatic and precarious because the hill's shale and sandstone layers have slipped away in places, leaving great, steep scars on the slopes. Unlike Gardom's Edge, Mam Tor contains plentiful evidence for settlement. Aerial photographs show around 100 platforms dug into the sloping ground within the enclosure's interior. When David Coombs and Frederick Thompson (1979) excavated several platforms during 1966–1969, they recorded post- and stakeholds, gullies, hearths and pits. They found late Bronze Age pottery (mainly undecorated, coarse jars) and a fragment from a bronze socketed axe.

Frederick Thompson excavated two sections through the bank and ditch that encloses Mam Tor (Coombs and Thompson 1979, 14–17). In one location, the bank was 3 metres in height, comprised of interleaving layers of earth, clay and stone, with traces of low retaining walls at the front and rear. The duration between the layers was sufficient on two occasions for a turf to form. Frederick Thompson admitted he misjudged the scale of the undertaking when excavating through the bank and ditch (Coombs and Thompson 1979, 14). It was a formidable structure. Combined with the steeply sloping ground on which the enclosure stood, there was a height difference of 9 metres from the base of the rock-cut ditch to the top of the bank. In a second trench excavated through the bank, 60 metres from the first, Thompson found a different sequence. The bank was lower, comprising layers of cut-turf and earth, with clear retaining walls and a posthole in front from what might have been a palisade. There was no evidence for turf-lines, which might have formed had there been years-long gaps in the process of building.

Mam Tor and Gardom's Edge are of comparable sizes (5 and 6 hectares). Both sit in prominent locations, whether on a hilltop or a scarp-edge. So far as excavations have determined, their banks varied in character along their lengths. The Gardom's Edge bank was slight by comparison with the formidable rampart constructed on Mam Tor. People built light dwellings and lived for a time within Mam Tor, which was not the case at Gardom's Edge. In spite of these differences, both sites are listed in the Atlas of Hillforts of Britain and Ireland (Lock and Ralston 2017). The atlas contains nearly 70 hillforts, distributed throughout Ireland and Britain, where there is occupation dated to 1200–800 BC (12 percent of all the hillforts recorded with later prehistoric dates). Of these sites, there are examples where the enclosing boundary is not dated precisely or the late Bronze Age activity on the hills precedes their enclosure. Accepting this imprecision, large enclosures of varied forms were built from late in the thirteenth century BC onwards in many regions of Ireland and Britain (Needham and Ambers 1994; O'Brien 2017), with earlier and contemporary hilltop enclosures recognised on mainland Europe (Primas 2002).

Breidden Hill, Powys, rises abruptly and steeply from the River Severn's floodplain. During the late tenth or ninth centuries BC, an earth, stone and timber rampart was constructed around the hill's less steep southeastern side (Musson et al. 1991). The northwestern side of the hill, now replaced by a deep quarry, had precipitous rocky slopes dropping 300 metres to the valley. The rampart was fronted by a double line of slender timber posts, which retained a bank of earth and stone. A low stone wall retained the back of the bank. It is likely the tenth- or ninth-century rampart extended for a kilometre, underlying a fourth- to second-century BC rampart. The rampart enclosed 28 hectares of land on the hilltop, which included a pond. The pond's sediments provided pollen and beetle remains that enabled a reconstruction of the environment and land use on the hill during the Bronze Age. Gilbert Smith (1991, 106–109) interpreted the pollen from sediments contemporary with the enclosure as evidence the hill was grazed in places, and largely wooded with alder and elm and smaller numbers of oak and lime. Alder's dominance probably reflects the damp conditions around the pond, where there was periodic and small-scale grazing by animals (Buckland et al. 2001).

If the palaeoenvironmental evidence points to limited human impact on the hill's vegetation, the excavated archaeological features indicate there were periods when intensive, localised activities occurred within the enclosure. These materials and features included pottery, hearths, four-post structures and considerable evidence for metalworking. There were no buildings that could be reliably dated to the tenth to ninth centuries. A small excavation on the southwestern end of the ridge and below a rock outcrop uncovered a concentration of 13 metalworking furnaces, associated with traces of slag and fragments of moulds and crucibles. Bronze items recovered during the excavations may have been scrap for melting down, including fragments of weapons and tools, as well as a socketed axe with the remains of a burnt willow haft.

A feature of Gardom's Edge and Breidden was their relative emptiness. The excavations and survey at Gardom's Edge found no evidence of settlement within the enclosure. The enclosure on Breidden was built one or two centuries later than Gardom's Edge. Traces of occupation were present in some areas although there were no definable houses. Mam Tor superficially presents a different character, as there are numerous small terraces indicating where structures had stood within the enclosure. Excavating these terraces, Coombs and Thompson (1979) found the arcs of shallow gulleys and scatterings of postholes. They did not find complete, convincing roundhouses. While people gathered within Mam Tor, they did not dwell within houses, as they did in the contemporary open and enclosed settlements that I described earlier, like Clonfinlough and Meyllteyrn Uchaf. Joanna Brück (2007, 30–31) proposes that British hilltop enclosures were used episodically, perhaps associated with the seasonal grazing of stock in the uplands. Sue Hamilton and John Manley (2001, 25) note 'sporadic' use at early hilltop enclosures in southeast England based on the small size and varied character of the pottery assemblages. The hilltop enclosures in Wessex generally lack evidence for sustained settlement. Balksbury, Hampshire, enclosed 18 hectares, it was constructed in the ninth century BC and the boundary was maintained for around 200 years (Ellis and Rawlings 2001). A large midden accumulated against the inside of the bank, but despite this evidence for intense activity the excavations only attributed a handful of four-post structures to the Bronze Age occupation.

Comparable enclosures are known from Ireland. Three circuits of stone banks encircle 11 hectares on the high point of a limestone ridge at Mooghaun South, County Clare (Grogan 2005a). The banks were built during the tenth or ninth century BC. The banks vary in height and width around the circuits, with linked, individually straight sections broadly following the bedrock's stepped profile. Eoin Grogan (2005a, 129) interpreted this pattern as evidence for separate gangs of workers building the enclosure. Grogan's excavations provided plentiful detail about the ways the banks were built: multiple walls retaining unstructured cores of stone. He found less evidence for people dwelling on the hill during the tenth to ninth centuries BC. There were small amounts of pottery and animal bone from layers beneath the inner and middle enclosure banks. A trench along a section of the middle enclosure produced animal bone, especially of cattle, pottery, flaked stone, hearths and traces of small circular structures from immediately inside the bank. The occupation debris was overlain in places where the stone bank had been widened. Debris from first-century AD metalworking and quern production was excavated from hollows in the limestone bedrock within the inner enclosure at Mooghaun South. Had it been present, tenth- and ninth-century occupation debris would have accumulated in the same hollows. It did not and it appears that the enclosure's central area was not occupied intensively at this time.

Access to the inner enclosure at Mooghaun South was through a gap less than a metre wide. The route passed diagonally through the wall, which prevented a sightline from outside in. The entrance was located on the side of the hill that was 'most difficult to approach' and furthest from the occupation area by the middle rampart (Grogan 2005a, 119). The uppermost, innermost area was set apart physically and visually. It was also empty of archaeological features and materials dating to the tenth to ninth centuries BC. Confined and secluded, the space might have served as brief refuge or for selective gatherings.

Bronze Age hilltop enclosures commonly occupy local topographic landmarks. Gardom's Edge, Mam Tor and Breidden are on steep-sided, distinctive hills, scarp edges or ridges. The hillfort on Parc-y-meirch, near Dinorben, Denbighshire, enclosed a promontory on the escarpment that overlooks the coastal plain of north Wales. A quarry has removed the hilltop and enclosure at Parc-y-meirch. The place's importance might be judged by the large offering of metalwork, including horse fittings, that was left at the base of the precipitous crag marking the enclosure's northwestern boundary (Gardner and Savory 1964, 16). Traprain Law, East Lothian, also attracted the interest of quarrying, which has consumed the hill's northeast side. Traprain Law is a volcanic plug that stands proud of the low-lying and rolling East Lothian coastal plain. The hill was enclosed by a revetted bank or rampart during the tenth or ninth century BC (Armit et al. 2005). Excavations during the early twentieth century uncovered contemporary metalwork and clay mould fragments, and more recent fieldwork excavated a group of four socketed axes buried on an exposed ledge. Traprain Law and Parc-y-meirch were suitable places for gifts of metalwork and for enclosures.

At Clashanimud, County Cork, the hilltop was enclosed during the twelfth or eleventh century BC by two circuits of ditches and banks (O'Brien and O'Driscoll 2017) (Figure 5.11). The inner ditch was cut into the bedrock, and the bank topped with a substantial palisade. Enclosing 9 hectares, Clashanimud's ramparts required months of digging through earth and rock. Three hundred and fifty oak posts were felled and erected as the framework for the inner palisade. This work inscribed the hilltop, it did not define or defend a dwelling place with houses. Archaeological excavations across the enclosure's interior found no traces of structures and no artefacts. Clashanimud's inner palisade was burnt down, leaving the timbers charred and the rocks fire-reddened and vitrified (Figure 5.12). Was the burning a community's failure or a place's spectacular transformation? O'Brien and O'Driscoll's (2017, 414) excavations at four hillforts in Munster and Leinster, although on a smaller scale than their work at Clashanimud, told similar stories: construction in the twelfth or eleventh century BC; an absence of material culture; and in the case of Toor More, County Kilkenny, the burning down of a timber boundary.

William O'Brien (in O'Brien and O'Driscoll 2017, 397) does not present the enclosures as defensive responses to insecurity and conflict—places for refuge. He interprets them as 'visual statement[s] of military power and dominion over

FIGURE 5.11 An aerial view of Clashanimud hilltop enclosure, County Cork, photographed in the 1970s by Daphne Pochin Mould. Image courtesy of William O'Brien.

a surrounding territory'. They were central places for regional chiefdoms. The enclosures' centrality and influence came from their topographic prominence, as visual nodes along trade routes. Chiefdoms expressed their strength through the mobilisation of the people and materials that were required to construct a hilltop enclosure (O'Driscoll 2017). Periodically, the competition between 'warlords' led to instability and short periods of intense and catastrophic conflict. In such circumstances, the burning of a hilltop enclosure was a 'highly visual statement of victory that marked the subjugation of a vanquished group in their ancestral homeland' (O'Brien and O'Driscoll 2017, 414). O'Brien and O'Driscoll join others (such as Armit 2007) in countering what they characterise as the pacification of later prehistory by placing hilltop enclosures within periods of endemic warfare. The shields, swords and plentiful spearheads recovered from wetlands and rivers were participants in these violent relations amongst individuals and between kin groups.

If the enclosures were centres for chiefly power, then how was that power expressed through the landscape before enclosures were being constructed in the twelfth century BC? The settlements dating from the later second millennium BC commonly comprised a few houses, and without obvious differentiation in size or wealth. It is curious that many locations chosen as sites for hilltop enclosures were not intensively occupied prior to enclosure, nor were they occupied intensively once the enclosures were constructed. In some instances, the hilltops

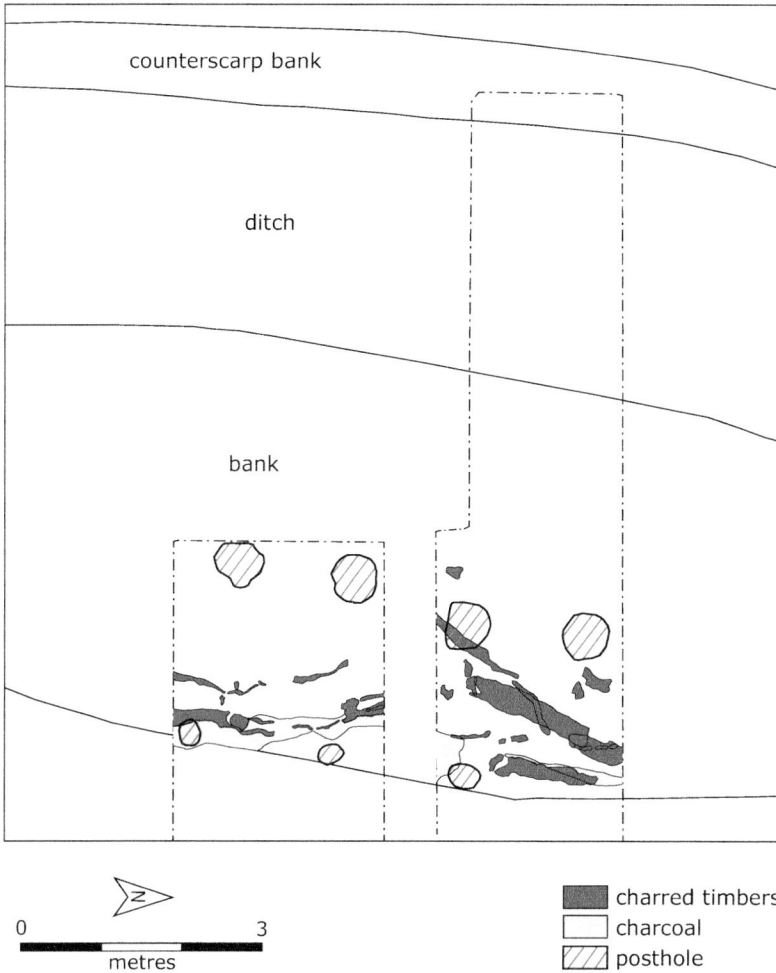

FIGURE 5.12 Features excavated within the inner bank at Clashanimud hilltop enclosure, County Cork. Adapted from O'Brien and O'Driscoll 2017.

remained 'empty gestures'—without buildings or material culture. Their emptiness may be deceptive. As landmarks, hills formed active places in cultural geographies. During the twelfth and eleventh centuries BC offerings of metalwork
were made in a variety of unmarked places, including hills, bogs and rivers.
Hilltops had, several centuries before, been suitable locations for constructing
funerary barrows. The hills were not neutral ground on which people might
project power or occupy for defence. The power lay not with the people or the
defences, but with the hills themselves. Enclosing was an act of topographic
veneration and appropriation. The acts of bounding drew the hills into different
domains of social life.

I am making a distinction between two conceptions of landscape. In one, hills were topographically convenient places from which communities could defend themselves or demonstrate power over their domain. Like today's quarries extracting stone from the slopes and edges, the hills were a passive resource. An alternative conception of landscape, and the one that I prefer, understands places as active participants in the formation of kin. Hills were known places within myths and histories, and powerful entities within kinwork. Enclosure, as a process, assembled new communities with the hills. It secured powerful alliances between a kin group and important, vibrant places.

We can find examples of these vibrancies amongst the folklore of Britain and Ireland, and by listening to communities' accounts of their places in more distant parts of the world. 'Do glaciers listen?' asked Julie Cruikshank (2005) in her study of local environmental knowledge in the Saint Elias Mountains. She found one answer to her question amongst Athapaskan and Tlingit elders who described the glaciers as sentient: 'animate (endowed with life) and as animating (giving life to) landscapes they inhabit' (Cruikshank 2005, 3). Keith Basso (1984) described places' animacy differently based on his fieldwork amongst the Western Apache. He explained how an elder recounted moral tales to a young person as chastisement for some act of delinquency or transgression. Placenames featured prominently in the stories, and each time the young person heard of or passed those same places, she would be reminded of her elder's admonishment. The stories and the places hunted the young person, as Nick Thompson told Keith Basso: 'It doesn't matter if you get old—that place will keep on stalking you like the one who shot you with the story' (Basso 1984, 42).

In the Bronze Age world, affirming or creating kinship bonds with powerful places affected the relations amongst all those participating in the building and use of enclosures. New groupings emerged because of the shared work required to construct the boundaries. Some kin took risks assembling the resources that such projects required. Niall Sharples (2010, 116–124) interprets the hillforts of the mid-first millennium BC, during the Iron Age of southern Britain, as acts of massive, conspicuous consumption. Accumulated food was offered at feasts in exchange for people's labour in constructing the hillforts' great ramparts. Communities competed, in the fashion of potlatch, to acquire sufficient surplus and attract ever larger gatherings. The size and elaboration of their enclosures reflected their communities' relative success in the cycles of accumulation, consumption and construction.

The gatherings and labour of building the enclosures formed the initial process through which people's relations with the hills were transformed. The enclosures I have described provide evidence their construction was cumulative, either through the contributions of separate groups or different times. On Gardom's Edge, the bank varied from a simple heap of stones to a more careful construction using orthostatic slabs to retain the bank. In one place, timber posts stood within the bank. There were breaks of sufficient duration for two layers of turf to form within the bank on Mam Tor. Eoin Grogan (2005a, 129) explains the variations in height and width of the banks around Mooghaun South as the contributions made by separate gangs of workers. Two sites on Bodmin Moor are candidates for Bronze Age hilltop enclosures: Roughtor and Stowe's Pound (Johnson and Rose 1994, 46–48). Both have a cumulative, slow architecture. Their banks are sinuous, varying in thickness and height, linking with stone outcrops and dense scatters of surface stone. There are three entrances into the enclosure on Roughtor and further narrower gaps through the banks. Each of the three substantial entrances is elaborated with external lines of banks and walled passages. Each entrance is quite different in character.

Countering the explanations of hillforts as defensive structures and symbols of power during periods of endemic warfare, Gary Lock (2011, 359) proposes that enclosures responded to an emotional insecurity rather than a physical insecurity: 'a defence against cosmological threats and thus metaphors for social cohesion, where bad emotions are transformed to the good life and emotional stability'. Lock's approach resembles Joanna Brück's (Brück 2000, 293–294) suggestion that the enclosing of Bronze Age settlements in Wessex and the Thames Valley was a strategy for establishing order on an unpredictable and changing world. These positions are necessary counterpoints to the raids and waring chiefdoms that take precedent in most accounts of Bronze Age hilltop enclosures.

The construction of enclosures punctuated the biographies of the hills. Life within or in sight of the walls, banks, ditches and palisades engendered novel forms of kinmaking in twelfth- to ninth-century landscapes. Some enclosures stayed empty of humans and animals. Others were used temporarily when animals and their people gathered for feasts and fairs, and perhaps refuge from vendettas and malign spirits. With time, some enclosures acquired resident communities. Knock Dhu, County Antrim, is a promontory enclosure on the edge of the Antrim Plateau, overlooking the coastal plain and the Irish Sea. The earliest ramparts across the promontory were built in the eleventh or early tenth century BC (Macdonald 2016). Surveys have identified more than 100 ring banks and platforms within the enclosure, and selective excavations demonstrated the features are the remains of roundhouses. The earliest calibrated radiocarbon dates for the houses are late tenth or ninth centuries BC, and the latest spans 800–550 BC. Stefan Bergh (2015) has identified similarly dense clusters of round buildings on hilltops at Mullaghfarna, County Sligo, and Turlough Hill, County Clare. Bergh (2015, 35) interprets the houses as 'part of activities linked to mountains as special places, places that reach the sky and where worlds meet'.

As hills lived well, they sometimes underwent spectacular transformations. Throughout most of the excavated sections of rampart on the Breidden, the timbers had burnt in their postholes, leaving charcoal and reddened stones (Musson et al. 1991, 177). The entire circuit of Clashanimud's inner palisade was burnt down, leaving the timbers charred and the rocks fire-reddened and vitrified. The thoroughness of these events is noteworthy. At Toor More, County Kilkenny, fire destroyed two concentric circuits of palisades, totalling 1.5 kilometres in length (O'Driscoll 2017, 519). This was achieved by careful fire setting and maintenance of the fires as they burned. Such an event might have involved as many people in the boundaries' destruction as participated in their construction. These were spectacular moments of transformation. They compare with the deliberate burning of houses and the cremation of humans during mortuary rites. Fire was integral to the fragmentation of metalwork (Knight 2018). I argued earlier that certain houses and objects existed as kin within the Bronze Age world. With the hilltop enclosures, it was the hill, the landmark, that gathered a community. The transformation of the place was a spectacle, a performance of timber, stone and fire.

If we accept the link with other examples of fiery transformations that made Bronze Age worlds, then the burning of the enclosures did not mark the end of the hills' or the enclosures' participation in kinwork. Cremated human remains were dispersed and deposited in pits and middens. Burnt and broken objects participated in exchanges between persons and with places. Hot, choking, dangerous performances encircled hills with fire, left them blackened and with the ashes and smells from burning timbers settling over the surrounding landscape. As cremated bone and burnt metalwork fragmented and dispersed, perhaps kin dispersed too with the burning of the hill. As with Keith Basso's tales of the Western Apache, the stories, the names and the places lived on in social life.

Performing places, 1150–700 BC

Three circuits of ditches and banks enclosed 14 hectares of a modest, locally prominent spur at Rahally, on the eastern edge of the Galway plain. The enclosure was excavated during the construction of the M6 motorway (McKeon and O'Sullivan 2014, 105–111). The new road corridor sliced through the middle of Rahally, enabling archaeologists to investigate around two-thirds of the inner enclosure and substantial sections of the middle and outer ditch circuits. They found no Bronze Age features apart from the ditches: no hearths or stakeholes, pits or postholes. Like Mooghaun South, which Rahally resembles in size and form, the enclosure lay empty of built structures.

Unlike Mooghaun South, where the innermost enclosure was accessed through a single narrow entrance on the hill's least accessible slopes, there were multiple gaps through the ditches at Rahally. The gaps were slightly offset from one another on the enclosure's northern and southern sides. They were paired in the outer and middle ditches, with opposed entrances across the inner ditch. The enclosure's architectural emphasis was on the outer and inner circuits of banks and ditches. The outer circuit comprised two concentric ditches with a medial bank. The ditch of the inner circuit was wider and deeper than the middle ditch circuit.

Animal bone, mostly cattle, and pottery were recovered in varying quantities from the middle and inner ditches. The degraded and fragmentary character of bone and pottery suggests it was on the surface for some time before deposition in the ditches. The pattern is blurred because re-occupation of the hill during the first millennium AD contributed material to the upper fills of the ditches (Hamilton-Dyer 2009). The bone from the middle ditch was more fragmentary than from the inner ditch. Proportionally there was more animal bone in the secondary sediments of the inner compared with the middle ditch. One explanation for the distributions of animal bone is that midden accumulated within the inner enclosure, from where some was collected and deposited in the ditches. Deposition within the ditches occurred as discrete events: two terminals of the middle ditch were marked, one with a concentration of mainly cattle bone, another with the burial of a large dog; three-quarters of the animal bone and the majority of pottery from the basal silts of the inner ditch were in one sector, on the west side, north of the western entrance—the majority of deer bone came from a secondary deposit in the same section of ditch.

Based on the material deposited in the ditches at Rahally, the hill's summit was a location for gatherings, where livestock, especially cattle, were consumed during the tenth and ninth centuries BC. The debris came from feasts in the enclosure's interior, from where some was collected and placed in the base of the inner and middle ditches. Material also eroded into the inner ditch as it silted. Access to the interior of the enclosure required passing across three boundaries, through entrances that were offset from one another. Distinctions could be made based on which entrances people, and animals, used when entering and leaving the enclosure. There was a performative aspect to the way the enclosure was used. Given the efforts that were taken to enclose the hill and the wider tradition of enclosing hilltops, I suggest that the place was an important participant in the gatherings—at Rahally's feasts.

The enclosure at Haughey's Fort is estimated to be a century or so older than Rahally. It too was a focal place for gatherings and feasts within an architecturally complex monument. Haughey's Fort lies in the rolling drumlin landscape west of Armagh city. Three concentric circuits of ditches enclosed (or partially enclosed, as sections in the north and west appear incomplete) the hill during the mid-twelfth to eleventh centuries BC (Mallory and Baban 2014) (Figure 5.13). The ditches were widely spaced (25–55 metres) from each other: over 2 metres deep, up to 4 wide, with v-shaped profiles and most likely water-logged. James Mallory's excavations within the innermost enclosure and on the hill's eastern side uncovered plentiful evidence for timber posts, stakes and pits. The difficulty lies in identifying structures amongst the dense clusters of features. Parallel curving lines of small postholes might be traces of a double palisade forming a small, innermost enclosure. Within this, several large pits could have held immense timber posts, forming a rectangular setting or building.

If the structures that stood within the enclosures are ambiguous, there is some patterning in the organisation of space. The three ditches were graded in depth, from the 2.25 metres of the outermost to 2.8 metres of the inner ditch. The innermost postholes and pits are larger and formed more substantial structures compared with the lines and clusters of stakeholes adjacent to the middle ditch, on the hill's east side. The distribution of animal bone, ceramics and metalwork

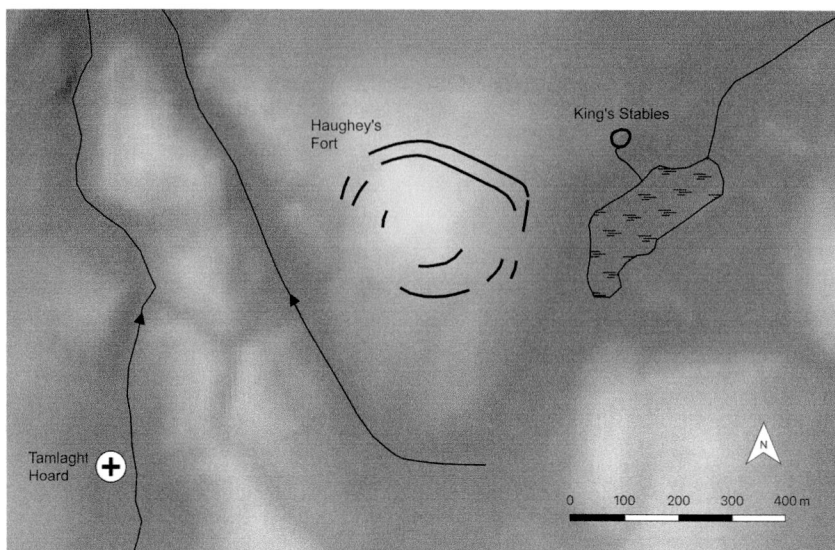

FIGURE 5.13 Map showing the locations of Haughey's Fort, King's Stables and the Tamlaght hoard. Adapted from Mallory and Baban 2014; Warner 2006. Map contains public sector information licensed under the Open Government Licence v3.0.

across the hill indicates a greater intensity of deposition within and around the inner enclosure. The inner ditch excavations recovered around 3,000 animal bone fragments. The middle ditch produced 37 fragments. Even allowing for the greater length of inner ditch that has been excavated, there was at least five times the density of animal bone in the inner compared with the middle ditch fill. A small number of bronze and gold fragments were excavated from features within the inner enclosure. A bronze disc-headed pin came from the upper levels of the inner ditch.

Large numbers of fully grown cattle and pigs were consumed at Haughey's Fort (Murphy and McCormick 1996). Extrapolating from the proportion of excavated inner ditch, James Mallory and Gina Baban (2014, 25) suggest the remains of approximately 1,700 cattle and 1,100 pigs might be buried at the site. This assumes quantities of deposition were uniform throughout the ditch, which is not the case at other excavated enclosures. Dogs are an interesting aspect of the faunal assemblage. They were consistently of a large size, including one skull that, when published in 1991, was the largest known from any archaeological collection in Ireland and Britain. The dog bones were disarticulated, broken and gnawed in similar ways to the cattle and pig bones, with Finbar McCormick (1991, 31) proposing the dogs were consumed as food. Dogs are commonly recovered from later Bronze Age sites, although evidence for their consumption is rare (Hambleton 2008, 75). Meriel McClatchie (2014) used the weed seeds amongst the charred grains, primarily naked barley, to identify a mix of intensive and extensive cultivation regimes. The weeds represented different local environments, from acidic to calcareous and wet to free-draining. McClatchie concludes that cereals were brought to Haughey's Fort from different locations, farms and communities in the surrounding area. The cereal may have been stored at the site, prepared and consumed during feasts in foods such as bread and alcoholic drinks.

Haughey's Fort gathered people, animals and crops from different places to one place. Food was prepared on the hill, based on the large quantities of pottery, the whole and broken querns and the fractured animal bone. Aspects of these activities were commonplace. They were made exceptional in their quantities and their diversity (cereals and presumably animals too from different places). There were exceptional acts, such as the consumption of dogs. And there were exceptional beasts: Eileen Murphy and Finbar McCormick (1996, 47) identified two large cattle amongst the animal remains. The hill and its architecture contributed to the place's separation from the everyday world. Three circuits of water-filled ditches constrained access to the hill's top. Timber palisades and posts stood within the inner enclosure, further defining the spaces at the hill's core.

Some materials from Haughey's Fort were deposited outside the enclosure. The enclosure's plan is teardrop-shaped, with the teardrop's apex, where there are breaks in the outer ditch, directed towards a contemporary artificial pool—the King's Stables (Hartwell 1991) (Figure 5.13). The pool was 25 metres across and originally 3 metres deep (Lynn 1977). It is surrounded by a broad, low bank, except on the west side, which is the direction of Haughey's Fort, 180 metres away. Chris Lynn excavated a small portion of the pool in 1975. Amongst the objects at the pool's base, Lynn's team found fragments of sword moulds, a portion of human skull and animal bone. Cattle were the most numerous species represented amongst the animal bone, as at Haughey's Fort. There were large numbers of dog bones, some of which were partially articulated. Red deer antlers were common. It is possible the mould fragments originated from Haughey's Fort, as small quantities of waste metal from casting were recovered from the enclosure's interior (Brandherm 2014) and the deposition of refractory waste in peripheral locations is a characteristic of other sites. The pollen at the pool's base indicates a surrounding of hazel, oak and alder. In comparison, the pollen from the inner ditch at Haughey's Fort and from Loughnashade, 1 kilometre to the east, indicates a relatively open environment, with pasture and cereals, during the final centuries of the second millennium BC (Weir 1993). One explanation for the difference is that the pool at King's Stables lay within woodland, which was conserved even as the surrounding landscape was cleared.

The gatherings at Haughey's Fort related the participants through their knowledge of and access to specialised objects for consuming food and liquid. The evidence for this is slight though important. A fragment of bronze from a large pit or posthole within the enclosure's interior is interpreted by Dirk Brandherm (2014, 62) as the handle from a small vessel, which copied in form if not in technology similar vessels originating in central Europe. There is corroboration for this close by. On a winter's day in 2004, a metal detectorist discovered a small collection of bronze objects in a boggy field in Tamlaght townland, 700 metres from Haughey's Fort: a leaf-shaped sword laid flat and oriented north south; in alignment with the sword and close to its hilt, a bowl contained a ring and the broken remains of a cup (Warner 2006). On stylistic grounds, the objects were placed in the marsh's edge during the twelfth or eleventh centuries BC— contemporary with the activity at Haughey's Fort and the King's Stables. The sword is a type found elsewhere in the north of Ireland. The vessels are not. They are a *Fuchsstadt* bowl and a *Jenišovice* cup, which are found in central Europe, sometimes together as at Tamlaght.

Vessels like the examples from Tamlaght are rare from Ireland and Britain. The few known examples are distinctive. A handled vessel or ladle was recovered from boggy ground at Corrymuckloch, Perthshire (Cowie et al. 1996) (Figure 1.4). The bronze vessel is graceful and carefully decorated with incised lines. Two identical cast bronze cups from beneath a cairn on the Hill of Knockie, Glentanar, have similar shaped terminals on their handles when compared with the Corrymuckloch vessel (Pearce 1970). The Glentanar vessels are, like Corrymuckloch, hard to parallel. Their allusions to vessels on mainland Europe connect them within a tradition of rare and ornate objects. The shale bowl with inlaid gold shields, oars and waves from Caergwrle is similarly distinctive (Davis and Townsend 2009). Like the Tamlaght and Corrymuckloch vessels, it too was buried in damp ground.

A connection is generally made between the cups or bowls, bronze buckets and cauldrons, and flesh-hooks. They are interpreted as the accoutrements for prestigious feasting customs (Coombs 1975; Needham and Bowman 2005), which derived inspiration from objects and practices in central Europe and the eastern Mediterranean (Gerloff 1986, 107). Two complete examples of the buckets have survived with handles that match or mimic those found on southeast European buckets: the one from Dowris, County Offaly, that I describe in Chapter 1, and another from the Mawddach estuary, northwest Wales—either Arthog or Nannau, the provenance is ambiguous (Gerloff 2010, 238–241). The Arthog bucket has a capacity of 35 litres and weighs around 4 kilograms (Figure 5.14). It is simply decorated with patterns of hammer-marks inside and out, with wear on the exterior through heavy use. One of the bucket's bronze sheets was reused from another vessel. Wear and repair, as on the Arthog bucket, characterises the other complete buckets and cauldrons. They had long lives before their deposition in wet ground or, in southern Britain, fragmentation and deposition with assemblages of other broken metalwork.

The flesh-hooks match the bronze vessels in their rarity and individuality. Stuart Needham and Sheridan Bowman (2005) identified 36 examples distributed across Atlantic Europe: Iberia, western France, Britain and Ireland. They range from hooks made from bent bronze rods and single socketed hooks, to elaborate designs with ferrules along and at the ends of the wooden shafts. Their chronology spans the thirteenth to ninth centuries BC. The flesh-hook found

FIGURE 5.14 The bronze vessel from Arthog, Gwynedd. Copyright: National Museum of Wales.

in a bog in Dunaverney, County Antrim, is an exceptional example, which dates to the late eleventh or tenth century BC (Bowman and Needham 2007) (Figure 5.15). When complete, the flesh-hook was over 70 centimetres long. Its oak shaft was inset with thin strips of bronze in repeating chevrons. The bronze hook has two curved prongs, which join a crossbar with a bobbin shape rather like the handles on the Glentanar and Corrymuckloch vessels. The central ferrule carries a 'family' of five cast-bronze swimming water birds, probably swans: three young birds and an adult, with a second adult set ahead of the others. The end ferrule carries two raven-like birds. The ravens are slightly angular and stylised, like the swans. Each bird on the flesh-hook has a tang that passes through the ferrule and shaft, with a coiled end holding a free-running ring. The Dunaverney flesh-hook exemplifies the individuality in design and in technological complexity found in feasting equipment. Stuart Needham and Sheridan Bowman (2005) propose that the individuality of the flesh-hooks had a totemic role. They were emblematic of specific polities and the 'particularities of local mythologies' (Needham and Bowman 2005, 122). It may not be a coincidence that the swans and ravens on the Dunaverney flesh-hook appear 1,700 years later as supernatural beings in early Irish epic tales.

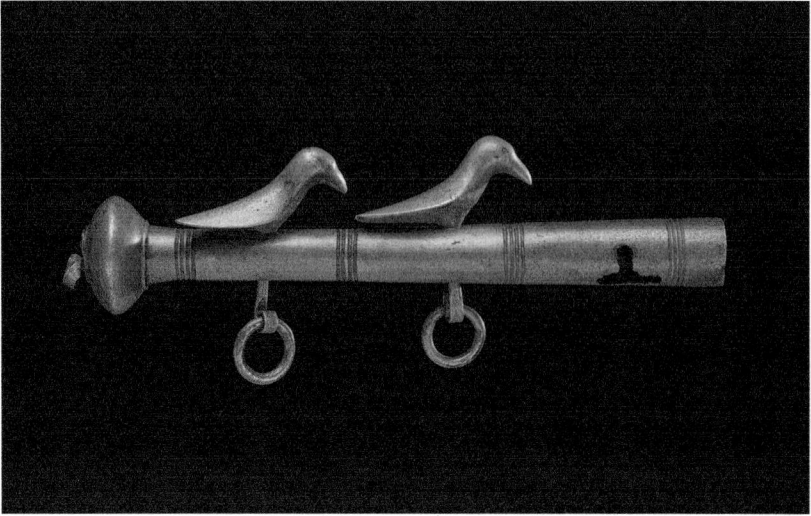

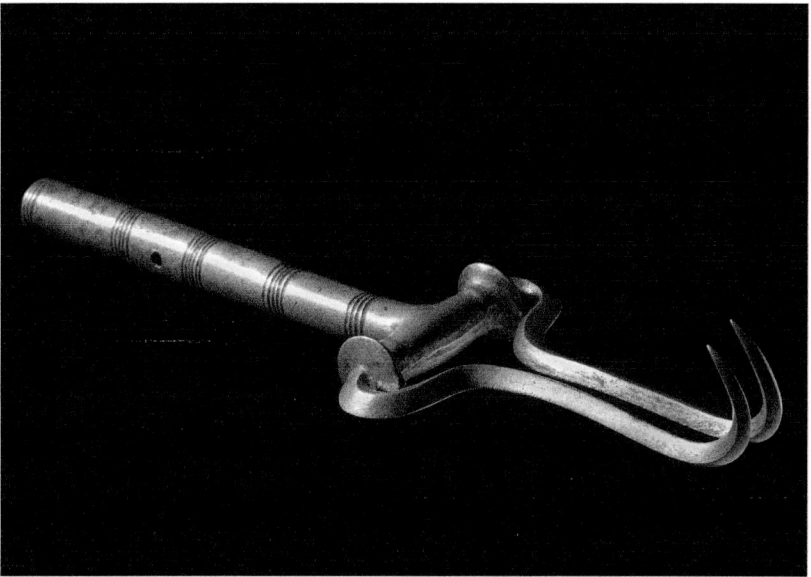

FIGURE 5.15 Two sections of the flesh-hook from Dunaverney, County Antrim: the curved prongs of the hook and the pair of raven-like birds on the end ferrule. © The Trustees of the British Museum. All rights reserved.

We do not know if flesh-hooks, cauldrons or buckets were ever present during gatherings at Haughey's Fort, although it is possible. The cup, bowl, ring and sword from Tamlaght probably were on the hill. Livestock, grain, dogs and people were there too, gathering together from the surrounding landscape. I suggest these gatherings were memorable events when feasts of food and drink generated the large quantities of animal bone and charred grain that now lie in the hill's ditches and pits. There were formalities—processions and votive ceremonies, perhaps—that connected the enclosure with the pool at King's Stables, and related the participants in the hill's feasts with the water's supernatural beings. The enclosure's boundaries were water-filled too. They formed protected and exclusive spaces that nested within one another, and categorised the hill's world from outside in.

Prehistorians routinely present Haughey's Fort and enclosures like it, such as Rathgall (Becker 2010) and Dún Aonghasa (Cotter 2012), as places of high status, as the residences of elites and as centres for chiefly power. The contemporary feasting equipment—cauldrons, buckets and the like—serviced a select and high status few who practised an etiquette that was understood across the high echelons of society in Atlantic Europe. A limitation with this interpretation is its narrow attention on an 'elite', around whom the remainder of social life revolved. It is difficult to escape the dependency of the model and the place: chiefdoms are known to have existed because of sites like Haughey's Fort; Haughey's Fort is interpreted as the centre of a chiefdom. Bruno Latour offers a critique for this way of thinking about social life which I find helpful. He argues that if we confuse the body politic for society, we begin with the structures we seek to understand premade for us: 'If [society] is already there, the practical means to compose it are no longer traceable' (Latour 2005, 160). When prehistorians assume the gravity of the Bronze Age world existed in chiefly power expressed at places like Haughey's Fort, they misread the wider complexity and variety of social life.

As a site of kinwork, Haughey's Fort assembled a diverse constituency of persons and materials. The enclosure's size, the complexity of its timber architecture and the quantities of food refuse all indicate that at times there were large numbers of people present. They brought animals, cereals, pottery and presumably much else that has not survived with them. These participants, human and nonhuman, made and shared kinship with each other and with the place. Kin made distinctions according to when and how they entered the enclosure, which spaces they occupied within the enclosure, which activities they enacted, how long they stayed and the materials they transformed and consumed. If we can say that Haughey's Fort exerted power, it did so through the kin who entered and then left the enclosure. Their status in the world was enhanced because of their kinship with the hill and its kindred. Cattle, pigs, dogs participated in the hill's social life, as part of the community and as food. Haughey's Fort was a powerful place, which hosted powerful events that created powerful kin. And yet those events can also be seen as bringing that place and the world into being. It was, to borrow from James Leach (2003, 206), 'a dramatic and sensory production of what a place is'.

This interpretation does not define specific roles or relative status amongst the enclosure's inhabitants. I have avoided using the words *chief*, *chiefdom* and *chiefly*. I do not refer to an *elite* or to *elite* culture. Distinctions between collective and personal identities are evident, although they do not align with expectations of hilltop enclosures as seats of individual power. At Haughey's Fort, arguably the likeliest indication of a preeminent person lies beyond the enclosure's bounds: the offering of a cup, bowl, ring and sword in the bog at Tamlaght. Stuart Needham and Sheridan Bowman (2005, 127) observe how the cauldrons and flesh-hooks, which are interpreted as related feasting equipment, were deposited separately from one another—the thirteenth-century BC cauldron and socketed flesh-hook from Feltwell, Norfolk, are the exception (Gerloff 1986, 89–90). Needham and Bowman (2005, 127) interpret this separation as derived from the associations the objects had with different beings: '[the cauldron] for divine provision, [the flesh-hook] for the earthly representative empowered to dispense food and largesse'. This difference can be expressed another way: the cauldrons assembled and transformed food into feast, as the buckets might have held liquids; the flesh-hooks and cups associated participants with the feasts. The wear and repairs on the cauldrons and buckets show they were long-lived and inherited objects. The flesh-hooks and cups were individualised, perhaps talismanic, and in the unique case of Dunaverney with its swans and ravens overtly implicated other powerful beings in the feasts. Both the hilltop enclosure and the feasting equipment drew together many different participants. A community's success lay in its capacities to draw together beings and energies of the living and other worlds. In whatever ways people understood themselves and others in kinship structures, those positions were made through diverse and powerful relations with human and other-than-human persons, through resources near at hand—cereals collected from the fields around Haughey's Fort—and distant—feasting culture and the supernatural.

Worlds apart: ringworks and islands, 1100–700 BC

From the twelfth century BC, constellations of large hilltop enclosures lit up the landscapes of Britain and Ireland. They often occupied landmarks, on promontories and distinctive hills. The ways that people inhabited the enclosures cannot easily be interpreted. Some were empty of built structures. In others, there were dwellings and evidence for temporary occupation. The hills were already powerful places, which were drawn into social life through the building of enclosures and as settings for gatherings. Fires marked spectacular moments of transformation in the lives of the hills and the communities. Small numbers of hilltop enclosures hosted intensive gatherings of people, animals and things. They were sites of making, votive rituals and feasts. I have argued these were powerful places and events for kinwork. Sharing food, exchanging animals and things, accessing and dwelling in powerful places: these were all processes whereby persons, human and other-than-human, became kin and changed their status as kin.

I have developed these interpretations with Haughey's Fort as a case study. There were other places where similar acts of kinwork took place, although in different forms. These included ringworks and islands. Ringworks were circular or near circular enclosures defined by earthen banks and ditches and palisades, often with more than one entrance and with a single central building or with a small group of houses in the interior (Manby 2007; Needham 1992). Ringworks were contemporary with the hilltop enclosures I have been describing, with chronologies spanning the mid-twelfth to eighth centuries BC. Most excavated examples are in eastern Britain, primarily around the lower Thames and its tributaries. Comparable enclosures have been identified in northern France, Germany and Denmark (Bradley et al. 2016, 223). Fieldwork and reinterpretations of excavations are extending the distribution westwards. Based on its size, shape and tenth- or ninth-century date, Andy Jones interprets the partially excavated circular enclosure at Tremough, Cornwall, as a ringwork (Jones et al. 2015, 202–225). Jones proposes several other yet to be investigated enclosures in the southwest might be of similar age. The south-western distribution extends into Pembrokeshire, with the late twelfth- to tenth-century BC ringwork at Bayvil Farm (Parker Pearson et al. 2018). For northwest Wales, Alex Gibson (2018) proposes that one of the circular enclosures at Llandegai, Gwynedd, is a ringwork of the early first millennium BC and not a settlement reusing a later Neolithic henge (Lynch and Musson 2004).

South Hornchurch in one of the ringworks in the lower Thames Valley and one of the few to be entirely uncovered. It lies just north of the Thames and adjacent to one of its tributaries, the Ingrebourne River. The archaeological excavations in 1996, in advance of a gravel quarry, revealed a dense area of tenth- to eighth-century BC settlement features and ditches (Guttmann and Last 2000). With few stratigraphic relationships and no radiocarbon dates, Erica Guttman and Jonathan Last mostly relied on variations in the pottery to distinguish between phases in the organisation of the South Hornchurch landscape. One feature, a ringwork, persisted throughout a major reorganisation of the boundary ditches and multiple occupations of open settlements in the surrounding fields. It was a circular ditch with two gaps in its circuit, to the south and northeast, and enclosing an area 32 metres in diameter. In the first phase of the ringwork's use, a large timber roundhouse (10–11 metres in diameter) stood in the middle of the enclosure. An elaborate porch marked the entrance to the roundhouse, aligning towards, if not exactly upon, the northeast gap in the enclosure ditch. Sometime later, although still within the currency of post-Deverel-Rimbury pottery, the circular enclosure ditch was recut, the roundhouse in the interior having by now been abandoned, and two new enclosures were constructed close by. These enclosures were circular and marked with posts or pits. Coarse and fineware jars, bowls and cups were recovered from the enclosures and features in the open settlements. Some of these vessels were placed in the ground intact, notably bowls at each of the ditch terminals by the entrance to the ringwork. There were numerous other instances of selective deposits of pottery and cremated bone elsewhere across the excavated area, and without clear distinctions between the practices in the ringwork compared with the open settlement areas.

Set apart from the surrounding unenclosed settlements, influencing the layout of the droveway, and with a large central roundhouse, South Hornchurch can be interpreted as a high-status farmstead. David Yates (2007) terms the ringworks 'aggrandised enclosures' and argues that their distribution marked the control of metalwork exchange by powerful elites. Christopher Evans prefers a similar interpretation for Mucking South: a farmstead that expressed its status through elaborate architecture, control of high-quality metalworking, feasting and other 'public actions' (Evans et al. 2016, 216). Terry Manby (2007, 418) describes the ringworks in the Yorkshire Wolds, the most closely studied of which is the site Manby excavated at Thwing, as 'strategic territorial centres' with strong aspects of symbolism and formality in their architecture. Guttmann and Last (2000, 353) conclude that the South Hornchurch ringwork provided 'a structure and order to events and a focal point for dispersed occupation'. This perspective was picked up by Timothy Darvill (2010, 234) when he describes ringworks and related sites as 'enclosed meeting places'.

The buildings, pits and artefacts support the interpretation of ringworks as dwelling places. Up to three roundhouses stood within the interior of Mucking North, along with four-post structures. A group of several round structures stood within Springfield Lyons, with a substantial porched roundhouse towards the enclosure's centre (Figure 5.16). Excavations at ringworks have recovered large quantities of pottery and fired clay, along with charred cereals and worked stone, although animal bone has not survived well in the main concentration of ringworks around the lower Thames, in Essex and north Kent. These assemblages

FIGURE 5.16 A digital reconstruction of the ringwork at Springfield Lyons, Essex. The eroded earthwork of a Neolithic causewayed enclosure is visible beyond the ringwork. There is a visual similarity between the ancient causewayed ditch and the ringwork's ditch. Drawn by Iain Bell; copyright: Essex County Council.

are similar to the material excavated at nearby unenclosed settlements. An oc-cupation area at Springfield Park contained a similar range of materials to the enclosure at Springfield Lyons, 200 metres to the west (Brown and Medlycott 2013, 159; Manning and Moore 2003). At South Hornchurch, the pits contain-ing pottery and cremated human bone were excavated amongst the unenclosed roundhouses, within the later post-built enclosures and the large ditched ring-work. A piece of briquetage and mould fragments from sword manufacture were excavated in locations outside the enclosure.

The special status of the ringworks might be judged on the enclosing boundaries that limited access to their interiors and increased their visual im-pact on the landscape. The banks and ditches were substantial though not mas-sive, even allowing for subsequent erosion of the ground surface: 1.7 metres wide and 1.35 metres deep at Tremough; 3 metres wide and 1.35 metres deep at Mucking North; Carshalton was 3.6 metres wide and 2.1 metres deep at its largest (Adkins and Needham 1985; Bond 1988; Jones et al. 2015). The timber palisades or ramparts at Thwing and Springfield Lyons formed formi-dable barriers, which were accessed through substantial entrance structures. Amongst the distinctions in the assemblages, Christopher Evans identifies metalworking and salt-making as critical to the identity of Mucking South, with metalworking in particular 'at the heart of the ringwork "phenome-non"' (Evans et al. 2016, 211). Fineware pottery, with smaller temper and burnished surfaces, formed a higher proportion of the assemblage within the ringwork at South Hornchurch compared with the occupation areas outside the enclosure (Guttmann and Last 2000, 352). A similar pattern is hinted at Mucking South, although this is based on a small sample of the material from external settlements (Brudenell 2016, 169–170). Timothy Champion's (2014) study of perforated clay plates, which were found at many late Bronze Age sites along the lower Thames, identifies the largest quantities of plates at ringworks. Champion proposes that people used the clay plates to make a novel food from spelt wheat—bread. The baking and consumption of bread was especially associated with feasting at the ringworks.

Metalworking debris is recorded from some ringworks. At Springfield Lyons, a selection of refractory waste produced from the casting of swords was placed in the northern terminals of the ditch at opposing, east and west, entrances to the enclosure. This positioning is not unique to ringworks, as I described earlier in the chapter. Mould and crucible fragments were deposited in pits at the entrance to a fenced pound at Kemerton. The sword moulds at South Hornchurch were excavated from a pit amongst a group of unenclosed roundhouses some distance away from the ringwork. The metalworking area at Thwing was located outside the earliest enclosure. The preponderance of sword moulds at Springfield Lyons is unusual. The refractory waste from Mucking South and North comprised parts of crucibles and mould fragments from making knives, spearheads, swords and sickles. The mould fragments from Tremough included patterns for a sword, a chisel and socketed axes.

The difficulties with interpreting the ringworks as high-status, defended farmsteads lie in several areas. The interiors of ringworks have layouts and structures that are unusual and do not look like contemporary unenclosed settlements. In its initial form, South Hornchurch had a single, central roundhouse with a distinctive porch or passage that continued into the house's interior. By the southern gap in the ringwork's ditch, which the excavators assigned to the later use of the enclosure, a line of pits led south before turning downslope and towards the nearby river. Large, central circular houses, post settings or ring ditches were excavated at other ringworks. In its first phase, Thwing enclosed a single roundhouse or unroofed enclosure surrounding a large irregular hollow with an upstanding 'boss' of chalk. A cremation in an urn was placed on the edge of the filled-in hollow, and a substantial circular structure, 26 metres diameter, with opposed entrances was raised. The central 'roundhouse' at Mucking South was defined by incomplete post rings and an unbroken circular gully which is unlike any contemporary buildings. At Mucking North, the roundhouses were screened from the enclosure's main, east-facing, entrance by an arc of posts. Similar 'screens' were identified within two of the ringwork's roundhouses. Richard Tabor (2008, 94) interprets a palisade across the eastern entrance of a ringwork at Sheep Slait, Somerset, as a similar structure that screened off the interior and controlled visual and physical access into the enclosure.

The unusual character of the internal structures is complemented by the distinctive form of the enclosures. When Margaret and Tom Jones began their pioneering landscape excavations at Mucking in 1965, they expected that the double-ring enclosure would be a later Neolithic henge. Their investigations quickly proved this interpretation was not correct. The mis-identification was understandable, and it continues to occur, as Mike Parker Pearson and colleagues (2018) found during their searches for Neolithic enclosures in Pembrokeshire. The inner, earlier enclosure at Thwing had a bank external to the ditch, which is a characteristic of many henges. The similarities with henges might have been a deliberate referencing of distant monumental traditions by the ringworks' builders. Springfield Lyons has an unusual segmented ditch, whose causeways were not matched by corresponding gaps in the bank. An inspiration for this curious design lies immediately east of the ringwork, where there were the ancient earthworks of a causewayed enclosure dating to the fourth millennium BC (Figure 5.16). Nigel Brown and Maria Medlycott (2013, 159) suggest the ringwork was a deliberate replication of the adjacent ancient monument, which connected the 'builders of the new circular enclosure to a mythic history, the meanings embodied in the old site being explicitly transferred to the new, enhancing the authority of those who created and used it'.

Like henges, ringworks endured in the landscape and they were subjected to periodic remodelling. Thwing, Mucking North, Mucking South, Springfield Lyons and South Hornchurch were all remodelled in ways that substantially altered the outer boundaries and the internal features. The chronological modelling at Springfield Lyons estimates that the duration of the occupation was

150–360 years, probably during the tenth and ninth centuries BC (Meadows et al. 2013, 145). This is three-times longer than the estimated duration of the longest occupied unenclosed settlement area at Bestwall Quarry, which was 40–120 years.

Ringworks were not settlements, nor can we describe them as 'defended farmsteads'. At times in their lives, like the hilltop enclosures, some ringworks might have been dwelling places with roundhouses and accompanying domestic structures. More commonly, the ringworks were set apart from daily life's routines. Their outer boundaries, the controlled access to their interiors and the monumental central buildings distinguished the events, the persons and the materials that entered and left the ringworks. The similarities between the assemblages from ringworks and unenclosed settlements reflect their interdependence in the landscape. The same people who lived in the nearby roundhouse settlements made and brought the things and produce that were used, processed and consumed in the ringworks. The ringworks made the ordinary extraordinary. These acts of accumulation and consumption may have continued after the boundaries decayed and collapsed. Matt Brudenell observes that the majority of the pottery at Mucking South was excavated from the ditches' upper fills. He estimates that 1,064 vessels were represented by the fragments. These Brudenell (2016, 187) interprets as accumulations of midden from within the enclosure that were subsequently re-deposited in the ditches: 'a build up of material generated in periodic group gatherings at the site'.

Inaccessibility was served in another way by riverine islands, crannogs and timber platforms. In Ireland, the construction of crannogs (small artificial or modified islands) began by the fifteenth century, with more dated to the eleventh century and after (O'Sullivan 2007). The crannogs were stone or timber platforms constructed in open water, they were up to 20–30 metres in size and most were enclosed by palisades. House structures were generally lacking, although hearths have been identified, as at Rathtinaun, County Sligo, where a hearth stone was surrounded by a clay-covered wicker basket (Fredengren 2002). As with other crannogs, Rathtinaun produced a large amount of metalwork and clay metalworking moulds, along with pottery, and wooden vessels. A hoard of objects placed in a wooden box next to the crannog contained a necklace of amber beads, a number of rings made from bronze, tin and lead, tweezers, a bronze pin and six boar tusks. Other finds from close to the crannogs on Lough Gara, where Rathtinaun is located, included human skulls and bronze metalwork, particularly swords.

The hoard at Rathtinaun and the deposits of metalwork and human bone in the lake led Christina Fredengren (2002) to interpret crannogs as special locations set aside for the preparation of objects for deposition. Moynagh Lough, County Meath, supports this interpretation (Bradley 2004). During the nineteenth or eighteenth century BC, a small islet was constructed with timber and stone. There were two timber buildings, a palisade and occupation debris. The islet was occupied again in the late tenth century BC, with a different character compared with the occupation eight centuries earlier. Although the excavations found hearths and a small circular structure, there were no traces of occupation. These features were covered by a layer of burnt stone, which was rich in artefacts: 20 broken querns, bronze objects including spearheads and pins, 32 amber beads and fragments of shale and lignite bracelets. John Bradley (2004, 98) concludes with a similar interpretation for Moynagh Lough as Christina Fredengren offers for the Lough Gara crannogs: 'a place where people assembled and ate preparatory to depositing offerings in the lake'.

While votive offerings were made in lakes during the Bronze Age in Britain, there have not been accompanying dates or material culture from crannogs. Many crannogs are recorded in Scotland, where their occupation occurred during the Neolithic and Iron Age, not the Bronze Age. An exception comes from Duncan Garrow and Fraser Sturt's (2019) research on the Isle of Lewis, which produced fourteenth- to twelfth-century BC calibrated radiocarbon dates from a stone structure on a crannog on Loch Langabhat. They did not find material culture contemporary with the islet's Bronze Age occupation. Instead, the islet was surrounded by large numbers of early Neolithic vessels, which were deposited when the islet was constructed during the mid-fourth millennium BC.

Richard Bradley (2019, 235–240) compares the Irish crannogs with the timber platforms and island sites found along the Thames Valley and the East Anglian fen edge. Places such as Runnymede Bridge (Needham and Spence 1996) and Wallingford (Cromarty et al. 2006), where middens accumulated from periodic inhabitation, craftwork and feasting. I would draw the connections still wider, to include ringworks and some of the hilltop enclosures. They were places physically separated from and closely related with their surroundings. People, animals and things journeyed or were carried to the sites, where they crossed tangible thresholds in order to participate in gatherings. They were places for the sharing and consumption of food and drink. They were places from where votive gifts were made into rivers, lakes and bogs, either immediately adjacent or close by. They reflected their surrounding world and were at the same time apart from it. They performed worlds into being. The formalities, the associations with gatherings and exchanges, suggest moments of transformation and transition, rites of passage such as marriage or naming rituals, and events at which genealogies might be retold and reimagined.

Conclusions—a gathering of relations

Towards the end of the previous chapter I proposed that people built and dwelt in more durable houses from the sixteenth century BC and the houses' durability supported a closer association between kindred and a locality. Dwelling places were vibrant and generative, and houses were amongst the kin that came to life during domestic routines. There were important continuities in roundhouse architecture and the organisation of settlements throughout the the sixteenth to eighth centuries BC. Houses were usually isolated or in clusters of two or three.

These places were abandoned after a generation or two and occupation shifted close by. In Yarnton, Oxfordshire, and Meadowend Farm, Clackmannanshire, the basic settlement form varied relatively little between the middle and later centuries of the Bronze Age. There were regional changes within this coarsely drawn picture. In parts of East Anglia and the English Midlands, more durable domestic architecture appears in the archaeological record alongside the transition to using post-Deverel-Rimbury ceramics.

An important if gradual change was a widening variety of activities and materials gathered within settlements. These were activities that previously took place away from settlements or had happened with less intensity in settlements. Archaeological excavations more commonly identify evidence for craft production relating to textiles, bone and leather working, pottery production and metal casting (Brück 2007, 34–36). Salt-making was associated with some coastal or estuarine settlements. Four-post settings appear alongside roundhouses at many locations, and while their purpose is not known, the straightforward explanation is that the posts supported raised storage for fodder or grain. At South Elmsall, West Yorkshire, a cluster of three roundhouses faced towards eight or more four-post structures arranged in roughly north–south rows—the same alignment as the three houses (Chadwick 2012; Grassam 2010). At Torber, County Offaly, two four-post structures stood immediately alongside the entrance to a single timber roundhouse (Walsh 2011).

The practices associated with the preparation and consumption of food changed too, with a diverse repertoire of ceramic vessels found in the post-Deverel-Rimbury traditions of midland and southern England. There were jars, bowls and cups, some of which were made with finer temper and with the outer surfaces burnished (Figure 5.17). Matt Brudenell (2012, 265) identifies two broad

FIGURE 5.17 Two post-Deverel-Rimbury vessels: a polished carinated bowl from Must Farm, Cambridgeshire; a coarseware jar from Striplands Farm, Cambridgeshire. Images courtesy of Matt Brudenell and Cambridge Archaeological Unit.

types of post-Deverel-Rimbury ceramic assemblage in eastern England. In fineware bowl-dominated assemblages, there were high frequencies of large jars and smaller burnished bowls, which suggested they enabled large-scale preparation of food and individual consumption. The coarseware jar-dominated assemblages contained more small jars, whose size made them suitable for cooking and serving daily meals amongst smaller numbers of people. These assemblage types did not map neatly to different forms of settlement. The distinctions in eating customs were probably determined by who participated and when, rather than the place where the meals occurred.

The twelfth and eleventh centuries brought a shift in the importance of households and houses as places of production, storage and consumption. Craft and consumption created relations outwards as much as within the settlements. As foci for production, households defined localities and distance through the materials they drew in, the things they crafted and the substances they transformed. The pottery from Tinney's Lane reached settlements up to 8 kilometres distant, which was not far. Perhaps the textiles made at the Reading Business Park settlements were exchanged more widely, as might the salt from Brean Down. The axes and swords made at Jarlshof could have travelled still further and passed through multiple exchanges and relations. Localities and their kin were defined by these relationships.

The traces of some crafts readily accumulated within and close to houses. Metalworking was unusual because its residues tended to be deposited in peripheral places or zones, close to settlements or on the margins of settlement. These locations may have been enclosing ditches as at Springfield Lyons, the waterholes and pits at Kemerton or the blocked-off niches in abandoned buildings at Jarlshof. These relationships reflected the status of metalworking as magical or otherworldly, although it was not so potent or dangerous as its residues could intermingle with domestic refuse, amongst middens, and in pits and ditches. During this same time, fragmentary human bone, burnt and unburnt, was more commonly mixed together with settlement debris, whether as specific depositions or accumulated within middens. In Kerri Cleary's (2018) review of human bone from settlements in Ireland, all her radiocarbon-dated sites post-date the twelfth century BC, with the exception of Chancellorsland. Dwelling places were empowered by and had sufficient power to control vibrant substances like human bone and metalworking debris.

Prehistorians routinely describe hilltop enclosures, which were widely constructed from the twelfth century BC, as high-status settlements that projected the power of their inhabitants and occupied the top tier in a hierarchy of open and enclosed sites. I suggest the enclosures were connected with while distinct from domestic life. The enclosures were large labour projects that monumentalised well-known and important places. Digging out the ditches, sourcing timber and raising the palisades gathered kin together and related them through their transformation of landmarks. Some enclosures remained empty of built structures, while others were only inhabited for short periods. The two circuits of low banks and shallow ditches at Ballylin, County Limerick, enclose 21 hectares with no evidence the enclosed area was occupied (O'Brien and O'Driscoll 2017, 142–159). Archaeological excavation of an entrance into the inner enclosure identified a five-metre gap flanked by large postholes. This was a grand gateway into a seemingly empty space. This emptiness, as defined archaeologically, is deceptive. The hills were powerful places, drawn into social life and landmarked through enclosure. Enclosure created spaces where people and animals could gather, and distinctions made according to access and association with powerful places. There was a making of kin, humans and animals, through assembly. On occasions the enclosures underwent spectacular transformations when their palisades were set alight and burnt to the ground. Charred and vitrified, the boundaries and the hills took on new meanings following these performances.

In cases where hilltop enclosures contained evidence for intensive occupation and at ringworks and crannogs, there appears to be a more straightforward equivalence with status and hierarchy. Applying terms like elite and chiefdom is unhelpful. These terms and the models they represent shortcut the necessary process of tracing connections between the places, their inhabitants and their worlds. The enclosures were firmly, knowledgeably separated from the lived-in landscape. The recurrence of three circuits of enclosing boundaries at Irish sites is a striking pattern: Dún Aonghasa, Rahally, Haughey's Fort, Rathgall are examples. Surrounding Haughey's Fort with water-filled ditches might have found a different expression in the use of crannogs and riverine islands. Enclosures also chose edgeland locations, with Dún Aonghasa the most dramatic instance. The ringworks mimicked the forms of ancient monuments with henge-like circular enclosures or causewayed ditches. These boundaries set the enclosed spaces apart from the domestic world. They were places for communicating with and drawing power from other worlds through performances: reciting genealogies, rites of passage, occasions of significant exchanges and so on.

The people, animals and things that gathered in hilltop enclosures, ringworks and crannogs were composed from their surroundings. The cereals consumed at Haughey's Fort came from fields throughout the landscape, as presumably did the animals and people. The pottery in ringworks was largely the same as that found in nearby open settlements, perhaps with a higher proportion of fineware. The distinctions lay in the amount and range of materials that accumulated in the enclosures, which were a consequence of the size and diversity of the gatherings. Central houses, or structures like houses, stood within a few of the excavated ringworks. They seemed to proclaim, Christopher Evans has written, 'that *the house*—and presumably its central hearth—lay at the core of everything' (Evans et al. 2016, 211). People and their relations with one another were transformed through the events, the performances and discourses, at enclosures. They took these differences and their relations out into the world. The swords made at Springfield Lyons were gifts that bound people and place together. New powerful kin emerged from enclosures. They went out into the world beyond the enclosure with their relations transformed.

References

Adkins, Lesley and Stuart Needham. 1985. New research on a Late Bronze Age enclosure at Queen Mary's Hospital, Carshalton. *Surrey Archaeological Collections* 76:11–50.

Andrews, Phil. 2006. A Middle to Late Bronze Age settlement at Dunch Hill, Tidworth. *Wiltshire Studies* 99:51–78.

Appadurai, Arjun. 1996. *Modernity at large: cultural dimensions of globalization*. University of Minnesota Press, Minneapolis.

Armit, Ian. 2007. Hillforts at war: from Maiden Castle to Taniwaha Pā. *Proceedings of the Prehistoric Society* 73:25–37.

Armit, Ian, Andrew Dunwell, Fraser Hunter and Eilmear Nelis. 2005. Traprain Law: archaeology from the ashes. *Past* 49:1–4.

Barnatt, John, Bill Bevan and Mark Edmonds. 2017. *An upland biography: landscape and prehistory on Gardom's Edge, Derbyshire*. Windgather, Oxford.

Barrett, John C, Richard Bradley and Martin Green. 1991. *Landscape, monuments and society: the prehistory of Cranborne Chase*. Cambridge University Press, Cambridge.

Basso, Keith H. 1984. "Stalking with stories": names, places, and moral narratives among the Western Apache. In *Text, play, and story: the construction and reconstruction of self and society*, edited by Edward M Bruner, pp. 19–55. Waveland Press, Prospect Heights, Illinois.

Bayliss, Alex, Christopher Bronk Ramsey, Gordon Cook, Lilian Ladle, John Meadows, Johannes van der Plicht, Robert Scaife and Ann Woodward. 2009. Radiocarbon dating. In *Excavations at Bestwall Quarry, Wareham 1992–2005. Volume 1: the prehistoric landscape*, edited by Lilian Ladle and Ann Woodward, pp. 126–153. Dorset Natural History and Archaeological Society, Dorchester.

Becker, Katharina. 2010. Heritage guide No. 51: Rathgall, Co. Wicklow. *Archaeology Ireland* 24(4).

Bell, Martin. 1990. *Brean Down: excavations 1983–87*. English Heritage, London.

Bergh, Stefan. 2015. Where worlds meet: two Irish prehistoric mountain-top 'villages'. *Il Capitale culturale: studies on the value of cultural heritage* 12:21–44.

Best, Joanne and Ann Woodward. 2011. Late Bronze Age pottery production: evidence from a 12th–11th century cal BC settlement at Tinney's Lane, Sherborne, Dorset. *Proceedings of the Prehistoric Society* 78:207–261.

Bond, Dermot. 1988. *Excavation at the North Ring, Mucking, Essex: a Late Bronze Age enclosure*. East Anglian Archaeology, 43. Essex County Council, Chelmsford.

Bowman, Sheridan and Stuart Needham. 2007. The Dunaverney and Little Thetford flesh-hooks: history, technology and their position within the Later Bronze Age Atlantic zone feasting complex. *Antiquaries Journal* 87:53–108.

Bradley, John. 2004. Moynagh Lough, Co. Meath, in the Late Bronze Age. In *From Megaliths to metal: essays in honour of George Eogan*, edited by Helen Roche, Eoin Grogan, John Bradley, John Coles and Barry Raftery, pp. 91–98. Oxbow, Oxford.

Bradley, Richard. 2019. *The prehistory of Britain and Ireland (second edition)*. Cambridge University Press, Cambridge.

Bradley, Richard, Roy Entwistle and Frances Raymond. 1994. *Prehistoric land divisions on Salisbury Plain: the work of the Wessex Linear Ditches Project*. English Heritage, London.

Bradley, Richard, Colin Haselgrove, Marc Vander Linden and Leo Webley. 2016. *The later prehistory of north-west Europe: the evidence of development-led fieldwork*. Oxford University Press, Oxford.

Brandherm, Dirk. 2014. Late Bronze Age casting debris and other base metal finds from Haughey's Fort. *Emania* 22:59–68.

Brossler, Adam, Robert Early and Carol Allen. 2004. *Green Park (Reading Business Park). Phase 2 excavations 1995—Neolithic and Bronze Age sites.* Thames Valley Landscapes, 19. Oxford University School of Archaeology, Oxford.

Brown, Nigel and Maria Medlycott. 2013. *The Neolithic and Bronze Age enclosures at Springfield Lyons, Essex: excavations 1981–1991.* East Anglian Archaeology, 149. Essex County Council, Chelmsford.

Brück, Joanna. 1997. *The Early–Middle Bronze Age transition in Wessex, Sussex and the Thames Valley.* PhD thesis, University of Cambridge.

Brück, Joanna. 1999. Houses, lifecycles and deposition on Middle Bronze Age settlements in southern England. *Proceedings of the Prehistoric Society* 65:145–166.

Brück, Joanna. 2000. Settlement, landscape and social identity: the Early–Middle Bronze Age transition in Wessex, Sussex and the Thames Valley. *Oxford Journal of Archaeology* 19(3):273–300.

Brück, Joanna. 2007. The character of Late Bronze Age settlement in southern Britain. In *The Earlier Iron Age in Britain and the near Continent*, edited by Colin Haselgrove and Rachel Pope, pp. 24–38. Oxbow, Oxford.

Brudenell, Matt. 2012. *Pots, practice and society: an investigation of pattern and variability in the Post-Deverel Rimbury ceramic tradition of East Anglia.* PhD thesis, University of York.

Brudenell, Matt. 2016. Late Bronze Age pottery. In *Lives in land. Mucking excavations by Margaret and Tom Jones, 1965–1978: prehistory, context and summary*, edited by Christopher Evans, Grahame Appleby, Sam Lucy, Jo Appleby and Matt Brudenell, pp. 158–188. Oxbow Books, Oxford.

Buckland, Paul C, Mike Parker Pearson, Andy Wigley and Maureen A Girling. 2001. Is there anybody out there? A reconsideration of the environmental evidence from the Breiddin hillfort, Powys, Wales. *Antiquaries Journal* 81:51–76.

Chadwick, Adrian. 2012. Routine magic, mundane ritual: towards a unified notion of depositional practice. *Oxford Journal of Archaeology* 31(3):283–315.

Champion, Timothy. 2014. Food, technology and culture in the Late Bronze Age of southern Britain: perforated clay plates of the Lower Thames Valley. *Proceedings of the Prehistoric Society* 80:279–298.

Clarke, Ann. 2006. *Stone tools and the prehistory of the Northern Isles.* BAR British Series, 406. Archaeopress, Oxford.

Cleary, Kerri. 2018. Broken bones and broken stones: exploring fragmentation in Middle and Late Bronze Age settlement contexts in Ireland. *European Journal of Archaeology* 21(3):336–360.

Cleary, Rose M. 1995. Later Bronze Age settlement and prehistoric burials, Lough Gur, Co. Limerick. *Proceedings of the Royal Irish Academy* 95C:1–92.

Cleary, Rose M. 2003. Enclosed Late Bronze Age habitation site and boundary wall at Lough Gur, Co. Limerick. *Proceedings of the Royal Irish Academy* 103C:97–189.

Cleary, Rose M. 2018. *The archaeology of Lough Gur.* Wordwell, Dublin.

Collins, A E Pat and Wilfred A Seaby. 1960. A crannog at Lough Eskragh, County Tyrone. *Ulster Journal of Archaeology* 23:25–37.

Coombs, David G. 1975. Bronze Age weapon hoards in Britain. *Archaeologia Atlantica* 1:49–81.

Coombs, David G and Frederick H Thompson. 1979. Excavation of the hill fort of Mam Tor, Derbyshire 1965–69. *Derbyshire Archaeological Journal* 49:7–51.

Cotter, Claire. 2012. *The Western Stone Forts Project: excavations at Dún Aonghasa and Dún Eoghanachta.* Wordwell, Dublin.

Cowie, Trevor. 2001. Galmisdale, Eigg, Highland (Small Isles parish): late Bronze Age metal working debris; flint cache. *Discovery and Excavation in Scotland* 2:63.

Cowie, Trevor, Mark Hall, Brendan O'Connor and Richard Tipping. 1996. The Late Bronze Age hoard from Corrymuckloch, near Amulree, Perthshire: an interim report. *Tayside and Fife Archaeological Journal* 2:60–69.

Cromarty, Anne Marie, Alistair Barclay, George Lambrick and Mark Robinson. 2006. *Late Bronze Age ritual and habitation on a Thames eyot at Whitecross Farm, Wallingford: the archaeology of the Wallingford bypass, 1986–92.* Thames Valley Landscapes, 22. Oxford Archaeology, Oxford.

Cruikshank, Julie. 2005. *Do glaciers listen? Local knowledge, colonial encounters and social imagination.* UBC Press, Vancouver.

Curle, Alexander O. 1931/1932. Interim report on the excavation of a Bronze Age dwelling at Yarlshof, Shetland, in 1931. *Proceedings of the Society of Antiquaries of Scotland* 66:113–128.

Curle, Alexander O. 1932/1933. Account of further excavations in 1932 of the prehistoric township at Jarlshof, Shetland, on behalf of H.M. Office of Works. *Proceedings of the Society of Antiquaries of Scotland* 67:82–136.

Curle, Alexander O. 1933/1934. An account of further excavation at Jarlshof, Sumburgh, Shetland, in 1932 and 1933. *Proceedings of the Society of Antiquaries of Scotland* 68:224–319.

Darvill, Timothy. 2010. *Prehistoric Britain.* Routledge, London.

Davis, Mary and Annette Townsend. 2009. Modelling the Caergwrle bowl: ancient, historic and modern methods. In *Holding it all together: ancient and modern approaches to joining, repair and consolidation*, edited by Janet Ambers, Catherine Higgitt, Lynne Harrison and David Saunders, pp. 177–183. Archetype, London.

Descola, Philippe. 1997. *The spears of twilight: life and death in the Amazon jungle*, London.

Dockrell, Stephen. 2007. *Tofts Ness, Sanday: an island landscape through 3000 years of prehistory.* The Orcadian, Kirkwall.

Downes, Jane and Raymond Lamb. 2000. *Prehistoric houses at Sumburgh in Shetland: excavations at Sumburgh Airport 1967–74.* Oxbow, Oxford.

Ellis, Chris J and Mike Rawlings. 2001. Excavations at Balksbury Camp, Andover 1995–97. *Proceedings of the Hampshire Field Club and Archaeological Society* 56:21–94.

Evans, Christopher, Grahame Appleby, Sam Lucy, Jo Appleby and Matt Brudenell. 2016. *Lives in land. Mucking excavations by Margaret and Tom Jones, 1965–1978: prehistory, context and summary.* Oxbow Books, Oxford.

Evans, Christopher, Jonathan Tabor and Marc Vander Linden. 2016. *Twice-crossed river: prehistoric and palaeoenvironmental investigations at Barleycroft Farm/Over, Cambridgeshire.* McDonald Institute for Archaeological Research, Cambridge.

Fredengren, Christina. 2002. *Crannogs: a study of people's interaction with lakes, with particular reference to Lough Gara in the north-west of Ireland.* Wordwell, Bray.

Gardner, Willoughby and Hubert N Savory. 1964. *Dinorben: a hill-fort occupied in Early Iron Age and Roman times.* National Museum of Wales, Cardiff.

Garrow, Duncan and Fraser Sturt. 2019. Neolithic crannogs: rethinking settlement, monumentality and deposition in the Outer Hebrides and beyond. *Antiquity* 93(369):664–684.

Gerloff, Sabine. 1986. Bronze Age Class A cauldrons: typology, origins and chronology. *Journal of the Royal Society of Antiquaries of Ireland* 116:84–115.

Gerloff, Sabine. 2010. *Atlantic cauldrons and buckets of the Late Bronze Age and Early Iron Age in western Europe.* Prähistorische Bronzefunde II/18, Stuttgart.

Gibson, Alex. 2018. Llandegai A—sanctuary or settlement? *Archaeologia Cambrensis* 167:95–108.

Gilmour, Nick, Sarah Horlock, Richard Mortimer and Sophie Tremlett. 2014. Middle Bronze Age enclosures in the Norfolk Broads: a case study at Ormesby St Michael, England. *Proceedings of the Prehistoric Society* 80:141–157.

Ginn, Victoria. 2012. *Settlement structure in Middle–Late Bronze Age Ireland.* PhD thesis, Queen's University Belfast.

Grassam, Alexandra. 2010. *Excavations on land between Field Lane and Doncaster Road, South Elmsall, West Yorkshire: excavation report.* Archaeological Services WYAS, Leeds.

Grogan, Eoin. 2005a. *The North Munster Project. Volume 1: the later prehistoric landscape of south-east Clare.* Wordwell, Bray.

Grogan, Eoin. 2005b. *The North Munster Project. Volume 2: the prehistoric landscape of north Munster.* Wordwell, Bray.

Grogan, Eoin and George Eogan. 1987. Lough Gur excavations by Seán P. Ó Ríordáin: further Neolithic and Beaker habitations on Knockadoon. *Proceedings of the Royal Irish Academy* 87C:299–506.

Guttmann, Erika B. 2005. Midden cultivation in prehistoric Britain: arable crops in gardens. *World Archaeology* 37(2):224–239.

Guttmann, Erika B and Jonathan Last. 2000. A Late Bronze Age landscape at South Hornchurch, Essex. *Proceedings of the Prehistoric Society* 66:319–359.

Hambleton, Ellen. 2008. *Review of Middle Bronze Age–Late Iron Age faunal assemblages from southern Britain.* Research Department Report Series, 71–2008. English Heritage, London.

Hamilton, John R C. 1956. *Excavations at Jarlshof, Shetland.* Her Majesty's Stationery Office, Edinburgh.

Hamilton, Sue and John Manley. 2001. Hillforts, monumentality and place: a chronological and topographic review of first millennium BC hillforts of south-east England. *European Journal of Archaeology* 4(1):7–42.

Hamilton-Dyer, Sheila. 2009. Animal bone report. In *N6 Galway to East Ballinasloe PPP scheme archaeological contract 3, phase 2 final report. ministerial directions: A041. Excavation registration No: E2006. Rahally, Co. Galway: hillfort, ringforts and field system,* edited by Gerry Mullins and Nóra Bermingham, pp. 272–310. CRDS Ltd, Dublin.

Hartwell, Barrie. 1991. Recent air survey results from Navan. *Emania* 8:5–9.

Haselgrove, Colin. 2009. *The Traprain Law Environs Project: fieldwork and excavations 2000–2004.* Society of Antiquaries of Scotland, Edinburgh.

Hearne, Carrie M and Neil Adam. 1999. Excavation of an extensive Late Bronze-Age settlement at Shorncote Quarry, near Cirencester, 1995–6. *Transactions of the Bristol and Gloucestershire Archaeological Society* 117:35–73.

Hey, Gill, Christopher Bell, Caroline Dennis and Mark Robinson. 2016. *Yarnton: Neolithic and Bronze Age settlement and landscape.* Thames Valley Landscapes, 39. Oxford University School of Archaeology, Oxford.

Hunter, Fraser, Trevor Cowie and Andrew Heald. 2006. Research priorities for archaeometallurgy in Scotland. *Scottish Archaeological Journal* 28(1):49–62.

Hurst, Derek. 2011. Middle Bronze Age to Iron Age: a research assessment overview and agenda. In *The archaeology of the West Midlands: a framework for research,* edited by Sarah Watt, pp. 101–126. Oxbow, Oxford.

Jackson, Robin. 2015. *Huntsman's Quarry, Kemerton: a Late Bronze Age settlement and landscape in Worcestershire.* Oxbow, Oxford.

Johnson, Nicholas and Peter Rose. 1994. *Bodmin Moor: an archaeological survey. Volume 1—the human landscape to c.1800.* English Heritage, London.

Jones, Andy M. 2015. Discussion: pits, deposition, metalworking and circularity. In *Settlement and metalworking in the Middle Bronze Age and beyond: new evidence from Tremough,*

Cornwall, edited by Andy M Jones, James Gossip and Henrietta Quinnell, pp. 159–225. Sidestone, Leiden.

Jones, Andy M, James Gossip and Henrietta Quinnell (editors). 2015. *Settlement and Metalworking in the Middle Bronze Age and Beyond: new evidence from Tremough, Cornwall.* Sidestone, Leiden.

Jones, Elizabeth, Alison Sheridan and Julie Franklin. 2018. Neolithic and Bronze Age occupation at Meadowend Farm, Clackmannanshire: pots, pits and roundhouses. *Scottish Archaeological Internet Reports* 77.

Jones, Glanville R J. 1996. The *gwely* as a tenurial institution. *Studia Celtica* 30:167–188.

Knight, Mark, Rachel Ballantyne, Iona Robinson Zeki and David Gibson. 2019. The Must Farm pile-dwelling settlement. *Antiquity* 93(369):645–663.

Knight, Matthew. 2018. *The intentional destruction and deposition of Bronze Age metalwork in south west England.* PhD thesis, University of Exeter.

Ladle, Lilian and Ann Woodward. 2009. *Excavations at Bestwall Quarry, Wareham 1992–2005. Volume 1: the prehistoric landscape.* Dorset Natural History and Archaeological Society, Dorchester.

Lambrick, George. 2009. Dividing up the countryside. In *The Thames through time: the archaeology of the gravel terraces of the Upper and Middle Thames. The Thames Valley in late prehistory: 1500 BC–AD 50*, edited by George Lambrick and Mark Robinson, pp. 53–90. Oxford Archaeology, Oxford.

Latour, Bruno. 2005. *Reassembling the social: an introduction to actor-network theory.* Oxford University Press, Oxford.

Leach, James. 2003. *Creative land: place and procreation on the Rai Coast of Papua New Guinea.* Berghahn Books, Oxford.

Lewis, John, Matt Leivers, Lisa Brown, Alex Smith, Kate Cramp, Lorraine Mepham and Chris Phillpotts. 2010. *Landscape evolution in the Middle Thames Valley: Heathrow Terminal 5 excavations. Volume 2.* Framework Archaeology, Oxford and Salisbury.

Lock, Gary. 2011. Hillforts, emotional metaphors, and the good life: a response to Armit. *Proceedings of the Prehistoric Society* 77:355–362.

Lock, Gary and Ian Ralston. 2017. Atlas of Hillforts of Britain and Ireland https://hillforts.arch.ox.ac.uk, accessed 30/11/19.

Lynch, Frances and Chris R Musson. 2004. A prehistoric and early medieval complex at Llandegai, near Bangor, North Wales. *Archaeologia Cambrensis* 150:17–142.

Lynn, Chris J. 1977. Trial excavations at the King's Stables, Tray Townland, County Armagh. *Ulster Journal of Archaeology* 40:42–62.

Macdonald, Philip. 2016. Excavations at Knock Dhu promontory fort, Ballyhackett, Co. Antrim 2008. *Emania* 23:33–52.

Mallory, James P and Gina Baban. 2014. Excavations in Haughey's Fort East. *Emania* 22:13–32.

Manby, Terry G. 2007. Continuity of monumental traditions into the Late Bronze Age? Henges to ring-forts, and shrines. In *Beyond Stonehenge: essays in honour of Colin Burgess*, edited by Christopher Burgess, Peter Topping and Frances Lynch, pp. 403–424. Oxbow, Oxford.

Manning, Andrew and Chris Moore. 2003. A Late Bronze Age site at Springfield Park, Chelmsford. *Essex Archaeology and History* 34:19–35.

Marshall, Will and Kevin Solman. 2015. Geochemical analysis of samples from Tremough. In *Settlement and Metalworking in the Middle Bronze Age and beyond: new evidence from Tremough, Cornwall*, edited by Andy M Jones, James Gossip and Henrietta Quinnell, pp. 107–110. Sidestone, Leiden.

McClatchie, Meriel. 2014. Food production in the Bronze Age: analysis of plant macro-remains from Haughey's Fort, Co. Armagh. *Emania* 22:33–43.

McCormick, Finbar. 1991. The animal bones from Haughey's Fort: second report. *Emania* 8:27–33.

McKeon, Jim and Jerry O'Sullivan (editors). 2014. *The quiet landscape: archaeological investigations on the M6 Galway to Ballinasloe national road scheme*. NRA Scheme Monographs, 15. National Roads Authority, Dublin.

Meadows, John, Gordon Cook and Christopher Bronk Ramsey. 2013. Radiocarbon dating In *The Neolithic and Bronze Age enclosures at Springfield Lyons, Essex: excavations 1981–1991*, edited by Nigel Brown and Maria Medlycott, pp. 141–147. East Anglian Archaeology, 149. Essex County Council, Chelmsford.

Miles, David, Simon Palmer, Gary Lock, Chris Gosden and Ann Marie Cromarty. 2003. *Uffington White Horse and its landscape: investigations at White Horse Hill, Uffington, 1989–95, and Tower Hill, Ashbury, 1993–4*. Thames Valley Landscapes, 18. Oxford Archaeology, Oxford.

Moloney, Aonghus. 1993. *Excavations at Clonfinlough, County Offaly*. Irish Archaeological Wetland Unit, Dublin.

Moore, Hazel and Graeme Wilson. 2011. *Shifting sands. Links of Noltland, Westray: interim report on Neolithic and Bronze Age excavations, 2007–09*. Historic Scotland, Edinburgh.

Moore, John and David Jennings. 1992. *Reading Business Park: a Bronze Age landscape*. Oxford University Committee for Archaeology, Oxford.

Morris, Elaine L. 1994. Production and distribution of pottery and salt in Iron Age Britain: a review. *Proceedings of the Prehistoric Society* 60:371–393.

Morris, Elaine L. 2004. Later prehistoric pottery. In *Green Park (Reading Business Park). Phase 2 excavations 1995—Neolithic and Bronze Age sites*, edited by Adam Brossler, Robert Early and Carol Allen, pp. 58–91. Thames Valley Landscapes, 19. Oxford University School of Archaeology, Oxford.

Muñiz-Pérez, Marta and Nóra Bermingham. 2014. Cremation cemetery and palisaded enclosure at Treanbaun. In *The quiet landscape: archaeological investigations on the M6 Galway to Ballinasloe national road scheme*, edited by Jim McKeon and Jerry O'Sullivan, pp. 122–129. NRA Scheme Monographs, 15. National Roads Authority, Dublin.

Murphy, Donald and Linda Clarke. 2001. 2001:1006—Site 17, Lagavooreen, Meath https://excavations.ie/report/2001/Meath/0006940/, accessed 05/12/18.

Murphy, Eileen and Finbar McCormick. 1996. The faunal remains from the inner ditch of Haughey's Fort. Third report: 1991 excavation. *Emania* 14:47–50.

Musson, Chris R, William J Britnell and A Gilbert Smith. 1991. *The Breiddin hillfort: a later prehistoric settlement in the Welsh Marches*. CBA Research Report, 76. Council for British Archaeology, London.

Needham, Stuart. 1980. An assemblage of Late Bronze Age metalworking debris from Dainton, Devon. *Proceedings of the Prehistoric Society* 46:177–215.

Needham, Stuart. 1992. The structure of settlement and ritual in the Late Bronze Age of south-east Britain. In *L'habitat et l'occupation du sol à l'Age du Bronze en Europe*, edited by Claude Mordant and Annick Richard, pp. 49–69. Edition du comité des travaux historiques et scientifiques, Paris.

Needham, Stuart and Janet Ambers. 1994. Redating Rams Hill and reconsidering Bronze Age enclosure. *Proceedings of the Prehistoric Society* 60:225–243.

Needham, Stuart and Sheridan Bowman. 2005. Flesh-hooks, technological complexity and the Atlantic Bronze Age feasting complex. *European Journal of Archaeology* 8(2):93–136.

Needham, Stuart and Susan Bridgford. 2013. Deposits of clay refractories for casting bronze swords. In *The Neolithic and Bronze Age enclosures at Springfield Lyons, Essex: excavations 1981–1991*, edited by Nigel Brown and Maria Medlycott, pp. 47–74. East Anglian Archaeology, 149. Essex County Council, Chelmsford.

Needham, Stuart and Tony Spence. 1996. *Refuse and disposal at Area 16 East, Runnymeade.* British Museum Press, London.

Ní Líonáin, Clíodhna. 2007. Life, death and food production in Bronze Age Ireland: recent excavations at Stamullin, Co. Meath. *Archaeology Ireland* 21(2):18–21.

Nowakowski, Jacqueline A. 2009. Living in the sands—Bronze Age Gwithian, Cornwall, revisited. In *Land and people: papers in memory of John G Evans*, edited by Michael J Allen, Niall Sharples and Terry O'Connor, pp. 115–125. Prehistoric Society Research Papers, 2. Prehistoric Society/Oxbow Books, Oxford.

Ó Ríordáin, Seán P. 1954. Lough Gur excavations: Neolithic and Bronze Age houses on Knockadoon. *Proceedings of the Royal Irish Academy* 56C:297–459.

O'Brien, William and James O'Driscoll. 2017. *Hillforts, warfare and society in Bronze Age Ireland.* Archaeopress, Oxford.

O'Sullivan, Aidan. 2007. Exploring past people's interactions with wetland environments in Ireland. *Proceedings of the Royal Irish Academy* 107C:147–203.

O'Brien, William. 2017. The development of the hillfort in prehistoric Ireland. *Proceedings of the Royal Irish Academy* 117C:3–61.

O'Connell, Aidan. 2013. *Harvesting the stars: a pagan temple at Lismullin, Co. Meath.* NRA Scheme Monographs, 11. National Roads Authority, Dublin.

O'Driscoll, James. 2017. Hillforts in prehistoric Ireland: a costly display of power? *World Archaeology* 49(4):506–525.

O'Neil, Tara. 2009. *M3 Clonee–Kells Motorway: report on the archaeological excavation of Skreen 3, County Meath.* Archaeological Consultancy Services Ltd, Drogheda.

Parker Pearson, Mike, Chris Casswell and Kate Welham. 2018. A Late Bronze Age ringfort at Bayvil Farm, Pembrokeshire. *Archaeologia Cambrensis* 167:113–141.

Parker Pearson, Mike, Niall Sharples and Jim Symonds. 2004. *South Uist: archaeology and history of a Hebridean island.* Tempus, Stroud.

Pearce, Susan. 1970. A Late Bronze Age hoard from Glentanar, Aberdeenshire. *Proceedings of the Society of Antiquaries of Scotland* 103:57–64.

Pearce, Susan. 2015. The moulds and metalwork. In *Settlement and metalworking in the Middle Bronze Age and beyond: new evidence from Tremough, Cornwall*, edited by Andy M Jones, James Gossip and Henrietta Quinnell, pp. 89–105. Sidestone, Leiden.

Powell, Andrew, Alistair Barclay, Lorraine Mepham, Chris Stevens and Phil Andrews. 2015. *Imperial College Sports Ground and RMC Land, Harlington: the development of prehistoric and later communities in the Colne Valley and on the Heathrow Terrace.* Wessex Archaeology, Salisbury.

Primas, Margarita. 2002. Taking the high ground: continental hill-forts in Bronze Age contexts. *Proceedings of the Prehistoric Society* 68:41–59.

RCAHMS. 2003. *Eigg the archaeology of a Hebridean landscape (RCAHMS Broadsheet 12).* Royal Commission on the Ancient and Historical Monuments of Scotland, Edinburgh.

Robinson, Mark and George Lambrick. 2009. Living off the land: farming, water, storage and waste. In *The Thames through time: the archaeology of the gravel terraces of the Upper and Middle Thames. The Thames Valley in late prehistory: 1500 BC–AD 50*, edited by George Lambrick and Mark Robinson, pp. 237–282. Oxford Archaeology, Oxford.

Robinson, Tim. 1990. *Stones of Arran: Pilgrimage.* Penguin, London.

Russell, Ian and Eoin Cocoran. 2001. *Northern motorway road project. Contract 7: Gormanstown–Monasterboice. Kilsharvan 16.* Archaeological Consultancy Services Ltd, Drogheda.

Sharples, Niall. 2010. *Social relations in later prehistory: Wessex in the first millennium BC.* Oxford University Press, Oxford.

Silvester, Robert J. 1980. The prehistoric open settlement at Dainton, South Devon. *Proceedings of the Devon Archaeological Society* 38:17–38.

Simpson, Ian A, Stephen J Dockrill, Ian D Bull and Richard P Evershed. 1998. Early anthropogenic soil formation at Tofts Ness, Sanday, Orkney. *Journal of Archaeological Science* 25(8):729–746.

Sites, Rachel. 2015. *Collapse, continuity, or growth? Investigating agricultural change through architectural proxies at the end of the Bronze Age in southern Britain and Denmark.* PhD thesis, University of Sheffield.

Smith, A Gilbert. 1991. Buckbean Pond: environmental studies. In *The Breiddin hillfort: a later prehistoric settlement in the Welsh Marches,* edited by Chris R Musson, William J Britnell and A Gilbert Smith, pp. 95–111. CBA Research Report, 76. Council for British Archaeology, London.

Tabor, Richard. 2008. *Cadbury Castle: the hillfort and landscapes.* History Press, Stroud.

Wainwright, Geoff J and Ken Smith. 1980. The Shaugh Moor Project: second report—the enclosure. *Proceedings of the Prehistoric Society* 46:65–122.

Walsh, Fintan. 2011. Excavation and conjecture of a late Bronze Age farmstead at Tober, Co. Offaly. *Journal of the Royal Society of Antiquaries of Ireland* 141:9–31.

Ward, Michael and George Smith. 2001. The Llŷn Crop Marks Project. Aerial survey and ground evaluation of Bronze Age and Romano-British settlement and funerary sites in the Llŷn Peninsula of North West Wales: excavations by Richard Kelly and Michael Ward. *Studia Celtica* 35:1–87.

Warner, Richard. 2006. The Tamlaght hoard and the Creeveroe axe: two new finds of Late Bronze Age date from near Navan, Co. Armagh. *Emania* 20:20–28.

Weir, David A. 1993. *An environmental history of the Navan area, Co. Armagh.* PhD thesis, Queen's University Belfast.

Wiggins, Ken, Bartosz Duszynski and Vicky Ginn. 2009. *M3 Clonee–North of Kells. Contract 2: Dunshaughlin–Navan. Report on the archaeological excavation of Ross 1, Co. Meath.* Archaeological Consultancy Services Ltd, Drogheda.

Williams, Brian B. 1978. Excavations at Lough Eskragh, County Tyrone. *Ulster Journal of Archaeology* 41:37–48.

Yates, David T. 2007. *Land, power and prestige: Bronze Age field systems in southern England.* Oxbow, Oxford.

PART III

Landmarks

6

ENCHANTING PLACES

2500–1500 BC

In John Hewitt's words, Ulster's rural landscape is a 'map of kinship…a chart of use…never at any level a fine view' (Hewitt 2007, 28). Hewitt used his poem, entitled 'Landscape', to emphasise work over recreation, and social networks over aesthetics—'landscape is families'. He reminds us that landscapes are constituted by people's labours alongside one another and with the environment in which they dwell. Henry Glassie, an ethnographer of rural life, related people, work and landscape in his description of turf cutting in County Fermanagh:

> 'Three men is the way for the bog', said Joe Murphy. Hugh Nolan put it like this: 'To work in comfort in the bog, you wanted to have three men, one cuttin, one liftin, one wheelin. I cut. I lifted. I wheeled.' Their agreement, termed 'swappin', arranged for each man's bog to be cut in turn by its owner with the help of two neighbours.
>
> *(Glassie 1995, 474)*

The social qualities of work make landscapes and they make kin. This happens during the co-presence of inhabiting places, and through exchanges of labour and knowledge about the environment.

The bogs where Joe Murphy and Hugh Nolan cut turf would once in a while reveal traces of the deep past, including worked timbers and (exceptionally) 'bog bodies', along with, more commonly, buried tree stumps. The diggers interpreted the stumps as evidence of the catastrophic impact of Noah's flood: 'strange and secret reminders of an ancient past' (Glassie 1995, 482). The bogs were ambivalent spaces, which people treated with caution and even fear: bottomless, unstable surfaces that were traps for unwary travellers and the homes of malign spirits and creatures (Meredith 2002). Bogs shift and appear to breath as their water table fluctuates and moves. Bogs are alive. Their bacteria digest vegetation and exhale methane and carbon dioxide (so-called 'marsh gas').

Bacterial methanogens could be responsible for the ethereal luminescence (will-o'-the-wisp or *ignis fatuus*) that has been observed over bogland. Written accounts of will-o'-the-wisp survive from the fourteenth century (Mills 1980). In most folk tales, the lights have a malign purpose, leading the unwary into danger. 'Will-o'-the-wisp' is widely used now when referring to a delusive concept that leads reasoning astray—like the traveller taken onto perilous ground by the wisp's beckoning glow. The problem with this metaphor is that *ignis fatuus* was precisely, consistently and reliably observed. It is 'manifestly real' (Edwards 2014, 4). Rather than a delusion, it is illusive. While academic works credit the ethereal bluish light to the combustion of marsh gas, this explanation remains unproven and problematic. There is no convincing mechanism for the methane's ignition nor a reason why first-hand accounts describe the flame as cool, when methane burns hot. Observations of *ignis fatuus* largely ceased at the end of the nineteenth century and scientists have been unable to replicate the phenomenon in laboratories. It has receded to folklore and metaphor.

The task in writing about Bronze Age landscapes is to retain these different facets of humanity's relations with land: as practice and mystery. Rather than beckoning us astray, I suggest that the will-o'-the-wisp leads us to interesting and productive ground. The will-o'-the-wisp acquired an identity in stories as a water sheerie, bog sprite, Jack-o'-lantern and *canwyll corff*. Irrespective of how it is identified in tales, the luminescence existed, albeit fleetingly, in relation to the assemblage of decaying vegetation, chemicals and water within the bog. We can imagine that when travellers saw the lights, they sought a closer look, became waylaid and wandered into treacherous parts of the wetland. The tales and the human experiences were related through the ways that the will-o'-the-wisp existed and acted.

Eduardo Kohn (2013) uses the word 'enchantment' to describe a worldview in which humans are one amongst many 'thinking selves'. Kohn challenges the idea that animism, amongst the Runa who live in the Ecuadorian Amazon, is solely a symbolic system that the Runa apply to an environment: 'the world beyond the human is not a meaningless one made meaningful by humans' (Kohn 2013, 72). The Runa's animism emerges through their attentiveness to the world they inhabit with other beings. It 'amplifies and reveals important properties of lives and thoughts' (Kohn 2013, 73). To apply this idea to the will-o'-the-wisp: it was a malign spirit in folklore because of when and where the luminescence appeared, how it moved and the ways it affected human behaviour.

This chapter seeks to integrate the practical and the mysterious. I use monuments to explore people's kinmaking with other humans and with beings in the land and sky. 'Monument' describes a wide variety of structures that were not, primarily, the settings for everyday domestic activities, and are best interpreted as places where rituals connected with death, rites of passage and seasonal observances might have been performed. Monuments include tombs and barrows, enclosures and settings of stones and timber posts. Chambered tombs were built in Britain and Ireland from early in the fourth millennium BC, around the time that people brought domesticated animals and plants to the islands. Subsequent centuries were punctuated by episodes of monument construction, sometimes on an extraordinary scale. Especially large numbers of monuments appeared throughout the landscape, often in association with human burials, during the twenty-second to sixteenth centuries BC. Monuments transformed places and endured throughout later prehistory.

Works in progress, 2500–2200 BC

The dwellings and settlements dating to the twenty-fifth to eighteenth centuries BC were neither architecturally complex nor enduring landmarks. Domestic buildings were primarily single, small round or oval structures, rarely more than five or six metres across. Scatters of flaked stone and pottery, clusters of pits, mounds of burnt stone and midden spreads were dispersed around the landscape. Inhabitation left fragile traces. These were the living ruins and residues of dwelling and of kinwork. There was considerable continuity in occupation practices throughout the third millennium BC (Pollard 1999).

By comparison, throughout much of the third millennium BC, communities committed considerable energies to building monuments that transformed places on an epic scale, involving gatherings of hundreds and sometimes thousands of people. The most spectacular monuments were constructed during the final centuries of the fourth millennium and the early to mid-centuries of the third millennium BC. These included the large passage tombs and earthen enclosures at Brú na Bóinne, County Meath, the stone circles in Orkney, at Stenness and Ring of Brodgar, the palisade enclosures at Forteviot and Meldon Bridge, and the remarkable concentration of immense enclosures, mounds and stone circles in Wessex, of which Silbury Hill, Avebury and Stonehenge are the most widely known.

As the chronology of large timber and earth monuments becomes better understood, prehistorians are gaining a better appreciation of their episodic histories and the short timescales over which some of the building projects were completed. Large monuments complexes have traditionally been viewed as phenomena of the 'Neolithic', but this label is unhelpful. The building and use of large monuments continued throughout the twenty-fifth to twenty-third centuries BC, in a period when unfamiliar people, ideas and technologies were transforming social life. Monuments were important places within this period of flux (Cleal and Pollard 2012).

The current chronological model for Stonehenge begins the story in the thirtieth century BC with the construction of a circular earthwork enclosure (Darvill et al. 2012). The erection of elaborate arrangements of sarsens and bluestones occurred during the twenty-sixth century BC. In the subsequent few centuries, a nearby stone circle was dismantled and its stones were possibly erected at

Stonehenge. An avenue was built that led from Stonehenge for 2.5 kilometres to the River Avon. The monument's final major remodelling began in the twenty-third or twenty-second century BC and was complete by 2000 BC. During these two or three centuries, the bluestone circles were dismantled and assembled afresh as a horseshoe setting at the centre of the monument and a circle between the two sarsen settings. The monument attained the alternating pattern of sarsens, bluestones, sarsens, bluestones, sarsens that we can experience today.

Stonehenge illustrates some recurring characteristics of these large monuments: people frequently altered, embellished and, occasionally, completely reworked them. They were foci for episodes of monument building over hundreds of years, during which times complexes of structures evolved. The large passage tombs at Knowth and Newgrange, County Meath, incorporated decorated stones from an earlier, dismantled monument, which had perhaps stood close by (Eogan 1998). Newgrange was subsequently enclosed by a stone circle and, around the twenty-ninth to twenty-fifth centuries BC, a large timber circle was constructed around an adjacent, smaller passage tomb (Carlin 2017). Plentiful beaker pottery indicates further activity over the timber circle and around the large passage tomb (Carlin 2018, 146–148). Dyffryn Lane, Powys, lies in the Severn Valley, at the confluence of the Rhiw and the Severn. By the early third millennium BC, it was a largely open landscape, with areas of scrub and woodland nearby (Gibson 2010). The denuded earthworks of centuries' old monuments, a long barrow and enclosure, would have been visible 500 metres north, at Lower Luggy. The first structure at Dyffryn Lane was a stone circle, which was then surrounding by a henge enclosure. Around the twenty-fifth to twenty-third centuries BC, a low mound of turf and soil roughly 40 metres in diameter was raised over the stones in the enclosure's interior. This sequence of an open circle followed by an enclosure is found at North Mains, Perth and Kinross (Barclay 2005). There were two phases of timber circles before enclosure by a henge after 2200–1900 BC. The interior was used for burials at around the same time.

Fieldwork at Silbury Hill, Wiltshire, has shown how a simple form, albeit of grand proportions, can have a complex history (Leary et al. 2013; Whittle 1997). On completion, the large chalk and earth mound was 140 metres in diameter and over 30 metres high (Figure 6.1). This was the final stage in a construction project that lasted a century or so, during the twenty-fourth century BC. The earliest structure was a small mound raised using gravel that was perhaps collected from the nearby River Kennet. A larger area was then demarcated with wooden stakes, and infilled with a mound of turf and clay. After a pause measured in years, people began to pile material onto the mound, this time a mix of soil, chalk, clay, gravel and turf. Five banks of chalk and clay encircled this new, larger mound, beyond which was a discontinuous ditch. The ditch was repeatedly backfilled and recut, its diameter widening in each case. The fifth and final ditch was vast, 5–9 metres deep, and provided the 235,500 cubic metres of chalk that formed the final mound. The crushed chalk in the mound was held in place with low roughly built walls, which gave the mound straight sides and radial

FIGURE 6.1 Silbury Hill, Wiltshire. Copyright: Bill Bevan.

lines 'something like a spider's web' (Leary and Field 2010, 111). Six hundred metres east, down the valley from Silbury Hill, a complex of timber palisade enclosures and alignments was built during the twenty-third or twenty-second century BC (Whittle 1997). If Silbury Hill and the palisade enclosures were built sequentially, as the scientific dating suggests, then the upper reaches of the river Kennet formed a focus for large-scale and quite diverse monument building over two or three centuries.

Silbury Hill and the West Kennet palisade enclosures illustrate the extraordinary scale that building projects continued to take into the twenty-fourth and twenty-third centuries BC (Figure 6.2). With the rapid cutting and back filling of the ditches at Silbury Hill, it seems as though the act of construction was more important than the ordered completion of a long-term plan. This shifts attention from the final architecture of the monuments, which dominates our experiences today, and foregrounds the many years, in some cases decades or centuries, during which they were works in progress. It is from this perspective that John Barrett advocates thinking about the complex architecture of the enclosure and stone circles at Avebury, located at a short distance from Silbury Hill, as the

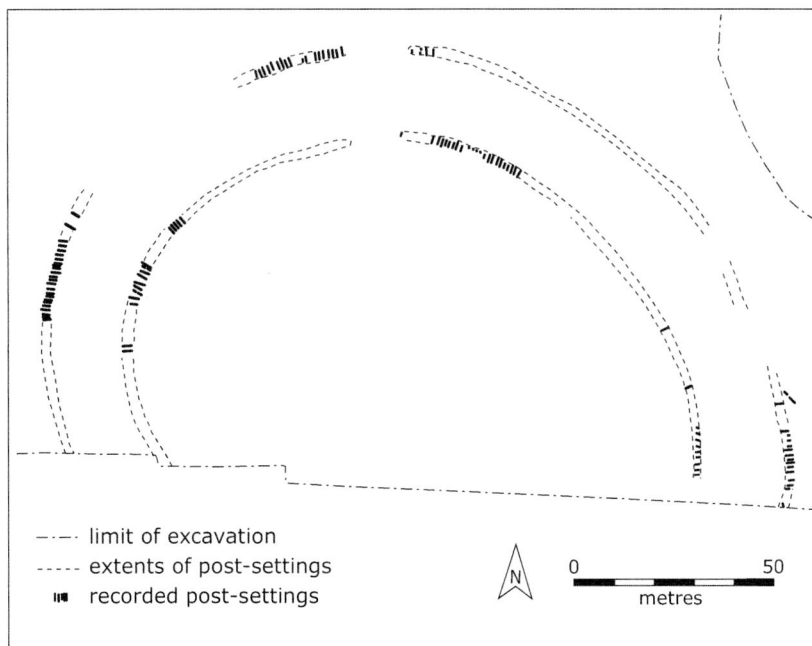

FIGURE 6.2 Excavations at Catterick, North Yorkshire, revealed two concentric sub-circular palisades of paired posts up to 200 metres in diameter. Construction of the enclosures began during the twenty-fifth to twenty-fourth centuries BC. Adapted from Hale et al. 2009.

'physical remnant of a number of abandoned projects and not the culmination of a series of planned phases' (Barrett 1994, 13), and Joshua Pollard (2013, 182–183) describes the Avebury monuments as 'places in motion'.

Colin Richards argues that the monuments at Stenness and Brodgar, Mainland, Orkney, were built piecemeal as groups took responsibility for finding, quarrying, moving and erecting individual stones (Richards 2004; 2013). The act of building was, he argues, more meaningful than the completed structure, and indeed an end to the project may never have been envisaged or desired. Social distinctions and particularly the establishment of respect and prestige would, for Richards, have been proven by leaders' abilities to generate the conditions for a large labour force to be assembled to quarry and erect one or perhaps more stones. The process of constructing the monuments was a material manifestation of the relationships that had been called into being to make the monuments possible. Authority might therefore have been relatively fragmented, with competing claims operating at a variety of scales. Particular individuals may have led projects or groups who drew on the obligations or debts felt by kin to assemble a workforce. This can be conceived in quite formal terms as evidence for large-scale social groupings, organised into chiefdoms, for instance. Alternatively, we could envisage a less hierarchical society, where groups collaborated in the common purpose of creating a monument. These communities of builders might have gained a sense of overall direction from a shared belief in the purpose and meaning of the monument rather than from the coercive leadership of one individual. In the melee of construction, there were many opportunities for risk-taking and for social status to be gained and lost. Labour brought people together and served as a setting in which political authority could be established, sustained and challenged.

The distances over which these large monuments drew their populations of builders can be reconstructed. The three henges close to the River Ure at Thornborough, North Yorkshire, were sited on a natural routeway across the Pennines, where stone axes from the Lake District might have been exchanged eastwards and till flint travelled west in return (Harding 2013). A study by Sarah Viner and colleagues of the cattle teeth from the henge at Durrington Walls, Wiltshire, provides a tangible measure of journeys (Chan et al. 2016, 36–37; Viner et al. 2010). Through their analysis of strontium and oxygen isotope ratios in the tooth enamel from the animals, the researchers demonstrate that the majority of the cattle were born and grazed in landscapes beyond the chalkland of Durrington Walls and its nearby monument at Stonehenge. The ratio of strontium's non-radiogenic to its radiogenic isotopes varies depending upon the geology where the animals spent their early lives. As the animals grazed, their bodies absorbed the strontium signature of the rocks and soils under their hoofs. Most of the cattle had strontium ratios that matched the geology close to but not on the chalkland, while 17 were raised much further afield, perhaps southwest England, Wales or northern Britain. The analysis does not pinpoint the animals' origins precisely. It does illustrate that some people gathering at Durrington Walls travelled long journeys of over 100 kilometres with their livestock.

These journeys were important in the way they expanded the constellation of places and kin related through Durrington Walls. These were not only the people, animals and things that moved, but the places and populations they passed through along the way. It is tempting to think of the monument not as the materialisation of these relations, but rather as the gravity that drew and held relations together. The communities perhaps acknowledged affinities through the assemblies and building projects occurring at the monuments. The size of the gatherings and the varied geographic origins of the participants made the social life at the monuments mutable and capable of absorbing cultural differences.

The major complexes are relatively dispersed and many are in river valleys and along natural routeways. This placement was key to integrating different forms of kinwork. There were the long journeys taken by materials, objects and some people that connected distant regions within the islands and to mainland Europe. These kinship networks enabled metallurgy and beakers, and the people who practised the technologies, to find their ways throughout Britain and Ireland during the twenty-fourth and twenty-third centuries. Monuments were powerful landmarks within these networks, as they had been in the preceding centuries. Key to the monuments' importance was also their capacity to create kin through gatherings for living, building, feasting and performance. The most recent excavations at Durrington Walls revealed houses and middens around the henge's south-eastern entrance. There were observable differences between food consumed within households and the intra-household feasting that created the deposits in the middens: 'As the integrity of households and smaller groups was maintained at one level, the sharing of foods across the community promoted unity amongst communities gathered from far and wide across Britain' (Craig et al. 2015, 1107). Kin gathered at monuments, and new kinships were made at monuments through common labour, sharing of food and participation in the rituals taking place within the spaces that had been built.

Becoming local, 2200–1500 BC

The monuments that were constructed from the twenty-second century BC continued the traditions of stone, timber and earthen mounds, circles and alignments. Expressed in the coarsest terms, the Bronze Age was defined by smaller, more numerous and geographically dispersed monuments when compared with the great circles and mounds constructed in the third millennium BC. The more typical sites categorised by prehistorians as Bronze Age comprise a wide variety of structures ranging from timber and stone circles and rows to barrows, cairns, chambered tombs and ring cairns. At their simplest, the monuments comprised individual and paired standing stones or propped boulders. Many were complex and composite structures, incorporating different materials and taking multiple forms during their lives. At Oddendale, Cumbria, two concentric rings of large posts were erected in around the twenty-sixth century BC (Turnbull and Walsh 1997). The posts were subsequently removed and the postholes capped with stones; a crouched inhumation burial with a beaker might have been deposited at around the same time. A ring of stones was then placed over the inner ring of capped postholes. Small deposits of cremated human bone and fragments of early Bronze Age pottery were recovered from the stone ring. While basic architectural forms—mounds of earth and stone, rings and rows of posts and stones—were widespread, there were regional monumental traditions. Chambered stone monuments were built in west and north Ireland (O'Brien 1999) and southwest England (Jones et al. 2010). Stone circles with a single 'recumbent' stone in the circuit were a feature of northeast Scotland and southwest Ireland (Welfare 2011).

The process of assigning a chronology to monuments is complicated by their complex biographies and their persistence in the landscape. Henges were built during the third millennium BC, with deposition and modification continuing into the second millennium BC. Timber and stone settings, such as circles and alignments, were built throughout the third and second millennia BC, continuing more rarely into first millennium BC (Gibson 1998). Scientific dating of standing stones in Scotland has produced measurements in the fourteenth to tenth centuries BC (Duffy 2007). In his review of the dating based on excavations at several Scottish stone circles, Richard Bradley concludes that monuments were being built and modified up to the thirteenth century BC, and there were a few examples of later additions to the monuments (Bradley and Nimura 2016).

It is difficult to place order on the monuments when moving beyond broadly defined labels such as barrows, cairns, rows and circles. Richard Bradley (1998) points out that many monuments contained elements of more than one category and, during their history, their forms may have changed from one archaeological type to another. An example of this creativity is the mischievously named 'wossit' at Street House on the north coast of Cleveland (Vyner 1988). The Street House monument was initially a small, sub-rectangular enclosure defined by closely set upright posts with four gaps broken by posts and stone orthostats or boulders (Figure 6.3). Two large posts, or perhaps an upturned tree stump as at the Holme-next-the-Sea circle that I will describe later, were erected in the interior and enclosed by a low stone bank. This seems to have been dismantled and the trenches in which the timbers had stood were backfilled, partly with oak charcoal (radiocarbon dated to the twenty-second century BC), which may have been the burnt remains of the dismantled timbers. Sometime later, stone was laid around the circumference and in the interior of the structure. Some of the stones were pecked with 'cup marks' or had been used as querns, while the central stone cairn contained a cremation in a collared urn. A jet button and fragment of a battle axe were also recovered.

The various materials, forms of architecture and deposited objects at Street House indicate the varied kin who participated in its making and remaking. The traces of their labour were marked by the contributions of stones and timbers, the worked stone objects that were added to the later cairn, and the burial of cremated remains. The monument was dismantled and re-built in a different form, and there was an interesting interplay of timber and stone architecture that went beyond the more common sequence of stone replacing timber. The small size of monuments like the Street House structure and its contemporary stone circles, ring cairns and funerary mounds could be interpreted as the monuments of stable, local communities, perhaps families or clans (Barnatt 2000). Alternatively, as in the preceding centuries, monuments might have places for making and unmaking kin through the shared labours and performances of building and rituals.

A distant example can help to illustrate what I mean by this creativity in kinship. Stefano Boni (2010) researched the funeral ledgers in the Akan area of West Africa (southern Ghana and southeastern Ivory Coast) to question previous ethnographers' translation of the term *abusua*, in Twi and Sefwi languages, as family or clan. The ledgers record the financial donations that relatives make at funerals. Instead of representing a stable unit of kinship, Boni found that *abusua* evoked varied forms of 'closeness': 'matrilineal ties, household relations, cognatic links, and … generic relatedness such as ethnic or village identity, same school attendance or friendship' (Boni 2010, 388). The funeral ledgers show the way this broader notion of relatedness breaks down into a taxonomy based on the contributions that people make to a funeral. There are distinctions between close

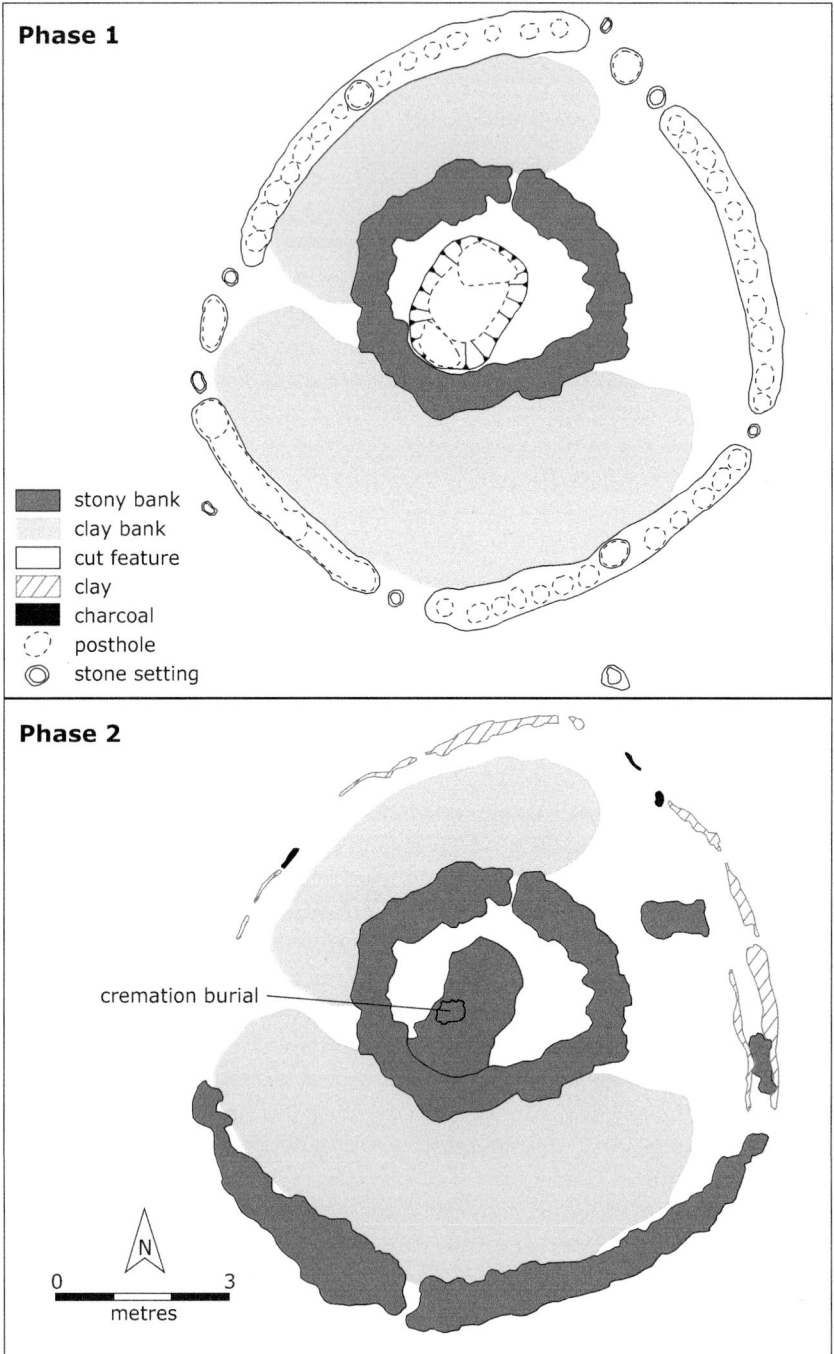

FIGURE 6.3 The phases of the timber, earth and stone monument at Street House, Cleveland. Adapted from Vyner 1988.

FIGURE 6.4   A reconstruction of the timber circle (Holme I) at Holme-next-the-Sea, Norfolk. Drawing by Julie Curl and David Dobson. Copyright: Norfolk Archaeological Unit.

kin and those more distantly related, through co-residency in the village, for instance. There are also opportunities for political manoeuvring: 'Funeral offerings are a crucial means of establishing kinship ties and of severing them in the endless process of redefining relations of parental affiliation and rank' (Boni 2010, 397). Kinship is not a free-for-all, open to unconstrained invention. Rather, norms and sanctions control creativity.

We might think in a similar way about the different forms of relatedness that existed within monument building and funerary rites during the Bronze Age: from the preparation of the body and goods that were gifted in the grave or pyre, to the labours involved in gathering stone, cutting turf and felling trees for the monuments. Following their excavation of four barrows in the Brenig Valley, Denbighshire, Frances Lynch and John Waddell estimated that it had taken a dozen people up to two weeks to cut and stack the turf used in the mounds (Lynch 1993, 186). The largest of the four mounds, Brenig 40, required the stripping of 2,100 square metres of turf. While this was undoubtedly a major undertaking, it is of an imaginable scale when compared with the labour consumed in monuments such as Silbury Hill. Crucially, it was within the capacities of a small group of people, in the tens rather than the thousands that might have gathered to build the great circles and mounds. The labour estimates for the Neolithic and Bronze Age monuments at Raunds, Northamptonshire, decline in size through time, with the early Neolithic long barrow requiring the greatest resource (470 worker-days) and the Bronze Age barrows the least (in the range of 10–100 worker-days) (Harding and Healy 2007, 184–187). The barrows' ditches were subpolygonal, which suggested that they were constructed in sections by different teams working at the same time or sequentially.

A pair of exceptionally preserved timber circles have been excavated near Holme-next-the-Sea, on Norfolk's north coast (Brennand and Taylor 2003; Robertson 2016) (Figure 6.4). Dendrochronology dates the building of both monuments to the spring or early summer of 2049 BC, when the area was an extensive saltmarsh. Holme I, the fully excavated of the two monuments, was an oval setting of timbers enclosing a large oak's upturned roots and lower trunk (Brennand and Taylor 2003). The preservation of the wood in the waterlogged silts meant that the marks of at least 51 metal axes were identified on the timbers. The 15–20 trees, mature oaks of 100–150 years old, were felled by two people working simultaneously from each side of the trunks. Each pair of axes seems to have been responsible for felling just one tree. Separate axes were then used for squaring off the top of each trunk and trimming the branches. If a different person used each axe, leaving aside the possibilities that an individual carried more than one tool or that axes were communal property, then separate groups of three to four people took responsibility for preparing each tree. It would have required a bigger team to haul and raise the central oak into position, and others could have been involved in making the rope and helping with splitting the timbers.

Holme I allows a clearer than usual glimpse of the relations of labour at a twenty-first-century monument. It highlights the extent of collaborations during the building of even a relatively small structure. This can be extended with the addition of the second monument, Holme II, built at the same time and possibly for mortuary rites that connected the two circles (Robertson 2016, 254). Might the evidence from Holme I be for kindred each contributing a tree to the project? If this was the case, then it is interesting that the circle was assembled in this way, as it need not have required such large numbers of people—a few teams could have completed the construction of the monument. The project was given added significance because of the numbers of participants and the short duration of its building.

The size of feasts and offerings undertaken at monuments offers another way to take the measure of gatherings. Two round barrows in the English Midlands, raised over single inhumation burials, have produced large numbers of animal bones, especially cattle. At Irthlingborough, Northamptonshire, 185 cattle skulls were piled over the burial chamber (Davis 2007). They were mixed with smaller numbers of bones from cattle, pigs, dogs and aurochs. The majority of the cattle skulls may have been brought to Irthlingborough in a defleshed state, with the cattle leg bones, representing perhaps 40 animals, resulting from feasts undertaken during the mortuary rituals. At Gayhurst, Buckinghamshire, 300 cattle were slaughtered, possibly from several different herds (Chapman 2007). Their defleshed skulls and limb bones were then spread across the mound, before being raked into the ditch around the barrow. These deposits hint at the communities of kin, both human and bovine, who assembled during the funerary rituals.

Jacqueline Towers and colleagues (2010) measured the strontium isotope ratios in the teeth enamel from the Irthlingborough and Gayhurst animals. The ratios for the Irthlingborough and Gayhurst cattle indicate that most were born, raised and probably then died on the local Jurassic geology. Only a few of the animals were non-local: one of the Irthlingborough cattle was born on older geology in western Britain, and came to the Jurassic region in its first year; one of the Gayhurst cattle was also born on older geology in western Britain, and another may have originated on chalkland to the south. In all three cases of non-local origins, the animals had travelled to and lived in the Jurassic region before their deaths. Towers and colleagues' sample was small, with only seven cattle from Irthlingborough and five from Gayhurst. Nonetheless, it appears that the large numbers of cattle (and people) gathered for the mortuary ceremonies were from the region around the monuments.

The faunal deposits at Gayhurst and Irthlingborough differ from the cattle that were analysed from Durrington Walls, where many of the animals travelled from long distances to the great henge (Chan et al. 2016, 36–37). The larger, twenty-sixth to twenty-fifth-century, monument gathered its communities of builders and celebrants from wider catchments than the smaller, later barrows. The labours of monument building continued, though they were dispersed across the landscape. Monuments from the fourth and third millennia BC remained powerful (Rogers 2013; Woodward and Woodward 1996). Clusters of Bronze Age monuments emerged with time with iterative acts of building and modification. The development of linear barrow groups offers one instance of these processes (Garwood 2007), as do the aggregations of stone-built monuments in the uplands throughout Ireland and Britain (Jones 2006; Moore 1995). Cumulatively, across several centuries, monuments occupied many more areas of landscape.

Cumulative architecture is expressed differently in the unusually complex groups of stone circles, alignments and cairns in mid-Ulster, the best known of these being Beaghmore and Copney, County Tyrone (May 1953; Pilcher 1969) (Figure 6.5). Beaghmore comprises three pairs of stone circles, each associated with a small cairn and one or more stone alignments. Further cairns lie in the immediate vicinity of the circles, along with an unusual 'stone circle' composed of 880 small stones closely packed together in an oval setting up to 18 metres across (Figure 6.6). None of the stones within the complex are particularly large, and both the circles and alignments are irregular in shape, giving the impression that the structures developed rather haphazardly. A similarly intricate arrangement of at least nine stone circles and associated alignments is located at Copney. As at Beaghmore, which is 11 kilometres to the northeast, the stones at Copney are buried within a layer of peat, although three circles were uncovered during archaeological investigations (Foley and MacDonagh 1998). Each of the circles has a small cairn at its centre, and all the cairns overlay cists that were disturbed in prehistory. The interiors of the circles are filled with over 1,000 small stones,

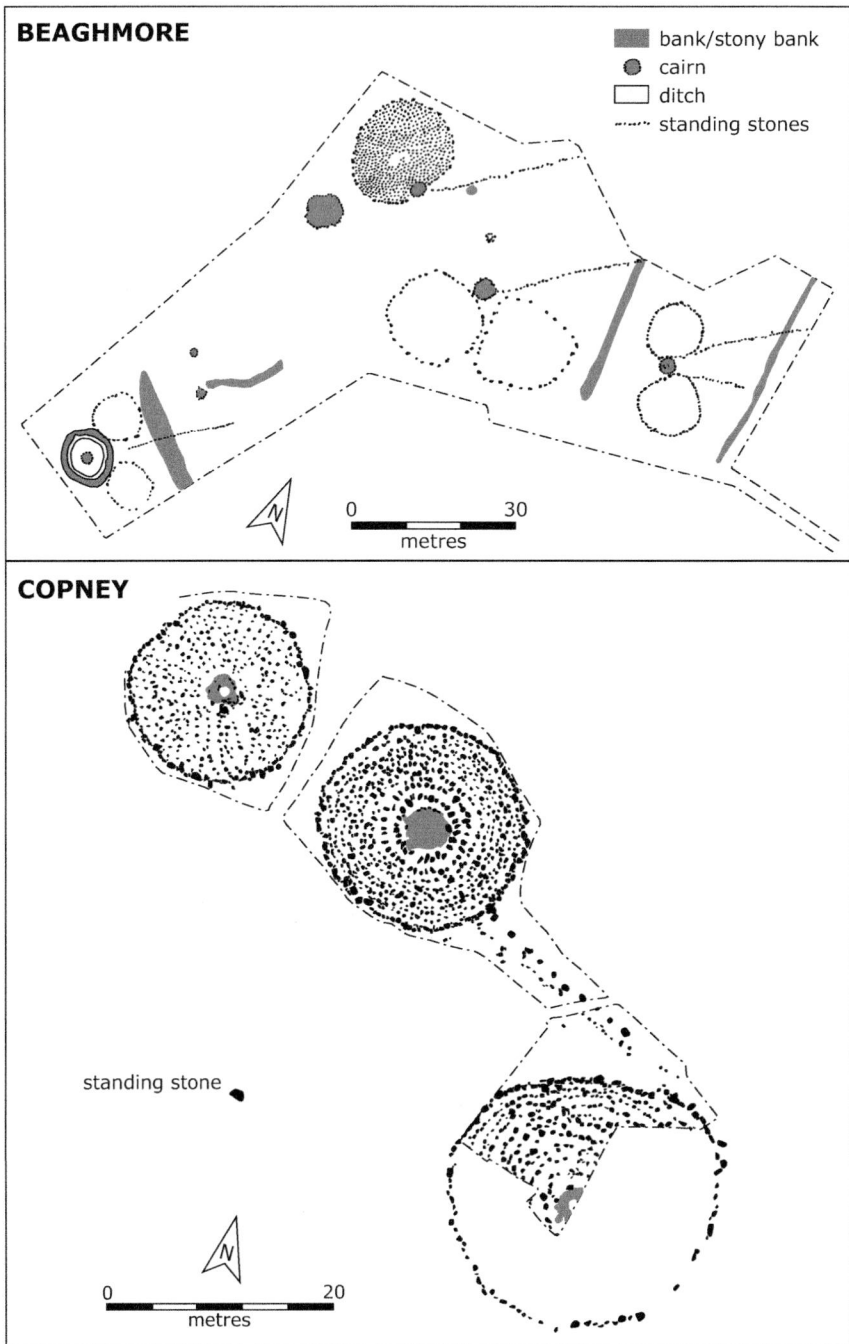

FIGURE 6.5 Plans of the stone circles, alignments and cairns at Beaghmore and Copney, County Tyrone. Adapted from Foley and MacDonagh 1998 and Pilcher 1969.

FIGURE 6.6 Concentric circles of small standing stones at Beaghmore, County Tyrone. Copyright: Bill Bevan.

which were mostly set upright or on edge and organised roughly concentrically around the cairns.

Although we do not know how long it took to build these monuments, they appear as accumulative architecture. Each ring of stones or perhaps every stone could have marked a person or group's contribution to the monument. It may not be coincidental that the patterns of circles and lines formed at Beaghmore and Copney find parallels in the motifs used in rock art, since they may be of similar date and they also emerged from a blending of cumulative patterns and com- posed designs. The densely packed, small stones are more unusual and find fewer parallels. One distant example is the 'stone setting' at Stackpole Warren, in which approximately 2,000 upright and edge-set stones and cobbles were laid around a large standing stone—the Devil's Quoit (Benson et al. 1990). Others may be the stone rows and settings on Dartmoor and Exmoor (Gillings 2015a) and the multiple stone alignments in Caithness and Sutherland, northeast Scotland (Burl 1993, 123–131). At Battle Moss, Caithness, where there are eight parallel alignments each comprising up to 21 small upright stones, there were subtle irregularities in the rows that the excavators interpreted as evidence for the incremental or phased formation of the monument (Baines et al. 2003). Based on his excavations of the Exmoor rows, Mark Gillings (2015b, 94) describes them as 'a composite or medley of individual stones raised by different people at different times'. At Lanacombe, the excavations found three different settings for holding the stones upright.

At every one of the thousands of Bronze Age monuments recorded through- out Ireland and Britain, people once gathered to build, undertake rites and make offerings. The kinwork that occurred at these places differed from the great en- closures and mounds of the third millennium BC. There were fewer participants, they travelled shorter distances to reach the monuments and the durations of their activities were briefer. The durations spent constructing timber and stone circles, barrows and cairns could be tallied in days, and perhaps experienced multiple times during a generation. These were labours that affected people's daily interactions and position within communities near-at-hand. They were opportunities for making, changing and breaking with kin, in places that were situated within people's day-to-day worlds. The dispersal of monumentality, temporally and spatially, changed the proximity of rituals to everyday life—it was a localisation of monumentality and rituals. This localisation dispersed the traditions and norms connected with building and performing rites at monuments throughout the landscape. In their durations and relations, monuments came closer to the domestic sphere, where dwelling created clusters of mounds and pits, scatters of debris and a gradual memorialising of place through iterative inhabitations and performances.

Stone that spoke, 3000–1500 BC

Over several days in September 2003, a wildfire swept across 240 hectares of moorland on the edge of the North York Moors, overlooking Robin Hood's Bay. Fylingdales Moor was ordinarily shrouded in a thick cloak of heather. The moorland after the fire was bare of vegetation and, most devastating from an ecological perspective, in places the peat had burnt off down to the mineral soil. After the ground cooled and as the wind blew away the ashes, archaeologists surveyed the damage to the moor's known monuments and looked for unrecorded sites (Brown and Chappell 2005; Oswald et al. 2005). Amongst the most numerous new discoveries were rock art, of which over 200 examples were identified by the completion of the surveys on the burnt and unburnt moorland (Brown and Chappell 2005, 63). Both earthfast and moveable stones were marked with cups, lines, rings and some with rarer geometric motifs.

Of 12 moveable marked stones identified during English Heritage's survey, 4 were incorporated into funerary cairns and 7 were found in stone banks, clearance cairns and in a water course (Oswald et al. 2005, 12). While these relationships may be a fortuitous circumstance of clearing stone from fields, the frequent presence of cup-marked stones in funerary cairns suggests otherwise. One example stands out from the others. The wildfire and subsequent erosion revealed an elliptical ring of stones on Stoupe Brow (Vyner 2011). The ring comprised two opposed standing stones, with smaller slabs and boulders set in a shallow gully. Two stones in the ring were marked with angular and curvilinear patterns and it is feasible that there were more, unexcavated, marked stones in the ring. One slab had a complex geometric pattern in its surface that is reminiscent of grooved ware pottery and passage tomb art. Blaise Vyner suggests that the stone might formerly have stood as a monument, before being shaped and incorporated into the stone ring. A portion of the stone was broken off and placed at its base. Smaller stones infilled the space marked out by the ring and some of these were also marked.

Open-air rock art, like the examples identified at Fylingdales, has a broadly western and northern distribution, with concentrations in southwest and northwest Ireland and in northern Britain (Beckensall 1999; O'Connor 2006). The markings are sparsely distributed in other areas, including Wales and southwest England (Darvill and Wainwright 2003; Jones and Kirkham 2013). The robustness of the stone plays a role in the survival of the markings, since chalk too was marked and carved, with the markings only surviving in buried contexts (Teather 2011). The motifs on open-air rock art overlap with though are largely distinct from the designs found at Neolithic-chambered tombs, stone-built houses and on pottery. The markings vary in form from simple circular hollows—termed 'cup marks'—to complex abstract designs mainly composed of circles, lines and cup marks. Figurative art, which is well known from elsewhere in western and northern Europe, is rare in Britain and Ireland: flat axes and a halberd on a cist at Ri Cruin, Kilmartin Glen (Needham and Cowie 2012), footprints and cup marks on a cist slab from West Harptree, Somerset (Coles et al. 2000), axe and dagger markings on the monoliths at Stonehenge (Field et al. 2015) are some examples.

The lack of representational designs makes it difficult to establish a chronology for British and Irish rock art. There are few depictions of objects that could be ascribed typologically to one period or another, and none on open-air, earthfast stones. Dating the earthfast rocks is challenging as they have few direct associations with other archaeological structures or artefacts. Andrew Jones and colleagues undertook excavations around earthfast rock art panels at Torbhlaren, Kilmichael Glen, Argyll (Jones et al. 2011). They found the remains of the stone hammers used to create the markings, along with charcoal which was radio-carbon dated to the early and mid-third millennium BC. Excavations amongst cup-marked stones at Backstone Beck, Ilkley Moor, produced possible hearths, grooved ware pottery and lithic scatters with a high proportion of definable objects—knives, arrowheads and scrapers (Edwards and Bradley 1999).

Rock markings continued to be created into the second millennium BC. Decorated stones were incorporated into standing stones, burial cists and cairns (Figure 6.7). In some instances, the designs were perhaps eroded before the stones were used to build monuments, as with the alignment of standing stones at Ballymeanoch in Kilmartin Glen (Barber 1977) and Drombeg stone circle, County Cork (Ó Nualláin 1984, 24–25). There are cases where stones with weathered symbols were later inscribed with new markings. The Cochno Stone, West Dunbartonshire, is profusely marked (Brophy 2018). An image of the stone produced by laser scanning reveals differential erosion of the markings and overlapping motifs, both of which indicate a prolonged sequence of carving at Cochno (Figure 6.8). Nearby, Euan MacKie identified two phases of markings amongst the complex arrangements of rock art on an outcrop at Greenland (MacKie and Davis 1988/1989). The second phase followed the quarrying of stone from the outcrop, which Richard Bradley suggests was removed and used in cists (Bradley 1997, 140). Blaze O'Connor (2006, 58) noted cup marks along the edge of a capstone in the Ballyhoneen wedge tomb, County Kerry. The cups were likely to have been marked after the tomb was built. Based on her review, O'Connor concluded that people ceased making the more

FIGURE 6.7 The cup and ring-marked standing stone at Nether Largie, Kilmartin Glen, Argyll. Copyright: Bill Bevan.

varied markings found on earthfasts towards the middle of the third millennium BC. The use of quarried rock art and marking stones with simple cup marks continued into the second millennium.

Taking into account these varied strands of evidence and arguments for chronology, rock art had its origins in the late fourth millennium BC, perhaps earlier, and continued in differing forms into the second millennium BC. This chronology is important because it means that rock art, like earth, timber and stone circles, endured within social life through the third and early second millennia BC. As with the monuments, rock art partially changed its place in the world during the centuries after 2200 BC. As people built smaller, more numerous and dispersed

FIGURE 6.8   A laser-scan image of the Cochno Stone, West Dunbartonshire. © Crown copyright: HES.

monuments, they sometimes detached, moved and incorporated marked stones into the structures. These acts can be interpreted as the destruction both of the physical panels—removing them from their 'natural' setting in earthfast outcrops—and of their power, by inverting them within mortuary contexts (Waddington 1998). They could have formed claims on land that associated individual dead, their lineages and monuments with ancient places and ways of marking land (Bradley 1997, 148–150).

The majority of rock art was created on open air, earthfast boulders and out-crops. The designs on the rocks range from, at their simplest, single or multiple cup marks, to the most complex involving arrangements of different elements, commonly multiple concentric rings and lines. The complex markings tend to be found at prominent or distinctive outcrops, and these are frequently also lo-cations that have wide views of the landscape (Bradley et al. 1993). The settings of the carved rocks vary between regions. In the Iveragh Peninsula, County Kerry, the decorated stones are commonly at the heads of valleys, at the interface between upland and lowland (O'Sullivan and Sheehan 1997). In his comparison of the rock art in Galloway and Northumberland, Richard Bradley concludes that the rock art in Galloway is sited around coastal valleys, close to areas of modern agricultural land, while the sites in Northumberland are on the fringes of higher ground, and often concentrated along natural routeways (Bradley 1997). The preferences for the interfaces between different topographies and at key points of access through the landscape might indicate that the marks related to journeys through or arriving to use the land.

It is an attractive idea to interpret the rock art as 'signposts'. It presents stone as a inert surface upon which people applied their symbolic schemes. Against this, there is the position that the later prehistoric world held animacies, 'lives' if you prefer, that participated in social life with people. The idea that rock markings were inscriptions onto convenient surfaces does not adequately explore the potential for the stones and places to have held power. We are a long distance from the later prehistoric world and our connections are partial. Applying twenty-first-century worldviews and ways of valuing does not address these disconnections. The approach I take in this book is to allow a wider range of beings and things to relate to people in forming social life. Antonia Thomas describes the later Neolithic-marked stones that she researched in Orkney as having 'animate qualities' and that the 'act of carving the stones and placing them as part of construction may have animated both the fragments and the buildings' (Thomas 2016, 209). Blaze O'Connor (2006) used the term 'living rock' when referring to the earthfast outcrops of stone where rock art was usually carved. The term has a long tradition in academic writing about rock art (Piggott 1939).

Following this position, inscription became a dialogue between makers and stones, between inhabitants and places. Andrew Jones (2007) observes that around Kilmartin Glen, the more complex panels are on rocks that are marked with natural fissures. The rock markings were 'woven' into the surfaces of the rocks by deliberately incorporating the fissures into the designs. Perhaps people explained the natural grooves and cracks as ancient carvings. The stones may have been ancestral guardians of land whose power was in some way controlled or released through the inscriptions. The placement of rock art in Kilmartin was inward-looking; the symbols formed a means for communities to socialise the landscape (Jones et al. 2011). Socialise means to come into relation with humans, or to participate in life with humans. By implication, the acts of marking rocks also brought humans into relation with places and stones—a process of naturalising.

Not only did rock art exist because of the rock's animacy, the art served to relate its makers to the rocks and the places—or the beings that lived within the rocks and the places. Acts of marking and of deposition were not laying a cultural schema onto the land; they were acts that related people to places and land that was already in life's flow and in a process of being. People were continuously in dialogue with places and beings. This involved making and remaking marks on rocks. It involved moving stones, or stones moving themselves; it was a landscape always in a process of becoming (Wallis 2009). Rock markings were amongst the varied traditions that people deployed in their efforts to relate to places and land.

Miriam Kahn's (1990) account of petrified ancestors in Wamira, Papua New Guinea, offers an example of stone's animacy within social life. The ancestral stones in Wamira vary in shape and size; they are found individually and in groups, set in clearings and amongst bushes, near the villages and in the surrounding forest: 'each stone has a name, a history, a life, we might even say a personality, resulting from the spirit enclosed within it' (Leenhardt quoted in Kahn 1990, 52). The people in Wamira explain that the stones move from place to place, as demonstrated in the story of the stone, Tauribariba, the ancestral leader of the Maibouni lineage (Kahn 1990, 55–59). Tauribariba originally formed part of a circle of stones located in the centre of a hamlet on the Wamira coast. The circle surrounded Tauribariba's sister, Tauanana, a larger boulder. The remainder of the circle consisted of numerous small stones, Tauanana's children, whose numbers varied as some left the circle and others were added when, on occasions, they appeared from the sea.

Missionaries removed Tauribariba from the circle in 1936 and cemented him into the pulpit wall of a new cathedral. That night, Tauribariba walked back to his circle. The following day, the priest returned, collected Tauribariba and cemented him back into the wall upside down and facing inwards. This inversion emptied the stone of power and he could not look towards Wamira. Tauribariba did not walk again. His sister returned to the sea with her children, grief-stricken. It took 50 years, so the story tells, before Tauanana resurfaced and the inhabitants of Irere could help her back into the circle where her children slowly began rejoining her. In Wamira, the stones are not personified; they are persons. They interact and they have the power to act. From the perspective of understanding how it is that the stones anchor myths and narratives spatially as well as temporally, Miriam Kahn argues that it is necessary to appreciate the stones as persons who can play a part with humans in social life.

Movement is a key factor in Kahn's account of Wamira's stones. Movement marks out the stones' personhood. It is the practical means through which people relate to the stones, in observing and facilitating the stones' movements. In his essay on animacy, Tim Ingold (2006, 14) identifies the 'primacy of movement': the 'animic world is in perpetual flux, as the beings that participate in it go their various ways'. The marked stones in Bronze Age Ireland and Britain moved too. They stood upright, both alone and in circles; they formed boxes for containing the human dead; they broke into pieces and joined unmarked stones in cairns. People helped the stones. That is how they, humans and stones, changed their relations with each other. Excavating the early Neolithic-chambered tomb at Cairnholy, Dumfriesshire, Stuart Piggott and Terrence Powell (1949, 118) came upon a small upright slab within the tomb's main chamber marked with two cups, multiple concentric rings and radial lines. The stone was propped up at its base with smaller stones. In the same part of the chamber, Piggott and Powell found fragments of food vessel pottery and cremated bone, which might have entered the tomb at the same time as the marked stone.

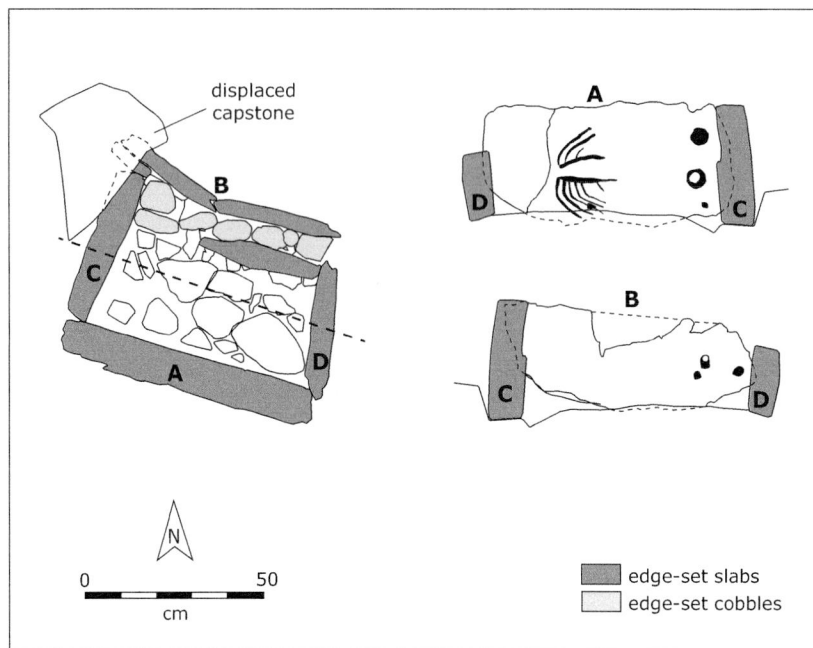

FIGURE 6.9   The cup and line-marked cist at Balblair, Highland. Adapted from Dutton et al. 2007.

Where the marks on earthfast rocks tended to be in visible if not always con-spicuous locations, the marks incorporated into cairns and cists were mostly hid-den. They were either incorporated into the bodies of the cairns or used as kerbs and cist slabs with the markings turned inwards. At Balblair, Highland, marked slabs formed three sides of a rectangular cist at the centre of a cairn (Dutton et al. 2007) (Figure 6.9). Fragments of food vessel pottery may have accompanied a long-decayed inhumation burial within the cist. The slabs were marked with cup marks, two of which were sufficiently deep to perforate the stones. One slab is marked with multiple parallel curving lines, in a paired pattern, rather like ribs. Parallels for these in motifs are found on later Neolithic-chambered tombs, and the excavators suggest that two of the slabs were orthostats in an earlier monu-ment before moving to the cist.

At Balblair, the decorated faces were turned inwards, and most, though not all, the motifs were buried beneath the cist's floor surface. At Kellah Burn, Northumberland, a small, polished stone pecked with unusual curvilinear lines was concealed behind a stone-lined pit containing a human cremation in an enlarged food vessel (Johnston and Pollard 1999). A piece of burnt human bone, possibly cranial, had been placed next to the marked stone. The stone and burnt bone only became apparent once the small cist was dismantled. In a few cases, cairns were built on top of decorated, earthfast rocks, obscuring all or part of the images. At Fowberry, Northumberland, a cairn overlay an area of simpler motifs and was framed by a band of complex art on the same outcrop (Beckensall 1983; Bradley 1997, 143–145).

The Fowberry cairn included cup-marked stones in the kerb and within the body of the cairn. The practice of including marked stones within the body of cairns, barrows and ring cairns was widespread. Reviewing material from northern England, Erin Watson (2011) identified more than 500 examples of small, moveable marked stones. Most were marked only with cups and excavated from barrows or cairns. On Ramsley Moor, Derbyshire, Derek Riley (1981) excavated a small cairn containing four cup-marked stones within the mound. A cist within the nearby embanked stone circle contained another cup mark on a cist stone (Barnatt 1990).

For Andy Jones and Graeme Kirkham (2013, 652), the cup marks in cairns had become 'powerful "ancient" symbols': 'talismans used to symbolize the presence of the ancestors, or simply as magical symbols, inviting good luck or warding off bad luck'. Richard Bradley (1997) attributes the placing of rock art within burial monuments to new forms of territorialisation, where claims to land were made through the appropriation of old carvings. Blaze O'Connor (2009) offered a fresh way of thinking about the instances of rock art in cairns based on a study of the worked and unworked stones found within cairns at Carn More, County Louth. O'Connor suggested that the working of stone might have been connected with the funerary process: a way of working through memories and emotions connected with bereavement.

O'Connor placed her emphasis on the making of the art rather than on the motifs as completed symbols. Hugo Lamdin-Whymark (in Jones et al. 2011) spent time replicating rock art during fieldwork in Kilmichael Glen, Argyll. He reflected on the auditory and visual performances that emerged as the rock was marked. The 'distinct high-pitched, repetitive and rhythmic sound of stone on stone … echoing around the landscape' appeared to come from other places, such as trees, rather than the rock itself (Lamdin-Whymark in Jones et al. 2011, 197). In Kenny Brophy's (2018) analysis of the Cochno Stone, he identifies carving that overlapped with and partially erased earlier marks. One of the marked stones at Reyfad, County Fermanagh, is so densely marked with cups, rings and lines that almost none of the recorded surface of the stone remains unmarked and there are many instances where markings intersect (Waddell 2010, 174).

Antonia Thomas (2016, 161) interprets the late Neolithic art in Orkney as a process of 'honouring' the stone. Thomas borrowed the idea of 'honouring' from Maurice Bloch's (1995) short and thoughtful paper about the traditional wood carving that decorates Zafimaniry houses in Madagascar. Bloch began his paper by musing on why it was that anthropologists', including his own, efforts to find out the meaning, sense or purpose of the carvings led only to banal responses from the carvers: the carvings were of nothing, there was no point to the carvings, they made the wood beautiful. Eventually, Bloch reached an understanding through a chance remark that one person made: the carvings 'honour the wood'.

It was then that Bloch appreciated that he should have begun his enquiries with the places where the symbols are carved—houses. A Zafimaniry house is created when a couple marry and begin settling down. The house's substance gradually hardens, through the replacement of softer with harder materials, and becomes more durable—bonier—as the marriage lasts, and children and then grandchildren are born. Carving forms a part of this hardening: 'the process of human maturation and settling down, of marriage and house creation' (Bloch 1995, 215).

Maurice Bloch, like Miriam Kahn who I quoted earlier, described things that transform along with their human kin. British and Irish prehistoric rock art also changed with the landscape and with visits from people. The numbers of markings on earthfast stones are impressively dense in some regions, representing many thousands of individual acts of carving. Some complex panels, such as the Cochno Stone or Reyfad in County Fermanagh, were places that rarely paused. Their form and the land around them morphed with new markings appearing and others changing. Fragments of stone hammers, quartz dust and small offerings accumulated on and then eroded from the stones. The excavations in Kilmichael Glen revealed that many stone hammers had been lightly used before discard (Lamdin-Whymark in Jones et al. 2011, 76). The marking was done collectively and iteratively. The markings participated in or facilitated a dialogue between people and places. This dialogue brought places into social life and brought people into places. It was kinwork.

The movement of stones into cists, cairns, barrows and circles was a furtherance of the landscape's animacy. Movement was a part of the stones' participation in the world. The marked rocks and the places with which they were associated did not cease to live because they were moved. Their movement was proof of their life and relevance in social life. Building monuments was an interaction with a world in flow, creating relations and putting them to work—creating kin and putting them to work. Marking perhaps continued at earthfast stones during the Bronze Age, though at a slower pace as monuments offered a new technology for naturalisation-socialisation. Places and people assembled themselves into monuments. The role of marked stones in circles, mounds and cists varied according to circumstance. Perhaps the cist slabs were powerful, honoured, stones that helped the dead in their journeys to other worlds. Perhaps the dead continued their dialogue with the stones and the markings from within the barrows and cists. Perhaps powerful stones were put to work controlling the dead and holding them in the monuments. Our speculations cannot, presently, be resolved any further.

Made with sky and earth, 2200–1500 BC

The earthfast stones on the lower slopes of Loch Tay's northern shore carry large numbers of carvings. Richard Bradley, Aaron Watson and Hugo Anderson-Whymark (2012) excavated test pits around some of the marked and unmarked earthfasts below Ben Lawers. They identified worked stone, primarily quartz flakes and hammerstones, in association with the marked boulders. The material was scattered around the stones, within fissures and, in one example, a natural bowl in the rock's surface. The largest assemblages of quartz at Ben Lawers were associated with outcrops of mica schist. Bradley, Watson and Anderson-Whymark observed that the mica within the rock reflects light and 'glitters' with sun and moonlight. They hypothesised that the mica dust created by pecking the rock might have been gathered and used in rituals at the carvings. At Kilmichael Glen, the rock art panels were once covered with quartz pieces and dust created as the stone hammers fragmented through use (Jones et al. 2011). The quartz gathered in the carvings' folds and hollows. Rainwater, too, collects within the cups and rings on flat and gently sloped stones. Drawing on this characteristic of the rock art, Vicki Cummings and Chris Fowler (2003) make a connection between quartz and water, suggesting that some forms of stone might have been understood as more fluid or water-like than others.

Quartz and water capture and reflect daylight and moonlight. They pool sky and land. The heavens and the earth may have been separate worlds, as in the tripartite cosmology proposed for the Nordic Bronze Age (Kaul 2005), but they existed in relation to one another. A characteristic of rock art and monuments was their capacity to assist these relations, connecting people and other beings on the land with persons and forces in the skies. Celestial beings inhabited other worlds, and they existed because of their relations with humans and their effects on the human world. Tim Ingold (2006, 17) challenges the separation of land and sky, where land offers the material place of life and sky a canopy overhead:

> In this world the earth, far from providing a solid foundation for existence, appears to float like a fragile and ephemeral raft, woven from the strands of terrestrial life, and suspended in the great sphere of the sky. This sphere is where all the lofty action is: where the sun shines, the winds blow, the snow falls and storms rage. It is a sphere in which powerful persons seek not to stamp their will upon the earth but to take flight with the birds, soar with the wind, and converse with the stars.

Making associations between land and sky with archaeological evidence can be fraught. At times, prehistorians have expressed suspicions about their capacities for defining these relations between monuments and celestial phenomena. Monuments, land and sky have all changed in the intervening millennia: stones have toppled, topographies and vegetation have altered, the precise paths of celestial bodies have shifted in relation to the earth. It can be difficult and sometimes impossible to decide which associations mattered and which did not. In rare cases, the principal orientations are unarguable, as with the midsummer and midwinter alignments for the final, stone phases at Stonehenge (Ruggles 1997). At Holme-next the-Sea, the primary posts in the timber circle align it between the midsummer rising sun on the one side and the midwinter setting sun on the other (Brennand and Taylor 2003). This alignment is perpendicular to the orientation of the roots in the upturned oak. The circle's entrance, through a forked timber on the southwestern arc, faced towards the midwinter setting sun.

The short stone rows form an important group since their alignments are evident, even if their preferred directions may not be. The rows' chronology is imprecisely grasped and a broad second millennium BC or Bronze Age attribution is the best we might claim. Clive Ruggles has examined the alignments of short stone rows in western Scotland and southwest Ireland (Ruggles 1999). They are aligned broadly north–south, and never east–west. Achieving this consistency required regular observation of or attentiveness to the heavens and the landscape. Ruggles did not find a pattern of precise celestial alignments amongst the Irish rows. He had more success with a sub-sample of Scottish monuments. The sites in northern Mull avoid places with wide horizons, instead choosing locations where the distant horizon is limited to a southern arc: from south-south-east to west-south-west. These locations are on the edge of the viewshed of Ben More, Mull's highest peak (Martlew and Ruggles 1996). This ensures that the movement of a low full moon can be observed rising, moving and setting across the southern sky at specific times and related to distant landscape features. Martlew and Ruggles (1996) link these associations between the stones, landmarks and the moon with ceremonies around the time of the summer solstice.

The celestial alignments adopted by circles and rows marked the times of year or even specific years (as with the moon's 18.6-year cycle) when the sun or moon would participate in monuments' rituals. The revelatory qualities of these experiences may have been important, perhaps acting as a catalyst for transformative rites during a ritual and through communication with supernatural beings. The solar alignments occurred year on year, and at tangible thresholds in the seasonal cycle and landscapes' slow transformations. This may have made the rituals seem that 'it has always been thus', which offered a stability and order that influenced everyday life. The sky was and is not stable. There are many bodies and energies (Ingold's 'lofty action') that influence what humans experience. Writing about the Gleninagh stone row, County Galway, Tim Robinson (1996, 201) describes a time when he watched the midwinter sun pass through a narrow cleft between two nearby mountains and in a direct alignment with the row of six quartzite boulders. 'Time, in our everyday experience, does not consist of such moments', he wrote afterwards, 'they are as rare in the general flux as grains of gold in the gravel of our Connemara streams'. People's labours and performances at monuments did not determine that a celestial body would participate. As any person familiar with the weather patterns of Ireland and Britain's western shores would explain, moments of revelation are unpredictable. They are all the more special for it.

Short stone rows were simple structures, without the protracted building sequences, changes in form and histories of deposition that are recognised at most Bronze Age monuments. The recumbent stone circles and Clava cairns in northeast Scotland illustrate how the relations between sky and land might have

FIGURE 6.10 The recumbent stone circle at Loanhead of Daviot, Aberdeenshire. The arc of an adjacent, later enclosed cremation cemetery is visible in the lower right of the image. © Crown copyright: HES.

evolved as monuments changed (Bradley 2002; Welfare 2011). Both the recumbent stone circles and Clava cairns were constructed and in use from the twenty-fifth century BC. There was often later activity, notably burials. They share structural similarities: a ring of standing stones, with the stones graded by size so that the largest lie on the west-south-west to south-south-east arc of the circle. The internal features and structural sequences are, however, different in each type, and the monuments have mutually excluding geographic distributions. The Clava cairns are known from the valley of the River Spey and the south side of the Moray Firth. The recumbent stone circles are found further east, in the lowlands of Aberdeenshire (Figure 6.10). The monuments' southerly orientations may have acknowledged the summer moon and in some cases the monuments aligned towards the midwinter sunset (Ruggles 2015). Celestial associations were important during the rituals at the monuments and integrated from the monuments' inceptions despite their architectural complexity.

Excavation of the recumbent stone circle at Tomnaverie, Aberdeenshire, demonstrated that the monument was built in a prescribed sequence or, as Richard Bradley (2005, 50) terms it, a 'narrative'. The narrative began in the twenty-fifth century BC when a cairn, retained by a kerb of large stones, was constructed at the top of a low hill, close to a tributary of the River Dee. The hill had been and continued to be used as a site for funeral pyres. It was also carefully chosen because every 18 years the summer moon, when viewed from the monument, passed across the top of the distinct outline of Lochnagar. Lochnagar is the highest and most prominent mountain on the skyline some 30 kilometres to the southwest. This alignment was accentuated when a ring of standing stones was placed around the cairn and two large standing stones flanking a still larger recumbent stone replaced the southwestern section of kerb. This arrangement framed the view towards Lochnagar, with the recumbent stone emulating the broad ridge of the distant mountain. The final form of the monument, with the recumbent stone blocking access to the monument, might have marked the end of rituals and specifically funeral pyres at Tomnaverie: 'The monument was closed to the living and only the light of the moon could illuminate the dead' (Bradley 2002, 136).

Stone circles similar in some respects to the Aberdeenshire circles were built in southwest Ireland during the Bronze Age. As with the Scottish monuments, the Irish recumbent circles have a limited geographical distribution, mainly to counties Kerry and Cork. They too incorporate a single recumbent stone within the southwestern arc of each circle, although the largest standing stones in the circles are placed diametrically opposite to the recumbent stones rather than flanking them. At Drombeg, County Cork, excavations uncovered five pits, one of which contained fragments of a human cremation burial, radiocarbon dated to 1125–795 BC. Other stone circles have produced similar late Bronze Age radiocarbon dates. There are no instances where the dates can be securely associated with the construction of the circles, and they may as easily relate to later activity, as with the Scottish recumbent stone circles. The distinctive 'portals' made from pairs of large standing stones and incorporated into the recumbent stone circles are found in isolation as paired standing stones, of which over 100 are known from the Cork and Kerry region, and part of a wider monumental tradition in Ireland and western Britain (Burl 1993, 181–202).

Alignments offer archaeologists with a tangible connector between land and sky. The alignments provided the paths along which people, whether alive or dead, and celestial beings moved between worlds, communicated, blended and became kin. There are associations that are more ambiguous, where the placements were less directive or the mediators appear metaphorical. Cairns and barrows frequently occupied high places: ridges and hill and mountain tops. These locations made the mounds and the burials within them more prominent in relation to the surrounding country. High places also offered points of access to the heavens or the sky, by virtues of their isolation and their altitude. Wigber Low, Derbyshire, might be instructive. While not especially high, Wigber Low is a short and steep-sided ridge in the southern limestone plateau of the Peak District (Figure 6.11). Its prominence makes it exposed to the weather, as John Collis and his team found when they began their excavations during a cold Easter in 1975

FIGURE 6.11   Wigber Low, Derbyshire: the cairn is on the left-hand prominence of the ridge. Copyright: Bill Bevan.

(Collis 1983). This exposure served a different purpose in the Bronze Age. Collis found a low circular stone platform scattered with human bone, mainly teeth and the small bones from hands and feet. Cow and pig bones, food vessel pottery and items of shale and jet were mingled amongst the cairn material. A deposit of human bone in the cairn contained the parts of three people.

John Collis concluded that Wigber Low was a place where people excarnated their dead, before removing the carrion-cleaned bones for cremation or burial elsewhere. While this makes sense of the archaeological material, there is more to say. Wigber Low brought together beings from the land and sky. Human flesh dissolved and was carried into air. Substances exchanged and persons transformed, Wigber Low facilitated the kinmaking between living people, their dead and other worlds. John Moreland (2001, 42) offered a similar assessment of the cairn's reuse for human burials during the seventh century AD: Wigber Low was a place 'where this world, and the otherworld, where past and present, intersected'. In the seventh century AD, the Wigber Low cairn provided a means to access an underworld of the dead or associate the burials with powerful forces and beings living within the mound (Semple 1998). In the Bronze Age, the ridgetop reached into the sky, and was a place where human and ethereal beings met and became kin.

Growing monuments, 2200–1500 BC

Following their excavations at the earthfast marked rocks in Strath Tay, Bradley, Watson and Anderson-Whymark (2012) noted, as others have done, that quartz gives off a luminescence when pieces are struck or rubbed together. Both Strath Tay and Kilmichael Glen provided examples where rock art and quartz, particularly fractured quartz, were associated. These associations continued into the Bronze Age and they can lead us to a wider appreciation of how the land, like the sky, could live and participate in social life. Andy Jones and Thomas Goskar (2017) excavated two stones at Hendraburnick, Cornwall, which were thought to form a ruinous quoit—chambered tomb. The stones were Greenstone, transported from the nearby river valley, and it turned out that they did not form a single structure. One stone, the smaller of the two, had stood upright and with a cup mark on its, now upper, surface. The much larger stone was marked with more than 100 cups and lines, some of which overlay one another. It was propped on a platform of slates edged with water-rolled quartz boulders. Jones and Goskar found more cup marks: on one of the slates in the platform and nearby on earthfast rock surfaces. Radiocarbon measurements of charcoal recovered from the stone holes give an indication of the chronology: twenty-sixth to twenty-fourth centuries BC for the stone platform, and eighteenth to seventeenth centuries BC for the standing stone.

In addition to worked flints, a macehead fragment, a whetstone and a segmented faience bead, the excavations at Hendraburnick produced 142 kilograms of broken quartz. The quartz had been smashed on the stones and spread around their bases. Jones and Goskar (2017, 289) propose that quartz was broken to release its triboluminescent glow, and the acts took place at night so that the luminescence would be visible. The resulting platform or arc of quartz then continued to reflect moonlight and created an 'aura' around the stones.

Quartz appears at many sites spanning later prehistory and beyond (Darvill 2002). Its presence has long been explained as an association between quartz, and white stone more generally, death and the moon (Burl 1980). The places where quartz was used and brought into association with structures were many and varied. People worked and used quartz as a sharp stone like chert and flint, and as hard hammers for making rock art. Quartz boulders formed kerb stones at Logie Newton and quartz pieces were packed around kerb stones at Fowlis Wester, two cairns in northeast Scotland (Ritchie and MacLaren 1972). Quartz pebbles were placed alongside cremated human remains in urns as at Edmondstown, County Dublin (Mount and Hartnett 1993), or as a stone 'bed' underlying the inhumation at Derry-Londonderry (McConway and Donnelly 2006), as offerings on the capstone of a cist containing a beaker burial at Porth Dafarch, Anglesey (Stanley 1878, 33), and on the large stone that covered cremated bone from 24 people in a pit within a henge at Whitton Hill, Northumberland, and dated to the thirteenth to eleventh centuries BC (Fowler 2013, 161). At Callestick, Cornwall, the doorway to a roundhouse was blocked with quartz blocks, the interior was infilled with material including quartz and a ring of quartz blocks was placed around the structure (Jones 1998/1999).

The underlying geology and the subsoil at Callestick are rich in quartz, and the roundhouse wall was built partially with quartz blocks. A risk in prehistorians' focus on quartz is essentialising its meaning across centuries and millennia and irrespective of geography. Dazzled by quartz's vibrancy, we miss or downplay other substances. Quartz becomes sacred, alive, while other materials remain mundane, mute. In reviewing the early Bronze Age burials of southeast Ireland, Charles Mount (1997, 141) noted seven examples where small pieces of rock crystal, limestone or quartz were present. At Mains of Scotstown, Aberdeenshire, 80 kilograms of water-rolled quartzite, gneiss and granite pebbles lined the cist floor, beneath an inhumation burial with a beaker (Ralston 1996, 124–125). A red clay, that might have been from up to 4 kilometres away, was used for filling the gaps between the cist slabs. In these instances, quartz was one of several materials that were assembled together. W E Griffiths (1960) found quartz fragments scattered across the interior of the Druids' Circle at Cefn Coch, Gwynedd. He excavated a cist placed near the circle's centre. The inverted vessel containing the cremation was immersed in white clay so that only its base was visible when Griffiths lifted the capstone.

At Olcote, Isle of Lewis, the kerb cairn built in the seventeenth or sixteenth century BC was 'carpeted' in broken and worked quartz amounting to some 15,000 pieces (Neighbour 2005; Warren and Neighbour 2004). It was intermixed in places with an underlying scatter of worked quartz, predating the cairn and relating to domestic occupation of the same location. The domestic material would have 'turned up' when the cairn's builders stripped the turf in preparation for the monument. They used the ash from burning turf, interleaved with layers of heather, to infill the cairn, before scattering freshly shattered quartz over the surface. Different forms of quartz, as tool and token, combined in forming a place at Olcote. When digging the ground before building the cairn, people revealed an ancient scatter of quartz that might then have influenced their decision to scatter fresh quartz across the completed monument. Turf and heather were important too. The peat was lifted, burnt and its ash used within the covering mound. At one of a pair of barrows excavated at Church Lawton, Cheshire, the ground was deturfed, and the turf stacked and burnt (Reid 2014) (Figure 6.12). The excavations recovered a small amount of cremated bone that seemed insufficient to indicate a pyre on the site. A ring of glacial boulders, laid in two connected arcs, encircled the burnt turf mound, before the surface was covered by an earth mound. A turf platform defined by a circuit of wooden stakes was excavated beneath a chalk-capped barrow at Buckskin, Hampshire (Allen et al. 1995). Burnt material, animal bone and broken pieces of collared urn were scattered across the platform, perhaps indicating ceremonies involving small feasts. The focus of this activity could have been a post standing centrally within the stake circle. The posthole was dug into an infilled tree bowl.

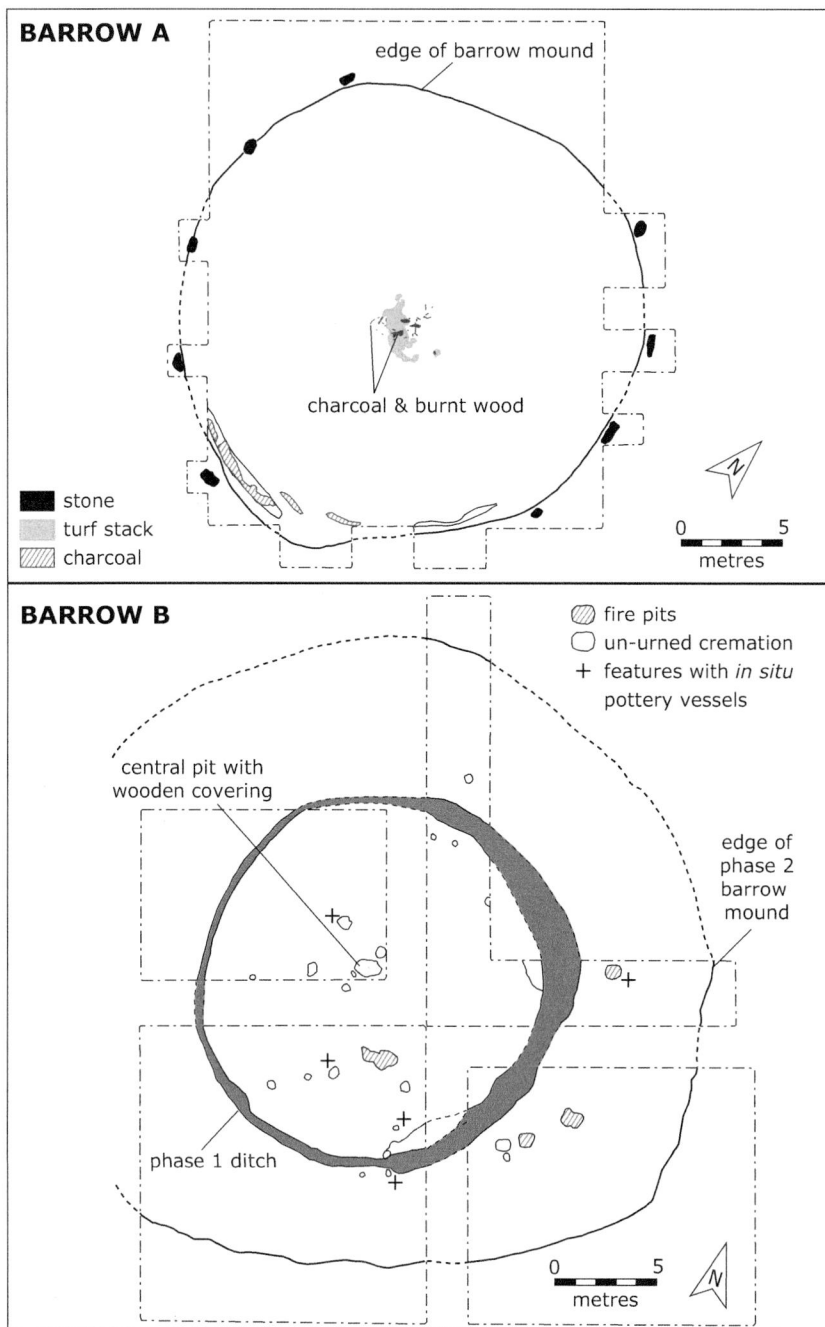

FIGURE 6.12 The two barrows excavated at Church Lawton, Cheshire. Adapted from Reid 2014.

Though lacking quartz's luminescence, turf and subsoils recur as important substances in the formation of monuments (Brittain 2015; Owoc 2004). While excavating barrows at Towthorpe, North Yorkshire, John Mortimer (1905, 2) observed that the mounds frequently contained clay that he thought had been carried from the valley bottoms up onto the ridges where the barrows were located. In one example, the first barrow that Mortimer ever opened, he noted a shallow mound of clay, over which a layer of burnt material and then local earth was heaped. At a barrow nearby, C39, Mortimer identified two types of clay, which he suggested came from separate sources more than 1.5 kilometres distant. The location of each type of clay in the mound broadly matched the direction from which Mortimer thought it was sourced. In her interpretation of barrow C39, Joanna Brück (2004, 184) offers the suggestions that the clay sources may have been places that were important in the life of the deceased or that they represented contributions from different kin groups, bringing materials from their home-ground. Sourcing the sediments may not be so straightforward. Clay could also come from dolines, or solution hollows, in the chalk, which were on the Wold tops and near to and sometimes overlain by barrows (Hayfield et al. 1995, 397–401). This leads to a different interpretation: the turf, chalk, flint and clay within the mounds were carefully assembled from the locality. The monuments were made from and grew from their immediate place in the landscape. Marcus Brittain (2015) argues that early Bronze Age monuments in Wales grew out of the substances that people assembled, which included tokens from distant places.

Gathering places into monuments might evoke ideas of harm and even desecration. Fierce storms blew across southern England in 1987 and 1990. The winds felled many trees including on and amongst the barrows on King Barrow Ridge, overlooking Stonehenge. The trees' roots tore holes in the barrows and archaeologists used these holes as opportunities to collect environmental samples and record the stratigraphy (Cleal and Allen 1994). Before the barrows were built, the downland had been grazed in varying intensities for several years, perhaps a few decades. The barrows were constructed of turf and soil, which was then capped with chalk from the surrounding ditches. Rosamund Cleal and Michael Allen (1994, 82) estimate that over a hectare of turf and soil contributed to each barrow. Multiplied across the barrows around Stonehenge, barrow-building exposed large expanses of chalk and transformed the soils. The removal of growing grass and organic-rich topsoil eroded the downland, revealing the land's under-layers. This might have been, Mike Parker Pearson and colleagues suggest (2006, 252), the destruction of valuable pasture that matched the ostentations consumption of cattle witnessed at other barrows, and what Barbara Bender (1992, 747) called 'a stronger—more aggressive—human intercession in the landscape'.

An alternative explanation is that the earth and chalk were in a metaphorical relation with flesh and bone (Parker Pearson et al. 2006, 252). The vegetation and soil were powerful substances incorporated into the barrows. The chalk that was dug from the surrounding ditches and used to cap the mounds created an inverted world of chalk, then turf and then the human dead. Jane Downes recognised practices of inversion during her excavations of cremation burials and pyres at Linga Fiold, Orkney (Downes 2009). At Linga Fiold, the pyres' layers were inverted in the cists: clean bone overlain with pyre debris. Inversion also structured the formation of the mounds covering the cists, with the lowest layers containing pyre debris, then turves, topsoil and subsoil. Downes suggests that the inverted world might have contained the generative and perhaps dangerous powers of the human dead. The barrows' edges at Linga Fiold were defined with stone kerbs and with the tools, stone mattocks and ards, that were used for breaking the ground. The kerbs and the tools, like the overlying subsoil that was unaffected by the pyre, were stable substances that could protect the living world from the mounds' contents.

Inversion recurred in monuments and in graves. The oak at Holme-next-the-Sea squatted, roots-to-the-sky, within its timber enclosure. Stones marked with rock art faced inwards when they were built into cists and placed on cairns. Collared and cordoned urns were commonly inverted, covering rather than containing the cremated bone. These inversions were not alike. Powerful, honoured, stones joined the dead within cists. Living stone retaining its vibrancy alongside the dead. The inverted urns took on different roles when they changed from containers into covers, along with a variety of technologies and substances that were employed for 'capping' burials (Cooper et al. 2019). The oak at Holme-next-the-Sea was 'planted' in wet ground from where it could grow downwards, with its earthly roots exposed to the sky. All the timbers except one in the enclosure had their bark-side facing outwards. The enclosure became the tree's outer skin, retaining a 'tree-ness' despite its human construction (Fahlander 2018).

The commonality amongst these interpretations is an allusion to growth or the generative qualities of different substances. The layers within the mounds on King Barrow Ridge and at Linga Fiold retained the land's topsoil-subsoil structure. The layers were retained and inverted within the space delineated by the barrows' outer ditches or kerbs. The layering was not only respectful and empowering, it was necessary (Jones 2010). To do otherwise would disrupt the body and the life of the land. Mounds transformed places as they emerged from the land. Humans participated in the process though they did not necessarily expect or believe that they could control it. People nurtured the growth of monuments. They assembled living substances in order that they might continue to participate in social life.

Conclusion

In the poem quoted at the beginning of the chapter, John Hewitt (2007, 28) described the sky as 'a handbook of labour or idleness' and observed that 'talk of weather is also talk of life'. Hewitt related people, land and sky within the routines of daily life. John Hewitt wrote about rural communities in twentieth-century Ulster. The landscapes of Ireland and Britain four millennia ago were alive with beings who in Hewitt's world were dismissed as subjects for superstitions and children's stories. I related the story of the will-o'-the-wisp as a phenomenon that was illusive and manifestly real. Theory and empirical evidence together make the argument for an entangled Bronze Age world where humans participated with other beings, who we define as mythical or natural, in the formation of social life. Prehistorians should not marginalise or ignore these actors and energies. They existed in language, things and places. They were brought into social life through stories and names, offerings and performances. Humans were not the only thinking beings in an enchanted world. To acknowledge that enchantment, we should write about the Bronze Age world as it was animate with humans, rather than how it was made animate by humans.

Monuments were places set apart for distinct acts of kinwork amongst human and nonhuman beings: in their unusual architectures, the presence of the human dead, their emphasis on transforming substances and marking celestial events. Monuments were the places where people performed rituals that were part of seasonal festivals or rites of passage connected with key stages in life—reaching adulthood, marriage or achieving affiliation to a group or role—and death. Monuments were places where exchanges made with other-than-human beings, and where humans and others went through transformations in states. These associations affected the mutuality of being, the constitution of persons and their world, and therefore monuments made and remade kin.

During the third millennium BC, large numbers of people gathered and built large and occasionally immense enclosures, avenues and mounds from earth, timber and stone. They transported objects and substances to the monuments, sometimes across considerable distances. The places where people gathered were already known and shaped by existing monuments and their associated histories. The palisade enclosures and timber settings at Ballynahatty, County Down, were built, then dismantled and burnt, during the first half of the third millennium BC (Hartwell 2002; Plunkett et al. 2008). The plateau overlooking the River Lagan was landmarked by several ancient passage tombs; it was largely cleared of woodland and farmed. A large earthen enclosure surrounding one of the passage tombs was built during or shortly after the use of the palisade enclosures. Across generations, kinship was established and sustained during visits to monuments and through the common labour, sharing of food and participation in the rituals taking place within the spaces that emerged.

People ceased building or altering most large monuments by around the twenty-second century BC and often a few centuries earlier. In the following centuries, their labours were more dispersed throughout the landscape, as many thousands of smaller monuments imitated the forms familiar from the Neolithic: circles, rows and mounds made from, timber, stone and earth. Distinctive regional architectures emerged alongside these dispersals, and were defined through the interplays of people, materials and places. On Bodmin Moor, Cornwall, stone banks and cairns surrounded some of the hilltop tors (rock outcrops). At

Tolborough Tor, a cairn rimmed with upright stones envelopes the tor and an alignment of five upright stones runs up to the monument (Johnson and Rose 1994, 39). Excavations commonly show that monuments evolved through their lives and there were complex histories of human burials and offerings. This seems to have been a particular feature of barrows during the twenty-second to nineteenth centuries BC (Garwood 2007). Neolithic monuments continued as powerful loci during the Bronze Age. People built new structures around the earlier monuments and in the surrounding country. Much older, upstanding chambered tombs were visited, reused for human burials and offerings, and sometimes modified. These practices recurred around Atlantic Europe (Gibson 2016). People took an interest in their landscape's history and, for want of better words, its folklore and vitalities.

Alongside the dispersal of monumentality, there was a shift in the size of the structures and the gatherings. Fewer people participated together in individual building projects during the Bronze Age compared with the preceding centuries. They travelled shorter distances to the monuments and their visits were briefer and more frequent. The labour estimates for the monuments at Raunds, Northamptonshire, decline in size from the early Neolithic to the Bronze Age (Harding and Healy 2007, 184–187). Around two or three cremations during each human generation would account for the 20 burials that clustered at Armadale Bay, Isle of Skye, during the twenty-first to eighteenth centuries BC (Krus and Peteranna 2016). Monuments remained collective projects. More than 50 axes were used to fell and prepare the trees used at Holme-next-the-Sea (Brennand and Taylor 2003).

Unlike the monuments of the early and mid-third millennium BC, Bronze Age monuments were closer in time and place to people's daily lives. The dispersal of monumentality localised rituals within familiar landscapes. Places acquired histories as monuments evolved and endured. The placements of human burials within barrows, together with the arrangements of mounds in the landscape, materialised kinship by positioning related events and persons in time and space. These were not stable genealogies that could always have been read from the land. They were not inscribed like text. Genealogies needed to be reworked and retold in order to remain alive and relevant. As with the funeral ledgers that Stefano Boni (2010) researched in the Akan area of West Africa, kinship comprised varied forms of 'closeness' that were ceaselessly under scrutiny. The building of and rites at monuments were critical fora for renegotiating kinship. Differences and relations could be noted by the contributions to the monuments' fabric, co-presences within ring ditches and palisades, and proximities to sensitive and revealing parts of rituals—as when a cup-marked cist slab was hefted into place.

Humans were not the sole participants in the labours and rituals performed at monuments. By defining certain structures as monuments, prehistorians recognise that they were places where people communicated with and transitioned between other worlds and beings. Open-air rock art provides an example of a practice through which humans related themselves with living rock and enchanted places that endured through the third and into the second millennium BC.

Alignments with celestial entities and events at stone rows and circles extended localities into the sky and drew the sky to the land. Mounds were made from the turf and clay in ways that respected the earth's order and retained its vitality. These acts bringing humans into relations with the land, sky and other beings were forms of kinmaking. In his ethnography of Te Waimana, a New Zealand Māori community, Sissons found kin-assemblages that comprised people, gods and ancestors. Some of the ancestors and gods existed as landscape features, such as springs. Sissons takes Marshal Sahlin's definition of kinship as a 'mutuality of being' to include 'human beings, their land and certain products of their collective labour' (Sissons 2013, 373). In making monuments, marking rock, and returning to and acknowledging these places, people were making kin between themselves and with other selves who inhabited the land and the sky. Monuments grew from a living land and vibrant sky. In an enchanted world, places as much as people made monuments.

References

Allen, Michael J, Michael Morris and R H Clark. 1995. Food for the living: a reassessment of a Bronze Age barrow at Buckskin, Basingstoke, Hampshire. *Proceedings of the Prehistoric Society* 61:151–189.

Baines, Andrew, Kenneth Brophy and Amelia Pannett. 2003. Yarrows Landscape Project / Battle Moss stone rows. *Discovery and Excavation in Scotland* 4:94–95.

Barber, John. 1977. The excavation of the holed-stone at Ballymeanoch, Kilmartin, Argyll. *Proceedings of the Society of Antiquaries of Scotland* 109:104–111.

Barclay, Gordon. 2005. The 'henge' and 'hengiform' in Scotland. In *Set in stone: new approaches to Neolithic monuments in Scotland*, edited by Vicki Cummings and Amelia Pannett, pp. 81–94. Oxbow, Oxford.

Barnatt, John. 1990. *The henges, stone circles and ringcairns of the Peak District.* Department of Archaeology and Prehistory, University of Sheffield, Sheffield.

Barnatt, John. 2000. To each their own: later prehistoric farming communities and their monuments in the Peak. *Derbyshire Archaeological Journal* 120:1–86.

Barrett, John C. 1994. *Fragments from antiquity: an archaeology of social life in Britain, 2900–1200 BC.* Blackwell, Oxford.

Beckensall, Stan. 1983. *Northumberland's prehistoric rock carvings.* Pendulum Press, Rothbury.

Beckensall, Stan. 1999. *British prehistoric rock art.* Tempus, Stroud.

Bender, Barbara. 1992. Theorising landscapes and the prehistoric landscape of Stonehenge. *Man* 27:735–755.

Benson, Don G, John G Evans, George H Williams, Timothy Darvill and Andrew David. 1990. Excavations at Stackpole Warren, Dyfed. *Proceedings of the Prehistoric Society* 56:179–245.

Bloch, Maurice. 1995. Questions not to ask of Malagasy carvings. In *Interpreting archaeology: finding meaning in the past*, edited by Ian Hodder, Michael Shanks, Alexandra Alexandri, Victor Buchli, John Carman, Jonathan Last and Gavin Lucas, pp. 212–215. Routledge, London.

Boni, Stefano. 2010. 'Brothers 30,000, sisters 20,000; nephews 15,000, nieces 10,000': Akan funeral ledgers' kinship and value negotiations, and their limits. *Ethnography* 11(3):381–408.

278 Landmarks

Bradley, Richard. 1997. *Rock art and the prehistory of Atlantic Europe: signing the land*. Routledge, London.
Bradley, Richard. 1998. *The significance of monuments: on the shaping of human experience in Neolithic and Bronze Age Europe*. Routledge, London.
Bradley, Richard. 2002. The land, the sky and the Scottish stone circle. In *Monuments and landscape in Atlantic Europe: perception and society during the Neolithic and Early Bronze Age*, edited by Chris Scarre, pp. 122–138. Routledge, London.
Bradley, Richard. 2005. *The moon and the bonfire: the investigation of three stone circles in north-east Scotland*. Society of Antiquaries of Scotland, Edinburgh.
Bradley, Richard, Jan Harding and Margaret Mathews. 1993. The siting of prehistoric rock art in Galloway, south-west Scotland. *Proceedings of the Prehistoric Society* 59:269–283.
Bradley, Richard and Courtney Nimura (editors). 2016. *The use and reuse of stone circles: feldwork at five Scottish monuments and its implications*. Oxbow, Oxford.
Bradley, Richard, Aaron Watson and Hugo Anderson-Whymark. 2012. Excavations at four prehistoric rock carvings on the Ben Lawers Estate, 2007–2010. *Proceedings of the Society of Antiquaries of Scotland* 142:27–61.
Brennand, Mark and Maisie Taylor. 2003. The survey and excavation of a Bronze Age timber circle at Holme-next-the-Sea, Norfolk, 1998–9. *Proceedings of the Prehistoric Society* 69:1–84.
Brittain, Marcus. 2015. Layers of life and death: aspects of monumentality in the early Bronze Age of Wales. In *The Neolithic of the Irish Sea*, edited by Vicki Cummings and Chris Fowler, pp. 224–232. Oxbow, Oxford.
Brophy, Kenneth. 2018. 'The finest set of cup and ring marks in existence': the story of the Cochno Stone, West Dunbartonshire. *Scottish Archaeological Journal* 40:1–23.
Brown, Paul M and Graeme Chappell. 2005. *Prehistoric rock art in the North York Moors*. Tempus, Stroud.
Brück, Joanna. 2004. Early Bronze Age burial practices in Scotland and beyond: differences and similarities. In *Scotland in ancient Europe: the Neolithic and Bronze Age of Scotland in their European context*, edited by Ian A G Shepherd and Gordon J Barclay, pp. 179–188. Society of Antiquaries of Scotland, Edinburgh.
Burl, Aubrey. 1980. Science or symbolism: problems of archaeo-astronomy. *Antiquity* 54(212):191–200.
Burl, Aubrey. 1993. *From Carnac to Callanish: the prehistoric stone rows and avenues of Britain, Ireland and Brittany*. Yale University Press, New Haven.
Carlin, Neil. 2017. Getting into the groove: exploring the relationship between Grooved Ware and developed passage tombs in Ireland c. 3000–2700 cal BC. *Proceedings of the Prehistoric Society* 83:155–188.
Carlin, Neil. 2018. *The Beaker phenomenon? Understanding the character and context of social practices in Ireland 2500–2000 BC*. Sidestone Press, Leiden.
Chan, Benjamin, Sarah Viner, Mike Parker Pearson, Umberto Albarella and Rob Ixer. 2016. Resourcing Stonehenge: patterns of human, animal and goods mobility in the Late Neolithic. In *Moving on in Neolithic studies: understanding mobile lives*, edited by Jim Leary and Thomas Kador, pp. 28–44. Oxbow, Oxford.
Chapman, Andy. 2007. A Bronze Age barrow cemetery and later boundaries, pit alignments and enclosures at Gayhurst Quarry, Newport Pagnell, Buckinghamshire. *Records of Buckinghamshire* 47(2):81–211.
Cleal, Rosamund M J and Michael J Allen. 1994. Investigation of tree-damaged barrows on King Barrow Ridge and Luxenborough Plantation, Amesbury. *Wiltshire Archaeological and Natural History Magazine* 87:54–84.

Cleal, Rosamund and Joshua Pollard. 2012. The revenge of the native: monuments, material culture, burial and other practices in the third quarter of the 3rd millennium BC in Wessex. In *Is there a British Chalcolithic? People, place and polity in the late third millennium BC*, edited by Michael J Allen, Julie Gardiner and Alison Sheridan, pp. 317–332. Prehistoric Society Research Papers, 4. Prehistoric Society/Oxbow, Oxford.

Coles, John, Hildur Gestsdóttir and Stephen Minnitt. 2000. A Bronze Age decorated cist from Pool Farm, West Harptree: new analyses. *Proceedings of the Somerset Archaeological and Natural History Society* 144:24–30.

Collis, John R. 1983. *Wigber Low, Derbyshire: a Bronze Age and Anglian burial site in the White Peak*. Department of Prehistory and Archaeology, University of Sheffield, Sheffield.

Cooper, Anwen, Duncan Garrow, Catriona Gibson and Melanie Giles. 2019. Covering the dead in later prehistoric Britain: elusive objects and powerful technologies of funerary performance. *Proceedings of the Prehistoric Society* 85:223–250.

Craig, Oliver E, Lisa-Marie Shillito, Umberto Albarella, Sarah Viner-Daniels, Ben Chan, Ros Cleal, Robert Ixer, Mandy Jay, Peter Marshall, Ellen Simmons, Elizabeth Wright and Mike Parker Pearson. 2015. Feeding Stonehenge: cuisine and consumption at the Late Neolithic site of Durrington Walls. *Antiquity* 89(347):1096–1109.

Cummings, Vicki and Chris Fowler. 2003. Places of transformation: building monuments from water and stone in the Neolithic of the Irish Sea. *Journal of the Royal Anthropological Institute* 9(1):1–20.

Darvill, Timothy. 2002. White on blonde: quartz pebbles and the use of quartz at Neolithic monuments in the Isle of Man and beyond. In *Colouring the Past: the significance of colour in archaeological research*, edited by Andrew Meirion Jones and Gavin MacGregor, pp. 73–92. Berg, Oxford

Darvill, Timothy, Peter Marshall, Mike Parker Pearson and Geoff Wainwright. 2012. Stonehenge remodelled. *Antiquity* 86(334):1021–1040.

Darvill, Timothy and Geoffrey Wainwright. 2003. A cup-marked stone from Dan-y-garn, Mynachlog-ddu, Pembrokeshire, and the prehistoric rock-art from Wales. *Proceedings of the Prehistoric Society* 69:253–264.

Davis, Simon. 2007. The Barrow 1 cattle bone deposit. In *The Raunds Area Project: a Neolithic and Bronze Age landscape in Northamptonshire*, edited by Jan Harding and Frances Healy, pp. 258–259. English Heritage, London.

Downes, Jane. 2009. The construction of barrows in Bronze Age Orkney—an 'assuagement of guilt'. In *Land and people: papers in memory of John G Evans*, edited by Michael J Allen, Niall Sharples and Terry O'Connor, pp. 126–135. Prehistoric Society Research Papers, 2. Prehistoric Society/Oxbow Books, Oxford.

Duffy, Paul R J. 2007. Excavations at Dunure Road, Ayrshire: a Bronze age cist cemetery and standing stone. *Proceedings of the Society of Antiquaries of Scotland* 137:69–116.

Dutton, Andrew, Kelly Clapperton and Stephen Carter. 2007. Rock art from a Bronze Age burial at Balblair, near Inverness. *Proceedings of the Society of Antiquaries of Scotland* 137:117–136.

Edwards, G and Richard Bradley. 1999. Rock carvings and Neolithic artefacts on Ilkley Moor, West Yorkshire. In *Grooved Ware in Britain and Ireland*, edited by Rosamund Cleal and Ann MacSween, pp. 76–77. Oxbow, Oxford.

Edwards, Howell G M. 2014. Will-o'-the-Wisp: an ancient mystery with extremophile origins? *Philosophical Transactions of the Royal Society A: Mathematical, Physical and Engineering Sciences* 372(2030):20140206.

Eogan, George. 1998. Knowth before Knowth. *Antiquity* 72:162–172.

Fahlander, Fredrik. 2018. The relational life of trees: ontological aspects of "tree-ness" in the Early Bronze Age of northern Europe. *Open Archaeology* 4:373–385.

Field, David, Hugo Anderson-Whymark, Neil Linford, Martyn Barber, Mark Bowden, Paul Linford and Peter Topping. 2015. Analytical surveys of Stonehenge and its environs, 2009–2013: Part 2—the stones. *Proceedings of the Prehistoric Society* 81:125–148.

Foley, Claire and Michael MacDonagh. 1998. Copney stone circles—a County Tyrone enigma. *Archaeology Ireland* 12(1):24–28.

Fowler, Chris. 2013. *The emergent past: a relational realist archaeology of Early Bronze Age mortuary practices.* Oxford University Press, Oxford.

Garwood, Paul. 2007. Before the hills in order stood: chronology, time and history in the interpretation of Early Bronze Age round barrows. In *Beyond the grave: new perspectives on barrows*, edited by Jonathan Last, pp. 30–52. Oxbow, Oxford.

Gibson, Alex. 1998. *Stonehenge and timber circles.* Tempus, Stroud.

Gibson, Alex. 2010. Excavation and survey at Dyffryn Lane henge complex, Powys, and a reconsideration of the dating of henges. *Proceedings of the Prehistoric Society* 76:213–248.

Gibson, Catriona. 2016. Closed for business or cultural change? Tracing the re-use and final blocking of megalithic tombs during the Beaker period. In *Celtic from the west 3. Atlantic Europe in the metal ages: questions of shared language*, edited by John Koch and Barry Cunliffe, pp. 83–110. Oxbow, Oxford.

Gillings, Mark. 2015a. Betylmania? Small standing stones and the megaliths of south-west Britain. *Oxford Journal of Archaeology* 34(3):207–233.

Gillings, Mark. 2015b. Fugitive monuments and animal pathways: explaining the stone settings of Exmoor. *Proceedings of the Prehistoric Society* 81:87–106.

Glassie, Henry. 1995. *Passing the time in Ballymenone: culture and history of an Ulster community.* Indiana University Press, Bloomington and Indianapolis.

Griffiths, W E. 1960. The excavation of stone circles near Penmaenmawr, North Wales. *Proceedings of the Prehistoric Society* 26:303–339.

Hale, Duncan, Andy Platell and Andrew Millard. 2009. A Late Neolithic palisaded enclosure at Marne Barracks, Catterick, North Yorkshire. *Proceedings of the Prehistoric Society* 75:265–304.

Harding, Jan. 2013. *Cult, religion, and pilgrimage: archaeological investigations at the Neolithic and Bronze Age monument complex of Thornborough, North Yorkshire.* Council for British Archaeology, York.

Harding, Jan and Frances Healy. 2007. *The Raunds Area Project: a Neolithic and Bronze Age landscape in Northamptonshire.* English Heritage, London.

Hartwell, Barrie. 2002. A Neolithic ceremonial timber complex at Ballynahatty, Co. Down. *Antiquity* 76(292):526–532.

Hayfield, Colin, John Pouncett and Pat Wagner. 1995. Vessey ponds: a 'prehistoric' water supply in East Yorkshire? *Proceedings of the Prehistoric Society* 61:393–408.

Hewitt, John. 2007. *Selected poems (edited by Michael Longley and Frank Ormsby).* Blackstaff Press, Belfast.

Ingold, Tim. 2006. Rethinking the animate, re-animating thought. *Ethnos* 71(1):9–20.

Johnson, Nicholas and Peter Rose. 1994. *Bodmin Moor: an archaeological survey. Volume 1—the human landscape to c.1800.* English Heritage, London.

Johnston, Robert and Joshua Pollard. 1999. Excavation and survey at Kellah Burn, Northumberland. *Universities of Durham and Newcastle Archaeological Reports* 22:17–23.

Jones, Andrew Meirion. 2007. *Memory and material culture.* Cambridge University Press, Cambridge.

Jones, Andrew Meirion. 2010. Layers of meaning: concealment, memory and secrecy in the British Early Bronze Age. In *Archaeology and memory*, edited by Dušan Boric, pp. 105–120. Oxbow, Oxford.

Jones, Andrew Meirion, Davina Freedman, Blaze O'Connor, Hugo Lamdin-Whymark, Richard Tipping and Aaron Watson. 2011. *An animate landscape: rock art and the prehistory of Kilmartin, Argyll, Scotland*. Windgather, Oxford.

Jones, Andy M. 1998/1999. The excavation of a Later Bronze Age structure at Callestick. *Cornish Archaeology* 37/38:5–55.

Jones, Andy M. 2006. Monuments and memories set in stone: a Cornish Bronze Age ceremonial complex in its landscape (on Stannon Down). *Proceedings of the Prehistoric Society* 72:341–365.

Jones, Andy M and Thomas Goskar. 2017. Hendraburnick 'Quoit': recording and dating rock art in the west of Britain. *Time and Mind* 10(3):277–292.

Jones, Andy M and Graeme Kirkham. 2013. From landscape to portable art: the changing settings of simple rock art in south-west Britain and its wider context. *European Journal of Archaeology* 16(4):636–659.

Jones, Andy M, Charles Thomas, Henrietta Quinnell, Anna-Lawson Jones, Kathleen McSweeney and Roger Taylor. 2010. Bosiliack and a reconsideration of entrance graves. *Proceedings of the Prehistoric Society* 76:271–296.

Kahn, Miriam. 1990. Stone-faced ancestors: the spatial anchoring of myth in Wamira, Papua New Guinea. *Ethnology* 29:51–66.

Kaul, Flemming. 2005. Bronze Age tripartite cosmologies. *Praehistorische Zeitschrift* 80(2):135–148.

Kohn, Eduardo. 2013. *How forests think: towards an anthropology beyond the human*. University of California Press, Berkeley.

Krus, Anthony and Mary Peteranna. 2016. Bayesian modeling of an Early Bronze Age cemetery at Armadale, Isle of Skye, Scotland. *Radiocarbon* 58(3):693–708.

Leary, Jim and David Field. 2010. *The story of Silbury Hill*. English Heritage, Swindon.

Leary, Jim, David Field and Gill Campbell (editors). 2013. *Silbury Hill: the largest prehistoric mound in Europe*. English Heritage, Swindon.

Lynch, Frances. 1993. *Excavations in the Brenig Valley: a Mesolithic and Bronze Age landscape in North Wales*. Cambrian Archaeological Association, Bangor.

MacKie, Euan W and A Davis. 1988/1989. New light on Neolithic rock carving: the petroglyphs at Greenland (Auchentorlie), Dunbartonshire. *Glasgow Archaeological Journal* 15:125–155.

Martlew, Roger D and Clive L N Ruggles. 1996. Ritual and landscape on the west coast of Scotland: an investigation of the stone rows of northern Mull. *Proceedings of the Prehistoric Society* 62:117–131.

May, Andrew McL. 1953. Neolithic habitation site, stone circles and alignments at Beaghmore, Co. Tyrone. *Journal of the Royal Society of Antiquaries of Ireland* 83(2):174–197.

McConway, Cia and Emma Donnelly. 2006. Daggers at dawn. *Archaeology Ireland* 20(2):5.

Meredith, Dianne. 2002. Hazards in the bog—real and imagined. *The Geographical Review* 92(3):319–332.

Mills, Allan A. 1980. Will-o'-the-wisp. *Chemistry in Britain* 16(2):69–72.

Moore, Michael J. 1995. A Bronze Age settlement and ritual centre in the Monavullagh Mountains, County Waterford, Ireland. *Proceedings of the Prehistoric Society* 61:191–243.

Moreland, John. 2001. *Archaeology and text*. Duckworth, London.

Mortimer, John R. 1905. *Forty years' researches in British and Saxon burial mounds of East Yorkshire*. A. Brown, London.

Mount, Charles. 1997. Early Bronze Age burial in south-east Ireland in the light of recent research. *Proceedings of the Royal Irish Academy* 97C(3):101–193.

Mount, Charles and Patrick J Hartnett. 1993. Early Bronze Age cemetery at Edmondstown, County Dublin. *Proceedings of the Royal Irish Academy* 93C(2):21–79.

Needham, Stuart and Trevor Cowie. 2012. The halberd pillar at Ri Cruin cairn, Kilmartin, Argyll. In *Visualising the Neolithic: abstraction, figuration, performance, representation*, edited by Andrew Cochrane and Andrew Meirion Jones, pp. 89–110. Oxbow, Oxford.

Neighbour, Tim. 2005. Excavation of a Bronze Age kerbed cairn at Olcote, Breasclete, near Calanais, Isle of Lewis. *Scottish Archaeological Internet Reports* 13.

Ó Nualláin, Seán. 1984. A survey of stone circles in Cork and Kerry. *Proceedings of the Royal Irish Academy* 84C:1–77.

O'Brien, William. 1999. *Sacred ground: megalithic tombs in coastal south-west Ireland*. Department of Archaeology, National University of Ireland, Galway.

O'Connor, Blaze. 2006. *Inscribed landscapes: contextualising prehistoric rock art in Ireland*. PhD thesis, University College Dublin.

O'Connor, Blaze. 2009. Re-collecting objects: carved, worked and unworked stone in Bronze Age funerary monuments. In *Materialitas: working stone and carving identity*, edited by Blaze O'Connor, Gabriel Cooney and John Chapman, pp. 147–160. Prehistoric Society Research Papers, 3. Prehistoric Society/Oxbow, Oxford.

O'Sullivan, Ann and John Sheehan. 1997. Prospection and outlook: aspects of rock art on the Iveragh Peninsula, Co. Kerry. In *Past perceptions: the prehistoric archaeology of southwest Ireland*, edited by Elizabeth Shee Twohig and Margaret Ronayne, pp. 75–84. Cork University Press, Cork.

Oswald, Al, Abby Hunt, Roger J Thomas and Jane Stone. 2005. *Analytical field survey of prehistoric and post-medieval remains on Fylingdales Moor, North Yorkshire*. Archaeological Investigation Report, AI/12/2005. English Heritage, Swindon.

Owoc, Mary Anne. 2004. A phenomenology of the buried landscape: soil as material culture in the Bronze Age of south-west Britain. In *Soils, stones and symbols: cultural perceptions of the mineral world*, edited by Nicole Boivin and Mary Anne Owoc, pp. 107–122. University College London Press, London.

Parker Pearson, Mike, Joshua Pollard, Colin Richards, Julian Thomas, Christopher Tilley, Kate Welham and Umberto Albarella. 2006. Materializing stonehenge: the Stonehenge Riverside Project and new discoveries. *Journal of Material Culture* 11(1/2):227–261.

Piggott, Stuart. 1939. The Badbury Barrow, Dorset, and its carved stone. *Antiquaries Journal* 19:291–299.

Piggott, Stuart and Terrence G E Powell. 1949. The excavation of three Neolithic chambered tombs in Galloway, 1949. *Proceedings of the Society of Antiquaries of Scotland* 83:103–161.

Pilcher, Jonathan. 1969. Archaeology, palaeocology and C14 dating of the Beaghmore stone circle site. *Ulster Journal of Archaeology* 32:73–91.

Plunkett, Gill, Faye Carroll, Barrie Hartwell, Nicki J Whitehouse and Paula J Reimer. 2008. Vegetation history at the multi-period prehistoric complex at Ballynahatty, Co. Down, Northern Ireland. *Journal of Archaeological Science* 35(1):181–190.

Pollard, Joshua. 1999. 'These places have their moments': thoughts on settlement practices in the British Neolithic. In *Making places in the prehistoric world: themes in settlement archaeology*, edited by Joanna Brück and Melissa Goodman, pp. 76–93. UCL Press, London.

Pollard, Joshua. 2013. From *Ahu* to Avebury: monumentality, the social, and relational ontologies. In *Archaeology after interpretation: returning materials to archaeological theory*, edited by Benjamin Alberti, Andrew Meirion Jones and Joshua Pollard, pp. 177–196. Left Coast Press, Walnut Creek, California.

Ralston, Ian. 1996. Four short cists from north-east Scotland and Easter Ross. *Proceedings of the Society of Antiquaries of Scotland* 126:121–155.

Reid, Malcolm. 2014. Once a sacred and secluded place: Early Bronze Age monuments at Church Lawton, near Alsager, Cheshire. *Proceedings of the Prehistoric Society* 80:237–277.

Richards, Colin. 2004. A choreography of construction: monuments, mobilization and social organization in Neolithic Orkney. In *Explaining social change: studies in honour of Colin Renfrew*, edited by John Cherry, Chris Scarre and Stephen Shennan, pp. 103–113. McDonald Institute for Archaeological Reseach, Cambridge.

Richards, Colin (editor). 2013. *Building the great stone circles of the north*. Windgather Press, Oxford.

Riley, Derek N. 1981. Barrow no. 1 on Ramsley Moor, Holmesfield. *Transactions of the Hunter Archaeological Society* 11:1–13.

Ritchie, J N Graham and Alastair MacLaren. 1972. Ring cairns and related monuments in Scotland. *Scottish Archaeological Forum* 4:1–17.

Robertson, David. 2016. A second timber circle, trackways, and coppicing at Holme-next-the-Sea beach, Norfolk: use of salt- and freshwater marshes in the Bronze Age. *Proceedings of the Prehistoric Society* 82:227–258.

Robinson, Tim. 1996. *Setting foot in Connemara and other writings*. Lilliput Press, Dublin.

Rogers, Alice. 2013. The afterlife of monuments in the English Peak District: the evidence of Early Bronze Age burials. *Oxford Journal of Archaeology* 32(1):39–51.

Ruggles, Clive L N. 1997. Astronomy and Stonehenge. In *Science and Stonehenge*, edited by Barry Cunliffe and Colin Renfrew, pp. 203–229. British Academy and Oxford University Press, Oxford.

Ruggles, Clive L N. 1999. *Astronomy in prehistoric Britain and Ireland*. Yale University Press, New Haven.

Ruggles, Clive L N. 2015. Recumbent stone circles. In *Handbook of archaeoastronomy and ethnoastronomy*, edited by Clive L N Ruggles, pp. 1277–1285. Springer, New York.

Semple, Sarah. 1998. A fear of the past: the place of the prehistoric burial mound in the ideology of middle and later Anglo-Saxon England. *World Archaeology* 30(1):109–126.

Sissons, Jeffrey. 2013. Reterritorialising kinship: the Māori "*hapū*". *Journal of the Polynesian Society* 122(4):373–391.

Stanley, W Owen. 1878. Notices of sepulchral deposits with cinerary urns, found at Porth Dafarch, in Holyhead Island, in 1848; and of recent excavations in the sand-mounds adjacent in 1875–6. *Archaeologia Cambrensis* 33:22–38.

Teather, Anne. 2011. Interpreting hidden chalk art in southern British Neolithic flint mines. *World Archaeology* 43(2):230–251.

Thomas, Antonia. 2016. *Art and architecture in Neolithic Orkney: process, temporality and context*. Archaeopress, Oxford.

Towers, Jacqueline, Janet Montgomery, Jane Evans, Mandy Jay and Mike Parker Pearson. 2010. An investigation of the origins of cattle and aurochs deposited in the Early Bronze Age barrows at Gayhurst and Irthlingborough. *Journal of Archaeological Science* 37:508–515.

Turnbull, Percival and Deborah Walsh. 1997. A prehistoric ritual sequence at Oddendale, near Shap. *Transactions of the Cumberland and Westmorland Antiquarian and Archaeological Society* 97:11–44.

Viner, Sarah, Jane Evans, Umberto Albarella and Mike Parker Pearson. 2010. Cattle mobility in prehistoric Britain: strontium isotope analysis of cattle teeth from Durrington Walls (Wiltshire, Britain). *Journal of Archaeological Science* 37:2812–2820.

Vyner, Blaise. 1988. The Street House wossit: the excavation of a Late Neolithic and Early Bronze Age palisaded ritual monument at Street House, Loftus, Cleveland. *Proceedings of the Prehistoric Society* 54:173–202.

Vyner, Blaise. 2011. A new context for rock art: a Late Neolithic and Early Bronze Age ritual monument at Fylingdales, North Yorkshire. *Proceedings of the Prehistoric Society* 77:1–23.

Waddell, John. 2010. *The Prehistoric Archaeology of Ireland*. Wordwell, Dublin.

Waddington, Clive. 1998. Cup and ring marks in context. *Cambridge Archaeological Journal* 8(1):29–54.

Wallis, Robert J. 2009. Re-enchanting rock art landscapes: animic ontologies, nonhuman agency and rhizomic personhood. *Time and Mind* 2(1):47–69.

Warren, Graeme and Tim Neighbour. 2004. Quality quartz: working stone at a Bronze Age kerbed cairn at Olcote, near Calanais, Isle of Lewis. *Norwegian Archaeological Review* 37(2):83–94.

Watson, Erin E. 2011. Not all monuments are megalithic: examining the cup and ring carved stones of northern Britain and the usefulness of the term 'portable art'. *Time and Mind* 4(3):337–353.

Welfare, Adam. 2011. *Great crowns of stone: the recumbent stone circles of Scotland*. Royal Commission on the Ancient and Historical Monuments of Scotland, Edinburgh.

Whittle, Alasdair. 1997. *Sacred Mound, Holy Rings. Silbury Hill and the West Kennet palisade enclosure: a Later Neolithic complex in north Wiltshire*. Oxbow, Oxford.

Woodward, Ann and Peter Woodward. 1996. The topography of some barrow cemeteries in Bronze Age Wessex. *Proceedings of the Prehistoric Society* 62:275–291.

7

AKIN TO LAND

2200–700 BC

Two standing stones at Llanbedr mark the beginning of an ancient trackway that, Colin Gresham proposed, stretched from the Irish Sea to the River Severn some 100 kilometres eastwards (Bowen and Gresham 1967, 56–61). Gresham traced the trackway from Llanbedr by following a discontinuous line of standing stones onto the nearby upland. Once inland and beyond the ring cairns at Moel Goedog, he mapped the route by linking old ways that respected the natural grain of the land, keeping clear of mires and the steepest ground, using rivers' easiest crossings. The occasional prehistoric landmark offered reassurance of the trackway's ancient origins: the cairn-circle at Bryn Cader Faner was one, the Llech Idris standing stone in Cwm Cain another (Figure 7.1).

Gresham's trackway joined other west–east routes that archaeologists had mapped across north Wales (Gresham and Irvine 1963; Griffiths 1960, 332–334). They were the mechanisms by which traders moved materials, especially metal, from the 'El Dorado of the West', as Arthur Evans (in Crawford 1912, 198) described Bronze Age Ireland, with the Wessex 'heartlands'. The trackways, marked with standing stones and other prominent monuments, offered safe and reliable passage across inhospitable and empty lands. Gresham and Irvine (1963, 54) conjured an intrepid image of an early traveller finding the way: 'crossing long stretches of sparsely inhabited upland, he would first have to be content with trial and error for his route, wandering as best he could over unknown hills and valleys'.

Frances Lynch (1984, 34–36) brings a different emphasis to her account of the uplands above Harlech. She wrote about Gresham's Llanbedr trackway after she excavated one of the two ring cairns at Moel Goedog. The ring cairns were within the first cluster of monuments on the route travelling eastwards. Lynch notes the presence of later prehistoric roundhouses and small fields on the hills' lower slopes. She observes how the ring cairns occupy subtly different positions

FIGURE 7.1 Bryn Cader Faner, Gwynedd: one of the monuments on Colin Gresham's 'Ardudwy trackway'. Copyright: Bill Bevan.

in the landscape, reflecting the builders' close knowledge of the topography. Sediments from the lowland several kilometres from the cairn adhered to two of the cremation deposits she excavated. In her report's conclusion, Lynch interprets the monuments as the ceremonial and funerary grounds for communities who lived 'relatively distant' and grazed their animals seasonally in the uplands. The monuments formed part of familiar localities, which were distanced by their status as places for funerary rituals.

John Roberts (2007) reviewed the shift from Gresham, Irvine and Griffiths' foot-weary long-distance travellers to Lynch's more local seasonal herders. Roberts identifies a ritualisation and distancing of monuments and upland landscapes in their accounts. What the accounts lacked, Roberts argues, was an appreciation of the practical context for people's inhabitation of the uplands. If the upland basins were grazed over centuries, as pollen records indicate, then the monuments held their primary meaning for the people and their livestock who moved around rather than through the landscapes. The circles and cairns were suitable places for marking arrivals and departures from grazing land, and negotiating tenure, perhaps between different kin sharing the pasture and with ancestral or supernatural beings who held the land.

I use this chapter to describe the ways that people's relations with the landscapes they inhabited transformed during the second and early first millennia BC. I begin in the uplands of north Wales and with the circles that W E Griffiths and Frances Lynch excavated. These were places embedded in routines of movement and pause as people established rights to occupy land and periodically remade their connections with places. New structures came to mediate people's relations with the land during the middle centuries of the second millennium: cairnfields, boundaries and field systems. Circles and barrows remained relevant, either built afresh or as places referenced through offerings and burials. Rectilinear field systems, limited to southern Britain during the middle and later centuries of the second millennium, were the most impressive (and monumental) of the new features ordering landscapes.

Field systems, like the roundhouses I described in Chapter 4, are presented by prehistorians as evidence for a fundamental change in people's worldviews. Landscapes formerly dominated by monuments and overtly ritualised were transformed through processes of domestication and agricultural intensification into political and economic capital. This portrayal misrepresents the process. After fields, people continued making offerings of objects and bodies in rivers, bogs, caves and at monuments. They undertook rituals that involved exchanges and communications with ancestral and supernatural beings. They inhabited a world that was as complex and animate in the fourteenth century BC as it was in the eighteenth century BC. I do not mean that worlds and kinship remained unchanged. They were transformed by fields and allied forms of landmarking.

The challenge for archaeologists is to describe the transformations of the second millennium BC in terms of all the participants in social life, human and nonhuman, living and supernatural. This includes the land itself, which was perhaps one of the most influential constituents of kinship. My approach to this task is to treat monuments and fields together as forms of landmarking and the means through which people related to land. The monuments were entangled with routine lives and landscapes. The field systems associated people with ancestors and supernatural beings. Monuments, pastures and fields were places for kinwork: between persons and with other selves who inhabited the land.

Emerging fields, 2200–1500 BC

I introduced the stone alignments, cairns and circles at Beaghmore, County Tyrone, in the previous chapter. Several low banks or 'causeways' of stone pre-dated the circles and alignments (May 1953). The banks may be the remnants of field boundaries or stone cleared during cultivation. They continue beyond the edges of the excavated area, and May (1953, 177) reported a further example in a peat cutting 800 metres to the southwest. Jonathan Pilcher (1969) reconstructed the environmental history at Beaghmore from pollen preserved in an infilled lake basin close by. He identified grassland with some cereals in a section of the profile dated to the later fourth millennium BC, at a time when the lake was surrounded by alder carr. The alder had reduced by the late third millennium BC, before the monuments were constructed sometime during the twentieth to seventeenth centuries BC. By this time, there were areas of open heath, grassland and woodland comprising oak, hazel and alder. The stone circles and alignments emerged in a locality where, for centuries, animals had grazed and people had managed woodland, cleared stone and cultivated small plots—a hearth with associated lithics and pottery found near one of the stone alignments dated to early in the third millennium BC (Pilcher 1975). The monuments did not stop people using Beaghmore for agriculture: animals continued to graze the land around the circles and there may have been intermittent cultivation close by.

Beaghmore illustrates that monuments could be active places within landscapes. The ring ditches in the Upper and Middle Thames Valley contain a layer of fine sediment that formed during a period of stable grassland (Robinson in Morigi et al. 2011, 186–187). Open areas seem to have been maintained through grazing, without cycles of clearance and regeneration that typified the Neolithic. Before the barrows were built on King Barrow Ridge, overlooking Stonehenge, the turf used in the mounds had been grazed in varying intensities for several years, perhaps a few decades (Cleal and Allen 1994). Charles French, Rob Scaife and Michael Allen's study of the wider Stonehenge-Durrington landscape identified a stable, grazed grassland that was established by the early third millennium BC and continued throughout the second millennium: 'a culturally desired, determined and managed landscape' (French et al. 2012, 30).

The many and widespread monuments dating after the twenty-second century BC could be interpreted as proxies for an opening up of woodland and a transformation in land use. Two henges have been located in the Peak District, both situated on the central limestone plateau. Nearer 1,000 barrows and open circular monuments marked a shift to a dispersed distribution of monuments that extended throughout the limestone and onto the sandstone areas to the north, east and west (Barnatt 1996). The fieldwork undertaken in Brecknock, south Wales, by the Royal Commission on the Ancient and Historical Monuments of Wales (RCAHMW 1997) revealed a contrast between the distribution of Neolithic chambered tombs, which are limited to a compact group on mainly lower land above the Usk-Llynfi basin, and Bronze Age monuments, which are distributed across most of the upland landscape. Funerary cairns are amongst the most common Bronze Age monuments on Brecknock's uplands, along with ring cairns, standing stones and stone circles.

Surveys in upland areas of Ireland are finding dense distributions of monuments (Moore 1995; Rice 2006). On the Beara Peninsula, southwest Ireland, William O'Brien (2009) used survey, excavation and palaeoenvironmental studies to investigate the history of a predominately upland landscape. There were marked changes in the formation of the landscape during the Bronze Age, particularly in the second half of the second millennium BC. This was when many of the standing stone pairs, stone circles, boulder burials and *fulachtaí fiadh* were built (Figure 7.2). This coincided with the widespread clearance of

FIGURE 7.2 Uragh stone circle, Beara Peninsula, County Kerry. Copyright: Bill Bevan.

woodland and the use of the landscape for pasture and some cultivation of cereals. The palaeoenvironmental record provides the only indication of land use
within these landscapes, since the earliest archaeologically visible settlement and
agricultural structures date from the late first millennium BC.

The large numbers of Bronze Age monuments, surviving especially in upland
areas, might represent periods when people began clearing and colonising what
are now characterised agriculturally marginal landscapes. Colin Burgess, in *The
Age of Stonehenge* (1980), presented a narrative of deepening encroachment into
the uplands throughout the second millennium BC as population rose and agricultural land in other ecological zones became exhausted. Burgess argued that
improved climatic conditions during the early second millennium facilitated this
expansion (Burgess 1985, 200). Compared with the 1980s, reconstructions of
climatic change are at a higher resolution and sensitive to regional differences.
We have a better appreciation of the complexities and imprecisions in the proxies used for researching past climates. The Bronze Age did not coincide with
a period of climatic amelioration in Ireland and Britain. Reviewing multiple
proxies, Dan Charman (2010, 1548) concludes that temperatures decreased and
stayed relatively low throughout the second millennium BC. Periods of wetter
conditions are recorded within the sedimentary records for the twenty-third to
nineteenth centuries BC (4260–4120 and 4030–3870 cal BP) and during the sixteenth to fourteenth centuries BC (3550–3300 cal BP). There is no evidence for
a large magnitude climatic downturn following 2200 BC in Britain and Ireland,
the so-called 4.2 ka event (Roland et al. 2014; Swindles et al. 2013).

Palynological studies indicate woodland clearance, pasture and, sometimes, cultivation predating the construction of monuments and lasting throughout the third and second millennia for many upland areas. Ralph Fyfe (2012) examined pollen sequences at three locations near barrows and stone rows high (400–450 metres altitude) on Exmoor. The Bronze Age was represented in two cores (Comerslade and North Twitchen Springs). Landscapes were semi-open with significant local woodland. At North Twitchen Springs, there was a century or so of grazing when the heathland transformed into pasture during the twentieth century BC. There was a general reduction in arboreal pollen from the fifteenth century BC, although this followed different processes with grassland reverting to heathland in one column and an expansion of grassland in another.

A similar pattern is present elsewhere. On Bodmin Moor, Ben Gearey's research identified a Bronze Age '"high tide" of upland settlement' (Gearey et al. 2000, 503). The episodes of major woodland clearance that Gearey recognised in his cores date from the later second and first millennia BC: 1650–1450 BC, Rough Tor South; 1150–950 BC, Tresellern Marsh; 750–400 BC, Rough Tor North. They were contemporary with the moor's field systems and roundhouses, rather than the funerary cairns and stone rows. The earlier parts of the cores indicate anthropogenic activity, though this was light and sporadic, perhaps related to seasonal land use. In Althea Davies' (2007) work in the upper (western) reaches of Glen Affric, a narrow valley deep in the northwest Highlands, she identified stock grazing in the valley from the thirtieth century BC, with more intensive grazing starting in the twenty-third century BC, which may have included some burning of heathland to encourage grassland. Barley cultivation did not occur until the nineteenth century BC and became consistent, together with weeds of cultivation, from the sixteenth century BC.

There are multiple difficulties with interpreting pollen diagrams because of the variations in their catchments and the differential dispersal of pollen taxa. This means that some pollen, especially arboreal taxa, can be over-represented in the data. Ralph Fyfe and colleagues (2013) modelled relative landscape openness across Britain and Ireland using over 70 pollen profiles. Their results are at a coarse resolution, working within 500-year intervals. The modelling uses a method that was developed for data from large lakes, which drew on pollen from the lakes' regions not their immediate localities. In Britain and Ireland, many sampling locations were smaller mires and bogs, where the dominance of heather might be more reflective of the immediate sampling location. The research concludes that local pollen studies tend to underestimate the degree of openness. For many regions, the landscape gradually became more open from the fourth millennium BC. There was variability between regions. Comparing the northeast and northwest uplands of England, heathland (heather) makes up a high proportion of the land cover from 3000 to 2500 BC in the northwest, while comparable proportions of heathland were not reached in northeast England until the first millennium AD. As a general trend, there was a gradual process of encroachment during 2500–1500 BC—a further opening up of what were already relatively open landscapes.

Pasture, circles and ring cairns, 2000–1500 BC

In this chapter's opening section, I described a long-distance trackway that Colin Gresham reconstructed from Llanbedr, north Wales. The route begins by the river's edge and two standing stones, from where it climbs for a few kilometres, steeply at first, onto leveller ground. It is here, with Foel Senigl as a backdrop and overlooking a broad, marshy basin, that the route picks up a line of standing stones. Carreg is the first stone. Several more, widely and evenly spaced, lead the way as far as a terrace below Moel Goedog and two ring cairns. Frances Lynch (1984) spent a wet, windswept month excavating one of the ring cairns in 1978 after it was mistakenly damaged. The monument (Moel Goedog I) stands on a small shelf that had been levelled into the hillslope. A second ring cairn is on another shelf a short distance upslope. Moel Goedog I originally comprised 12 stones, upright and standing no more than a metre in height, arranged in a rough circle seven metres across (Figure 7.3). A stony bank formed an outer ring around the standing stones. Lynch identified ten pits within the circle's small interior: one central within the ring and the others towards the periphery. The pits were mostly small, capped with stones and filled with dark earth and charcoal. Four pits included small quantities of cremated human bone from young adults. The bone accompanied an inverted enlarged food vessel and a collared urn. A second inverted collared urn contained dark earth and charcoal, with no cremated bone.

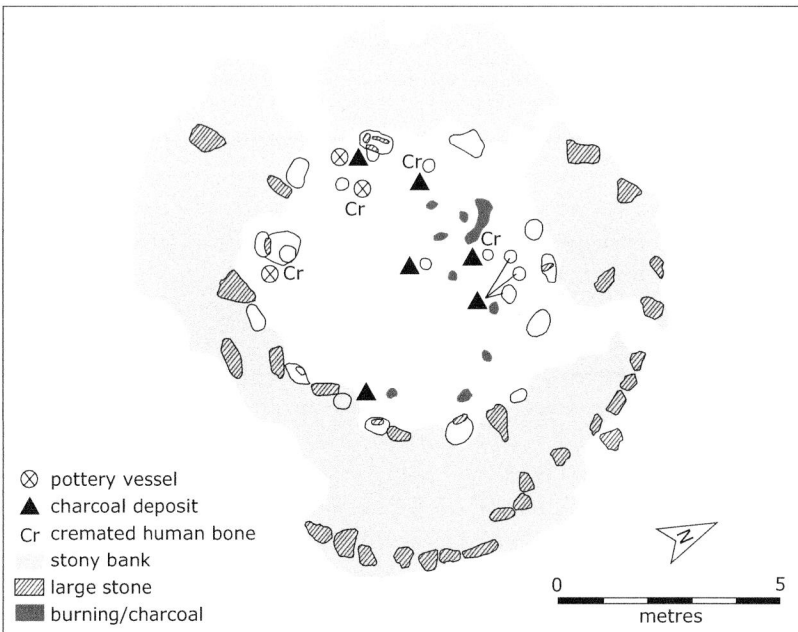

FIGURE 7.3 Excavation plan of Moel Goedog I ring cairn, Gwynedd. Adapted from Lynch 1984.

The offerings at Moel Goedog occurred at different times during the twentieth to seventeenth centuries BC. The calibrated radiocarbon dates lack the precision needed to limit the duration more precisely. The pit containing the enlarged food vessel was cut alongside a stone hole and filled before the stone was raised. The pot and pit contained clean yellow clay, which is the local subsoil. The pit with the collared urn, charcoal and earth was dug against the face of an upright stone. The other pits re-emerged at different levels during the excavation, suggesting that they were originally dug periodically as a soil formed within the circle. The sediments adhering to two deposits of cremated bone were not from Moel Goedog. The bone had previously been buried elsewhere, with the nearest source for the sediment located to the south, in the direction taken by the alignment of standing stones. Frances Lynch (1984, 36) concludes the report on her excavations at Moel Goedog by characterising the landscape as a seasonal grazing area and as a burial or ceremonial area that was 'distant' from lowland settlements. Pollen analysis of a core from the basin east of Moel Goedog identified a phase of decreased woodland (primarily alder and hazel), together with an increase in heath and taxa of open country, beginning around the twenty-third to twentieth centuries BC (Chambers and Price 1988). The basin perhaps lost much of its skirt of alder carr, allowing sedges, with meadowsweet and dropwort, to increase. These changes preceded or were contemporary with the establishment of the excavated Moel Goedog ring cairn and its neighbouring monument.

Rather than a ritual landmark on a long-distance routeway, the Moel Goedog circle lay within a regularly visited and grazed landscape. Given the location's exposure to weather, it is likely the visits were seasonal, when the meadowsweet flowered around the basin's margins. John Roberts (2007) offers a similar interpretation of the clusters of monuments and small cairns at Cefn Coch and Waun Llanfair, above Penmaenmawr, on Wales's north coast (Figure 7.4). The relatively intimate, low-key rituals that took place at the monuments underpinned people's persistent associations with and rights of access to pasture. The monuments make more sense, Roberts argues, as evidence for the establishment and maintenance of grazing areas that groups inhabited with their animals.

Waun Llanfair is a broad upland basin adjacent to Graig Lwyd, where stone was quarried for ground-stone axes from the mid-centuries of the fourth millennium BC. Substantial landscape changes occurred during the twenty-eighth century BC (Caseldine et al. 2017). Hazel and then alder declined as heath and grassland increased. Small cairns at Waun Llanfair and Graig Lywd have produced material dated to the third millennium BC, contemporary with the more extensive grazing around the basin. Around the twentieth to eighteenth centuries BC, there was a further decline in hazel and alder, preceded by a peak in microscopic charcoal. Grassland expanded around the same time. The twentieth century BC brought a change in the ways people marked their inhabitation in the landscape. The deposition of human burials and offerings within the stone circle and ring cairn at Cefn Coch began around this time, as did activity at one of the two excavated burnt stone mounds located by small streams in Waun Llanfair.

FIGURE 7.4   Aerial photograph of the monuments at Cefn Coch and the upland basin of Waun Llanfair, Gwynedd. The Druid's Circle is visible close to
the plateau's edge, in the lower left of the image. © Crown copyright:
RCAHMW.

W E Griffiths (1960) excavated two circles at Cefn Coch, a short distance northeast from Waun Llanfair. The Druid's Circle is the larger and more prominent monument: a ring of standing stones set along the inner edge of a stone bank, with an entrance in the circle's southwest arc. Four deposits clustered around the circle's central area, within the limits of where Griffiths excavated. A cist filled with white clay contained an inverted enlarged food vessel, which was filled with the same white clay and a young person's cremated remains. Next to the cist, under a flat stone, an inverted food vessel contained some cremated bones from a young person and a small bronze knife. The vessel's mouth was sealed with clay. Two more offerings comprised a partial and broken food vessel wedged upright in a pit, and a scoop lined with whetstones and with a small quantity of cremated bone.

The second circle Griffiths excavated is a ring cairn, a little over 150 metres from the Druid's Circle. Despite their proximity, the circles are not inter-visible. The ring cairn is a low, substantial bank of stones with its inner edge marked with boulders. One stone within the inner kerb was larger than the others, edge-set and embedded in the subsoil. The ring cairn sprang from this grounded rock. A fire or fires had burnt at the stone's base and a fragment of cremated bone was placed into the bank at the stone's edge. A small pit had been dug against the edge in the opposing arc of the circle. A fire was lit around and in the pit; the ashes and burnt soil were scooped up and placed in the small collared urn; the vessel was placed upright in the pit, capped with a stone, and a second fire was set over the stone. People made varied though uncomplicated offerings within the circles at Cefn Coch and at Moel Goedog. The offerings comprised cremated human bone—all young adults—and the remains of fires, whether cleaned charcoal, gathered ash or burnt soil. Pottery vessels were sometimes used for holding the bone, charcoal and sediments.

Related practices are recorded at circles elsewhere. Anthony Ward (1988) surveyed the ring cairns in south Wales, on the Gower Peninsular west of Swansea and in the hills north of Llanelli. The ring cairns tended to occupy small terraces, overlooked by higher ground and with limited horizons. Ward excavated an adjacent pair of ring cairns on Cefn Bryn, Gower. Both had gaps through the rings that were subsequently infilled and in one case the entire ring was infilled. A pit in one cairn's interior contained a few grams of cremated bone. In the other cairn, a fire had been set against a stone on the circle's inner kerb. At Carnkenny, County Tyrone, 17 pits clustered in the circle's interior contained charcoal, earth and small quantities of poorly preserved cremated bone (Lynn 1973/1974). The ring cairns excavated in southwest England contain simple deposits of material, including charcoal and quartz. Six monuments were investigated during the rescue excavations undertaken in 1977 on Shaugh Moor, on Dartmoor's southwestern fringe (Wainwright et al. 1979): three ring cairns and three small cairns, enclosing or covering various deposits of charcoal and material culture both in pits and on the ground surface. Two of the ring cairns enclosed earthfast boulders. On Farway Hill, Dartmoor, two adjacent ring cairns were associated with 38 pits filled with charcoal along with deposits of cremated bone in a cist (Pollard 1971).

The three ring cairns and two 'tailed' cairns excavated by Andy Jones (2006) on Stannon Down, Bodmin Moor, Cornwall, contained deposits of charcoal and quartz and incorporated large earthfast stones ('grounders'). The monuments were periodically transformed with additions of stone and upright posts. Jones grouped the five monuments into two clusters, which had differing landscape settings and depositional associations. The eastern group—a tailed cairn and a ring cairn—incorporated large grounders in their form and there were offerings of broken pottery, charcoal, pieces of quartz and slate, and faience and amber beads. The monuments in the western group incorporated alignments on Rough Tor, a prominent rocky hill skylined to the northeast, and they did not contain offerings of portable objects. Jones (2006, 360) interprets the small offerings, incorporation of grounders and erecting of large boulders, and the alignments on Rough Tor as rituals that connected people with the place—enabling 'the control of natural landscape features'.

People's activities at Stannon Down's monuments occurred during a time (the twentieth to fifteenth centuries BC) when a largely wooded, oak-hazel landscape opened up and the first permanent grasslands were established (Heather Tinsley in Jones 2004/2005, 66). Plants associated with grazing and disturbance are visible in the pollen record: ribwort plantain, sheep's sorrel, thistle and dandelion. Clearings and pasture were parts of the moor's ecology in a minor way in previous centuries, and always followed by woodland recovery. The environmental history on Stannon Down has similarities with the pollen records that I described from Waun Llanfair and Moel Goedog. New landscapes were being created by people and animals, in which woodland played a smaller part that it once had, and pastures were maintained and periodically expanded. Reviews of excavated faunal assemblages from Ireland and southern Britain identify a decline in the proportions of pigs alongside increases in cattle and sheep/goat around this time (McCormick 2007; Serjeantson 2011). Sheep or goats were cremated along with humans in three of the deposits in a ring cairn at Cloburn Quarry, Lanarkshire (Lelong and Pollard 1998).

Mark Gillings (2015) has connected the stone rows or settings on Exmoor with grazing and animals' journeys through the landscape. The rows were active structures. Their stones were periodically lifted, dropped and reset in different ways. Some stone holes contained 'triggers', which were larger than normal chock stones that could ease the placement and displacement of stones. Gillings noticed that the rows are sited at places where the bedrock is closer to the surface and where the vegetation is more open. The stones are attractive to livestock, as rubbing posts and somewhere to shelter. During the Bronze Age, the rows were good places to encourage stock to pause on their movement through the landscape—presumably sheep, given the stones' diminutiveness. The stones were set *with* rather than *for* animals.

Unlike Exmoor's stone settings, the circles I described in this section were circumscribed spaces. The low banks, standing stones and timber posts marked the distinction between inside and outside. Their landscape settings sometimes invited approaches from particular directions, as Frances Lynch (1984, 34) speculated in the case of the Moel Goedog circles. Their entrances defined the way for entering and leaving the circles. In the case of Cefn Bryn, the entrances were blocked during the monument's history. The same occurred at Barbrook II, Derbyshire, where a low cairn filled an original gap in the circle (Barnatt 1990, 57). In other examples, the circles' interiors were infilled with stone. Richard Bradley (1998) argues that the permeability of the open circles enabled those performing rituals inside the monuments to make reference to the world framed by the standing timber posts and stones. Monuments oriented themselves upon celestial bodies and landmarks drew otherworldly beings and forces into the performances. The ceremonies may have involved selective esoteric knowledge and made participants attentive to the surrounding landscape.

Fire, bone, earth and stone formed some of the processes and substances that shaped the monuments. Cremated bone, mainly though not always human, was deposited in comparable ways to the burials in mounds and cemeteries. Commonly, the cremated bone was dispersed to and incorporated with multiple places. Small quantities of bone were taken into and left in the circles. Two of the cremated bone deposits excavated at Moel Goedog spent time buried elsewhere, before being excavated and taken to the ring cairn. The cremated bone may have had generative qualities that were both potent and dangerous. The offerings at the circles connected those performing the rites with the place and the land. The gift of cremated bone was then repaid with access to rich pasture or there was, as John Evans (Evans 2003, 59) and Jane Downes (2009) have suggested for different contexts, an 'assuagement of guilt' for the harm wrought on woodland. Small fires were burnt within the circles and sometimes elsewhere, possibly nearby, in other monuments or domestic structures. The remains of the fires were deposited in pits, cists and vessels. The timber burnt in the fires was characteristic of the woodland in the surrounding landscape, unlike pyres, which were dominated by oak. The fires that burnt in ring cairns were closer to domestic hearths than the pyres I discussed in Chapter 3.

A group of barrows and cairns cluster within a broad basin near the headwaters of the Afon Brenig, a tributary of the Alwen and the Dee, Denbighshire. Amongst the monuments, there is a ring cairn with an annular turf bank, faced and capped with stone, and formerly encircled by a ring of posts (Lynch 1993, 117–143) (Figure 7.5). Cremated bone and charcoal were deposited at different times during the monument's use in the twentieth to fifteenth centuries BC. Hazel, willow, birch, oak and alder were burnt within the circle and deposited in pits. The cremated remains of three people were buried in two inverted collared urns in a pit on the east arc of the cairn, together with clay 'ear-studs', a flint knife and an accessory vessel. The pit was then filled with charcoal of hazel, oak, willow and alder, and covered with burnt stones. Two of the burnt stones were halves of a single slab. The slab had been burnt on one side, broken in two and placed on the pit with one burnt-side upwards and the other burnt-side

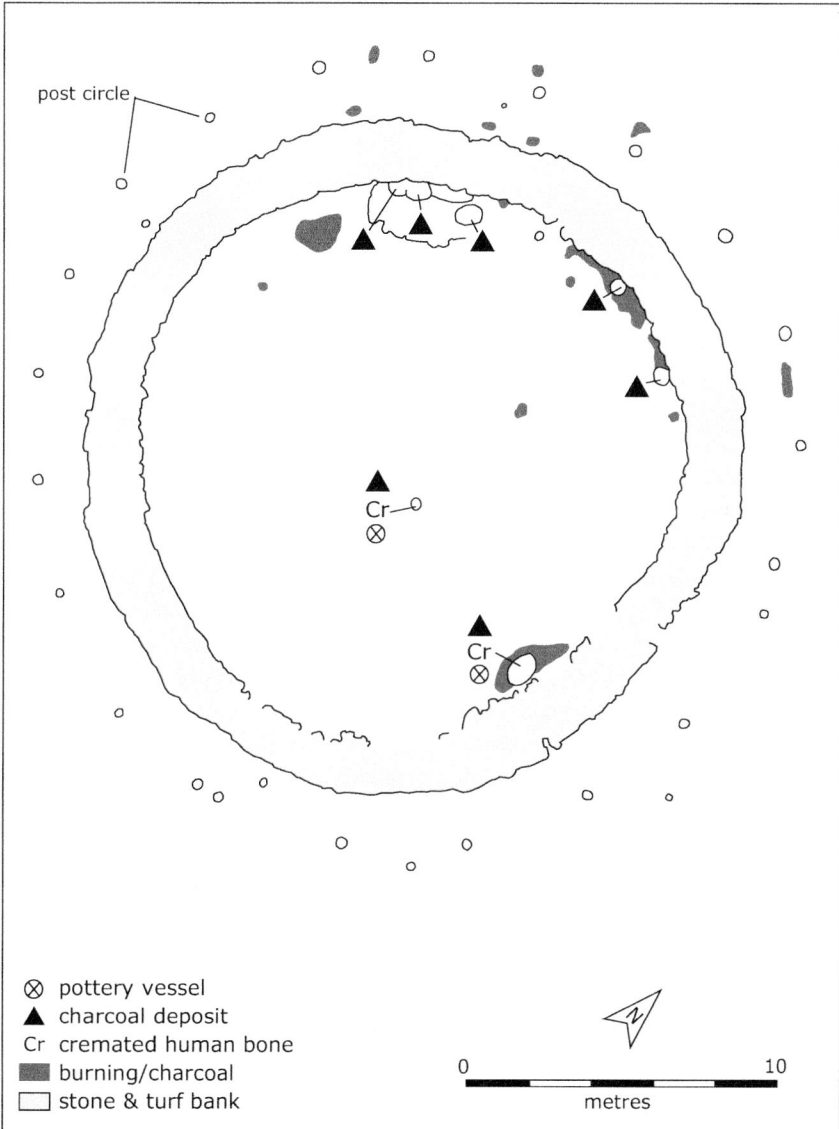

post circle

⊗ pottery vessel
▲ charcoal deposit
Cr cremated human bone
■ burning/charcoal
☐ stone & turf bank

0   10
metres

FIGURE 7.5 Excavation plan of the ring cairn at Brenig, Denbigh Moors. Adapted from Lynch 1993.

downwards. The same process was followed with a stone covering a pit on the opposite side of the circle. The Brenig ring cairn gained a history and complexity as people's relations with the valley deepened. The turves in the bank were cut from nearby pasture and cultivated land and then taken to an area of heather moorland where the cairn was built. People gathered brushwood from the surrounding landscape and set fires within the cairn. Burnt-out, the fires' remains were buried at points on the cairn's circumference. The slabs covering two of the pits may have been the stones on which fires were set. Once broken, like the ring cairn, the slabs faced inwards and outwards: out to the landscape and into the pit where the residues from the rites were buried in the earth.

There may have been centuries-long associations between communities and the land where ring cairns were sited. Iterative offerings were made within some ring cairns and they were located amongst groups of other monuments, including complex funerary monuments with multiple burials. During his surveys on the Eastern Moors in the Peak District, Derbyshire, John Barnatt (2000) frequently discovered monuments in compact clusters: stone circles, ring cairns, standing stones and barrows. He interprets these clusters as the ceremonial areas used by small communities who farmed and lived adjacent to the monuments. John Roberts (2007) describes a less settled world in north Wales during the early second millennium BC. The people who built and used the monuments were pastoralists who moved between grazing areas according to season and tradition. Willy Kitchen (2001) envisages more heterogeneous kinwork occurring at monuments. People's journeys with their animals might have extended over long distances and converged on large grazing areas such as the Peak District's limestone plateau—the focus of Kitchen's research. The pastures used by different communities overlapped in space and time. People used monuments as temporary tethering places at which to negotiate and mark their access to land at particular times.

The flint that people used for flaked stone during the Bronze Age in the Peak District was from east Yorkshire and East Anglia, at distances greater than 100 kilometres (Kitchen 2001, 118). When available, the flint was used in preference to the chert found on the limestone. Kevin Cootes and Patrick Quinn (2018) examined the petrography of a sample of Bronze Age ceramics from the Peak District. The clays contain tempers from specific igneous outcrops that were collected from sometimes tens of kilometres from the locations where the clays were sourced and the pots were buried. John Llewellyn Williams and David Jenkins (2004) undertook a petrographic analysis of early Bronze Age ceramics from north Wales. They found that the clays and fillers were sourced from varying distances from the places where the pots were deposited. The vessels from Anglesey used igneous rock temper from a select few sources within 10 kilometres of the burials. In Ardudwy (the ring cairn at Moel Goedog), igneous tempers were sourced from up to 30 kilometres away. At Brenig, the source for the temper was more distant, somewhere from Wrekin as far south as the Malvern Hills.

There are different ways to explain the displacement of rock used in ceramic temper and in flaked stone tools. They may be added to the variety of materials that moved with people and during exchanges: copper, tin, bronze and gold; jet, shale, amber and faience. Alternatively, as Kitchen (2001) and Cootes and Quinn (2018) suggest, the rock was collected during more routine journeys, when moving livestock between grazing areas. The consistency with which sources of temper align with different regions in north Wales and the Peak District lends support to the latter explanation. Mobility was important and may, depending on region and community, have involved relatively long distances. This did not mean that people and animals were disconnected or unfamiliar with the landscapes they visited. The monuments were attentive to their localities and grew out of places. The turf and stone, the alignments on landmarks, charcoal composed from nearby woodland and cremated human bone: these were gatherings from parts of places, practices and people. They composed kinship from humans and places. People were not taking control of land and pasture; they were negotiated tenure with places in moments of arrival and departure, by the duration of their presence and the activities of their animals. In these ways, a dimension of kinship grew from the inhabitation of pasture.

Harvests of stone: cairnfields, 2500–1500 BC

> These mounds, which are almost invariably wanting in any signs of an interment beyond pieces of charcoal and burnt stone … are usually found associated in groups, sometimes in very considerable numbers. They are of small size and slight elevation, and frequently have one or more of much larger size placed amongst them, these latter being generally found to contain cists. They are clearly artificial, and are sometimes very carefully constructed, with stones overlapping one another in a regular series commencing from the centre.
>
> *(Greenwell 1877, 420)*

The ring cairns and stone circles I described in the previous section are recorded alongside relatively compact groups of small cairns, as observed by William Greenwell in this section's epigraph. The cairns tend to be less than five metres across and without obvious evidence for the outer kerbs or internal cists than occur within funerary monuments (Figure 7.6). Over 20 small cairns are scattered across the drier ground of the upland basin at Waun Llanfair, close to the circles at Cefn Coch (Caseldine et al. 2017). A dense grouping of 30 small cairns is located down the valley from the ring cairn and barrows at Brenig (Frances Lynch and Richard Kelly in Lynch 1993, 161–163). These associations between small cairns and monuments are widespread if not ubiquitous. John Barnatt recognised groups of small cairns and irregular field systems accompanied by stone circles and ring cairns on the Eastern Moors, Derbyshire (Barnatt 1986). Michael Moore's (1995) survey in the Monavullagh Mountains, County Waterford, recorded several groups of small cairns in a landscape rich with structured cairns, ring cairns and standing stones.

The cairnfields, as the groups are termed, can comprise hundreds of cairns at their largest, with around 30 or fewer more normal (Yates 1984, 225). Cairnfields are commonest in southern Scotland and northern England: in the Border Hills of Dumfriesshire and Lanarkshire, the sandstone uplands of Northumberland, the

FIGURE 7.6 The cairnfield at Barnscar, Cumbria. Copyright: Oxford Archaeology.

Lakeland fells in Cumbria and on the North York Moors. Their distributions within landscapes favour locations suitable for agriculture. This has been examined systematically in Dumfriesshire and the North York Moors where the cairnfields are found on flat or gentle south-facing, well-drained land below around 300 metres in altitude (Fleming 1971; Yates 1984). Archaeological excavations of the small cairns support their association with agricultural activity. The cairns commonly comprise heaped fieldstone with limited structural complexity and few artefacts.

Given their simplicity and ubiquity, cairnfields cannot reliably be assigned a precise chronology based on morphology alone. Farmers pile fieldstone around trees, onto outcrops and into the corners of fields in today's landscapes. The majority of the cairnfields that survive in the British and Irish uplands originated in later prehistory, as the examples I describe later will demonstrate. Not all are of this date. On Dartmoor, the majority of clearance cairns are found within medieval fields, and there are only a small number of cairnfields which may be prehistoric in date (Fleming 1980). Prehistoric and medieval clearance features were excavated at Callaly Moor, Northumberland (Macklin et al. 1991). The date of the cairns was distinguished partly by their association with other, datable, archaeological features. Apart from these associations, there was little to distinguish between later prehistoric and medieval cairns. Seventh- to fourteenth-century AD calibrated radiocarbon dates were measured from samples beneath a cairn at Devoke Water, Cumbria (Quartermaine and Leech 2012, 200).

Many small cairns are unstructured, simple mounds of stone, sometimes piled around earthfast boulders. Occasionally, cairns contain formal structural elements—kerbs of larger stones, cists and pits. On Danby Rigg, North Yorkshire, there are around 850 cairns interspersed with linear banks of stone, a large barrow and several ring cairns (Harding and Ostoja-Zagórski 1994). The excavated small cairns comprised unsorted stones that had been collected from the surrounding ground and heaped around earthfast boulders. At Crawley Edge, County Durham, the 41 cairns are distributed in small clusters on a south-facing spur of land overlooking the River Wear. Robert Young and Adam Welfare (1992) excavated two adjacent cairns, one large and one small, at Crawley Edge. Under the larger cairn, he found two adjoining oval settings of upright stones, like a flattened '8'. There was a cremation burial in a collared urn within a pit in one of the ovals, and the second enclosed a small deposit of animal bone and three jet beads. A broken saddle quern was found in the cairn. Charcoal from small oak branches beneath the cairn perhaps resulted from the clearance of young trees before the cairn was built. The small cairn comprised a loose pile of stones built up against an earthfast boulder. In spite of its small size and relative simplicity, it too contained artefacts—30 pieces of flint—and the base of the cairn was lined with flat stones, in a similar way to the larger monument.

Eight small cairns were excavated at Elvanfoot, South Lanarkshire (Kirby 2009). The cairnfield, two banks and an enclosure were located in the valley floor, near to a group of roundhouse platforms and a field system. The cairns were evaluated and then removed mechanically. All the cairns were unstructured piles of fieldstone. In one, slightly larger than the others if otherwise undistinguished, the mechanical excavator uncovered a central, sub-rectangular pit. Sherds from a slender, low-carinated beaker lay grouped in the pit's base. The pit's size and east-west alignment suggest that it could have held an inhumation burial that has not survived. Around four kilometres along the valley from Elvanfoot, Jane Downes (2001) excavated part of a cairnfield comprising over 50 cairns at Fall Kneesend. Of three simple heaps of stones, one contained a rough cist and overlay a pyre with mainly oak charcoal and burnt human bone. A calibrated radiocarbon date of 2560–2200 BC from pyre charcoal is similar to the date from Elvanfoot (2470–2200 BC). Another two cairns were built on prepared or levelled ground, with pieces of flaked chert and pottery recovered from around the cairns. Others had structures, including a kerb, outer ditch and bank, and a cist. Charred material was recovered from several contexts within and outside the cairns. The timber had been gathered from open woodland on drier ground. Barley may have cultivated as a few charred grains were identified.

Investigations on Arran, above Machrie Bay on the west of the island, targeted a large number of structures, which included three small cairns sited amongst a group of agricultural terraces (Barber 1997). The cairns looked similar until excavations revealed that they each had a different character: one was a compact mass of small stones piled around five earthfast boulders; another was a looser spread of stone, which had probably been disturbed; and the third cairn overlay a low earth mound containing a cist with a short-necked beaker and a small quantity of cremated bone. A late third millennium BC radiocarbon date was obtained from beneath the first cairn, raising the likelihood that stone was being cleared from fields and piled around earthfast boulders and burials at about the same time.

Archaeologists have repeatedly discussed the distinctions between clearance cairns and burial cairns based on the presence or absence of human remains and the degree to which the cairns were complex structures, incorporating features such as kerbs (Graham 1959; Yates 1984). The examples I have described, amongst many others, illustrate the overlap between these categories, with some simple cairns and ill-defined clearance features overlying human burials, and structured cairns offering no evidence for funerary activity (Johnston 2001). At Eaglestone Flat, Derbyshire, the cremated remains of 16 people were buried in pits amongst a gradually accumulating group of clearance cairns and banks (Barnatt 1994). The fieldstone was probably created when cereals were cultivated in the adjacent fields.

The ambiguities between clearance and mortuary features can be explained by archaeologists' inability to identify sometimes subtle distinctions in function. Another approach is to accept that the ambiguity existed in the Bronze Age just as it does now, and that cairns emerged through a variety of activities that related people with land. The gathering of fieldstone into cairns and banks occasionally occurred alongside human burials, offerings of cremated human bone and artefacts, and the creation of structures for undertaking low-key rituals. In these respects, the cairnfields have parallels with the circles I discussed in the previous section.

Unlike the circles, clearance cairns did not provide an enclosed space within which rites and offerings occurred. The cairns developed in fields, as stone was thrown and carried in baskets and dumped into heaps. Cairnfields expanded with the labour of stone clearance and the transformation of land. The cairns with human burials and offerings were barely distinguishable from the cairns without. After time, the distinction may have been irrelevant. The generalised presence of the cremated human bone in the fields was sufficient. Of three excavated small cairns at Birrel Sike in western Cumbria, two had evidence for a kerb of larger stones (Richardson 1982). One of these cairns was built around two earthfast boulders, and deposited within the mound were 12 pieces of worked flint and a polished shale blade. The other cairn overlay a large stone slab that was placed on top of a deposit of charcoal. These structured elements were minor events in the lives of the cairns.

Especially large and dense areas of cairnfields are located on the western and southwestern fells of the Cumbrian Lake District. The Lake District National Park Survey covered 78 square kilometres of unimproved upland, with a large majority of the survey's 10,300 archaeological features accounted for by small cairns (Quartermaine and Leech 2012). The cairnfields are located at altitudes between 150 and 300 metres. These parameters reflect the 'tideline' of historic clearance and enclosure and an upper altitudinal limit to the land use within the cairnfields. The small cairns have not survived the stone clearance and ploughing of modern fields that generally lie below 150 metres altitude.

The landscapes south of Eskdale, in the foothills of the southwest Lake District fells, contribute the most to understanding cairnfields because there have been complementary surveys, excavations and palaeoenvironmental studies (Figure 7.7). The cairnfields are on the broad, gently sloping and therefore rather wet ridge of Barnscar, on the west-facing slopes below Birkby and Stainton Fell, and around Devoke Water. The largest cairnfield is at Barnscar, with the main concentration comprising some 400 small cairns of varying sizes and shapes spread over 25 hectares (Figure 7.6). Barnscar's field archaeology is complex, with multiple periods of use represented, which includes small cairns, stone banks and enclosed settlement. In the nineteenth century, Charles Dymond (1893) was the first to systematically survey and excavate the cairns. Dymond excavated 14 cairns, finding several inverted urns—the surviving examples are collared urns—and 'some burnt bone'. Donald Walker (1965) excavated at Barnscar in the 1950s. He investigated a further ten cairns without finding any human bone or pottery vessels. There were numerous hollows or pits that may have been where stones were dug out. The hollows were filled with burnt stone and charcoal-flecked sediment, and then capped with a layer of clay that continued beneath the cairns.

The pollen recovered from the sediments beneath the cairns excavated by Walker at Barnscar were rich in tree species: birch, oak, alder and hazel. Walker

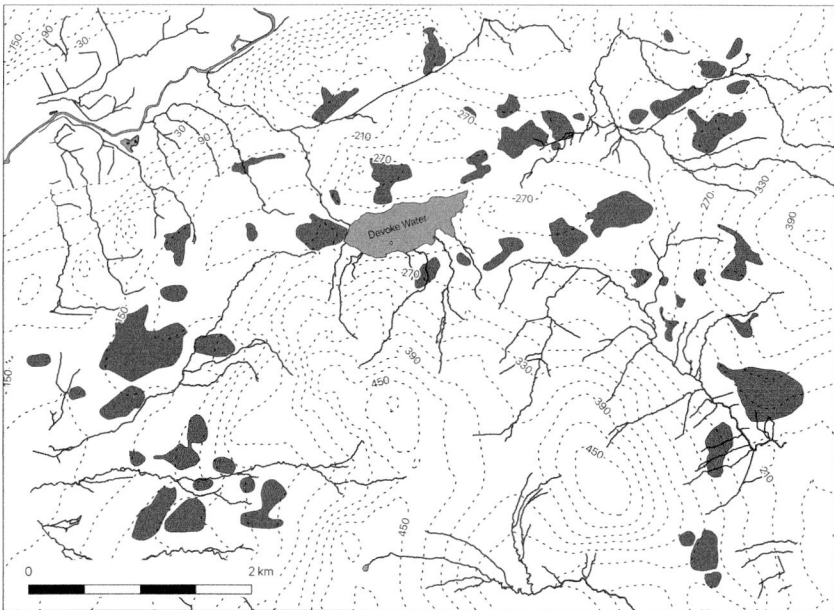

FIGURE 7.7 The distribution of cairnfields (shaded areas) amongst the fells south of Eskdale, Cumbria. Adapted from Quartermaine and Leech 2012. Cartographic data: © Crown copyright and database rights 2020 Ordnance Survey (100025252).

interpreted this as evidence the cairnfield was associated with pioneer clearance of woodland. Quartermaine and Leech (2012, 318) similarly attribute the cairnfields to forest clearance and pioneer agriculture, and they interpret the pits that Walker excavated beneath the Barnscar cairns as hollows where tree roots were dug out. The pollen records from mires amongst the cairnfields below Birkby Fell and Stainton Fell, within 1 kilometre of Barnscar, present a more complex sequence (Quartermaine and Leech 2012, 178–179). Anthropogenic woodland clearance first occurred in the late fourth millennium BC with some subsequent woodland regeneration. Cores were studied from Devoke Water by Winifred Pennington (1964) and from the nearby Tewit Moss (research by Guy Wimble summarised in Quartermaine and Leech 2012, 201–204). Devoke Water and Tewit Moss are close to Barnscar and surrounded by cairnfields. The mire core showed a decline in the proportion of tree taxa compared with grass and heathland during the late third and second millennia BC. There were spikes in microscopic charcoal that might have marked more intense episodes of clearance. Tree taxa begin rising as a proportion of the identified pollen during the mid-second millennium BC. Cereal-type pollen appears in the pollen record from the fourth millennium BC, and following a hiatus reappears in around the late third to early second millennia BC. The cereal-type pollen may be wild grasses, rather than cultivated plants. A similar environmental history can be traced into the lowlands of southwestern Cumbria, where mires record small-scale clearance of woodland during the late third and early second millennia BC (Appley 2013; Wimble et al. 2000). Altitude alone might not have been a factor in determining how landscapes were occupied.

The environmental histories associated with the Cumbrian cairnfields are similar to the pollen records I described for the circles in the last section. Anthropogenic woodland clearance, grazing and cereal cultivation occurred in the centuries preceding the cairnfields. The inception of cairnfields, probably after the mid-third millennium BC, accompanied more sustained though still extensive land use. Grazing animals prevented woodland from recolonising and there were episodes of more short-term intensive use. Andrew Hoaen and Helen Loney (2007) excavated within a cairnfield and analysed pollen records close to Ullswater, in the eastern Lakeland fells. They interpret the high instances of birch and hazel in the pollen record as indications that ground lay fallow for sufficiently long periods to allow the regeneration of scrub and light-loving species. Grazing and clearance recurred with enough frequency to prevent the regeneration of dense woodland. In the Bowmont Valley in the northern Cheviot Hills, Richard Tipping (2010, 172–174) identified barley cultivation during the mid-third and second millennia BC within the catchments of the pollen sampling sites above 300 metres altitude. Greater quantities of sediment collected in upland river valleys from around 2500 BC. The sediment presumably eroded from cleared, cultivated ground.

Quartermaine and Leech (2012) suggest that cairnfields formed during the production of hay fodder rather than cultivation. They argue that fieldstone was cleared to prevent damaging sickles, and the random scattering of small cairns in many cairnfields precluded the use of ards for cultivation. A single explanation for the cairns is unnecessary. The vegetation histories indicate some variability, with heath, a mix of ancient and regenerating woodland, grassland and possibly cultivated plots. Fieldstone might be harvested as plots were periodically hand-dug for cultivating barley. As fallow land, the cairnfields would provide pasture—and fodder, if collected. Plots could be cleared and sown in spring, around the time that, if used seasonally as assumed, the partially wooded uplands provided grazing for livestock. Minded cattle and sheep could be kept well apart from fields, and away from trampling and chewing crops or hay.

It can be difficult to imagine the places occupied by cairnfields in the now entirely unwooded and exposed grassland of the western fells in the Lake District or Scotland's southern uplands. The cairnfields survive on land that is now agriculturally marginal. They are made from stone, which means that they have not decayed or eroded. Their substance ensures their persistence in the landscape. Stone's resilience is largely what led to its clearance from soils in the Bronze Age. It also ensured the cairns' continuing place in today's landscapes. People's labours in assarting, breaking turf and gathering stone accumulated a texture and memories in the fields (Hoaen and Loney 2013). These labours did not transform land as a passive resource. The burials and small offerings occasionally left in cairns, as with the intensities of rites practised in ring cairns, reveal an enchanted land which people and their animals inhabited.

Caroline Humphrey's account of pastoral communities and their landscapes in Mongolia's recent past offers an illustration:

> The Mongols do not take over any terrain in the vicinity and transform it into something that is their own… they let it pervade them and their herds, influencing where they settle, when they move, and what kinds of animals they keep.
>
> *(Humphrey 1995, 135)*

The Mongol's landscape is vibrant with natural and supernatural beings and energies. Humphrey did not find a coherent cosmology in the way that people relate to landscape's energies and spirits. There are differences in how landscapes are 'put together', which depend upon the identities of the persons shaping the world and communicating with supernatural entities: chiefs and shamans are the most influential; midwives, smiths, bone-setters, diviners, hunters and astrologers play their parts. Their worldviews overlap, yet with distinct ecologies and domains of life. Chiefly power is more successful in the wide-open steppe. The shamans have more influence in the ecologically and topographically diverse forested, mountainous regions, in which they acknowledge the 'infinite multiplicity of beings which people feel to have power' (Humphrey 1995, 151).

The upland landscapes with cairnfields and monuments that I have described in this and the previous section were inhabited in a sustained way from the closing centuries of the third millennium BC. The clearance cairns complemented contemporary practices of marking and monumentality: rock art, cairns and circles, standing stones. Cairnfields were not produced by an 'agricultural sensibility' in the way people perceived their landscape when contrasted with a 'monumental landscape'. The monuments were part of inhabited landscapes in which people tended to stock and cultivated fields. Clearance cairns emerged in those same lands. Both monuments and clearance cairns can be interpreted as the means through which kin groups, of varying scales, periodically defined their connection to places and landscape. The irregular texture of clearance cairns spread discontinuously and gradually across thousands of hectares in the uplands.

Uncommon ground: cellular fields, 1700–1100 BC

Tim Robinson (2011, 153) wrote: 'There are places where place itself proliferates'. His subject was Carna, on Connemara's southern shore, and specifically a group of stone-walled fields—an 'amoeboid clustering'—at An Seangharraí (the old garden or old plot). Robinson found names and stories associated with each of the little fields:

> One plot is called Garraí Thaidhg Mhóir; here Tadhg the robber, who was either Tadhg na Buile, the monster of Caisleán na hAirde, or has been amalgamated with him by time, lurked in An Scailp Mhór, the big cleft, under a prominent slab of rock, and leaped out to terrorize passers-by. In an adjacent field called Garraí Pholl an Chiste, the treasure-hole garden, a man unearthed a pot of gold; there was an ugly serpent coiled around it, and he was afraid and covered it up again.
>
> *(Robinson 2011, 154)*

The 'amoeboid clustering' that Robinson describes is a cellular pattern found amongst landscapes throughout the west and north of Ireland and Britain, and with origins at various times during the last 5,000 years. At Scord of Brouster, on the west side of Mainland, Shetland, oval houses, small fields and clearance cairns were occupied from the middle centuries of the third millennium BC (Whittle 1986). Similar groups of fields are recorded elsewhere on the island and their use may span up to a millennium (Turner 2012). Large areas of West Penwith, Cornwall, especially in the north of the peninsula, are enclosed by fields with later prehistoric origins (Nowakowski 2016). The patterns persist within modern working farms, as at Zennor. The great stones and deep histories that form the foundations for some of west Cornwall's field banks led to their folkloric origins as giants' hedges (Crawford 1936).

A helpful aspect of Robinson's deep mapping of lore and land is the way he broadens our attention to the field as narrative rather than as acreage. The histories, names and associations of fields exist because they were maintained across years, generations and centuries. Boundaries played a critical role in this process.

It is common throughout the world to cultivate plots without boundaries, and for changing land use—as between arable, pasture and woodland—to make fields. Constructed and grown boundaries of hedge, ditch, earth and stone perpetuate the patterns of fields in the long term. The boundaries materialise agricultural and tenurial practices. Bounded fields inherit and anticipate. The knowledge of how to and who should inhabit a field is exchangeable, inherited, between the field's generations of human and animal inhabitants. The work done in clearing stone, improving soil and maintaining boundaries anticipates future seasons of growth and grazing.

Richard Feachem (1973) reviewed the knowledge about early agricultural landscapes of western and northern Britain, based on decades of survey undertaken by the Ordnance Survey Archaeology Division and the Royal Commissions on Ancient Monuments in England, Scotland and Wales. Feachem proposed three categories of field system: 'amorphous walled enclosures'; irregular field banks, lynchets and clearance cairns; and regular rectangular field systems. Feachem placed these categories in a chronological order, with the walled enclosures being the earliest and dating from the third and second millennia BC. Peter Fowler (1983, 128–144) identifed five types for categorising the fields throughout Britain. Like Feachem, Fowler's categories were partly chronological and partly based on differences in geographic distribution. Researchers have subsequently drawn out the developmental characteristics of these schemes, emphasising a sequence from pastoralism through to fixed-field, mixed agriculture (Quartermaine and Leech 2012, 327–334).

These schemes are idealised and not intended to chart the development of all landscapes. Nonetheless, they assume that the complexity of some archaeological landscapes emerged from a gradual and inevitable rationalisation in how people used the land. 'Simple', mobile pastoralism marked the beginning of these landscape transformations. Year-round settlement and fixed-field cultivation marked their end. In a Bronze Age world that humans inhabited with other 'thinking selves', people did not make decisions about how to live in a place according to rationales familiar to us or with a mind to an idealised conception of agriculture's future development. Marked edges and enclosed areas emerged in a variety of circumstances and with differing historical consequences.

The clearance of stone into banks occurred amongst some cairnfields. The banks lack the coursing or structure associated with walls, they vary in length and many are discontinuous. They barely define an edge, never mind bound areas of land. On Bootle Fell, south of Barnscar, the banks are aligned roughly perpendicular to the hillslope (Quartermaine and Leech 2012, 121–139). They are segmented, with small cairns sometimes continuing the banks' paths. The fields surveyed by the Royal Commission on the Ancient and Historic Monuments of Wales in the uplands of south Wales are described by Stephen Briggs as 'so fugitive or incomplete as to scarcely merit distinction as "field systems"' (RCAHMW 1997, 203). The 'discontinuous serpentine rubble wall[s]' on the east of Dyffryn Nedd offer a good example of the 'fugitive systems' that Briggs describes. The bank of fieldstone weaves a sinuous line along the hillside, apparently formed at the limits of cleared land further upslope. Each segment of the bank has a distinctive concave shape as though episodes of clearance were tacked one onto the other across the hillslope. The linear banks defined fields' edges with stone.

It is difficult to disentangle the sequence with which these landscapes developed. In general, when both are present, clearance cairns were built earlier than stone banks. At Tulloch Wood, Moray, the cairns lie outside an area demarcated by parallel, stone boundaries, leading Stephen Carter (1993) to suggest that an earlier cairnfield was cleared as the field system developed. The calibrated radiocarbon dates, from charcoal in the buried soils, support this sequence. The cairns were built after the twenty-third century BC, while the stone banks were built after the sixteenth century BC. On Kilearnan Hill, Sutherland, a calibrated radiocarbon measurement from an excavated clearance cairn estimated its use in the early second millennium BC (McIntyre 1998). The later prehistoric dates from roundhouses span the thirteenth to sixth centuries BC. At Gardom's Edge, Derbyshire, landscape surveys discovered what appeared to be a coherent pattern of monuments, cairns and field plots (Barnatt et al. 2017). The dating of features following their excavation lengthened this chronology: the first cairns were built in the late third millennium BC, while the houses and boundaries all seem to be later, and date to the early first millennium BC.

The chronology of linear clearance banks and fields generally begins from the middle centuries of the second millennium BC. This makes them broadly contemporary with the shift to durable domestic architecture that I describe in Chapter 4. The banks and fields that predate the mid-second millennium BC are exceptional: the enclosures on Shetland that I introduced earlier, and the extensive systems of rectilinear fields buried under blanket peat in northern County Mayo, whose inception probably began in the thirty-seventh century BC (Caulfield et al. 2011).

At several excavated upland settlements in northern England and southern Scotland, the excavated houses were surrounded by loose and unstructured banks of stone similar in construction to adjoining field boundaries (Johnston 2001) (Figure 7.8). Standrop Rigg is located deep in Northumberland's Cheviot Hills. George Jobey (1983) investigated a late second-millennium BC settlement comprising six roundhouse platforms dispersed amongst fields defined by banks and lynchets. Low banks of stone surrounded some of the house platforms. The banks formed during the houses' lives, and in one case the bank continued as a site for gathering stone after the house's abandonment. Standrop Rigg's roundhouse platforms are connected together by the field banks.

Jobey (1981) excavated the roundhouse platforms at Green Knowe in the years immediately prior to working at Standrop Rigg. The platforms are strung along a gentle slope overlooking the Meldon Burn, Peeblesshire, and are now hemmed in by forestry plantations. The timber buildings were surrounded by banks of stone originating from the surrounding fields. As the fields were farmed, people

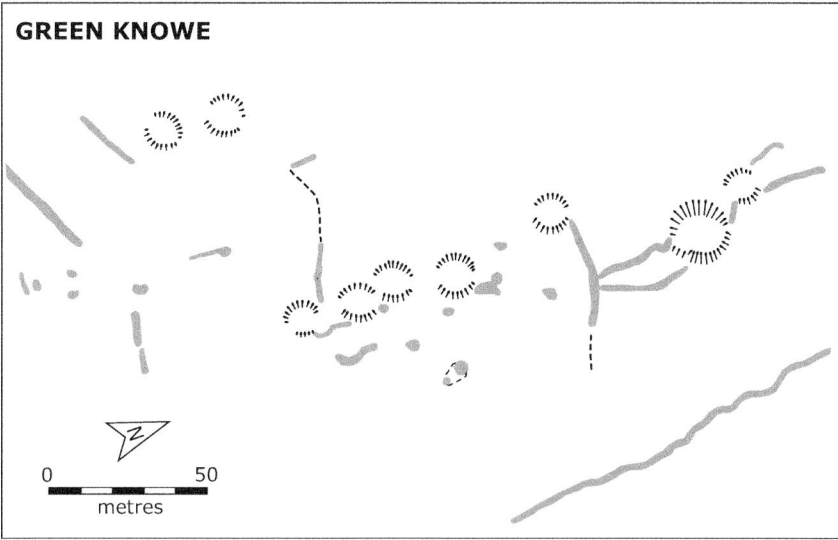

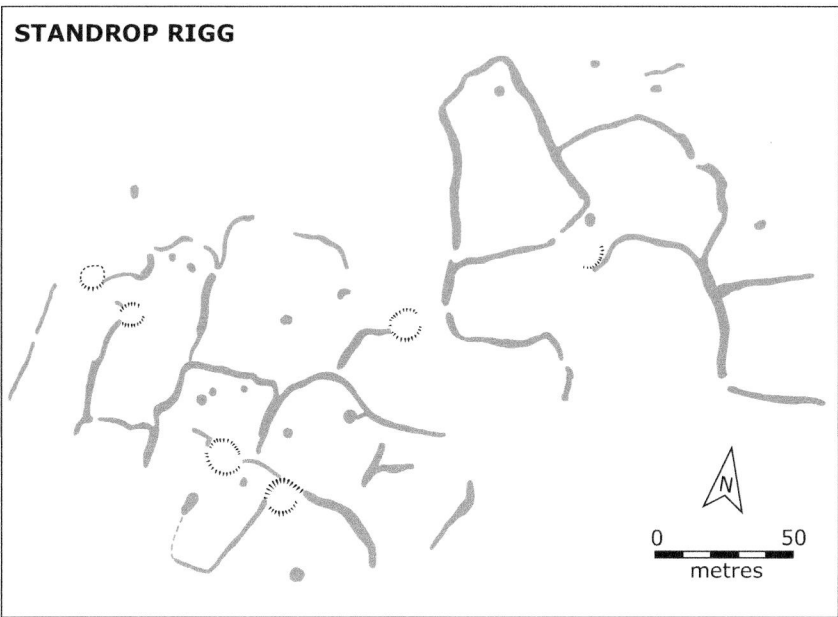

FIGURE 7.8   Plans of the roundhouse platforms, small cairns and fields at Green Knowe, Peeblesshire, and Standrop Rigg, Northumberland. Adapted from Jobey 1981 and 1983.

cleared stone and piled it around the houses' walls with gaps left for the entrances. On one of the platforms, the bank of stone was particularly large where there had been at least two structures built one after another on the same terrace. Amongst the stones, by the entrance, there was a substantial quantity of debris interleaved with the stone: broken pottery, fragments of two shale objects and worked stone. The midden and stone gathered around the platform during the lives of the building and the field. The field banks were composed from the same material and in the same way as the house banks: they never stood as walls, nor was there evidence for hedges or fences. The low fieldstone banks marked the edges of farmed land in the same way as the stone rings marked the houses.

Extensive areas of fields and buildings were mapped as part of major archaeo-logical surveys of moorland in southwest England (Herring et al. 2016; Newman 2011). On Bodmin Moor, Cornwall (Johnson and Rose 1994), the surveyors identified different patterns of boundaries and buildings. There are small en-closures associated with buildings that are likely to have been settlements with stock pens, yards and small gardens. There are also extensive areas of 'aggregate' or 'cellular' field systems (so-called because they appear to have developed in-crementally). The fields are relatively small, 0.25–0.5 hectares, the majority are found in small clusters together with a few roundhouses and they are likely to have served a variety of purposes, including for crops and livestock. Across the western and central parts of Bodmin Moor, the groups of fields and buildings are dispersed across the landscape, each separated by an area of moorland. In the northwest, there are subsequent phases of aggregated settlements, in some cases with large numbers of round huts densely packed within enclosures, which the surveyors have tentatively argued marked a later phase of purely pastoral agri-culture. The settlements, enclosures and cellular fields date from the fifteenth century BC and into the first millennium BC based on excavations (Bender et al. 2007; Jones 2004/2005), and the environmental history that indicates this was the period when the moorland began being grazed most extensively (Gearey et al. 2000). Cereals were cultivated amongst some of the field systems, where they probably formed a minor component of the land use compared with pasture and wood-pasture.

On Leskernick Hill, Bodmin Moor, the houses and fields were inhabited for times during the fifteenth to ninth centuries BC on a hillside with varying den-sities of surface stone, locally termed 'clitter' (Bender et al. 2007; Johnson and Rose 1994, 59–62). The forms of the enclosures and houses vary around the hill's western and southern slopes: cellular field systems that emerge from clusters and lines of roundhouses; single roundhouses with appended enclosures; and a loose cluster of houses enclosed by a sinuous boundary in the densest area of clitter. In places, the stone banks spring from roundhouses and form an arc of lobe-like enclosures (Figure 7.9). Other roundhouses are tied into the field system by short banks that closed the gaps between houses and field edges. Houses incorporate large earthfast stones (grounders) in their walls, opposing the entrances. Bounda-ries emerge from and disappear into the clitter. Christopher Tilley and colleagues

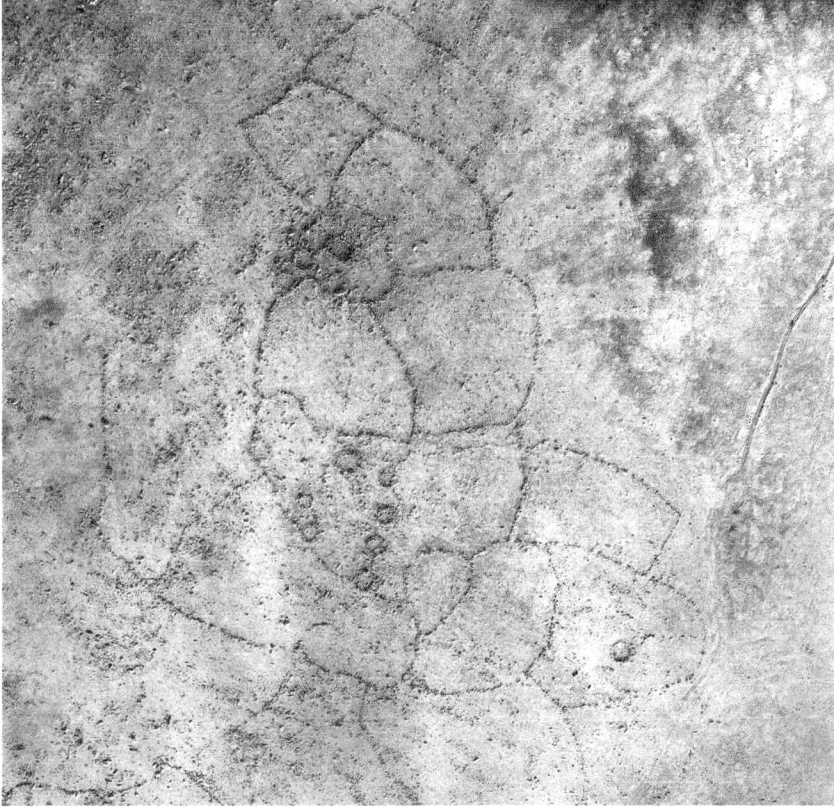

FIGURE 7.9 Aerial photograph of the cellular fields and roundhouses at Leskernick, Bodmin Moor. © Crown copyright; Historic England Archive.

(2000, 220) interpret the stones in the Bronze Age world of Leskernick Hill as imbued with animacy: the 'social world was co-existent with the stones which were themselves a foundation for the cosmos'.

There is a biological patterning to the enclosures at Leskernick: like the cells of a simple organism. This organic quality reflects the way the fields emerged from and changed the land's texture. The densities of clitter, grounders, the topography and soils, patches of scrubland and trees affected people's labours and decisions when forming the fields' edges and the banks' paths. The stone banks kinked and curved around obstacles that are long gone. They took their cues from grounders that were easier to incorporate than to avoid or move. The patterns emerged from animals' ways of inhabiting the moor. The gaps in the banks lay towards the corners of fields, sometimes with a subtle funnelling of the boundaries or a large grounder by the gap to gather the stock. The fields' varied sizes and proximities to the houses acknowledged the differing intensities in the relations between people and animals. Pregnant ewes and cows, dairy stock, animals ready for slaughter or exchange: each required different levels of attentiveness, routines and enclosure. An engrained knowledge of place emerged amongst and structured the development of the settlements within the animate world.

This longevity and attachment to place was reflected in the durability and persistence of inhabitation. Field systems dating to the second millennium BC, some like the examples I describe earlier, are known from western and northern Ireland: on the Burren, County Clare (Jones et al. 2011; Plunkett-Dillon 1985), Inishark, County Galway (Quinn et al. 2019), and north Mayo (Caulfield et al. 2011). Carleton Jones (2019) has mapped an extensive area of field walls on Roughan Hill, County Clare. The earliest walls survive in fragments across the hill. In places, they form irregular-shaped fields, and some walls radiate from large multi-celled enclosures. Jones excavated heavily fragmented and mixed midden material within the enclosures, including animal bone, worked stone, and beaker and food vessel pottery. The animal bones are mostly cattle, with smaller numbers of sheep/goat and pig. The calibrated radiocarbon dates from the middens span the twenty-third to fifteenth centuries BC, which corresponds with the chronology that Jones (2016) has estimated for the pedestals of uneroded limestone preserved beneath the field walls. Unlike the cellular fields on Bodmin Moor, there are no roundhouses visible amongst Roughan's fields and it is the enclosures and the middens within them which formed the focal points for boundaries.

The rectilinear field systems buried beneath blanket peat on Céide Hill, County Mayo, originated in the mid-fourth millennium BC (Caulfield et al. 2011). After a period when woodland recolonised the landscape, people began extensively clearing ground and grazing livestock from the twenty-fourth century BC. There are spreads of occupation debris dating to the early Bronze Age excavated from several locations, and the relic boundaries of the Neolithic field system were rebuilt and expanded. The pollen record shows an increased pastoralism with some evidence for cultivation during the early and middle second millennium BC (Molloy and O'Connell 1995). At Belderg Beg, west of Céide, small plots adjacent to a stone-built roundhouse were cultivated perhaps over several centuries during the late second millennium BC. Lucy Verrill and Richard Tipping (2010a) used a combination of soil micromorphology and pollen analysis to show that the productivity of arable fields was maintained through the addition of domestic midden debris, including ash and animal bone. These practices seem to have been adopted at a time when the ground was becoming increasingly prone to water logging, although peat growth only followed after cultivation had ceased.

People worked hard and used their environmental knowledge to sustain inhabitation at Belderg Beg during the late second millennium BC. This persistence is in contrast to the occupation of the Céide landscape during the fourth millennium BC, where wetter climatic conditions and soil degradation seem to have been factors in its abandonment by people (Verrill and Tipping 2010b). The durable organisation of fields and roundhouses emerged from and reproduced resilient kinship with localities. A fragment of cellular field system at Black Moss, Argyll, was first recorded in 1968 as peat was cut away on the Moss of Achnacree (Carter and Dalland 2005). The moss occupies a stump of coastal lowland and lochans at the western end of Loch Etive. A zigzag pattern of banks has been traced for 750 metres through excavation and probing in the peat. The banks are composed of sediment dug from shallow flanking ditches, and faced with stones that were lifted from the surrounding land and possibly from the nearby shore of Loch Etive. The banks were built during the second millennium BC in heather-covered heathland, with heavily podsolised soils. The field system developed eastwards, as enclosures were appended one onto another, encroaching and possibly 'improving' the heathland. Stephen Carter and Magnar Dalland (2005) conclude their assessment of four decades' research at Black Moss by drawing parallels between people's encroachment onto and sustained use of heathland during the second millennium BC and the crofting communities that reoccupied the land during the early 1800s. In both cases, environmental conditions constrained though did not determine how and where people lived.

The study of Bronze Age soils in the Western and Northern Isles of Scotland has provided evidence for the maintenance and enrichment of soils using domestic waste and human manure (Guttmann et al. 2006). One interpretation of the evidence is that the soils were formerly household middens and were dispersed and cultivated. Animal manure may have been collected as a fuel. At Tofts Ness, Sanday, Orkney, anthropogenic soils of around one hectare were identified close to three settlement mounds (Simpson et al. 2007). The soils were created through the addition of ash and human manure. Later, during the first millennium BC, plaggen soils developed when turf was cut, used as animal bedding, composted and then added to fields. In her review of soil enrichment in later prehistoric Britain, Erika Guttmann (2005) found evidence for the use of household midden and not animal manure in cultivated soils during the Bronze Age. In regions where people had ready access to woodland and peat for fuel, animal manuring could have taken place 'on-the-hoof', in the plots and paddocks appended onto houses amongst the cellular field systems I described earlier. The smaller fields could have been cultivated periodically if not intensively.

At Gwithian, a long-lived settlement and its fields were uncovered beneath sand dunes on Cornwall's north coast (Nowakowski 2009; Nowakowski et al. 2007). The first cultivated fields were established at Gwithian from the eighteenth century BC. During the fifteenth to thirteenth centuries BC, after a period of decreased activity, a field system defined by hedge banks was established and maintained. The fields were ploughed and emmer wheat was cultivated. Sheep or goat and cattle were grazed in fallow fields or on nearby pasture. The inhabitants contended with windblown sand and managed the thin, unstable soils. The hedge banks were helpful barriers for controlling erosion and there is evidence that soils were enhanced with domestic midden and seaweed. Jacqueline Nowakowski (2009) connects the longevity and tenacity of people's inhabitation of Gwithian with a deepening, familial attachment to land. In support of this interpretation, Nowakowski notes a line of four pits laid close to and parallel with one of the field banks. Each pit contained the partial remains of a human cremation and cremated animal bone.

The deepening attachment to land that Nowakowski recognises at Gwithian occurred elsewhere in Ireland and Britain in the cellular field systems, associations of houses and fields, and the efforts people made to transform soils and manage livestock. These processes can be traced in time from the monuments and cairnfields during the early second millennium BC, although the bounded fields were not an inevitable consequence in the evolution of farming and social life. After about the sixteenth century BC (the chronologies are imprecise), fields increasingly became a means of relating soil, plants, animals and people. Animals were ordered within fields according to their roles in life, much like people's domestic routines were structured by buildings. Soils and plants were transformed through the mixing of potent substances: domestic middens with earth.

These processes worked within and transformed the animate landscapes and enchanted places that I described in Chapter 6. Circles and mounds decreased in importance as the sites through which people negotiated their relations with ancestors, beings and energies. These discourses, transactions and amalgamations happened in fields, in houses and throughout the landscape. The long stone dykes on Tofts Ness are overlain by numerous small cairns, some of which have visible cists and with reports they contained burials (Lamb 1980, 8–9). The box-like structures of the orthostats in some of the dykes are themselves cist-like (Dockrell 2007, 6). The changes did not align with similar ways of living. So far as we can reconstruct, forms of seasonal pastoralism continued for some communities. They made use of coastal and upland grasslands that may have been impractical or inhospitable at times during the year. Cultivating and gathering plants played their parts too, both in sustained ways at locations like Gwithian or Belderg Beg and, less certainly, amongst the cellular fields on Bodmin Moor. Bounded fields changed how agricultural traditions and knowledge persisted and how people anticipated their futures in landscapes.

Hedges, hooves, grains: rectilinear fields, 1700–1100 BC

In May 1972, John Collis and Andrew Fleming, who were then two young academics at the University of Sheffield, led a student fieldtrip on Dartmoor (Fleming 2008). During a break for lunch, Collis and Fleming walked along the line of what they understood to be a medieval land boundary. The boundary, a vegetated stony bank, was one of several adjoining one another and traceable for over 4 kilometres across the hillside. Collis and Fleming were initially confused and then excited to discover that a D-shaped prehistoric enclosure had been appended to one of the walls. The enclosure's straight side used the existing 'medieval' boundary. Clearly, the system of long boundaries was likely to be prehistoric and, as it later turned out, Bronze Age in date. Over the coming decade, Fleming discovered and mapped hundreds of kilometres of the Bronze Age boundaries.

Twelve months previously, in an entirely different setting on the outskirts of Peterborough, Francis Pryor began excavating two parallel ditches running towards what would once have been fenland. He expected the ditches to be Roman and contain large amounts of pottery. When he checked the excavators' finds trays by the trenches, there were just a few crumbs of hand-made pottery with the texture of wet biscuit. Pryor decided that he needed a more ambitious approach if he was to understand the ditches—he would retain the mechanical digger for the remainder of the season and 'think in terms of whole landscapes' (Pryor 2001, 31). Opening large area excavations did not change the quality or number of finds from the ditches, as they remained stubbornly empty. But the larger excavations did, with the help of aerial photographs, reveal the extraordinary scale and regularity of the field systems. Gradually, Pryor began to appreciate what he was dealing with: an extensive system of Bronze Age fields and droveways (Figure 7.10).

The rectilinear field systems that Andrew Fleming mapped across Dartmoor and Francis Pryor unearthed at Fengate were widespread throughout southern Britain during the middle centuries of the second millennium BC. David Yates's (2007)

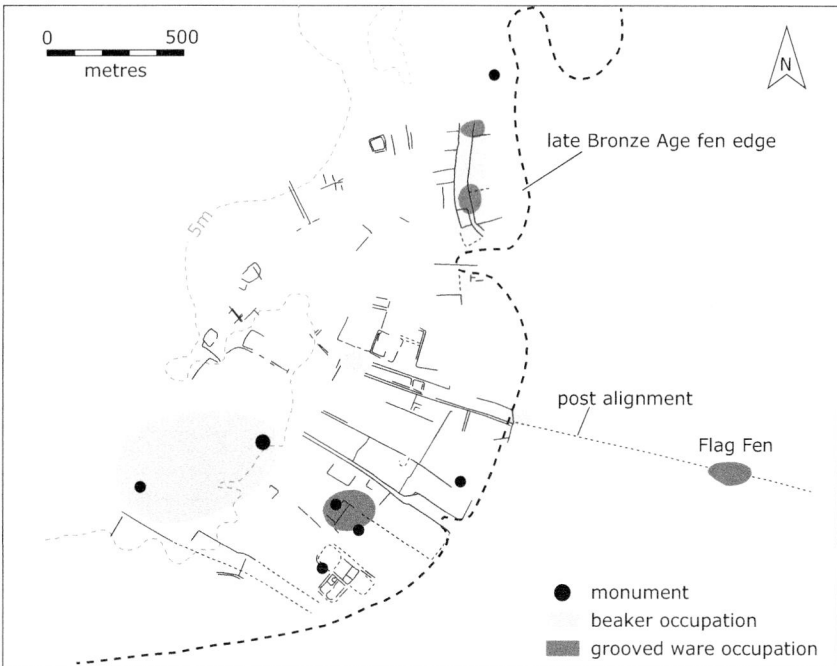

FIGURE 7.10   The Fengate landscape as revealed after 50 years of archaeological investigations: areas of occupation during the third millennium BC (grooved ware and beaker), funerary barrows, rectilinear fields and droveways, and the Flag Fen platform and post alignment. Adapted from Evans et al. 2009.

synthesis of excavated Bronze Age rectilinear field systems reveals the contributions development-led investigations have made to the known distribution of rectilinear field systems. Yates identifies examples in many regions of southern England, occupying land south of a line drawn from the Wash to the Bristol Channel. Rectilinear fields are not limited to a horizon in the second millennium BC or to southern Britain. Similar mid-second-millennium rectilinear fields, some with roundhouses, have been excavated in northern France.

Coaxial land enclosure occurred at different times and places during the last 6,000 years (Fleming 2008; Løvschal 2020). The form occurs later in prehistory in Britain and the northwest European lowlands (Chadwick 2016; Løvschal 2014). The rectilinear fields on Céide Hill, County Mayo, were reoccupied and possibly extended during the second millennium BC (Caulfield et al. 2011). Linear ditches dating to the later second millennium BC were excavated at Ask, County Wexford (Stevens 2007), and Lismullin, County Meath (O'Connell 2013, 50–51). Ask and Lismullin were uncovered during road developments, which constrained the excavated area within a narrow corridor and limited the potential to understand the ditches. The advances in understanding of lowland rectilinear fields have come from major area investigations, as first exemplified in Britain by Margaret Jones at Mucking and Francis Pryor at Fengate (Evans et al. 2009, 12–13).

The rectilinear fields vary in morphology, the character of their boundaries and the land use within the fields. Variation aside, most share important characteristics: their layouts follow dominant axes, which has led to the descriptive terms 'linear' and 'coaxial', and the field systems tend to extend across large areas, sometimes in the hundreds of hectares. The boundaries vary between regions. In southwest England, notably on the granite upland of Dartmoor, they were constructed earth banks and low walls, perhaps topped with hedges. Excavations have demonstrated that some banks replaced timber fences. On the downland of Wiltshire, Dorset and Sussex, the boundaries survive as earth lynchets, where sediment eroded from the fields built up against barriers downslope. In the gravels and claylands of the Thames Valley and the fen-edge of East Anglia, the boundaries were marked with ditches and earth banks, probably topped with hedges and fences.

Dartmoor, Devon, offers the most complete and impressive patterns of Bronze Age rectilinear fields (Butler 1997; Fleming 2008). Cellular and rectilinear field systems have been recorded on the moor, together with long cross-moor boundaries, all likely dating from the second millennium BC. Based on archaeological surveys and excavations, the cellular fields had a longer history both pre- and post-dating the long boundaries and rectilinear fields (Newman 2011, 77–80; Wickstead 2008, 109). The rectilinear field systems are mainly distributed around the southern and eastern sides of the moor. They can be traced from the open moorland into the alignments of the present-day enclosed land. Fragments of rectilinear fields have been recorded on the limestone upland to the south and in the lowland river valleys to the east (Fitzpatrick et al. 1999; Gallant et al. 1985).

FIGURE 7.11   Schematic map depicting the main areas of linear field systems on Dartmoor. The shaded areas depict land above 200 and 400 metres altitude. Adapted from Fleming 1983, 221.

Andrew Fleming uses the local Devon term 'reave' to describe the boundaries in the rectilinear systems. His surveys of the moorland reaves reveal distinct and internally coherent systems, which at their largest enclosed 3,000 hectares (Fleming 2008) (Figure 7.11). The spines are long reaves that follow watersheds or contour along slopes. The longest stretch for 10 kilometres. The rectilinear fields lie perpendicular to the spines, and in the classic pattern they use the spine as a terminal for multiple parallel strips. The strips are further sub-divided by traverse banks, amongst which are scattered small enclosures and roundhouses. Some reave systems are keyed into larger sub-divided moorland blocks, as on Shovel Down. Others adhere to the coaxial structure on an epic scale, with the parallel fields stretching for 6 kilometres across hills and valleys, as at Dartmeet, on the moor's east side. Andrew Fleming carefully dissected the reave systems, proposed theories for how and why they developed, and reviewed the phenomenon of coaxiality in later prehistoric and historic landscapes. In Fleming's (2008) account, people were using the moor as common pasture in the centuries prior to enclosure. They claimed and negotiated access to grazing using funerary barrows, stone rows and stone circles, and the finest of these monuments acted as pivotal places in landscapes. The communities living around the moor's edges applied the idea of coaxial land division relatively rapidly, and perhaps motivated by pressures on their common grazing lands from groups living off-moor. Each block of fields represented a 'large terrain' that emerged out of existing territories marked by the distributions of stone circles, rows and barrows.

Vegetational change during the third and early second millennia BC on Dartmoor is poorly understood (Caseldine 1999). It is likely, as elsewhere on southwest England's moorlands, that the monuments were built and used at a time when there was more extensive and sustained grazing of animals on the moor, with areas of open land, woodland pasture and established woodland. From the eighteenth century BC, when the first reaves may have been built, there was open grassland above and amongst the fields with woodland nearby. The pollen record from Shaugh Moor, on the south of Dartmoor, includes evidence for cereal cultivation, which probably occurred on a small scale amongst the fields (Balaam et al. 1982). Analysis of the pollen and fungal spores from peat associated with an excavated reave on Shovel Down identified relatively low grazing pressures and localised hazel and alder woodland during the early second millennium BC (Fyfe et al. 2008). This was followed by ample evidence for species-rich grassland and grazing from the fourteenth century BC. The analysis of pollen within an undated bank under a reave wall on Walkhampton Common recorded predominately grasses and ribwort plantain, indicative of grazing, together with fungal spores associated with animal dung (Mairead Rutherford in Simmonds and Champness 2015, 84). Cereal-type pollen may indicate cultivation in the nearby fields.

The chronology for Dartmoor's reaves remains imprecise. People probably began building rectilinear field systems on the moor from the eighteenth or seventeenth century BC, with the process continuing over several centuries. The phase of sustained grazing on Shovel Down is estimated to end in the eleventh century BC. This broadly corresponds with the chronology for rectilinear fields elsewhere in southern Britain. Many are associated with Deverel-Rimbury pottery and, in the southwest, Trevisker pottery, whose use spans the sixteenth to twelfth centuries BC. As on Dartmoor, some rectilinear fields predate the sixteenth century BC. Radiocarbon measurements on cereal from ditches excavated at Minster, Isle of Thanet, Kent, placed the initial use of the fields in the nineteenth or eighteenth century BC

(Martin et al. 2012). Ditch and hedged fields could have formed part of the Fengate landscape as early as the nineteenth to eighteenth centuries BC, with a seventeenth- or sixteenth-century BC inception more likely on the balance of the evidence (Evans et al. 2009, 256). The earliest ditches at Bestwall, Dorset, were probably in use contemporaneously with domestic activity radiocarbon dated to the seventeenth or sixteenth century BC (Bayliss et al. 2009, 140–142).

While some rectilinear field systems continued to be maintained into the first millennium BC, there are many more instances of the boundaries falling into disuse before the final century or two of the second millennium BC. At Broom, Bedfordshire, many of the field ditches were silted up before the use of post-Deverel-Rimbury pottery (Cooper and Edmonds 2007, 89). At Fengate, pits dating to the twelfth to tenth centuries BC were dug into the silted-up ditches at the Elliot Site (Figure 7.12), and large pits and a metalled surface overlay the ditch system at Edgerley Drain Road (Evans et al. 2009, 85 and 145). One of the pits on top of a silted ditch contained the burial of a cow and unborn calf dated to 1630–1450 BC. At Raunds, Northamptonshire, a circular structure, an enclosure and pits occupied space within one of the droveways, and the pits spread beyond the ditched boundaries (Harding and Healy 2007, 193). Calibrated radiocarbon dates for the features span the fourteenth to ninth centuries BC. At Heathrow, where Framework Archaeology excavated 75 hectares of rectilinear field systems, grazing and some cereal cultivation continued in the landscape during the late Bronze Age (Lewis et al. 2010). There were fewer archaeological deposits dated to the late Bronze Age, with the calibrated radiocarbon dates for some 'farmsteads' (groups of related boundaries and waterholes) indicating an end to activity before the twelfth century BC and in other cases before the tenth century BC. The sequence at Heathrow, with field systems going out of use by the twelfth to eleventh centuries BC, is found more widely in the Middle and Upper Thames Valley (Davies 2016, 67). In the Lower Thames, at South Hornchurch, the excavators assigned the first phase of a ringwork and rectilinear field system to the tenth century BC. An alternative interpretation of the layout is that the ringwork disrupts the line of an existing trackway, perpendicular to the field system, suggesting that the trackway and its fields were abandoned. The ninth-century BC ringwork at Mucking South overlies an earlier field system and it is likely that the fields to the north went out of use at the same time (Evans, Appleby, et al. 2016).

There are exceptions where rectilinear fields were built or in use during the late Bronze Age, and many more instances where the dating information is insufficiently precise to judge. At Harlington, north of Heathrow, a rectilinear field system and associated settlement evidence is dated to the late Bronze Age on the basis of post-Deverel-Rimbury pottery (Elsdon 1996; Yates 2007, 35). With allowance for these examples, people began building and using rectilinear field systems in southern Britain from the eighteenth century BC. The process accelerated during the sixteenth and fifteenth centuries BC. Most fields were maintained and respected until the twelfth to eleventh centuries BC, with some

FIGURE 7.12 The transformation of the droveway and ditches at Elliot Site, Fengate, Peterborough. Adapted from Evans et al. 2009.

abandoned earlier. While this chronology is speculative, I suggest that the main episode of boundary-building and field-use lasted around four centuries.

For a long time, prehistorians have explained the rectilinear field systems and the associated ample evidence for livestock and arable farming as an agricultural revolution in the countryside. An old order of land management was 'swept away' by a new imperative to maximise economic production: a 'major phase of economic expansion … accompanied by a fundamental shift in regional power and wealth towards the lowlands of southern England' (Yates 2007, 107). The surplus of resources generated by this aggressive exploitation of the landscape supported an unstable political system in which power and status were achieved by participating in the competitive exchange of gifts with both nearby and distant communities (Earle 2002; Rowlands 1980). The maximisation of economic production was achieved through more intensive methods of farming within field systems. Intensification, in these accounts, meant deliberate efforts to improve agricultural productivity by increasing the labour and capital applied to land. People used field boundaries to manage land more efficiently so that animals were grazed at higher densities and to ensure that fallow ground was manured effectively, so making short fallow periods sustainable.

The accounts that identify agricultural intensification and link it to political competition can be challenged. The 'aggrandised enclosures', primarily ringworks, that David Yates interprets as elite settlements (and which I interpret differently in Chapter 5) were constructed from the eleventh or tenth century BC, after most rectilinear field systems were no longer maintained. Structures for storing cereal and fodder, which might be associated with the forms of accumulation and exchange described by Rowlands (1980) and Earle (2002), were not a routine feature of domestic life until after the twelfth century BC. Based on their review of excavated sites in the Upper and Middle Thames Valley, Mark Robinson and George Lambrick (2009, 262–263) argue that the shift towards a greater reliance on arable farming and the more intensive management of the landscape emerged over many centuries, from the middle of the second millennium BC to the late first millennium BC.

Dale Serjeantson (2011) and Ellen Hambleton (2008) reviewed faunal remains from excavated later prehistoric sites in southern Britain. There was a gradual increase in the importance of sheep during the second millennium BC, perhaps alongside a shift to breeds carrying wool. Cattle were important and became smaller during the second millennium BC. The changes in cattle may have been a consequence of selection for dairy rather than meat, which is supported by evidence that pottery was used for processing milk (Copley et al. 2005). The ages at which livestock were killed varied to a degree that makes specialisation by communities, in dairying or textiles, unlikely. Francis Pryor argues that the boundaries, droveways and paddocks at Fengate, Peterborough, formed a system for managing large flocks of sheep, with different communities having their own group of stockyards (Pryor 1996). Christopher Evans questions the ubiquity of this model: some double-ditched paddocks were more likely hedge banks, not drafting races; faunal and pollen records indicate that cattle and cereals were as present as sheep in the life of Fengate's inhabitants; the multiple droveways at Fengate were more likely to be used for the routine movement of cattle and for access to seasonal pastures on the fen marshes (Evans et al. 2009, 243–246).

Chris Stevens and Dorian Fuller (2012) identify a rapid increase in the numbers of directly dated cereal remains during the fifteenth and fourteenth centuries BC. They interpret the spike in radiocarbon dates as a proxy for an inward migration of people who favoured cultivation over pastoralism. Stevens and Fuller do not account for the impact of formation processes and the bias caused by major excavation projects in their interpretations. The shift to durable domestic architecture and year-round settlements played a part in the concentration and preservation of archaeological deposits. Large excavation projects with strong archaeobotanical and radiocarbon dating programmes influence the data too. More than 50 per cent (24) of Stevens and Fuller's middle Bronze Age dates for cereals are from two excavation projects: Heathrow and Bestwall Quarry.

After softening the spikes in Stevens and Fuller's (2012, 714) distribution of dates (to allow for the biases of Heathrow and Bestwall Quarry), there was a gradual trend upwards in dated cereals during the twenty-fifth to tenth centuries BC. Cereal cultivation was an aspect of life in the rectilinear field systems, although arable was complementary with, rather than a replacement for, grazing livestock. The middle and late centuries of the second millennium BC witnessed agricultural innovation and diversification in how people lived with animals, plants and soil. In the previous section, I described some of the evidence for the enhancement of soils through the addition of household waste and perhaps manuring by animals in small fields. The changes in livestock, sometimes favouring textile production and dairying, involved selective breeding and choices about where and how to live with animals. Certain plants were adopted or became more common during the later second millennium BC: spelt wheat, oats, rye, Celtic bean and flax (Fuller et al. 2014; Hall and Huntley 2007; Treasure and Church 2017). Changes occurred in different ways across Britain and Ireland. Bounded field systems were, for southern Britain, the loci for evolving relations between people and domesticated species of animals and plants.

Living with lines, 1700–1100 BC

Rectilinear fields were not essential for the transformations in agriculture that I described in the previous section. People could have sustained more settled, mixed farming regimes within the relatively open landscapes of southern Britain without constructing and maintaining durable boundaries. The longevity or persistence of the boundaries, the large extents of enclosed land and the regularity of the field systems were all characteristics that emerged from relations alongside and beyond the routine lives of people with their livestock and crops.

Communities began dwelling in durable domestic dwellings and year-round settlements at around the same time that rectilinear field systems were established. The processes of settlement and agricultural change have been closely linked in prehistorians' narratives (Barrett et al. 1991; Bradley 1980). An influential idea is that the larger and more fluid social networks of the third millennium BC fragmented into smaller and more rigidly defined kin groups (Barrett 1994; Brück 2000). The foundations for these lineages were in the funerary ceremonies of the early centuries of the second millennium BC, which sought to represent lines of genealogical descent by physically placing the dead in relation to earlier burials in linear cemeteries and as multiple interments within individual barrows. John Barrett (1994, 147) argues that people's concern with genealogy and inheritance engendered different senses of time, history and tenure: 'households or household clusters were the products of a lineal history in which their individual identities were fixed historically and also in relation to the land'. These transformations occurred alongside the intensification and enclosure of fields, to which communities claimed historical rights of tenure. Joanna Brück (2000) describes a process of fragmentation in the organisation of early Bronze Age communities and the extensive genealogical lineages through which they defined themselves. This fragmentation and the foundation of permanent settlements disrupted traditional subsistence strategies and required more intensive cultivation of land and management of animals within organised field systems. Bounded spaces, whether in settlements or the surrounding agricultural landscapes, enabled the people living in new configurations to deal with change: 'By structuring space, life can be made more predictable in the face of a changing world' (Brück 2000, 294).

The associations between rectilinear field systems and permanent settlements were more complex than Barrett's and Brück's narratives allow for. Settlements were loosely integrated into the rectilinear field systems, suggesting that the relations that defined the fields were not the same as the relations shaping the settlements. Boundaries around settlements were not commonplace and they could often be created late in settlements' histories. The rectilinear fields in some regions lack evidence for contemporary settlements, or the domestic evidence is suggestive of more transient occupation compared with the stability of the field boundaries. The kinship made through rectilinear field systems was distinct from the kinship made in dwelling places.

On the chalk downs, roundhouse settlements occupied spaces within existing field systems. The alignments and development of the field systems could be unaffected by the cycles of establishing and abandoning settlements. Itford Hill and Black Patch, Sussex, were placed within cultivated and grazed fields (Burstow and Holleyman 1957; Drewett 1982). The settlement at South Lodge, Dorset, was established within an existing field system defined by shallow lynchets (Barrett et al. 1991). The roundhouses stood within the fallow corner of a field. The downland settlements did not influence the layout of the field systems. The lynchets on Cranborne Chase and the South Downs preceded the establishment of the settlements and they maintained their coaxial structure irrespective of the settlements. The history was a little different on the Marlborough Downs. Christopher Gingell (1992, 156) argues that the lynchets were deeper around the settlements, suggesting that cultivation was more sustained in these areas.

Large open area excavations have traced the movement of settlements within the field systems. At Bestwall Quarry, Dorset, the field ditches had silted up before the first roundhouses were built—a gap of about a century (Ladle and Woodward 2009). It is likely that the banks and hedges of some boundaries were maintained, while buildings overlay the ditches in parts of the system. In the Upper and Middle Thames Valley, the settlements could be ephemeral when compared with the tangibility and persistence of the field systems in which they were placed (Lambrick 2009b). The excavated settlements comprise concentrations of debris resulting from domestic occupation, with roundhouses and settlement enclosures being rare. Contemporary settlements are largely illusive amongst the excavated field systems of eastern England (Evans et al. 2009, 66). In Anwen Cooper and Mark Edmonds's (2007) account of the landscapes at Broom, Bedfordshire, they contrast the fluidity of settlement practices with the more rigid layout of the field boundaries.

Unusually for a fen-edge setting, roundhouses were excavated amongst the rectilinear field system on O'Connell Ridge, Cambridgeshire (Evans, Tabor, et al. 2016, 245). As at Bestwall, the houses appear unconnected with the fields' layout, as though they had been scattered and allowed to settle randomly in the landscape. Andrew Fleming (2008, 84–85) makes a similar observation about the roundhouses distributed amongst the rectilinear fields on Holne Moor, Dartmoor. He describes the distribution of roundhouses and the enclosure of land as 'two quite unrelated patterns'. Fleming infers from this pattern that the houses related to each other, in neighbourhood groups, and not to the organisation of the reaves. Helen Wickstead's (2008) research on Dartmoor corroborates Fleming's observations. She demonstrates that houses did not influence the layout of the rectilinear fields. The generational relocation of houses would have disrupted any trajectory of sedentism, allowing for a more fluid, 'transactional' form of tenure within the fields.

Roundhouses were attentive to the boundaries even if they did not deflect the layout of the field systems. On Dartmoor, the houses were sited close to the coaxial boundaries, and they were often either joined by short lengths of wall or connected within small cellular field systems (Figure 7.13). Wickstead's (2008, 106–107) statistical analysis of the surveyed houses and boundaries within three of Dartmoor's rectilinear field systems supports this observation. The boundaries established a relation with the land, which the building and occupation of roundhouses then respected.

Andrew Fleming employs the phrase 'terrain oblivious' to describe the ways that some of the boundaries on Dartmoor seemed to disregard the impracticalities of crossing deeply cut river valleys. He likens the fields to Neolithic cursus monuments in the way they imposed an order onto the land: structures that acted 'as mnemonics and reference points in the landscape, helping to perpetuate the belief systems which gave rise to them' (Fleming 1987, 199). The rectilinear field systems on Salisbury Plain generally conform to a northeast–southwest axis, irrespective of the local topography (McOmish et al. 2002, 54–55). David Field (2008) offers

FIGURE 7.13 Aerial photograph of the rectilinear fields on Horridge Common, Dartmoor. © Crown copyright; Historic England Archive.

a few suggestions why these alignments were influential: cosmological beliefs, the practicalities of ensuring good access to sunlight and protection from prevailing winds, and as part of a method for apportioning agricultural land. Chris Green and Chris Gosden (in press), working on the English Landscape and Identities Project, analysed rectilinear field systems with prehistoric and early historic origins from across England. They found that the field systems with the strongest adherence to axiality commonly respected a northeast–southwest alignment, for which a likely explanation would be an acknowledgement of the summer or winter solstice. Letty Ten Harkel and colleagues (2017) interpret the alignments as attempts by the fields' builders to involve spiritual forces in the future fertility and sustainability of life in the field systems.

For Jane Downes and Antonia Thomas (2013), the fields' coaxiality structured the safe movement of animals and people between enclosed and unenclosed (outfield) land. Drawing on the Nordic concept of *utmark*, Downes and Thomas suggest that the outfield, usually upland, open pasture, was a more dangerous and magical part of the landscape. Access had to be negotiated safely by following north–south axes of movement through the fields, which respected a vertical ordering of the world found in northern European Bronze Age cosmologies (Kristiansen and Larsson 2005). Joanna Brück (2019, 175–178) makes a case for this same worldview in Britain and Ireland during the Bronze Age.

The regularity with which the boundaries were inscribed and the prominence of the shared axes can be compared with patterns in other settings. Parallel lines were selectively used to mark pottery and metalwork. Lateral zonation, especially with horizontal scored and impressed lines, was commonplace on early Bronze Age ceramics. It continued on Deverel-Rimbury vessels in southern Britain. Some of the globular urns from Bestwall are marked with bands of horizontal grooves or incised lines that run in parallel around the vessels (Woodward 2009). Narrow bands of multiple parallel lines decorate the lowest sections of some spearhead sockets and the shafts of bronze pins. Speculatively, parallel lines may have marked human and animal bodies too, whether painted or tattooed, and formed decorative schemes on textiles.

Were the regularity and the axiality of rectilinear field systems an outcome of applying similar marking practices to land? In the previous chapter, I proposed that monuments emerged as much as they were built from the land. Humans nurtured the growth of monuments by respectfully ordering substances (turf, stone and wood) and making offerings to places. The rectilinear fields may have applied a related, if geometrically different, logic to retaining land's powerful participation as kin in social life. Maurice Bloch's (1995) use of the term 'honouring' could be a helpful way to imagine the process. Bloch describes how the replacement of softer with harder woods and the application of carvings to the timbers in Madagascan houses occurs alongside the maturation of the human relations amongst the household. The carving honours the wood and participates in its hardening. Rectilinear field systems wrapped the land in lines. This process honoured the land as powerful kin and hardened a locality alongside a maturation of its human and animal inhabitants.

Comparative analysis can reduce rectilinear fields to their dominant alignments and their basic patterns (although this is not always the case: Green and Gosden in press; Wickstead 2008). The variability and detail that are lost through this process remove some of the relations that can be important. The parallel reaves that cross the River Dart epitomise a strict, terrain-oblivious, adherence to an alignment in spite of steep and complex topography (Fleming 1983). They terminate or begin (depending on your viewpoint) perpendicular with a long boundary on Holne Moor. The long boundary distinguishes the high moorland to the south, which was unenclosed, from the Upper Dart Basin and East Moor to the north, which were sub-divided. The boundary precisely respects the position and orientation of a stone row. On Shovel Down and Kestor, the rectilinear fields reference the positions and alignments of the hilltop tors, the North Teign River and a group of stone rows (Johnston 2005). On Shaugh Moor, the primary reave followed a route defined by an earlier trackway and fences. The Shovel

Down and Shaugh Moor fields took account of existing, powerful landmarks and histories engrained through people's and animals' routines within the landscape.

At Over and Barleycroft, Cambridgeshire, on either side of the River Ouse, ring ditches were used as the nodes for networks of field boundaries (Evans and Knight 2000; Evans, Tabor, et al. 2016). The ring ditches were probably all earlier than the boundaries, although in some cases they remained a focus for the deposition of burials while the field systems and settlements were inhabited. A similar arrangement was identified at Broom, Bedfordshire, where the alignments of the boundaries developed from a landscape structure that was partly defined by earlier ring ditches (Cooper and Edmonds 2007). Barrows were located at critical locations and respected by boundaries in other regions, notably on Salisbury Plain and on Dartmoor. With the construction of rectilinear field systems, the barrows remained active, visible places in the landscape where human burials had recently been placed and in cases they continued to be deposited.

Fields were given a vibrancy and relevance by physically connecting with or respecting the presence of barrows. It could be said that the barrows too were 'held in place' by their incorporation within the fields' patterns (Cooper 2016). However radical the rectilinear fields' linearity and parcelling of land may have been, it was a process that acknowledged and carried forward relations from a landscape's past. Writing about Broom, Bedfordshire, Anwen Cooper and Mark Edmonds describe the laying out of field systems as 'a *process* of reworking rather than a *moment* of reinvention' (Cooper and Edmonds 2007).

People worked to keep rectilinear fields enmeshed in social life. The boundaries and the fields ordered agricultural activities and mobilities. Ditches, hedges and walls were recut, relaid and repaired. Offerings of metalwork, and human and animal burials were occasionally placed in boundaries and in the waterholes within the fields (Brück 2019, 199–200; Harding and Healy 2007, 193; Wickstead 2008, 124–125). The field systems did not appear in moments, intact and immutable. They were built over time, worked, adapted, expanded and abandoned. These processes can be grasped from the different phases of boundary construction along the line of the primary reave on Shaugh Moor, Dartmoor, which included sections of bank, hedge, fence and wall (Smith et al. 1981). Christopher Evans and Emma Beardsmore describe some of the ditches at the Elliott Site, Fengate, as 'ropey' (Evans et al. 2009, 80). The ditches like those elsewhere within the Fengate system had been recut in a variety of ways: parallel additions, enlarged segments, minor straightenings.

Work on the boundaries and work in the fields were means of connecting kin and making kin with rights (tenure) to grazing and soil. Different forms of kinship were drawn into the making, dividing, extending and re-ordering of field systems. This kinmaking operated alongside and in relation to households, but the fields were not household property and they were not inherited as property. This conclusion is based on the shifting character of settlements within the fields and the weak influence of settlements on the organisation of the boundaries. The alignments adopted by the boundaries related fields and the activities within them to supernatural sources of tenure, with vibrant or enchanted landmarks, and with genealogically referenced patterns of movement through landscapes. The sub-division and re-ordering of fields may have accumulated and embodied complex genealogies (Gosden 2013, 114) that emerged from 'labile and shifting interpersonal and intercommunity relationships' (Brück 2019, 198). Helen Wickstead (2008, 148) argues that the relative ease and regularity with which rectilinear field systems could be sub-divided, and then sub-divided again and again, enabled people to perpetuate exchanges of tenure with one another. In Wickstead's account, land and kin could be made through these exchanges of tenure. The boundaries defined a relation between kin rather than delimiting an area of property.

Rectilinear fields brought a monumental change in the landscapes of southern England. They ordered land, cultivation, grazing and movement for several centuries, primarily during the sixteenth to twelfth centuries BC. The fields held the capacity to honour the land, its histories and supernatural forces. Tenurial claims and exchanges were a malleable political resource. The fields charted the histories of these exchanges through the work done by people, animals and plants in transforming soils and boundaries, and in the sub-divisions, additions and re-ordering of the fields. Like the narratives that I offered for the monuments with which I began this chapter, life's routines and flows were intrinsic to the formation of the fields. The success of rectilinear field systems lay in their capacities to remain relevant to daily life and to the deeper kinwork involved in maintaining and building relations with the land.

Linear earthworks and pit alignments, 1100–700 BC

On Louden, Bodmin Moor, two stone banks cross the cellular fields against the grain of the slope, reusing some of the earlier boundaries and connecting wet ground on either side of the hill (Johnson and Rose 1994, 65–70). Similar banks were created close by on Rough Tor, where again they cut across and in places reuse the edges of cellular fields. One of the long boundaries on Rough Tor survives to over a metre in height and originally could have been a wall two or three metres in width. Nicholas Johnson and Peter Rose interpret the boundaries as territorial divisions in areas used as seasonal pasture. Clusters of small roundhouses provided dwellings for people living on the moor with their animals during the summer. The shift to seasonal grazing within large land blocks replaced the mixed agricultural strategies marked by the earlier cellular fields and settlements.

There is a relative chronology for the changes on Bodmin Moor. Johnson and Rose's (1994, 73) preferred model is that a reorganisation of the landscape occurred towards the end of the second millennium BC and in the early centuries of the first millennium BC. One reason for estimating this date range is that comparable changes in the ordering of land using long boundaries occurred elsewhere in Britain at around this time. On Berkshire and Wiltshire's chalk downlands, long interconnected linear earthworks were built along watersheds and following contours on 'false-crest' positions (Ford 1982; Kirkham 2005; McOmish et al. 2002). Where stratigraphic relationships can be identified by field survey, the ditches and banks usually cut across the lynchets of rectilinear field systems and preceded the construction of hilltop enclosures. Barry Cunliffe (2004) places the inception of the Wessex linear earthworks in the ninth to eighth centuries BC. Excavations on Salisbury Plain found plain post-Deverel-Rimbury ceramics beneath the banks and within the ditches (Bradley et al. 1994, 58–60). Samples of bone from deposits deliberately placed in the ditches after their initial silting produced radiocarbon measurements spanning the eighth to fifth centuries BC. An extensive network of linear earthworks criss-crosses the chalkland of the Yorkshire Wolds (Stoertz 1997). The ditches have produced late Bronze Age pottery, and they predated and were closely integrated into mid- and late first-millennium BC settlements. Further north, on the Cleveland, Hambleton and Tabular Hills, the linear earthworks form similar although less extensive patterns to those in the Wolds (Spratt 1989). Large linear earthworks, known as 'treb dykes', survive on several areas of Orkney, and Raymond Lamb (1983) assigned them to the Bronze Age based on their form and associations. A network of long walls on the Antrim Plateau are interpreted as major land divisions dating to the twelfth to ninth centuries BC (Gardiner et al. 2019) (Figure 7.14). There may be similar boundaries surviving elsewhere in Ireland's uplands. Nick Hogan's (2009, 83) survey at Ardgroom, County Cork, recorded long parallel walls aligned perpendicular to the hillslope and possibly continuing through the modern enclosed land to the coast.

Pit and post alignments may be characterised within the same broad tradition as the linear earthworks. Pit alignments precede, run parallel with and continue the alignment of some linear earthworks in the Yorkshire Wolds (Stoertz 1997 40–41). Long lines of closely spaced pits have been recorded and excavated in the Thames Valley (Lambrick 2009a, 60–61) and the English East Midlands (Boutwood 1998). Clusters of pit alignments and cross-ridge linear earthworks are known from aerial surveys in the central Welsh Marches (Wigley 2007). Lines of pits containing burnt stone and with evidence for burning within the pits are recorded in Denmark and northern Germany (Løvschal and Fontijn 2019). The 'fire pit lines', as they are called, originate during the early first millennium BC and were broadly contemporary with the pit alignments in Britain.

As with the cairnfields and field systems that I describe elsewhere in this chapter, linear earthworks and pit alignments have long and diverse chronologies. They cannot be placed in time based on their morphologies alone. Pit and post alignments are known from much earlier, Neolithic, settings and they have been dated to the eighth to fourth centuries BC at St. Ives, Cambridgeshire (Pollard 1996), and fourth to first centuries BC at Gardom's Edge, Derbyshire (Barnatt et al. 2017). The long spinal reaves and cross-ridge boundaries on Dartmoor have a lot in common with the linear earthworks on the Wessex downland, except that the reaves consistently complement rather than slight the rectilinear fields

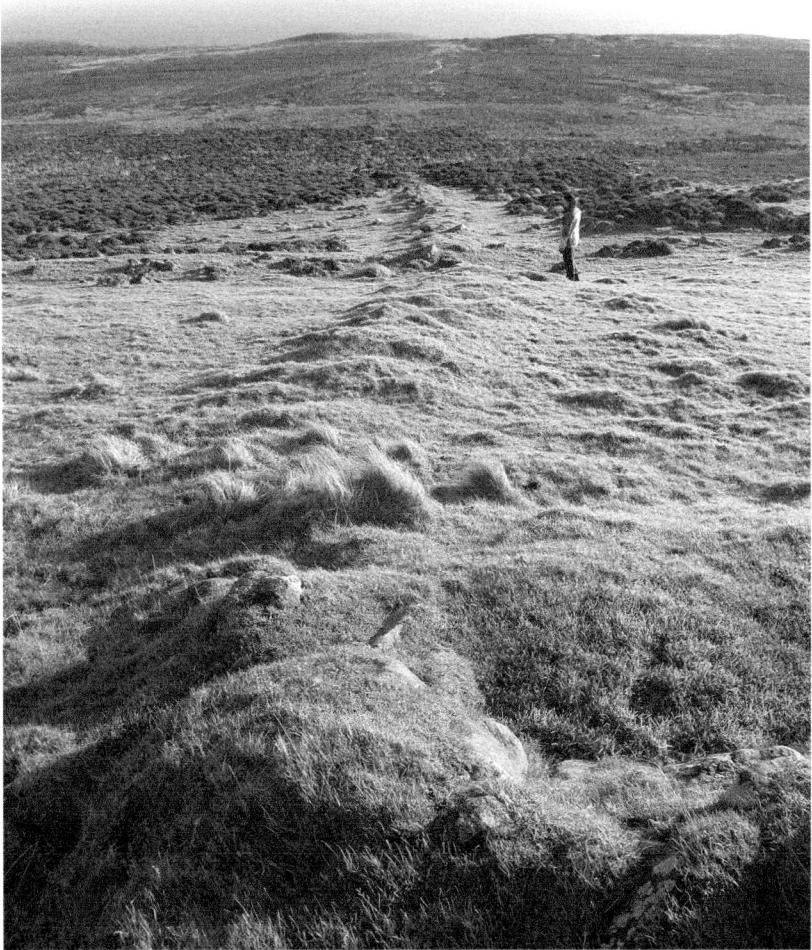

FIGURE 7.14 A late Bronze Age linear boundary above Garron on the Antrim Plateau. Image courtesy of Mark Gardiner.

and the available dating places them in the mid-second millennium BC. In the Cheviot Hills, Northumberland, linear earthworks are assigned to the later centuries of the first millennium BC (Topping 2008).

Since their earliest recognition by archaeologists, the linear earthworks have been interpreted as territorial boundaries, primarily for the demarcation and defence of land and livestock. This view has gradually shifted away from a defensive or territorial status for the earthworks towards a role in managing livestock (Bowen 1978). Barry Cunliffe (2004) associates the linear earthworks with a change to pastoralism on the Wessex downland during the early first millennium BC. This pastoral economy developed, Cunliffe argues, in correspondence with more intensive live-stock management and specialisation in textiles and dairying.

The linear earthworks on the Yorkshire Wolds sometimes extend for distances of over 10 kilometres, and they are located on the slopes and ridges parallel to watercourses or across the heads of valleys (Fenton-Thomas 1999; Stoertz 1997). The features at the entrances to the earthworks are flaring or funnelled (Stoertz 1997, 43), which would have facilitated the movements of herds and flocks. The earthworks were principally on higher ground, which was open, grazed grass-land during the first millennium BC. Some earthworks run towards though do not enclose water sources. This might be because access to the scarce water sources remained in common, while grazing was territorial.

This simplifies a complex picture. The earthworks take different forms de-pending on their locations within the landscape (Dent 2010, 31–33). The banks and ditches could be porous, interrupted with gaps, and they could be osten-tatiously elaborate. At Huggate, six parallel lines of banks and ditches cross a narrow neck between two deep-cut valleys. Excavations and aerial survey have shown that pit alignments preceded the construction of linear earthworks in some places and flanked others (Powlesland 1988). West of Burton Fleming, three linear earthworks with flanking pit alignments cross the valley of the Gypsey Race. While roughly contiguous, the earthworks subtly weave across the floodplain within a zone defined by the pit alignments. Several linear earth-works converge on this location from the surrounding higher ground. Melanie Giles (2012, 56–57) interprets the linear earthworks on the Wolds in terms of flows rather than territories. She argues that the earthworks did not circumscribe areas of land. They delineated ways onto and around areas of higher pasture, and the more routine routes taken by people and animals to water sources. The earthworks defined 'ingress and egress' rather than demarcating permanently settled blocks of land.

Marcos Llobera (1996) analysed the visibility to and from the linear earth-works on Salisbury Plain. The boundaries follow false crests along prominent landscape features such as watersheds, which led to the interpretation that they were positioned to be visible from within territories rather than to appear prom-inent from outside. Llobera argues differently. He found that the visibility tended to be segmented and primarily alongside or close to the earthworks. The earth-works would be 'stumbled across' and followed and not sighted from afar. They were 'linearities' rather than territories. Mette Løvschal and David Fontijn (2019) take a similar approach to the fire pit lines and pit alignments of northern Europe. The lines were forms of accumulative architecture that offered connections and directions, not divisions.

Writing in 1888, Maule Cole observed that the linear earthworks on the Yorkshire Wolds were not Roman: 'there is not a straight line amongst the whole lot' (quoted by Mortimer 1905, 368). Cole continued: 'They may look straight on paper, but not on the ground itself'. The variation in the forms of the earthworks comes partly from the multiple phases of construction, as pit alignments were replaced with ditches and banks, and contiguous lines of earthworks were added subsequently. Melanie Giles (2012, 53) describes how the earthworks acquired histories and legitimation through labour: '[the linear earthworks] became mnemonics of labour and sweat: "congealed histories" through which people traced their rights of place'. Richard Sennett (2012, 6) sets out in *Together* that successful cooperation 'emerges from practical activity'. The pit alignments at Four Crosses, Powys, form parallel and perpendicular arrangements that respected existing ring barrows and the, albeit indistinct, topography of the floodplain (Havard et al. 2017; Owen and Britnell 1989) (Figure 7.15). Andy Wigley (2007) considers how the alignments may have defined a community through the shared labour of construction, while making distinctions between individual contributions in the digging of separate pits. The pits were rectangular, with variations in size, orientation and positioning. This creates the impression of irregularities in the alignments, which acknowledged the frictions and eccentricities between times and people.

The linear earthworks and pit alignments defined kin, land and places through the affirmation of routeways, edges and directions. The largest networks of earthworks have been recognised on downland in north-eastern and southern England. These respected the routes and edges of pastures, which were shaped by livestock and people. Constructing pit alignments and continuous earthworks along these lines was an ongoing means of negotiating access and affirming presence in the landscape. In places, like Four Crosses, the pits formed parallel and perpendicular arrangements that were the essence if not the function

FIGURE 7.15 An aerial photograph showing an area of the pit alignments and ring ditches at Four Crosses, Powys. © CPAT. Photo Number: 79-CT-0000.

of rectilinear fields. They reduced the idea of rectilinear fields to its most basic element, without the messiness of fields, without the intensities of occupation that fields required and without the rigidity that had perhaps led to contestation and conflict within fieldscapes.

Linear earthworks and pit alignments followed in the 'aftermath' of rectilinear fields (Bradley and Yates 2007). This was not the replacement of one technology for land apportionment with another. The linear earthworks have a considerably wider geographical distribution that overlaps with the rectilinear fields. Even if the chronologies remain unhelpfully imprecise, there was probably a time gap between the end of rectilinear field systems (by which I mean the end of their maintenance and relevance) and early linear earthworks. Speculatively, it was a duration of two or three centuries, around the twelfth to tenth centuries BC. Far from marking a decline in agricultural activity, the palaeoenvironmental evidence indicates an extension of grazing and cultivation across Britain and Ireland (Plunkett 2008; Tipping 2015). This occurred in regions irrespective of whether linear earthworks and alignments would be built (Groves et al. 2012; Spencer et al. 2020).

Conclusion—mending kin

Spring was the time for closing gaps in Robert Frost's (1973, 43–44) poem, 'Mending Wall'. The mending was a joint labour Frost carried out with his neighbour, walking their respective sides of the wall's line and repairing as they went. In one section, the wall divided orchard from pinewood. Practically, the wall seemed unnecessary amongst the trees and Frost said so. A tension entered their conversations and their work. The neighbour twice responded with his father's reasoning: 'good fences make good neighbours'. The wall created its own need. It held the walls' menders in a particular relation with one another. Leaving the wall to ruin would, in turn, disrupt the relationship. Perhaps it was this disruption, or its unforeseen consequences, that made Frost's neighbour mistrustful. Perhaps it was Frost's goading about the apparent futility of the repairs that touched a nerve.

Boundaries of many kinds appeared throughout Britain and Ireland during the early to middle centuries of the second millennium BC, and especially from the sixteenth century. Walls, fences, ditches, banks and hedges were raised, dug and grown alongside fields and against the edges of settlements. Boundaries were not everywhere; they were commonplace and they proliferated in some landscapes. Frost's poem offers a reminder that boundaries held things in relation, in relations of difference and of similarity. Boundaries and relations were maintained and mended through labour (Figure 7.16). The act of building acknowledged an affinity. The boundaries participated in these processes. Even when the original intentions for the boundaries were forgotten, the boundaries continued to affect how people interacted with places.

It is tempting to cast theories about field systems based on modern conceptions of boundary-making, property and agriculture. A wall is a wall, after all.

FIGURE 7.16 Drystone walling, Teignhead Newtake, Dartmoor. © Chris Chapman 1981.

A field is a field. And yet, the boundaries that people built and the field systems that emerged during the second millennium BC had entirely different histories to Frost's New England walls or, indeed, the 'amoeboid clustering' of fields in Tim Robinson's deep maps of Connemara. Bronze Age field systems were built in landscapes animated by a variety of human and nonhuman beings. Land was inspirited or active; it was not alienable property. The approach I took across this chapter and the last was to treat monuments and fields as comparable means of landmarking and ways through which people related to land. The monuments were connected with routine lives and landscapes. The fields connected people with ancestors and supernatural beings. In making monuments, pasture and fields, people were making kin between themselves and with other selves who inhabited the land. Monuments and fields grew from a living land. Changes in land and tenure mattered because they were part of how persons and kindred were constituted: 'the incorporation of land and places into a history of social relations is where life exists' (Leach 2003, 29).

The dispersal of monuments across wide areas of countryside during the later centuries of the third millennium and the early second millennium BC hints at more extensive land use and a changing connection with places. Pollen records support this interpretation. Vegetation gradually became more open and grazing was sustained in areas for decades and centuries—sufficiently long to change the ecology of grassland and woodland. People negotiated access to land in part by building and making offerings in monuments. The human dead and cremated human bone played roles in these processes of landmarking and kinmaking with places. Monuments accumulated histories alongside the transformed ecologies. Land was itself transformed as people harvested stone into cairns. People continued to move with their livestock reproducing seasonal and longer routines. The distances that people moved and the durations over which they settled in localities varied between communities and regions. Kinwork depended on these seasonal routines and the associations, perhaps over several generations, with localities. People understood their history, their genealogy, with reference to a network of places across regions, and perhaps a generalised sense of emergence from a particular land. Monuments were an acknowledgement that places held people.

Bounded fields became widespread after the sixteenth century BC. Cellular field systems were built and farmed alongside and physically connected with roundhouses. The biographies of buildings, households and fields intersected. The passing of time was represented in the accumulation of stone on banks, the rebuilding of boundaries and the extension of field systems. Fields increasingly regionalised the land, as communities iteratively defined their kinship in relation to localities. Kin groups were gradually caught in localities' webs. The webs were made from decades of labour in the fields, the ordering of land according to the behaviours of animals and plants, the persistent and sustained transformation of soils, and the myths and supernatural beings that inhabited landscapes with people. Kin defined themselves according to the places they inhabited, whether year-round or seasonally. They may have anticipated future generations inhabiting the same localities, if not the same fields. Household kin and localities belonged together.

Rectilinear field systems extended across tens, hundreds and occasionally thousands of hectares of land in southern Britain around the same time as the cellular fields. Both forms of landmarking could co-exist, as they did on Dartmoor. They co-existed because they expressed different kinships with land. The lines that formed rectilinear fields honoured land, its histories and supernatural forces. They monumentalised and claimed a kinship with extensive areas. They emerged from correspondingly extensive kin networks. Life's routines and flows were intrinsic to the formation of the fields, as the cultivation of soil created lynchets and the alignments of droveways respected animals' journeys to and from pasture. Tenurial claims and exchanges were a malleable resource. The fields charted the histories of these exchanges, their longevities and successes, in the work done by people, animals and plants in transforming soils and boundaries, and in the sub-divisions, additions and re-ordering of the fields. Rectilinear field systems were not routinely sustained in the long term. Many boundaries were not maintained after the twelfth and eleventh centuries BC, even when the land continued to be cultivated and grazed. Perhaps the purposes of the lines, in honouring land and holding kin in place, were forgotten, misunderstood or became politically malign.

Lines returned as a form of landmarking during the ninth or eighth centuries BC across a wider geographic region than the rectilinear fields. Linear earthworks and pit alignments reworked the idea of rectilinear fields, which by then survived in some landscapes as patchworks of lynchets, ruined walls and grown-out hedges. The linears reduced the rectilinear fields to their most basic elements—lines. Ditches, banks and pits related kin, land and places through the affirmation of routeways, edges and directions. The earthworks respected the routes to and the edges of pastures, which were themselves shaped by live-stock and people. Kin networks came together in order to share the labour of constructing pit alignments and continuous earthworks. The linear earthworks emerged from and contributed to the persistence of these extensive kin networks.

References

Appley, Craig. 2013. *The prehistoric environment of Furness: palaeoenvironmental influences upon human activity during the Neolithic and Bronze Age of the Furness Peninsula, South Cumbria, UK*. PhD thesis, University of Sheffield.

Balaam, Nicholas D, Ken Smith and Geoff J Wainwright. 1982. The Shaugh Moor Project: fourth report—environment, context and conclusion. *Proceedings of the Prehistoric Society* 48:203–278.

Barber, John (editor). 1997. *The archaeological investigation of a prehistoric landscape: excavations on Arran 1978–1981*. Scottish Trust for Archaeological Research, Edinburgh.

Barnatt, John. 1986. Bronze Age remains on the East Moor. *Derbyshire Archaeological Journal* 106:18–100.

Barnatt, John. 1990. *The henges, stone circles and ringcairns of the Peak District*. Department of Archaeology and Prehistory, University of Sheffield, Sheffield.

Barnatt, John. 1994. Excavation of a Bronze Age unenclosed cemetery, cairns, and field boundaries at Eaglestone Flat, Curbar, Derbyshire, 1984, 1989–1990. *Proceedings of the Prehistoric Society* 60:287–370.

Barnatt, John. 1996. Barrows in the Peak District: a review and interpretation of extant sites and past excavations. In *Barrows in the Peak District: recent research*, edited by John Barnatt and John R Collis, pp. 3–94. Sheffield Academic Press, Sheffield.

Barnatt, John. 2000. To each their own: later prehistoric farming communities and their monuments in the Peak. *Derbyshire Archaeological Journal* 120:1–86.

Barnatt, John, Bill Bevan and Mark Edmonds. 2017. *An upland biography: landscape and prehistory on Gardom's Edge, Derbyshire*. Windgather, Oxford.

Barrett, John C. 1994. *Fragments from antiquity: an archaeology of social life in Britain, 2900–1200 BC*. Blackwell, Oxford.

Barrett, John C, Richard Bradley and Martin Green. 1991. *Landscape, monuments and society: the prehistory of Cranborne Chase*. Cambridge University Press, Cambridge.

Bayliss, Alex, Christopher Bronk Ramsey, Gordon Cook, Lilian Ladle, John Meadows, Johannes van der Plicht, Robert Scaife and Ann Woodward. 2009. Chapter 6: radiocarbon dating. In *Excavations at Bestwall Quarry, Wareham 1992–2005. Volume 1: the prehistoric landscape*, edited by Lilian Ladle and Ann Woodward, pp. 126–153. Dorset Natural History and Archaeological Society, Dorchester.

Bender, Barbara, Sue Hamilton and Chris Tilley. 2007. *Stone worlds: narrative and reflexivity in landscape archaeology*. Left Coast Press, Walnut Creek, Ca.

Bloch, Maurice. 1995. Questions not to ask of Malagasy carvings. In *Interpreting archaeology: finding meaning in the past*, edited by Ian Hodder, Michael Shanks, Alexandra

Alexandri, Victor Buchli, John Carman, Jonathan Last and Gavin Lucas, pp. 212–215. Routledge, London.

Boutwood, Yvonne. 1998. Prehistoric linear boundaries in Lincolnshire and its fringes. In *Lincolnshire's archaeology from the air*, edited by Robert Bewley, pp. 29–46. Occasional Papers in Lincolnshire History and Archaeology, 11. Society for Lincolnshire History and Archaeology / RCHME, Lincoln.

Bowen, Emyrs G and Colin A Gresham. 1967. *History of Merioneth. Volume I. From the earliest times to the age of the native princes.* The Merioneth Historical and Record Society, Dolgellau.

Bowen, H Colin. 1978. 'Celtic' fields and 'ranch' boundaries in Wessex. In *The effect of man on the landscape: the lowland zone*, edited by Susan Limbrey and John G Evans, pp. 115–123. CBA, London.

Bradley, Richard. 1980. Subsistence, exchange and technology: a social framework for the Bronze Age in southern England c.1400–700 BC. In *Settlement and society in the British later Bronze Age*, edited by John C Barrett and Richard Bradley, pp. 57–76. BAR British Series, 83. British Archaeological Reports, Oxford.

Bradley, Richard. 1998. *The significance of monuments: on the shaping of human experience in Neolithic and Bronze Age Europe.* Routledge, London.

Bradley, Richard, Roy Entwistle and Frances Raymond. 1994. *Prehistoric land divisions on Salisbury Plain: the work of the Wessex Linear Ditches Project.* English Heritage, London.

Bradley, Richard and David T Yates. 2007. After 'Celtic' fields: the social organisation of Iron Age agriculture. In *The Earlier Iron Age in Britain and the near continent*, edited by Colin Haselgrove and Rachel E Pope, pp. 94–102. Oxbow, Oxford.

Brück, Joanna. 2000. Settlement, landscape and social identity: the Early–Middle Bronze Age transition in Wessex, Sussex and the Thames Valley. *Oxford Journal of Archaeology* 19(3):273–300.

Brück, Joanna. 2019. *Personifying prehistory: relational ontologies in Bronze Age Britain and Ireland.* Oxford University Press, Oxford.

Burgess, Colin. 1985. Population, climate and upland settlement. In *Upland settlement in Britain: the second millennium BC and after*, edited by Don Spratt and Colin Bugess, pp. 195–230. BAR, Oxford.

Burgess, Colin B. 1980. *The age of Stonehenge.* Dent, London.

Burstow, George P and George A Holleyman. 1957. Late Bronze Age settlement on Itford Hill, Sussex. *Proceedings of the Prehistoric Society* 23:167–212.

Butler, Jeremy. 1997. *Dartmoor atlas of antiquities. Volume 5: the second millennium BC.* Devon Books, Exeter.

Carter, Stephen. 1993. Tulloch Wood, Forres, Moray: the survey and dating of a fragment of prehistoric landscape. *Proceedings of the Society of Antiquaries of Scotland* 23:215–233.

Carter, Stephen and Magnar Dalland. 2005. Bronze Age banks at the Black Crofts, North Connel, Argyll, a synthesis and re-assessment. *Proceedings of the Society of Antiquaries of Scotland* 135:191–212.

Caseldine, Astrid E, Catherine J Giffiths, John Griffith Roberts, George Smith and John Ll Williams. 2017. Land use and environmental history of Waun Llanfair, an upland landscape above Penmaenmawr, north Wales. *Archaeologia Cambrensis* 166:89–140.

Caseldine, Christopher J. 1999. Archaeological and environmental change on prehistoric Dartmoor—current understandings and future directions. *Quaternary Proceedings* 7:575–583.

Caulfield, Seamus, Gretta Byrne, Noel Dunne and Graeme Warren. 2011. *Excavations on Céide Hill, Behy & Glenulra, north Co. Mayo, 1963–1994.* UCD School of Archaeology and the Irish Strategic Archaeological Research Programme (INSTAR), Dublin.

Chadwick, Adrian M. 2016. Foot-fall and hoof-hit. Agencies, movements, materialities, and identities; and later prehistoric and Romano-British trackways. *Cambridge Archaeological Journal* 26(1):93–120.

Chambers, Frank M and S-M Price. 1988. The environmental setting of Erw-wen and Moel y Gerddi: prehistoric enclosures in upland Ardudwy, north Wales. *Proceedings of the Prehistoric Society* 54:93–100.

Charman, Dan J. 2010. Centennial climate variability in the British Isles during the mid–late Holocene. *Quaternary Science Reviews* 29:1539–1554.

Cleal, Rosamund M J and Michael J Allen. 1994. Investigation of tree-damaged barrows on King Barrow Ridge and Luxenborough Plantation, Amesbury. *Wiltshire Archaeological and Natural History Magazine* 87:54–84.

Cooper, Anwen. 2016. 'Held in place': round barrows in the later Bronze Age of lowland Britain. *Proceedings of the Prehistoric Society* 82:291–322.

Cooper, Anwen and Mark Edmonds. 2007. *Past and present: excavations at Broom, Bedfordshire 1996–2005.* Cambridge Archaeological Unit, Cambridge.

Cootes, Kevin and Patrick Quinn. 2018. Prehistoric settlement, mobility and societal structure in the Peak District National Park: new evidence from ceramic compositional analysis. *Archaeometry* 60(4):678–694.

Copley, Mark S, Rob Berstan, Vanessa Straker, Sebastian Payne and Richard P Evershed. 2005. Dairying in antiquity. II. Evidence from absorbed lipid residues dating to the British Bronze Age. *Journal of Archaeological Science* 32(4):505–521.

Crawford, O G S. 1912. The distribution of Early Bronze Age settlements in Britain. *The Geographical Journal* 40(2):184–203.

Crawford, O G S. 1936. The work of giants. *Antiquity* 10(38):162–174.

Cunliffe, Barry. 2004. Wessex cowboys? *Oxford Journal of Archaeology* 23(1):61–81.

Davies, Alex. 2016. *Social organisation in the Upper and Middle Thames Valley from the Late Bronze Age to the Middle Iron Age.* PhD thesis, Cardiff University.

Davies, Althea L. 2007. Upland agriculture and environmental risk: a new model of upland land-use based on high spatial-resolution palynological data from West Affric, NW Scotland. *Journal of Archaeological Science* 34:2053–2063.

Dent, John. 2010. *The Iron Age in eastern Yorkshire.* BAR British Series, 508. Archaeopress, Oxford.

Dockrell, Stephen. 2007. *Tofts Ness, Sanday: an island landscape through 3000 years of prehistory.* The Orcadian, Kirkwall.

Downes, Jane. 2001. The investigation of a Bronze Age cairnfield and later buildings at Fall Kneesend, Clydesdale. *Scottish Archeological Journal* 23(1):33–66.

Downes, Jane. 2009. The construction of barrows in Bronze Age Orkney—an 'assuagement of guilt'. In *Land and people: papers in memory of John G Evans,* edited by Michael J Allen, Niall Sharples and Terry O'Connor, pp. 126–135. Prehistoric Society Research Papers, 2. Prehistoric Society/Oxbow Books, Oxford.

Downes, Jane and Antonia Thomas. 2013. Where mythical space lies: land ownership versus land use in the northern Bronze Age. In *An archaeology of land ownership,* edited by Maria Relaki and Despina Catapoti, pp. 70–92. Routledge, London.

Drewett, Peter. 1982. Later Bronze Age downland economy and excavations at Black Patch, East Sussex. *Proceedings of the Prehistoric Society* 48:321–400.

Dymond, Charles W. 1893. Barnscar: an ancient settlement in Cumberland. *Transactions of the Cumberland and Westmoreland Antiquarian and Archaeological Society (First Ser)* 12:179–187.

Earle, Timothy. 2002. *Bronze Age economics: the beginnings of political economies.* Westview, Oxford.

Elsdon, Nicholas. 1996. *Cranford Lane, Harlington, London Borough of Hillingdon: post excavation assessment report*. Museum of London Archaeology Service, London.

Evans, Christopher, Grahame Appleby, Sam Lucy, Jo Appleby and Matt Brudenell. 2016. *Lives in land. Mucking excavations by Margaret and Tom Jones, 1965–1978: prehistory, context and summary*. Oxbow Books, Oxford.

Evans, Christopher, Emma Beadsmore, Matt Brudenell and Gavin Lucas. 2009. *Fengate revisited: further fen-edge excavations, Bronze Age fieldsystems and settlement and the Wyman Abbott/Leeds archives*. Cambridge Archaeological Unit, Cambridge.

Evans, Christopher and Mark Knight. 2000. A Fenland delta: later prehistoric land-use in the lower Ouse Reaches. In *Prehistoric, Roman and post-Roman landscapes of the Great Ouse Valley*, edited by Michael Dawson, pp. 89–106. CBA, London.

Evans, Christopher, Jonathan Tabor and Marc Vander Linden. 2016. *Twice-crossed river: prehistoric and palaeoenvironmental investigations at Barleycroft Farm/Over, Cambridgeshire*. McDonald Institute for Archaeological Research, Cambridge.

Evans, John G. 2003. *Environmental archaeology and the social order*. Routledge, London.

Feachem, Richard W. 1973. Ancient agriculture in the highland of Britain. *Proceedings of the Prehistoric Society* 39:332–353.

Fenton-Thomas, Chris. 1999. *Forgotten Wolds: late prehistoric and early historic landscapes on the Yorkshire chalk*. PhD thesis, University of Sheffield.

Field, David. 2008. The development of an agricultural countryside. In *Prehistoric Britain*, edited by Joshua Pollard, pp. 202–224. Blackwell, Oxford.

Fitzpatrick, Andrew P, Christine A Butterworth and Jan Grove. 1999. *Prehistoric and Roman sites in east Devon: the A30 Honiton to Exeter improvement DBFO scheme, 1996–9. Volume 1: prehistoric sites*. Wessex Archaeology Report, 16. Wessex Archaeology, Salisbury.

Fleming, Andrew. 1971. Bronze age agriculture on the marginal lands of north-east Yorkshire. *Agricultural History Review* 19:1–24.

Fleming, Andrew. 1980. The cairnfields of north-west Dartmoor. *Proceedings of the Devon Archaeological Society* 38:9–12.

Fleming, Andrew. 1983. The prehistoric landscape of Dartmoor part 2: north and east Dartmoor. *Proceedings of the Prehistoric Society* 49:195–241.

Fleming, Andrew. 1987. Coaxial field systems: some questions of time and place. *Antiquity* 61(232):188–202.

Fleming, Andrew. 2008. *The Dartmoor reaves: investigating prehistoric land divisions [second edition]*. Windgather, Oxford.

Ford, Steve. 1982. Linear earthworks on the Berkshire Downs. *Berkshire Archaeological Journal* 71:1–20.

Fowler, Peter J. 1983. *The farming of prehistoric Britain*. Cambridge University Press, Cambridge.

French, Charles, Rob Scaife, Michael J Allen, Mike Parker Pearson, Joshua Pollard, Colin Richards, Julian Thomas and Kate Welham. 2012. Durrington Walls to West Amesbury by way of Stonehenge: a major transformation of the Holocene landscape. *Antiquaries Journal* 92:1–36.

Frost, Robert. 1973. *Robert Frost: selected poems. Edited with an introduction by Ian Hamilton*. Penguin, London.

Fuller, Dorian Q, Chris Stevens and Meriel McClatchie. 2014. Routine activities, tertiary refuse, and labor organization: social inferences from everyday archaeobotany. In *Ancient plants and people: contemporary trends in archaeobotany*, edited by Marco Madella, Carla Lancelotti and Manon Savard, pp. 174–217. University of Arizona Press, Tucson.

Fyfe, Ralph M. 2012. Bronze Age landscape dynamics: spatially detailed pollen analysis from a ceremonial complex. *Journal of Archaeological Science* 39:2764–2773.

Fyfe, Ralph M, Joanna Brück, Robert Johnston, Helen Lewis, Thomas P Roland and Helen Wickstead. 2008. Historical context and chronology of Bronze Age land enclosure on Dartmoor, UK. *Journal of Archaeological Science* 35:2250–2261.

Fyfe, Ralph M, Claire Twiddle, Shinya Sugita, Marie-Jose Gaillard, Philip Barratt, Christopher J Caseldine, John Dodson, Kevin J Edwards, Michelle Farrell, Cynthia Froyd, Michael J Grant, Elizabeth Huckerby, James B Innes, Helen Shaw and Martyn Waller. 2013. The Holocene vegetation cover of Britain and Ireland: overcoming problems of scale and discerning patterns of openness. *Quaternary Science Reviews* 73:132–148.

Gallant, Louise, Norah Luxton and Morris Collman. 1985. Ancient fields on the south Devon limestone. *Proceedings of the Devon Archaeological Society* 43:23–38.

Gardiner, Mark, William P Megarry and Gill Plunkett. 2019. A Late Bronze Age field system and traces of settlement on the Antrim Plateau. *Journal of Irish Archaeology* 28:49–57.

Gearey, Benjamin R, Dan J Charman and Martin Kent. 2000. Palaeoecological evidence for the prehistoric settlement of Bodmin Moor, Cornwall, southwest England. Part II: land use changes from the Neolithic to the present. *Journal of Archaeological Science* 27:493–508.

Giles, Melanie. 2012. *A forged glamour: landscape, identity and material culture in the Iron Age.* Windgather, Oxford.

Gillings, Mark. 2015. Fugitive monuments and animal pathways: explaining the stone settings of Exmoor. *Proceedings of the Prehistoric Society* 81:87–106.

Gingell, Christopher. 1992. *The Marlborough Downs: a later Bronze Age landscape and its origins.* Wiltshire Archaeology and Natural History Society, Devizes.

Gosden, Chris. 2013. Fields. In *Counterpoint: essays in archaeology and heritage studies in honour of Professor Kristian Kristiansen*, edited by Sophie Bergerbrant and Serena Sabatini, pp. 111–117. BAR International Series, 2508. Archaeopress, Oxford.

Graham, Angus. 1959. Cairnfields in Scotland. *Proceedings of the Society of Aantiquaries of Scotland* 90:7–23.

Green, Chris and Chris Gosden. in press. Field systems, orientation and cosmology. In *English landscapes and identities: investigating landscape change from 1500 BC to AD 1086*, edited by EngLaId Team. Oxford Univerity Press, Oxford.

Greenwell, William. 1877. *British barrows: a record of the examination of sepulchral mounds in various parts of Britain.* Clarendon, Oxford.

Gresham, Colin A and H C Irvine. 1963. Prehistoric routes across North Wales. *Antiquity* 37(145):54–58.

Griffiths, W E. 1960. The excavation of stone circles near Penmaenmawr, North Wales. *Proceedings of the Prehistoric Society* 26:303–339.

Groves, Jon A, Martyn P Waller, Michael J Grant and J Edward Schofield. 2012. Longterm development of a cultural landscape: the origins and dynamics of lowland heathland in southern England. *Vegetation History and Archaeobotany* 21:453–470.

Guttmann, Erika B. 2005. Midden cultivation in prehistoric Britain: arable crops in gardens. *World Archaeology* 37(2):224–239.

Guttmann, Erika B, Ian A Simpson, Donald A Davidson and Stephen J Dockrill. 2006. The management of arable land from prehistory to the present: case studies from the Northern Isles of Scotland. *Geoarchaeology* 21(1):61–92.

Hall, Allan R and Jacqueline P Huntley. 2007. *A review of the evidence for macrofossil plant remains from archaeological deposits in northern England.* Research Department Report Series, 87/2007. English Heritage, Swindon.

Hambleton, Ellen. 2008. *Review of Middle Bronze Age–Late Iron Age faunal assemblages from southern Britain.* Research Department Report Series, 71–2008. English Heritage, London.

Harding, Anthony F and Janusz Ostoja-Zagórski. 1994. Prehistoric and early medieval activity on Danby Rigg, North Yorkshire. *Archaeological Journal* 151:16–97.

Harding, Jan and Frances Healy. 2007. *The Raunds Area Project: a Neolithic and Bronze Age landscape in Northamptonshire.* English Heritage, London.

Havard, Tim, Timothy Darvill and Mary Alexander. 2017. A Bronze Age round barrow cemetery, pit alignments, Iron Age burials, Iron Age copper working, and later activity at Four Crosses, Llandysilio, Powys. *Archaeological Journal* 174(1):1–67.

Herring, Peter, Nicholas Johnson, Andy M Jones, Jacqueline Nowakowski, Adam Sharpe and Andrew Young. 2016. *Archaeology and landscape at the land's end, Cornwall: the West Penwith surveys 1980–2010.* Cornwall Archaeological Unit, Truro.

Hoaen, Andrew and Helen L Loney. 2007. Cairnfields: understanding economic and ecological practice during the Bronze Age of central Britain. In *Studies in northern prehistory: essays in memory of Clare Fell*, edited by Peter J Cherry, pp. 189–210. Cumberland and Westmoreland Antiquarian and Archaeological Society, Carlisle.

Hoaen, Andrew and Helen L Loney. 2013. Landesque Capital and the development of the British uplands in later prehistory: investigating the accretion of cairns, cairnfields and ancient agricultural landscapes. In *Memory, myth and long-term landscape inhabitation*, edited by Adrian M Chadwick and Catriona D Gibson, pp. 124–145. Oxbow, Oxford.

Hogan, Nick. 2009. The Ardgroom landscape. In *Local worlds: early settlement landscapes and upland farming in south-west Ireland*, edited by William O'Brien, pp. 69–87. The Collins Press, Cork.

Humphrey, Caroline. 1995. Chiefly and shamanist lanscapes in Mongolia. In *The anthropology of landscape: perspectives on place and space*, edited by Eric Hirsch and Michael O'Hanlon, pp. 135–162. Clarendon Press, Oxford.

Jobey, George. 1981. Green Knowe unenclosed platform settlement and Harehope cairn, Peeblesshire. *Proceedings of the Society of Antiquaries of Scotland* 110:72–113.

Jobey, George. 1983. Excavation of an unenclosed settlement on Standrop Rigg, Northumberland, and some problems related to similar settlements between Tyne and Forth. *Archaeologia Aeliana (5th Ser)* 11:1–21.

Johnson, Nicholas and Peter Rose. 1994. *Bodmin Moor: an archaeological survey. Volume 1—the human landscape to c.1800.* English Heritage, London.

Johnston, Robert. 2001. 'Breaking new ground': land tenure and fieldstone clearance during the Bronze Age. In *Bronze Age landscapes: tradition and transformation*, edited by Joanna Brück, pp. 99–109. Oxbow, Oxford.

Johnston, Robert. 2005. Pattern without a plan: rethinking the Bronze Age coaxial field systems on Dartmoor, south-west England. *Oxford Journal of Archaeology* 24(1):1–21.

Jones, Andy M. 2004/2005. Settlement and ceremony: archaeological investigations at Stannon Down, St Breward, Cornwall. *Cornish Archaeology* 43/44:1–140.

Jones, Andy M. 2006. Monuments and memories set in stone: a Cornish Bronze Age ceremonial complex in its landscape (on Stannon Down). *Proceedings of the Prehistoric Society* 72:341–365.

Jones, Carleton. 2016. Dating ancient field walls in karst landscapes using differential bedrock lowering. *Geoarchaeology* 31(2):77–100.

Jones, Carleton. 2019. Climate change and farming response in a temperate oceanic zone—the exploitation of a karstic region in western Ireland in the third and second millennia BC. *Journal of Island and Coastal Archaeology.* DOI: 10.1080/15564894.2019.1614115

Jones, Carleton, Olive Carey and Clare Hennigar. 2011. Domestic production and the political economy in prehistory: evidence from the Burren, Co. Clare. *Proceedings of the Royal Irish Academy* 111C:33–58.

Kirby, Magnus. 2009. The evaluation of a Beaker period cairnfield at Elvanfoot, South Lanarkshire. *Scottish Archaeological Journal* 31(1/2):33–48.

Kirkham, Graeme. 2005. Prehistoric linear ditches on the Marlborough Downs. In *The Avebury landscape: aspects of the field archaeology of the Marlborough Downs*, edited by Graham Brown, David Field and David McOmish, pp. 149–155. Oxbow, Oxford.

Kitchen, Willy. 2001. Tenure and territoriality in the British Bronze Age. In *Bronze Age landscapes: tradition and transformation*, edited by Joanna Brück, pp. 110–120. Oxbow, Oxford.

Kristiansen, Kristian and Thomas Larsson. 2005. *The rise of Bronze Age society: travels, transmissions and transformations*. Cambridge University Press, Cambridge.

Ladle, Lilian and Ann Woodward. 2009. *Excavations at Bestwall Quarry, Wareham 1992–2005. Volume 1: the prehistoric landscape*. Dorset Natural History and Archaeological Society, Dorchester.

Lamb, Raymond G. 1980. *Sanday and North Ronaldsay: an archaeological survey of two of the North Isles of Orkney*. Royal Commission on the Ancient and Historical Monuments of Scotland, Edinburgh.

Lamb, Raymond G. 1983. The Orkney Trebs. In *Settlement in north Britain, 1000 BC–AD 1000: papers presented to George Jobey, Newcastle upon Tyne, December 1982*, edited by John C Chapman and Harold C Mytum, pp. 175–184. BAR British Series, 118. British Archaeological Reports, Oxford.

Lambrick, George. 2009a. Dividing up the countryside. In *The Thames through time: the archaeology of the gravel terraces of the Upper and Middle Thames. The Thames Valley in late prehistory: 1500 BC–AD 50*, edited by George Lambrick and Mark Robinson, pp. 53–90. Oxford Archaeology, Oxford.

Lambrick, George. 2009b. Hearth and home: buildings and domestic culture. In *The Thames through time: the archaeology of the gravel terraces of the Upper and Middle Thames. The Thames Valley in late prehistory: 1500 BC–AD 50*, edited by George Lambrick and Mark Robinson, pp. 133–178. Oxford Archaeology, Oxford.

Leach, James. 2003. *Creative land: place and procreation on the Rai Coast of Papua New Guinea*. Berghahn Books, Oxford.

Lelong, Olivia and Tony Pollard. 1998. Excavation of a Bronze Age ring cairn at Cloburn Quarry, Cairngryffe Hill, Lanarkshire. *Proceedings of the Society of Antiquaries of Scotland* 128:105–142.

Lewis, John, Matt Leivers, Lisa Brown, Alex Smith, Kate Cramp, Lorraine Mepham and Chris Phillpotts. 2010. *Landscape evolution in the Middle Thames Valley: Heathrow Terminal 5 excavations. Volume 2*. Framework Archaeology, Oxford and Salisbury.

Llobera, Marcos. 1996. Exploring the topography of mind: GIS, social space and archaeology. *Antiquity* 70(269):612–622.

Løvschal, Mette. 2014. Emerging boundaries: social embedment of landscape and settlement divisions in northwestern Europe during the first millennium BC. *Current Anthropology* 55(6):725–750.

Løvschal, Mette. 2020. The logics of enclosure: deep-time trajectories in the spread of land tenure boundaries in late prehistoric northern Europe (2000–50 BCE). *Journal of the Royal Anthropological Institute* 26(2): 365–388.

Løvschal, Mette and David Fontijn. 2019. Directionality and axiality in the Bronze Age: cross-regional landscape perspectives on 'fire pit lines' and other pitted connections. *World Archaeology* 51(1):140–156.

Lynch, Frances. 1984. Moel Goedog circle I: a complex ring cairn near Harlech. *Archaeologia Cambrensis* 133:8–50.

Lynch, Frances. 1993. *Excavations in the Brenig Valley: a Mesolithic and Bronze Age landscape in North Wales*. Cambrian Archaeological Association, Bangor.

Lynn, Chris J. 1973/1974. The excavation of a ring-cairn in Carnkenny townland, Co. Tyrone. *Ulster Journal of Archaeology* 36/37:17–31.

Macklin, Mark G, David G Passmore, A C Stevenson, David C Cowley, N Edwards and Colm F O'Brien. 1991. Holocene alluviation and land-use change on Callaly Moor, Northumberland, England. *Journal of Quaternary Science* 6(3):225–232.

Martin, Jon, Jörn Schuster and Alistair J Barclay. 2012. Evidence of an Early Bronze Age field system and spelt wheat growing, together with an Anglo-Saxon sunken featured building, at Monkton Road, Minster in Thanet. *Archaeologia Cantiana* 132:43–52.

May, Andrew McL. 1953. Neolithic habitation site, stone circles and alignments at Beaghmore, Co. Tyrone. *Journal of the Royal Society of Antiquaries of Ireland* 83(2):174–197.

McCormick, Finbar. 2007. Mammal bones from prehistoric Irish sites. In *Environmental archaeology in Ireland*, edited by Eileen M Murphy and Nicki J Whitehouse, pp. 77–101. Oxbow, Oxford.

McIntyre, Alison. 1998. Survey and excavation at Kilearnan Hill, Sutherland, 1982–3. *Proceedings of the Society of Antiquaries of Scotland* 128:167–201.

McOmish, David, David Field and Graham Brown. 2002. *The field archaeology of the Salisbury Plain Training Area*. English Heritage, Swindon.

Molloy, Karen and Michael O'Connell. 1995. Palaeoecological investigations towards the reconstruction of environment and land-use changes during prehistory at Céide Fields, western Ireland. *Probleme der Küstenforschung im südlichen Nordseegebiet* 23:187–225.

Moore, Michael J. 1995. A Bronze Age settlement and ritual centre in the Monavullagh Mountains, County Waterford, Ireland. *Proceedings of the Prehistoric Society* 61:191–243.

Morigi, Anthony, Danielle Schreve, Gill Hey, Paul Garwood, Mark Robinson, Alistair Barclay and Philippa Bradley. 2011. *Thames through time. The archaeology of the gravel terraces of the Upper and Middle Thames. Early prehistory: to 1500 BC*. Thames Valley Landscapes Monograph, 32. Oxford Archaeology, Oxford.

Mortimer, John R. 1905. *Forty years' researches in British and Saxon burial mounds of East Yorkshire*. A. Brown, London.

Newman, Phil. 2011. *The field archaeology of Dartmoor*. English Heritage, Swindon.

Nowakowski, Jacqueline A. 2009. Living in the sands—Bronze Age Gwithian, Cornwall, revisited. In *Land and people: papers in memory of John G Evans*, edited by Michael J Allen, Niall Sharples and Terry O'Connor, pp. 115–125. Prehistoric Society Research Papers, 2. Prehistoric Society/Oxbow Books, Oxford.

Nowakowski, Jacqueline A. 2016. Prehistoric settlement—roundhouses and fields, 2nd to 1st millennia BC. In *Archaeology and landscape at the land's end, Cornwall: the West Penwith surveys 1980–2010*, edited by Peter Herring, Nicholas Johnson, Andy M Jones, Jacqueline Nowakowski, Adam Sharpe and Andrew Young, pp. 138–159. Cornwall Archaeological Unit, Truro.

Nowakowski, Jacqueline A, Henrietta Quinnell, Joanna Sturgess, Charles Thomas and Carl Thorpe. 2007. Return to Gwithian: shifting the sands of time. *Cornish Archaeology* 46:13–76.

O'Brien, William. 2009. *Local worlds: early settlement landscapes and upland farming in southwest Ireland*. The Collins Press, Cork.

O'Connell, Aidan. 2013. *Harvesting the stars: a pagan temple at Lismullin, Co. Meath*. NRA Scheme Monographs, 11. National Roads Authority, Dublin.

Owen, Glyn and William J Britnell. 1989. Pit alignments at Four Crosses, Llandysilio, Powys. *Montgomeryshire Collections* 77:27–40.

Pennington, Winifred. 1964. Pollen analyses from the deposits of six upland tarns in the Lake District. *Philosophical Transactions of the Royal Society of London. Series B, Biological Sciences* 248(746):205–244.

Pilcher, Jonathan. 1969. Archaeology, palaeocology and C14 dating of the Beaghmore stone circle site. *Ulster Journal of Archaeology* 32:73–91.

Pilcher, Jonathan. 1975. Finds at Beaghmore stone circles, 1971 and 1972. *Ulster Journal of Archaeology* 38:83–84.

Plunkett, Gill. 2008. Land-use patterns and cultural change in the Middle to Late Bronze Age in Ireland: inferences from pollen records. *Vegetation History and Archaeobotany* 18:273–295.

Plunkett-Dillon, Emma. 1985. *The field boundaries of the Burren, Co. Clare.* PhD thesis, Trinity College, Dublin.

Pollard, Joshua. 1996. Iron age riverside pit alignments at St Ives, Cambridgeshire. *Proceedings of the Prehistoric Society* 62:93–115.

Pollard, Sheila H M. 1971. Seven prehistoric sites near Honiton, Devon. Part II: three flint rings. *Proceedings of the Devon Archaeological Society* 29:162–180.

Powlesland, Dominic. 1988. Staple Howe in its landscape. In *Archaeology in eastern Yorkshire*, edited by Terry G Manby, pp. 101–107. Department of Archaeology and Prehistory, Sheffield University, Sheffield.

Pryor, Francis. 1996. Sheep, stockyards and field systems: Bronze Age livestock populations in the Fenlands of eastern England. *Antiquity* 70(268):213–324.

Pryor, Francis. 2001. *Seahenge: a quest for life and death in Bronze Age Britain.* Harper Collins, London.

Quartermaine, Jamie and Roger H Leech. 2012. *Cairns, fields, and cultivation: archaeological landscapes of the Lake District uplands.* Oxford Archaeology North, Lancaster.

Quinn, Colin P, Ian Kuijt, Nathan Goodale and John Ó Néill. 2019. Along the margins? The later Bronze Age seascapes of western Ireland. *European Journal of Archaeology* 22(1):44–66.

RCAHMW. 1997. *An inventory of the ancient monuments in Brecknock (Brycheiniog): the prehistoric and Roman monuments. Part i: later prehistoric monuments and unenclosed settlements to 1000 AD.* RCAHM(Wales), Aberystwyth.

Rice, Kim. 2006. *The prehistory of Piperstown: a reassessment of an upland landscape.* MA thesis, University College Dublin, Dublin.

Richardson, Colin. 1982. Excavations at Birrel Sike, near Low Prior Scales, Calder Valley, Cumbria (NY 0702 0735). *Transactions of the Cumberland and Westmoreland Antiquarian and Archaeological Society* 82:7–27.

Roberts, John G. 2007. Short journeys, long distance thinking. In *Prehistoric journeys*, edited by Vicki Cummings and Robert Johnston, pp. 102–109. Oxbow, Oxford.

Robinson, Mark and George Lambrick. 2009. Living off the land: farming, water, storage and waste. In *The Thames through time: the archaeology of the gravel terraces of the Upper and Middle Thames. The Thames Valley in late prehistory: 1500 BC–AD 50*, edited by George Lambrick and Mark Robinson, pp. 237–282. Oxford Archaeology, Oxford.

Robinson, Tim. 2011. *Connemara: a little Gaelic kingdom.* Penguin, London.

Roland, Thomas P, Chris J Caseldine, Dan J Charman, Chris S M Turney and Matthew J Amesbury. 2014. Was there a '4.2 ka event' in Great Britain and Ireland? Evidence from the peatland record. *Quaternary Science Reviews* 83:11–27.

Rowlands, Michael. 1980. Kinship, alliance and exchange in the European Bronze Age. In *Settlement and society in the British later Bronze Age*, edited by John C Barrett and Richard Bradley, pp. 59–72. BAR British Series, 83. British Archaeological Reports, Oxford.

Sennett, Richard. 2012. *Together: the rituals, pleasures and politics of cooperation.* Allen Lane, London.

Serjeantson, Dale. 2011. *Review of animal remains from the Neolithic and Early Bronze Age of southern Britain (4000 BC–1500 BC).* Research Department Report Series, 29–2011. English Heritage, Portsmouth.

Simmonds, Andrew and Carl Champness. 2015. Excavation of a transect across the Great Western Reave at Walkhampton Common, Dartmoor. *Proceedings of the Devon Archaeological Society* 73:75–89.

Simpson, Ian A, Stephen J Dockrill, Erika B Guttmann, Ian D Bull and Richard P Evershed. 2007. Soils and the early cultural landscape. In *Investigations in Sanday, Orkney. Vol 2: Tofts Ness, Sanday. An island landscape through three thousand years of prehistory*, edited by Stephen J Dockrill, pp. 239–252. The Orcadian and Historic Scotland, Kirkwall.

Smith, Ken, J Coppen, Geoff J Wainwright and Stephen C Beckett. 1981. The Shaugh Moor Project: third report—settlement and environmental investigations. *Proceedings of the Prehistoric Society* 47:205–273.

Spencer, Daisy Eleanor, Karen Molloy, Aaron Potito and Carleton Jones. 2020. New insights into Late Bronze Age settlement and farming activity in the southern Burren, western Ireland. *Vegetation History and Archaeobotany* 29:339–356.

Spratt, Don A. 1989. *Linear earthworks of the Tabular Hills of northeast Yorkshire.* University of Sheffield Department of Archaeology and Prehistory, Sheffield.

Stevens, Chris J and Dorian Q Fuller. 2012. Did Neolithic farming fail? The case for a Bronze Age agricultural revolution in the British Isles. *Antiquity* 86(333):707–722.

Stevens, Paul. 2007. Burial and ritual in late prehistory in north Wexford: excavation of a ring-ditch cemetery in Ask townland. In *New Routes to the Past: proceedings of a public seminar on archaeological discoveries on national road schemes, August 2006*, edited by Jerry O'Sullivan and Michael Stanley, pp. 35–46. National Roads Authority, Dublin.

Stoertz, Catherine. 1997. *Ancient landscapes of the Yorkshire Wolds.* RCHME, Swindon.

Swindles, Graeme T, Ian T Lawson, Ian P Matthews, Maarten Blaauw, Timothy J Daley, Dan J Charman, Thomas P Roland, Gill Plunkett, Georg Schettler, Benjamin R Gearey, T Edward Turner, Heidi A Rea, Helen M Roe, Matthew J Amesbury, Frank M Chambers, Jonathan Holmes, Fraser J G Mitchell, Jeffrey Blackford, Antony Blundell, Nicholas Branch, Jane Holmes, Peter Langdon, Julia McCarroll, Frank McDermott, Pirita O Oksanen, Oliver Pritchard, Phil Stastney, Bettina Stefanini, Dan Young, Jane Wheeler, Katharina Becker and Ian Armit. 2013. Centennial-scale climate change in Ireland during the Holocene. *Earth-Science Reviews* 126:300–320.

Ten Harkel, Letty, Tyler Franconi and Chris Gosden. 2017. Fields, ritual and religion: holistic approaches to the rural landscape in long-term perspective (c. 1500 BC–AD 1086). *Oxford Journal of Archaeology* 36:413–437.

Tilley, Christopher, Sue Hamilton, Stephan Harrison and Ed Anderson. 2000. Nature, culture, clitter: distinguishing between cultural and geomorphological landscapes; the case of the hilltop tors in south-west England. *Journal of Material Culture* 5(2):197–224.

Tipping, Richard. 2010. *Bowmont: an environmental history of the Bowmont Valley and the northern Cheviot Hills, 10,000 BC – AD 2000.* Society of Antiquaries of Scotland, Edinburgh.

Tipping, Richard. 2015. 'I have not been able to discover anything of interest in the peat': landscapes and environments in the later Bronze and Iron Ages of Scotland. In *Scotland in later prehistoric Europe*, edited by Ian Ralston and Fraser Hunter, pp. 103–117. Society of Antiquaries of Scotland, Edinburgh.

Topping, Peter. 2008. Landscape narratives: the south-east Cheviots Project. *Proceedings of the Prehistoric Society* 74:323–364.

Treasure, Edward R and Mike J Church. 2017. Can't find a pulse? Celtic bean (*Vicia faba* L.) in British prehistory. *Environmental Archaeology* 22(2):113–127.

Turner, Valerie. 2012. *Location, form and function in Shetland's prehistoric field systems.* PhD thesis, University of Stirling.

Verrill, Lucy and Richard Tipping. 2010a. A palynological and geoarchaeological investigation into Bronze Age farming at Belderg Beg, Co. Mayo, Ireland. *Journal of Archaeological Science* 37:1214–1225.

Verrill, Lucy and Richard Tipping. 2010b. Use and abandonment of a Neolithic field system at Belderrig, Co. Mayo, Ireland: evidence for economic marginality. *The Holocene* 20:1011–1021.

Wainwright, Geoffrey J, Andrew Fleming and Ken Smith. 1979. The Shaugh Moor Project: first report. *Proceedings of the Prehistoric Society* 45:1–33.

Walker, Donald. 1965. Excavations at Barnscar, 1957–58. *Transactions of the Cumberland and Westmoreland Antiquarian and Archaeological Society* 65:53–65.

Ward, Anthony H. 1988. Survey and excavation of ring cairns in SE Dyfed and on Gower, West Glamorgan. *Proceedings of the Prehistoric Society* 54:153–172.

Whittle, Alasdair. 1986. *Scord of Brouster: an early agricultural settlement on Shetland.* Oxford Committee for Archaeology, Oxford.

Wickstead, Helen. 2008. *Theorising tenure: land division and identity in later prehistoric Dartmoor, south-west Britain.* BAR British Series, 465. Oxford, Archaeopress.

Wigley, Andy. 2007. Pitted histories: early first millennium BC pit alignments in the central Welsh Marches. In *The Earlier Iron Age in Britain and the near continent*, edited by Colin Haselgrove and Rachel E Pope, pp. 119–134. Oxbow, Oxford.

Williams, John Ll and David A Jenkins. 2004. Petrographic analysis and classification of prehistoric pottery from northern Wales: Neolithic and Bronze Age. *Studia Celtica* 38:1–48.

Wimble, Guy, Colin E Wells and David Hodgkinson. 2000. Human impact on mid- and late Holocene vegetation in south Cumbria, UK. *Vegetation History and Archaeobotany* 9:17–30.

Woodward, Ann. 2009. Chapter 8: the pottery. In *Excavations at Bestwall Quarry, Wareham 1992–2005. Volume 1: the prehistoric landscape*, edited by Lilian Ladle and Ann Woodward, pp. 200–271. Dorset Natural History and Archaeological Society, Dorchester.

Yates, David T. 2007. *Land, power and prestige: Bronze Age field systems in southern England.* Oxbow, Oxford.

Yates, Michael J. 1984. Groups of small cairns in northern Britain—a view from SW Scotland. *Proceedings of the Society of Antiquaries of Scotland* 114:217–234.

Young, Robert and Adam T Welfare. 1992. Fieldwork and excavation at the Crawley Edge cairnfield, Stanhope, Co. Durham. *Durham Archaeological Journal* 8:27–49.

8

CONCLUSION

A social prehistory

"Listen for different stories."
(Mrs Annie Ned, Yukon, quoted by Julie Cruikshank 2005, 76)

This book is a narrative synthesis of the Bronze Age in Ireland and Britain shaped by a new way of thinking about kinship in archaeology. The narrative emerges from an ambition voiced in this chapter's epigraph: to listen for different stories. *Listening for* is a more acute, attentive and searching process than listening to. It reaches beyond what is familiar, and acknowledges that other, different perspectives lie on the margins of our experiences of the world. Annie Ned was in her late eighties when she told a conference of scientists and First Nations elders in southern Yukon to listen for different stories if they wished to understand indigenous relations with the environment. Translating this idiom to a prehistory written of Britain and Ireland may appear contrived. I disagree. The message is simple: the Bronze Age world was unlike our own. In order to write prehistories of the Bronze Age, we should accept our partial connections with the past and listen for the differences. There are three aspects of my approach that respond to this task and which, I hope, produce a distinctive account of the Bronze Age in Britain and Ireland.

The first relates to my treatment of chronology. I have eschewed the established schemes for organising the Bronze Age, whether the coarser quadripartite system (Chalcolithic, Early, Middle and Late Bronze Age) or finer periodisations based on metalwork or a combination of artefact classes (Needham 1996). In their place, I have followed centennial, and occasionally decadal where available, timescales. A calendrical framework is more sensitive to the different resolutions of archaeological chronologies and the historical processes I am describing. The times of funerary assemblages are scientifically measured more frequently and with considerably more precision compared with the durations of settlements and the transformations of monuments. Periodised schemes are dependent upon the material culture from which they are constructed. A calendrical framework has the advantage that it is independent of the archaeological material and social processes that compose the narrative. It can accommodate the different rhythms and asynchronies of persons' lives, things and processes. A narrative prehistory has become a realistic proposition because of the wide application of radiocarbon dating and Bayesian modelling, even if our grasp of Bronze Age chronologies remains behind the advances achieved in research about the Neolithic (Whittle 2018).

The book's geographical focus is Europe's western archipelago: Ireland, Britain and the nearby islands. These diverse landscapes had distinct histories. None were ever in isolation. People were widely connected with kin in patterns that respected certain hard-to-define geographies, and took no account of our present-day administrative and national boundaries. The Channel, North Sea and Irish Sea proved important connectors throughout the period (Lehoërff and Talon 2017). Bracketing the islands from mainland Europe keeps the synthesis within a manageable project, but it limits my capacities to represent the considerable cultural continuities that existed across northwest Europe (Bradley et al. 2016). In compensation for this narrowing in one respect, I have given attention to material from throughout the islands, and especially to areas that are commonly left on the margins of syntheses. Thirty years of development-led fieldwork have made immense contributions to the archaeological data from Ireland and Britain. The negative impact has been an accentuation of the geographic inequalities in archaeological knowledge, with regions of the west and north especially under-represented. It is worth listening for these different stories because places and localities mattered. I disagree with Kristiansen and Larsson's (2005, 369) assessment that the study of localities brings a static and inward-looking perspective. The local and the distant mutually constituted one another, rather than representing separate, hierarchically organised and perhaps contrary realities. I introduced the terms 'insensitive landscape' and 'worlding' in Chapter 1 to describe the way that a study of localities is also a study of the world as it was.

A third way in which the book is distinct from other prehistories of the Bronze Age is my attention on kinship as the relations that connected people with one another and their worlds. Kinship is an aspect of how all humans inhabit and make worlds. Its ubiquity can confound attempts to define it. Like other elements within social life, place being one example, kinship varies markedly in how it is constituted by different societies. There are different research strategies for dealing with this variability. One is to reduce kinship to a quantifiable attribute—the genetic relations between humans created through sexual reproduction. A different position is to define kinship as a rich and inventive sphere of culture that incorporates biological relations but is not determined by them (Sahlins 2013). I have taken the second position.

My approach to kinship responds to the criticisms of relational theories in archaeology, that relational theory has exorcised depth and humanness from our narratives (Barrett 2016). I adopt kinship as a distinct form of relation, and kinwork as a distinct practice of relating with and amongst humans. Kinship can be discriminated from other forms of relatedness through degrees of intensity and mutuality. Kinship describes the close relations and practices of relating that constitute humans as persons and groups. These relations include those generated through procreation and established through creative acts of naming, gift exchange, sharing substances and co-presence. Kinship formed personhood and collective belonging, and associated people with nonhuman beings, things and landscapes. To recast Nigel Thrift's (1996, 92) formulation for relating society, space and time: social life was 'always and everywhere' kin.

Kinwork in Bronze Age worlds

My task with this concluding chapter is to connect the book's themes of Gifts, Dwellings and Landmarks within a single narrative for the period 2500–700 BC. I organise the narrative around six centuries in order to illustrate change across the span of the Bronze Age, without prioritising a single periodised chronology. The centuries are not chosen arbitrarily; they are in parts representative and in parts exceptional.

The twenty-fourth century brought continental populations and the widespread making, use and deposition of beaker pottery to Ireland and Britain. The twenty-first century marked a period of localisation as people's kinship with localities emerged and regions took on distinct characters in mortuary rites and ceramics. The seventeenth century BC witnessed a flourishing of circular monuments and associated mortuary rituals, together with the beginnings of widespread durable domestic buildings and rectilinear field systems. The domestic domain of kinship developed in importance over the remaining centuries of the Bronze Age. By the fourteenth century, settlement architecture was widespread and varied, with heterogenous kinship founded on people's relations with landscapes, settlements and through exchanges of gifts. By the eleventh century, settlements had acquired greater intensity and complexity, with imposing enclosures becoming powerful places for selective performances such as feasts. During the eighth century, and with the widespread availability of iron, the kinship created around metalwork exchange and prestigious feasting rituals was weakened, and new collective labour projects and prominent domestic settlements dominated social life.

Twenty-fourth century—worlds in flux

Social life underwent a period of profound disruption during the twenty-fourth century BC. The process began a few decades earlier. By the century's close, people were sourcing, working and wearing copper and gold, making and consuming food from beaker pottery, and choosing to bury some of the dead without cremation and in graves. People, things and ideas from Europe's lowlands were amongst the catalysts for these transformations. The process involved some degree of population replacement (in a genetic sense), with the timescale for this process currently unclear. A biological perspective contributes a lot to our understanding although alone it is insufficient. Objects in continental styles were crafted from Ireland and Britain's clay, stone and metal. The cultural and demographic catalysts were eastern. At the same time, copper and gold aligned people's worlds to the southwest of Ireland and Britain as metals became intrinsic substances in social life. The regional connections established during the twenty-fourth century changed lives and landscapes.

Novelties in culture, ethnicity, technology and language blended rapidly within Irish and British landscapes. There were not deep attachments between communities and territories or places. Large scatters of worked stone and pottery accumulated during periodic and short-lived settlement within locales throughout the third millennium BC. The shared consumption of food and drink, whether in settlements, at burnt mounds and at monuments brought dispersed and new kin together in a world characterised by mobility and a mutability of social life. People absorbed the flux of the wider world in daily life's routines and their inhabitations of landscapes. Beaker pottery rapidly and relatively widely became a part of how food was shared and consumed in domestic settings, and its close association with the kinwork of living together. These practices bound novel people and ideas through the intimacies of sharing food and co-presence. The mobilities and flux of twenty-fourth-century life offered the conditions for kin to be made afresh as readily from the familiar as from the unfamiliar.

Kinship's malleability emerged from the freedoms with which ideas, places, things and people could become entangled and separated. People were not closely bound to large group identities or territories. They understood the depth of their kinship in terms of the extent and richness of connections across landscapes and during gatherings, not through reference to histories of dead relations. Kinship was derived from contemporary connections amongst the living and with other worlds. The great circles and mounds gathered populations and materials from far and near. The times that people spent together in rituals, the labours and feasts they shared, and the gifts they exchanged formed kinship. Unfamiliar people, pottery and metals rapidly found associations in these places. The times when people were together and their journeys between places were important. The rare beaker inhumation burials during the twenty-fourth century BC were performances that gathered aspects of this diverse kinship, codified within a continental mortuary rite, and assembled persons for lives in another world. These were pauses during lives and worlds in flux.

Twenty-first century—forming ecologies with the dead

Over the course of two to three centuries, people of times increasingly became people of places. There was a process of localisation in a world that remained dense with long-distance connections and mobilities. The efficacy of the kin networks that stretched across Ireland, Britain and the near continent ensured that tin-bronze was rapidly and widely made, exchanged and deposited. Copper was sourced from west Wales and tin from southwest England, adding to the relations that had enabled copper and gold to circulate in the preceding centuries. Jet and faience joined a variety of substances that moved as gifts between kin and made persons. Strong regional distinctions in ceramics and mortuary traditions were in place by the twenty-first century. These included notable concentrations of beaker-accompanied burials in eastern regions of Britain, and the food vessel bowls in northern Ireland and northern Britain. Kinship was founded from associations within localities and by maintaining relations with more distant kin through journeys and gifts.

The process of localisation can be traced in varied ways. Sustained grazing of pastures and the longer-term management and clearance of woodland changed the ecologies within landscapes. These changes occurred as people returned routinely to familiar localities, while retaining aspects of seasonal or longer rhythms of residential relocation. The clearance of fieldstone from small, hand-dug plots created cairnfields. Cooking and crafts using burnt stone technology left troughs and mounds along stream and bog edges. These were examples of a dispersal of landmarking across the landscape. Small monuments composed from earth, timber and stone proliferated in many regions. Circles and mounds grew from materials near-at-hand: turf, clay, oak, chalk, granite and quartz found within short distances of the monuments. The varied rituals performed at monuments drew supernatural beings and energies associated with localities into kinwork.

The deposition of human inhumation and cremation burials contributed to the creation and transformation of monuments. Monuments and their localities gathered generations of the dead into remembered and mythical histories. Burials were positioned vertically above one another and in horizontal arrangements that allowed for different orderings within kinship narratives. Kinship was made from narrative histories and the places with which those histories were associated. The intrinsic qualities of locality and distance are vividly represented by burials such as Gristhorpe, North Yorkshire, where an elderly man's kin marked his death with elaborate burial rites, grave goods and a prominent monument (Melton et al. 2013). The man's body bore the traces of a life as a craftworker, a rich diet and illness late in life that impaired his speech and movement. The bronze dagger and the oak trunk coffin marked the man's burial as unusual, and comparable with the treatment of small numbers of other individuals in Britain around this time. The careful wrapping of the body in cattle hide and the double ribband placed across the man's lower breast were tendernesses born of familiarity. Persons, however senior and skilled, drew their kinship from their near community and their more distant associations. The burial drew these different relations together into a large earth barrow on an exposed headland overlooking the North Sea.

Seventeenth century—honouring with lines

Across four centuries, complex cemeteries and composite mounds had landmarked many regions. The more regularly arranged barrow groups formed distinct lines that structured narratives of kinship and legitimised claims on authority. History and place mattered in the constitution of kinship. Barrows, cemeteries and circles inhabited the pastures that livestock grazed. The dead, named and mythologised, maintained a co-presence with the living. Cremation was commonplace during mortuary rites, with ceramic vessels, bags and pits used for containing the cremated bone. Cremation transformed the substance of the body. Cremated bone could be curated and incorporated with other substances. The quantities of cremated bone buried in graves decreased as it became more common to disperse bodies between locations. Ring cairns and stone circles were places to where cremated bone was carried and deposited. Cremated bone was one of the substances that people exchanged during their ongoing negotiations with places.

Houses brought new spaces and things into the formation of kinship during the seventeenth century. Small round and oval buildings had been features of people's lives in earlier centuries. The insubstantiality of most structures meant that they did not endure as landmarks. From the seventeenth century, materials and labours assembled larger, more robust structures, which unambiguously played important roles in the formation of settlements. High timbers, deep stone walls and sheltering turves created monuments for the living. Routines of daily life stabilised within and around the buildings. Someone's kinship depended on which spaces they occupied and the tasks they undertook. Houses hardened the relations within settlements and made the settlement a fixed place and a distinct identifier within social life. Kindred's associations with localities were becoming defined through the presence of the living kin and their houses, and less through the gifts left within barrows and cairns. Early houses, while more durable than their predecessors, did not immediately disrupt the established domestic configurations and rhythms of settlement and mobility. Houses were isolated in seasonally grazed uplands and by lakeshores, and paired together amongst fields that were cultivated and grazed year-round.

Other domains of kinwork retained greater influence than domestic life on people's kinship. Feasts and craftworking continued at burnt mounds, in places set apart from houses. The elaborate costumes that accompanied some grave assemblages hint at the richness and idiosyncrasies of status and rituals. Heavily worn, often fragmentary objects, such as the shale and amber cups or the fragments of gold from the Mold cape, were communal heirlooms that created powerful kinship through the sharing of substances and their access to supernatural beings and worlds. People could trace their kin directly and by associations across Ireland, Britain and onto the European mainland. The seas retained their importance as flows rather than as barriers. The linear field systems that began appearing in southern Britain during the seventeenth century BC related people to the land as it was known and organised through barrows and monuments, and not how it was settled by houses. The linear fields honoured the land's animacy and the histories of generations buried in its monuments, and not in the tasks and co-presences around houses. Fields organised livestock and cultivation, and relied upon powerful and successful relations amongst groups and with supernatural realms. Houses had little influence on these relations. For the moment, kinwork around settlements lacked influence upon the more powerful domains of kinship in land and gift exchange. This imbalance gradually changed.

Fourteenth century—a kaleidoscope of relations

Kinship was at its most heterogenous during the fourteenth century BC, with powerful kin made in landscapes, settlements and through exchanges of gifts across long distances and with other worlds. By the early fourteenth century, houses, settlements and field systems had been shaping some landscapes for two or three hundred years. In southern Britain, linear field systems hardened the land, and ordered the routines and relations of agricultural life: where animals moved, grazed and drank from water sources, the spaces for crops and for dwellings. Kinship categories emerged from these extensive networks of boundaries and the associations they created between people and land's supernatural agencies. This kinship between people of a locality and the land was maintained in different ways: the sub-divisions of fields, the recutting of ditches, the offerings made within waterholes and the gifts of metalwork and human and animal burials in boundaries. There was not a simple nesting of households within localities. Localities and co-resident-kindred derived their kinship from different associations and practices, and they retained different forms of authority within social life.

Kinship derived from living together in settlements grew in importance within social life. This occurred in different ways: through aggregation, as houses clustered within groups; duration, with the inhabitation of the same locales by several generations of kin; and definition, as boundaries were placed around settlements, sometimes sufficient to form defensive barriers. These processes of aggregation, longevity and enclosure sometimes occurred together at a settlement, as at Chancellorsland, County Limerick (Doody 2008). The concentric enclosures at Meyllteyrn Uchaf, Gwynedd, enclosed a pair of roundhouses and sufficient space where livestock might be penned and grazed close to the buildings (Ward and Smith 2001). Aggregation and enclosure responded to a variety of local circumstances, such as vendettas and supernatural hazards, rather than reflecting the adoption of a particular identity or status. Aggregation, longevity and enclosure brought transformations to the kinwork within settlements. Where people lived and with whom they shared their lives, their kindred, combined to become a more powerful identifier in social life.

Personal and collective kinship was also formed through the gifts that people exchanged during longer journeys and in the offerings made in the landscape. The offerings give us glimpses of the ways that identities were made with things: gold and bronze body ornaments that carried associations with localities and continental customs; spears, rapiers and shields composed a warrior aesthetic and gave persons agency through violence. These objects were critical in the ways that people made kinship with supernatural beings. The metalwork deposited in rivers and bogs was dominated by spearheads and blades. Small groups of body ornaments were frequently deposited during the fourteenth century in

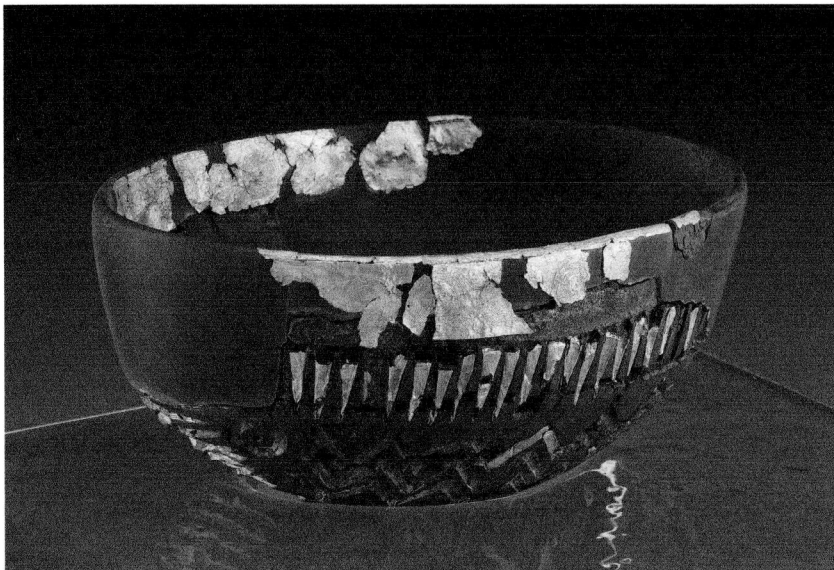

FIGURE 8.1 The Caergwrle bowl. The vessel is 177 mm in length and 75 mm in height. Copyright: National Museum of Wales.

southern Britain. The metalwork and the manner of its deposition associated people within European networks and traditions.

The idiosyncrasies of rituals that characterised earlier centuries were less apparent during the fourteenth century. The bowl uncovered when workers excavated a drain through a boggy field at Caergwrle, Flintshire, may be an exception (Davis and Townsend 2009). The bowl is oval like a coracle, with traverse lines carved into the base denoting wooden ribs and three deeply incised, wave-like lines, inlaid with gold, decorating the lower section (Figure 8.1). Coracles are simple vessels for one or two people. The Caergwrle vessel had grander, perhaps magical pretensions. Rows of blades (whether oars or weapons), each an elongated triangular piece of tin wrapped in a thin layer of ribbed gold, are arranged above the zigzag pattern. A broad strip of gold-covered tin capped the upper part of the vessel, carefully engraved with discs, similar to shields. It was a 'war coracle' for other worlds. The vessel took its life from the pair of engraved ocular circles looking out from the lower 'prow'. The kin who drank together from the vessel gained from the journeys that it made into other worlds.

Eleventh century—performance and alchemy

The personal and political merged with the domestic realms of kinwork during the eleventh century BC as settlements supported diverse activities and sometimes provided the settings for performances. Pottery production, saltmaking and textile processing occurred in and close to buildings. Four-post structures may have allowed grain and fodder to be stored and displayed amongst the houses. There were some specialisations in the crafts that settlements produced, which gave kindred particular roles amongst networks of surrounding settlements. This was not commodified exchange nor were there regional authorities controlling production. Kinship categories emerged from where people lived, with whom they shared their lives, and the things that they made.

Metalworking was an unusual craft because it ordinarily happened on the margins of settlement areas. The practices, substances and persons that constituted metalworking operated in relations of otherness, physically removed and existentially separated from the kinship within settlements. Metalworking debris could be incorporated within the fabric of places at the margins of settlements. The potency of the craft and its substances could not be contained within the spaces of everyday life. The exceptions in this pattern were hilltop enclosures and ringworks, where metalworking sometimes occurred within the enclosures. The enclosures could include elements familiar from settlements, with roundhouses, and middens of broken pottery and animal bone. The enclosures were not domestic settlements. They alluded to domestic life while emerging from more specialised, selective and performative kinwork. They took prominent landscape positions, occupying landmarks or close to the principal routes along which people travelled (Figure 8.2). They were enclosed by monumental boundaries, including water-filled ditches and by occupying islands. The feasts, exchanges and co-presences within the enclosures created powerful kinship. They may have formed a distinct cadre within social life, which comprised persons with access to

FIGURE 8.2 George Petrie's painting of Dún Aonghasa, Árainn, evokes the spectacle of the stone fort's setting on land's edge. Photo © National Gallery of Ireland.

and the means (in kinship and through gifts to exchange) to participate in gatherings. The participants were familiar and unfamiliar. Wonderful and magical objects may have played their roles, with the bronze cups, large vessels and flesh hooks likely to be present during some occasions. Persons and things re-entered the world beyond the enclosures with their kinship transformed.

The eleventh-century world was made through cycles of fragmentation, dispersal, exchange and amalgamation. Destruction played a part in the transformation and formation of substances and in processes of exchange, and therefore in the making of kin. Mortuary rites transformed the human dead into parts of unburnt and cremated bone that were deposited in a variety of places, including small amounts within settlements and in middens. Objects made from bronze and more rarely gold, amber and jet were deliberately broken before their exchanges between people and with supernatural beings. Landmarks were created through first the labours of building large enclosures and then the energies needed to burn their palisades to the ground. Places, things and persons were composed from fragments of others. In a world saturated with meanings, an alchemy of complex and fragmented exchanges created kinship.

Eighth century—a world made in decay

The domestic domain of kinwork broadened and increased its importance in social life by the eighth century BC. Many kindred lived in small clusters of roundhouses, with provision for storing grain and fodder adjacent to the houses. A return to decorating pottery used in daily life across southern and midland Britain offered differentiations between practices, persons and substances within settlements. Enclosure was becoming widespread in Britain, both around small aggregations of roundhouses and on the grander scale of ramparts and palisades enclosing hilltops and promontories. The hilltop enclosures included communities who were resident together for part or all of the year. The communal labour that gathered to build hilltop enclosures found different expressions in the creation of linear boundaries and pit alignments, and in the accumulations of large middens. The trajectory in Ireland, characterised broadly, provides an exception with a marked decline in settlements after the mid-ninth century BC.

The large-scale accumulation of domestic debris occurred within some enclosures and riverine islands during the tenth to eighth centuries BC. In the eighth century, comparable middens began accumulating across substantial areas in open settlements, with examples identified in southern and midland England and south Wales (Waddington et al. 2019). At their most monumental, the middens became broad mounds, two or three hectares in extent and with several metres' depth of material—food, animal bone and manure, broken pottery, metalworking debris and human bone. The middens grew during year-round settlement and seasonal aggregations of people and livestock. Animals were corralled, butchered and feasted on in large numbers, with differences in the species and forms of husbandry depending on the location. The deposits merged the residues of different facets of domestic and ritual life, from every-days and fair-days, into a compound that celebrated the vibrancy of communal kinwork. They were fragments of the world collected and given to the land—a world made in decay.

The middens shared the fragmentary character although not the selective characteristics of the votive offerings made with metalwork during the preceding few centuries. The places where the middens accumulated also lacked the restrictive and imposing architecture of earlier enclosures. The more performative and politically selective forms of kinship were formed elsewhere or without the same spatial distinctions as before. The eighth century brought a wider acceptance of and access to iron as an everyday material. The votive offerings of bronze metalwork declined during the century. Iron's availability transformed the kinship that had been created and sustained through bronze exchange. By the eighth century, bronze was moving in carefully choreographed exchanges, with objects sometimes cast especially for the occasions. This formality found its richest expression in the identical tin-bronze axes found in groups in Wessex and northwest France. The large deposits of identical axes, most impressively at Langton Matravers (Roberts et al. 2015), occurred when the choreographed exchanges that had made kinship between persons moved to new domains. The axes became gifts to gods. Briefly, a new, supernatural kinship was required in response to uncertain times.

Other worlds, different kin

My account of kinship during the twenty-fourth to eighth centuries BC identifies long-term processes that transformed social life. Localisation describes the process through which people increasingly belonged to landscapes and places. This occurred alongside and shaped the growing distinctions between regions in Ireland and Britain. A gradual empowerment of relations within domestic life occurred as houses replaced monuments as landmarks. This process progressed at different rates depending on how people dwelt in landscapes. For some regions, aspects of domestic life, including sharing food and craft, took on public and selective roles in kinwork within ringworks and enclosures. The performative and public aspects of kinwork were founded on relations with the supernatural, in personal and communal rituals, and in acts of raiding, collective labour and feasting.

Archaeology is gaining new perspectives on the relations that textured social life. We are presently benefiting from new capacities in the life sciences to understand the lifeways of human and animal populations. Palaeogenetics and isotopic analyses have proved especially influential in the past decade as research has given unprecedented clarity to accounts of population mobility and replacement within Eurasia during the third millennium BC. These methods are now being turned to regional studies, the examination of individual cemeteries, the reconstruction of diet and the recognition of disease. We are on an exciting journey towards a richer account of human life in prehistory. Kinship is emerging again in archaeological discourse, largely shaped by biological data. Palaeogeneticists and archaeologists are reviving concepts such as family and lineage, and practices of matri- and patrilocality. The risk is that the models from which these terms are derived constrain our narratives within the limits of the genealogical method. And kinship returns as a synonym for biological relatedness, despite the immense breadth of cultural enquiries that have demonstrated otherwise. Kinship is more complex, interesting and important than the genealogical method alone can accommodate.

I will conclude by returning to the community hall in 1982 at Haines Junction, southern Yukon, where I started this chapter: 'Where do these people come from?' Mrs Annie Ned asked the assembled academic researchers and elders. She was referring to the researchers. 'Outside? You people talk from paper' (Cruikshank 2005, 76). Annie Ned's instruction was to listen for different stories. *Listening for* is more acute, attentive and searching. It reaches beyond the familiar and acknowledges other ways of knowing. The Bronze Age comprised worlds unlike our own. A social prehistory composes these other worlds from different kin.

References

Barrett, John C. 2016. The new antiquarianism? *Antiquity* 90(354):1681–1686.

Bradley, Richard, Colin Haselgrove, Marc Vander Linden and Leo Webley. 2016. *The later prehistory of north-west Europe: the evidence of development-led fieldwork*. Oxford University Press, Oxford.

Cruikshank, Julie. 2005. *Do glaciers listen? Local knowledge, colonial encounters and social imagination*. UBC Press, Vancouver.

Davis, Mary and Annette Townsend. 2009. Modelling the Caergwrle Bowl: ancient, historic and modern methods. In *Holding it all together: ancient and modern approaches to joining, repair and consolidation*, edited by Janet Ambers, Catherine Higgitt, Lynne Harrison and David Saunders, pp. 177–183. Archetype, London.

Doody, Martin. 2008. *The Ballyhoura Hills Project*. Wordwell, Bray.

Kristiansen, Kristian and Thomas Larsson. 2005. *The rise of Bronze Age society: travels, transmissions and transformations*. Cambridge University Press, Cambridge.

Lehoërff, Anne and Marc Talon (editors). 2017. *Movement, exchange and identity in Europe in the 2nd and 1st millennia BC: beyond frontiers* Oxbow, Oxford.

Melton, Nigel, Janet Montgomery and Christopher Knüsel (editors). 2013. *Gristhorpe Man: a life and death in the Bronze Age*. Oxbow, Oxford.

Needham, Stuart. 1996. Chronology and periodisation in the British Bronze Age. *Acta Archaeologica* 67:121–140.

Roberts, Benjamin, Dorothee Boughton, Michael Dinwiddy, Nisha Doshi, Andrew P Fitzpatrick, Duncan Hook, Nigel Meeks, Aude Mongiatti, Ann Woodward and Peter J Woodward. 2015. Collapsing commodities or lavish offerings? Understanding massive metalwork deposition at Langton Matravers, Dorset during the Bronze Age–Iron Age transition. *Oxford Journal of Archaeology* 34(4):365–395.

Sahlins, Marshall. 2013. *What kinship is—and is not*. University of Chicago Press, Chicago.

Thrift, Nigel. 1996. *Spatial formations*. Sage, London.

Waddington, Kate, Alex Bayliss, Thomas Higham, Richard Madgwick and Niall Sharples. 2019. Histories of deposition: creating chronologies for the Late Bronze Age–Early Iron Age transition in southern Britain. *Archaeological Journal* 176(1):84–133.

Ward, Michael and George Smith. 2001. The Llŷn Crop Marks Project. Aerial survey and ground evaluation of Bronze Age and Romano-British settlement and funerary sites in the Llŷn Peninsula of north west Wales: excavations by Richard Kelly and Michael Ward. *Studia Celtica* 35:1–87.

Whittle, Alasdair. 2018. *The times of their lives: hunting history in the archaeology of Neolithic Europe.* Oxbow, Oxford.

INDEX

Note: *Italic* page numbers refer to figures.

MYTHS &
LEGENDS
ABOUT
KRAKOW

1 A man-eating dragon once lived in a cave beneath Wawel Castle—he supposedly exploded after eating a sheep filled with sulfur. **1**

2 The "Smok Wawelski" dragon statue by the Vistula River actually breathes real fire—activated by SMS. Not a joke. **2**

3 St. Mary's Church has two unequal towers because two brothers competed—one murdered the other. **3**

4 A trumpeter plays every hour from the tower but abruptly stops the tune—to honor a guard shot mid-signal. **4**

5 A river of tears from sacrificed maidens supposedly flows beneath Krakow. **5**

6 As a child, Pope John Paul II is said to have explored the dragon's cave with friends—playing dragon hunter. **6**

7 The mighty Sigismund Bell grants wishes—if you touch it at the first strike. **7**

8 A Polish king is buried in a side altar—allegedly without his head. **8**

9 A buried treasure lies beneath Kazimierz—but it's cursed. **9**

10 A herbal witch allegedly fought the plague with garlic, vodka, and powdered toad. **10**

11 A falling wine barrel in the royal cellar is said to foretell regime changes. **11**

12 A white knight made of salt supposedly appears when Poland is in danger. **12**

13   A mysterious stone on the market square must not be moved—or risk the wrath of spirits.   **13**

14   Ghostly monks are said to fly over the city on brooms once a year.   **14**

15   In one of the oldest houses in the Old Town, a bricked-up window is said to have belonged to a witch who cursed people from it.   **15**

16 In Nowa Huta, there was once a bell that rang by itself when someone in the neighborhood died – it was later removed for being "too accurate." **16**

17 In the Wieliczka Salt Mines near Krakow, the ghosts of former miners are said to guard the tunnels – especially when tourists try to steal salt. **17**

18 Visitors to the Barbican, Krakow's old city gate, often report hearing "voices" at night – despite the halls being empty. **18**

19 Parts of Krakow's city wall were never completed – a superstition says the city would fall if the wall was ever closed. **19**

20 At the Słowacki Theatre, a former actor is said to haunt the building – he died during a performance and has since been seen as a shadow figure. **20**

21 Beneath the artificial lake in Nowa Huta lies a buried church – supposedly flooded during construction to prevent religious uprisings under communism. **21**

CURIOSITIES
&
HISTORY

22 The Cloth Hall on the Main Square was the first shopping mall in Europe during the Middle Ages. **22**

23 Krakow's Main Square is one of the largest medieval squares in Europe – 200 by 200 meters. **23**

24 Beneath the Main Square lies a modern museum showcasing real excavations of the medieval city. **24**

25 Floriańska Street was once Krakow's most splendid street – part of the royal coronation route. **25**

26 The Barbican – the round defensive tower in front of the city wall – once hosted knight tournaments. **26**

27 The Planty Park encircles the Old Town – where the city wall once stood, there's now a green haven. **27**

28 The oldest street in Krakow is Kanonicza Street – once home only to clergy members. **28**

29 The tower of St. Mary's Basilica is a Krakow landmark – but only the left tower is open to the public. **29**

30 Wawel Hill was settled over 1,000 years ago – one of Poland's oldest royal seats. **30**

31

The Wawel Castle has a secret underground tunnel that once served as an escape route.

31

32

The Sigismund Bell tower has walls that are 10 meters thick.

32

33

In the courtyard of the Jagiellonian University, every whisper echoes to the farthest corner.

33

34 In Krakow, there's a street with no houses: "Ulica Bracka" just ends in nothing. **34**

35 The Collegium Maius has a clock with moving figures that dance daily at 1 p.m. **35**

36 The Wawel Cathedral was once rumored to contain a stone with extraterrestrial energy. **36**

37 Benches around the Main Square play classical music when you sit on them. **37**

38 There's a lantern in the Old Town said to never go out – an eternal light of love. **38**

39 The Franciscan Church has stained glass windows made from Murano glass – a gift from Venice. **39**

40 The Town Hall tower bears not a rooster but a knife – as a warning to traitors. **40**

41 On Sławkowska Street stands Krakow's oldest inn – where even Goethe once drank. **41**

42 The "Window Without a Wall" is a famous optical illusion on a house near Wawel Hill. **42**

SECRETS, LEGENDS & SUPERSTITION IN KRAKÓW

43 In St. Mary's Church, a trumpeter plays a tune every hour – abruptly ending. Legend says the first trumpeter was struck by an arrow. **43**

44 It's said that a dragon lived in a cave under Wawel – once threatening Krakow. **44**

45 The Wawel Dragon was supposedly defeated by a cobbler's apprentice using a clever trick. **45**

46 It is believed that beneath Wawel lies an Earth Chakra – a place of mystical energy. **46**

47 An old legend says Krakow was founded by King Krak – after he killed the dragon. **47**

48 In the Old Town, there's a house whose window always stays shut – said to be haunted. **48**

49 A legend tells of two brothers building St. Mary's towers – one murdered the other. **49**

50 The Vistula River was once said to carry golden fish – a sign of luck and wealth. **50**

51 In Wawel's crypt lie Polish kings – some believe their spirits watch over the city. **51**

52 Many believe there's a secret underground tunnel system under Krakow – reaching even to the Tatras. **52**

53 The "Stone of Misfortune" in Planty Park is said to bring bad luck to anyone who touches it. **53**

54 A white lady is said to appear at night in a fountain near the Franciscan Church. **54**

55 Those who get lost at night in Rakowicki Cemetery supposedly hear whispers from the graves. **55**

56 An old Krakow tradition is to toss coins into the fountain at the Main Square – for a wish. **56**

57 In an alley near Wawel Cathedral, there's a supposedly cursed door knocker. **57**

58 During storms, people in Krakow avoid old church towers – due to alleged demon lightning strikes. **58**

59 Some pilgrims believe that touching the wall of the Dominican monastery brings healing. **59**

60 Legend says a treasure is hidden in a house in Kleparz – guarded by a sleeping dog. **60**

61 Some claim to hear singing from the past at night in front of the Barbican. **61**

62 The Wawel Dragon at the Vistula Riverbank breathes real fire – every 15 minutes. **62**

63 In Krakow, it's believed that carrying a coin in your pocket during exams brings luck. **63**

FOOD, DRINK & CULINARY TRADITIONS

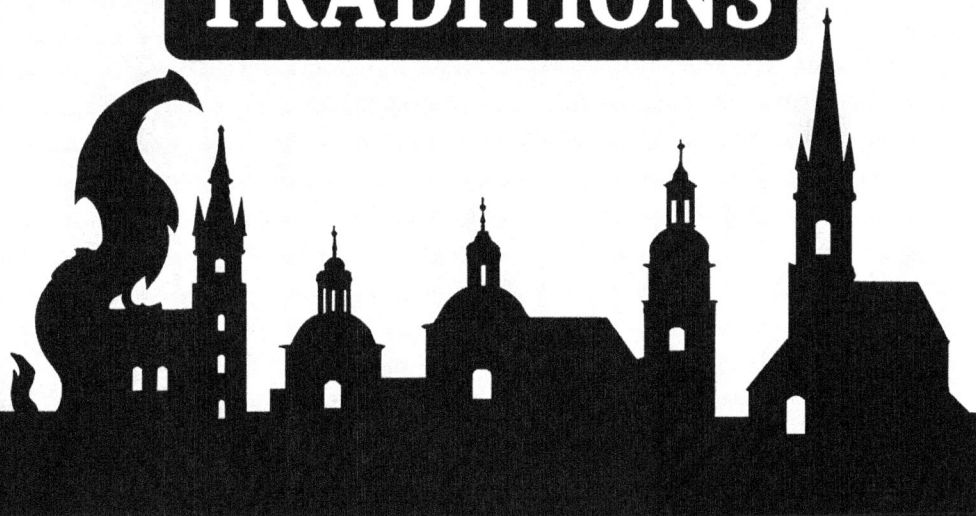

64 The "Obwarzanek Krakowski" – a ring-shaped bread – is the city's unofficial symbol. **64**

65 Pierogi – stuffed dumplings – are a national dish and especially popular in Krakow. **65**

66 Krakow has its own culinary traditions: dishes like "Zurek" (sour rye soup) are classics. **66**

67 "Zapiekanka" – a baked baguette – is Krakow's street food, especially popular at Plac Nowy. **67**

68 In Krakow, sauerkraut, beets, and mushrooms are traditional staples. **68**

69 Krakow's cuisine blends Polish, Jewish, Austrian, and Hungarian influences. **69**

70 "Barszcz" – a beetroot soup – is often served with small dumplings (Uszka). **70**

71 The dessert "Sernik" – a creamy cheesecake – is especially loved in Krakow. **71**

72 Many restaurants in Krakow serve seasonal game dishes – like venison or wild boar. **72**

73 In Krakow's Old Town, you can try kosher specialties – especially in the Jewish district Kazimierz. **73**

74 Krakow locals enjoy "Kompot" – a sweet fruit drink made from boiled fruits. **74**

75 Polish vodka is also very popular in Krakow – often served in small glasses and ice-cold. **75**

76

Many Old Town cellars house traditional restaurants with vaulted ceilings.

76

77

"Stary Kleparz" is one of Krakow's oldest food markets – offering fresh fruit, vegetables, and cheese.

77

78

Krakow has many "milk bars" ("Bar Mleczny") – cheap restaurants serving traditional home-style food.

78

79 A traditional Krakow feast begins with soup – usually Zurek or Barszcz. **79**

80 A typical Krakow specialty is "Kielbasa z grilla" – grilled sausage sold at street stands. **80**

81 Many cafés serve traditional poppy seed cake ("Makowiec"). **81**

82 Krakow locals enjoy fruit liqueurs like Wiśniówka (cherry liqueur) – often as a digestif. **82**

83 Many places also serve vegetarian versions of classic dishes. **83**

84 In Krakow, breakfast is often hearty – with bread, cheese, eggs, and sausage. **84**

NATURE, PARKS & RECREATION

85 The Vistula, Poland's longest river, flows right through Krakow. **85**

86 The Planty Park surrounds the Old Town like a green belt on the former city walls. **86**

87 The Krakus Mound offers one of the best panoramic views of Krakow. **87**

88 There are over 40 large parks and green spaces in Krakow. **88**

89 Jordan Park is one of the oldest and most popular city parks. **89**

90 You can walk, jog, or cycle along the Vistula riverbanks. **90**

91 Twardowski Rock Park is a nature reserve with an old legend. **91**

92 Las Wolski (Wolski Forest) is a vast forest area in western Krakow. **92**

93 The Krakow Zoo is also located in the Wolski Forest. **93**

94 The Kościuszko Mound is an artificial hill with a great view. **94**

95 Lake Bagry is a popular spot for swimming, sailing, and relaxing. **95**

96 Zakrzówek Lake lies in a former quarry and features turquoise water. **96**

97 The Botanical Garden of the Jagiellonian University is the oldest in Poland (since 1783). **97**

98 Lasek Mogilski is a natural forest area on the eastern edge of the city. **98**

99 The Krakow Zoo houses over 1,400 animals from more than 270 species. **99**

100 Krakow hosts several urban gardening projects in parks and courtyards. **100**

101 Many parks in Krakow offer free outdoor fitness equipment. **101**

102 Park Lotników is a modern recreational park with playgrounds, a skate park, and relaxation zones. **102**

103 The Dębniki meadows on the southern Vistula bank offer peaceful walks with a view of Wawel. **103**

104 Krakow has its own beekeeping project – with urban beehives on rooftops. **104**

105 The city promotes biodiversity through flower meadows in public green areas. **105**

FAMOUS
PEOPLE
&
CURIOUS
STORIES
FROM KRAKOW

106 Pope John Paul II was Archbishop of Krakow before becoming pope in 1978. **106**

107 Oskar Schindler, known from "Schindler's List", saved over 1,000 Jews – his factory still stands in Krakow. **107**

108 The famous scientist Nicolaus Copernicus studied at the Jagiellonian University. **108**

109 Helena Rubinstein, the cosmetics pioneer, was born in Krakow in 1872. **109**

110 Poet Wisława Szymborska received the Nobel Prize in Literature in 1996 and lived in Krakow until her death. **110**

111 The Wawel Dragon was supposedly defeated by a poor shoemaker – with a sheep filled with sulfur. **111**

112 The Krakow Lajkonik, a man in Tatar costume on a wooden horse, stars in an annual parade. **112**

113 Polish King Sigismund III had a huge bell cast in Krakow – it weighs over 11 tons. **113**

114 The "Zygmunt" Bell at Wawel rings only on very special occasions. **114**

115 Famous actor Daniel Olbrychski is from Krakow. **115**

116 Kraka, a legendary princess, is said to have founded the city. **116**

117 Polish film director Andrzej Wajda, an Oscar winner, was born in Krakow. **117**

118 Opera singer Ada Sari, famous in the 1930s, was born in Krakow. **118**

119 Krakow has a Museum of Galician Jewish Culture. **119**

120 The legendary medieval alchemist Sendivogius is said to have worked in Krakow. **120**

121

The famous composer Krzysztof Penderecki lived and taught in Krakow.

121

122

Former Queen Bona Sforza brought many Italian influences to Krakow.

122

123

Polish writer Stanisław Lem ("Solaris") lived for many years in Krakow.

123

124 Karol Wojtyła (John Paul II) worked as a young man in a quarry in Zakrzówek. **124**

125 Poet Adam Zagajewski was a major literary voice of modern Krakow. **125**

126 The legendary wizard Twardowski is said to have made a pact with the devil – and supposedly lived in Krakow. **126**

CULINARY KRAKÓW

—

FOOD & DRINK

127 The "Obwarzanek" – round twisted bread rings – are Krakow street food classics. **127**

128 The oldest recipe for Obwarzanek dates back to 1394. **128**

129 Zapiekanka, a toasted half-baguette, became a popular meal during communism. **129**

130 The best place for Zapiekanka is Plac Nowy in the Kazimierz district. **130**

131 Krakow is famous for its sausage stands – especially at night. **131**

132 The "Kiełbaski z Nyski" van has been selling sausages from an old car for decades. **132**

133 Pierogi – filled dumplings – come in sweet, savory, or vegetarian varieties. **133**

134 The most popular type of Pierogi are filled with potatoes and cheese (Ruskie). **134**

135 Krakow's cheesecake is often much fluffier than German versions. **135**

136 Barszcz czerwony – a beetroot soup – is often served with dumplings in Krakow. **136**

137 Żurek, a sour rye soup with sausage, is a Krakow comfort food. **137**

138 In Krakow, people often drink from clay mugs – especially during festivals. **138**

139 Oscypek, a smoked cheese from the Tatra mountains, is also popular at Krakow's markets. **139**

140 Krakow offers many vegan alternatives to traditional dishes. **140**

141 Many traditional recipes in Krakow come from Jewish cuisine. **141**

142 Krakow's cuisine blends Polish, Hungarian, Austrian, and Jewish influences. **142**

143 At the Rynek there is a "chocolate street" with several chocolate cafés. **143**

144 Krakow has many traditional bakeries with handmade pastries. **144**

145 Galaretka – a meat jelly – is an acquired taste and a Krakow classic. **145**

146 Raw beef tartare is popular even in fine Krakow restaurants. **146**

147 The people of Krakow love tea almost as much as coffee – often with lemon and sugar. **147**

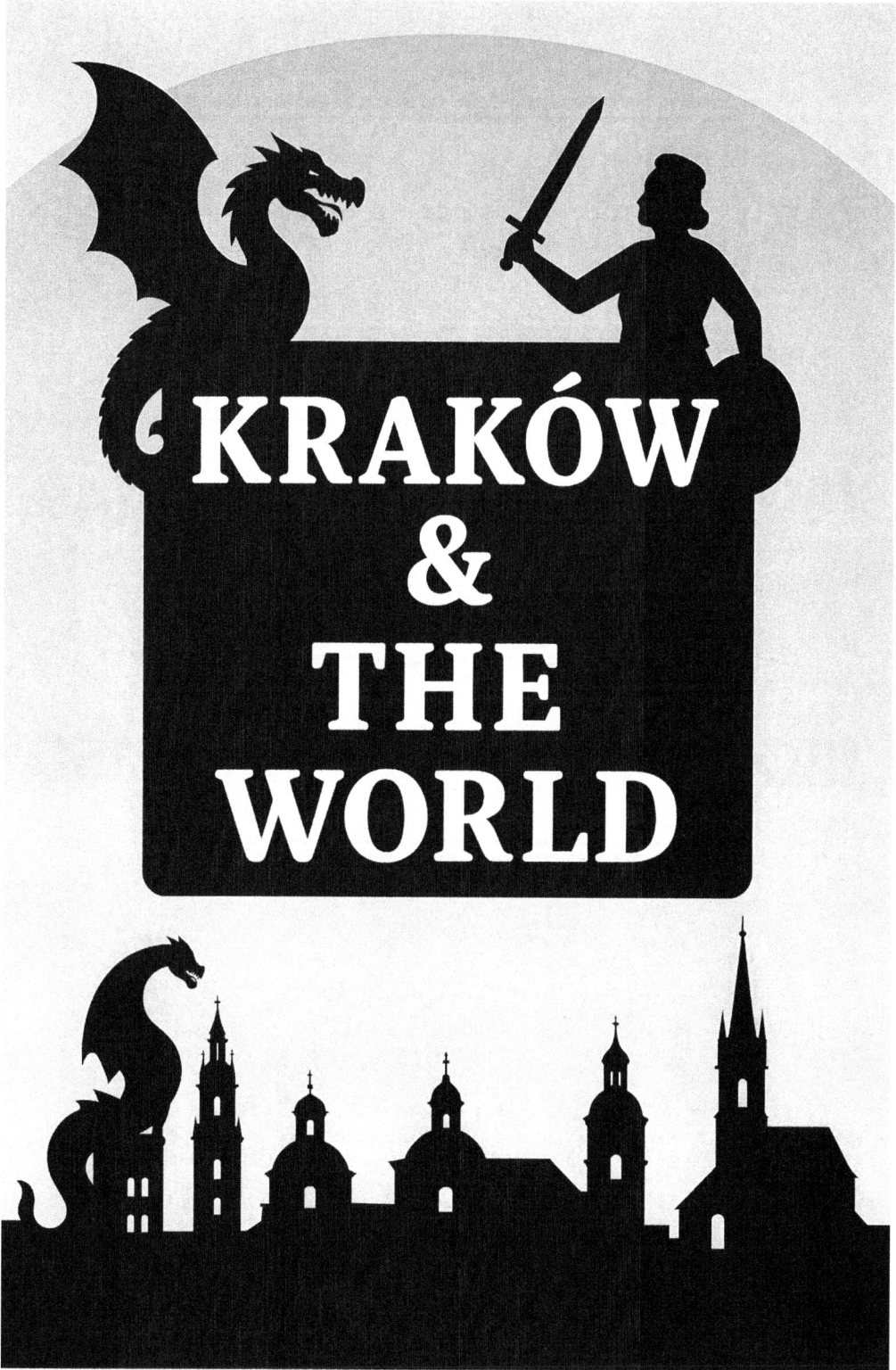

148 Krakow has been a UNESCO World Heritage Site since 1978. **148**

149 Krakow was European Capital of Culture in 2000. **149**

150 The city is twinned with Nuremberg, Rochester, Lviv, Bordeaux, and many others. **150**

151 The Jagiellonian University attracts students from over 80 countries. **151**

152 The Pope's visit in 1979 made Krakow internationally famous. **152**

153 Krakow has over 30 international sister cities around the world. **153**

154 Over 1 million foreign tourists visit Krakow every year. **154**

155 Krakow Airport is one of the fastest-growing in Eastern Europe. **155**

156 The city hosts many international conferences and trade fairs. **156**

157

Krakow hosted World Youth Day in 2016 with over 2 million visitors.

157

158

The famous film "Schindler's List" was partly filmed in Krakow.

158

159

Many people in Krakow speak fluent English, especially in the city center.

159

160 The city is known for its openness toward international students. **160**

161 Krakow is a member of the UNESCO City of Literature network. **161**

162 Many cafés in Krakow offer menus in English, German or French. **162**

163 Krakow cooperates closely with the EU on cultural funding projects. **163**

164 The city has hosted multiple international film and jazz festivals. **164**

165 Krakow's Christmas market attracts many international visitors every year. **165**

166 Krakow actively supports international cultural exchange, e.g. with Japan, Israel, and France. **166**

167 The "Kraków Live" festival brings international music stars to the city every year. **167**

168 Krakow is considered one of Poland's most international cities – culturally, academically, and in tourism. **168**

CURIOSITIES
&
FUN FACTS
ABOUT
CITY LIFE

169 Krakow is said to have more pigeons than people – at least, that's what some locals claim. **169**

170 In Krakow, some pedestrian lights show female figures – as a symbol of equality. **170**

171 Students throw coins into a fountain at the Jagiellonian University – for luck in exams. **171**

172 On Plac Nowy, cheese is sold during the day – at night, it's party time with Zapiekanka. **172**

173 Krakow has a bar located entirely inside a former public toilet. **173**

174 Many street corners have small religious figures in niches – some with LED lighting. **174**

175

There's a café in Krakow inhabited entirely by cats – and yes, they're allowed on the tables.

175

176

Krakow locals often wear sneakers even in winter – yes, even below freezing.

176

177

Krakow's pub density rivals Berlin's – especially in the Kazimierz district.

177

178 Some ticket machines are only in Polish – a real puzzle for tourists. **178**

179 The "Red Double-Decker" is a pub – and also a real London bus. **179**

180 Krakow has its own craft beer scene – with brews like "Smok" or "Wawel IPA." **180**

181
A cinnamon bun café in Krakow sells only five varieties daily – usually sold out by afternoon.
181

182
On Plac Szczepański there's a modern glass toilet – fully transparent until you lock the door.
182

183
Many bakeries hand out free candy with your order – just because.
183

184 There's a café that changes theme daily – from jazz bar to board game night. **184**

185 It's said that Wawel Hill attracts strange dreamers and mystics – due to its "energy." **185**

186 Most Krakow locals drink their coffee black – milk is often seen as unnecessary. **186**

187 Le café «Alchemia» possède une porte secrète menant à une autre salle – presque magique. **187**

188 On peut garer les trottinettes électriques partout en centre-ville – même en plein trottoir. **188**

189 Les magasins cracoviens adorent les autocollants de prix – même sur les bananes, les petits pains et le chocolat. **189**

THE 21 CRAZIEST, MOST USELESS & SURPRISING KRAKOW FACTS

190 Krakow has a church with a crooked tower – but no one knows when or why it tilted. **190**

191 The city council officially keeps a collection of lost gloves. **191**

192 Once a year, Krakow holds a parade in honor of... nothing – it's pure tradition. **192**

193 There's a street officially named "Street Without a Name." **193**

194 Some locals claim Krakow has its own microclimate – especially during romantic dates. **194**

195 A park in Krakow features a monument to a... shoe. **195**

196 The longest recorded Zapiekanka in Krakow was over 1.5 meters long. **196**

197 Krakow has an "invisible" café – with a completely darkened interior. **197**

198 A lecture on "Useless Knowledge" at the university drew over 500 attendees. **198**

199 There's a Krakow club where entry is only granted in pajamas. **199**

200 A city fountain once accidentally played techno music for six hours straight. **200**

201 Krakow has a cinema where you lie in beds instead of sitting in chairs. **201**

202 There's an alley so narrow that two Krakow locals allegedly got married there – without moving. **202**

203 A survey revealed: The most-missed smell in Krakow is that of Obwarzanek. **203**

204 Krakow locals sometimes open beer bottles with their phones – no one knows why. **204**

205

One park bench bears the inscription: "Sit down, you've earned it."

205

206

A street musician became famous for playing the exact same note every day – for 5 years.

206

207

A drunk man once hijacked a tram in Krakow – thankfully, only for two stops.

207

208 There's a flat in Krakow that's been empty for 30 years – purely out of stubbornness. **208**

209 An old Krakow elevator has no "stop" button – only "go" or "fate." **209**

210 The most popular Instagram spot is a wall that reads: "I survived Krakow." **210**

legal notice

Printed in Dunstable, United Kingdom

63823272R00047